THE HERAKLEOPOLITE NOME

AMERICAN STUDIES IN PAPYROLOGY

Series Editor
Ann Ellis Hanson

Number 37
THE HERAKLEOPOLITE NOME
by
Maria Rosaria Falivene

THE HERAKLEOPOLITE NOME

A Catalogue of the Toponyms
with
Introduction and Commentary
by
MARIA ROSARIA FALIVENE

SCHOLARS PRESS
ATLANTA, GEORGIA

THE HERAKLEOPOLITE NOME

by
MARIA ROSARIA FALIVENE

© 1998
The American Society of Papyrologists

Library of Congress Cataloging in Publication Data
The Herakleopolite Nome : a catalogue of the toponyms with
 introduction and commentary / by Maria Rosaria Falivene.
    p. cm. — (American studies in papyrology ; no. 37)
   Includes index.
   ISBN 0-7885-0412-6 (cloth : alk. paper)
   1. Names, Geographical—Egypt—Heracleopolite Nome.
2. Herakleopolite Nome (Egypt)—Historical geography.
3. Manuscripts, Greek (Papyri)—Egypt. 4. Manuscripts (Papyri)—
Egypt. I. Falivene, M. Rosaria (Maria Rosaria) II. Series:
American studies in papyrology ; v. 37.
DT137.H47 1997
916.2—dc21   97-35621
                                            CIP

Printed in the United States of America
on acid-free paper

To my Parents

Contents

Preface	xi
Note on Conventions and Abbreviations	xv

PART ONE	Introduction	1
1	*In insula Nili*	3
2	Toparchies and *Pagi*	7
3	Documents mentioning Herakleopolite Toponyms: Time-distribution, Provenance and Contents	13

PART TWO	The Toponyms of the Herakleopolite Nome	35
1	Catalogue	37
2	Fossil Kleroi	273
3	Other Kleroi	289

INDEXES		291
1	Villages arranged by Toparchy	293
2	Chronological Index	295
3	Reverse Index	305
4	Variant Spellings	323

Map	*at end of volume*

Acknowledgements

The Herakleopolite Nome is a thoroughly revised version of the second part of a doctoral dissertation approved in 1987. It is a pleasure to remember the occasion on which Professor Herwig Maehler first suggested that I could do research on this topic. In the final year of my stay in London my research was made possible by a British Council scholarship. Dr. Dorothy J. Thompson, FBA, and Professor Ludwig Koenen were among the first readers of my work: I wish to thank them for their comments and encouragement at that very early stage. I also wish to thank an anonymous reader who more or less at the same time contributed stimulating criticism. When my work began, volume XIV of the *Berliner Griechische Urkunden* had only just come out: its editor, Dr. William M. Brashear, was the first of many colleagues to whom I have written asking to check readings on the originals, or to procure photographs for me. They have been invariably helpful, and their contribution is gratefully acknowledged at the appropriate places. Dr. Katelijn Vergote gave expert advice on the etymologies of Egyptian toponyms. In the final stages of my work, comments and criticism from Professor Ann Ellis Hanson, Professor Willy Clarysse, Professor Roger Bagnall, and the anonymous readers of the American Society of Papyrology offered me the opportunity to clarify several points.

The excellent library of the Istituto Papirologico Vitelli, in Florence, has been essential for the completion of the present work: my thanks are due to the colleagues and members of staff there. Finally, I wish to thank all my colleagues and members of staff at the Istituto di Filologia Classica, Università di Urbino, for their support and friendship during all these years.

Precious help has also been provided by Valentina Calderai (whenever I had a problem with computers), Riccardo Lucignani (in drawing the map at the end of the volume), Kathleen Cann and Patrick Downey (in revising my English style), Massimo Saltarelli (in preparing the camera-ready copy), Maria Gabriella Colantonio (in checking the final details).

Preface

No book is ever finished, only abandoned[1] - and I must now finally abandon this book. It has accompanied me for a sizeable part of my life, since I was a part-time PhD student in Classics at the University of London (Birkbeck College), with a job in cataloguing the manuscripts of the British and Foreign Bible Society, an interest in Alexandrian poetry, and a fascination with Alexandria. At the time, it was not yet fashionable to call a city like Alexandria (or London) «multicultural», but I can now see very clearly that that was what attracted me to Alexandria (and London): cosmopolitan places where so many different ways of life co-existed, often ignorant of each other, often in the same individual.

I turned to papyrology when I began wondering what happened south of Alexandria, in the χώρα whence the city drew the wealth that made it possible for such a wonderfully complex capital to exist. The abundance of material was astonishing, indeed disorientating for a young would-be scholar with little experience of documentary papyri. Following a suggestion of Herwig Maehler, I selected the Herakleopolite nome as the special subject for my research: new material from that district had just been published by William Brashear[2]. I had only recently read Dorothy Crawford's *Kerkeosiris*[3], so I gave my PhD thesis the provisional title: «Life in the Herakleopolite nome, a district in Middle Egypt during the Ptolemaic period»[4].

The present book is one result of that decision of many years ago. It is essentially based on the Greek papyri, dating from the third century B.C. to the eighth century A.D., which mention Herakleopolite place-names. It aims both at mapping the nome territory, and at investigating the provenance of these papyri, the vast majority of which can be traced back to a limited number of sites. These two aims, which have required analysing and evaluating each papyrus that appears in the *Catalogue*, are not pursued in the standard work of reference for geographical names in Graeco-Roman Egypt[5].

The Greek language was adopted and kept in use, long after the end of the Macedonian dynasty in Egypt, by the administrators of a country whose mother-tongue was very much alive, and prestigious, throughout the so-called Graeco-Roman millennium. For the Ptolemaic period, in particular, Demotic papyri have often been found together with Greek ones at the same Herakleopolite sites[6]: Demotic (and Coptic) sources may in any case be expected to provide important, indeed essential information on the historical geography of the Herakleopolite nome in the long period of time that interests us here. Much work remains to be done on this part of the evidence: I have done my best to take into account those sources

---

[1] As Paul Valéry apparently once said: I found this allusion in GABRIEL JOSIPOVICI, «Neither love nor friendship. Marcel Proust and the discovery of a vocation» (Review of JEAN-YVES TADIÉ, *Marcel Proust. Biographie*, Paris 1996), *Times Literary Supplement*, October 4, 1996, p.4.

[2] *Ägyptische Urkunden aus den Staatlichen Museen Berlin. Griechische Urkunden, XIV.Band. Ptolemäische Urkunden aus Mumienkartonage*, bearbeitet von WILLIAM M. BRASHEAR, Berlin 1980.

[3] DOROTHY J. CRAWFORD (THOMPSON), *Kerkeosiris. An Egyptian Village in the Ptolemaic Period*, Cambridge 1971.

[4] My PhD thesis (*The Herakleopolite Nome in the Ptolemaic Period*) was approved in May 1987.

[5] ARISTIDE CALDERINI-SERGIO DARIS, *Dizionario dei nomi geografici e topografici dell'Egitto greco-romano*, Cairo-Madrid-Milano 1935-1987; *Supplemento 1*, Milano 1988; *Supplemento 2*, Bonn 1996.

[6] Cf. *P.Hib.* I, *Introduction*, p.11: «... the proportion of Greek to demotic in the Hibeh cartonnage is distinctly smaller than in that discovered by Flinders Petrie at Gurob and Hawâra, and apparently smaller than that found by Jouguet and Lefebvre at Magdola, though it is larger than in the cartonnage found by us at Tebtunis, the demotic papyri from which outnumber the Greek by two to one».
I wish to thank Willy Clarysse and Mark Depauw, for information on published Demotic papyri originating from the Herakleopolite nome.

that are referred to in the secondary literature [1], but first-hand work will need an Egyptologist.

There are, of course, many more documents (Greek, Demotic and Coptic) from the Herakleopolites, dating from the third B.C. to the eighth A.D., than those actually mentioning Herakleopolite toponyms: a «Guide to the documents from the Herakleopolite nome», compiled along the lines of the *Guide to the Zenon Archive* [2], is conceivable, though this goes far beyond my present purposes.

Greek and Latin literary sources referring to Herakleopolite localities are few: I have listed [3], but only occasionally discussed them; they would in fact require an altogether different approach from that adopted for documentary papyri. A thorough inspection of the volumes of the *Patrologia Graeca* could prove fruitful here [4].

Before the third century B.C., the history of Egypt is intimidatingly long, and richly documented. The *Wilbour Papyrus*, dating from the twelfth century B.C., is a survey of the land granted to temples in an area largely coinciding with the Herakleopolite and Oxyrhynchite nomes of a later age: some of the many toponyms mentioned in it can be recognized in the Greek documents of one or two thousand years later [5]. Throughout the Graeco-Roman millennium, the apparently insignificant village of Πιακερ is attested by a single document dating from the sixth century A.D. (*Stud.Pal.* X 228): it does however recur in the *Wilbour Papyrus*, which proves its continuing existence, under the same name (*Pr-Jqr*: «Pi-Ōker» [6]), since the twelfth century B.C. at least.

The case of Πιακερ should inspire prudence when attempting to draw conclusions on the basis of the number and time-distribution of sources relating to any single toponym, and to the toponyms of a district as a whole. The cases of Tilothis and Ταχονπαχνουβ are equally instructive. Tilothis, the main centre of its own toparchy in the Ptolemaic period, received a new, or rather a second name (Νείλου πόλις) in the Roman period, as it increased in importance, eventually becoming the metropolis of an independent nome. But it is its Egyptian name that we find in the *Suda*, and that still survives in modern Dalās [7]: Νείλου πόλις obviously existed primarily in the documents of the Roman administration. The Egyptian place-name Ταχονπαχνουβ was translated into Greek: it is Ἰβιῶν Πάχνουβις in a document of 131 A.D., presumably an indication of the interest, on the part of the new settlers, in the Egyptian ibis-cult.

A good number of place-names found in the Greek papyri can be identified, one or two thousand years later, in the modern Arabic names of the same localities. These can be traced on the *Egypt Survey Map* of 1917, thus making it possible to locate a number of Herakleopolite villages on the *Map* which is found at the end of this volume [8].

The capital of the nome was called Ἡρακλέους πόλις by the Greeks, who equated the Egyptian Ram-god Harsaphes (*Hrj-šf*), the chief divinity of the nome, with the Greek hero. For the native Egyptian, however, the town had always been H*w.t-nn-nsw*, the «Mansion of the Royal Child»: *Nn-nsw*, «the Royal

---

[1] For Coptic sources, STEFAN TIMM, *Das christlich-koptische Ägypten in arabischer Zeit*, Wiesbaden 1984-1994, is a mine of information.

[2] PIETER W. PESTMAN ET ALII, *A Guide to the Zenon Archive*, Leyden 1981.

[3] See *Catalogue*, s.vv. ΑΓΚΥΡΩΝ ΠΟΛΙΣ, ΘΜΟΙΝΕΨΙ, ΙΠΠΩΝΩΝ ΚΩΜΗ, ΙΣΙΟΝ, ΚΑΙΝΗ, ΚΟΜΑ, ΠΕΕΝΑΜΕΥΣ, ΣΙΝΑΡΥ, ΧΟΡΤΑΣΩ..

[4] The starting point here must be the *Einleitung* to TIMM, *Das christlich-koptische Ägypten* (vol.I, pp.1-33); see also the discussion of the literary sources relating to the Hermopolite nome by MARIE DREW-BEAR, *Le nome Hermopolite. Toponymes et sites*, Ann Arbor 1979, pp.4-10. The book by JOHN BALL, *Egypt in the Classical Geographers*, Cairo 1942, though somewhat confused, may still be of some use.

[5] See *Catalogue*, s.vv. ΘΜΟΙΑΜΟΥΝΕΩΣ and ΠΙΑΚΕΡ. The geographical information contained in the *P.Wilbour* has been thoroughly exploited by FAROUK GOMAÀ, RENATE MÜLLER-WOLLERMANN, WOLFGANG SCHENKEL, *Mittelägypten zwischen Samalūṭ und dem Gabal Abū Ṣīr*, Wiesbaden 1991.

[6] See *Catalogue* s.v. ΠΙΑΚΕΡ.

[7] See *Catalogue*, s.v. ΤΙΛΩΘΙΣ.

[8] Cf. *Introduction*, pp.4-10.

PREFACE

Child», being one name of *Ḥrj-šf*. Another name was Somtous, *Sm3-t3.wj*, «he who unites the two countries» [1], well suited to the god of a city that had twice been the capital of Egypt. The Coptic sources preserve the Egyptian name (*Hnes*), which actually survives to this day (Ihnāsiyā al-Madīna) for us to ponder on the limits of reciprocal understanding between Greeks and the natives in Egypt. Even at the time when the Greeks called it Herakleopolis, this was an important town, deserving a special study which cannot be attempted here.

«Egyptian names always have a meaning» [2], which can often be recovered; in the case of Egyptian toponyms known from Greek documents, this can only be done once the Egyptian spelling has been retrieved through (or at times in spite of) the Greek transliteration. A sound methodological basis for this kind of work has been provided by Jean Yoyotte and Jan Quaegebeur (often in cooperation with Willy Clarysse) [3]; more ground-breaking work is being done by Katelijn Vandorpe [4]. Once interpreted, Egyptian toponyms tell us of gods to whom places were once sacred, of important persons to whom they once belonged, of features in the natural landscape after which they were called, of the work and life of people who lived there. The same is true of the Greek and Latin names given to places that were either newly founded, or re-named by the Greek (and Roman) new-comers. Much work also remains to be done in this field.

---

[1] The child-god of H*w.t-nn-nsw*/Herakleopolis has been recognized in a bronze statuette of a Belgian private collection, and in several other statuettes (one of them from Al-Hība / Ἀγκυρῶν πόλις) by JAN QUAEGEBEUR, «Somtous l'Enfant sur le lotus», *CRIPEL* 13, 1991, pp.113-121. Somtous was «l'avatar juvenile d'Hérishef» (JEAN YOYOTTE - PIERRE CHUVIN, «Le Zeus Casios de Péluse à Tivoli. Une hypothèse», *BIFAO* 88, 1988, p.176).

[2] PIETER W. PESTMAN, *The New Papyrological Primer*, Leiden-New York-København-Köln 1990, p.44.

[3] See especially JAN QUAEGEBEUR, «Documents grecs et géographie historique. Le Mendésien», *L'Égyptologie en 1979. Axes prioritaires de recherches (Colloques Internationaux du Centre National de la Recherche Scientifique. N. 595*, Paris 1982, Tome I, pp.267-272). Quaegebeur refers, among others, to several articles by Jean Yoyotte, who may rightly be considered the εὑρετής of this branch of studies: «Il a notamment très bien montré la position intermédiaire de la documentation papyrologique entre, d'une part, les données proprement égyptologiques et, d'autre part, les sources coptes et arabes, qui n'appartiennent plus aux époques qui constituent l'objet de l'égyptologie» (p.267).

[4] She was so kind as to put a copy of her unpublished thesis on *Egyptische geografische elementen in Griekse transcriptie* (Leuven 1988) at my disposal. I am most grateful to Willy Clarysse, who read through the (almost) final version of the present work, and certainly succeeded in making me feel less a stranger to Demotic studies.

Note on Conventions and Abbreviations

The *Catalogue* lists all toponyms of the Herakleopolite nome as attested in the Greek (and Latin) literary sources and in the Greek (and Latin) papyri published up to 1997, to the exclusion of the *metropolis* (Herakleopolis Magna).

Toponyms are listed in alphabetical order: those whose beginning is lost or damaged are found at the end of the catalogue. The main entries consist of the toponyms in the nominative case, if this is attested in, or may be unambiguously deduced from one or more sources: otherwise, the toponym is given as it appears in the source(s). In indicating dates, I have basically followed the criteria adopted in Eric G. Turner's *Greek Manuscripts of the Ancient World*[1].

As a rule, I have refrained from imparting accents (and breathings) to Egyptian toponyms transliterated into Greek. This is a risky, and perhaps superfluous undertaking: the criteria adopted by Preisigke in his *Namenbuch* were aimed, by the author's own admission, at internal consistency rather than scientific accuracy[2], while a quite bewildering variety prevails in the editions of Greek documentary papyri. Willy Clarysse has convincingly argued that toponyms with an –ις ending should be proparoxytonous, where possible (following the declension of δύναμις, genitive δυνάμεως: thus, Φέβιχις, *not* Φεβῖχις as in Preisigke, followed by all later editors of Greek documents) and that toponyms ending in –ευς should be oxytonous (as in ἱππεύς or Ἀχιλλεύς, gen. –έως)[3]. These two are indeed among the most common endings in hellenised Egyptian place-names, but there are many other less straightforward instances, and establishing a new set of rules for Greek accents on Egyptian names[4] could by no means be my task here.

Under each main entry, the relevant sources are listed in chronological order: abbreviations are those adopted in JOHN F. OATES ET AL., *Checklist of Editions of Greek and Latin Papyri, Ostraca and Tablets*, 4th ed. (*BASP* Suppl. 7, 1992); dates are as in the *editio princeps*, unless otherwise indicated. For each source, the toponym is quoted as given in the *editio princeps*, unless the reading has been later improved: in

---

[1] ERIC G. TURNER, *Greek Manuscripts of the Ancient World*. Second Edition revised and enlarged. Edited by PETER J. PARSONS, University of London, Institute of Classical Studies, *BICS Supplement* 46, 1987, p.VII: «When a precise date cannot be offered, the date suggested is usually a century, indicated by a ... roman figure preceding the abbreviation B.C. or A.D. Thus II B.C. means second century before Christ; III/II B.C. means third to second century B.C. (i.e. about 225-175 B.C.)».

[2] Cf. FRIEDRICH PREISIGKE, *Namenbuch enthaltend alle griechischen, lateinischen, ägyptischen, hebräischen, arabischen und sonstigen semitischen und nichtsemitischen Menschennamen, soweit sie in griechischen Urkunden (Papyri, Ostraka, Inschriften, Mumienschilder usw.) Ägyptens sich vorfinden*, Heidelberg 1922, p.4: «Was die Akzentfrage anbetrifft, so sind vom wissenschaftliche Standpunkte aus diejenige Gelehrten zweifellos im Rechte, welche die Akzente für griechisch geschriebene ägyptische und semitische Namen überhaupt ablehnen; aber die griechischen Urkunden Ägyptens werden nicht bloß von Orientalisten, sondern auch, und zwar in überwiegenden Maße, von Gräzisten benutzt, welche der orientalischen Sprachen unkundig sind, und diese sind gewohnt, beim Aussprechen eines Namens den Ton auf irgend eine Silbe zu legen. Aus rein praktischem Grunde hat sich daher, wie viele Papyrusausgaben zeigen, die Gepflogenheit herausgebildet, Akzente zu setzen. Auch in diesem Namenbuche wollen die Akzente der nichtgriechischen Namen nur als Notbehelf angesehen werden; der Gegner möge sie als nicht vorhanden betrachten, die übrigen Gelehrten aber mögen sie als Andeutung dafür annehmen, welche Silbe von den ägyptischen Griechen vermutlich betont worden sein wird, und wie wir heute praktisch das Wort aussprechen wollen. Daß ich dabei immer das Richtige getroffen habe, darf ich keinesfall behaupten».

[3] It is sometimes impossible to decide whether a toponym (attested e.g. in the genitive only) had an –ις, or an –ευς ending in Greek. When in doubt, I have indicated an (-ις) ending.

[4] A paper by WILLY CLARYSSE on this topic has been kindly made available to me by its author in March 1996: see now his article on «Greek Accents on Egyptian Names», *ZPE* 119, 1997, pp.177-184.

the latter case, reference is made to the *Berichtigungsliste der Griechischen Papyrusurkunden aus Ägypten (BL)*, volumes 1-9, or (in a footnote) to the relevant publication (the abbreviations adopted are those of the *Bibliographie Papyrologique*). The contributions of colleagues who kindly checked the readings for me against the originals are also acknowledged in the footnotes. I have myself suggested a number of new readings, which I have checked against the originals or from photographs. *New readings* are signaled by an asterisk marking the relevant entries in the *Reverse Index* (see below).

When it seemed appropriate, I have quoted more than just the place-name: e.g. when reference is made to the status of a locality (κώμη, ἐποίκιον, χωρίον, τόπος, etc.[1]), or when officials, trades, other place-names and the like are mentioned in connection with the toponym under consideration. I have *not* repeated the toponym when it is given in the source as it appears in the main entry. A question mark preceding the reference to a source indicates that this may not refer to a Herakleopolite village.

The list of sources is followed by secondary entries for the *toparchy* of the village under consideration, the *etymology* of its name, and the *modern Arabic name* (whenever the identification with an ancient locality is possible). One or other, or indeed all of these secondary entries may be missing, when no relevant information is available.

A short *comment* usually follows, mainly discussing the nature of the sources and the location of the village under consideration.

A list of *Fossil Kleroi* and a list of *Other Kleroi* in the Herakleopolite Nome are appended at the end of the *Catalogue*.

There follow a list of *Villages arranged by Toparchies*, a *Chronological Index* of the papyri referred to in the *Catalogue* (arranged by centuries), a *Reverse Index* of the papyri referred to in the *Catalogue* (which is organized according to the papyrus edition in which each text mentioned appears) and an *Index of Variant Spellings*.

A *Map* is also appended.

The following *Abbreviations* are employed:

BL = *Berichtigungsliste der Griechischen Papyrusurkunden aus Ägypten*, Bände I-IX, 1922-1995.

CALDERINI-DARIS, *Dizionario* = ARISTIDE CALDERINI-SERGIO DARIS, *Dizionario dei nomi geografici e topografici dell'Egitto greco-romano*, Cairo-Madrid-Milano 1935-1987; *Supplemento 1*, Milano 1988; *Supplemento 2 (1987-1993)*, Bonn 1996.

CRUM, *Coptic Dictionary* = W.E. CRUM, *A Coptic Dictionary*, Oxford 1939.

DREW-BEAR, *Le nome Hermopolite* = MARIE DREW-BEAR, *Le nome Hermopolite. Toponymes et sites*, Ann Arbor 1979.

L.Ä. = W. HELCK, E. OTTO, W. WESTENDORF, *Lexikon der Ägyptologie*, Wiesbaden 1972-1992.

LSJ = *A Greek-English Lexicon*. Compiled by HENRY GEORGE LIDDELL and ROBERT SCOTT. Revised by HENRY STUART JONES. With the assistance of RODERICK MCKENZIE *et al*. Ninth edition, Oxford 1940; *A Supplement*. Edited by E.A. BARBER. With the assistance of P. MAAS, M. SCHELLER and M.L. WEST, Oxford 1968.

PREISIGKE, *Namenbuch* = FRIEDRICH PREISIGKE, *Namenbuch enthaltend alle griechischen, lateinischen, ägyptischen, hebräischen, arabischen und sonstigen semitischen und nichtsemitischen Menschennamen, soweit sie in griechischen Urkunden (Papyri, Ostraka, Inschriften, Mumienschilder usw.) Ägyptens sich vorfinden*, Heidelberg 1922.

PPt = WILLY PEREMANS - EDMOND VAN'T DACK, *Prosopographia ptolemaica*, vol. I-VII, Louvain-

---

[1] On these denominations, see MARIE DREW-BEAR, *Le nome Hermopolite. Toponymes et sites*, Ann Arbor 1979, pp. 41-42; PAOLA PRUNETI, *I centri abitati dell'Ossirinchite. Repertorio toponomastico*, Firenze 1981, pp. 10-12.

NOTE ON CONVENTIONS AND ABBREVIATIONS

Leiden 1950-1975; *Addenda et corrigenda*, vol.VIII, 1975; vol.IX, 1981.

PRUNETI, *Centri abitati* = PAOLA PRUNETI, *I centri abitati dell'Ossirinchite. Repertorio toponomastico*, Firenze 1981.

P.Wilbour = *The Wilbour Papyrus*. Edited by ALAN H. GARDINER, vols I-III, Oxford 1948; vol. IV (*Index*, by RAYMOND O. FAULKNER), Oxford 1952.

SB = *Sammelbuch Griechischen Urkunden aus Ägypten*, Bände I-XX, 1915-1997.

SEM = *Survey of Egypt Map* (1917 and 1930; scale 1:100,000).

TAVO B 69 = FAROUK GOMAÀ, RENATE MÜLLER-WOLLERMANN, WOLFGANG SCHENKEL, *Mittelägypten zwischen Samalūt und dem Gabal Abū Ṣīr. Beiträge zur historischen Topographie der pharaonischen Zeit* (Beihefte zum *TAVO, Tübinger Atlas des Vorderen Orients*, Reihe B [Geisteswissenschaften], Nr. 69), Wiesbaden 1991.

TIMM, *Das christlich-koptische Ägypten* = STEFAN TIMM, *Das christlich-koptische Ägypten in arabischer Zeit. Eine Sammlung christlicher Stätten in Ägypten in arabischer Zeit, unter Ausschluß von Alexandria, Kairo, des Apa-Mena-Klosters (Dēr Abū Mina), der Skētis (Wādi n-Natrūn) und der Sinai-Region* (Beihefte zum *TAVO, Tübinger Atlas des Vorderen Orients*, Reihe B [Geisteswissenschaften], Nr. 41/1-6), Wiesbaden 1984-1992.

Abbreviations for periodicals are those adopted in *SB* and *L.Ä.*

PART ONE
Introduction

1 In insula Nili

At the time of the Pharaohs, the Herakleopolites was called the Nome of the tree *naret (n^cr.t)*: its main divinity was the Ram-god Harsaphes (*Hrj-šf*, originally meaning «he who is upon his lake» [1]), whom the Greeks identified with Herakles [2]. The Greek re-naming of the district and of its capital Herakleopolis Magna evidently took place *via* this identification; the Egyptian name was *Hw.t-(n-)nn-nsw* or, in its compressed form, H*w.t-nsw*, sometimes abbreviated as *Nn-nsw*, «Mansion of the Royal Child». Herakleopolis, about 80 kms south of Memphis, was an important town in Pharaonic Egypt [3]: its site, one of the largest in Egypt, was first excavated by Naville [4], then by Petrie [5] and, with different (papyrological) interests, by Wilcken [6]; there followed members of the Beni Suef Antiquities Service and, since 1966, the Spanish Archaeological Mission, who have been digging at Herakleopolis until the present day [7]. The city stood where the Nile valley was at its widest (about 25 km) in southern Egypt: it is no more than 10 km wide near Dahmarū/Τααμωρου, in the border-area between the Herakleopolite and the Oxyrhynchite nomes (approx. 46 km south of Herakleopolis). The ancient Herakleopolites extended over the modern province of Beni Suef and beyond, its southernmost toparchy (the Koites) corresponding roughly to the northern part of the modern province of Al-Minya.

During their 1981 survey of the region comprised between Samalūt and the Gabal Abū Ṣir, the authors

---

[1] See HERMANN KEES, *Ancient Egypt. A Cultural Topography* (Edited by T.G.H. James. Translated by Ian F.D. Morrow), London-Chicago 1977 (1961¹; original title: *Das alte Aegypten*), pp.212-230 («Herakleopolis and the Fayum»). See also *L.Ä.* II 1015-1018; JOZEF VERGOTE, «Note sur ΕΣΗΦ», *JJP* 11/12, 1957/58, pp.93-96; more recently: JAN QUAEGEBEUR, «Une statue égyptienne représentant Héraclès-Melqart?», in *Phoenicia and the east Mediterranean in the First Millennium B.C.* (Studia Phoenicia V = OLA 22), Leuven 1987, pp.157-166; IDEM, «Somtous l'Enfant sur le lotus», *CRIPEL* 13, 1991, 113-121. Somtous was «l'avatar juvénile d'Hérishef»: cf. JEAN YOYOTTE - PIERRE CHUVIN, «Le Zeus Casios de Péluse à Tivoli. Une hypothèse», *BIFAO* 88, 1988, pp.172-176. The dissertation by KATELIJN VANDORPE, *Egyptische Geografische Elementen in Griekse Transcriptie*, Leuven 1988 (unpublished), has also been of great use to me, here and elsewhere.

[2] The identification might rest upon a later interpretation of Harsaphes' name, apparently implying a reference to (Harsaphes') «virile courage» (τὸ ἀνδρεῖον: cf. PLUT. *Is. et Os.* 37): a quality the Greeks would certainly see as Herakles' own. See VERGOTE, «Note sur ΕΣΗΦ», *cit.*, p.94 f.

[3] MOHAMED GAMAL EL-DIN MOKHTAR, *Ihnâsya El-Medina (Herakleopolis Magna). Its Importance and its Role in Pharaonic History* (BdE 40), Cairo 1983.

[4] EDOUARD NAVILLE, *Ahnas El Medineh (Herakleopolis Magna)*, in *Eleventh Memoir of the Egypt Exploration Fund*, London 1894.

[5] WILLIAM MATTHEW FLINDERS PETRIE, *Ehnasya*, London 1905; cf. also WILLIAM MATTHEW FLINDERS PETRIE-GUY BRUNTON, *Sedment*, London 1924.

[6] See below, p.27.

[7] For a brief history of the Spanish excavations see MARIA DEL CARMEN PEREZ DIE - PASCAL VERNUS, *Excavaciones en Ehnasya El Medina (Herakleópolis Magna)*, Madrid 1992 (vol.I); 1995 (vol.II). See also EADEM, «Discoveries at Herakleopolis Magna (Ehnasya el-Medina)», *Egyptian Archaeology. The Bulletin of the Egypt Exploration Society*, No.6, 1995, pp.23-25. On the town-quarters of Graeco-Roman Herakleopolis see DIETER HAGEDORN-PIETER J. SIJPESTEIJN, «Die Stadtviertel von Herakleopolis», *ZPE* 65, 1986, pp.101-105.

of supplement (*Beiheft*) *B 69*[1] to the *Tübinger Atlas des Vorderen Orients* were able to detect the remains of nine ancient dykes in what used to be the territory of the Herakleopolite nome. Parts of these dykes are to this day in use as roads, or paths, and the modern names of some villages in their proximity can be identified with ancient toponyms appearing in the documents of the Greek, Roman and Byzantine periods. In at least some cases the dykes may also have functioned as land-marks, defining the boundaries between toparchies within the nome. All dykes but one extended from the Nile to the Old Baḥr Yūsuf, crossing the Nile valley at a distance of approximately 8-11 kms from each other: the one dyke built at right angles to the others ran roughly parallel to, and midway between the Nile and the Old Baḥr Yūsuf; its remains are recognisable to the east of Ṣaft Rašin[2]. In what follows, these dykes will occasionally serve as reference points in locating villages and toparchies.

Strabo, Ptolemy and Pliny the Elder[3] agree in stating that the Herakleopolite nome was an island, and if Pliny's assertion is bound to be second-hand, Strabo declares that he travelled «as far as the frontiers of Ethiopia»[4], while Ptolemy, an inhabitant of Egypt and a geographer, is on both grounds likely to give an accurate description of a district in Middle Egypt[5].

Strabo concentrates upon the northern part of the island:

«... the Herakleote (*sic*) nome, on a large island where, on the right, is the canal which leads into Libya to the Arsinoite nome, so that the canal has two mouths, a part of the island intervening between the two»[6].

Further on, he describes how

«... locks have been placed at both mouths of the canal, by which the engineers (οἱ ἀρχιτέκτονες) regulate both the inflow and the outflow of the water. ... Near the first entrance to the canal, and on proceeding thence about thirty or forty stadia, one comes to a flat, trapezium-shaped place, which has a village, and also a great palace composed of many palaces - as many in number as there were nomes in earlier times ...»[7]

Important water-control works at Πτολεμαὶς Ὅρμου (modern Al-Lāhūn) are repeatedly referred to in the *Petrie Papyri*: these should perhaps be identified with a six-gate sluice mentioned in some documents

---

[1] The region described in *TAVO B 69* corresponds to that surveyed by the *P.Wilbour*; on the dyke and basin system, see esp. pp.49-52. The survey was based on the maps drawn by Schouani, Martin and Linant de Bellefonds (see pp.29-44, with the Tables at the end of the volume, especially Tables XXIII-XXV), as well as those published by the Survey Department of Egypt, at various stages in the course of the 20th century (cf. the *Verzeichnis der benutzten Landkarten*, pp.XIX-XX).
See also RENATE MÜLLER-WOLLERMANN, «Zur Lokalisierung von Orten in Mittelägypten», *Proceedings of the 19th International Congress of Papyrology (Cairo 1992)*, vol. I, pp.713-721.

[2] See below, p.10.

[3] STRAB. *Geogr.* 17,1,35; PTOL. *Geogr.* IV, 5, 55-59 ; PLIN. *H.N.* 5,9,50 (*Heracleopolites est in insula Nili longa passuum quinquaginta M, in qua et oppidum Herculis appellatum.*).

[4] STRAB. 2,5,11: ἐπήλθομεν ... ἐπὶ μεσημβρίαν ... μέχρι τῶν τῆς Αἰθιοπίας ὅρων.

[5] Any number of papyri prove that this region was easily reached from Alexandria, where Ptolemy lived: «De la vie de Ptolémée, nous ne savons presque rien, mais nous connaissons grâce à la *Syntaxe Mathématique* le lieu de ses observations, Alexandrie, et leur date: la plus ancienne, portant sur une éclipse de lune, remonte à la neuvième année du règne d'Hadrien (141)» (GERMAINE AUJAC, *Claude Ptolémée astronome, astrologue, géographe. Connaissance et représentation du monde habité*, Paris 1993, p.9). Ptolemy may well have visited the region himself.

[6] STRAB. 17,1,35. Translations by H.L. Jones (in the Loeb edition, Cambridge Mass.-London 1959). The «part of the island intervening between the two (mouths of the canal leading to the Arsinoite nome)» may correspond to the Μέση toparchy of the Herakleopolites: see below, p.9 f.

[7] STRAB. 17,1,37.

INTRODUCTION

of the Roman period[1]; it is likely that the same were meant by Strabo, too[2].

Ptolemy's «coordonnées ... sont là pour permettre à quiconque de dresser une carte qui soit imitation très approximative, mais utile, de la réalité»[3]. Here is his description[4]:

«The country south of the Great Delta and of the Northern Land is called Ἑπτὰ Νομοί (or Ἑπτανομίς): and the first nome, west of the river, is the Memphites, with its metropolis Memphis. Also west of the river (inland) is Akanthon Polis.
Then the river divides into two separate branches, forming an island, the Herakleopolite nome, and in the island (inland) is Niloupolis, at 62° (long.), 29° 30/60' (lat.). The metropolis is near the western branch of the river: Herakleopolis, a large town: 61° 50/60'(long.), 29° 10/60' (lat.). And within the island there is Niloupolis (inland)[5].
West of the island is the Arsinoite nome, with its metropolis Arsinoe (inland) and the port of Ptolemais[6].
East of the island is the Aphroditopolite nome, with the metropolis bearing the same name, Aphroditopolis.
There follows, again east of the island, Ankyron Polis[7]. The river-branches forming the island flow together again at 62° (long.), 29° 45/60' (lat.).
West of the river lies the Oxyrhynchite nome with its metropolis Oxyrhynchos. There follows, on the same side of the river, the Kynopolites with its metropolis, west of the river, Kō[8]. And facing it, on the island, there is Kynon Polis».

The course of the Baḥr Yūsuf, and of the Nile, have altered over the centuries, as a result of the combined work of nature and man. Thus, a 2.5 km shift eastwards of the Nile in the post-Roman period certainly occurred in the Memphite region[9]. The hydro-geographical reality described by Strabo and Ptolemy for the Herakleopolite nome clearly differs from that shown on the 1917 Survey of Egypt Map[10]:

---

[1] O.M. PEARL, «ΕΞΑΘΥΡΟΣ. Irrigation Works and Canals in the Arsinoite Nome», *Aegyptus* 31, 1951, pp.223-230.

[2] Strabo also reports (17,1,39) that the inhabitants of Herakleopolis worshipped the ichneumon; cf. also AELIAN., *N.A.* 1,47.

[3] GERMAINE AUJAC, *op.cit.*, p.155. Ptolemy himself (*Geogr.* II,1,2) warned his reader about possible inaccuracies. Cf. also JOHN BALL, *Egypt in the Classical Geographers*, Cairo 1942, pp.117-119: «Out of the total of a hundred and sixty-seven places in Egypt of which the sites or probable sites have been identified in the foregoing lists, the positions given by Ptolemy prove to be correct to within half a degree in both latitude and longitude in seventy-nine cases, or 47%, and to within one degree of both latitude and longitude in 126 cases, or 75% of the total of places identified ... . As was only to be expected from the circumstance that there existed in those days no satisfactory method for determining longitudes by astronomical observations, Ptolemy's errors in longitude are larger both in number and in magnitude than his errors in latitude ...». Furthermore, Ptolemy's figures will have been liable to incorrect transcription on the part of the scribes in the course of manuscript transmission.

[4] CLAUD.PTOL. *Geogr.* 4,5,55-60 (ed. C.F.A. NOBBE, Leipzig 1843-1845; repr. Hildesheim 1966). I only report Ptolemy's co-ordinates for Herakleopolite localities.

[5] Different figures are apparently given in locating Niloupolis: I take the first (62° long.; 29° 30/60' lat.) to refer to the point at which the Nile divided into two branches (i.e. the northern extreme of the Herakleopolite island); and the second (62° long.; 29° 45/60' lat.) to refer to the actual location of Niloupolis.

[6] This is of course Πτολεμαΐς Ὅρμου/Al-Lāhūn.

[7] The measurements (62° 15/60' long.; 29° 20/60' lat.) given for Ἀγκυρῶν πόλις (to be identified with Al-Hība: see *Catalogue, s.v.*) locate it too far north (e.g. in relation to Herakleopolis) in the nome.

[8] On the relation between Kω and Κυνῶν πόλις, and of both with the Koites, see *Catalogue, s.v.* ΚΩ.

[9] KATELIJN VANDORPE, «'The Dockyard Workshop' or the Toachris Village», *Enchoria* 22, 1995, p.159.

[10] From now on: *SEM*.

indeed, *SEM* records the traces of a «Baḥr Yūsuf Old», near Al-Gafadūn and immediately west of Ṣaft Rašin[1]. These continuous, if slow, alterations in the course of the Nile, and of its branches, were caused by the "new land" formations: fluvial deposits accumulated to form what was called in Egyptian *m3j*, a term which was either transliterated as (Θ)μοι/υ(ν)-, or translated as νῆσος in Greek[2]. The high incidence of toponyms compounded with the prefix *m3j* = (Θ)μοι/υ(ν), or translated into Greek as Νήσων, Τεχθὼ Νῆσος, Ἱερὰ Νῆσος, shows that such formations were typical of the Herakleopolite nome[3].

Perhaps the «Baḥr Yūsuf Old» silted up, entirely or in part(s), while the Nile made its progress eastwards; at the same time, the new Baḥr Yūsuf was formed. In the process, the Herakleopolite island, as known to some ancient authors, disappeared. If so, the fact that the region of the Herakleopolite nome is no longer *in insula Nili* need not mean that our literary sources were mistaken, or not telling the truth. Rather, it would mean that the hydro-geographical setting of this district has altered over the centuries.

---

[1] Cf. *TAVO B 69*, pp.44-45: «Die *Description de l'Égypte* zeigt offensichtlich in diesem Bereich, wie dies sonst im Ganzen Untersuchungsbereich der Fall war und ist, einen Verlauf des Baḥr Yūsuf nahe am Wüstenrand. Dieser ältere Baḥr Yūsuf ist noch heute gut zu verfolgen ... als Bahr Yusef Old bzw. el-Qadîm bezeichnet»; cf. also p.50: «nicht der heutige Flußlauf ... sondern ein noch bei Linant de Bellefonds an Deichen erkennbarer älterer Flußlauf westlich Ṣaft Rašin». On the alterations in the course of the Baḥr Yūsuf (including a major one in 1870) see *L.Ä.* I 601 *s.v.* «Bahr Jussuf». On the ancient name of the Baḥr Yūsuf (*Tmt*, "Teme", Τῶμις ποταμός) see DIETER KESSLER, *Historische Topographie der Region zwischen Mallawi und Samalūṭ*, Wiesbaden 1981, p.28.

[2] Cf. VANDORPE, «'The Dockyard Workshop'», p.160: «Newly-gained or alluvial land (*m3j*) came into being by the deposit of silt on a bank in the Nile, thus creating an island which could be attached to the main land later on, or by the deposit of silt on the shore, thus creating a peninsula. The term *m3j* could also be used outside the agrarian environment to denote a real and lasting island...». Much the same process can be observed in the formation of an *Altwasser*, in the Bavarian Altmühltal (Germany): a branch of the river slowly silts up at its downstream end, so as to be cut out from the main stream (initially in the low-ebb periods only); this allows for vegetation to grow thicker both under water and on the banks, which in turn makes further silting up easier etc. This process can be artificially accelerated, in order to obtain more cultivable (and very fertile) land.

[3] Cf. *TAVO B 69*, pp.118-119 (with special regard to the so-called Zone II, around Ψῦχις/Absūg).

2. Toparchies and Pagi[1]

«Audit the revenue accounts, if possible, village by village (κατὰ κώμην) - and we think it not to be impossible, if you devote yourself zealously to the business - if not, by toparchies (κατὰ τοπαρχίαν)...» (*P.Tebt.* III 703,117-123)[2].

The wording of this instruction (addressed by the dioiketes to an oikonomos in the late third century B.C.) suggests that an oikonomos would be inclined to adopt the toparchy (or τόπος), rather than the village, as the smallest unit, when assessing taxes for the nome he was in charge of, no matter what the preferences of his superiors were. The obvious counter-move on the part of his superiors, aiming at ensuring a more pervading, village-by-village administrative control, was to make the toparchies smaller by increasing their number. Thus, the Ἄγημα toparchy was divided into a Northern, a Central and a Southern Ἄγημα already in the Ptolemaic period, while the Neilopolites (probably coinciding with the northern part of the nome) was given the status of independent district from the middle of the second century A.D. - a time at which the Koites, at the other end of the Herakleopolites, was split into Κάτω and Ἄνω Κωίτης[3].

In the later Ptolemaic period, which is also the time for which we have the largest amount of evidence on this subject, the following toparchies (in alphabetical order) are attested in the Herakleopolite nome: Ἄγημα Ἄνω, Ἄγημα Κάτω, περὶ Κόμα, Μέση[4], Πέραν, περὶ Πόλιν, περὶ Τεκμι, Τεχθω Νῆσος, περὶ Τίλωθιν[5], περὶ Φέβιχιν/Κωίτης[6].

Some villages can be identified with their modern namesakes[7] on the basis of (1) phonetic similarity[8],

---

[1] See the *Map* at the end of the volume.

[2] *P.Tebt.* III 703 comes from the Herakleopolites, being among the papyri obtained from the cartonnage of mummies found at Umm Al-Baragat (see below, p.17 f.). This passage was quoted by EDMOND VAN'T DACK, «La Toparchie dans l'Égypte ptolémaïque», *Chr.Ég.* 23, 1948, p.158; he also remarked that the larger villages only are likely to have had their own administrators, who must have been in charge of the smaller nearby villages, too (e.g. the komogrammateus of the main village in a τόπος may well have acted as the komogrammateus of the smaller surrounding villages, too, thereby coinciding in effect with the topogrammateus).

[3] See *Catalogue*, s.vv. Κωίτης and Νείλου πόλις.

[4] In *BGU* VIII 1827, ἐν τ[οπαρ]χίᾳ Φνεβιεῖ is an uncertain reading: in any case, the toparchy of Φνεβιεύς (see *s.v.*) should coincide with the Μέση.

[5] *BGU* VIII 1780 does probably *not* refer to the ὑποστράτηγος Artemidoros as based at Τάγχαις (see *s.v.*): this village was in fact in the Tilothis toparchy, and is nowhere else referred to as the main centre in a toparchy of its own.

[6] See *Catalogue*, s.vv. Cf. *BGU* XIV, pp.220-221.

[7] The specific reasons for assigning a village to a particular toparchy, or for identifying it with a modern one, are discussed in the *Catalogue*, under the relevant entry.

[8] The modern toponym must be «meaningless» in Arabic, this being an important countercheck against arbitrary identifications based solely on phonetical similarity; cf. MÜLLER-WOLLERMANN, «Zur Lokalisierung von Orten», p.713: «Der heutige Ortsname ist nicht genuin arabisch, könnte also auf einen altägyptische griechischen oder koptischen zurückgehen». On the criteria for reliable identification between ancient and modern toponyms see also JEANNE and LOUIS ROBERT, «La persistance de la toponymie antique dans l'Anatolie», in *La toponymie antique. Actes du Colloque de Strasbourg (12-14 Juin 1975)*. Université des Sciences Humaines de Strasbourg. Travaux du Centre de recherche sur le proche-Orient et la Grèce antiques.4, pp.11-63.

in combination with (2) archaeological evidence and/or (3) information regarding the location of villages in a particular toparchy, as provided by *(a)* Greek and Latin papyri or *(b)* literary sources, or *(c)* similar information offered by ancient Egyptian, Demotic, Coptic and Arabic sources[1]. These identifications of the sites of ancient villages also enable us to locate the different toparchies in relation to each other.

The identification of Abū Sir al-Malaq (where most first-century B.C. documents from the Herakleopolite nome were found[2]) with Bousiris shows that the Koma toparchy, to which Bousiris is assigned in the first-century B.C. sources[3], was the northernmost toparchy in the district. Just over 9 km NE of Abū Sir al-Malaq, Qimān Al-ʿArûs should be ancient Koma itself[4]; modern Al-Maimûn must be ancient Thmoiamoun(is): this is near the Nile, 10 km away from Abū Sir al-Malaq, and slightly to the south of it.

Tilothis (modern Dalās, approx. 7 km south of Al-Maimûn, and again not far from the Nile) was the main centre of the next toparchy (περὶ Τίλωθιν). In the Roman period, Tilothis had its name changed to Νείλου πόλις, as it became the capital of an independent district, the Neilopolites, which must have comprised the whole of the northern Herakleopolites. About 4 km south of Tilothis/Νείλου πόλις/Dalās, Būš should be ancient Pois, often connected to Tilothis in the documents; Tansa Al-Malaq, less than 4 km NW of Dalās/Τίλωθις, and Ishmant, less than 5 km NE of it, can be identified with the ancient Tanchais and Σχμῶνθις, respectively, both in the Tilothis toparchy.

Ἡρακλέους πόλις (modern Ihnāsiya al-Madīna), the nome capital, was at the western extreme of dyke no.14, running over Noeris (modern An-Nuwaira) to Banī Suwaif. Its toparchy was called περὶ Πόλιν: it may have comprised Πεενη = modern Bāha (9 km NE of the capital) and Τίντηρις = Dandīl (less than 4 km further NE).

Dimšuwīya (about 8 km east of Herakleopolis; immediately south of dyke no.14[5]) has been convincingly identified with Μοῦχις[6], a well attested village in the Tekmi toparchy[7]; less than 7 km SW of it, Ṭuwa could be the modern equivalent of Τωυ, in the same toparchy. North of Dimšuwīya, other identifications may be suggested for villages of the Tekmi toparchy: the second part of the place-name Banī Bikhīt (a little more than 3 km to the north) may preserve the ancient toponym Βιχινθωυθ. About 8 km north of Banī Bikhīt, by the Gabal Abū Ṣīr, Al-Barqī = Πυργωτός is also a possibility. Neighbourhood relationships between the Koma, Tekmi and Tilothis toparchies are revealed by the fact that quite a few of their villages are repeatedly listed together in documents such as *P.Lille* I 59, *P.Cair.Zen.* IV 59782 (b) and *BGU* XIV 2370[8].

The northernmost village in the Ἄγημα toparchy which can be identified with a modern one is Πεεναμεύς (modern Bahnamūh), assigned to Ἄγημα κάτω in the first century B.C., but to the Μέση

---

[1] On the combination of these criteria, cf. JAN QUAEGEBEUR, «Documents grecs et géographie historique. Le Mendésien», *Colloques internationaux du C.N.R.S. N° 595. L'Égyptologie en 1979. Axes Prioritaires de recherches*, Paris 1982, Tome I, pp.267-272.

[2] See below, pp.21 ff.

[3] It was in its own toparchy (περὶ Βούσιριν) in the Roman period.

[4] As suggested by TIMM, *Das christlich-koptische Ägypten*, vol.V, p.2154.

[5] «Verläuft von südlich Banī Suwaif nördlich ausholend über an-Nuwaira nach Ihnāsiyā al-Madīna. Im Gelände ohne Vorwissen wohl kaum zu erkennen» (*TAVO B 69*, pp.49-52).

[6] *TAVO B 69*, § 4.3 (M 109).

[7] *Stud.Pal.* X 211, 212 and 213 suggest connections between the Tekmi, Agema and Techtho toparchies: see *Catalogue*, s.v. ΚΟΛΛΑΣΟΥΧΑ.

[8] *P.Lille* I 59 and *P.Cair.Zen.* IV 59782 (b) date from the third century B.C., *BGU* XIV 2370 from the first century B.C. See also *Catalogue*, s.v. ΒΟΥΣΙΡΙΣ.

INTRODUCTION

in the third century A.D.[1]. The modern village is on the Baḥr Yūsuf, but the Coptic *Life of the Apa Epima* suggests that in ancient times it was the village of Πεενσαμοι that functioned as its port[2]: this in turn can be identified with modern Al-Bahsamūn (about 4.5 km SW of Πεεναμεύς/Bahnamūh) or, more precisely, with the nearby Al Kōm Al Ahmar. The modern Baḥr skirts this village, which the documents assigned to the Πέραν toparchy, «on the other (i.e. western) side» of the ancient canal: Peensamoi must have been near the northern limit of this toparchy, which extended to Σιναρυ/Sinara, almost 30 km south of Al-Bahsamūn (just east of the Old Baḥr Yūsuf, as shown on *SEM*) a border-line village between the Herakleopolite and Oxyrhynchite nomes[3].

We may assume that the Old Baḥr Yūsuf, running near Peensamoi, separated the Πέραν toparchy from the northern (κάτω) Ἄγημα toparchy, while the (shifting) boundary between Ἄγημα κάτω and Μέση must have been near Peenameus. The links between Πέραν and Ἄγημα were close[4]: both toparchies extended in a north-south direction, along the opposite sides of the Old Baḥr Yūsuf. The Ἄγημα toparchy (on the eastern side) was divided into a Northern (κάτω) and a Southern (ἄνω) Ἄγημα; dyke no.12[5] may have marked the boundary between the two. The southernmost Ἄγημα village should be Κορφοτοι/Al-Gafādūn, about 27 km south of Πεεναμεύς/Bahnamūh, east of the ancient course of the Baḥr Yūsuf (though modern Al-Gafādūn is west of the present course of the Baḥr)[6]. Other identifications are possible, with varying degrees of certainty: Νινω (in the κάτω Ἄγημα toparchy) is Nina, 6 km SE of Πεεναμεύς/Bahnamūh; the best preserved dyke (dyke no.13) ran about one km north of it[7]. Alilais (in the ἄνω Ἄγημα) could be Hillīya, a now dismantled archaeological site 9 km south of Νινω/Nina; 3.5 km west of Hillīya, Badahl could be ancient Πεταχορ. In the first century B.C., the village of Peenameus is assigned to the Ἄγημα κάτω in *BGU* XIV 2437, but to the Μέση toparchy in *CPR* I 64 and *Stud.Pal.* XX 28 (which date from about three centuries later): while this is an indication that the toparchy called the Μέση bordered on the Ἄγημα κάτω, it seems difficult to conclude that the name Μέση actually stood for (Ἄγημα) Μέση. For one thing, the full name Ἄγημα Μέση is not attested in any document among those published to this date; furthermore, there is very little space left for the Ἄγημα κάτω north of Peenameus/Bahnamūh and south of Herakleopolis/Ihnāsiya al-Madīna. I think we may safely conclude that the Ἄγημα toparchy was divided into Northern (Κάτω) and Southern (Ἄνω) Ἄγημα, while the Μέση was probably east of the Ἄγημα κάτω, and bordered on the Arsinoite nome. In fact, one or more villages of the Μέση toparchy may have been identical with those bearing the same names, and appearing elsewhere in an Arsinoite setting: in such cases we should assume that these villages changed loyalties, as it were, at different times, or even just in different documents, but under different circumstances[8]. Φνεβιεύς, for example, is well attested as the main centre of the Μέση toparchy in

---

[1] A similar "shifting" (from Ἄγημα to Μέση) occurs in the case of Sisine (see *Catalogue, s.v.* ΣΙΣΙΝΗ) .

[2] See *Catalogue, s.v.* ΠΕΕΝΑΜΕΥΣ.

[3] Only documents of the Ptolemaic period assign this village to the Herakleopolites: in later times, Sinary is invariably recorded for the Oxyrhynchites,

[4] See *Catalogue, s.vv.* ΝΙΣΕΥΣ, ΤΕΡΤΟΝΠΕΤΕΧΩΝΣ, ΠΕΤΑΧΟΡ.

[5] «Verläuft über Abu Surbān weiter südlich von Ṣaft Rašin nach Santūr. In Westteil noch einigermaßen zu erkennen» (*TAVO B 69*, pp.49-52).

[6] Cf. *TAVO B 69*, pp.44-45: «Die *Description de l'Égypte* zeigt offensichtlich in diesem Bereich, wie dies sonst im ganzen Untersuchungsbereich der Fall war und ist, einen Verlauf des Baḥr Yūsuf nahe am Wüstenrand. Dieser ältere Baḥr Yūsuf ist noch heute gut zu verfolgen ...».

[7] «Der Deich erstreckt sich über ca.8 km Luftlinie vom Baḥr Yūsuf über Kafr Abū Sahba [*via* Al-Mašariqa] zum Muḥīt-Drain. Nur am östlichen und westlichen Ende des Deichs sowie im Dorf Kafr Abū Sahba ist der Deich stärker abgetragen, z.T. bis auf Fruchtlandniveau, ansonsten ist der Erhaltungszustand sehr gut. Teilweise (insbesondere im Bereich der westlichen Teiche) sind sogar die schrägen Böschungen jedoch bis zur Senkrechten seitlich abgegraben, um zusätzlich Ackerflächen zu gewinnen. Der Deich dient über die gesamte Länge als Fahrweg» (*TAVO B 69*, pp.49-52): it is marked in Sheet 68/60 of the 1917 Egypt Survey Map.

[8] For instance: it appears that the nomarchy of Achoapis «did not coincide with nome boundaries, but included parts of

various documents of the first century B.C.: the same place-name, however, first appears in two *Petrie Papyri* (*P.Petr.* III 43 (2); *P.Petr.* III 62 b) in association with a number of Arsinoite villages, all of them involved in the work of canal-maintenance, under the supervision of the nomarch Achoapis. And the place-name Thmoinothis, attested for the Μέση toparchy in the Herakleopolites[1], may perhaps also be detected in *P.Petr.* III 43 (2). The *Petrie Papyri* were extracted from mummy-cases found by Sir Flinders Petrie at Sidmant al-Gebel, 10 km SW of Hawwārah ʿAdlān. In the same area, Πτολεμαῒς Ὅρμου (modern Al-Lāhūn, east of dyke no.17) is invariably assigned to the Arsinoites, but Hawwārah ʿAdlān and Kōm Madīnat Gurāb (both west of the same dyke) could be identified with the Herakleopolite Αὔηρις (which a document assigns to the Μέση toparchy) and Magdola, respectively[2]. As for Thmoinothis, this could be modern Mayyāna, about 7 km south of Sidmant. Another place mentioned in the *Petrie Papyri* is Ἱερὰ Νῆσος τῆς Πο(λέμωνος μερίδος) (*P.Petr.* III 66, col.III,15): this is distinguished, in the same document, from the homonymous village in the Herakleides division of the same (Arsinoite) nome, but may well have been the Ἱερὰ Νῆσος which some documents connect to Herakleopolite villages[3]. *P.Tebt.* III 828 (about 139 B.C.) shows the Ἱερὰ Νῆσος in the Polemon division to have been by the Μοντιλα ποταμός, possibly the name of the canal flowing from the Old Baḥr Yūsuf towards the Arsinoites. It could be that Phnebieus and Θμοινωθις/Mayyāna also lay by this canal, where it was still within the territory of the Herakleopolite nome, while Ἱερὰ Νῆσος was further down, therefore administratively belonging to the Polemon meris of the Arsinoites. If so, these villages would have common obligations, regardless of nome boundaries, with respect to canal-maintenance. The documents do not tell us which toparchy Τρικωμία[4], Λευκόγιον and Δικωμία belonged to, but the contexts in which they are mentioned make it clear that they, too, must have been in the area we are dealing with. These all are homonymous with Arsinoite localities: likewise, Tebetny of the Πέραν toparchy certainly was a different village from its Arsinoite namesake (modern Dafadnu)[5].

The well-attested links between the Πέραν toparchy, particularly Πεενσαμοι/Al-Bahsamūn, and Τεχθω (main centre of its own toparchy) support the phonetically likely identification Τεχθω = Daštūt (6 km south of Al-Bahsamūn, almost in direct line). The full name of this toparchy was Τεχθω Νῆσος, denoting a "new land" formation: the traces of a dried-up canal (the Old Baḥr Yūsuf, presumably[6]) are still to be seen, midway between Daštūt and Ṣaft Rašīn; parallel to the canal, an ancient dyke ran in a north-south direction[7]. Ṣaft Rašīn (an important archaeological site, about 4 km east of Daštūt/Τεχθω, and about 5 km south of Nina/Νινω) was built on slightly raised ground, like Νινω/Nina and all other villages that

---

more than one nome» (*P.Hib.* II 205,27 adn.), namely the northern part of the meris of Herakleides (Arsinoites), but also part of the Memphite and Herakleopolite nomes. In other words: «Even administrative subdivisions did not always follow the nome boundaries» (WILLY CLARYSSE, «Philadelpheia and the Memphites in the Zenon Archive», in *Studies on Ptolemaic Memphis (Studia Hellenistica 24)*, p.99). See also WILLY PEREMANS - EDMOND VAN'T DACK, «Hérakleia, Hiera Nésos, Kerkéésis, Niseus, villages homonymes», in *Prosopographica (Studia Hellenistica 9)*, Louvain-Leiden 1953, pp.62-66.

[1] CPR I 64 attests a connection between Thmoinothis and Peenameus.

[2] Homonymous villages are very well attested for the Arsinoites, and identified with modern localities in the Fayūm: the Arsinoite Αὔηρις is now called Hawwārah Al-Makta; Magdola of the same name is Madīnat Nehas.

[3] See *Catalogue*, s.v. See CALDERINI-DARIS, *Dizionario*, s.v. ΙΕΡΑ ΝΗΣΟΣ, for a complete list of papyri mentioning this place-name.

[4] Trikomia occurs once with Hiera Nesos and several Herakleopolite villages in the same document (*BGU* VIII 1808); see *Catalogue, s.vv.*

[5] In general, the frequent occurrence of homonyms among Egyptian place-names can be explained by their referring to recurring features in the natural and human landscape.

[6] Cf. *TAVO B 69*, p.50: «... nicht der heutige Flußlauf [of the Baḥr Yūsuf] ... sondern ein noch bei Linant de Bellefonds an Deichen erkennbarer älterer Flußlauf westlich Ṣaft Rašīn».

[7] Cf. *TAVO B 69*, pp.49-52: «... bedeutender Deich ... ein Stück weit östlich Ṣaft Rašīn in süd-nördlicher Richtung verlaufend - nach Linant de Bellefonds zum vor-neuzeitlichen Bestand gehören muß».

INTRODUCTION

were situated halfway between the Nile and the Baḥr Yūsuf[1]. Like several other places in Egypt that bear the name Ṣaft, it should be identified with an ancient Σῶβθις[2]: one is in fact well attested in the περὶ Πόλιν toparchy, and could be made to coincide with Ṣaft Rašin by assuming that the περὶ Πόλιν toparchy was long and narrow, like the Πέραν and Ἄγημα toparchies[3].

Πάπα = Bibā is the northernmost identifiable village in the περὶ Φέβιχιν toparchy, which was also called Κωίτης[4]. The area north of Papa was probably split between the Tekmi and Phebichis toparchies: the villages of Peentechy and Tanaso (both in the Tekmi toparchy) and that of Tosachmis (Phebichis toparchy), which were apparently a short distance from each other, must have been in this part of the nome. Τάβοκλις seems to have been in a similar location: it was in the Tekmi toparchy and associated with Τοχοντωυ, but also connected with Ψελέμαχις, which was in the Phebichis toparchy. Given the proximity of Τοχοντωυ to Τωυ (the two villages share the same komogrammateus in *BGU* XVI 2597), and provided that the identification Τωυ/Tuwa is accepted, it follows that the border between περὶ Τεκμι and περὶ Φέβιχιν was not too far from here. Phebichis itself should in my opinion be identified with Al-Fašn, to this day the main centre in this area. Modern Ṭalā, in a central location 7.5 km NW of Al-Fašn/Φέβιχις, could be identified with ancient Ταλαη, also in the Phebichis toparchy, which the documents connect with Ψῦχις (modern Absūg[5], about 4 km SE of Ṭalā); but an identification Ṭalā = Ταλαώ (in the Northern toparchy of the Oxyrhynchites)[6] has also been suggested, in view of the equation Talt wal-Qulīya (3.5 km SW of Ṭalā) = Θῶλθις. Tholthis was in the Northern toparchy of the Oxyrhynchites, like Ταλαώ and a few other villages, Σεσφθα and one of the three Oxyrhynchite localities called Ψῶβθις among them[7]. The identification of Ṣaft al-Hirsa with this Ψῶβθις also seems safe[8], while Ṣaft al ʿUrafā (2.5 km east of Ṣaft al-Hirsa/Ψῶβθις, and 5 km SW of Absūg/Ψῦχις) could be equated with Ψεβθονεμβη[9], but also with Ψεβθονπένουφις (both these villages were in the Phebichis

---

[1] These are the «leichte Höhenrücken im Bassingebiet die in Nord-Südrichtung verlaufen und die Deiche queren» (*TAVO B 69*, p.69).

[2] The identification of Ṣaft Rašin with Σεσφθα (in the Northern toparchy of the Oxyrhynchite nome) has been tentatively suggested in *TAVO B 69* § 4.3, p.92 (M 91), and dubitatively accepted by JANE ROWLANDSON, *Landowners and Tenants in Roman Egypt. The Social Relations of Agriculture in the Oxyrhynchite Nome*, Oxford 1996, p.XIII and p.15 n.35. In order to justify this identification phonetically, *TAVO B 69* needs to postulate that: «Bei Ṣaft Rašin liegt ein Spezialfall vor», which would allow Ṣaft to derive in this case from Se(s)phta (rather than from Sobthis, as is normally the case): see however the different etymology proposed by Jan Quaegebeur, *OLP* 4, 1973, p.90, n.47 (detecting the name of the god Ptah as the second component in this toponym: «le bois/ la place ou le bassin de Ptah»; Quaegebeur further refers to an article by JEAN YOYOTTE, *Annuaire de l'EPHE, Section des Sciences Religieuses* 79, 1971-1972, p.192). From the topographical point of view, the Northern toparchy of the Oxyrhynchites did probably form a wedge between the Koites and the southernmost villages of the Herakleopolites which were near the Baḥr Yūsuf (Korphotoi, occasionally Sinary): it seems unlikely, however, for this wedge to extend as far as Ṣaft Rašin (see below, p.12).

[3] The proximity of the περὶ Πόλιν to the Ἄγημα, but also to the Tekmi toparchy (and the Koites?) seems to be implied by *P.Select.* 17 (for περὶ Πόλιν and Ἄγημα) and *Stud.Pal.* XX 26 (see *s.vv.* ΤΑΝΑΣΩ and ΤΟΚΩΙΣ). Again, these multiple neighbourhood relationships are best explained by assuming long and narrow toparchies. This assumption, however, is not reconcilable with the tempting identification of Qilla (about 11 km NE of Ṣaft Rašin) with Κέλλα, a village attested in just one document, which apparently assigns it to the northern (κάτω) Ἄγημα toparchy: its identification with Qilla would require the Ἄγημα to extend well beyond the limits that are compatible with a long and narrow περὶ Πόλιν.

[4] The Koites must have derived its name from Ko, a locality only rarely attested in the Greek documents, and apparently superseded by Phebichis as the main centre in the toparchy. On the location of Ko, see *Catalogue, s.v.* ΚΩ.

[5] As in *TAVO B 69* § 4.3 (M 68).

[6] Cf. *TAVO B 69* § 4.3 (M 73).

[7] Cf. *P.Oxy.* XLVII 3333 (92 A.D.); XIV 1659 (218-222 A.D.); XXIV 2422 (290 A.D.); X 1285 and XII 1529 (III A.D.).

[8] Cf. *TAVO B 69*, § 4.3 (M66, M71).

[9] *TAVO B 65* § 4.3 (M 65), following JEAN YOYOTTE, *RdE*, 15, 1963, p.108.

toparchy); the name of one or other of these two may survive as 'Izben Ṣaft (a little more than 2 km south of Ṣafṭ al 'Urafā). It appears then that the Oxyrhynchites (more precisely, the Κάτω toparchy of this nome) here formed a wedge between the Phebichis toparchy and the southern end of Ἄγημα (where Κορφοτοι/Al-Gafādūn was), and that the border between the Herakleopolites and the Oxyrhynchites ran exactly between Ṣaft al-Hirsa and Ṣaft al 'Urafā, then east of Tholthis to the Old Baḥr Yūsuf. Ptolemy's description of a river-branch rejoining the Nile at 'Αγκυρῶν πόλις/Al-Hība might even be accommodated here, by assuming the existence of a canal also serving as a border between the two districts. The hydro-geographical situation in this area was in any case different from the one recorded in *SEM*, and this should account for the shifting boundary between the two districts, whereby Σιναρυ/Sinarā and Τααμωρου/Dahmarū (just 2 km north of Πάλωσις/Bilhasā, which the sources invariably locate in the Oxyrhynchites[1]) were at different times assigned to one or the other nome. Malatiya, 5 km east and about 2 km north of Τααμωρου/Dahmarū, could be ancient Μόλωθις, attested by one first century B.C. document which locates it in the Koites.

The Koites may have at least partly coincided with the "uncanonical" Nineteenth Nome ("of the He-Goat"), which appears in some pre-Ptolemaic lists of nomes, immediately south of the Herakleopolites (this used to be the Twentieth Nome)[2]; and part of the northern Oxyrhynchites (in particular the Κάτω toparchy) may well have been included in the Nome of the He-Goat. An ancient tradition of autonomy for this area could account for the later variability of the boundaries in the region.

On the east bank of the Nile, the Herakleopolites clearly extended south far beyond the border with the Oxyrhynchites on the west bank: Ἱππώνων/Qarāra is invariably assigned by the sources to the Koites which, on this side of the river, may well have bordered on the Kynopolites.

In 313/314 A.D., just six years after toparchies had been superseded by *pagi*[3], *P.Michael*. 28 assigns some villages of the Koites (Pselemachis, Thelbo, Thneis and Philonikou) to the 12th *pagus*; other sources assign Koba to the same (12th) *pagus*, Phebichis to the 11th *pagus*. This information is interesting for different reasons: first, it shows that the numbering of the *pagi* was obviously continued from the 10th and northernmost *pagus* of the Oxyrhynchite nome; secondly, the fact that the villages of the Koites were distributed between two *pagi* is consistent with the distinction between a Northern and a Southern Koites, as attested in the documents of the Roman period. As the numbering of the *pagi* proceeded from south to north, we may conclude that the Southern Koites corresponded to the 11th *pagus*, the Northern Koites to the 12th *pagus*: consequently, the villages of the 12th *pagus* must have been to the north of Phebichis/Al-Fašn (as Papa/Bibā in fact is). A third conclusion concerns the location of the 10th and 11th *pagi*, which may have more or less adjoined one another: the 10th *pagus*, roughly coinciding with the Northern toparchy of the Oxyrhynchites, will have faced towards the Old Baḥr Yūsuf; the 11th *pagus*, corresponding to the Southern Koites, fronted on the Nile. The village of Sesphtha (which we know to have been in the 10th *pagus*) will have been approximately on the same latitude as Phebichis, and in any case certainly not farther north than Papa/Bibā (which was in the 12th *pagus*): its identification with Ṣaft Rašin seems therefore impossible. Πεενσαμου/Al-Bahsamūn and Καινή, two villages that used to be in the Πέραν, came to belong to the 13th *pagus*, which can thus be located next to, and east of the 12th *pagus*.

---

[1] See PRUNETI, *Centri abitati*, s.v.

[2] Cf. *TAVO B 69*, pp.12-13; the «Ziegengau» is «unkanonisch» because «oft übergangen» in the pre-Ptolemaic lists of nomes: *ibid.*, p.11 n.28.

[3] Cf. J. LALLEMAND, *L'Administration civile de l'Égypte de l'avènement de Dioclétien à la création du diocèse (284-382)*, Bruxelles 1964, p.97 f.

3 Documents mentioning Herakleopolite toponyms: Time-distribution, provenance and contents[1]

An integrated analysis of the time-distribution, provenance and contents of the papyri mentioning Herakleopolite toponyms makes it possible to sort out what may at first seem a bewildering mass of material into groups of papyri, each consisting of documents found at one particular site, though later dispersed. Clearly, in terms of proving the existence of a certain place, a large number of documents, if coming from the same site and dating from the same time, weigh as much as a single source from another site and/or a different time. The same provenance for most, or even all sources for one village, then, may account for its being attested only within a limited time-span: it would be misleading to deduce from this that the village did not exist before, or ceased to exist afterwards.

In what follows, I shall take *provenance* to mean the *place where a papyrus was found*. Thus defined, the *provenance* does not necessarily coincide with, indeed it often differs from the place where a papyrus was written, which I shall call its *origin*. Moreover, both *provenance* and *origin* may differ from places mentioned in the text (*internal evidence*). In many cases, of course, the *origin* and *provenance* of a document, as defined above, may be one and the same place, which in turn may well coincide with, or be near or somehow related to places the text refers to (*internal evidence*)[2].

Documents that mention Herakleopolite toponyms, but have no, or no certain Herakleopolite origin, are considered separately. Such papyri (more numerous for the Roman and Byzantine periods) while contributing *internal evidence* on various Herakleopolite villages, actually originate from neighbouring nomes (Arsinoites and Oxyrhynchites) or, in a few cases, from more distant sites.

1. Documents from the Herakleopolites. From the third to the first century B.C.

1.1. Documents of the third century B.C.

Most information concerning the Herakleopolite nome in the third century B.C. derives from two major cartonnage finds, in the southern (Al-Hība) and northern (Kōm Madīnat Gurān) parts of the district, respectively. Both finds go back to the beginning of the twentieth century. The information provided by the Kōm Madīnat Gurān texts is supplemented by a few papyri from the Zenon archive, besides two or three *Petrie Papyri* (Kōm Madīnat Gurāb find). Recent additions to our documentation for the third century B.C. appeared on the antiquities market around 1980.

P.Hib. II 198 has a completely different character from the other sources under consideration here: it «is not cartonage and was not found at El-Hibeh, but was bought at Illahun in the winter of 1902-3. Its provenance is therefore uncertain»[3]; this is a royal ordinance on security measures to be taken along the Nile: it mentions Techtho, where a guard-post is also attested by *P.Strasb.* II 103 and 104[4].

---

[1] See the *Chronological Index*, pp.295-304.

[2] Conversely, a papyrus may have a *first origin* (e.g. in the case of a letter: the place where it was written) and a *second origin* (at the recipient's end), neither of which coincides with its *provenance*.

[3] *P.Hib.* II, p.74 f., where the Editor adds that: «Its provenance is therefore uncertain, but a number of indications ... suggest that it was a place on the river Nile between Memphis and Hermopolis».

[4] The provenance of *P.Strasb.* II 103 and 104 is discussed on p.14 n.6.

THE HERAKLEOPOLITE NOME

1.1.1. Documents from Al-Hība.

When Grenfell and Hunt came to Al-Hība, in March 1902, somebody had already been there:

«By far the greater part [of the necropolis] had been dug out before our arrival, principally in 1895-1896, when, as report states, an Arab dealer from the Pyramids, known as Shêkh Hassan, excavated the cemetery on a large scale. From the assertions of an inhabitant of Hibeh who was then employed as a *reis*, it appears that the dealer met with much success ... Quantities of mummies of the Ptolemaic period with papyrus-cartonnage were also unearthed, but thrown away as worthless. This is the usual fate of cartonnage found in the Nile valley proper, where, except at one or two places, native tomb-diggers until quite recently attached no value to papyrus apart from large rolls. A handful of small fragments, however, found their way to Cairo, where they were bought by us in 1896 [1]. During the next few years much plundering continued at Hibeh ...» [2].

Much material was sold to other buyers [3] as well, particularly to the Deutsches Papyruskartell [4]. Three criteria may be defined, which in combination guarantee that a document originates from Al-Hība: (1) a date in the third century B.C.; (2) re-use for the manufacturing of papyrus-cartonnage; (3) reference to one or more villages of the southern Herakleopolites [5] (or of the northern Oxyrhynchites). All three apply not just to a large number of the *Hibeh Papyri*, but also to many documents in the Strasbourg collection [6], to the papyri of the Gradenwitz collection (later sold to the Fuad I University in Cairo) [7], and to papyri in

---

[1] These were published as part of *P.Grenfell* II in the following year.

[2] *P.Hib.* I, *Introduction*, p.2. See also the report by AHMED BEY KAMAL, *ASAE* 2, 1901, pp.84-91, who was sent to Al-Hība by the Egyptian authorities the year before Grenfell and Hunt were authorized to excavate there.

[3] Cf. *P.Hib.* II, *Preface*, p.VI: «It is clear ... that apart from the documents formerly at Berlin, published in *BGU* VI, a not inconsiderable number of texts from this site are now in the collections at Hamburg and at Heidelberg. A few pieces are at Manchester, and possibly El-Hibeh is the origin of some of the texts in Strasbourg». See also *L.Ä.* II 1180-1181.

[4] On the acquisitions by the Deutsches Papyruskartell, on behalf of various German Universities, between 1906 and the beginning of the First World War, see: KARL PREISENDANZ, *Papyrusfunde und Papyrusforschung*, Leipzig 1933, p.210 f.; ERWIN ARNOLD, «Die Papyrussammlung der Bayerischen Staatsbibliothek. Ein historischer Abriß», in *P.Münch.* I (repr. 1986), pp.*11-12; OLIVER PRIMAVESI, «Zur Geschichte des Deutschen Papyruskartells», *ZPE* 114, 1996, pp.173-187.

[5] Connections with other parts of the nome account for the fact that villages of other toparchies are mentioned in three *P.Hib.* documents (see *Catalogue, s.vv.* ΣΙΣΙΝΗ, ΦΥΣ, ΒΟΥΣΙΡΙΣ): these documents are too few, in fact, to suppose that they were part of a batch originating from another part of the nome, and re-cycled for mummy-cartonnage.

[6] The connection between *P.Strasb.* VII 641-643 and some *P.Hib.* documents is recognized in the introduction to *P.Strasb.* VII 641; see also the introduction to *P.Strasb.* IX 802: under the same inventory number (P.gr.2354) «quatre fragments de cartonnage, dont un démotique, provenant visiblement de Hibeh» are also recorded. Three of the Strasbourg papyri in our *Chronological Index* (II 111; II 113; V 563) belong to the archive of Harmachis, which was reassembled by WILLY CLARYSSE, *Anc.Soc.* 7,1976, pp.185-207: he observes (p.191 f.) that «all belong to a group of papyri formerly in the possession of the Wissenschaftliche Gesellschaft ... all come from the same mummy cartonnage, which also included *P.Strasb.* II 103-108». *P.Strasb.* 103 and 104 appear in our *Chronological Index*.

[7] See *Vorbemerkung* to *P.Grad.* (p.5): «Die folgenden Texte ... haben offensichtlich mit den *P.Hibeh* die gleiche Herkunft und gehören, abgesehen von den meist aus der Regierung von Philopator stammenden Vorträgen, z.T. sicher, zum andern Teil vermutlich, zu den Akten des aus den *P.Hibeh* bekannten Κλείταρχος τραπεζίτης τοῦ Κωίτου»; cf. also the *Introduction* to *P.Fuad Crawford* (p.I): «In 1938 the Fuad I University bought a collection of ancient papyri which had belonged to the late Professor O. Gradenwitz. A few of those published by Plaumann [the *P.Grad.*] are now missing».
The documents from the ex-Gradenwitz collection in our *Chronological Index* are: *P.Fuad Crawford* (*App.* I) 3 and 4; *P.Fuad Crawford* (*App.* II) 66 *recto* (mentioning Psebthonembe, which also appears in *P.Hib.* I 33); *P.Grad.* 3; *SB* III 6301. *P.Fuad Crawford* 5, containing a list of villages in the Koites much like that of *P.Strasb.* IX 802, is in my opinion likely to come from Al-Hība, too: I therefore propose to re-date it to the middle of the third century B.C., as opposed to the first century B.C. dating tentatively proposed in the *ed.pr.* Note that its Gradenwitz inventory number (Grad. 198) places this papyrus immediately after the fragment of a letter to the banker Kleitarchos (*P.Fuad Crawford*, App.II, 20 = inv. Grad.197); the Gradenwitz inventory nos. of *P.Grad.* 3 and *P.Fuad Crawford,* App.I, 3 and 4 are Grad.159 and 160, respectively.

INTRODUCTION

Heidelberg [1], Hamburg [2], Berlin [3], besides other German collections [4].

SB X 10447 (*P.Sorbonne* inv. 2073; previously in the Reinach collection) must have the same provenance [5], although no reference to cartonnage origin is made in the *editio princeps*. This document can be dated to the third century B.C., and it mentions three localities in the Koites; like the *P.Reinach*, it may have been bought «au cours d'un voyage assez rapide que j'ai fait en Egypte pendant l'hiver 1901/1902» [6], just when material from Al-Hiba appeared on the market, alerting Grenfell and Hunt to the potentialities of the site.

Like *SB* X 10447, *P.Ross.Georg.* II 3 provides internal evidence of its provenance from Al-Hiba: it is dated to 226/225 B.C., and it refers to the Koites; besides, there exist very close links between *P.Ross.Georg.* II 1-2 and a cartonnage papyrus now in Jena (inv.nr. 901) [7].

BGU XIV 2391 and 2392 were obtained, like *BGU* XIV 2380 (contract drawn at Κυνῶν πόλις in 265 B.C.) «aus Probeauflösungen kleinerer Sargfragmente, die in den sechziger und siebziger Jahren durch J. Hofmann und seinen Vorgängner, M. Brzyski, erfolgten»: the village there mentioned (Νεχιση) is not elsewhere attested, so that there is no means of knowing whether it too was in the Kynopolites. In view of the connections between this nome and the Koites, it would not be surprising to find Kynopolite localities mentioned in papyri from Al-Hiba cartonnage.

Finally, the numerous literary papyri also obtained from the Al-Hiba mummy-cases testify to a quite refined level of Greek cultural life in this area during the early Ptolemaic period [8].

1.1.2. Documents from Kōm Madīnat Gurān.

These documents were obtained from the cartonnage of mummy-cases found at Kōm Madīnat Guran («Ghorân» in the edition; at the western edge of the Bahr al-Gharāq basin, in the southern Fayūm) during the excavations there and at Madīnat en-Nahas by Pierre Jouguet and Gaston Lefebvre in 1901 and 1902 [9]. Their present location is at the Sorbonne in Paris; other material from the same find is in Cairo [10]. At least three documents in our *Chronological Index* were obtained from the same mummy-case

---

[1] In our *Chronological Index*: *P.Bad.= VBP* IV 82. See *P.Bad.* IV, *Einleitung*, p.6: «Es ist ein merkwürdiger Zufall, daß, während wir ... keine Papyruskartonage fanden, die Heidelberger Universitätsbibliothek eine Anzahl solcher Kartonagefetzen besitzt, die offenbar den Raubgrabungen von Schêch Hassan in Hîbeh entstammen. Es sind meistens literarische Stücke, doch auch einige Urkundenfetzen».

[2] In our *Chronological Index*: *P.Hamb.* III 202. See also next footnote.

[3] In our *Chronological Index*: *BGU* X 1911, mentioning the village of Δικωμία, which also appears in *P.Hib.* I 47. In his *Vorwort* to *BGU* X (p.5), Wolfgang Müller noticed that: «Diese überwiegend aus dem Gau von Oxyrhynchos stammenden Urkunden stehen sachlich in enger Beziehung zu ähnlichen, aus Mumienkartonage gewonnenen Verträgen in *BGU* VI, *P.Hib.* I und II, *P.Hamb.* II, *P.Grad.*, *P.Frankfurt* u.a. und können dadurch in vielen Fällen sinngemäß ergänzt werden».

[4] *SB* VIII 9841 (247 B.C.; from cartonnage; reference to a village of the Koites: therefore included in our *Chronological Index*) is at Jena, together with three more papyri belonging, like *BGU* X 1911 (see n.10), to Kallistratos' correspondence. Jena owns an abundance of papyri from Al-Hiba cartonnage: cf. FRITZ UEBEL, «Die Jenaer Papyrussammlung», *Proceedings of the twelfth International Congress of Papyrology*, Toronto 1970, pp.491-495.

[5] Like *P.Sorbonne* 9-12: cf. UEBEL, «Die Jenaer Papyrussammlung», p.493.

[6] *P.Reinach*, *Préface*, p.I. The internal evidence of *P.Rein.* 98 (109 A.D.) points in fact to the Koites (see *s.v.*): see below, pp.25 f., 28 f., for documents of the second and third century A.D. also originating from Al-Hiba.

[7] UEBEL, «Die Jenaer Papyrussammlung», p.493.

[8] MARIA ROSARIA FALIVENE, «The Literary Papyri from Al-Hiba: a new approach?», *21. Internationaler Papyrologenkongress* (Berlin, 13.-19. August 1995), forthcoming.

[9] Cf. *P.Lille*, *Préface*, p.1. Excavations report: PIERRE JOUGUET, *BCH* 25, 1901, pp.380-411.

[10] *P.Enteux.*, *Préface* (by Pierre Jouguet), pp.V-VI: «Selon l'usage alors en vigueur [the documents from Kōm Madīnat Gurān and Madīnat en-Nahas] ont été partagés entre l'Égypte et la France; les uns sont à l'Institut de Papyrologie de Paris, les

(«Ghorân 288»): *P.Enteux.* 61 (mentioning a village called Φαινίππου), *SB* III 7176 (φορτία λιβανωτικά to the Koites) and *SB* III 7179 (maintenance work on the canals to be paid for with money from the bank at Phys). The last two documents belong to the correspondence of Kresilaos, who could be the agent of the oikonomos Ammonios, appearing in two more documents from mummy «Ghorân 288» and also known from the Zenon archive[1]. The same Kresilaos may be the addressee of *P.Lille* I 6, reporting an episode of brigandage: the writer has been assaulted on his way from Tebetny to Korphotoi. An act of piracy against a boat sailing to Τμοιένετις (= Θμοίνωθις?) is reported in *P.Coll.Youtie* I 7, the most recent addition to the group[2]. In view of the provenance of these documents, it is not surprising that many of them should refer to villages in the Ἄγημα κάτω, Μέση and Πέραν, probably the three Herakleopolite toparchies most easily connected with the Arsinoites[3]: *P.Lille* I 31 mentions Niseus and Tertonpetechon, and *SB* III 7203[4] has entries for Thmoinothis and Phys. The provenance of *P.Lille* I 59 is said to be «Magdôla» (i.e. Madînat en-Nehas), not «Ghorân»: the document mentions place-names of the Koma, Tilothis and Tekmi toparchies.

Literary papyri were also obtained from the mummy-cases of Kōm Madînat Gurān[5].

1.1.3. Documents from Kōm Madînat Gurāb.

The mummy-cases of the *Petrie Papyri* were found by Petrie in 1899 at Kōm Madînat Gurāb[6], a site in the area between the Herakleopolite and the Arsinoite nomes: Thmoinothis and Phnebieus[7] (both probably in the Μέση toparchy) are mentioned in *P.Petrie* III 43 (2), which deals with maintenance work on a canal possibly connecting the two nomes. *P.Petrie* III 99 has a reference to Φιλονίκου (in the Koites).

1.1.4. Documents from (?) now in Vienna and Genoa.

The following four papyri, now in the possession of different institutions[8], may, I suspect, come from one

---

autres au Musée du Caire». Unpublished papyri from this find are at the Sorbonne (information from Willy Clarysse).

[1] *P.Pt.* I 1008 + add.; see also *Guide to the Zenon Archive. Prosopography, s.vv.* In *P.Cair.Zen.* III 59368 (see below, p.24) the oikonomos Ammonios again appears in a Herakleopolite setting. *SB* III 7178 (one of the documents in Kresilaos' correspondence) is written to Ammonios by an agent of Sosibios. This Sosibios, obviously a high-ranking person (judging from the tone of this letter), could be the estate-holder known from *P.Tebt.* III 860. He could also be the Sosibios celebrated by Callimachus (*PPt* VI 17239), but later receiving a bad press in Polybius (cf. PAUL COLLART - PIERRE JOUGUET, «Petites recherches sur l'Economie Politique des Lagides», *Raccolta di scritti in onore di Giacomo Lumbroso*, Milano 1925, pp.109-134).

[2] Cf. *P.Coll.Youtie*, p.79: the document was obtained from the «chaussure d'un cartonnage de momie provenant de Magdôla ou de Ghorân (rien, dans l'inventaire, ne permet de decider entre ces deux sites)», but the reference to Τμοιενετις (if this may be taken as a variant spelling for Θμοινωθις) may make the provenance from Kōm Madînat Gurān more likely.

[3] See above, pp.8 ff.

[4] No mention of cartonnage is made in the *editio princeps* (MARCEL HOMBERT, *Revue Belge de Philologie et d'Histoire* 4, 1925, pp.633-676), but the inventory number (P.Sorbonne inv.572) suggests the same provenance as for *SB* III 7176-7179 (inv.578, 582, 581, 580).

[5] «Ce sont des momies de Ghorân qui contenaient les fragments de Comédies publiés en 1906» in *BCH*, pp.103-149 (these correspond to nos.1656 and 1657 Pack: New Comedy). A fragment of the *Odyssey* (no.1081 Pack), and ll.1-103 of Euripides' *Hippolytos* (no.393 Pack) have the same provenance. I wish to thank Tiina Purola (University of Helsinki) for providing me with this information.

[6] Cf. WILLY CLARYSSE, *The Petrie Papyri.* I, *Introduction*, p.11.

[7] Also mentioned in *P.Petrie* III 62 b.

[8] *P.Rain.Cent.* 40 and 44 (inv. P.Vindob G 40587 and 40586) are from the "Kauf Fackelmann 1979": cf. HELENE LOEBENSTEIN, «Vom "Papyrus Erzherzog Rainer" zum Papyrussammlung der Österreichischen Nationalbibliothek. 100 Jahre Sammeln, Bewahren, Edieren», in *P.Rain.Cent.*, vol.I, p.22 n.129. *PUG* III 114 was «acquistato sul mercato antiquario ...

INTRODUCTION

find. They are all obtained from cartonnage and acquired more or less at the same time; besides, they all mention villages in the northern part of the Herakleopolites. *P.Rain.Cent.* 40 mentions Hiera Nesos and Kollasoucha; *SB* XVI 12387 refers to Tanchais; *PUG* III 114 indicates Peentechy, Taemsis and Tanaso as intermediate stations in the transport of corn to Alexandria. *P.Rain.Cent.* 44, also dealing with the transport of corn, refers to Onnes, Thmoiobastis and Bousiris.

1.2. Documents of the second century B.C.

It is a likely hypothesis [1] that *P.Tebt.* III 703 contains the instructions of a dioiketes to an oikonomos: this is supported by the nature and contents of several papyri published in the same volume, also probably originating from the office of the oikonomos in the Herakleopolite nome. Further intriguing connections can be detected between certain *P.Tebt.*III documents and other papyri of the second century B.C. obtained from cartonnage, which have been more recently acquired on the antiquities market by different institutions (*P.Hels.*, *P.Duke*).

1.2.1. Documents from Umm al-Baragāt (P.Tebt. III)

The documents published in the third volume of the *Tebtunis Papyri* come from the cartonnage of human mummies found by Grenfell and Hunt at Umm al-Baragāt (the ancient Tebtynis) in the winter of 1899/1900 [2]. The site is «in the south of the Fayyûm on the desert side of the Bahr Gharak» [3]: discarded papyri from the Herakleopolites had already travelled along the same waterway to Kōm Madînat Gurān [4].

«Mummy 38» gave back a few receipts for police-tax (*P.Tebt.* III 838; 986-989; 991; 992) paid to the sitologoi of various Herakleopolite villages (in the toparchies Ἄγημα, περὶ Τεκμι, περὶ Πόλιν and Koites): all date from 139 B.C. and were issued by two officials called Apollodoros and Herakleides. *P.Tebt.* III 860, from the same mummy-case and dated about 138 B.C., originates probably from the same office [5]: it is an account recording payments for rent, use of pasture and various taxes (including the police-tax) from various villages, mostly in the Koites (though there is also an entry for Tilothis): the Σωσιβίου δωρεά is often referred to [6]. This office was probably that of the oikonomos in Herakleopolis: the contents of the other documents from the same mummy-case, all dated between 140/139 and 135/134 B.C., are consistent with this hypothesis [7].

---

nell'anno 1981» (*PUG* III, p.5 n.). *SB* XVI 12387 is a *P.Moen.*: this siglum designates papyri belonging to a Dutch private collection, several of which have been published by P.J. Sijpesteijn: cf. *Chr.Ég.* 54, 1979, p.273 («The provenance of these papyri is probably - like that of the other papyri of this collection which are like the papyri published here regained from mummy-cartonnage - the Arsinoite nome»).

[1] It has already been put forward in the introduction to the *editio princeps* of this document.

[2] See *P.Tebt.* IV, *Introduction*, p.1.

[3] BERNARD P. GRENFELL-ARTHUR S. HUNT, *APF* 1, 1901, p.376. On the recent excavations at Umm al-Baragāt see CLAUDIO GALLAZZI, «Fouilles anciennes et nouvelles sur le site de Tebtynis», *BIFAO* 89, 1989, pp.179-191.

[4] See above, p.15 f.

[5] Cf. especially l.38, which presumably refers to payments cashed by a sitologos but not conveyed «to us» (*sc.* Apollodoros and Herakleides?): [sitologos' name?] σιτολόγου ὧν οὐ προεῖται ἡμῖν.

[6] See above, p.16 n.1 (about Sosibios).

[7] *P.Tebt.* III 723 concerns pay and provisions to soldiers (cf. *P.Hels.* I 6, where the oikonomos appears in charge of this); *P.Tebt.* III 917 is similar to *P.Tebt.* III 723, though not so well preserved; *P.Tebt.* III 810 (referring to the Herakleopolite nome) contains a declaration on oath by the captain of a ship; *P.Tebt.* III 930 is addressed to an ἐπιμελητὴς Ἡρακλεοπολίτου. *P.Tebt.* III 913 mentions a σιτολόγος; *P.Tebt.* III 1006 lists various classes of cleruchs; *P.Tebt.* III 1013 and 1052 contain accounts, in wheat and in kind respectively; *P.Tebt.* III 929 is concerned with the payment of the diartaba, one of the taxes mentioned in *P.Tebt.* III 860.

A group of three papyri (*P.Tebt.* III 857[1]; 1044; 1045[2]) from «Mummy 6» have in common: (i) a date of *c.* 164 B.C., the crucial time in the struggle between Philometor and Euergetes II[3] (both *P.Tebt.* III 857 and *P.Tebt.* III 1044 refer to a seventh year, which must be the last of the joint reign of these two sovereigns); (ii) a reference to the village of Peensamoi. Their connection with the *P.Hels.*I papyri will be discussed below.

1.2.2. Papyri Helsingienses I. Their relation to P.Tebt.III

P.Hels. I 4-47 come from the head of a mummy-case acquired on the antiquities market in 1977: other material from the same cartonnage had been bought by the Österreichische Nationalbibliothek in 1976[4]. This group of documents originates from the archive of the oikonomoi of the Herakleopolite nome between about 165 and 159 B.C.[5] The oikonomoi whose names are preserved are Philippos(?) (164 B.C.; *P.Hels.* I 6), Dionysios (163/162-162/161 B.C.; *P.Hels.* I 9-20), Straton (160 B.C.; *P.Hels.* I 30-32) and Alexandros (159 B.C.; *P.Hels.* I 36-37), all of them previously unknown. The βασιλικὸς γραμματεύς Erasychis[6], however, who was already known from *P.Tebt.*III 857 (see above), reappears in *P.Hels.* I 6 and 7, which date from the same years; to these *P.Hels.* I 26[7] should be added, which has an entry for Peensamoi. Do *P.Tebt.* III 857, 1044 and 1045[8] originate from the same oikonomos' office as *P.Hels.* I 6,7 and 26?

1.2.3. The Duke papyri. Their relation to P.Tebt. III

SB XVIII 13304 (= *P.Duk.* inv.602) is a letter from a komogrammateus (with apparently no address) reporting the transfer of troops, led by the strategos Euphranor, from Papa (in the Koites) to Tekmi - more precisely, to the military establishment in nearby Βιχινθωυθ[9]. Other papyri from the same piece of cartonnage (purchased in 1974)[10] also come from the Herakleopolites. *SB* XVIII 13304 can be dated to 149 or 138 B.C.[11], and the other documents from this cartonnage date from the same period: the same

---

[1] Report (addressed to the oikonomos?) on the results of an inspection at the granary of Pois (perhaps in other places, too: see l.29): various sitologoi, and the βασιλικὸς γραμματεύς Erasychis (of whom more later), are mentioned.

[2] *P.Tebt.* III 1044 and 1045 are probably parts of the same document, an account of advances of wheat and barley to the cleruchs of some Herakleopolite villages: these may well have been compiled in the oikonomos' office.

[3] Cf. THEODORE C. SKEAT, *The Reigns of the Ptolemies*, München 1954, pp.33-34.

[4] *P.Hels.* I, p.3 (*Vorwort*) and p.31: «Es ist wahrscheinlich, daß Papyri aus demselben Fund oder sogar aus demselben Ökonomen-Archiv noch in anderen Sammlungen oder Veröffentlichungen entdeckt werden». *P.Hels.* I 19,20,26,34 are in Wien.

[5] The reviews by WILLY CLARYSSE, *JHS* 109, 1989, pp.246-247, and EDMOND VAN'T DACK, *BiOr* 48, 1991, pp.842-844 offer useful comments and improvements on the texts.

[6] *PPt* I 442.

[7] Dated to the 19th year of Philometor (163/162), to which reference is made in *P.Tebt.* III 857. Another coincidence is the recurrence, both in *P.Tebt.* III 1045 and in *P.Hels.* I 26, of the personal name Patamousos (see *Catalogue, s.v.*), apparently typical of Peensamoi and its surroundings.

[8] *P.Tebt.* III 827 (dated to about 170 B.C.; report on unproductive land mentioning a φυλακίτης of Herakleopolis; on the *recto*: *P.Tebt.* III 1031, account of receipts in kind), also from «Mummy 6», may well originate from an oikonomos' office, too.

[9] See also *Catalogue, s.v.* ΒΙΧΙΝΘΩΥΘ.

[10] Most of these are still unpublished: see PETER VAN MINNEN, *BASP* 31, 1994, pp.89-99, who offers a preliminary edition of *P.Duk.* inv.600 and 620 *recto*, besides some information on the provenance of the Duke papyri.

[11] See GREGG W. SCHWENDNER, *ZPE* 72, 1988, pp.275-276.

officials recur in different documents, e.g. the strategos Euphranor reappears in *P.Duk.* inv.598 (unpublished)[1], together with the βασιλικὸς γραμματεύς Pesouris, who in turn is the addressee of *P.Duk.* inv.600, a declaration of property (wheat) similar to *P.Hels.* I 10-20 (these, however, date from 163/162 B.C. and were addressed to the oikonomos). The nearest parallel to *P.Duk.* inv.600[2] is *P.Tebt.* III 806 (139 B.C.; declaration of a horse), also addressed to a βασιλικὸς γραμματεύς[3]. *P.Duk.* inv.620 *recto* (abstracts of declarations of livestock) represents a «further stage of digestion of the full information»[4] contained in documents such as *P.Tebt.* III 806, and is dated to a 31st year that can be either 151/150 or 140/139 B.C.

A further possible link between the Duke and the Tebtynis papyri is offered by *P.Tebt.* III 723. Like some other documents discussed above, this papyrus is from «Mummy 38» and probably from the oikonomos' office[5]; it is dated to the 33rd year, «doubtless that of Euergetes II, the documents accompanying [it] ranging from the 31st year to the 36th»[6]. The Euphranor appearing at l.15 presumably forwarded this order for the monthly payment of soldiers, to an addressee whose name and title are lost at the beginning of *P.Tebt.* III 723. In my opinion, this Euphranor could be the strategos of that name, who leads troops from Papa to Bichinthouth in *SB* XVIII 13304 (and, if the identification is accepted, *SB* XVIII 13304 must be dated to 138, rather than 149 B.C.).

I think that the Duke papyri, obtained from cartonnage and dating from the same years as many *P.Tebt.* III (e.g. those from «Mummy 38»), may also originate from the oikonomos' office of the Herakleopolite nome: *SB* XVIII 13304, in particular, may have been destined for the oikonomos, so that he should know where the provisions for the troops were to be sent. *P.Duk.* inv.600, sent by mistake to the βασιλικὸς γραμματεύς, may have been forwarded by him to the appropriate (i.e. the oikonomos') office; the same thing may have happened in the case of *P.Tebt.* III 806. The oikonomos' office also seems to me the likely place for abstracts to be compiled (like *P.Duk.* inv.620 *recto*) from such declarations of property.

1.2.4. Hypothesis on the provenance of P.Hels. and P.Duk.

A number of coincidences connect certain Tebtynis papyri to some papyri now in Helsinki and at Duke University. These documents

(1) date from the same periods: namely, (a) *P.Hels.* and a part of *P.Tebt.* III (including those from «Mummy 6») date from the time of the power struggle between Philometor and Euergetes II; (b) another part of *P.Tebt.* III (including those from «Mummy 38») and *P.Duk.* date from approximately twenty-five to thirty years later;

(2) are all obtained from cartonnage;

(3) originate from the Herakleopolites, as is shown by the fact that: (a) they mention Herakleopolite toponyms; (b) the same officials (operating in the Herakleopolite nome) recur;

(4) may be said with certainty (in the case of *P.Hels.*) or with good probability (in the case of the *P.Tebt.* III, and perhaps in the case of *P.Duk.*[7]) to have come from the oikonomos' office at Herakleopolis, apparently in two separate batches: presumably these were delivered to the Tebtynis manufacturers of mummy-cases on two different occasions;

---

[1] This papyrus is briefly referred to by VAN MINNEN, *cit.*, p.92.

[2] *Editio princeps* in VAN MINNEN, *cit.*, pp.91-94.

[3] See *BL* 7,273 (the name of the βασιλικὸς γραμματεύς is almost entirely lost at l.2: [....]υνι, in the dative). There is only one other declaration of property (a horse, again) addressed to a βασιλικὸς γραμματεύς: *P.Petr.* III 72 (= *Chr.W.*222), of the third century B.C.

[4] VAN MINNEN, *cit.*, p.90.

[5] Cf. the above-mentioned *P.Hels.* 6 (an order for payment addressed by the oikonomos(?) Philippos to the βασιλικὸς γραμματεύς Erasychis).

[6] *P.Tebt.* III.1, p.127.

[7] For the Duke papyri, this hypothesis needs of course to be verified once all documents are published.

(5) were purchased (at least as regards the *P.Hels.* and the *P.Duk.*) in the same years (1974, 1976, 1977) on the antiquities market.

My guess is that *P.Hels.* and *P.Duk.*, like the *P.Tebt.* III, come from Umm al-Baragāt.

1.2.5. Documents from (?) now in Strasbourg, Hamburg, Berlin, Munich, Geneva, Milan.

The editors of *P.Strasb.* VIII 781 have noted «l'identité du "decoupage"» of this document and of *P.Hamb.* I 57, 91 and 92 (*P.Hamb.* I 91 mentions the Herakleopolite villages of Tebetny and Pois): these documents are also related by their contents (they are all addressed to the strategos Kydias[1]) and were acquired in the same years, presumably through the Deutsches Papyruskartell[2].

BGU VI 1244 is said to belong to the «Alter Bestand», having been bought (through the Papyruskartell, presumably) in the Fayūm: it relates to a pronouncement by the χρηματίσται in a case of assault (the claimant is from Φνεβιεὺς καὶ Πεενσχω, in the Μέση toparchy: somebody had broken into his house), and its contents connect it to *P.Yale* I 57, also referring to a pronouncement by the χρηματίσται in a case of assault in the Μέση toparchy (people breaking into a vineyard at Peenpibykis). *P.Mert.* 59 (acquired in 1924) must have the same provenance, too: this is a divorce agreement before the χρηματίσται at Κροκοδείλων πόλις; the parties are to meet for the final settlement at Bousiris.

No information is offered in the edition on the provenance of *SB* XIV 12089 (now in Cologne): was it also acquired through the Deutsches Papyruskartell? *P.Münch.* I 49, 51 and 55 (referring to the Herakleopolite villages of Tebetny and Thmoinache) probably were, and were definitely purchased not later than 1913; *P.Münch.* I 55, in particular, is said to have been bought at El-Ashmunein: the inventory numbers suggest that all three documents were purchased at the same time[3].

Seventy years later, in 1992 and 1993, new material (in two «Papyruskonvolute»), related to some *P.Münch.*, was acquired by the Papyrussammlungen of Heidelberg, Cologne and Vienna[4].

Unpublished cartonnage papyri from the Herakleopolites are also in the possession of the universities of Geneva[5] and Milan, both at the Università Cattolica (purchase of 1990)[6] and at the Università Statale (purchase of 1992). The Università Statale, in particular, acquired a papyrus roll (*P.Mil.Vogl.* inv.1295) containing the epigrams of Posidippus, besides five documents, all from the same cartonnage[7]: the documents date from the early second century B.C.; two of them (*P.Mil.Vogl.* inv. 1299 and 1300)

---

[1] *PPt* I 274; also in L. MOOREN, *The Aulic Titulature in Ptolemaic Egypt. Introduction and Prosopography*, Bruxelles 1975, Prosopography no.095. The strategos Kydias is attested from 167 to 160 B.C.: he is attested, among other documents, in *P.Hels.* I 26A and *UPZ* I 9-11, which mention Herakleopolite toponyms.

[2] See above, p.14 n.4.

[3] Inv.nos.122, 114 and 116, respectively. On the papyrus acquisitions of the Bayerische Staatsbibliothek (which begun in 1899/1900) see ERWIN ARNOLD, «Die Papyrussammlung der Bayerischen Staatsbibliothek», in *P.Münch.* I (repr. 1986), pp.*10-12. About 110 papyri were reckoned by Wilcken to be in the first lot bought by Hermann Thiersch for the Staatsbibliothek of Bavaria in 1900 (ULRICH WILCKEN, *APF* 1, 1901, pp.468-491; see also LEOPOLD WENGER, *Chr. Ég.* 7, 1932, pp.335-348). The three documents in our list were probably part of one of the later purchases, made through the Deutsches Papyruskartell between 1909 and 1913.

[4] As reported by James M.S. Cowey at the 21st International Congress of Papyrologists (Berlin, 13-19 August 1995). These papyri, to be published by Cowey himself and by Demokritos Kaltsas, also refer to several Herakleopolite localities.

[5] See PAUL SCHUBERT, «Nouveaux Papyrus Ptolémaïques dans la collection de Génève», *Proceedings of the 20th International Congress of Papyrologists* (Copenhagen, 23-29 August 1992), Copenhagen 1994, pp.273-274.

[6] Cf. SERGIO DARIS, «La serie P.Med. inv. 90.14-90.60», *Aegyptus* 75, 1995, pp.17-25.

[7] See for the time being GUIDO BASTIANINI - CLAUDIO GALLAZZI, «Il papiro ritrovato. Scoperti gli epigrammi di Posidippo in un pettorale di mummia», *Rivista Ca' de Sass* 121, 1993 (offprint).

INTRODUCTION

mention the Herakleopolite villages of Koma and Petachor, respectively[1].

1.3. Documents of the first century B.C.

1.3.1. Documents from Abū Sīr al-Malaq

The documents in our *Index* come from the necropolis in the Gabal Abū Sīr, which was excavated by Otto Rubensohn during three campaigns, in 1903, 1904 and 1908[2]; nearby Abū Sīr al-Malaq is the ancient Bousiris, one of the northernmost Herakleopolite villages. The cartonnages of the mummies found there (dating from the first century A.D.[3]) gave back, beside the remains of a lawyer's archive in Alexandria[4]:

(1) a large number of documents from the office of the strategos and the βασιλικὸς γραμματεύς at Herakleopolis (published in *BGU* VIII), mostly mentioning villages in the northern part of the nome;

(2) a series of tax-lists, accounts and land-survey documents (published in *BGU* XIV), which offer the most comprehensive available information on Herakleopolite villages and toparchies[5].

BGU VI 1216 (also from cartonnage, but now unfortunately lost) is a special case: its editor dated it to 110 B.C., and its internal evidence mostly points to the Memphite nome, but also to the Herakleopolites (see *s.v.* περὶ Αὐλήν).

1.3.2. BGU VIII and some related documents.

These documents are mostly related to the judicial activity of the strategos of the Herakleopolites (and of his staff): they are petitions addressed by inhabitants of the district to various strategoi who held office between 61/60 and 47 B.C., besides correspondence within the administration concerning inquiries to be made and decisions to be put into effect on matters of divorce, inheritance[6], conflicts between tax-payers and various officials, cases of assault and robbery[7], and so on. There are requests for tax-release, sometimes claiming a condition of ἀσθένεια for a whole village, and a number of transfers of catoecic land[8]. Another group of

---

[1] See *Catalogue, s.vv.* I wish to thank Guido Bastianini for information concerning these two documents.

[2] See KARL PREISENDANZ, *Papyrusfunde und Papyrusforschung*, p.179 f. The site had already been inspected by Heinrich Schäfer in 1899 (see ULRICH WILCKEN, «Die Berliner Papyrusgrabungen in Herakleopolis magna», *APF* 2, 1903, p.325), on the occasion of the ill-starred excavations conducted by Wilcken at Ihnāsiyā al-Madīna, of which more will be said later.
On more recent discoveries from the Saite and Graeco-Roman periods (apparently no papyri, though) at Abū Sīr al-Malaq see *Orientalia* 55, 1986, p.263 (reporting a piece of news from *Al Ahram* of September the 28th, 1985).

[3] PREISENDANZ, *Papyrusfunde und Papyrusforschung*, p.179.

[4] See WILHELM SCHUBART, *APF* 5, 1913, pp.35-81.

[5] A number of orders for payment addressed to bankers, now in the possession of Florida State University, are obviously from the same find (related documents have appeared as *BGU* XIV 2401-2416): they were published by ROGER S. BAGNALL-RAYMOND BOGAERT, *Ancient Society* 6, 1975, pp.79-108 (now *SB* XIV 11309-11328). These papyri were bought in 1973 from «a private collector in Holland, from whom information was received that the papyri had been the property of her family since early in this century. A note with the texts stated that they came from the mummy cartonnage found at Abou Sir Al-Malaq» (*ibid.*, p.79). *BGU* XIV 2401-2416 are documents of exactly the same type. Is there any connection between the Florida papyri and the Visser papyri (see below, p.22 n.5)?

[6] *BGU* VI 1285 (a cleruch's testament concerning his house at Thmoiphtha) probably belongs here (unless it can be connected to *BGU* VI 1244: see above, p.20) and so do two documents published outside the *BGU* series, but also from Abū Sīr al-Malaq: *SB* VI 9065 and VIII 9790.

[7] *SB* V 7609 falls within this category.

[8] Ἀσθένεια: *BGU* VIII 1815 (61/60 B.C.), submitted by the inhabitants of Machor. Three more documents of this kind date from 51/50 B.C. (*BGU* VIII 1779, for Peenepsy; *BGU* VIII 1835, for Hiera Nesos) and 50/49 B.C. (*BGU* VIII 1843, for Tinteris). Land-transfers: see, in our *Chronological Index*, *BGU* VIII 1771 and 1772, and cf. *BGU* VIII 1731-1740.

documents (*BGU* VIII 1741-1755) comprises orders for the shipping of wheat to Alexandria[1], or for payments to soldiers or priests[2]. *SB* V 8755 and 8756, authorising seed-loans to the βασιλικὸς γεωργός of Phys, and to a κάτοικος of Mouchis, were published later.

BGU VIII 1768 is a report on a visit by a high official, possibly at Herakleopolis: he landed at Ἱερὰ Νῆσος, and thence proceeded to visit a locality provided with a temple of Herakles, an Arsinoeion and a γυμνάσιον: one is reminded of the itinerary followed by an οὐραγία to be escorted to Ἱερὰ Νῆσος (*BGU* VIII 1784)[3].

1.3.3. BGU XIV documents.

The *BGU* XIV documents that appear in our *Chronological Index* come mostly from a single mummy-case, the head of which had been dismantled before World War II, while the remaining part was disassembled in 1975[4]. *BGU* XIV 2419, 2420, 2425 and 2431 are so-called Visser papyri[5]; *BGU* XIV 2435 comes from yet another piece of cartonnage[6]. Finally, *BGU* XIV 2376 and 2377 (copies of the same document) were obtained from a mummy-case otherwise containing material from the Augustan period (see below).

BGU XIV 2370, 2436, 2437, 2439 and 2440 were all re-used on the verso by one scribe, the one who wrote *BGU* XIV 2440, as shown in the following Table:

Recto	*Verso*
BGU XIV 2370	*BGU* XIV 2433
BGU XIV 2436	*BGU* XIV 2436 *verso*
BGU XIV 2437	*BGU* XIV 2438
BGU XIV 2439	*BGU* XIV 2432
BGU XIV 2440	*BGU* XIV 2434

None of these documents is dated, except for *BGU* XIV 2370 (not exactly dated, but containing references to a 34th and a 33rd year). Furthermore, *BGU* XIV 2370 and 2436 were written by the same hand that compiled *BGU* XIV 2374, a petition to Soter II, to be dated between 88 and 81 B.C. This is also consistent with the dating (82 and 81 B.C.) of some orders for payments (*BGU* XIV 2401-2416) from the same cartonnage[7]. The 34th year referred to in *BGU* XIV 2370 is therefore 84/83 B.C. (34th year of Soter

---

[1] In our *Chronological Index*: *BGU* VIII 1742 (wheat shipped from the granary of Tilothis to Alexandria).

[2] *BGU* VIII 1747-1749 (payments to soldiers); *BGU* VIII 1752-1753 (assignments of wheat to priests at Tilothis and in περὶ Πόλιν, respectively).

[3] Both documents (written by different hands) are undated; compare the list of ships in *BGU* VIII 1807, where reference is made (as in *BGU* VIII 1784) to the Troites (i.e. the region around Troia, in the Memphites: see *Catalogue, s.v.* ἹΕΡᾺ ΝῆΣΟΣ).

[4] See *BGU* XIV, *Einleitung*, pp.V-VII.

[5] The Visser papyri, also from Abū Sīr al-Malaq cartonnage, were entrusted to C.E. Visser before World War II, and eventually appeared in *BGU* XIV.

[6] See *BGU* XIV, *Einleitung*, p.VIII: «aus Probeauflösungen kleinerer Sargfragmente, die in den sechziger und siebziger Jahren durch J. Hofmann und seinen Vorgänger, M. Brzyski, erfolgten».

[7] See p.21 n.5.

INTRODUCTION

II's reign)[1]. The chronological gap between *BGU* XIV 2370 and 2436, on the one hand, and *BGU* XIV 2440, 2433, 2436 *verso*, 2438, 2432 and 2434, on the other, may perhaps be assessed to approximately 25-30 years. *BGU* XIV 2441-2448 and 2449-2450 (two sets of land-survey documents written by two different hands) are probably nearer in time to the more recent of the documents listed above (i.e. those written on the *verso* and *BGU* XIV 2440): as a matter of fact, there is a single (undeciphered) line of writing on the back of *BGU* XIV 2449, apparently by the same hand that wrote *BGU* XIV 2440; and the handwriting of *BGU* XIV 2441-2448 is similar to that of *SB* VI 9065[2], which is dated to 50/49 B.C., besides mentioning a Herakleopolite Ἰβιών locality[3]. *BGU* XIV 2437 and 2439, both written on *recto* sides, may be thought to be nearer in time to *BGU* XIV 2370 and 2436.

BGU XIV 2441-2448 and 2449-2450 preserve portions of what must have been a complete survey of all agricultural land in each village of the Tekmi toparchy, and probably of the whole nome. *BGU* XIV 2370 includes a report on the administration of two oikonomoi, whom their (unnamed) colleague presently in charge considers responsible for certain tax-arrears: this must have been addressed to a higher authority, presumably the strategos, who would also be in a position to grant the requested tax-release[4]. In fact all the above-mentioned *BGU* XIV documents may originate from the strategos' office. Possible links between *BGU* XIV 2441-2448 and *BGU* VIII documents may also be detected, if the γεωργός-entrepreneur Hierax of *BGU* XIV 2444,86-91 and 2448,11 is identified with the homonymous ἐκλογιστής of *BGU* VIII 1821 and 1823[5]. Similarly, the γεωργός-entrepreneur Κιαλῆς ὁ Ἡρακλείου of *BGU* XIV 2449,70-73 could be identical with Κίλλης ὁ Ἡρακλείτου[6] of *BGU* VIII 1813: like the orphans of *BGU* VIII 1813, the κάτοικος Straton, son of Demetrios of *BGU* XIV 2449 was unable, or unwilling to cultivate his kleros (he cedes 55 arourae to Kiales/Killes, while leaving 39 more arourae mostly uncultivated[7]).

1.4. Documents from the beginning of the Roman Period from Abū Sīr al-Malaq.

All papyri dating from the Augustan period in our list come from Abū Sīr al-Malaq. The most recently published are the *BGU* XVI papyri[8]: almost all of these were extracted from a single coffin fragment. The

---

[1] The other possibilities for year 34 are: 148/147 B.C. (year 34 of Ptolemy VI Philometor) and 137/136 B.C. (year 34 of Ptolemy VIII Euergetes II). A dating to the second century B.C. is favoured by Reinhold Scholl (*C.Ptol.Sklav.*, p.977) on the ground that Exakon (an official in charge of the admission to the rank of κάτοικος ἱππεύς) and Archinos (his secretary) appear both in *BGU* XIV 2441 (ll.149 and 153, respectively) and in *P.Tebt.* III 739, which certainly dates from the middle of the second century B.C. However, a different explanation is possible for the recurrence of both names in the two documents, while accepting the first century B.C. date for *BGU* XIV 2441 (cf. MARIA ROSARIA FALIVENE, «Exakon and Archinos in *P.Tebt.* III 739 and *BGU* XIV 2441» (forthcoming). Objections to Scholl's opinion are already raised in *BL* 9,34: «Es sei aber aufgemerkt, daß 2436 von derselben Hand geschrieben ist als 2374: eine Eingabe an Ptolemaios IX. Vgl. auch die ebenfalls aus derselben Kartonage stammenden *BGU* 2401-2416».

[2] As observed by William Brashear (*BGU* XIV, p.165), who also notes the similarity between the handwriting of *BGU* XIV 2441-2448 and that of the *Laterculi Alexandrini* (= 2068 Pack), also obtained from cartonnage found at Abū Sīr al-Malaq.

[3] References to a 6th year are found in *BGU* XIV 2444,24 and 2449,36; to a 40th (or 20th +) year in *BGU* XIV 2441,119; to a queen and a king in *BGU* XIV 2444,25 and *BGU* XIV 2441,100, respectively: these pieces of information are not easy to pin down to any particular sovereign (cf. *BGU* XIV 2441,119 n.).

[4] Compare similar requests addressed to the strategos and published in *BGU* VIII (see above, p.21 n.8).

[5] As suggested by JEAN BINGEN, «Les cavaliers catoeques de l'Héracléopolite au Ier siècle», in *Egypt and the Hellenistic World. Proceedings of the International Colloquium* (Leuven, 24-26 May 1982), Leuven 1983, pp.8-9. Bingen stresses «l'ambiguité du terme γεωργός, désignant celui qui pour les autorités se reconnaît comme responsable de l'exploitation, quelle que soit la manière dont il mène la chose, qu'il soit grand entrepreneur agricole ou petit fermier» (*ibid.*, p.8).

[6] In *BGU* XIV 2449, α and λ are often indistinguishable, and so they are in the case of this personal name.

[7] Cf. ll.66-69.

[8] I wish to thank William M. Brashear, for allowing me to browse through the final draft of *BGU* XVI before it was published.

remaining ones, retrieved from boxes in the Berlin Ägyptisches Museum, are connected with some *BGU* IV documents: *BGU* XVI 2665, for instance, belongs to a small private archive of letters published as *BGU* IV 1203-1209, while *BGU* XVI 2674 is written in the same script as *BGU* XVI 2672 (and maybe 2673), which contains a list of priests mostly coinciding with *BGU* IV 1196 (ll.65-83 and 101-123)[1].

BGU XVI 2578-2587 are a group of declarations of property (sheep and goats): with the exception of *BGU* XVI 2586 (dated 5 B.C.), they are all dated to 14/13 B.C., and addressed to a subordinate of the supervisor of the pasture-tax (ὁ πρὸς τῷ ἐννωμίῳ) in the Herakleopolites.

A large majority of the documents obtained from this coffin fragment, however, belong, or may be affiliated to the archive of Athenodoros (*BGU* XVI 2600-2668), who operated in the Herakleopolites as dioiketes, epistates, and also overseer of the affairs (φροντιστής) of a certain Asklepiades[2].

Three of the documents extracted from this piece of cartonnage date from the pre-Augustan period: besides the already mentioned *BGU* XIV 2376 and 2377 (from 36/35 B.C.: see above), there is the still unpublished *P.Berol.* inv.25263 (oath by a κάτοικος ἱππεύς dated 52 B.C.).

The same coffin fragment also produced literary papyri: a magical text, a Greek-Latin word-list, and a speech of Demosthenes (part of which had been extracted at an earlier time)[3].

2. Documents of the Ptolemaic period from outside the Herakleopolites.

2.1. Documents of the third century B.C.

2.1.1. From the Arsinoites (Zenon archive).

Certain connections between documents from Kōm Madīnat Gurān and some papyri from the Zenon archive have been noted above: coincidences are not surprising between two sets of papyri having both date (early Ptolemaic period) and provenance (Fayūm) in common. Besides, Zenon's enterprises extended to the Herakleopolites. *P.Cair.Zen.* IV 59782 (b) records payments to Egyptian men from various Herakleopolite villages as wages for the manufacturing of flax: the list of place-names (in the Koma, Tilothis and Tekmi toparchies) largely coincides with the one in *P.Lille* I 59[4], but also includes Meia (in the Memphites) and Thmoiobastis, a locality in the Koma toparchy which is again mentioned in *P.Lond.* VII 1972. Bee-keeping[5] on a large scale is attested in *P.Cair.Zen.* III 59368 (complaints against the oikonomos Ammonios, whom we met in Kresilaos' correspondence): a thousand bee-hives are leased out to Egyptians in the Herakleopolite and Memphite nomes. *P.Cair.Zen.* IV 59753 (a trading cruise connecting Memphis, Aphroditopolis, Herakleopolis, Bousiris and Ptolemais Hormou) defines a wider context within which the northern Herakleopolites should be viewed. Connections to the Koites, *via*

---

[1] They resulted from *Probeauflösungen* made before World War II: cf. *BGU* XVI, *Preface*, pp.V-VI. William Brashear informed me that *BGU* XVI 2588, also from cartonnage, once belonged to Wilcken's private collection (letter of October 12, 1995).

[2] At the beginning of the Roman period, and throughout the first century A.D., the title of διοικητής designated a subordinate local official: cf. DIETER HAGEDORN, «Zum Amt des διοικητής im römischen Ägypten», *YCS* 28, 1985, pp.188-191.

[3] See *BGU* XVI, *Preface*. The magical text (*P.Berol.* inv.21243) was published by WILLIAM M. BRASHEAR, *ZPE* 33, 1979, pp.261 ff. The Greek-Latin word list (*P.Berol.* inv.21246; on the back of a register recording land-holdings) was also published by W. M. BRASHEAR, «A Greek-Latin Vocabulary», *Proceedings of the XVI International Congress of Papyrology* (New York, 24-31 July 1980), Chico 1981, pp.31-41. The Demosthenes papyrus contains *De Chersoneso* 60-67: cf. IDEM, *ZPE* 48, 1982, pp.61-65. To these may be added the six lines of iambic trimeter (in Doric: instructions for the toasting of deities at a symposion) written along the fibres in *P.Berol.* inv.21285, and apparently surrounded by accounts at a later stage (*BGU* XVI 2673: see Ed. *ad loc.*); the poem was published by W. M. BRASHEAR, «Symposion Rules», *Proceedings of the XVIII International Congress of Papyrology* (Athens, 25-31 May 1986), vol.II, pp.107-111.

[4] See *Catalogue*, s.v. ΒΟΥΣΙΡΙΣ.

[5] Bee-keepers from Bousiris: *P.Cair.Zen.* II 59151 and *PSI* V 510.

INTRODUCTION

Moiethymis and Onnes, are attested by *PSI* V 587.

2.1.2. From Memphis.

With one exception, all *UPZ* documents in our *Chronological Index* pertain to Ptolemaios, son of Glaukias, the recluse in the Serapieion who came from Psychis in the Herakleopolite nome: his archive was discovered at Saqqara, and dispersed throughout Europe, in the 1820s[1]. The exception is *UPZ* I 122, a petition addressed to Poseidonios, strategos of the Memphite nome[2], by a follower of Serapis from Παανᾰμεύς (*scil.* Πεενᾰμεύς), in the Herakleopolite nome. Wilcken already noticed that «authentische Nachrichten über den Speziellen Ort, an dem die Texte gefunden sind, und über die genaueren Fundumstände sind ... nicht bekannt»[3]: as regards *UPZ* I 122, he suggested (*ad loc.*) that the petition may have been found among the ruins of the Anoubieion in Memphis.

3. Documents from the Herakleopolites. From the first to the fifth century A.D.

No papyrus mentioning Herakleopolite toponyms and dating from a time later than the Augustan period comes from cartonnage; also, many of these documents were found by clandestine diggers and sold on the antiquities market to buyers from all over Europe (as far as Tbilisi), the United States, and Australia. These two facts make it much more difficult to sort them out into groups of papyri that can be traced back to their common provenance. The provenance of those papyri that stayed in, or eventually went back to Egypt is often equally unknown. However, the fact that certain papyri (1) date from the same period, and (2) refer to the same places in the Herakleopolites, does offer a clue to their possibly common origin. This possibility may then be checked against any information (if available) on where, when, by or through whom, and for which institution(s) or private individual(s) these papyri were bought. Moreover, the inventory-numbers may offer useful indications as to which papyri in a collection were found, or at least bought together.

3.1. Documents of the first and first/second century A.D. from Al-Hība

In the winter of 1914, ten years after Grenfell and Hunt had last been there, Friedrich Bilabel went to Al-Hība. He was well aware that his could only be «eine Nachlese zu den Raubgrabungen und den englischen Ausgrabungen». Nevertheless, he was able to report that «[es] traten an den verschiedensten Stellen der Stadt Fetzen zutage, die von der Perserzeit (ägyptische Stücke) bis etwa ins 2./3. Jahrhundert n.Chr. reichen. Byzantinisches habe ich nicht gefunden, aber einige kleine koptische Fetzen. In den Häusern ... sind ... meines Erinnerns nur römische Texte gefunden worden ... Das spricht dafür ... daß ungefähr seit dem 3. Jahrh. p.Chr. die Stadt wohl nur mehr dürftig bewohnt war. Aus koptischer Zeit sind einige Gräber von uns ausgedeckt worden»[4]. Of the documents dating from late first or early second A.D. that mention Herakleopolite toponyms (Ἀγκυρῶν πόλις and other places, for the most part in the Koites), *P.Heid.* IV 326 was certainly found during Bilabel's excavations, while *P.Hib.* II 218, 272 and 275 were among those recovered by Grenfell and Hunt: «A few houses on higher ground in the south-east quarter of the town had some *afsh*, but had already been much dug, and we found little save *some second or third century fragments*»[5].

---

[1] Cf. DOROTHY J. THOMPSON, *Memphis under the Ptolemies*, Princeton 1988, pp.213-231.

[2] There are four more petitions to strategoi of the same nome among the *UPZ*: *UPZ* I 123, also addressed to Poseidonios; *UPZ* I 124 (to the strategos Krateros); *UPZ* I 7 and 8 (to the strategos Dionysios).

[3] *UPZ* I, *Einleitung*, pp.1-2.

[4] *P.Bad.*=*VBP* IV, *Einleitung*, p.5 f. On the «Raubgrabungen» and the «englische Ausgrabungen» see above, p.14 f.

[5] *P.Hib.* I, *Introduction*, p.7 (italics mine); see also *P.Hib.* II, *Preface*, pp.V-VI.

The papyri coming from this site as a result of the *Raubgrabungen* of Shêkh Hassan had been on the market at least since 1896, and it is conceivable that one or more of the papyri of unknown provenance that mention Herakleopolite toponyms may have come from Al-Hïba (especially as the houses inspected by Grenfell and Hunt «had already been much dug»), particularly if it mentions a locality in the Koites, and if it was acquired not much later than 1896[1]. This could be the case for *P.Ross.Georg.* II 11, in which reference is made to Ἀγκυρῶν πόλις and Μουχινπαγει, the second village being also mentioned in a of the third century B.C. papyrus from Al-Hïba (*P.Hib.* I 112). In his *Vorwort* to *P.Ross.Georg.* I, Zereteli wrote that an edition of the papyri acquired for him in Egypt by B. Turaiev and M. Rostovtzeff was planned just before World War I broke out; in 1900 Zereteli was still learning the papyrologist's job in Berlin[2]: at some point between 1900 and 1914 he must therefore have asked Turaiev and Rostovtzeff to purchase papyri for him; at that time, some documents from Al-Hïba may have still been around[3]. On the other hand, the date of *P.Ross.Georg.* II 11 is rather earlier than that of other papyri from the Roman period definitely found at Al-Hïba, none of which is earlier than the second half of the first century A.D.[4]

3.2. Documents of the second and third centuries A.D.

3.2.1. From the first and second «Fayūm finds».

Some 40,000 papyri went to Vienna either in 1881/1882 (so-called *first Fayūm find*: mostly, but not exclusively Byzantine documents) or in 1884/1885 (the *second Fayūm find*). They came from a site north of Medinet al-Fayūm (ancient Arsinoe) but also, in large quantities, from Ihnāsiya al-Madīna/Herakleopolis. The first Fayūm find also comprised papyri from Hermopolis[5].

The Roman, as well as the (much more abundant) Byzantine documents in the Vienna collection that mention Herakleopolite toponyms may thus be assumed to come mostly from Herakleopolis, while others may be from the Arsinoite nome. For the second and third centuries A.D. these also include, besides the *CPR*, *Stud.Pal.* and *P.Vind.* documents included in our *Chronological Index*, the following papyri (all from the third century A.D.): *P.Rain.Cent.* 64; *P.Select.* 17; *SB* I 4370; *SB* XIV 11643; *SB* XVI 12241; *SB* XVIII 13858; *P.Vindob.* G 23035[6].

However, not all papyri from the Fayūm finds went to Vienna: though the vast majority of them did, others found their way to Berlin, Oxford, Paris, London, and elsewhere[7]. The provenance from the second Fayūm find is virtually certain for *P.Aberd.*, also represented by one document in our list[8], and *SB* XVI

---

[1] It is difficult to tell, however, for how long papyri from Al-Hïba were to be found on the antiquities market: the Ptolemaic literary papyri must have gone very quickly, but a document of the Roman period may have taken longer to sell (see also p.28 n.9). See below, p.28 f., on *BGU* XI 2073, acquired at El-Ashmunein in 1908, but possibly from Al-Hïba. There are many cases of separate groups of documents from the same find being sold at different stages, either to the same or to different buyers: the case of the Petaus archive is particularly striking (see *P.Petaus*, *Vorwort*, p.5).

[2] ISAAK F. FIKHMAN, «G.F. Zereteli und die Berliner Papyrussammlung», *APF* 34, 1988, pp.43-52.

[3] See above, p.15, on some papyri of the third century B.C. from Al-Hïba cartonnage published in *P.Ross.Georg.* II.

[4] Oxyrhynchus is the other possible provenance for this document: see below, p.30.

[5] See HELENE LOEBENSTEIN, «Vom "Papyrus Erzherzog Rainer" zur Papyrussammlung der österreichischen Nationalbibliothek. 100 Jahre sammeln, bewahren, edieren», in *P.Rain.Cent.* (Wien 1983), pp.3-39.

[6] The toponym Kerkytos, well attested for the Herakleopolites, appears in *P.Vind.Tand.* 10: despite its early date (54 A.D.), the inventory number of this papyrus relates it to documents from the Fayūm finds published in the same volume, which pertain to the Arsinoites.

[7] As stated by Grenfell and Hunt in *P.Fayûm*, p.18; they also added that «enormous quantities of papyrus rolls of the Roman period» were found in the houses at Dimê (ancient Soknopaiou Nesos), and that «during this period, 1887-1894, dealers' agents were busy at other sites, especially at Kôm Ushîm ... and other places on the east side of the Fayûm, which had been deserted since the fourth century» (*ibid.*, p.19).

[8] Cf. *P.Aberd.*, *Preface*, p.V: «From internal evidence it seems clear that the bulk of the documents come from Dimê ...

INTRODUCTION

12612 was also «recovered by the University of Michigan at Dime»[1].

It is not easy to point to a published Berlin papyrus, among those in our list, which may have come from the first or second Fayūm finds[2]. *BGU* XIII 2326, for example, might be one of them (this is a customs house register mentioning Κεφαλαί, Λευκόγιον and Bousiris, the last two places at least being in close relation to the Arsinoites)[3].

3.2.2. Lost documents from Ihnāsiya al-Madīna.

In the winter 1898/1899, Ulrich Wilcken led an excavation at the site of Herakleopolis: *BGU* III 927 and 958a, two of the papyri found on that occasion, were published on the basis of Wilcken's preliminary transcriptions, after the originals had been destroyed, with all else that had been brought from Egypt, «durch eine elementare Katastrophe im letzten Augenblick ...: auf dem Schiff, das die Papyruskisten von Ägypten bis Hamburg sicher gebracht hatte, brach zuletzt im Hamburger Hafen ein Feuer aus, dem auch unsere Kisten bis auf einige wertlose Rest zum Opfer fielen»[4].

3.2.3. Documents from (?)

In the 1920s and early 1930s different institutions bought papyri of the second and third centuries A.D.: their editors offer very little information on the provenance of these documents, but it should be noted that the Herakleopolite villages they mention were in the northern part of the nome, namely in the Koma, Tekmi and Μέση toparchies. In my opinion, there is a strong probability that all, or most of these papyri may come from the same find: did Wilcken leave something behind, at Ihnāsiya al-Madīna?

The documents in question are: *P.Bon.* 18 and 25, acquired in 1930 and mentioning, respectively, Machor and Phys[5]; *P.Iand.* III 33, mentioning Bousiris[6]; *P.Mert.* II 78 (acquired in 1930[7]; place-name almost entirely lost in a lacuna); *P.Mil.Vogl.* VI 287 (toponym mentioned: Tekmi)[8]. With the exception of *P.Bon.* 18 (a census declaration dated 138 A.D., like *P.Oslo* III 98, which refers to Herakleopolis) the

---

several pieces in this collection are closely related to others, now preserved in London and Berlin, which are known to have come from the Fayyūm ... I have not discovered that any of the Aberdeen fragments connect with pieces in the Rainer collection at Vienna, though in certain texts the same persons appear».

[1] LOUISE C. YOUTIE, *ZPE* 37, 1980, p.205.

[2] In the *Einleitung* to *BGU* XI reference is made to the Sammlung Brugsch (1891), as part of the Berlin collection: this could well include documents of the first and second Fayūm finds. However: «Nur die Bestände, die aus den Grabungen der Berliner Museen (1899-1910) stammen, tragen meist Grabungsdatum und Herkunftsangabe; was jedoch damals von einheimischen Händlern erworben wurde, was auch aus den Sammlungen Brugsch (1891), Reinhard und Carl Schmidt stammt, enthält nur selten entsprechende Angaben; fast alle aus dem Fayûm stammenden Papyri kommen aus Mappen oder Kästen ohne jede Angabe...» (*ibid.*, p.VI).

[3] See *Catalogue, s.vv.*

[4] ULRICH WILCKEN, «Die Berliner Papyrusgrabungen in Herakleopolis Magna im Winter 1898/1899», *APF* 2, 1903, p.333 f.

[5] *P.Bon., Avvertenza*, p.5: «La raccolta dei papiri bolognesi fu acquistata nel 1930 ... presso M. Nahman, antiquario del Cairo».

[6] Cf. HANS GEORG GUNDEL, «Papyri Iandanae. Eine Einführung», *Kurzberichte aus den Gießener Papyrus-Sammlungen* 29, 1971, pp.1-2, whence it is possible to deduce that *P.Iand.* III 33 may have been bought either in 1905/1906 or in 1927; perhaps the fact that another papyrus in the same collection (*P.Iand.* VI 124, of the fourth century A.D.), also mentioning a Herakleopolite toponym, was certainly bought in 1927, makes the later date more likely for *P.Iand.* III 33, too.

[7] Wilfred Merton took part in the consortium set up by Kelsey, on which see below, p.29 n.5.

[8] «Acquistato nell'anno 1934 probabilmente al Cairo» (Ed. *ad loc.*).

documents all date from the last twenty years or so of the second century A.D. (*P.Mil.Vogl.* VI 287 bears no exact date). To these *P.Oslo* III 82 (third century A.D.; reference to Koma) may be added: we only know that it was acquired between 1920 and 1936[1]. The villages appearing in *P.Köln* II 98 (second century A.D.), II 99 (second/third century A.D.) and II 88 (third century A.D.) are from the same area: no information seems to be available on their provenance[2], but this may be the same as for the preceding documents. *SB* XIV 11277[3] could also come into this group.

3.2.4. Documents from Al-Hība.

To begin with, a source of a different kind from Al-Hība may be mentioned: this is *SB* I 2246, a funerary inscription.

The papyri published in *P.Hib.* II, *P.Bad.= VBP, P.Heid.* IV, and *SB* XII 11262 (a re-edition of *P.Bad.= VBP* IV 79), besides *SB* XVI 12836-12837 (now in Vienna), certainly come from Al-Hība[4]. To these *P.Corn.* 17 should be added, being a census declaration from the same place ('Αγκυρῶν πόλις) and the same year (147 A.D.) as *P.Bad.= VBP* IV 75a-b, and perhaps also *P.Gen.* I 9 and *P.Lond.* II 171: both mention Phebichis and were acquired between 1891 and 1895, just when material from this site must have become more abundant on the market[5]. *P.Ross.Georg.* V 20, mentioning localities of the Ἄγημα, Τεχθω Νῆσος toparchy, and the Koites (including Phebichis), may be suspected of having the same origin, especially if this is attributed to *P.Ross.Georg.* II 11, too[6]. The same point can be made for *P.Hamb.* I 17 (bought in the Fayūm[7]), as other papyri now in Hamburg come from Al-Hība.

Other papyri in our *Chronological Index* mention 'Αγκυρῶν πόλις and/or other villages in the Koites and could come from Al-Hība: *P.Ryl.* II 225 and 87 are among these[8], as well as *P.Strasb.* V 356[9], and perhaps *PSI* I 32, VI 928, XII 1229. *BGU* XI 2073 contains a list of inhabitants of 'Αγκυρῶν πόλις, the personal names being the same as in certain papyri of the second and third centuries A.D. from Al-Hība[10]:

---

[1] *P.Oslo* III 82 is said in the edition to come from the Oxyrhynchites: however, it contains official correspondence destined for the strategos of the Arsinoites.

[2] The Editors note that they have «benachbarte Inventarnummern». On the *recto* of *P.Köln* II 99, a tax-list for the Polemon meris is found: «Vermutlich ist der Papyrus nach der Erstbeschriftung auf dem Rekto vom Arsinoites in den Herakleopolites gebracht worden, wo er wahrscheinlich auch gefunden wurde. Nr.88, mit einem benachbarten Inventarnummer stammt ebenfalls aus dem Herakleopolites» (*P.Köln* II 99, p.141).

[3] Cf.the *editio princeps* of this document in *Aegyptus* 54, 1974, p.52: «Il papiro ... potrebbe provenire dall'Herakleopolites e, più precisamente, dai dintorni di Hawara».

[4] Cf. *SB* XVIII, p.486 f. See above, p.25 f.

[5] The first lots of Geneva papyri were acquired through Édouard Naville (then the agent of the Egypt Exploration Fund in Egypt) in the 1880s and early 1890s; cf. CLAUDE WEHRLI, «L'état de la collection papyrologique de Genève», *Actes du XVe Congrès International de Papyrologie*, Troisième Partie, Bruxelles 1979, pp.20-24.

[6] See above, p.26.

[7] Grenfell and Hunt also bought most of the literary *Hibeh Papyri* in the Fayūm: see *P.Hib.* I, *Introduction*, p.1.

[8] Cf. *P.Ryl.* I, *Preface* (dated 1910): Grenfell and Hunt, who acquired the Rylands papyri «on behalf of Lord Crawford or the late Mr. Rylands», give no indication of their provenance or date of purchase.

[9] Only the beginning of a toponym is preserved (Θμοι[). Most place-names formed with this prefix, however, were in the Herakleopolites (and almost all in the Koites), while the Strasbourg collection possesses a good number of cartonnage papyri of the third century B.C. found at Al-Hība (see above, p.14 f.): one of the Roman documents found in the houses could have been bought at the same time as these. The inventory number of *P.Strasb.* V 356 (inv.2537a) is consistent with this hypothesis, being between e.g. *P.Strasb.* VII 662 (inv.2352) and *P.Strasb.* VII 642 (inv.2569), both dating from the third century B.C.

[10] See *Catalogue*, s.v. 'Αγκυρῶν πόλις, p.43 n.3.

INTRODUCTION

this suggests that it may originate from there, too, although it was bought at El-Ashmunein in 1908.

3.3. Documents of the fourth and fourth/fifth centuries A.D.

The papyri in this group have the usual provenances: a novel type of document is represented by archives from μοναί in the southernmost part of the district.

3.3.1. Documents from Ihnāsiya al-Madīna.

CEL 231-233 (Latin papyri now in Vienna, mentioning a fort at *Psoftis*) must come from the so-called Fayūm finds. *BGU* III 938 and 949 (mentioning Sobthis and Papa) were among the papyri found by Wilcken at Ihnāsiya and burnt in the port of Hamburg. Again, it is conceivable that a number of documents appearing in our lists of sources for the fourth and fourth/fifth centuries A.D. may be "left-overs" which, having escaped Wilcken, were found by local diggers and eventually acquired by different buyers, more or less at the same time. These may include *P.Athen.* 34, *P.Iand.* VI 124, *P.Lond.* III 985, *P.Oxf.* 6 (referring to villages in the περὶ Πόλιν or Tekmi toparchies), *P.Michael.* 28 and *SB* XIV 11615 (both mentioning Papa), *P.Med.* I² 66 and *P.Batav.* XXV 65 (mentioning Νείλου πόλις and Bousiris, respectively)[1].

3.3.2. Documents from Al-Hība.

A couple of documents from Al-Hība (*P.Hib.* II 219 and 220) date from the fourth century A.D.; to these *P.Ahm.* II 142 and 147[2] and *P.Ross.Georg.* V 61b might be connected (unless their provenance is Oxyrhynchus) as well as *P.Gen.* I 10, containing a reference to Phebichis[3].

3.3.3. The Nepheros archive.[4]

A novel group of sources for this period is provided by the Nepheros archive: these documents reveal the existence of a number of μοναί in the southern Herakleopolites and in the neighbouring area of the Kynopolites. There were μοναί at Ankyron, Pselemachis, Taamorou, (P)hathor: they followed the Meletian confession, and *P.Lond.* VI 1913-1929 report episodes of their struggle with the Alexandrian bishop Athanasius. No information is available about the provenance of these papyri: *P.Lond.* VI 1913-1929 were «acquired on two occasions, in 1922 and 1923, each time as part of a quite miscellaneous collection»[5]; the Nepheros archive was bought on the antiquities market in 1982[6].

---

[1] On the provenances of these papyri we have little, if any, information. *P.Iand.* VI 124 was acquired in 1926 through Carl Schmidt; Aristide Calderini seems to indicate that *P.Med.* I² 66 was purchased around 1927 as part of the Collezione Jacovelli-Vita; *P.Leid.Inst.* 65 was acquired in 1930.

[2] The *Amherst Papyri* were «bought for Lord Amherst by us [Grenfell and Hunt] at various places in Egypt during the last three years» (*P.Ahm.*, Preface [dated 1900]).

[3] Like *P.Ross.Georg.* V 20 and *P.Gen.* I 9: see above, p.28.

[4] On the dating of this archive see ROGER S. BAGNALL, «Fourth-Century Prices: New Evidence and Further Thoughts», *ZPE* 76, 1989, p.74 f.

[5] *P.Lond.* VI, p.43; see also Preface (p.III): «... acquired as a part of a joint purchase by the Museum and certain American and other universities, in which Prof. F.W. Kelsey of Michigan was the moving spirit» (see below, p.31). One wonders whether *SB* VIII 9683 (a papyrus now in Oxford, in which a monk reports the theft of an anchor, and Ἀγκυρῶν πόλις and Thelbo are mentioned) was also acquired at that time.

[6] Cf. *P.Neph.*, Vorwort. See also BÄRBEL KRAMER, «Neuere Papyri zum frühen Mönchentum in Ägypten», in

In 1981, the Macquarie University also made a purchase «comprising, or at least including an archive from the 330's and 340's A.D. The most substantial pieces are linked by their subject matter and by reference to Aspidas of Ἱππώνων and/or his family»[1]: perhaps there are links between this archive and that of Nepheros.

4. Documents from outside the Herakleopolites. From the first to the fifth century A.D.

4.1. Documents from the first and first/second century A.D.

4.1.1. From Oxyrhynchus.

Another possible provenance for *P.Ross.Georg.* II 11, beside Al Hība[2], could be Oxyrhynchus. A number of *P.Oxy.* are in fact included in our list for the first century A.D.: Grenfell and Hunt excavated there from 1896/1897 to 1906/1907; in 1910 the Italians (Ermenegildo Pistelli and Giulio Farina) took over, operating for the *Società per la ricerca dei papiri* promoted by Vitelli in Florence, and Evaristo Breccia went back there about twenty years later (from 1927/1928): *PSI* VIII 967 must come from on or other of these excavations[3], as well as *PSI* VIII 897, where the same fossil kleros is mentioned as in *P.Oxy.* II 348[4]. In the long intervals between one authorized excavation and the next, however, local diggers may have tried their hand at Oxyrhynchus: if they found any papyri, these would have ended up, of course, on the antiquities market.

As may be expected, the sources from Oxyrhynchus mainly (though not exclusively: see *P.Oxy.* XXIV 2412 and XLII 3052) record toponyms of the neighbouring Koites. *SB* XVI 12762 (a re-edition of *P.Oxy.* II 352), mentioning the village of Ko[5], is from Oxyrhynchus: it is now in New York (Columbia University) as a result of the distributions of papyri to several American universities made by the Egypt Exploration Fund in 1901, 1907, 1914-1915 and 1922. Princeton was one of these universities, and one wonders whether *P.Princ. inv.* AM 15960 B(1) may have been among the papyri from Oxyrhynchus thus distributed, or whether it was bought at another time, either on the occasion of the joint purchase of papyri by the universities of Michigan, Cornell, Princeton, Geneva and the British Museum organized by Francis W. Kelsey in 1921, or in one of the three later cooperative purchases funded «through the generosity of

---

Philanthropia kai eusebeia. Festschrift für Albrecht Dihle zum 70. Geburtstag, hrsg. von G.W. Most, H. Petersmann und A.M. Ritter, Göttingen 1993, pp.217-233.

[1] ALANNA M. EMMETT, «An unpublished Petition to Flavius Olympius (*P.Macquarie* inv. 358)», *Atti del XVII Congresso Internazionale di Papirologia*, vol.III, p.825.

[2] See above, p.26.

[3] Cf. ERIC G. TURNER, *Greek Papyri*, Princeton 1968, pp.27-31 (Grenfell and Hunt at Oxyrhynchus). On the provenance of the papyri now in Florence (*PSI*, *P.Flor.* and *P.Laur.*) see ROSARIO PINTAUDI, «Per una storia della papirologia in Italia: i papiri laurenziani (*P.Laur.*)», *Miscellanea Papyrologica* (Papyrologica Florentina VII), a cura di Rosario Pintaudi, Firenze 1980, pp.391-409; *Cinquant'anni di Papirologia in Italia. Carteggi Breccia-Comparetti-Norsa-Vitelli*, a cura di Donato Morelli e Rosario Pintaudi, con una premessa di Marcello Gigante, Napoli 1983 (at the end of the second volume, p.867 f., there is a list of the «Campagne di scavo» led between 1903 and 1940: this also records Girolamo Vitelli's and Medea Norsa's trips to Egypt, which were the occasions for the purchase of papyri); ROSARIO PINTAUDI, «Documenti per una storia della papirologia in Italia», *Analecta Papyrologica* 5, 1993, pp.155-176. On the excavation campaign led by Evaristo Breccia at Al-Hība in 1934/1935, during which some papyri were found (*PSI* VIII 967 could have been among them), see also ENRICO PARIBENI, «Rapporto preliminare su gli scavi di Hibeh», *Aegyptus* 15, 1935, p.398: «Di papiri non abbiamo raccolto altro che minuti frammenti tra la terra che riempiva le case e nelle vie tra una casa e l'altra. Quelli rinvenuti nella parte Nord dello scavo sono per lo più di scrittura greca corsiva di età romana, mentre quelli raccolti dalle case della zona Sud ... sono tutti demotici».

[4] See the list of *Fossil Kleroi in the Herakleopolite Nome*, s.v. Ἡρακλείδου τοῦ Καλλιστράτου.

[5] See *Catalogue*, s.v.

INTRODUCTION

Mr. Robert Garrett»[1]. Other Princeton papyri bear inventory numbers "neighbouring" *P.Princ. inv.* AM 15960 B(1), and are assigned dates ranging between the third and the sixth/seventh A.D.: some of these also mention Herakleopolite toponyms (they are listed in the appropriate sections of the *Chronological Index*) and are likely to have been acquired at the same time. Its nearest "neighbour", *P.Princ. inv.* AM 15960 B(2), on the other hand, contains a reference to the Arsinoite village of Kerkeusiris[2]: on this basis, the possibility cannot be ruled out that both this papyrus and *P.Princ. inv.* AM 15960 B(1) may come from the Fayūm.

4.1.2. From the Fayūm.

Fayūm provenance is certain in the case of *P.Mich.* II 121, acquired in Cairo in 1921 through the agency of Kelsey: this is an abstract of contracts drawn at the γραφεῖον of Tebtynis, and the party to one of these contracts is from the otherwise unattested Herakleopolite village of Φεναμενι. Like the preceding document, *P.Cornell* 22 contains a possible incidental reference to a Herakleopolite village (being a list of people living at Philadelphia but having their ἰδία somewhere else, it includes two Σοβθῖται: the nearest Sobthis to the Arsinoites was in the Herakleopolites); it was acquired in the same year (or the next), again through Kelsey. *P.Tebt.* II 535, «found in the houses of the town [Tebtynis] during the first month of the excavations» led by Grenfell and Hunt in 1899/1900[3], contains an order for an arrest to be put into effect by the ἀρχέφοδος of Thelbo.

In the 1920s and 1930s, the coptologist Carl Schmidt was very active as a purveyor of papyri to German universities[4]: through him were acquired *P.Giss.Univ.* 19[5] and the papyri now in the collection of Erlangen University (including *P.Erl.*58, with a much abraded Herakleopolite toponym).

P.Osl. III 151 was acquired between 1920 and 1936[6]; there is no means of knowing whether the Νεί[λου πόλις] there mentioned (assuming that this is the right supplement) was in the Arsinoites or in the Herakleopolites[7], but in both cases the Fayūm would be a likely provenance for this papyrus: its acquisition, then, may date from 1923, when a consortium formed by Oslo University with the British Museum, and other European and American universities, purchased papyri from different Fayūm villages through the agency of H.I. Bell. More papyri, this time from Oxyrhynchus, were bought by the same consortium in 1928[8].

---

[1] Cf. *P.Princ.* I, *Preface*, p.VII. No information seems to be available on the provenance of *P.Princ.* inv. AM 15960 B(1) (see the *ed.pr.* by PIETER J. SIJPESTEIJN, *Aegyptus* 70, 1990, p.36); however, since the policy of the Egypt Exploration Fund seems to have been to distribute the papyri only when they had been published, this papyrus is more likely to have been acquired in 1921, or later.

[2] Cf. also *P.Princ.* inv. AM 15960 A(1) and A(2).

[3] *P.Tebt.* II, *Preface*, p.V.

[4] On Carl Schmidt as a supplier of papyri to many collections in Germany and northern Europe, see ISABELLA ANDORLINI, «Scavi e acquisti di papiri negli anni '30: il caso dei PLund», *Istituto Papirologico «G.Vitelli». Firenze. Comunicazioni*, 1995, p.47 f. and n.11 (with further bibliography).

[5] All documents edited in this publication were bought at Madînat al-Fayūm: cf. *P.Giss.Univ.*, *Vorwort*, p.3. The village referred to in this papyrus, however, is probably the Arsinoite Kos:]νοιτην, on the *verso*, is probably to be restored as εἰς τὸν Ἀρσι]νοίτην.

[6] As stated in the *Preface* to *P.Osl.* III.

[7] See *Catalogue*, s.vv. ΝΕΙΛΟΥ ΠΟΛΙΣ and ΤΙΛΩΘΙΣ.

[8] See *P.Osl.* II, *Preface*.

4.2. Documents of the second and third century A.D.[1]

4.2.1. From the Fayūm.

The *Wilcken Ostraka* were found by Adolf Erman in 1886 at Sidmant Al-Gebel[2]: not surprisingly, they record traffic between the Arsinoite and the Herakleopolite nomes. The *O.Meyer* 51, *O.Mich.* I 68, and the ostraka published as *SB* I 1492-1517 (several of which are in our *Chronological Index* for the third century A.D.) belong to the same class of documents, but date from about 50 years later: they all emanate from the sitologos-office at Theadelphia[3].

Our list also includes some documents that come from the Fayūm and were bought (or found) during the first ten years or so of the twentieth century. Thus, *P.Berl.Leihg.* I 2 and *SB* V 7515, both in Berlin, may come from Theadelphia[4]; their inventory numbers are not too distant from that of *BGU* VII 1568 (dealing with the "abduction" of a female donkey from the Neilopolites into the Arsinoites). *P.Laur.* IV 174 was bought, with all other texts published in this series, «in Egitto nel primo decennio del secolo»[5]: it contains a reference to the village of Τοου, as does *SB* XVIII 13151 (now in Cairo; no information on its provenance); *P.Flor.* III 364, published in a much earlier series, must have been acquired in the same years as the *P.Laur.*: its provenance from the Fayūm is suggested by the mention of Καινή. The same locality appears in *P.Fayum* 23, which Grenfell and Hunt found at Harît/Theadelphia, and in *P.Mil.Vogl.* IV 214 (from Tebtynis). *P.Tebt.* II 301 and 575 mention Herakleopolite localities only incidentally; it is less obvious why *P.Tebt.* III 353 (a receipt for tax-arrears paid to the agent of the komogrammateus of Peensamoi) should have been found, like the other two, in a house at Tebtynis[6]. The *Papyri Pragenses*, once the private possession of Carl Wessely, were bought in 1904[7]: they, too, relate mostly to the Arsinoite nome.

P.Mich. IX 551, *O.Mich.* 179 and *SB* XIV 11341 come from Karanis: they were found during the excavations led there by the expedition of the University of Michigan in 1924-1934.

Phebichis (main centre of the Koites) and Thmoinache (Techtho toparchy) are mentioned in *P.Petaus* 28, an "intruder"[8] bought in 1954 with the half of Petaus' archive which is now in Cologne: it is not apparent what this letter is doing among the papers of the komogrammateus of five villages in the Arsinoite nome.

---

[1] Two documents in our III A.D. list of documents mentioning Herakleopolite toponyms come from Thebes (*O.Theb.* 132) and Panopolis (*P.Beatty Panop.* 1). *SB* XIV 12193 is a mummy-label, like the *Ét.Fouad* 2 (to which no date is assigned).

[2] Cf. *O.Wilck.* I, p.22; a few of the *Wilcken Ostraka* were already in the Berlin collection before «etwa 1880» and are said to belong «zu den alten Beständen»: these may have been from the first or second Fayūm finds.

[3] See PIERRE JOUGUET, *BIFAO* 2, 1902, p.91 (about *SB* I 1492-1517): «... achetés chez un marchand grec de Médinet, mais leur contenu ne laisse aucun doute sur leur origine: ils émanent tous du ... grenier publique de Théadelphie et ont dû être ramassés à Hârit, sur les ruines du village antique». The *O.Meyer* were acquired through Carl Schmidt between 1904 and 1912 (see *Vorwort* to the edition, pp.III-IV).

[4] See *BGU* IX, *Einleitung*, pp.V-VI; also *P.Col.* V, *Introduction*, p.XV. *SB* V 7515 came to Berlin as one of seven rolls (bought by Schubart in 1912): more texts from these rolls were published in *BGU* IX; besides, the texts published in *P.Col.* II and *P.Col.* V come from the same find. Inventory numbers of the Berlin papyri: *P.Berl.Leihg.* I 2 (inv.11541); *SB* V 7515 (inv.11652); *BGU* VII 1568 (inv.11473).

[5] *P.Laur.* I, *Introduzione*, p.9. See also above, p.30 n.3.

[6] During the excavations of 1899/1900: see *P.Tebt.* II, *Preface*, p.V. On *P.Tebt.* II 353 see also *Catalogue, s.v.* ΠΕΕΝΣΑΜΟΙ.

[7] *P.Prag.* I, *Introduzione*, p.3: «Relativamente alle origini della sua collezione Wessely ci informa ... che acquistò i suoi papiri nel 1904 da un mercante ... Mihram Sivadjian».

[8] See Edd. *ad loc.*: «Eine sichere Angabe darüber, ob die Urkunde ein Bestandteil des Petaus-Archivs war, oder gar, aus welchem Grunde sie in das Archiv hineingekommen ist, läßt sich nicht machen».

4.2.2. From Oxyrhynchus.

Other *PSI* papyri in our *Chronological Index*, as well as *P.Erl.* 48[1] and *P.Lund* VI 8-9[2], probably come from Oxyrhynchus, and the same provenance may be guessed for *P.Alex.* inv.563 (note that *PSI* VI 928, mentioned above, is also at Alexandria: inv.247)[3].

Besides the *P.Oxy.* included in our *Chronological Index*, an Oxyrhynchite provenance is established for *P.Wash.Univ.* I 18[4] and for *SB* XIV 11958 and 11959, which their editor rightly connected to *P.Oxy.* XX 2272[5]. The last three documents were in fact all part of a τόμος συγκολλήσιμος recording expenses for the re-furbishing of sacred buildings in the Herakleopolites, which was later re-used on the *verso* by an official in the Oxyrhynchite nome: this, then, is their *provenance* and also their *second origin*.

4.3. Documents of the fourth and fourth/fifth century A.D.

4.3.1. From Oxyrhynchus.

There is no information on the provenance of *SB* XVIII 13260, but it seems reasonable to connect it with another papyrus in the same collection, *P.Mich.* XV 722 (both mention localities in the Koites), which was received from the British Museum in 1926. Both may well come from Oxyrhynchus, and so may (besides, of course, *P.Oxy.* XIV 1708) *PSI* III 222 and IX 1037, *P.Flor.* I 11 and *P.Laur.* II 42. All villages mentioned in these documents were in the Koites.

4.3.2. From the Fayūm.

A large number of our sources for the IV A.D. originate from Karanis[6]: these include, besides *P.Mich.* IX 573 and several *O.Mich.*, *P.NYU* 4 and 11 and *SB* VI 9632[7]. Two documents belonging to Fayūm archives (*P.Abinn.*[8] 11 and *P.Sakaon* 22) refer to the harbour of Λευκόγιον.

5. Documents of the fifth/sixth and sixth century A.D.

More documents concerning monks are in our list, mentioning much the same places as in *P.Lond.* VI 1913-1929 and in the Nepheros archive: these include *P.Köln* III 151 (no information on provenance) and

---

[1] Bought through Carl Schmidt: see above p.31.

[2] No information on provenance is offered in the *ed.pr.*

[3] No information on provenance. The Graeco-Roman Museum of Alexandria was officially opened on September the 26th, 1895. It was endowed with papyri given by the Direction Générale du Service des Antiquités, or donated by E. Glymenopoulo and by A. Cattavi; more papyri were bought by the direction of the museum.

[4] *P.Wash.Univ.*, *Preface*, p.II: «In return for contributions to aid in his excavations at Oxyrhynchus in the 1920s Sir Flinders Petrie sent to Washington University several hundred papyri...».

[5] ANNA ŚWIDEREK, «Deux Papyrus de la Sorbonne relatifs à des travaux effectués dans des temples de l'Héracléopolite», *JJP* 11/12, 1957/1958, pp.59-91.

[6] On these excavations see A.E.R. BOAK - E.E. PETERSON, *Karanis: topographical and architectural report of excavations during the seasons 1924-8*, Ann Arbor 1931.

[7] See *P.NYU*, *Preface*, p.IX; *P.Col.* VII, *General Introduction*, p.3.

[8] On the acquisition of the Geneva part of the Abinnaeus archive through Édouard Naville, see *P.Abinn.*, *Introduction*, pp.2 ff.

SB XII 10939, a letter addressed to the bishop of Oxyrhynchus[1], perhaps also *P.Heid.* III 246 (a list of payments including a reference to a κλῆρος Ἀθωρ; provenance unknown).

Apart from some Oxyrhynchite documents[2], all other sources in this list come from the first and second Fayūm finds, comprising a vast number of documents from Ihnāsiya al-Madīna now in Vienna.

6. Documents of the sixth, seventh and eighth century A.D.

Almost all papyri from the Herakleopolites dating from the late Byzantine and early Arabic period are now in Vienna, being the fruit of the first and second Fayūm finds. We know, however, that some documents from the same finds went to Berlin[3]: this may explain the presence in our list of *P.Berl. Zill.* 7, *SB* XX 14123, 14705, 14236, 14234[4], *SB* I 5337, 5338 and 5681. Others went to Paris, London (*P.Lond.* II 392; III 1097[5]) and *via* London, perhaps, to Dublin[6] and Michigan (*P.Mich.* inv.489[7]). One may even have stayed in Egypt (*SB* VI 9262: reference to Leukogion). *P.Erl.* 67, *P.Köln* III 158 and VII 319-323 may have the same provenance, too, judging by internal evidence[8].

The other possible provenance for the documents mentioning Herakleopolite toponyms, at this late stage, is again Oxyrhynchus: besides several *P.Oxy.*, we may include in this group *P.Mich.* X 591, *P.Princ.* II 105, *P.Wash.Univ.* II 103, *SB* I 1967 and XVIII 13949, *P.Laur.* II 47[9], *SB* VI 8987.

P.Bad. IV 55 (found at Qarāra)[10], *SB* XVIII 13888 and perhaps *P.Batav.* XXV 80B should perhaps, again because of internal evidence, be related to earlier documents pertaining to the monasteries in the southern Herakleopolites.

---

[1] This document is now at the Beinecke Library (Yale). Its editor offers no information on provenance. In any case, it is not among those given to Yale by the Egypt Exploration Fund (cf. *P.Yale* II, pp.XV ff.; also *P.Yale* I, *Preface*, p.VII).

[2] These include *PSI* I 80, III 183, *SB* I 1945, besides *P.Oxy.* XVI 1834, XX 2268 and *P.Mert.* 46 (the last three documents, all referring to the village of Γεσσιάς, must originate from the same archive).

[3] See above, p.26.

[4] The last two (*SB* XX 14236 and 14234; *ed.pr.* GÜNTER POETHKE-PIETER J. SIJPESTEIJN, *Archiv* 38, 1992, pp.33-38) «gehörten einst zu den Sammlungen von Heinrich Brugsch und Rudolf Mosse und gelangten mit einer größeren Zahl von Faijum Papyri in den Jahren 1891, 1893 und 1894 in die Berliner Papyrus-Sammlung» (*ibid.*, p.33).

[5] *PUG* I 50 was given to Lumbroso by Grenfell in 1896, who bought it together with documents published in *P.Grenf.* II (cf. *PUG* I, p.103). Its date, and the toponym mentioned (Leukogion), would seem to relate it to the papyri we are discussing.

[6] *P.Dub.*, *Preface*, p.IX: «In most cases ... no record of their acquisition ... This, of course, does not apply to the Oxyrhynchus documents, whose arrival from Oxford as a gift from the Egypt Exploration Fund was duly recorded» - but not, apparently, in the case of the documents mentioning Herakleopolite toponyms. On the other hand, it should be noted that the only other loan with Christian invocation, besides *P.Dub.* 28, now in Berlin (*BGU* I 314), dates from the same period (630 A.D.), and also originates from the Herakleopolites. Herakleopolis itself is mentioned in *BGU* I 314, while the *P.Dub.* in our list refer to Leukogion and Onnes (Tekmi toparchy, which bordered upon the περὶ Πόλιν). It seems very likely for all these documents to be from the first or the second Fayūm find.

[7] Unless it comes from Oxyrhynchus: but the reference to Leukogion rather relates this document to the others we are discussing here.

[8] Note that *P.Köln* II 99, for which a provenance from Herakleopolis has been suggested (see above, p.28 n.2), mentions Peenpibyk(is) along with other villages: Peenpibyk(is) also recurs in *P.Köln* VII 319 and 321, suggesting the same provenance for these documents, too. The inventory numbers, however, differ widely.

[9] *P.Laur.* II 47 is among the papyri bought by Girolamo Vitelli for the Biblioteca Laurenziana in January 1904 in Cairo, Ghizeh, Madînat al-Fayūm and El-Ashmunein: cf. ROSARIO PINTAUDI, «Per una storia della papirologia in Italia» (cited on p.30 n.3), pp.405, 406 (and n.23), also p.395.

[10] According to Bilabel, in his introduction to this document: «In meinem Privatbesitz (... in Maghagha zusammen mit einigen Altertümern, unter denen ein Bronzeschöpflöffel hervorragt, gekauft). Die Gegenstände weisen deutlich auf das benachbarte Qarâra als Fundort hin».

PART TWO

The Toponyms of the Herakleopolite Nome

1 Catalogue

A.[±3]

VII/VIII A.D.	*Stud.Pal.* X 17,8	ἀπὸ χ'ω'(ρίου) Α.[±3]

The villages of Pkommatoei, Koma and Poinami (= Peenameus) are listed in the same document.

ΑΓΗΜΑ (toparchy)

25 Feb.-25 March 261 B.C.	*P.Hib.* I 101,3	σιτόλογος τοῦ Ἀγήματος
about 250 B.C.	*BGU* XIV 2392,2	Ἀγήματος
139 B.C.	*P.Tebt.* III 987,5	ὁ σιτολογῶν [........] τοῦ Ἀγήματος (4-5)
I B.C. (after 84/83 B.C.)	*BGU* XIV 2370,37	Ἀγήματος
63/62 B.C.	*BGU* VIII 1771,13	τοῦ Ἀγήματος
24 October 50/49 B.C.	*SB* V 7611,1	παρ' Ἀρχακρέους τοπογραμματέως τοῦ Ἀγήμ[ατος]
29 July 25 B.C.	*SB* XVI 12312, col.II,5-6	Ἡρακλείῳ τοπάρχῃ Ἀγήματος
8/7 B.C.	*BGU* XVI 2562,6	περὶ ῎Αγ'η'(μα)
about 7-4 B.C.	*BGU* XVI 2662,13	Ἀγήματος
6/5 B.C.	*BGU* XVI 2572,3	῎Αγημα
218-222 A.D.	*CPR* I 61,4	[δι' ἐπιτηρητῶν ἀγορανομίας μερῶν τ]οπαρχίας Ἀγήμ[ατος (2-3)
221 A.D.? 225/226 A.D.?	*CPR* I 78,4	δι' ἐπιτηρητῶν ἀγορανομίας Ἀγ[ήματος (3-4)

2 July 225 A.D.[1]	*P.Vind.Bosw.* 7,11	δι' ἐπιτηρητῶν ἀγορανομίας Ἀγήματος
222 A.D.	*Stud.Pal.* XX 26,40; [49]	ἐπὶ τὴν ἀγορ(ανομίαν) Ἀγ[ή]ματ(ος)
222-235 A.D.	*CPR* VI 73,4-5	δι' ἐπιτηρητῶν ἀγορα[νομίας Ἀγή]ματος (4-5)
236 A.D.? (cf. *BL* 7,259)	*Stud.Pal.* XX 47,3-4 (= *MPER* V p.96 = *CPR* I 6)	δι' ἐπι[τ]ηρητ[ο]ῦ ἀγορανομίας μερῶν τ]οπαρχίας Ἀγή[μ]ατος
first half of III A.D.	*CPR* I 86,3	[..... Ἀγήμα]τος
first half of III A.D.	*CPR* I 88,1 (+ *CPR* I 132[2])	ἀγορανομίας Ἀ]γήματος
first half of III A.D.	*CPR* I 96,2	[... Ἀγήματ]ος
first half of III A.D.	*CPR* I 98,3	ἀγορανομίας Ἀγήμα]τος
mid-III A.D.	*P.Select* 17,4	Ἀγή[μ]ατος[3]
III A.D.	*CPR* I 87,2-3	

See also *s.vv.* ΑΝΩ (ΑΓΗΜΑ); ΚΑΤΩ (ΑΓΗΜΑ).

ETYMOLOGY: τὸ Ἄγημα (or τὸ Μακεδονικόν) was the name of a special unit in the Ptolemaic army: see *PPt* II 4394-4414 (with the *Addenda* in *PPt* VIII), and cf. WILLY PEREMANS, «Les indigènes égyptiens dans l'armée de terre des Lagides. Recherches anthroponymiques», *Ancient Society* 9, 1978, pp.98-99. See also *s.vv.* οἱ Ἀρχαῖοι, περὶ Αὐλήν.

A list of the villages that can be assigned to this toparchy will be found on p.293.

P.Hels. I 6 assigns the village of Alilais to the Ἄνω toparchy: *BGU* XIV 2370, on the other hand, refers to Alilais as being in the Ἄγημα, immediately after an entry concerning Peensemtheus, which it locates in the Κάτω toparchy. Other documents (*BGU* XIV 2437 and 2438, from the same find) place this same village in the Ἄγημα κάτω. It follows that (a) the κάτω toparchy of *BGU* XIV 2370 coincides with the Ἄγημα κάτω (because Peensemtheus is assigned both to the κάτω and to the Ἄγημα κάτω in different documents); (b) the references, in a few other documents, to a Κάτω τοπαρχία must be to the (Ἄγημα) κάτω (see *s.v.*); (c) the Ἄνω toparchy of *P.Hels.* I 6 is in fact the (Ἄγημα) ἄνω toparchy (as Alilais is assigned to the Ἄνω toparchy in *P.Hels.* I 6, but to the Ἄγημα in *BGU* XIV 2370).

It seems safe to conclude that the Ἄγημα toparchy was divided into Northern (Κάτω) and Southern

---

[1] On this dating, see JEAN A. STRAUS, *Chr.d'Ég.* 69, 1994, pp.305-307.

[2] Cf. *P.Rain.Cent.* p.88, n.10.

[3] Reading checked for me by Johannes Diethart: «Z.4 scheint mir (und auch H. Harrauer) Ἀγή[μ]ατος sehr unsicher, aber aus dem Zusammenhang heraus durchaus passend» (letter from Johannes Diethart, 9 September 1994).

("Ανω) Ἄγημα, and that these two toparchies were sometimes also more simply called Ἄνω and Κάτω τοπαρχία.

The Agema, Bousiris, and Tilothis toparchies appear in consecutive lines in *BGU* XVI 2662.

ΑΓΗΡΜΕΙ [1]

V A.D.	*Stud.Pal.* X 233, col. II,21

ΑΓΚΥΡΩΝ ΠΟΛΙΣ

about 260 B.C.	*P.Hib.* I 112,74	[᾽Αγκ]υρῶν π[ό]λ]ις
239 (238) or 214 (213) B.C.	*P.Hib.* I 117,15-16	ἐξ ᾽Αγ[κυρῶν πόλεως] [2]
237 B.C. (cf. *BL* 2.2,183)	*P.Bad.* (=*VBP*) IV 82,8	᾽Αγκυ(ρῶν) πόλεως
228 (227) B.C.	*P.Hib.* I 67,4	τοῖς ἐν ᾽Αγκυρῶν πόλει [ὑ]πογεγραμμένοις ὑφάνταις (4-5)
mid-III B.C. [3]	*P.Fuad Crawford* 5,*verso*,7	Αγκυρων.....
2 Sept. 162 B.C.	*P.Hels.* I 26,A,31	᾽Ανκυ(ρῶν) πό(λεως)
13 Dec. 19 A.D.	*CPGr* II 3, 5;6;15 (= *P.Ross.Georg.* II 11)	ἀπὸ κώμης ᾽Αγκυρῶνος (5), ἐπὶ τῆς ᾽Αγκυρῶν (6), κωμογραμματεὺς ᾽Αγκυρῶν καὶ τῶ[ν συν]κυρουσῶν κωμῶν μετ᾽ ἐπιτρό[π]ου Ἡρακλ[είδου] τοῦ πατρός (15-17)
July/August (?) 98 A.D.	*P.Heid.* IV 326,2	ἀπὸ κώ]μης ᾽Αγκυ[ρῶ]νο[ς τοῦ ὑπὲρ Μέμφιν Ἡρα]κ[λεοπολεί[του] νομ[οῦ (2-3)
late I or early II A.D.	*P.Hib.* II 218,9;13	᾽Αγκυρώνων (9,13)
Sept.-Nov. 117 A.D.	*SB* XIV 11958,27;29	ἀπὸ ᾽Αγκυρώ(νων) (27); λατομίας ᾽Αγκυρώ(νων) (29)

---

[1] «Kol. II 21 ist wahrscheinlich Αγηρμει zu lesen» (letter from Johannes Diethart, of February 25, 1994).

[2] «Very likely one or both words were abbreviated» (Edd. *ad loc.*).

[3] On the re-dating of this document see *Introduction*, p.14 n.7.

133 A.D.	*P.Bad.(=VBP)* 75a,3	ἀπὸ κώμης Ἀγκ[υρώνων]
3 July 138 A.D.	*P.Heid.* IV 320,9-10	ἀπ[ὸ] Ἀγκυ]ρώνων
23 July 138 A.D.	*P.Bad.(=VBP)* IV 74,7;12	ἀπὸ κώμης Ἀγκυρῶν τοῦ Ἡρακλεοπολ(ίτου) νομοῦ (6-8); ἀπὸ τῶν αὐτῶν Ἀγκυρῶν (11-12)
19 June 139 A.D.	SB XII 11262 (=*P.Bad.* IV 79),11;18	ἀπὸ κώ(μης) Ἀνκυρ(ῶνος) τοῦ Ἡρακλεοπ(ολίτου) νο(μοῦ) (11-12); ἀπὸ μὲγ τῆς προκ(ειμένης) Ἀνκυρῶνο(ς) (17-18)
8 March 147 A.D.	SB XX 14304 = *P.Corn.* 17,3	ἀπὸ κώμ(ης) Ἀγκυρώ(νων)
11 March 147 A.D. (cf. *ZPE* 107,1995,p.95)	*P.Bad.(=VBP)* IV 75b,5	ἀπ[ὸ] κώμ(ης) Ἀγκυρώνων (4-5)
171-176 A.D. (cf. *BL* 9,103)	*P.Heid.* IV 297,4	ἀπὸ κώμη[ς Ἀ]γκυρῶ[ν]
177-180 A.D.	*P.Hib.* II 237+217,17 [1]	ἀπὸ κώμης [Ἀγκυ]ρώνων (16-17)
9 June, 20 July, 26 August 182 A.D.	*P.Heid.* IV 322 (= *VBP* IV 81),5	ἀπαιτη(τῇ) πρ(άκτορος) ἀργ(υρικῶν) Ἀ[γ]κυρώνων καὶ ἄλ(λων) κωμ(ῶν) (4-5)
II A.D.	*P.Bad.(=VBP)* IV 77,8	ἐν κ]ώμῃ Ἀγκυρώνων
II/III A.D. [2]	BGU XI 2073,2	Ἀγκυρώνων
II/III A.D.	PSI VI 928,12	περὶ κώμην Ἀνκυρώνων τοῦ ὑπὲρ Μέμφιν Ἡρακλεοπολείτου νομοῦ (12-13)
208 A.D.	PSI I 32,3;8	ἀπὸ κώμης Ἀγκυρώνων (2-3); περὶ τὴν αὐτὴν Ἀγκυρώνων ἐκ νότου τῆς κώμης (8-9)

---

[1] These two papyri were joined by DIETER HAGEDORN, *ZPE* 97, 1993, pp.97-101.

[2] See below p.43 n.3

217 A.D.	*Stud.Pal.* II p.28, 6;11;12;13-14	ἀπὸ κώμ(ης) Ἀγκυρώνων (6); Ἀγκυρώνων (11); κώμ[ης] Ἀγκυρώνων(12); ἀπὸ [κώ]μης Ἀγκυρώνων (13-14)
7 Oct. 225 A.D. (cf. *BL* 9,293)	*SB* XVI 12836 (=*CPR* I 243),2-3;7;37	ἀπὸ Ἀγ[κυρώ]νων (2-3); ἐν τῇ προκειμένῃ Ἀγκυρώ[νων] (7); ἀ[πὸ Ἀγκυρ]ών[ων] (37)
225-233 A.D.	*SB* XVI 12837,8	ἐν κώμῃ Ἀνκυρώνων
early III A.D.	*P.Ryl.* II 87,5	πεδία Ἀγκυ[ρ]ώνων
309 A.D.	*P.Hib.* II 219,4;12	τοῖς [ἀπὸ Ἀγκυρ]ώνων λινούφοις (3-4); [Ἀγκυρ]ώνων (12)
335 A.D.	*P.Hib.* II 220,5	κωμαρχῶν κώμης Ἀγκυ[ρ]ώνων (4-5)
IV A.D.	*P.Neph.* 3,11	τοῦ μονα[χο]ῦ μονῆς Ἀγκυρῶνος (10-11)
IV A.D.	*P.Neph.* 6,24	τοῦ μοναχοῦ τοῦ ἐν Ἀγκυρῶνγει
end of IV A.D.	*SB* VIII 9683,6;12	Ἀγκυρωνίτης (?) (6); μονῆς Ἀγκυρωνίτης (?) (12)
29 Sept. 457 A.D.	*P.Rain.Cent.* 101,10	ἐ[ν π]εδίοις Ἀνκυρ(ώνων) [πόλ]εως[1]
VI A.D.	*Stud.Pal.* III 453,2	ἀπὸ ἐποικ(ίου) Ἀγκυρ(ῶνος)

Literary Sources

I B.C.	ALEXANDR. POLYHIST. *ap.* STEPH. BYZ. *s.v.* (= ALEXANDR. POLYHIST. 273F10 Jacoby)	
II A.D.	PTOL. IV,5,57	Ἀγγυρῶν ἢ Ἀγκυρῶν πόλις
V A.D.	STEPH. BYZ. *s.v.*	Ἀγκυρῶν <πόλις>
VII A.D.	AN. RAV. III,2,2	*Angiopolis*[2]

---

[1] The denomination compounded with πόλις is otherwise only attested in the Ptolemaic period.

[2] Cf. *Abh. Ak. Berlin, Phil.-hist. Kl.*, 1858, p.131 n.154.

See also:]ωνος.

TOPARCHY: Koites.

ETYMOLOGY: «So called because they cut the stones(?) which they used as anchors from the nearby quarries. This was a traditional Egyptian craft» (ALEX. POLYHIST. ap. STEPH. BYZ. s.v. Ἀγκυρῶν <πόλις>)[1]. At some point during the Roman period, this πόλις was downgraded to κώμη, possibly as part of a general reorganisation of the nome at the beginning of the Roman domination (conversely, Tilothis was promoted from κώμη to πόλις, and actually renamed Νείλου πόλις: see s.v.).

The alteration (first attested in *P.Heid.* IV 326, of year 98 A.D.) of the original name Ἀγκυρῶν πόλις, typically preserved in the literary sources, to Ἀγκυρώνων κώμη, is perhaps best accounted for by assuming that the place-name was usually rendered Ἀγκυρῶν (as in Stephanus of Byzantium), and that this genitive plural came to be felt as a nominative singular, on the analogy of Greek words such as ἱππών, from which Ἱππώνων (or Ἱππῶνος) κώμη was derived (see s.v.).

MODERN ARABIC NAME: Ankyron was identified with Al-Ḥiba by Bilabel, who found papyri mentioning it among the ruins of houses of the Roman period, a few hundred yards to the north of the modern hamlet[2]. This identification was already deemed possible, but not certain, by Grenfell and Hunt, who also found some Roman papyri (referring to a large number of places in the Koites, among them Ἀγκυρῶν) in the ancient town[3]; they also pointed out that «the quarries at Hibeh would well accord with [Stephanus' of Byzantium] explanation of the name Ἀγκυρῶν πόλις»[4]. Ptolemy's *Geographia* located it on the east bank, a little to the north (one quarter longitudinal degree) of the point at which the two branches of the river joined, after forming what he describes as the Herakleopolite island[5].

Near the modern hamlet of Al-Ḥiba, *Teudzoi* (*T3j.w-ḏ3j.t*: «Their wall») was an important fortress in the late Pharaonic period[6]: in 1902 and 1903 its remains were searched by Grenfell and Hunt (who had been preceded by the Arab dealer Shêkh Hassan). They describe the site as follows: «The town was built on rising ground, which reaches its highest point at the north-west corner of the site. The most conspicuous feature is the *massive wall* of crude brick, some metres thick, which protects it from attack on the north and east sides, the east wall running in a south-westerly direction to meet the river, so that the area enclosed

---

[1] Ἀγκυρῶν· πόλις Αἰγύπτου, ὡς Ἀλέξανδρος ἐν [ι]γ Αἰγυπτιακῶν, ὠνόμασται δὲ οὕτως, ἐπειδὴ λιθι....ας ἔτεμνον αἷς κατεχρῶντο ἀκκύρα<ι>ς ἐκ † δὲ τῆς παρακειμένης λατομίας. [τὸ ἐθνικὸν] ἡ τέχνη ἐκ τοῦ Αἰγυπτίων ἤθους. (τὸ ἐθνικὸν is apparently anticipated from the following sentence which, according to Stephanus' normal practice, should be: <τὸ ἐθνικὸν Ἀγκυροπολίτης>, ὡς γὰρ Κυνῶν πόλις Κυνοπολίτης κτλ).

[2] FRIEDRICH BILABEL, «Der griechische Name der Stadt El-Hibe», *Philologus* 77 (1921), pp.422-425. See also *P.Bad.* (= *VBP*) IV, *Einleitung*, p.7, where these papyri are listed: *P.Bad.* = *VBP* IV 74; *P.Bad.* = *VBP* IV 75a and 75b (two census declarations recently re-examined by ROGER S. BAGNALL, *BASP* 27, 1990, pp.2-3); *P.Heid.* IV 321 (re-ed. of *P.Bad.* = *VBP* IV 76); *P.Bad.* = *VBP* IV 77; *SB* XII 11262 (re-ed. of *P.Bad.* = *VBP* IV 79); *P.Heid.* IV 322 (re-ed. of *P.Bad.* = *VBP* IV 81); *P.Bad.* = *VBP* IV 88. Many more literary and documentary papyri were obtained, as is well known, from the cartonnage of the mummies found in the vast local necropolis: MARIA ROSARIA FALIVENE, «The Literary Papyri from Al-Ḥiba: a new approach», in *Akten des 21. Internationalen Papyrologenkongresses*, Stuttgart-Leipzig 1997, pp.273-280.

[3] Listed in the *Introduction* to the first volume of the *Hibeh Papyri* (published in 1906), p.8; they are now all published: *P.Hib.* II 272; 220; 278; 218 *recto* and *verso* (following the order in which they were mentioned by Grenfell and Hunt).

[4] *P.Hib.* I, *Introduction*, p.9 (cf. p.1: «The high desert at this point approaches the river edge, leaving only a narrow strip a few yards in width available for cultivation, and providing suitable places for quarrying limestone»).

[5] See *Introduction*, p.5. This location is in fact too far north in relation to Herakleopolis; it is also incorrect if compared with the identification of Ankyron with Al-Ḥiba: cf. *Introduction*, p.12.

[6] The identification of *T3j.w-ḏ3j.t* with Techtho (see s.v.) is not tenable, both on phonetical and on geographical grounds.

forms with the river a kind of acute-angled triangle[1]. ..... Opposite the ruins, and separated only by a channel which becomes dry in the summer, is an *island* about 2 miles long, which was already there in early times, for it is mentioned in the demotic papyri from Hibeh of Darius' reign. The modern village of El-Hibeh is a poor hamlet a few hundred yards to the south of the ruins, and is combined for administrative purposes with another village on the island which contains a few hundred feddans of cultivated ground, while on the main land there is practically none»[2].

Ankyron is assigned to the Koites in *P.Hib.* I 112; *P.Hib.* I 117; *P.Hib.* I 67; *P.Hels.* I 26 A; *P.Heid.* IV 320. More documents associate it with other villages in the same area (*P.Fuad Crawford* 5, *P.Ross.Georg.* II 11, *P.Hib.* II 218, *P.Ryl.* II 87, *P.Hib.* II 219, *P.Neph.* 3 and 6, *SB* VIII 9683, *P.Rain.Cent.* 101, *Stud.Pal.* III 453).

A number of papyri of the second century A.D. deal with local quarrying, and the related activity of Ankyron as a port: local naukleroi (their names all Egyptian)[3] conveyed stone (also worked stone), and other materials, to various destinations: nine columns (their bases already dressed, the capitals not yet worked) to Herakleopolis (*P.Hib.* II 237 + 217); one hundred columns to the ὅρμος Ἀρτέμιδος θεᾶς μεγίστης (*SB* XIV 11958); materials for the building of a theatre from Ankyron to Ptolemais Hormou (*SB* XII 11262); chaff from the Oxyrhynchites to Antinoupolis (to be employed in the building of a theatre there) is also carried by naukleroi from Ankyron (*P.Bad.* = *VBP* IV 74).

In the III B.C. weavers (ὑφάνται[4]) and, more specifically, carpet-weavers (ταπιδυφάνται) are attested at Ankyron in *P.Hib.* I 67 and 112, respectively; the local λινούφοι are provided with λινά from the neighbouring villages in the second half of the IV A.D. (*P.Hib.* II 219).

Cultivated land (πεδία) is attested near the Μεσσαλινιανὴ οὐσία: here was, in the Ptolemaic period, the kleros granted to Μενέλαος (*P.Ryl.* II 87, *SB* XVI 12836; the second document records land now assigned to the veteran soldier Aelius Syron: cf. also *SB* XVI 12837). Another reference to the same πεδία is found in *P.Rain.Cent.* 101.

In the IV A.D., *P.Neph.* 3 and 6 mention a μονὴ Ἀγκυρῶνος, one establishment in a net of (probably Meletian[5]) monasteries in the same area: μοναί at Pselemachis[6], Taamorou;[7] and Phathor (or Hathor) are also attested in the Nepheros archive.

---

[1] A map of the site may be found in the report by AHMED BEY KAMAL, *ASAE* 2, 1901, p.84 f.

[2] In the *Introduction* to the first volume of the *Hibeh Papyri* (pp.1-2; italics mine). See also *P.Ryl.dem.*, pp.37-39.

[3] Pareitis, the son of Pausiris (*SB* XIV 11958); Pausiris, the son of Hatres, and Heron, the son of Pisys (*P.Bad.* = *VBP* IV 74); the same Heron, son of Pisys (*SB* XII 11262); Pamunis, the son of Pamunis, and Pausiris, the son of Paneus (*P.Hib.* II 237 + 217: recently unified by DIETER HAGEDORN, *ZPE* 97, 1993, pp.97-101). Some of these names (like Pareitis) must have been typical of Ankyron and its neighbourhood: cf. *P.Heid.* IV 297,3 n.; cf. also the comments by the Editor of *BGU* XI 2073. In two, perhaps three cases, the same people may actually be mentioned in *P.Heid.* IV 320 and *BGU* XI 2073: Pnephoros son of Psenamunis (ll.5 and 11, respectively), Pareitis son of Pnephoros (ll.8 and 13, respectively) and Pareitis son of Ta[peteamunis] (l.9, and ll.7 and 14, respectively). Should these identifications stand, the dating of *BGU* XI 2073 would have to be revised accordingly, as *P.Heid.* IV 320 dates from 138 A.D.

[4] Ὑφάνται are similarly attested at Choinotmis (also in *P.Hib.* I 68), a village connected to Ankyron in other documents, too (*P.Hib.* I 112; *P.Fuad Crawford* 5; *P.Heid.* IV 320).

[5] See BÄRBEL KRAMER, «Neuere Papyri zum frühen Mönchtum in Ägypten», in *Philanthropia kai eusebeia. Festschrift für Albrecht Dihle zum 70. Geburtstag*, hrsg. von G.W. Most, H. Petersmann und A.M. Ritter, Göttingen 1993, pp.217-233.

[6] In the same document with Ankyron: *P.Hib.* I 112; *P.Fuad Crawford* 5.

[7] Also recurring with Ankyron in *P.Fuad Crawford* 5.

ΑΓΥΦΑΛΟΣ

| 138-161 A.D. | P.Hib. II 277,19 | ἀπὸ Αγυφαλος κώ[μης [1] |

TOPARCHY: Koites.

P.Hib. II 277 was written by Herakleides from Choinothmis (in the Koites), on account of an illiterate man ἀπὸ Αγυφαλος κώ[μης.

ΑΙΛΙΑΝΟΥ [2]

V-VI A.D.	P.Rain.Cent. 133,2	εἰς τὸ ἐποίκιον Αἰλιανοῦ
26 April, 629 or 644 A.D. [3]	CPR VIII 51,2	ἀπὸ ἐπ(οικίου) Αἰλιανοῦ (1-2)
VII/VIII A.D.	CPR IV 2,17	χ(ωρίον) Αἰλιαν'οῦ'
VII-VIII A.D.	Stud.Pal. X 230,3	χ(ωρίον) Αἰλιαν'οῦ'

ETYMOLOGY: an ἀρχιδικαστής called Ailianos, the son of the ex-ἐξηγητής Euphranor, is known from *P.Oxy.* XII 1472 (136 A.D.): this document may have the same provenance as *PSI* VIII 962(b), of A.D. 132, also addressed to a (different) ἀρχιδικαστής, in which reference is made to Herakleopolis and Thmoiphtha.

Another seemingly important Ailianos (possibly the epistrategos of the Thebaid) is known from *P.Oxy.* IV 708.

P.Rain.Cent. 133: delivery of wood εἰς οἰκοδομὴν τοῦ μοναστηρίου.
Stud.Pal. X 230: other villages listed: Ἁλμυρά (Koites?), Αναβαλε() and Kollintaathyr (Tekmi toparchy).
CPR IV 2 (a bilingual document in Coptic and Greek) lists many villages of the central toparchies of the Herakleopolite nome (toponyms in Greek) [4].

---

[1] Very uncertain reading.

[2] An ἐποίκιον Αἰλιανοῦ is also attested in the Hermopolite nome (cf. JEAN GASCOU, *Bibliotheca Orientalis* 42, 1985, p.335): this may have taken its name from the landowner often mentioned in the archive of Apollonios from Pesla (in the Hermopolites), which was published in *CPR* VI. This Ailianos has been tentatively identified with Sostratos Ailianos, strategos and exactor, who is known from *P.Cairo Preisigke* 4 and 8 (of A.D. 320 and 321, respectively): cf. *CPR* VIII, pp.69-73.

[3] Cf. RENATE ZIEGLER, *ZPE* 91, 1992, pp.91-94.

[4] See *s.v.* ΝΙΝΩ.

ΑΙΛΟΥΤΟΣ

VI-VII A.D.   *CPR* VIII 68,9-10   ἐν κλήρῳ καλου(μένῳ) Πιααε.[.]ευ ἤτοι λάκκου Αἰλοῦτος

TOPARCHY: περὶ Πόλιν.

See *s.v.* Πιααε.[.]ευ.

ΑΚΑΚΙΗΤΗ

VII-VIII A.D.   *Stud.Pal.* X 206,14   Ακακιητη Πμανκεμ

Listed as a κλῆρος with several others (see the *Reverse Index* at the end of this volume): it is not clear whether Πμανκεμ is the name of a separate place.

ΑΚΕΕΙΣ

574 A.D   P.Berl. Zill. 7 *recto*,13; *verso*,1   μηχανὴν καλουμ(ένην) ᾽Ακεεῖς (*recto*,13); μηχανῆς καλουμ(ένης) ᾽Ακεεῖς (*verso*,1)

See: ΚΩ.

ΑΚΩΤΟΥ

683/684 A.D.   *CPR* X 135,10   ᾽Ακώτου

Land ἐν διαφόροις κλήροις: the toponym Μικρουαλιχ recurs on the same line.

(?)ΑΛΗ

VII-VIII A.D.   *Stud.Pal.* X 200,5   χ'ω'(ρίον) προσχ'ω' αλη [1]

Listed with Magdola, Notinon, Peene.

---

[1] «Scheint durchaus zu stimmen» (Johannes Diethart, letter of February 25, 1994).

ΑΛΙΛΑΙΣ

18 August 164 B.C.	P.Hels. I 6,7	ἐν 'Αλιλάει
after 84/83 B.C.	BGU XIV 2370,38	πρὸς κώμην 'Αλιλᾶϊν
after 52/51 B.C.	BGU VIII 1808,21	'Αριλάεως [1]
I/II A.D.	P.Hib. II 218,33	'Αλιλάεως
12 July 192 A.D.	P.Vind.Sal. 6,7	ἀπὸ κ[ώ]μης 'Αλιλάεως
early III A.D.	P.Ryl. II 87 recto, col. II,9	'Αλιλάεως [2]

TOPARCHY: Ἄγημα ἄνω.

ETYMOLOGY: $^{c}l^{c}l$ («shrew-mouse») also attested in the personal name P3-$^{c}l^{c}l$, P3-^{c}lyl, Gk. Πελ(ε)ιλις[3]. The variant spelling 'Αριλάεως is consistent with the common interchangeability of *l* and *r* in Egyptian (see also *s.v.* ΤΙΝΤΗΡΙΣ).

MODERN ARABIC NAME: Hillīya?
The location of the modern village could be consistent with this identification: cf. *TAVO* B 69, p.169 («Wir wissen, daß eine ganze Reihe von Ruinenstätten praktisch abgetragen worden ist»), and p.210: «Im Dorf existierte früher ein Kōm, der jedoch heute abgetragen ist: An der Stelle liegen jetzt noch Steinblöcke, darunter ein über 3 m. langer, in zwei Teile zerbrochener Steinbalken. Ein anderer Steinblock trägt koptische (?) Ornamente. Die im Dorf aufgesammelten Keramikscherben sind in spätantike und arabische Zeit zu datieren».

P.Hels. I 6: a letter from a certain Philippos (the oikonomos?) to the basilikos grammateus encloses a copy of the letter to Philippos from the σιτολογοῦντές τινας τόπους τῆς ἄνω 'Αγήματος, concerning the delivery of corn provisions for the army from the θησαυρός at Alilais to the φρούριον at Hiera Nesos, «as usual, and besides because the place (i.e. Alilais) is poorly guarded» (ll.8-9)[4]. In *BGU* VIII 1808, Hiera Nesos and Alilais appear in two consecutive lines (20-21): two more villages of the Agema toparchy follow (Kollasoucha and Korphotoi: ll.22 and 23); Petachor, also in the Agema, follows.
Troubles at Alilais are again reported by the oikonomos Phames in *BGU* XIV 2370 (ll.37 ff.), which also assigns this village to the Agema. The preceding section (ll.26-36) deals with the (Ἄγημα) κάτω toparchy: the village Peensemtheus is mentioned (l.34).
P.Vind.Sal. 6: Aspheus son of Horus, from Alilais, acknowledges a 500 drachmae loan from Nemesianus son of Nemesianus, ex-gymnasiarches and ἀρχιερεύς of Herakleopolis.
P.Hib. II 218 lists Alilais, Kollasoucha and Petachor in three consecutive lines (33-35). These three villages are also found together in *BGU* VIII 1808 (see above).

---

[1] Reading checked for me by Günter Poethke (letter of April 14, 1994: «ρ ist sicher; ι ist besser als τ»); the Editors offered 'Αρτλαεως (but 'Αργαλαῖς in their Index of geographical names). The same exchange between liquid consonants (ρ for λ: 'Αριλάεως = 'Αλιλάεως) e.g. in *Stud.Pal.* X 44,6 (Τιντήλ[ε]ως for Τιντήρεως) dating from the VI A.D.

[2] «The *recto* contains two incomplete columns of official accounts of some sort» (see the *Introduction* to this document, p.51). I have checked this reading on a photograph kindly provided by the Audio-Visual Office of the Rylands University Library of Manchester.

[3] Cf. WILLY CLARYSSE, «Some Egyptian Tax-Payers in Early Roman Thebes», *JJP* 23, 1993, p.36; also CRUM, *Coptic Dictionary*, p.6/a (*s.v. Alil*, «field mouse»). On the cult of the shrew-mouse (also at Herakleopolis): *L.Ä.* V, coll.1160-1161.

[4] For a couple of important new readings, and an interpretation of this document, see DIETER HAGEDORN, *ZPE* 71, 1988, p.285 f.

ΑΛΜΥΡΑ

V A.D.	*Stud.Pal.* X 8,4	
V-VI A.D.	*Stud.Pal.* XX 124,1 (= *Stud.Pal.* III 578 p.122)	δι(ὰ) τῶν κεφαλαιωτῶν Ἀλμύρας
VII A.D.[1]	*Stud.Pal.* VIII 1309,4	ἀπὸ χ(ωρίου) Ἀλμύρας
VII-VIII A.D.	*Stud.Pal.* X 230,2	χ(ωρίον) Ἀλμέρας
VIII A.D.	*Stud.Pal.* X 72,11;12;14	[χ(ωρίον) Ἀ]λμ[ύρ]ας (11); [χ(ωρίον)] Ἀλμύρας (12); χ(ωρίον) Ἀλμύρας (14)
VIII A.D.	*Stud.Pal.* X 223,1	ἀπὸ χ(ωρίου) Ἀλμύρας
Byz.	*SB* I 5338,15	Ἀ[λμυ]ρᾶς (?)

ETYMOLOGY: this name presumably refers to «salt» land in the surroundings of the village. Cf. Ἀπαλά (*q.v.*), another village apparently named by an adjective referring to the quality of the land in its vicinity.

Stud.Pal. VIII 1309: inhabitants of this village and of Διασημωτ(άτων) act as testimonies for an inhabitant of Psychis ἡ μεγάλη (in the Koites).

It recurs in lists of Herakleopolite villages belonging to various toparchies, along with Kollintaathyr (*Stud.Pal.* X 230,5); Koma and Onosis (*Stud.Pal.* X 223); Ogou and Pyrgotos (*Stud.Pal.* X 72); Choinotmis, Techtho, Phnebieus (*Stud.Pal.* X 8).

ALYI/AIY

about 300 A.D.	*Itin.Anton.* 168,3	*Alyi*
V A.D.	*Not.Dign.Or.* 28,44	*Aiy*

MODERN ARABIC NAME: JOHN BALL, *Egypt in the Classical Geographers*, Cairo 1942, p.143, locates Alyi on the east bank of the Nile, opposite Geziret el-Wahliya.

Itin.Anton. 168: military station, located between *Hipponon* (see *s.v.* Ἱππώνων) and *Thimonepsi* (see *s.v.* ΘΜΟΙΝΕΨΙ).

According to *Not.Dign.Or.* 28, the *cohors secunda Itureorum* of the *provincia Augustamnica* was stationed at *Aiy*. Following an apparently southward itinerary, it is listed after Aphroditopolis (*Afrodito*, l.43: station of the *cohors quarta Iuthungorum*), and before *Muson* (l.45: *cohors secunda Thracum*) and *Narmunthi* (l.46; this is Narmouthis, in the Oxyrhynchite nome: station of the *cohors quarta Numidarum*).

ΑΜΗΤΙΑΝΟΣ

V A.D.	*Stud.Pal.* X 50,4	κ]ώμης Ἀμητιανος

---

[1] «Quittung wohl aus dem 7. Jh.» (Johannes Diethart by letter of February 25, 1994). Wessely dated it to the VII-VIII A.D.

ETYMOLOGY: «... eine fehlerhafte Schreibung für den Personennamen ʼΑμυντιανός» (JOHANNES DIETHART, *Tyche* 10, 1995, p.237). Or perhaps a personal name ʼΑμητιανός was derived from ἄμητος, «harvest, harvest-time», or «crop, harvest gathered in» (*LSJ s.v.* I 2; II).

Gemoun(is) (Koites) is listed in the same document, which also mentions a χέρσος Βουνων.

AMMIAN[..]

V A.D.	*Stud.Pal.* X 233, col. II,15	Αμμιαν[..][1]
VII A.D.	*Stud.Pal.* X 66,2	χ(ωρίον) ʼΑμια...[2]

Phebichis (Koites) follows Αμμιαν[..] in *Stud.Pal.* X 233; Philonikou (Koites) is among the villages mentioned in *Stud.Pal.* X 66.

ΑΜΜΩΝΙΑΝΟΥ

3 (?) April 541 A.D.   *SB* XVIII 13949,5   ἀπὸ ἐποικίου ʼΑμμωνιανοῦ τοῦ Ἡρακλε[ο]πολίτου νο[μοῦ] (5-6)

BIBLIOGRAPHY: PIETER J. SIJPESTEIJN, «Five Byzantine Papyri in the Michigan Collection», *ZPE* 62, 1986, pp.133 ff.

SB XVIII 13949 is a deed of surety addressed to two *scholastici*.

ΑΜΦ.Δ( )

late III A.D.   *BGU* XIII 2365,1   Αμφ.δ( )[3]

---

[1] Cf. CALDERINI-DARIS, *Dizionario*, vol. I, p.14: «Nelle carte del Grenfell trovo la proposta di integrazione ʼΑμμιαν[ῆς]».

[2] «Z.2 ist wohl χ(ωρίον) ʼΑμια...statt χ(ωρίον) .μι.[der *ed. pr.* für ʼΑμμιαν(οῦ/ῆς) zu lesen» (Johannes Diethart, letter of February 25, 1994).

[3] ʼΑμφίω(νος), though attractive, does not seem to fit the traces (reading checked by me on the photograph, and by William Brashear on the original).

ΑΝΑΒΩΛΙΑ

96-94 or 63-61 B.C.	*BGU* XIV 2429,8	Ἀνα(βώλια?)
V A.D.	*Stud.Pal.* X 233, col.III,2	Ἀναβώλια [1]
VII-VIII A.D.	*(?) Stud.Pal.* X 230,4	χ(ωρίον) Ἀναβαλ'ε' (= Ἀναβώλια?)

ETYMOLOGY: this place-name is probably derived from the Greek word ἀναβολή, which designated the «throwing up» of the earth in the process of clearing the canals and repairing the dykes (cf. *P.Mich.* XI 612,20 n.). The word ἀναβόλια (in the genitive: τιμῆς ἀναβολίω(ν) τοῦ ε ἔτους) was doubtfully read by the Editor in *O.Fayyum* 49,5 (tax-receipt of A.D. 19) [2].

TOPARCHY: Tekmi.

BGU XIV 2429 records Ἀνα(βώλια) in the same line with Mouchis (Tekmi toparchy).
Stud.Pal. X 230: Ἀναβαλ'ε' recurs in the same list with (besides other villages) Kollintaathyr, which was in the Tekmi toparchy.

ΑΝΑΤΙΕΥ

| 267 (266) B.C. | *P.Hib.* I 100,12 | ἐξ Ἀνατιεύ (?) |

TOPARCHY: Koites [3]?

P.Hib. I 100: receipt for payment εἰς τὰ ἐκφόρια τοῦ Ἀλεξάνδρου κλήρου.

ΑΝΙΠΙΑΡ

| 522 A.D. | *Stud.Pal.* XX 137,9 | ἀπὸ ἐποικίου Ἀνιπιάρ |

BIBLIOGRAPHY: TIMM, *Das christlich-koptische Ägypten* III, p.1088 (s.v. Hanepioor I).
Rough copy of a contract drawn up at Herakleopolis between an inhabitant of the town and an inhabitant of Anipiar.

---

[1] Ἀναβώλια ed. pr.: Ἀναβολίου Grenfell *apud* CALDERINI-DARIS, *Dizionario*, s.v.

[2] Wilcken (*BL* 1,113) proposed to read ἀναβολικ(ῶν).

[3] See *P.Hib.* I 39, Introduction.

ΑΝΝΗΣ

51/50 B.C.　　　　　　　　*BGU* VIII 1831,9　　　　περὶ Αννης¹

The petitioner (a Macedonian katoikos hippeus) complains of damage he has suffered from Theophilos son of Nikobios, «one of those from the Σαδαλεῖον», apparently as a consequence of an assault on the land he cultivates περὶ Αννης on account of Hierax (who also owns land near Tokois, in the Polis toparchy).

ΑΝΝΙΑΝΟΥ

V A.D.　　　　　　　　*Stud.Pal.* X 94,2　　　　ἐποίκ(ιον) ᾿Αννιανοῦ

ETYMOLOGY: cf. JOHN R. REA, «Letter of a Recruit: P.Lond. III 982 Revised», *ZPE* 115, 1997, p.190, for possible identifications.

The other villages listed in the same document include Gessias (5; Koites), Peenameus (6; Μέση toparchy), Daphne (7), Tosachmis (8; Koites).

ΑΝΩ (ΑΓΗΜΑ)

18 Aug. 164 B.C.　　　　*P.Hels.* I 6,2　　　　Ἡρώιδης καὶ
　　　　　　　　　　　　　　　　　　　　　᾿Αλέξαν(δρος)
　　　　　　　　　　　　　　　　　　　　　σιτολογοῦντές τινας
　　　　　　　　　　　　　　　　　　　　　τόπους τῆς ἄνω
　　　　　　　　　　　　　　　　　　　　　᾿Αγή(ματος)

II B.C.　　　　　　　　*P.Münch.* III 56,6　　　τῆς ῎Ανω τοπαρχίας

See also *s.v.* ΑΓΗΜΑ.

As the ῎Αγημα κάτω was also called simply the Κάτω τοπαρχία, it seems reasonable to assume that the same could happen for the (῎Αγημα) ῎Ανω. *P.Münch.* III 56 is likely to refer to the Herakleopolite nome, and thus to the (῎Αγημα) ῎Ανω toparchy, as other papyri «mit benachbarten Inventarnummern» (Ed. *ad loc.*) originate from this district.

ΑΠΑΛΑ

VII A.D.　　　　　　　　*SB* VI 9590,4;16;22　　　γῄδια ᾿Α[π]αλά (4);
　　　　　　　　　　　　　　　　　　　　　[᾿Απα]λά (16);
　　　　　　　　　　　　　　　　　　　　　᾿Απαλά (22)²

---

¹ Reading checked for me by Günter Poethke (letter of April 14, 1994): «α ist ziemlich sicher». One might otherwise be tempted to suggest the reading Ουνην: is this a different vocalisation of the same place-name?

² ᾿Απαλᾶ *ed. pr.*: but if this is a Greek place-name we should write ᾿Απαλά (plural neuter of ἁπαλός, referred to γῄδια).

ETYMOLOGY: this name may refer to «soft» land in the surroundings of the village, or perhaps to the quality of the produce obtained on that land (thus ἁπαλοτάτη, which the writer then substituted with χλωροτάτη, qualifies κριθή in *P.Cair.Zen.* I 59129,9).

Cf. Ἁλμυρά (*q.v.*), another village apparently named using a Greek adjective referring to the quality of the land in its vicinity.

Two arourae which Anatolios cedes to Pamoûn are apparently split between Makaitonos, Tebetny (Peran toparchy) and Chortaso, and situated to the west of the γῄδια Ἀπαλά, ἐν κλήρῳ καλουμένῳ Τσαβα.

ΑΠΕΡΙΟ(Υ) (?)

V A.D.	*Stud.Pal.* X 233, col. II,5	Απεριο(υ) καὶ Χορτασω[1]

Chortaso is elsewhere (*SB* VI 9590) connected with Tebetny (Peran toparchy).

ΑΠΙ( )

162 B.C.	*P.Tebt.* III 857,37 (fr.1, col.V)

Other villages in the same papyrus: Peensamoi, Pois.

ΑΠΙΩΝΟΣ

497 A.D.	*Stud.Pal.* XX 129,2	[παρὰ Αὐρηλίου Πτο]λεμαίου παραλή[μπ]του οὐσίας Ἀπίωνος τοῦ ἐνδοξοτάτου
17 April 677 or 707 A.D.	*SB* XVIII 13771,10	[ἀπὸ χωρίου] Ἀπίωνος παγαρχ(ίας) Ἡρακλε(οπολίτου)
VII A.D.	*Stud.Pal.* X 4,3	
VII-VIII A.D.	*Stud.Pal.* X 208,2	χω(ρίον) Ἀπίωνος

TOPARCHY: the estates of the Apion family in the V and VI centuries are mostly attested in the Oxyrhynchites, but also in the Herakleopolites.

---

[1] A very uncertain reading; «Απεριο(υ) καὶ Χορτασω durchaus möglich» (Johannes Diethart, letter of February 25, 1994).

BIBLIOGRAPHY: JEAN GASCOU, *Les grands domaines, la cité et l'état en Égypte byzantine* (Collège de France, Centre de recherche d'histoire et civilisation de Byzance, Travaux et Mémoires 9), Paris 1985, pp.61-75. See also BERNHARD PALME, «Flavius Strategius Paneuphemos und die Apionen»; IDEM, «Die *domus gloriosa* des Flavius Strategius Paneuphemos» (forthcoming)[1].

Stud.Pal. X 4: villagers from Apionos (1), Poinami (2; variant spelling for Peenameus, in the Ἄγημα κάτω toparchy), Thmoiamounis (4; Koma toparchy) and Pkommatoei (5) are requested for compulsory work to be done on the dyke (παράχωμα) at Κόμα.

ΑΠΡΗΛ( )

I B.C.   *BGU* XIV 2450 (fr.17),39

TOPARCHY: Tekmi ?

Two fossil kleroi are mentioned in this fragment: the one in l.41 cannot be deciphered, but a kleros Πτολεμαίου (l.40) is also found in *BGU* XIV 2441 (ll.125, 198, 258), where it is located in the surroundings of Pyrgotos (Tekmi toparchy).

ΑΡΡΙΑΝΟΥ

384/385 A.D. (cf. *BL* 7,16)   *BGU* III 938,4   τοῦ χωρίου Ἀρριανοῦ

BGU III 938 is a lease contract for land in the surroundings of Ἀρριανοῦ, near the Sobthis plain.

ΑΡΣΕΜΘΕΩ[Σ]   (ΤΑ)

215-214 B.C.   *P.Strasb.* II 111,20-21   τὰ Ἀρσεμθέω[ς]

TOPARCHY: Πέραν[2].
ETYMOLOGY: «the (mansions of) Harsemtheus»[3]

Ἀρσεμθεύς is presumably the same person who appears in *P.Hib.* I 74 as an agent of Teos, who in turn may be the same person (a tax-farmer?) who pays the δωδεκαχαλκία (the same tax which the γεωργοί are refusing to pay in *P.Strasb.* II 111) in *P.Hib.* I 112,30.

---

[1] Reference from Todd Hickey.

[2] εἰς τὸ Πέραν can, I think, be read above l.21 (checked on the photograph provided by Willy Clarysse: see next note).

[3] See WILLY CLARYSSE, *Ancient Society* 7, 1976, p.203.

ΑΡΤΕΜΙΔΟΣ ΟΡΜΟΣ

117 A.D. SB XIV 11958,17-18; 29-30 εἰς τὸν τῆς Ἀρτέμ[ιδ]ος
θεᾶς μεγίσ(της) ὅρμον
(17-18); εἰς ὅρμον
Ἀρτέμιδος θεᾶς
μεγίσ(της) (29-30)

TOPARCHY: περὶ Πόλιν.

ETYMOLOGY: Herodotus (II 59,89) equated Artemis to the goddess Bast. One is reminded of the place-name Thmoiobastis («the new land of Bast», in the Koma toparchy): see s.v.

This could be the port of a temple dedicated to Artemis, in the Herakleopolite nome[1]. One hundred columns from the quarry of Ankyron are shipped to the ὅρμος Ἀρτέμιδος θεᾶς μεγίσ(της), and repair works are in progress in September-November 117 A.D., following the instructions of Aquilius Polion, strategos of the Herakleopolite nome in that year[2]; seven seats (ἴκρια) from a theatre are re-adapted to support the statues carried in the procession at the Νεμεσεῖα (ll.33-37). The reason for celebration of this festival here must lie with the triple identification Nemesis = Artemis = Bast[3]. The temple of Nemesis at Herakleopolis, of which Wilcken suspected the existence[4], is presumably the same as the Artemis temple of SB XIV 11958.

It is worth remembering that references to the cult of the Νεμέσεις καὶ Ἀδράστειαι, θεαὶ μέγισται, in the Herakleopolites are also found in BGU IV 1216 (110 B.C.; ll.49-50 and 162-163) and BGU VIII 1753, II (64/63 B.C.; instructions from the strategos for the daily provision of ἀθήρα[5] are forwarded to the antigrapheus of the θησαυρός of the περὶ Πόλιν toparchy).

ΑΡΧ(ΑΓΓΕΛΟΥ) ΜΙΧ(ΑΗΛ)

VIII A.D. Stud.Pal. X 218,6 χ(ωρίον) ἀρχ(αγγέλου)
Μιχ(αήλ)[6]

TOPARCHY: Techtho Nesos (?)[7]

BIBLIOGRAPHY: cf. TIMM, Das christlich-koptische Ägypten I, p.1259, s.v. «Kirche des Erzengels Michael»; p.1268, s.v. «Kirche des (hl.) Michael(ios)».

---

[1] Cf. ANNA ŚWIDEREK, JJP 11/12, 1957/58, p.70 (ed. pr.): «... il s'agit probablement du port du temple (le nom d'une localité serait plutôt simplement ὅρμος Ἀρτέμιδος et non ὅρμος Ἀρτέμιδος θεᾶς μεγίστης; il en résulte que le temple était situé non loin du Nil ou d'un canal».

[2] Also attested in P.Oxy. IX 1189.

[3] See PAULI-WISSOWA, R.E., Bd.II, col.1372; Bd. XVI, col.2377.

[4] APF 2, 1903, p.318.

[5] Cf. FRANÇOISE PERPILLOU-THOMAS, «Une bouille de céréales: l'athèra», Aegyptus 72, 1992, pp.103-110.

[6] Παρ'χ' Μι'χ' Wessely. Reading checked for me on the original by Johannes Diethart (letter of February 25, 1994).

[7] Cf. TIMM, Das christlich-koptische Ägypten, VI, p.2469 f. (s.v. Tahtūt) noting, among other things, that «Im Livre des perles enfouies ... findet sich die Notiz, daß es in Tahtūt eine Kirche des (Erzengels) Michael gäbe» (for the identification Techtho = Daštut, see s.v. ΤΕΧΘΩ).

Other villages listed in the same document include Onosis (1.2; περὶ Πόλιν toparchy) and Tinteris (1.7; Koma toparchy).

ΟΙ ΑΡΧΑΙΟΙ

63/62 B.C. BGU VIII 1771,14 περὶ Πεενεψῶμφιν ἐν τοῖς Ἀρχαίοις

TOPARCHY: Ἄγημα.

BIBLIOGRAPHY: οἱ Ἀρχαῖοι was the name of a special detachment in the regular army of the Ptolemies: cf. *PPt* II 4257-4274 (with the *Addenda* in *PPt* VIII), and cf. WILLY PEREMANS, «Les indigènes égyptiens dans l'armée de terre des Lagides. Recherches anthroponymiques», *Ancient Society* 9, 1978, pp.98-99 [1]. See also *s.vv.* Ἄγημα and οἱ περὶ Αὐλήν.

This was a settlement of Greek katoikoi near Peenepsomphis, in the Ἄγημα toparchy, contiguous to another such settlement called οἱ περὶ Αὐλήν, near Βιχινθωυθ in the Tekmi toparchy. Two ἀρχαῖοι κάτοικοι ἱππεῖς appear in *BGU* XIV 2441 (ll.135-148), within the land-survey of the Pyrgotos area (Tekmi toparchy). In *BGU* XIV 2437 Pyrgotos is connected to περὶ Αὐλήν and both are assigned to the Tekmi toparchy.

ΑΣΚΑΙΑΤΑΣ

I B.C. BGU XIV 2437,13 περὶ Ασκαιατας

TOPARCHY: Tekmi.

Mentioned together with Pyrgotos as administratively subordinated to περὶ Αὐλήν (Tekmi toparchy).

ΑΣΣΥΑ

about 260 B.C.	P.Hib. I 112,5;12;52	Ἀσσύας
239 (238) or 214 (213) B.C.	P.Hib. I 117,12	περὶ Ἀσσύαν
139 B.C.	P.Tebt. III 991,8	[περὶ Ἀσ]σύαν (?)
I B.C.	BGU XIV 2435,26	Ἀσσύας
I/II A.D.	P.Hib. II 218, col. III	Ἀσσύας
176-180 A.D.	P.Hib. II 278,2-3	ἐν κ[ώ]μῃ Ἀσσύᾳ τοῦ Κωίτου

---

[1] See also JEAN LESQUIER, *Les Institutions militaires de l'Égypte sous les Lagides*, Paris 1911, p.181.

218-222 A.D.	*CPR* I 62,4	ἀπὸ κ]ώμης Ἀσσύας¹
III A.D.	*P.Oxy.* XII 1529,11	Ἀσσύας
IV A.D.	*P.Rain.Cent.* 147,8	Ἀσσύας
V/VI A.D.	*P.Vind.Tand.* 16,24	Ἀσσύας
VIII A.D.	*Stud.Pal.* X 199,4	χ(ωρίον) Ἀσσύας²

TOPARCHY: Koites.

BIBLIOGRAPHY: ARISTIDE CALDERINI, *Aegyptus* 6, 1925, p.87; PRUNETI, *Centri abitati*, pp.36-37.

P.Hib. I 117, *BGU* XIV 2435: Assya is subordinated to Tale for administrative purposes. In *P.Vindob. Tand.* 16 Kerkesephis is also listed (as in *BGU* XIV 2435), while in *Stud.Pal.* X 199 Philonikou is also mentioned.

P.Oxy. XII 1529: all other villages appearing in this document belong to the Northern toparchy of the Oxyrhynchite nome. Assya, however, is consistently assigned to the Koites by sources dating from the III B.C. to the VIII A.D.

ΑΤ..[

28 Sept.-27 Oct.54 A.D.	*P.Vind.Tand.* 10,3;61	ἀπὸ κώμης Ατ..[(3); ἀπὸ κώ]μης Ατ.[(60-61)

See also: Ατρτ..

TOPARCHY: Μέση?

According to the Editors, the οὐσίαι referred to in this document were in the vicinity of Euhemeria (Arsinoites).

Part of a τόμος συγκολλήσιμος containing oath-declarations by the προστάται γεωργῶν in the οὐσίαι belonging to the Emperor Claudius and to Agrippina Augusta Minor. In the better preserved declaration, two προστάται ἀπὸ κώμης Κερκύτου (l.32; attested in the Μέση toparchy) appear.

ΑΤΡΤ..

IV-V A.D.	*MPER* XV 91,5

See also: Ατ..[

TOPARCHY: Μέση.

---

¹ New reading, checked for me on the original by Johannes Diethart (letter of February 25, 1994): «Keine κώμη Ἀσίας in *CPR* I 62: in dieser Urkunde aus den Jahren 218-222 ist in Z.4 das bereits einige Male belegte Dorf Ἀσσύας zu lesen. Ἀσία als Dorfname ist in CALDERINI, *Dizionario*, Bd. 1, 1966, zu streichen».

² Reading checked for me by Johannes Diethart (letter of February 25, 1994).

Phys (Μέση toparchy) is also mentioned (l.3). Further on in the same document, references to the πεδ(ίον) Βουσίρεως (ll.34,37) and the μερὶς Ἡρακλείδου of the Arsinoite nome (l.35) are found.

ΑΤΤΟΝ( )

III A.D.   *BGU* XIII 2365,4

TOPARCHY: Koites?

BGU XIII 2365: list of tax-revenues from sixteen villages, three of which are known to be in the Koites (ll.12-14: Techtho, Papa, Thelbo). Also mentioned: Magdola (l.3; a village by this name is attested in the Πέραν toparchy) and Θμοιχ() (l.15: Θμοι- is a common prefix for villages of the Koites).

ΑΥΗΡΙΣ

after 84/83 B.C.	*BGU* XIV 2370 (fr. 1),80	ἐξ Αὐήρ(ι)εω[ς¹
I B.C.	*BGU* XIV 2438,100	Αὐ.ρεω[ς]²

TOPARCHY: Μέση.

ETYMOLOGY: *Ḥw.t-wr.t* (*Ḥw.t* = «Great mansion»)³.

MODERN ARABIC NAME: Hawwārah ʿAdlān? A place by the same name is well attested for the Arsinoites (Herakleides division): this should be identified with Hawwārah al-Makta, 9 km. NW of Hawwārah ʿAdlān, along the Baḥr Yūsuf, and in a somewhat off-limit location⁴. It may be that both villages derived their name from the celebrated «Labyrinth», which no Greek literary source since Herodotus (II 148) fails to mention when describing the entrance to the Fayūm⁵.

Listed in *BGU* XIV 2438 with other villages known to be in the Μέση toparchy (Phnebieus, Peenpibykis, Chennis), and again recurring after Phnebieus in *BGU* XIV 2370, fr. 1⁶.

---

¹ Αὐήρ(ι)εω[ς *ed. pr.*: a hard breathing is requested by the Egyptian *Ḥw.t-wr.t*.

² Αὐήρεω[ς] seems to fit the traces (as suggested in the *ed. pr., ad loc.*; see preceding note for the hard breathing which is needed here).

³ Information from Katelijn Vandorpe (letter of July 18, 1995).

⁴ On the Arsinoite village, see *P.Ashm.dem., Introduction*, esp. pp.12-22 («The Fayyum Town of Hawara»): some of these documents qualify it as Αὐῆρις τῶν ἔξω τόπων τῆς Ἡρακλείδου μερίδος. See also *L.Ä.* Bd.II, 1072-1074, *s.v.* «Hawara»).

⁵ Cf. *L.Ä.*, Bd.III, 1072-1074.

⁶ Note that in this document Phnebieus is connected to the Ἄγημα κάτω τοπαρχία.

CATALOGUE

περὶ ΑΥΛΗΝ

110 B.C.	*BGU* VI 1216,68-70 [1]	κατοίκων τῶν περὶ Αὐλήν (68); ἀπὸ περὶ Αὐλ(ήν) (70)
63/62 B.C.	*BGU* VIII 1771,16	περὶ Τέκμι περὶ Βιχινθῶυθ ἐν τοῖς περὶ Αὐλήν
I B.C.	*BGU* XIV 2433,71	περὶ Αὐλήν
I B.C.	*BGU* XIV 2437,12	περὶ Αὐλήν

TOPARCHY: Tekmi.

ETYMOLOGY: the expression οἱ περὶ Αὐλήν designated a special detachment of the Royal Guard[2] in the Ptolemaic army: cf. *PPt* II 4367-4368 (with the *Addenda* in *PPt* VIII); and LEON MOOREN, *The Aulic Titulature in Ptolemaic Egypt. Introduction and Prosopography* (Verhand. Kon. Academie v. Wetenschappen van Belgie. Kl. Lett. XXXVII, Nr.78), 1975, Nr.279.

See also *s.vv.* Ἄγημα and οἱ Ἀρχαῖοι.

BIBLIOGRAPHY: WILHELM SPIEGELBERG, «Ägyptologische Beiträge», *APF* 7, 1923, p.184 (on *BGU* VI 1216); JEAN LESQUIER, *Les Institutions militaires de l'Égypte sous les Lagides*, Paris 1911, p.23 f.

BGU VIII 1771 indicates that this was a settlement of Greek katoikoi near Βιχινθωυθ, in the Tekmi toparchy, bordering on another such settlement called ἐν τοῖς Ἀρχαίοις, near Peenepsomphis, in the Ἄγημα toparchy. In *BGU* XIV 2437 Pyrgotos is connected to it. A settlement of κάτοικοι ἱππεῖς called οἱ περὶ Αὐλήν in the Herakleopolites is also referred to in *BGU* VI 1216: the cult of the Νεμέσεις καὶ Ἀδράστειαι there mentioned (ll.49-50 and 162-163) is again attested for the same nome in *BGU* VIII 1753; it must have been a favourite of these κάτοικοι ἱππεῖς.

ΑΥΞΩΝΙΟΣ

V A.D.	*P.Vind.Sijp.* 9,2	εἰρηνάρχου ἐ[ποι]κίου Ὀσυτεος (?) καὶ Αὐξώνιος (1-2)

TOPARCHY: Μέση.

---

[1] The goddess Ἀθερνεβθφῆι (ll.89 and 100) was identified by W. SPIEGELBERG (*APF* 7, 1923, p.183 f.; see also *P.Batav.* XX 50, p.190) with Ḥ.t-Ḥr-nb.(t).tpj-ᶜḫw, «Hathor, Herrin von Aphroditopolis»; he therefore suggests a provenance from the Aphroditopolites for this document, where an Aphroditopolite toponym also recurs (Τοῦφις, read by Wilcken at l.41); failing a different indication in the text itself, all other place-names should be referred, according to Spiegelberg, to the same nome. He then proceeds to interpret the document as a whole as a «Steuerauseinandersetzung zwischen dem Tempelland (ἱερὰ γῆ) von Aphroditopolis und dem Fiskus (τὸ βασιλικόν)». However, the fact that the Νεμέσεις καὶ Ἀδράστειαι (appearing at ll.49-50 and 162-163) were worshipped in the Herakleopolites (as shown by *BGU* VIII 1753) may support an identification of περὶ Αὐλήν mentioned in *BGU* VI 1216 with the Herakleopolite locality thus named.

[2] See already CALDERINI-DARIS, *Dizionario*, vol. I, *s.v.*: «luogo così chiamato dal permanere di un posto di guardia reale»; «sede di milizie, diventato poi sede stabile di abitanti».

Aurelios Dorotheos, police officer (εἰρηνάρχης) of the ἐποίκιον Ὀσυτεος (?) καὶ Αὐξώνιος, leases 3/4 ar. of land in the plain of Phys (Middle toparchy).

It is not clear whether the ἐποίκιον Ὀσυτεος and Αὐξώνιος should be considered as two different settlements[1].

ἈΦΛΩΘΕΩΣ

after 52/51 B.C.   BGU VIII 1808,27   Ἀφλώθεως

MODERN ARABIC NAME: an Aflatūn canal is recorded on the *ESM*, running not far east of Sidmant El Gebel.

This village is entered after Phnebieus (Μέση toparchy), and before Tanchais and Pois (Tilothis toparchy): a location in the northern part of the nome seems likely, especially if the possible survival of this name as the designation of the Aflatūn canal is taken into account.

Β[..]ΟΥ

after 84/83 B.C.   BGU XIV 2370 (fr.1),77

ΒΑΣΙΛ( )

late III A.D.   BGU XIII 2365,8

TOPARCHY: Koites?

BGU XIII 2365: list of tax-revenues from sixteen villages, two of which are known to be in the Koites (Papa, Thelbo). Other villages mentioned in this document include Magdola (l.3; a village by this name was in the Πέραν), Techtho (l.13) and Θμοιχ ( ) (l.15: Θμοι- is a common prefix for villages in the Koites).

ΒΑΥΚΑΛΙ[2]

V A.D.   Stud.Pal. X 233, col.III,1

ETYMOLOGY: βαυκάλιον was the name of a «narrow-necked vessel, that gurgles when water is poured in or out» (*LSJ, s.v.*): the term is used in *P.Oxy.* VI 936,6;8 (III A.D.).

---

[1] Cf. JOHANNES DIETHART, ZPE 76, 1989, p.108: «Αὐρήλιος Δωρόθεος kann εἰρηνάρχης eines ἐποίκιον x und von Αὐξῶνις sein (Αὐξώνιος, gen.); Ortsname nicht belegt; vgl. schon Sijpesteijn - Worp, ZPE 29 (1978), S.273, wobei ἐποίκιον als fester Bestandteil zu dem ersten Ortsnamen zu zählen ist».

[2] «Kol. III 1 ist eine Lesung Βαυκαλι - es ist keine Kürzung angezeigt - wahrscheinlich; die *ed. pr.* hat Βουκολι, Βουκολι(), vgl. CALDERINI-DARIS, *Dizionario*, Bd. 2, 1973, S.62» (letter from J. Diethart, 25 February 1994).

BE( )

about 160 B.C.　　　　*P.Hels.* I 40,1;2;4;6　　　ἀ[π]ὸ Βε( ) (1);
　　　　　　　　　　　　　　　　　　　　　ἀπὸ Βε( ) (2;4;6)

The document is a list of tax-payments.

ΒΕ[.]Υ

I B.C.　　　　　　　　*BGU* XIV 2433,53

ΒΙΧΙΝΘΩΥΘ

149 or 138 B.C.[1]　　　*SB* XVIII 13304,2　　　κωμογραμματέως Τέκμι
　　　　　　　　　　　　　　　　　　　　　καὶ Βιχινθωύθ[2]

63/62 B.C.　　　　　　*BGU* VIII 1771,16　　　περὶ Τέκμι περὶ
　　　　　　　　　　　　　　　　　　　　　Βιχινθῶυθ ἐν τοῖς περὶ
　　　　　　　　　　　　　　　　　　　　　Αὐλήν

TOPARCHY: Tekmi.

ETYMOLOGY: the second element in this toponym is the name of the god Thoth (*Dhwty*).

MODERN ARABIC NAME: Bani Bikhīt (phonetically and geographically compatible: see *Introduction*, p. 8).
BIBLIOGRAPHY: DIETER HAGEDORN, *ZPE* 68, 1987, pp.84-85

The military settlement of οἱ περὶ Αὐλήν (*scil.* κάτοικοι: see *s.v.*) was established «near Bichinthouth in the Tekmi toparchy» (*BGU* VIII 1771). It must be to this place that the strategos Euphranor led his troops from Papa (in the Koites), as reported in *SB* XVIII 13304 by the komogrammateus of Tekmi and Bichinthouth. The fact that Bichinthouth had the same komogrammateus as Tekmi proves that it was adjacent to the main centre of its toparchy.

ΒΟΑΦΡΕΩΣ

VIII A.D.　　　　　　*Stud.Pal.* X 199,1　　　χωρ[ί]'ου' Βοάφρε'ω'(ς)

ETYMOLOGY: the second component in this toponym is the personal name *w3h-ib-Re*, which was rendered in the Greek documents as Ὀαφρῆς (the same name as Ἀπριῆς, which is already found in Herodotus).

BIBLIOGRAPHY: TIMM, *Das christlich-koptische Ägypten* I, p.417.

---

[1] The date 157 B.C., suggested by the first Editors (*BASP* 22, 1985, pp.243-246) is probably wrong: cf. GREGG W. SCHWENDNER, *ZPE* 72, 1988, pp.275-276, where the dates 157 or (preferably) 138 B.C. are proposed.

[2] Cf. DIETER HAGEDORN, *ZPE* 68, 1987, pp.84-85.

Herakleopolis is referred to in the same line with the present village; two villages of the Koites (Assya and Philonikou) appear at ll.4-5.

ΒΟΥΝΩΝ

V A.D.   *Stud.Pal.* X 50,6   χέρ(σου) Βουνῶν

ETYMOLOGY: the Greek word βουνός, «hill», first attested in HDT. 4,199, is also found in LXX *Ex.* 17,9, *al.* It is used in *BGU* IV 1129,14;16 (I B.C.), where βουνοί are mentioned as a reference point to mark the borders of two plots of land.

Gemoun(is) (Koites) mentioned in the same document.

ΒΟΥΣΙΡΙΣ

8 Oct. 256 B.C.	*P.Cair.Zen.* II 59151,1	Βουσίριος
254/3 B.C.	*PSI* V 510,4;11	ἐμ Βουσίρει (4); ἐγ Βουσίρεως (11)
mid-III B.C.[1]	*P.Cair.Zen.* IV 59753,14;51	εἰ]ς Βουσ<ῖρ>ιν (14); ἐγ Βουσίρεως (51)
mid-III B.C.[2]	*P.Cair.Zen.* IV 59767,6	ἐ[γ Βουσί]ρεως
mid-III B.C.[3]	*P.Cair.Zen.* IV 59782(b),53;78	Βουσιρίτης (53); Βουσιρ(ίτης) (78)
247/246 B.C.	*SB* III 7203,11	ἐν Βουσίρει
about 245 B.C.	*P.Hib.* I 116,2	Βουσείρεως
26 July 240 B.C.	*P.Cair.Zen.* III 59368,23	ἐν Βουσείρει
239/238 B.C.[4]	*P.Rain.Cent.* 44,9-10;13	ἐγ Βουσίρεως (9-10); ἐν Βουσίρει (13)[5]

---

[1] Σπίνθηρ, οἰκονόμος of the household, appears in *P. Cairo Zen.* IV 59753 and in other documents of the Zenon archive, including *P.Lond.* VII 2004 (l.32), which is dated to 248 B.C. Σάτυρος (ὁ παρὰ Ζήνωνος) also appears in both documents.

[2] Reference to Θεόφιλος (ὁ ζωγράφος) also appearing in other mid-III B.C. documents of the Zenon archive: cf. MARIA NOWICKA, *Chr.d'Ég.* 53, 1978, pp.152-153.

[3] *P.Cair.Zen.* IV 59782 (a), on the other side of the same papyrus, mentions Panakestor, who was manager of the δωρεά in Philadelphia in 257/256 B.C., and afterwards (256/255 and 255/254 B.C.) ὁ πρὸς ταῖς ἀποστολαῖς in the Memphites (cf. *P.Batav.* XX, p.4; *P.Batav.* XXI, *Prosopography*, p.286).

[4] In my opinion, this document should be dated to the 9th year of Euergetes (239/238 B.C.). See the Editor's note at l.11; *P.Rain.Cent.* 44 comes from the same cartonnage as *P.Rain.Cent.* 43, which is dated to 236 B.C.

[5] At l.13, ἐν is my reading: ἐγ *ed. pr.*

CATALOGUE

212/211 B.C.	*P.Lille* I 59, 6;16;20;21;34;42; 102;106;120;125	ἐν Βουσίρει (6); Βουσίρεως (16;20;21;34;42; 102;106;120;125)
about 170 B.C.(?)	(?)*P.Tebt.* III 1043, *Intro.* [1]	ἐν Βουσίρει
163 B.C.	*P.Hels.* I 12,7	ἐν κώμῃ Βουσίρει (6-7)
August 160 B.C.	*P.Hels.* I 32,4	περὶ Βουσῖριν
154 or 143 B.C.	*P.Mert.* II 59,20	εἰς Βουσῖριν
about 111 B.C.	*P.Tebt.* III 878,22	ἐπὶ Βουσίρεως
after 84/3 B.C.	*BGU* XIV 2370 (fr. 2),92	Βουσίρεως
after 62/1 B.C.	*BGU* VIII 1813,6;8	ἐν κώμῃ Βουσίρει (6); περὶ τὴν Βουσῖριν (8)
59/8 B.C.	*BGU* VIII 1773,[5];8	π[ερὶ Βουσῖριν] (5); ἐν τῇ Βουσίρει (8)
after 52/1 B.C.	*BGU* VIII 1808,13	Βουσίρεως
18 B.C.	*BGU* IV 1202,1	περὶ Βουσῖριν
14 B.C.	*BGU* IV 1061,8	ἐν Βουσίρει
12/11 B.C.	*BGU* IV 1197,I,4	ἐν κώ[μῃ] Βουσίρι
*ca.*11/10 B.C.	*BGU* IV 1196,27	Βουσέρεως
17 Dec. 10 B.C.	*BGU* XVI 2611,6;8	ἐν τῇ Βουσίρει (6); εἰς Βουσίρ(ε)ιν (8)
21 Dec. 10 B.C.	*BGU* XVI 2630,11	ἐν Βουσίρ<ε>ι
9/8 B.C.	*BGU* XVI 2643,10	ἐν Βουσίρ<ε>ι
21 March 8 B.C.	*BGU* XVI 2647,9	εἰς Βουσῖριν
28 Jan. 5 B.C.	*BGU* XVI 2586,12	περὶ Βουσῖριν
about 7-4 B.C.	*BGU* XVI 2662,14	[πε]ρὶ Βουσῖριν
5/4 B.C.	*BGU* IV 1198,6	ἐν Βουσίρι
12 May 3 B.C.	*BGU* XVI 2646,14	περὶ Βουσῖριν
2/1 B.C.	*BGU* IV 1200,[3]	ἀπ]ὸ κ[ώμης Βουσίρεως] [2]
ca. 1 A.D.	*BGU* IV 1189,3;9	κώμης Βουσίρεως (3); περὶ Βουσί[ριν] (9)

---

[1] As noted by the Editor, this is «an account of wheat for which various cultivators were responsible. [...] From one of the entries, τοῦ (*scil.* πυροῦ) ἐν Βουσίρει κτλ., it may be inferred that the account comes from the Herakleopolite nome». FRITZ UEBEL, *Die Kleruchen Aegyptens unter den ersten sechs Ptolemäern*, Berlin 1968, p.283, n.2, also thought that this papyrus might originate from the «Gegend von Busiris».

[2] Bousiris, supplied at l.3, is nowhere else mentioned in this document, but «die Ergänzung des Namens Busiris ist nach den übrigen Priesterurkunden dieser Gruppe sehr wahrscheinlich» (*ed.pr.*, ad loc.).

2 A.D.	*BGU* IV 1201,4	κώμης Βουσίρεως
I/II A.D.	*P.Hib.* II 218,65;76	Βουσ[είρε]ως (65); [Βουσ]είρεως (76)
142 A.D.	*SB* XIV 11959,12;23	ἐν λατομί[αι]ς Βουσί(ρεως) (12); [ἐν λατομίαις] Βουσί(ρεως) (13)
169-177 A.D. (cf. *BL* 9,32)	*BGU* XIII 2326 a,13	Β]ουσείρειν
180-192 A.D.	*P.Iand.* III 33,7	ἀπὸ κώμης Βουσείρεως (6-7)
II A.D.	*P.Oxy.* XX 2272,13;16	ἀπὸ Βουσείρεως (13); ἀπὸ ὅρμ[ο]υ Βουσείρεως (16)
27 Dec. 200 A.D.	*P.Köln* II 88,4	περὶ Βουσῖ(ριν)
200 A.D.	*P.Oxy.* VI 899,22	περί τε κώμην Βουσεῖρ[ι]ν
292 A.D.	*PSI* III 184,4	κώμ[ης] Β[ουσ]είρεως (cf. *BL* 1,392)
II/III A.D.	*O.Wilck.* II 1125,3	Βουσίρεως
IV A.D.	*MPER* XV 101,2;13	πεδ(ίου) Βουσίρεως
late IV/early V A.D.	*P.Batav.* XXV 65,9	βοηθ(ὸς) Βουσίρ(εως)[1]
late IV/early V A.D.(cf. *BL* 9,368)[2]	*P.Vind.Tand.* 18,16	ἀπὸ Βουσίρεως
IV/V A.D.	*MPER* XV 82,3;4	ἀπὸ Βουσίρεως
IV/V A.D.	*MPER* XV 91,34;37	πεδ(ίου) Βουσίρεως
9 Oct. 492 A.D.	*P.Rain.Cent.* 124,6-7;9-10	ἐν κώμῃ Βουσίρει (6-7); ἀπὸ κώμης Βουσίρεως (9-10)
V A.D.	*MPER* XV 13,2	π[ε]δ[ίου] Βουσίρεως
V A.D.	*Stud.Pal.* X 233, col.I b,11	Βουσίρεως
V/VI A.D.	*SB* XVIII 14004,2 (=*Stud.Pal.* III 479 a)	κώμης Βουσίρεως
V/VI A.D.	*SB* XVIII 14005,2 (=*Stud.Pal.* III 479 b)[3]	κώμης Βουσίρεως

---

[1] As pointed out by the Editor, because of a striking similarity in handwriting between this text and *P.Vind.Tand.* 18, it is attractive to regard Bousiris in l.9 as the Herakleopolite village; the hand is of the type identified by HERMANN HARRAUER-BRIGITTE ROM, *ZPE* 54, 1984, pp.95-96.

[2] See *P.Leid.Inst.* p.276 n.3.

[3] Cf. also *SB* XVIII 14002 (= *Stud.Pal.* III 479 c). *Stud.Pal.* III 479 a,b,c have been re-edited by PIETER J. SIJPESTEIJN, *ZPE* 65, 1986, pp.160 ff.

CATALOGUE

V/VI A.D.	*P.Vind.Sijp.* 16,4	ἀπὸ κώμης Βο'υ'σίρεως (3-4)
VI/VII A.D.	*CPR* XIV 36,1;5;9;13	ἀ[πὸ Βουσί]ρ[ε(ως) (1); ἀπὸ Βουσίρε(ως) (5;9;13); cf. ἀπὸ τῆς αὐτ(ῆς) (2;6;10;11)

TOPARCHY: in the Roman period, Bousiris appears to have been the main centre in its own toparchy (*BGU* IV 1202 and 1189; *BGU* XVI 2662)[1]. Previously, it probably pertained to the Koma toparchy.

This was a common place-name: there was a Bousiris in the Arsinoites (division of Polemon). The Bousiris of DIOD.SIC. I 85 was probably in the Delta (modern Abū Sir Bana, on which cf. *LÄ* I, 883-884), like the Νείλου πόλις also mentioned there.

ETYMOLOGY: «House of Osiris» (*Pr-Wsir*)[2]. Bousiris of the Herakleopolite nome is already attested in the «inscription of Shoshenq I» (*Journal d'entrée du Musée égyptien du Caire* no.39410, l.20; mid-X B.C.)[3] and in *P.Ryl.dem.* 9,10/10 (VI B.C.).

MODERN ARABIC NAME: Abū Sir Al-Malaq.

BIBLIOGRAPHY: *P.Ryl.dem.*, p.85, n.5.

According to documents of the early Roman period, Bousiris had its own toparchy, but already in the III B.C. it rather seems to be at the centre of a wider region comprising the northern part of the Herakleopolites, as defined by the largely coinciding lists of *P.Lille* I 59 and *P.Cair.Zen.* IV 59782 (b): this region in turn had close ties with the Arsinoite and the Memphite nomes, involving the transport of wheat (by boat), cattle-breeding, bee-keeping and quarrying.

Besides Bousiris, *P.Lille* I 59 and *P.Cair.Zen.* IV 59782 (b) list villages of the Koma toparchy (Koma, Krekis, Machor; in addition, *P.Cair.Zen.* IV 59782 (b) mentions Thmoiobastis and Toou), of the Tilothis toparchy (Tilothis and Tanchais; in addition, *P.Lille* I 59 mentions Peenpasbyt(is) and Schnomthis) and of the Tekmi toparchy (Onnes; in addition, *P.Lille* I 59 has Peenepsy). Many of these villages are recorded in *BGU* XIV 2370, fr.1: Koma, Toou, Machor, Thmoiobastis (under the main entry Κάτω τοπαρχίας), Onnes, Tilothis, Tanchais. A second fragment (*BGU* XIV 2370 fr.2) has a reference to Bousiris. Much the same connections are shown in the following documents:

P.Rain.Cent. 44 (corn transport; Onnes, Thmoiobastis, Bousiris);

BGU XVI 2611 (letter concerning the transport of wheat to Alexandria: the sender operates between Bousiris and Tilothis);

BGU VIII 1808 (Tekmi, Koma, Onnes, Thmoiobastis, Bousiris, again recur in a sequence; Tanchais appears a few lines below);

BGU IV 1189 (the gymnasiarch of Bousiris petitions the strategos on account of two inhabitants of the same village, among whose titles is that of δεκανοί of the χῶμα κατὰ Κόμα);

P.Hib. II 218 (listing Koma, Krekis, Bousiris, Thmoiamoun(is), Thmoiobastis in a sequence comprising ll.63-67);

BGU XIII 2326 (customs house register) also mentions Κεφαλαί and Λευκόγιον;

---

[1] References to a toparches (*BGU* IV 1189) and a topogrammateus (*BGU* IV 1202) of the Bousiris toparchy are only found at the beginning of the Roman period. In *BGU* VIII 1813,8, περὶ τὴν Βουσῖριν (*scil.* κώμην) does not designate the toparchy, but only locates the land belonging to Herakleides' children.

[2] Cf. JOHN D. RAY, *The Archive of Hor*, London 1976, *Index*, p.183.

[3] Cf. PAUL TRESSON, «L'inscription de Chechanq Ier, au Musée du Caire», *Mélanges Maspero* I. *Orient Ancien* (*MIFAO* 66), Le Caire 1935-1938.

Stud.Pal. X 233 (col.I B, 8-11: Thmoiobastis, Thmoiamoun(is) and Bousiris one after another).

P.Cair.Zen. IV 59782 (b) also mentions a Memphite village (Meia): trade relations between the northern Herakleopolites, the Arsinoites and the Memphites are confirmed by *P.Cair.Zen.* IV 59783 (itinerary of a boat trading between Memphis, Aphroditopolis, Herakleopolis, Bousiris and Ptolemais) and *P.Cair.Zen.* III 59368 (Kleon and Sostratos own 1000 bee-hives that are distributed between the two districts [1]; 15,000 bundles of hay are deposited at Bousiris), besides *BGU* XVI 2630 (the second part of this letter deals with the transport of grain: Tanchais, but also the Troites[2] and the Arsinoites are mentioned).

PSI V 510 concerns taxes to be paid by a bee-keeper from Bousiris upon request of the οἰκονομῶν in the Κάτω toparchy, where the bee-hives were presumably kept (ll.1-2: παρ' Ἀπολλωνίου τοῦ [ο]ἰκονομ[ο]ῦντος τὴν κάτω τοπαρχίαν); the payment may be effected either at Bousiris or at Herakleopolis.

BGU XVI 2586 is a declaration of 3200 sheep and 53 goats[3] in the possession of a single owner περὶ Βουσῖριν καὶ δι' ὅλου τοῦ νομοῦ (ll.11-12): these were tended by three shepherds, two of them guarding respectively 780 sheep (and 16 goats) and 1275 sheep (plus 16 goats) in the Πέραν toparchy (ll.15-17).

Stone and plaster used for repairs at the Herakles/Eseph temple at Herakleopolis came from Bousiris as shown by *SB* XIV 11959 (mentioning the local λατομίαι) and *P.Oxy.* XX 2272 (γύψος to be conveyed from the port of Bousiris): both these papyri may in fact have been part of the same τόμος συγκολλήσιμος)[4].

A number of documents refer to a temple at Bousiris: assaults against it are reported in *BGU* IV 1061 (no less than sixteen assailants from Sinary; the pastophoros' wife had been killed) and *BGU* IV 1201 (overnight assault; this papyrus shows that the temple was dedicated primarily to Sarapis: cf. l.9). *BGU* IV 1197 and 1200 reveal a conflict between the priests from Bousiris and those from Line and Koma about government allowances. According to *BGU* IV 1202 (18 B.C.) subsidies were granted to priests from Onnes (Tekmi toparchy). *BGU* IV 1198 indicates that Isis and Asklepios were also worshipped in the Sarapis temple at Bousiris. *BGU* IV 1196 contains a list of 133 priests.

ΓΑΠΑΣΩΕΩΣ

I/II A.D.	*P.Hib.* II 218,47;68	Γαπασώ[εω]ς (47); Γαπ[ασώ]εως (68)

TOPARCHY: Koites?

Most villages listed in *P.Hib.* II 218 were in Koites: a reference to Phebichis immediately precedes (l.46) the entry for this village.

ΓΕΛ[

VI-VII A.D.	*Stud.Pal.* X 5,10	τὸν βοηθ(ὸν) Γελ[[5]

---

[1] Cf. *P.Cair.Zen.* 59151 (fragment of a petition from a bee-keeper owning 5000 bee-hives apparently distributed between three nomes at least, including the Herakleopolites and the Oxyrhynchites).

[2] This must be the area, or toparchy around Troia, in the Memphite nome.

[3] «By far the largest number of sheep and goats ever registered for one individual» (Ed. *ad loc.*).

[4] See ANNA SWIDEREK, *JJP* 11/12, 1957/58, p.64.

[5] A reading Γεμ[, supplied to Γεμ[ούνεως, may be tempting but is «m.E. auszuschliessen» (Johannes Diethart, letter of February 25, 1994).

CATALOGUE

TOPARCHY: περὶ Πόλιν?

Other villages listed in the same document used to be in the Koma toparchy (Tinteris, l.5), in the περὶ Πόλιν (Onosis, l.4), in the Ἄγημα (Nino, l.7) and in the Tekmi toparchy (Kollintaathyr, l.6).

ΓΕΜΟΥΝΕΩΣ

| about 138 B.C. | P.Tebt. III 860,65 | Γεμούνεως |
| V A.D. | Stud.Pal. X 50,1;5 | πεδί(ον) Γεμούνεως (1); π]αλαιᾶς κώμης Γεμού[νεως (5) |

TOPARCHY: Koites.

*P.Tebt.*III 860: Sosibios' δωρεά comprises land at Koba (Koites), Gemoun(is) (listed immediately after Koba), and other villages.

ΓΕΣΣΙΑΣ

V A.D.	Stud.Pal. X 94,5	Γεσσιάδος[1]
late V A.D.	P.Oxy. XX 2268,6	ἐν τῇ αὐτῇ Γεσσιάδι
late V or early VI A.D. (cf. BL 8,208)	P.Mert. I 46,2	Γεσσιάδα
late V or early VI A.D.	P.Oxy. XVI 1834,3;5	τὴν Γεσσιάδα (3); ἀπὸ Γεσσιάδος (5)

Stud.Pal. X 94: other villages listed include Peenameus (l.6; Ἄγημα toparchy) and Tosachmis (l.8; Koites).
P.Oxy. XX 2268; *P.Mert.* I 46; *P.Oxy.* XVI 1834: *riparii* at work near Gessias. The last two documents contain complaints against the same person (Philoxenos), *P.Oxy.* XVI 1834 being delivered by people living at Palosis, in the eighth *pagus* of the Oxyrhynchites[2], which was apparently near Gessias.

ΔΑΦΝΗ

| V A.D. | Stud.Pal. X 94,7 | ἐποί]κ(ιον) Δάφνης |

---

[1] In the genitive case. «Γ ist jetzt nach der Restaurierung ganz zu sehen, vgl. *BL* 7,258».

[2] See PRUNETI, *Centri abitati, s.v.*

VI/VII A.D.	(?)*SB* XX 15072,7 [1]	Δάφνης ὅρμου Νεμάρεως
VI-VII A.D.	*Stud.Pal.* X 237,3	
VII A.D.	*Stud.Pal.* X 220,2	ἀπὸ χ(ωρίου) Δάφνης
VII-VIII A.D.	*Stud.Pal.* X 217,1	ἀπὸ χ(ωρίου) Δάφ[νης] παγαρχίας Ἡρακλεοπολίτου

TOPARCHY: Μέση.

ETYMOLOGY: in Greek, «bay, laurel». But this could also be an Egyptian word: *T3-chm-p3-t3*, «servant (fem.) of the land» (cf. KARL-TH. ZAUZICH, *Enchoria* 13, 1985, pp.115-116).

The κλῆρος Ψαννε, which is connected to Daphne in *Stud.Pal.* X 217, was in the πεδίον of Phys, i.e. in the Μέση toparchy, according to *P.Vind.Sijp.*9. Villages listed in *Stud.Pal.* X 94 include, beside Daphne, Gessias (5; Koites), Peenameus (6; Ἄγημα and Μέση toparchy) and Tosachmis (8; Koites).

ΔΙΑΣΗΜΟΤΑΤΟΥ [2]

V A.D.	*Stud.Pal.* X 233, col.II,17	Διασημοτάτου [3]
VII A.D. [4]	*Stud.Pal.* VIII 1309,4	ἀπὸ χ(ωρίου) Διασημωτ(άτου)
VII/VIII A.D.	*CPR* IV 2,17	Διασημο'τ'(άτου)

ETYMOLOGY: διασημότατος is a title, corresponding to Latin *perfectissimus*: cf. *P.Oxy.* XLIII 3124, 1-2 n. (about A.D. 322).
BIBLIOGRAPHY: TIMM, *Das christlich-koptische Ägypten* II, p.855.

Stud.Pal. VIII 1309: inhabitants of Διασημοτάτου and of Ἁλμυρά act as testimonies for an inhabitant of Psychis ἡ μεγάλη (in the Koites).
CPR IV 2 (a bilingual document in Coptic and Greek) lists many villages of the central toparchies of the Herakleopolite nome (toponyms in Greek) [5].

---

[1] This document has been published by PIETER J. SIJPESTEIJN, *ZPE* 81, 1990, pp.245-251: it is not certain that it deals (at least not entirely) with Herakleopolite villages.

[2] CARL WESSELY, *Topographie des Fayum in griechischer Zeit*, Wien 1904, p.56, assigned this village to the Arsinoites (followed by CALDERINI-DARIS, *Dizionario, s.v.*).

[3] New reading, checked for me by Johannes Diethart (letter of February 25, 1994).

[4] «Quittung wohl aus dem 7. Jh.» (Johannes Diethart by letter of February 25, 1994). Wessely dated it to the VII-VIII A.D.

[5] See *s.v.* ΝΙΝΩ.

CATALOGUE

ΔΙΔΥΜΙΑΝΟ[

227 A.D.   *Stud.Pal.* XX 29,23

TOPARCHY: Koites.

One of several κλῆροι, including some fossil kleroi[1], referred to in a sale contract for land near Tosachmis.

ΔΙΚΩΜΙΑ

256 (255) B.C.	*P.Hib.* I 47,29	εἰς Δικωμίαν
III B.C.	*BGU* X 1911,7	ἐν Δικωμίαι
27/26 B.C.	*BGU* IV 1208,21	εἰς Δικωμίαν
about 26-28 A.D.(?)	*P.Oxy.* LV 3807,35	εἰς Δικωμί(αν)
II/III A.D.	*P.Oxy.* LIX 3993,7	ἀπὸ Δικωμίας
about 250 A.D.	*SB* I 1495,4	Δικωμί[ας]
about 250 A.D.	*SB* I 1497,1	Δικωμίας
about 250 A.D.	*SB* I 1511,4	Δικωμία(ς) ὄνοι

TOPARCHY: Herakleopolite or Arsinoite nome?

ETYMOLOGY: this toponym obviously refers to the συνοικισμός of two originally separate villages: in view of the new *Greek* toponym, this must have taken place in the Ptolemaic period.

Other toponyms compounded with –κωμία: Τρικωμία (also in the Herakleopolite nome; but another Τρικωμία, as well as a Τετρακωμία, are also attested in the Arsinoites).

The sources offer no clue as to the location of this village, except that *BGU* IV 1208 (a private letter)[2] was found at Abū Sīr al-Malaq.

P.Hib. I 47: letter from Leodamas (an official involved with corn-revenues) to his subordinate Lysimachos; ll.25-32 deal with calves to be sent to Δικωμία.

BGU X 1911: part of the correspondence between Kallistratos and his subordinate Akestias (cf. the *Einleitung* to this document).

P.Oxy. LIX 3993: acknowledgement of the receipt of a letter and a package containing gold leaves (for gilding? for writing magical texts?) delivered by an ἐπιστολαφόρος; as noted by the Editor (on l.7), «it may be that the goods were sent direct from Dikomia, but it is perhaps more likely that this was a point on the journey where they changed boats, i.e. the sender paid freight to their boatman as far as his destination, Dikomia. From that point the next carrier worked for "cash on delivery". Dikomia may also have been a customs station».

SB I 1495, 1497, 1511 are receipts (issued at the θησαυρός of Theadelphia) for the transport of corn by donkeys belonging to inhabitants of Δικωμία.

---

[1] See below, *s.vv.* Μάρωνος, Νεπωτιανοῦ, and the list of *Fossil Kleroi* (pp.273 ff.).

[2] See BROR OLSSON, *Papyrusbriefe aus der frühesten Römerzeit*, Uppsala 1925, pp.36 ff.

ΔΙΩΡΥΞ Η ΟΜΦΑΛΟ.ΝΙΑ

36/35 B.C.	*BGU* XIV 2376,18-19; 38 (= XIV 2377, 44)	διῶρυξ καλουμένη ἡ ὀμφαλο.νια
36/35 B.C	*BGU* XIV 2377, 44	διῶρυξ καλουμένη ἡ ὀμφαλο.νια

A piece of garden-land near Sobthis is located by reference to this διῶρυξ (south) and to the ὁδὸς βασιλική (north).

ΔΙΩΡΥΞ

VI A.D.	*P.Oxy.* XVI 1917, 111-112	δι(ὰ) τῶν πρωτοκ(ωμητῶν) Τααμώρου ὑπὲρ τῆς ἀνωρυχθ(είσης) διώρ(υγος) ἐξ ἀπηλιώτου Ψελεμάχεως

A canal originating east of Pselemachis apparently reached Taamorou.

Ε....[

I B.C.	*BGU* XIV 2440,63	περὶ Ε....[

TOPARCHY: Ἄγημα? Πέραν?

Berenike cedes land to Herakleia (ll.62-66): some of it is περὶ Ε....[, some more near Peene. The total drawn at ll.64-66 indicates that the land near Ε....[was περὶ Πέραν καὶ Νισέα (Niseus was also in the Ἀγημα).

Ε[...]ΕΡ( )

V A.D.	*Stud.Pal.* X 233, col.II,3	ἐποίκ(ιον) Ἐ[...]ερ(

Ε...ΦΕ (?)

I/II A.D.	*P.Erl.* 58,2-3	...τ]οῦ Ἡρακλ[ε]ο[πολ]ίτ(ου) ...] κώμη Ε...φε [1]

---

[1] The reading is very uncertain.

CATALOGUE

ΕΕΒΗΚΙΣ[1]

| 190/191 A.D. | O.Wilck. 1104,3 | διὰ ὄνων Ἡρακλεοπολίτου Ἐεβῆκις |

TOPARCHY: Koites?

ETYMOLOGY: the element *byk* («the regular term for falcon in the animal cult»[2]) can perhaps be detected in this toponym.

O.Wilck. 1104: sitologos receipt for corn transport ; the fact that it was released by the sitologoi of Oxyrhynchus makes it likely that this village was in the Koites.

ΕΛΑΣΙΜΗΣ

| 161/160 B.C. | P.Hels. I 29,19 | Ελασ.( )[3] |
| V A.D. | Stud.Pal. X 94,3 |] Ἐλασίμης |

TOPARCHY: Πέραν?

A village of the Πέραν toparchy (l.24: Thmoiphtha) is found in *P.Hels.* I 29.
Other localities listed in *Stud.Pal.* X 94: Gessias (5; Koites), Peenameus (6; Ἄγημα toparchy), Daphne (7; Μέση toparchy), Tosachmis (8; Koites).

ΕΤΩΝ

| VI A.D. | Stud.Pal. III 399,1 | βοηθὸς] κώμης Ετων τοῦτ'ἔστιν Νήσων |

See *s.v.* ΝΗΣΩΝ (κώμη).

ΗΛΙ( )

| VII-VIII A.D. | Stud.Pal. X 211,5 | το'ῦ' χ(ωρίου) Ηλι( ) |

TOPARCHY: Tekmi.

---

[1] «Schrift kaum noch erhalten, vielleicht auch Σεβηκις» (Günter Poethke, letter of April 14, 1994).

[2] WILLY CLARYSSE - JAN QUAEGEBEUR, «Ibion, Isieion and Tharesieion in two Oslo Papyri», *Symbolae Osloenses* 57, 1982, pp.69-85, n.36 (with reference to *L.Ä.*, Bd.I, col.516).

[3] My reading (checked on photograph); ελυση() *ed.pr.* («wohl ein Dorfname»).

Other villages mentioned in the same document: Ogou (3) and possibly Pyrgotos (4), both in the Tekmi toparchy.

Θ[±3 ?]

VII-VIII A.D.   *Stud.Pal.* X 227,8   ἀπὸ χ(ωρίου) Θ[±3 ?]

Tale (Koites) is among the villages listed in this document.

ΘΑΛΛΟΥΣ[1]

VII-VIII A.D.   *Stud.Pal.* X 203,3   [χ(ωρίον)] Θαλλους

ETYMOLOGY: possibly the genitive of a Greek name (Θαλλώ, -οῦς was the name of a Greek divinity of increase: see *LSJ s.v.*).

The document lists Herakleopolite villages (belonging to various toparchies) whose names begin with the same letter: Thmoiobastis, Thoiamoun(is) (both in the Koma toparchy), Thelbonthis (Polis toparchy), Thmoinothis (Middle toparchy), Thelbo (Koites), Thmoinepsi, etc.

ΘΑΛΜΙ

VII A.D.   *Stud.Pal.* X 214,5   ἐν π(ε)δ(ί)ῳ Θαλμι

Peroe (Koites) is on top of the list in this document.

ΘΑΛ...ΚΑΡΕΙ

18 B.C.   *BGU* IV 1202,11   ἐν Θαλ...καρει (11-12)[2]

TOPARCHY: Bousiris?

BGU IV 1202 (a letter from the topogrammateus of the Bousiris toparchy) relates to the monthly ratios of ὄλυρα to the priests of Mendes, Amun, Chonsis and Harpochrates at Onnes.

---

[1] Cf. DREW-BEAR, *Le nome Hermopolite*, p.108: «(Θάλλους) appartient vraisemblablement à l'Héracléopolite, car il figure sur une liste de villages connus, pour la plupart, dans ce nome. En revanche, le toponyme Θαλλοῦ, cité par le *Stud.Pal.* X 190,3, est certainement situé dans le nome Hermopolite, comme les autres toponymes du texte».

[2] «In Edition richtig gelesen» (Günter Poethke, letter of April 14, 1994). But it is not clear where exactly the toponym ends.

ΘΕΛΒΩ

probably 17/18 A.D.	(?)P.Oxy. IV 814 descr.[1]	ἀπὸ Θελβωι
early I A.D.	SB XX 15130,2 = P.Tebt. II 535 descr.[2]	ἀρχεφόδωι Θελβωι (ll.1-2)
I/II A.D.	P.Hib. II 218,52	
late II or III A.D.	P.Ryl. II 225,36	περὶ Θελβώ
223 A.D.	P.Ross.Georg. V 20 verso, col. II,2	
III A.D.	(?)P.Ryl. II 351 descr.	ἀ]πὸ κώμης Θελβ.[[3]
late III A.D.	BGU XIII 2365,14	
313/314 A.D.	P.Michael. 28,9	κώμης Θελβώ
IV A.D.	P.Neph. 20,6;8;13	ἀπὸ Θελβώ (6); τοὺς τῆς Θελβὼ εἰρηνάρχους (8); οἱ προειρημένοι εἰρή[ναρχοι] τῆς Θελβώ (13)
end of IV A.D.	SB VIII 9683,16	εἰς Θελβώ
VII A.D.	Stud.Pal. X 231,1	χ'ω'(ρίου) Θελβώ
VII/VIII A.D.	SB XVIII 13888,7	[χ(ωρίου) Θ]ελβω
VII-VIII A.D.	Stud.Pal. X 203,2	χ(ωρίον) Θελβώ
VIII A.D. (cf. BL 8,439)	Stud.Pal. III 343,1	ἀπὸ χωρίου Θελβώ

TOPARCHY: Koites (XII *pagus*: P.Michael. 28).

ETYMOLOGY: cf. JEAN YOYOTTE, *MDAIK* 16, 1958, p.423: «Dans l'histoire légendaire d'Anusis, telle que la rapporte Hérodote (II, 140), on trouve mention d'une grande île qui était située dans les marais côtiers du Delta et qui se nommait Ελβω. Il est assez probable que cette forme recouvre le même mot égyptien que le terme Θελβω, le Θ initial représentant dans cette dernière transcription l'article féminin *t3*. ... En dépit de l'analogie frappante, il est difficile de voir dans *Telbo/Elbo* une abréviation de *Telbont/Elbont*. ... le plus simple est sans doute de supposer l'existence d'un vocable *elbo*, tout différent de *elbont* et dont la forme égyptienne reste à découvrir». Yoyotte also wonders (*ibid.*, n. 3) whether: «Une

---

[1] According to PIETER J. SIJPESTEIJN, *ZPE* 87, 1991, p.260 (see also CALDERINI-DARIS, *Dizionario*, p.252) P.Oxy. IV 814 descr. should refer to the same Thelbo (in the Arsinoite nome) as *P.Mil.Vogl.*IV 212 verso, col. XI,7 (109 A.D.). It is perhaps more likely for the Thelbo appearing in a papyrus from Oxyrhynchus to have been in the Oxyrhynchites: if so, this is likely to be the same village attested in *P.Ryl.* II 351 (see below). As the Herakleopolite village by the same name was in the southern part of the Koites, there is a possibility that this was in fact the same village.

[2] The document has been edited by PIETER J. SIJPESTEIJN, *ZPE* 87, 1991, pp.259-260.

[3] «Oxyrhynchite nome. Fragment of a contract (?). The villages *Thelbon* and *Pakerke* occur» (descr.). The document is still unpublished; on a photograph of this papyrus (kindly provided by the Audio-Visual Office of the Rylands University Library of Manchester) it is possible to decipher (1.2): ἀ]πὸ κώμης Θελβ.[. The traces after β seem compatible with an ω. In l.3, ἀπὸ κώ]μης Πακερκη is straightforward: according to PRUNETI, *Centri abitati*, *s.v.*, there were two villages by this name in the Oxyrhynchites. See also P.J. SIJPESTEIJN, *ZPE* 87, 1991, p.260.

explication par *t3 rbt* (terbe), "Le Parc" mérite-t-elle d'être prise en considération? Θελβω serait *t3 rbt ᶜ3t*, "Le Grand Parc" (soit *t-erb(e)-o*)».

P.Tebt. II 535: beginning of a letter from the τοπάρχης Artemidoros to the ἀρχέφοδος of Thelbo.
Listed with other Herakleopolite villages (mainly in the Koites) in *P.Hib.* II 218, Thelbo appears together with villages of the Koites in later documents, too: Thelbo and Philonikou, in particular, appear both in *P.Ryl.*II 225 and in *P.Michael.* 28.

SB VIII 9683: the monastery of Ankyron has been robbed of an anchor by a certain Paulus; it is requested that the matter be settled at Thelbo with the deacon Horus.

The village by this name in *P.Ryl.* II 351 and *SB* XVIII 13888 is most likely the same Thelbo, near the border with the Oxyrhynchites: *SB* XVIII 13888 mentions it along with Kalamou, Ostrakinou (both in the Oxyrhynchites)[1], but also Nokle, Hipponon and Phathor (southern Koites). Nokle and Thelbo also recur together in *P.Ryl.* II 225.

Thelbo and Thelbonthis are different villages: they are both listed, in consecutive lines, in *Stud.Pal.* X 203, ll.1-2.

(Θ)ΕΛΒΩΝΘΙΣ

2 Sept. 162 B.C.	*P.Hels.* I 26,A,13;21	Ἐλβώνθεως
I B.C.	*BGU* XIV 2440,98	[π]ερὶ [Θε]λβῶνθιν
VII-VIII A.D.	*Stud.Pal.* X 202,11	χ(ωρίον) Θελβον'θ'( )
VII-VIII A.D.	*Stud.Pal.* X 203,1	χ(ωρίον) Θελβ[ων]θ( )
VII-VIII A.D.	*Stud.Pal.* X 212,2	χ(ωρίον) Θελβώνθ'ε'(ως)

TOPARCHY: Techtho Nesos.
Localities by this name are attested in the Delta[2], in the Hermopolites and in the Oxyrhynchites[3].

ETYMOLOGY: Elbonthis and Thelbonthis (with the addition of the Egyptian article *t3*) are variant spellings for the same place-name. According to JEAN YOYOTTE, *MDAIK* 16, 1958, pp.419-423, «ce vocable désignait une entité topographique bien définie, mais fort commune, soit une catégorie particulière de terrains, soit une forme spéciale de construction ou d'agglomeration». See also *s.v.* ΘΕΛΒΩ.

P.Hels. I 26: tax-arrears from the Koites, Techtho Nesos and Πέραν; payments for the Techtho Nesos area are made through the *logeutes* of Elbonthis (ll.12-13); the association between these two localities is confirmed at l.21.

BGU XIV 2440: Archetime's holding is distributed between Thelbonthis and Thmoin-, while both these villages are made to depend on ....λσίου[4].

Note that *Stud.Pal.* X 211, 212 and 213, though published as separate documents, are in fact fragments of the same text, so that the villages mentioned in *Stud.Pal.* X 211 (Ogou, in the Tekmi toparchy), 212 (Thelbonthis) and 213 (Petachor and Kollasoucha) may have been near each other.

---

[1] See PRUNETI, *Centri abitati, s.v.* ΘΕΛΒΩ/ΘΕΛΒΩΙ.

[2] *BGU* IV 1138 (19/18 B.C.; from a cartonnage found at Abū Sīr al-Malaq) also refers to Σᾶϊς (l.12), which was in the Western Delta. This should be the same Ἔλβονθις found in the lexicon of Stephanus of Byzantium (πόλις μεταξὺ Αἰγύπτου καὶ Κυρήνης).

[3] Cf. M. DREW-BEAR, *Le nome Hermopolite, s.v.* Τελβῶνθις; PAOLA PRUNETI, *Centri abitati, s.v.* Θελβῶνθις.

[4] The preceding reference to Ολωνθεως, in the περὶ Πόλιν toparchy, is separated from these entries by a blank space: it seems reasonable to assume that these belonged to a different toparchy.

Thelbo and Thelbonthis were different villages: they are both listed, in consecutive lines, in *Stud.Pal.* X 203, ll.1-2.

ΘΕΡ

| 2 Sept. 162 B.C. | *P.Hels.* 26,B,19 | Θερ [1] |
| 25 July 396 A.D. | *CPR* 107a, [5?];9 | ἐν τῇ αὐτῇ Θέρ |

TOPARCHY: Μέση?

P.Hels. 26: Ther (if correctly read) is connected to Techtho, to which reference is made in the same line. *CPR* 107a: Aurelius Nemesianus could be the same person (from Herakleopolis) who leases out 3/4 ar. ἐν πεδίῳ Φῦς (Μέση toparchy) in *P.Vind.Sijp.*9. Connections between Techtho and the Μέση toparchy are attested elsewhere (see *s.vv.*).

ΘΜΟ( )

| III/IV A.D. | *P.Mich.* XV 722, 1;3;4;7;8;15;22 |

TOPARCHY: Koites [2].

ETYMOLOGY: *t3-m3j* («new, newly gained land») is the first component of several Herakleopolite toponyms.

ΘΜΟΙ[

| II A.D. | *P.Strasb.* V 356,3 | συνορία Θμοι[|

ETYMOLOGY: Egyptian *t3-m3j* («new, newly gained land»): see *s.v.* ΘΜΟ().

In the Editor's description, this is a «fragment cadastral, concernant une subdivision territoriale, à l'échelon d'un village». The surveyed area is connected to the Πτο]λεμαικὸς ποταμός (l.4), mentioned in *BGU* VIII 1784, where Ἱερὰ Νῆσος also appears.

---

[1] Ε̣.ρα() *ed.pr.*, but see note *ad loc.*: «Vielleicht könnte man Θερ lesen». The photograph seems to support this reading.

[2] Cf. the Editor's introduction to this document (p.70): «The text ... lists the amounts of land possessed by different people in either Θμο() and/or Περο(). A village Περόη is known from the Herakleopolite nome and more particularly from the Koites in which several villages starting with Θμο() are also to be found. There are a few villages in other nomes starting with Περο() and Θμο() but the combination of the two names seems to me to be significant».

ΘΜΟΙΑΜΟΥΝΕΩΣ

about 14/13 B.C.	*BGU* XVI 2670, col.III,1	Θμοιαμούνεως
I/II A.D.	*P.Hib.* II 218,66	Θμοι[αμούνεως[1]
IV A.D.	*PSI* III 222,7	κώμης Θμοιαμούνε[ως
IV A.D.	*P.Oxy.* XVI 2017,1;2;4;6;12	ὅρμου Θμοιαμούνεως (1;12); κώμης Θμοιαμούνεως (2;4); ἀπὸ θ[η]σαυροῦ Θμοιαμούνεως (6)
V A.D.	*Stud.Pal.* X 233, col.I b,10	Θμοιαμούνεως
V A.D.	*SB* VI 9146,5;13	ἀπὸ χωρίου [Θ]μοιαμούνεως (4-5); ἀπὸ τ(οῦ) αὐτ(οῦ) Θμοια(μούνεως) χωρίου (13)
VI/VII A.D.	*Stud.Pal.* X 4,6	Θμοιαμούν'ε'(ως)
VII A.D.	*Stud.Pal.* X 232,1	χ(ωρίου) Θμοιαμ[ούνεως
VII/VIII A.D.	*Stud.Pal.* X 203,6	χ(ωρίου) Θμοιαμούν'ε'(ως)
VII-VIII A.D.	*Stud.Pal.* X 208,3	χω(ρίου) Θμοιαμουν'ε'(ως)

See also *s.vv.* ΘΜΟΥΑ...[; [±8]ΟΥΝΕΩΣ.

TOPARCHY: Koma.

ETYMOLOGY: «the new land of Amun» (*T3-m3j-(n-)Imn*)[2]; first component (*t3-m3j*): see *s.v.* ΘΜΟ(). This toponym is already found in *P.Wilbour* A 76,42; 79,37.

MODERN ARABIC NAME: Al-Maimūn (on phonetical and topographical grounds: see *Introduction*, p.8).

BIBLIOGRAPHY: TIMM, *Das christlich-koptische Ägypten*, VI, p.2636, *s.v. Thmoiamounis*.

BGU XVI 2670 is an account of contributions from individuals and groups of workers and artisans, in preparation for the visit by a certain Lupus (presumably the nome strategos); the place-name Phainippou (Tekmi toparchy) appears at the top of the preceding column.

P.Oxy. XVI 2017: corn from various villages (including Machor, in the Koma toparchy) is conveyed to Thmoiamoun(is), which had an ὅρμος and a θησαυρός.

Stud.Pal. X 4 includes Thmoiamoun(is) in a group of villages (also including Pkommatoei and Poinami = Peenameus) which must send workers to Koma, for repair-works on a dyke.

---

[1] My supplement; a village of the Koma toparchy is required (see below), so that Θμοι[ναχ(ῆς)] of the *ed.pr.* cannot be maintained, as this was a village of the Techtho Nesos toparchy. Thmoiamoun(is) is the only other village (beside Thmoibastis, also appearing in this list) whose name begins with Θμοι–, to be attested for the Koma toparchy.

[2] Information from Katelijn Vandorpe (letter of July 18, 1995).

Stud.Pal. X 233, col.I B, enters Thmoiamoun(is) between Thmoiobastis and Bousiris, thus supporting the supplement Θμοι[αμούνεως in *P.Hib.* II 218, within a group of villages (ll.63-67) belonging to the area around Koma and Bousiris: Koma, Krekis, Bousiris, Thmoiamoun(is), Thmoiobastis.

SB VI 9146: at least three inhabitants of Thmoiamoun(is) stand surety for a whole family from the same village.

P.Hib. II 280 also mentions Mouchis (Tekmi toparchy), which also recurs not far away from Thmoiamoun(is) in *Stud.Pal.* X 233, col.I B (see above).

ΘΜΟΙΝ( )

VII-VIII A.D.	*Stud.Pal.* X 203,5	χ(ωρίον) Θμοιν( )

ETYMOLOGY: prefix *t3-m3j*, «new, newly gained land»: see *s.v.* ΘΜΟ().

The document lists Herakleopolite villages (belonging to various toparchies) whose name begins with the same letter: Thmoiobastis, Thoiamoun(is) (both in the Koma toparchy), Thelbonthis (Polis toparchy), Thmoinothis (Middle toparchy), Thelbo (Koites), Thmoinepsi, etc.

ΘΜΟΙΝ( )

VII-VIII A.D.	*Stud.Pal.* X 208 *verso*,1

ETYMOLOGY: prefix *t3-m3j*, «new, newly gained land»: see *s.v.* ΘΜΟ().

Mentioned with Phnebieus (Middle toparchy) and Pselemachis (Koites); on the *recto*, reference is made to Thmoiamoun(is).

ΘΜΟΙΝ( )

VII A.D.	*Stud.Pal.* X 22,5	χ(ωρίον) Θμοιν( )
VIII A.D.	*Stud.Pal.* X 218,5	χ(ωρίον) Θμοιν( )
VIII A.D.	*Stud.Pal.* X 223,3	ἀπὸ χ(ωρίου) Θμοιν( )

TOPARCHY: περὶ Πόλιν.

ETYMOLOGY: prefix *t3-m3j*, «new, newly gained land»: see *s.v.* ΘΜΟ().

Onosis (περὶ Πόλιν toparchy) and a village of the Koma toparchy (Tinteris) are also mentioned in *Stud.Pal.* X 218. As Onosis and Koma also recur in *Stud.Pal.* X 223, it seems likely that the same Θμοιν– is meant in both documents.

Θμοιν- in *Stud.Pal.* X 22, where two more villages of the περὶ Πόλιν toparchy (Sobthis and Tokois) are listed, could well be the same village.

ΘΜΟΙΝ.( )[1]

beginning of III A.D.   *P.Erl.* 48,23

TOPARCHY: Koites?

ETYMOLOGY: prefix *t3-m3j*, «new, newly gained land»: see *s.v.* ΘΜΟ().

Two important villages of the Koites, Psychis and Phebichis, are included in the same list.

ΘΜΟΙΝΑΥΣΙΡΙΣ

172 B.C.	*BGU* XIV 2389, [2]; 17	ἐκ κ[ώμης Θμοιναυσίρεως] (2); ἐκ κώμης Θμοιναυσίρεως (17)
163 B.C.	*P.Hels.* I 11,11	περὶ κώ(μην) Θμοιναυσῖριν τοῦ Πέραν
163 B.C.	*P.Hels.* I 14,7-8	περὶ κώμην Θμοιναυσῖριν τοῦ Πέραν (7-8)
2 Sept. 162 B.C.	*P.Hels.* I 26 A,20;29	Θμοιναυσίρεως
mid-II B.C.	*P.Duke* inv.605 (unpubl.)[2]	
I B.C.	*BGU* VIII 1888,3	Θμοιναυσίρεως

TOPARCHY: Πέραν.

ETYMOLOGY: «the new land (of the people?) of Osiris» (*T3-m3j-(na?)-Wsir*)[3]; first component *t3-m3j*: see *s.v.* ΘΜΟ().

P.Hels. I 11, *P.Hels.* I 14 and *P.Hels.* I 26 assign Thmoinausiris to the Πέραν toparchy. *P.Hels.* I 11 and 14 are ἀπόμοιρα declarations by tax-payers, whose vineyards are at Thmoinausiris, in the fossil kleros Σωστράτου.

The komogrammateus of Thmoinausiris is mentioned in *BGU* VIII 1888.

---

[1] Θμοινη() *ed. pr.*: η not detectable on the photograph provided by Egert Pohlmann and the Universitätsbibliothek Erlangen-Nürnberg.

[2] See PETER VAN MINNEN, *BASP* 31, 1994, p.92 (the κωμογραμματεύς of Thmoinausiris is mentioned in this document: he also appears in another unpublished document: *P.Duke* inv.599).

[3] Etymology suggested by Katelijn Vandorpe (private communication: September 12, 1996).

ΘΜΟΙΝΑΧΗ

II B.C.	*P.Münch.* III 55,3	εἰς Θμοιναχήι
I B.C.	*BGU* XIV 2440,97	περὶ Θμοιν(αχή)
about 14/13 B.C.	*BGU* XVI 2602,12	ἐκ Θμοναχή
I/II A.D.	*P.Hib.* II 218,51;84	Θμοιν[άχ(ης)] (51); Θμοινάχ(ης) (84)
2 Sept. 162 A.D.	*P.Hels.* I 26,A,14;17;B,20	Θμοιναχῆι
II A.D.	*CPR* I 115 + 145, 1;18;19 [1]	ἀπὸ κώμης Θμοινα[χη (1-2); περὶ Θμοιναχη (18);]ν Θμοιναχη (19)
II A.D.	*P.Petaus* 28,6;20	τῷ ναυτικῷ τῷ ἀπὸ Τμουναχῆ [2]
222 A.D.	*PSI* XV estr. 1546, [5]; 14	Θμο]ι̣[ν]αχή (5); ἀπὸ Θμοιναχ[ή (14)
223 A.D.	*P.Ross.Georg.* V 20,*verso*,col. II,1	Θμοιναχή
early III A.D.	*P.Ryl.* II 87, *recto*,col. II,12	Θμοιναχῆ [3]
V A.D.	*Stud.Pal.* X 233, col. I A,8	Θμοιναχη

TOPARCHY: Τεχθὼ Νῆσος.

ETYMOLOGY: «the new land of reed» (*T3-m3j-n-3hj*): see also CRUM, *Coptic Dictionary*, p.XVI, *Add.*25a, s.v. Tmounahi [4]. First component: *t3-m3j* («new, newly gained land»): see s.v. ΘΜΟ().

BGU XVI 2602: οἱ ἀπὸ Τεχθὼ γεωργοί write to Athenodoros, in his capacity as epistates and dioiketes, informing him that an agent of the strategos has tried to compel them to do canal work; one of Athenodoros' men has come to the rescue from Thmoinache.

Not far from Techtho (on account of *BGU* XVI 2602 and *P.Hels.* 26), Thmoinache is connected to Phebichis (and other villages) in *P.Ross.Georg.* V 20, and in *P.Petaus* 28. It is also associated with villages of the Ἄγημα toparchy, namely Korphotoi (*P.Ross.Georg.* V 20 *recto*) and Alilais (*P.Ryl.* II 87 *recto*).

In *BGU* XIV 2440, ll.97-100, Thelbonthis and Thmoin() are made to depend on a third village (....λσίου): the supplement Thmoinache is supported by the fact that this village, like Thelbonthis, belonged to the Techtho toparchy; it also recurs in the line after (T)elbonthis in *P.Hels.*I 26 [5].

---

[1] «*CPR* I 115 ist mit *CPR* I 145 vereinigt» (letter from Johannes Diethart, of February 25, 1994).

[2] Cf. the Editor's note *ad l.* 6: «Τμουναχῆ ist sicher identisch mit Θμοιναχῆ».

[3] «The *recto* contains two incomplete columns of official accounts of some sort» (see *Introduction* to this document, p.51). I have checked this reading on a photograph provided by the Audio-Visual Office of the Rylands University Library of Manchester.

[4] Information from Katelijn Vandorpe (letter of July 18, 1995).

[5] This seems the most likely supplement to me. However, another possibility should be mentioned: Θμοιν(έφθα), which was in the Πέραν toparchy but is found on the same line with Thelbonthis in *Stud.Pal.* X 202; Thmoiphtha appears in *P.Hels.* I 26, where the connection of Thelbonthis to the Πέραν is also shown.

ΘΜΟΙΝΕΘΥΜΙΣ

251/250 B.C.(?)	*SB* X 10540,3 (= *P.Hib.* I 154 descr.)	ἐκ Θμ[ο]ινεθύμεως
250 B.C.	*P.Hib.* I 80,7-8	ἐκ Θμ[οι]νεθύμεως
7 Jan. 229 B.C.	*P.Hib.* I 163 descr.	περὶ κώμην Τμοινεθῦμιν
about 228 B.C.	*P.Hib.* I 70 (b),8-9	περὶ κώμην Τμοινεθῦμιν
mid-III B.C.[1]	*P.Fuad Crawford* 5,verso,3	Θμοινεθῦμις
mid-III B.C.	*P.Strasb.* IX 802,3;24	Θμοινεθῦμις
2 Sept. 162 B.C.	*P.Hels.* I 26,A,9;B,[9]	Θμοινεθύμεως
beginning of III A.D.	*P.Erl.* 48,28	Θμοινετ(ῦμις)[2]

TOPARCHY: Koites.

ETYMOLOGY: «the new land of Atum» (*T3-m3j-n-Itm*); first component (*t3-m3j*): see *s.v.* ΘΜΟ().[3]

In *P.Hels.* 26, *P.Strasb.* 802, *P.Fuad Crawford* 5 and (if correctly resolved) *P.Erl.* 48, Thmoinethymis is listed with various villages of the Koites (around Phebichis).

P.Hib. 70 (b): sale of vine-land near Thmoinethymis, bought by a μάχιμος of Herakleopolis from Aspheas son of Horus.

P.Hib. 80, 6-12, and *SB* X 10540 deal with deliveries of wine from Thmoinethymis to Hiera Nesos.

ΘΜΟΙΝΕΠΤΕΙ

227/226 B.C.	*P.Grad.* 3,6; [20] (*SB* III 6277)	ἐν κώμηι Θμοινέπτει
227/226 B.C.	*SB* III 6301,6[4]	ἐν κώμηι Θμοινέπτ[ει

TOPARCHY: Koites

ETYMOLOGY: the first component of this toponym is *t3-m3j* («new land»): see *s.v.* ΘΜΟ().

P.Grad. 3, a surety document drawn up at Thmoineptei, is addressed to Kleitarchos, τραπεζίτης τοῦ Κωίτου.

---

[1] On the re-dating of this document see *Introduction*, p.14 n.7.

[2] This seems a likely resolution to me: Θμοινετ(ῆ?) *ed. pr.*; Θμοιναχῆ Daris: but Θμοινετ() is the correct reading (checked on a photograph).

[3] Cf. JEAN YOYOTTE, *RdÉ* 15, 1963, p.88.

[4] «Der Papyrus stellt die Außenschrift dar, deren Innenschrift *SB* III 6277 (= *P.Grad.* 3) ist» (*ed. pr., ad loc.*).

ΘΜΟΙΝΕΨΙ

late IV/early V A.D. (cf. *BL* 9,368)	*P.Vind.Tand.* 19,6;7	κορνικουλαρ(ίῳ) κάστρ(ων) Θμοινέψει (6); ἀκτουαρ(ίῳ) κάστρ(ων) Θμοινέψει (7)
V A.D.	*Stud.Pal.* X 233, col.II,14	Θμοινεψι
V/VI A.D.	*SB* I 1945,6 [1]	Θμουνέψ(εως)
VI A.D.	*P.Mich.* X 591,1	πρωτοκ(ωμήταις) καὶ εἰρηνάρχ(αις) Θμοινέψι; cf.l.3: κώμης [2]
VI A.D.	*Stud.Pal.* III 66,1	ὅρμου Θμοινεψ( ) (cf. *BL* 9,332)
VI A.D.	*P.Wash.Univ.* II 103,6	ἀπ[ὸ] Θμονεψ.[
VI/VII A.D.	*P.Oxy.* LVI 3870,3	ἐν τῇ Θμοινέψι
VII/VIII A.D.	*CPR* IV 2,12	χ(ωρίον) Θμοιγέ( )
VII-VIII A.D.	*Stud.Pal.* X 203,7	χ(ωρίον) Θμοινεψ( )
VIII A.D.	*Stud.Pal.* X 84,7	χ(ωρίον) Θμοινεψι [3]

Literary Sources

about 300 A.D.	*Itin. Anton.* 168,4	*Thimonepsi*
V A.D.	*Not. Dignit. Or.* XXVIII 31	*Thinunepsi*

ETYMOLOGY: «the new land of the lake» (*T3-m3j-n-p3-šj*)[4]; first component *t3-m3j*: see *s.v.* ΘΜΟ().

MODERN ARABIC NAME: the identification with Banī Sulaimān Aš Sarqīya, suggested in *TAVO* B 69, § 4.3 (O 22; see also p.185), is consistent with the information contained in *Itin. Anton.* (see below).

The *Itin. Anton.* identifies *Thimonepsi* as one of the stations of the Roman army on the east bank of the Nile (preceded, from south to north, by *Hipponon* and *Alyi*), approximately 16 miles south of Aphroditopolis, i.e. roughly on the same parallel as Herakleopolis. The *ala prima Tingitana* was stationed there (cf. *Not.Dign.*, and the reference to κάστρα Θμοινέψει in *P.Vindob.Tand.* 19).

Stud.Pal. X 84 lists Thmoinepsi after Noeris (περὶ Πόλιν toparchy), Pois (Tilothis toparchy) and Peensamoi (Πέραν toparchy).

---

[1] *SB* I 1945 includes a list of toponyms (all of them χωρία, apparently) found on vases. See BERNARD P. GRENFELL - ARTHUR S. HUNT, *Egypt Exploration Fund. Arch. Report* 1904/1905, p.15.

[2] L.3: [μὴ ἀμ]ελήσατε ἐκπέμψαι εἰς τὴν πόλιν μετὰ ἑνὸς πεδιοφύλακος τῆς ὑμῶν κώμης.

[3] The supplement I suggested, [Θμ]οινεψι, based on [ ]οινεψι of the *ed. pr.* has been confirmed by Johannes Diethart: «Z.7 ist nach der Restaurierung jetzt Θμοινεψι zu lesen» (letter of September 13, 1994).

[4] Etymology proposed by Katelijn Vandorpe (private communication, September 12, 1996).

CPR IV 2 (a bilingual document in Coptic and Greek) lists many villages of the central toparchies of the Herakleopolite nome (toponyms in Greek)[1]: it is therefore likely that Thmoinepsi is meant here (Thmoinethymis or Thmoineptei are the only other options, but both were in the Koites).

ΘΜΟΙΝΠΕΣΛΑ

320/21-321/22 A.D.	*P.Neph.* 45,19	ἀπὸ Θμοιπέσλα[2]
334 A.D.	*P.Lond.* VI 1913,10	ἀπὸ Θμοινπέσλα (cf. *BL* 9,148)
IV/V A.D.	*P.Rain.Cent.* 153,10	ἀπὸ Θμοινπέσλα
24 July 423 A.D.	*P.Köln* III 151,34	ἀπὸ κώμης Θμοινπέσλα[3]

TOPARCHY: Koites.
A village called Πέσλα is well attested in the Hermopolites (see DREW-BEAR, *Le nome Hermopolite, s.v.*).

ETYMOLOGY: «the new land of the cultivated land» (*T3-m3j-n-p3-dl*^{C} [4]; first component *t3-m3j*: see *s.v.* ΘΜΟ().

P.Rain.Cent. 153: Thmoinpesla is listed with Tale and Thneis (Koites), Phys and Peempibyk(is) (Μέση toparchy), Palosis (Northern toparchy of the Oxyrhynchites).
P.Neph. 45, *P.Lond.* VI 1913: net of monasteries at Hipponon, Phathor, Thmoinpesla, in the proximity of the Kynopolite nome (cf. also *P.Köln* III 151).
Stud.Pal. III 66: ὅρμος of Thmoinpesla.

ΘΜΟΙΝΩΘΙΣ

247/246 B.C.	*SB* III 7203,8	κωμάρχηι Θμοινότιτος
17 Jan. 245 B.C.[5]	*P.Petr.* III 43 (2), col. III,28	τὴν γέφυραν τήν ἐν Θμοινώτιδι (cf. *BL* 3,146)[6]
mid-II B.C.	*P.Strasb.* VIII 781,8	ἐκ Θμοινώθεως

---

[1] See *s.v.* ΝΙΝΩ.

[2] «Zum Schwund des Nasals vor Labial vgl. GIGNAC, I, p.117» (Edd. *ad loc.*).

[3] Cf. *P.Neph.* 45,19 n.: Θμοινπέλλα ed. pr.

[4] Cfr. DIMITRI MEEKS, *Le grand texte des donations au temple d'Edfou*, Cairo 1972, pp.113-114; see also SERGE SAUNERON, «Phthla, le terrain cultivé», *BIFAO* 67, 1969, pp.117-119.

[5] See ALAN E. SAMUEL, *Ptolemaic Chronology*, München 1962, p.92.

[6] A very uncertain reading, checked for me by Brian McGing (Trinity College, Dublin; letter of September 8, 1994): «The trace of ink after Θμοιν would certainly fit omega, but after that the traces are extremely faint».

I/II A.D.	*P.Hib.* II 218,58	Θμοινώθ(εως)
II/III A.D.	*P.Köln* II 99,5	Θμοινώθεω[ς
227 A.D.	CPR I 64,9;15	[ἀπὸ] κώμης Θμοινώθεως (8-9); [περ]ὶ Θμοινῶθιν (15)
VII/VIII A.D.	*Stud.Pal.* X 203,8	χ(ωρίον) Θμοινω'θ'( )

TOPARCHY: Μέση.

ETYMOLOGY: first component *t3-m3j* («new, newly gained land»): see *s.v.* ΘΜΟ().

MODERN ARABIC NAME: Mayyāna (see *Introduction*, p.10). This is site W 38 (Mayyāna/Sidmant) in *TAVO B 69*: «Auf halbem Weg zwischen Mayyāna im Süden und Sidmant im Norden befindet sich eine ausgedehnte Nekropole. Sie liegt am Rand der Anhöhe, die das Fayyūm vom Niltal trennt ... und wurde schon zu Beginn dieses Jahrhunderts ausgegraben ... Diese ausgedehnte Nekropole gehört zu ... Herakleopolis magna» (p.240).

CPR I 64: παραχώρησις contract between Aurelios Sarapammon (from Herakleopolis but apparently living at Kerkytos) and a woman living at Thmoinothis; the woman acquires 9.5 arourae near Phys (in the fossil kleros of Ἄμμων) and a few more near Thmoinothis (in the fossil kleros Ἀριστομάχου). The contract is recorded at the agoranomos office of the Μέση toparchy at Peenameus.

P.Strasb. VIII 781 is from the same cartonnage as *P.Hamb.* I 91 [1], where the villages of Tebetny and Pois are mentioned.

In *P.Köln* II 99 the three places mentioned above (Kerkytos, Thmoinothis, Phys) appear in a group of villages which also includes Phnebieus and Peempibyk(is): each of these is assigned to the Μέση toparchy by other documents. In *P.Hib.* II 218 Thmoinothis is entered between Pois and, again, Phnebieus.

A location in the Μέση is consistent with *P.Petr.* III 43 (2), also referring to Phnebieus [2]. In *SB* III 7203 Bousiris is also mentioned.

ΘΜΟΙΟΒΑΣΤΙΣ

27 March 254 B.C.	*P.Lond.* VII 1972,1	εἰς Θμοίβαστιν [3]
mid-III B.C. [4]	*P.Cair.Zen.* IV 59782 (b),24;63;81;88(?)	ἐκ Τμοιβάστεως (24); ἐκ ⟦Κ..ας⟧ Τμοιβάστιος (63); ἐκ Τμοι[βάστεως] (81); ἐκ [Τμοιβά]στιος (88) [5]

---

[1] See *Introduction*, p.20.

[2] See *Introduction*, p.10.

[3] As Willy Clarysse points out to me, one expects Θμοιόβαστιν, or else Θμοιούβαστιν (on the analogy of Πετύβαστις, Ψενόβαστις), as a small *omikron* might be easily missed by the Editor, but I have not been able to check this reading. The reference to this village is found in «the right-hand fragment, containing the ends of the lines, [which] is in Cairo» (cf. *P.Lond.* 1972, Introduction, p.61: the fragment was in fact first published as *P.Cair.Zen.* 59197).

[4] On the dating of this document see above, p.60 n.3.

[5] Again, a small *omikron* could easily have been missed by the Editor, but I was unable to check these readings on the original.

239/238 B.C.[1]	*P.Rain.Cent.* 44,6	ἐκ Θμοιοβάστεως
6 June 130 B.C.	*SB* XIV 12089,2	ἐν Θμοιοβάστει
after 84/3 B.C.	*BGU* XIV 2370 (fr.1),78	Θμοιοβά(στεως)
I B.C.	*BGU* XIV 2432,22	Θμοιοβά(στεως)
I B.C.	*BGU* XIV 2440,58	Θμοιοβά(στεως)
after 52/1 B.C.	*BGU* VIII 1808,12	Θμοι⟦..α⟧'ο'βάσ'τ'εως (cf. BL 8,49)
I/II A.D.	*P.Hib.* II 218,67	Θμο[ιοβ]άσ̣τ̣[εως (cf. *BL* 8,151)
V A.D.	*Stud.Pal.* X 233, col.I B,8	Θμοιουβαστεως
VI A.D.	*Stud.Pal.* X 258,2	πρὸς χῶμ(α) Θμοιο[υ]β(εστι)
VI-VII A.D.	*P.Vind.Tand.* 17,17;18	Θμοιιουβεστεως
VII A.D.	*Stud.Pal.* X 263,1	ἀπὸ χω(ρίου) [Θμ]ουιουβ[έστ]εως
VII-VIII A.D.	*Stud.Pal.* X 203,4	χ(ωρίον) Θμοιο[υ]β(εστι)
VIII A.D.	*Stud.Pal.* X 119,2	ἀπὸ χ(ωρίου) Θμοιουβ(εστι)

See also: ΤΙΩΒΑΣΤΙ.

TOPARCHY: Koma.

ETYMOLOGY: «the new land of the goddess Bast» (*T3-m3j-n-B3st.t*)[2]. First component (*t3-m3j*): see *s.v.* ΘΜΟ().

In the Herakleopolites, the cat-goddess Bast[3] was closely associated with the goddess Âayt (*c3t*): cf. OLIVIER PERDU, *RdÉ* 40, 1989, pp.195-197[4].

This village is assigned to the Koma toparchy in *BGU* XIV 2440. In *P.Lond.* VII 1972 Zenon instructs Sosos to go to Thmoiobastis, so that he may collect olive plants and vines «which have been [...] by Theon on the river» (1.4: ἐπὶ τοῦ ποταμοῦ, designating either the Baḥr Yūsuf or the Nile). Thmoiobastis must have been a station on the route to Lower Egypt: cf. *P.Rain.Cent.* 44 (corn transport: 525 artabae from Onnes, 200 from Thmoiobastis and, on a different boat, 725 from Bousiris).

---

[1] In my opinion, this document should be dated to the 9th year of Euergetes (239/238 B.C.). See the Editor's note at l.11; *P.Rain.Cent.* 44 comes from the same cartonnage as *P.Rain.Cent.* 43, which is dated to 236 B.C.

[2] See also CRUM, *Coptic Dictionary*, p.160b, *s.v. Tmoui oubesti* (information from Katelijn Vandorpe: see above, *s.v.* ΘΜΟΙΑΜΟΥΝΕΩΣ). Cf. above, *s.v.* ΑΡΤΕΜΙΔΟΣ ΟΡΜΟΣ, on the triple identification Bast = Artemis = Nemesis.

[3] An amulet «de fayenza verde de Bastet representada con cuerpo humano y cabeza de gata» was found at the site of Herakleopolis during the 1989 Spanish excavations there; it bears the inscription: «Bastet, mistress of heaven» (MARIA DEL CARMEN PEREZ-DIEZ - PASCAL VERNUS, *Excavaciones en Ehnasya el Medina*, vol. I, Madrid 1992, p.75). On this goddess, see also *s.v* .ΑΡΤΕΜΙΔΟΣ ΟΡΜΟΣ.

[4] I owe this reference to Luc Limme.

P.Cair.Zen. IV 59782 (b) lists Thmoiobastis with Bousiris and other villages of the Koma toparchy (Koma, Krekis, Machor, Toou), of the Tilothis toparchy (Tilothis, Tanchais) and of the Tekmi toparchy (Onnes). Many of these villages are also recorded in *BGU* XIV 2370, fr.1 (under the main entry κάτω τοπαρ[χ]ίας): Koma, Toou, Machor, Thmoiobastis, Onnes, Tilothis, Tanchais. A second fragment (*BGU* XIV 2370 fr.2), written by the same hand, has a reference to Bousiris.

In *BGU* XIV 2432 Thmoiobastis appears after Toemesis (Koites) and Ibion Techtho. A comparison with *BGU* VIII 1808 may be instructive: Koma, Onnes, Thmoiobastis and Bousiris again appear in a series, preceding an entry for Techtho.

Θμοιουβεστις in *P.Vind.Tand.* 17 (VI/VII A.D.), where this village appears in an Arsinoite context, should be the same as Θμοιο[υ]β() of *Stud.Pal.* X 258 (VI A.D.), *Stud.Pal.* X 263 and *Stud.Pal.* X 119 (VIII A.D.): its identification with the Herakleopolite Thmoiobastis was suggested by Edgar (in his comment to *P.Cair.Zen.* II 59197).

ΘΜΟΙΟΝΠΡΟΦ[[1]

early II A.D.   *P.Köln* II 98,40

ETYMOLOGY: first component *t3-m3j* («new, newly gained land»): see *s.v.* ΘΜΟ().

Other place-names in the same document: Sobthis, Patamousou, Temenkyrkis (Koites).

ΘΜΟΙΟΥΘΙΣ

about 260 B.C.	*P.Hib.* I 112,56;88	Θμοιοῦθις
mid-III B.C. [2]	*P.Fuad Crawford* 5 verso,12	Θμοι[.].θις [3]
IV A.D.	*P.Amh.* II 142,4	[περὶ ἐποίκ]ι[ο]ν Θμοιούθεως

TOPARCHY: Koites.

ETYMOLOGY: first element *t3-m3j* («new, newly gained land»): see *s.v.* ΘΜΟ().

Most villages mentioned in *P.Hib.* I 112 and *P.Fuad Crawford* 5 *verso* belong to the Koites. In *P.Amh.* II 142, reporting an assault upon the land of Aurelius Germanus at Thmoiouthis, the πραιπόσιτος τ[ῶ]ν κάστρων Ἱππώνων is requested to intervene.

---

[1] .μοιονπροφ[*ed. pr.*: the trace at the beginning can hardly have belonged to any other letter but θ or τ of the prefix (Θ/Τ)μοι–.

[2] On the re-dating of this document see *Introduction*, p.14 n.7.

[3] Cf. Ed. *ad loc.*: «Either Θμοινῶθις (*P.Hib.* I, Intro. p.8) or Θμοιοῦθις (*P.Hib.* 112,56 and 88). More probably the latter».

ΘΜΟΙΤΑΩΥΣ

mid-III B.C.   *P.Strasb.* IX 802,4

TOPARCHY: Koites?

ETYMOLOGY: first component *t3-m3j* («new, newly gained land»): see *s.v.* ΘΜΟ().
All villages listed in *P.Strasb.* IX 802 were apparently in the Koites.

ΘΜΟΙΤΟΘΙΣ

| about 260 B.C. | *P.Hib.* I 112,39 | Θμοιτόθις |
| about 138 B.C. | *P.Tebt.* III 860,22 | περὶ Θμοιτόθιν [1] |

See also *s.v.* ΤΟΘΙΣ (which could well be the same place).

TOPARCHY: Koites.

ETYMOLOGY: «the new land of Thoth» (*T3-m3j-(n-)Dhwty*)[2]; first component *t3-m3j*: see *s.v.* ΘΜΟ().

Most villages mentioned in *P.Hib.* I 112 and *P.Tebt.* III 860 belong to the Koites.

ΘΜΟΙΦΘΑ

215/214 B.C.	*P.Strasb.* II 111,23	Θμοι[έ]φθ[α][3]
2 Sept. 162 B.C.	*P.Hels.* I 26 A,27	Θμοῖφθα
161/160 B.C.	*P.Hels.* I 29,24	Θμοῖφθα
I B.C.	*BGU* VI 1285,9	ἐν κώμῃ Θμοίφθαι
I B.C.	*BGU* XIV 2432,17	
I B.C.	*BGU* XIV 2437,36	
131/132 A.D.	*PSI* VIII 962 (b),25	ἀπὸ κώμης Θμοινέφθα
VII-VIII A.D.	*Stud.Pal.* X 202,7	χ(ωρίον) Θμοιεφ'θ'()

See also: Ἰβιὼν Θμοίφθα

TOPARCHY: Πέραν.

---

[1] This reading seems compatible with the traces (checked on a photograph) : περὶ Θμόιτος ἐπ(οίκιον) *ed. pr.* (see note *ad loc.*: «Θμοιτόθιν, which *P.Hib.* 112 might suggest, cannot be read»).

[2] As suggested by Katelijn Vandorpe (letter of July 18, 1995).

[3] My reading; Θμοι[.]φ[..] was deciphered by WILLY CLARYSSE, who re-edited this document in *Ancient Society* 7, 1976, pp.200-203. After φ, the remnants of a round letter are clearly detectable on the photograph.

ETYMOLOGY: «the new land of Ptah» (*T3-m3j-(n-)Pth*) [1]; first component *t3-m3j*: see *s.v.* ΘΜΟ().

BGU XIV 2432 and 2437 indicate that this village was in the Πέραν toparchy. This is confirmed by *P.Hels.* I 26, where it is listed with Tebetny, Peensamoi, Thmoinausiris. In *P.Hels.* I 29 Kerkytos (l.28; Μέση toparchy) is also mentioned.

Thmoiphtha should also be supplied at *P.Strasb.* II 111,23, again in connection with Peensamoi (here spelt Πεονταμουν): farmers on strike have apparently fled from the first to the second village. The oikonomos' agent (called Harmachis) who is in charge at Techtho in the Koites (*P.Strasb.* II 563 and 113), also supervises affairs at Thmoiphtha and Peensamoi (both villages of the Πέραν toparchy) [2]. The same oikonomos deals with tax-arrears from the Koites, Techtho Nesos and the Πέραν in *P.Hels.* I 26 (*P.Hels.* I 21 almost certainly belongs to the same document).

Stud.Pal. X 202 lists together Thmoiphtha and Thelbonthis (Techtho Nesos toparchy).

PSI VIII 962 (b) is a contract between a man from Herakleopolis and another from Thmoiphtha.

ΘΜΟΙΧ( )

| late III A.D. | *BGU* XIII 2365,15 | |

TOPARCHY: Koites.

ETYMOLOGY: first component *t3-m3j* («new, newly gained land»): see *s.v.* ΘΜΟ().

Other villages mentioned in the same document: Techtho, Papa, Thelbo (all in Koites).

ΘΜΟΥΑ...[

| middle or late II A.D. | *P.Hib.* II 280,3 | ἐν κώ(μῃ) Θμουα...[|

ETYMOLOGY: first component *t3-m3j* («new, newly gained land»): see *s.v.* ΘΜΟ().

ΘΝΗΙΣ

mid-III B.C.	*P.Strasb.* IX 802,5	Θνηῖς
about 163 B.C.	*P.Hels.* I 20,13	ἐν κώμηι Τνήει
161/160 B.C.	(?)*P.Hels.* I 29,18	Θνῆς[3]
286 A.D.	*P.Wash.Univ.* I 18,17	ἀπὸ Τνήεως

---

[1] Information from Katelijn Vandorpe (letter of July 18, 1996).

[2] See Clarysse's article (cited on p.84, n.3), pp.185-207.

[3] This could be a place, rather than a personal name (as suggested in the *ed.pr.*).

313/314 A.D.	*P.Michael.* 28,9	κωμάρχοις κώμης Τνήεως¹
IV/V A.D.	*P.Rain.Cent.* 153,12	ἀπὸ Τνήεως
V A.D.	*Stud.Pal.* X 233, col. I A,2	Τνήεως
VIII A.D.	*Stud.Pal.* X 109,9	ἀπὸ χ(ωρίου) Τνήεως

See also: Την...[

TOPARCHY: Koites (XII *pagus*: *P.Michael.* 28).

P.Strasb. VII 802: list of Herakleopolite villages, most of them in the Koites.
P.Michael. 28: the other villages mentioned in this document (Papa, Phebichis, Pselemachis, Thelbo, Philonikou: all belonging to the Koites) are here assigned to the XII *pagus*.
P.Rain.Cent. 153: Thneis is listed with Tale and Thmoinpesla (Koites), Phys and Peempibyk(is) (Middle toparchy), Palosis (Northern toparchy of the Oxyrhynchites).
Stud.Pal. X 109: other villages listed: Taamorou, Pyrgotos, Tinteris, Philonikou (which also follows immediately after Thneis in *Stud.Pal.* X 233), Phnebieus.
P.Hels. 20 is the ἀπογραφή for a dove-cote at Thneis.

ΘΡΥΩΝΟΣ

VII/VIII A.D.	*Stud.Pal.* X 17,1	ἀπὸ χ'ω'(ρίου) Θρυωνο[
VII-VIII A.D.	*Stud.Pal.* X 208,4	χ'ω'(ρίον) Θρυωνος

ETYMOLOGY: the Greek word θρύον («reed, rush»), declined in the genitive plural (θρύων), may have been the original toponym: compare the Byzantine toponym Ἀγκυρῶνος, which modifies the original Ἀγκυρῶν (πόλις; see *s.v.*).

Stud.Pal. X 17 also lists Koma (3), Poinami (= Peenameus) (10), Pkommatoei (12), the last two villages being in the Μέση toparchy. *Stud.Pal.* X 208 lists villages assigned to the διοίκησις of the διάκονος Λεόντιος: these include Apionos (1) and Thoiamoun(is) (2; Koma toparchy); on the *verso*, Phnebieus (2; Μέση toparchy) and Pselemachis (3; Koites) are mentioned.

ΙΒΙΧΕΩΣ

487 A.D.	*P.Oxy.* XVI 1961,9	ἀπὸ κώμης Ἰβ[ί]χεως το[ῦ Ἡ]ρακλεοπολίτου νομοῦ²

---

¹ Τίκεως *ed. pr.* The new reading is mine (checked on a photograph).

² Ἰβ[ί]χεως *ed. pr.*, but «Ἰβίχεως looks acceptable» (reading checked for me by Revel A. Coles, letter of August 8, 1994).

P.Oxy. XVI 1961: two inhabitants of Oxyrhynchus lease part of a house ἐν τῇ αὐτῇ πόλει (1.14); the house belongs to a woman ἀπὸ κώμης Ἰβ[ί]χεως.

ΙΒΙΩΝ (1)

IV/V A.D. *MPER* XV 91,4 Ἰβιῶνος

ETYMOLOGY: see *s.v.* ΙΒΙΩΝ ΑΡΣΑΜΟΥ.

BIBLIOGRAPHY: see *s.v.* ΙΒΙΩΝ ΑΡΣΑΜΟΥ.

Other villages mentioned are Phys (3; Μέση toparchy) and Ατρτ.. (5); there follow references to the πεδίον of Bousiris (34, 37) and the μερὶς Ἡρακλείδου in the Arsinoites (35).

ΙΒΙΩΝ (2)

28/29 A.D. *P.Oxy.* XXIV 2412,72 Ἰβίωνος

TOPARCHY: Tekmi.

ETYMOLOGY: see *s.v.* ΙΒΙΩΝ ΑΡΣΑΜΟΥ.

BIBLIOGRAPHY: see *s.v.* ΙΒΙΩΝ ΑΡΣΑΜΟΥ.

The document mentions six villages, presumably all in the Tekmi toparchy: Ogou, Tekmi, Kollintaathyr, Pyrgotos, Mouchis, Ibion.
In *BGU* XIV 2436 Ogou is perhaps connected with Ἰβιὼν Ἀρσάμου. In *BGU* XIV 2449, where land in the Tekmi toparchy is surveyed (see ll.39-40), an ἰβιών is referred to at 1.26.

ΙΒΙΩΝ (3)

50/49 B.C. (cf. *BL* 8,338) *SB* VI 9065,11 περὶ κώμην Ἰβιῶνα[1]

See also: Ἰβιὼν ... (5)

TOPARCHY: περὶ Πόλιν

ETYMOLOGY: see *s.v.* ΙΒΙΩΝ ΑΡΣΑΜΟΥ.

BIBLIOGRAPHY: see *s.v.* ΙΒΙΩΝ ΑΡΣΑΜΟΥ.

A widow describes her dead husband's possessions περὶ κώμην Ἰβιῶνα and ἐν τῇ μητροπόλει:

---

[1] περὶ κώμην Ἰβιῶνα [Ἀρσάμου (?) ...] *ed.pr.*: Ἰβιὼν Ἀρσάμου, however, was in the Koites.

the temple of Eseph referred to at l.14[1] was probably at Herakleopolis. An ἰβιών is attested at Sobthis (περὶ Πόλιν toparchy) in *BGU* VIII 1753, I, 1.6 (64/63 B.C.).

ΙΒΙΩΝ ... (4)

    mid-III B.C.[2]   *P.Fuad Crawford* 5, verso,10

TOPARCHY: Koites.

ETYMOLOGY: see *s.v.* ΙΒΙΩΝ ΑΡΣΑΜΟΥ.

BIBLIOGRAPHY: see *s.v.* ΙΒΙΩΝ ΑΡΣΑΜΟΥ.

Several villages known to be in the Koites appear in this document, including Pselemachis. Other Ἰβιών localities near Pselemachis: Ἰβιὼν Ἀρσάμου, Ἰβιὼν Πάχνουβις.

ΙΒΙΩΝ ... (5)

| I B.C. | *BGU* XIV 2429,6 | Ἰβι(ῶνος) ... |
| I B.C. | *BGU* XIV 2436,2 | Ἰβιῶνα ... |

ETYMOLOGY: see *s.v.* ΙΒΙΩΝ ΑΡΣΑΜΟΥ.

BIBLIOGRAPHY: see *s.v.* ΙΒΙΩΝ ΑΡΣΑΜΟΥ.

The second part of this place-name is written exactly in the same (abbreviated and very cursive) manner in *BGU* XIV 2429 and 2436[3].

BGU XIV 2429 lists several villages, many in the Ἄγημα toparchy: Peenameus (2), Peenepsomphis (3), Korphotoi (4), Nino (6), Kollasoucha and Magdola (7).

BGU XIV 2436 surveys a holding split among the following villages: Magdola (1), Ἰβιών (2), Pois (2), Peensamoi and Ogou (3). Magdola also recurs in *BGU* XIV 2429.

ΙΒΙΩΝ ΑΡΣΑΜΟΥ

    about 138 B.C.   *P.Tebt.* III 860,103   Ἰβιὼν Ἀρσάμου

See also: ΙΒΙΩΝ ... (4).

TOPARCHY: Koites.

---

[1] ἱερῶι τοῦ Εσηπ (cf. *BL* 8,339).

[2] On the re-dating of this document see *Introduction*, p.14 n.7.

[3] The decipherment is extremely uncertain (reading checked by me on a photograph, and by William Brashear on the original). Ἰβιὼν Φα() or Δια() *ed. pr.* Ἰβιὼν Ἀρσ(άμου) is rather tempting, but this was a place in the Koites, whereas the Ἰβιών in question must have been in the central part of the nome.

ETYMOLOGY: Ἰβιών is the Greek translation for the Egyptian word (in other place-names simply transliterated as Ταχο/ε = *t3-ᶜhj*: : see *s.v.* Ταχονπαχνουβ) referring to a sanctuary of the Ibis cult[1]. Here it is combined with a (Persian) personal name (Ἀρσάμης: clearly the founder/sponsor of this sanctuary)[2]; it can also be associated with the name of a village in such toponyms as Ibion Thmoiphtha and Ibion Techtho (see *s.vv.*).

BIBLIOGRAPHY: KATELIJN VANDORPE, «Les villages des Ibis dans la toponymie tardive», *Enchoria*, 18, 1991, pp.115-122, esp. p.119.

P.Tebt. III 860: under the entry for Ἰβιὼν Ἀρσάμου, a tax-payment by the owner of a vineyard near Pselemachis (Koites) is recorded.
Another centre named after an ibis sanctuary near Pselemachis was called Ibion Pachnoubis.

ΙΒΙΩΝ ΘΜΟΙΦΘΑ

I B.C.   *BGU* XIV 2437,38

TOPARCHY: Πέραν (see *s.v.* ΘΜΟΙΦΘΑ).

ETYMOLOGY: see *s.v.* ΙΒΙΩΝ ΑΡΣΑΜΟΥ.

BIBLIOGRAPHY: see *s.v.* ΙΒΙΩΝ ΑΡΣΑΜΟΥ.

Sacred land of an Hermes temple is mentioned in connection with this Ἰβιών: sacred ibises were in fact dedicated to Thot[3], whom the Greeks identified with Hermes.

ΙΒΙΩΝ ΠΑΧΝΟΥΒΙΣ

See *s.v.* ΤΑΧΟΝΠΑΧΝΟΥΒ.

ΙΒΙΩΝ ΤΑΜΜΩΡ[Ο]Υ

301 A.D.   *PSI* IX 1037,9   παρὰ διαφόρων κωμῶν,
                                         Ἰβιῶνος Ταμμώρ[ο]υ
                                         καὶ Κόσμα καὶ ἄλλων
                                         (8-9; cf. *BL* 8,405)

---

[1] See K.A.D. SMELIK, «The Cult of the Ibis in the Graeco-Roman Period with Special Attention to the Data from the Papyri», in *Studies in Hellenistic Religions* (EPRO 78), 1979, pp.225-243.

[2] Cf. Ἀρσάκης, also a Persian personal name (PH. HUYSE, *Iranisches Personennamenbuch* V 6a, p.34, no.16); see also *s.v.* ΣΙΣΙΝΗ (Σισίνης is another Persian personal name).

[3] See WILLY CLARYSSE - JAN QUAEGEBEUR, «Ibion, Isieion and Tharesieion in two Oslo Papyri», *Symbolae Osloenses* 57, 1982, p.80.

TOPARCHY: Koites.

ETYMOLOGY: see *s.v.* ἸΒΙΩΝ ἈΡΣΆΜΟΥ.

BIBLIOGRAPHY: see *s.v.* ἸΒΙΩΝ ἈΡΣΆΜΟΥ.

See *s.v.* ΤΑΑΜΟΡΟΥ.

ΙΒΙΩΝ ΤΕΧΘΩ

I B.C.   *BGU* XIV 2432,20

TOPARCHY: Techtho Nesos (see *s.v.* ΤΕΧΘΩ).

ETYMOLOGY: see *s.v.* ΙΒΙΩΝ ΑΡΣΑΜΟΥ.

BIBLIOGRAPHY: see *s.v.* ΙΒΙΩΝ ΑΡΣΑΜΟΥ.

Listed with Toemesis (l.18; Koites) and Thmoiobastis (l.22; Koma toparchy), this Ἰβιών was obviously near Τεχθώ.

ΙΕΡΑ ΝΗΣΟΣ

about 270 B.C.	*P.Hib.* I 110 recto, 21; 22	ἐφ' Ἱερᾶι Νήσωι (21); ἀφ' Ἱερᾶς Νήσου (22)
251/250 B.C.(?)	*SB* X 10540 (= *P.Hib.* I 154 descr.),3	εἰς Ἱε[ρὰν Νῆ]σον (4-5)
22 Jan. 223 B.C.[1]	*P.Rain.Cent.* 40,7	ἐν Ἱερᾶι Νήσωι
early II B.C.	*P.Tebt.* III 1082,31	ἐν Ἱερᾶι
18 August 164 B.C.	*P.Hels.* I 6,6	ἐν Ἱερᾶι Νήσωι
96-94 or 63-61 B.C.	*BGU* XIV 2429,11	Ἱερὰ Νῆ(σος)
later than 52/51 B.C.	*BGU* VIII 1808,20	Ἱερᾶ[ς] Νήσου

---

[1] New dating by Willy Clarysse (letter of July 7, 1994): «The two letters (*P.Rain.Cent.* 40 and 41) are written by different scribes, but they are very similar and of a rather unusual type. Their inventory numbers also show that they were found or at least bought together. *P.Rain.Cent.* 41 is dated to 5 Choiak of a 24th year, *P.Rain.Cent.* 40 to 7 Choiak of a 29th year. On the photograph, however, the reading κθ in *P.Rain.Cent.* 40 is far from certain: the top of the *theta* is in fact a large ink blot. If this ink blot is not taken into account, *delta* is a perfectly sound reading here. In our opinion both texts should therefore be dated to the same 24th year (ἔτους κδ) and they were written only two days apart. If so, the reign of Philadelphos is no longer the only possibility. The writing rather suggests a date toward the end of the third century, most probably under Euergetes *i.e.* 20 and 22 January 223 B.C.».

CATALOGUE

later than Mesore 51/50 B.C.	*BGU* VIII 1835,3-4	παρὰ τῶν ἱερέων τοῦ ἐν Ἱερᾶς Νήσου ἱεροῦ Σεμαρποχράτου θεοῦ κραταίου (3-5)
I B.C.	*BGU* VIII 1768,1	μέχρι Ἱερᾶς Νήσου
I B.C.	*BGU* VIII 1784,5	μέχρι Ἱερᾶς

Literary Sources

V A.D.	STEPH. BYZ. s.v.[1]

TOPARCHY: the place-name Hiera Nesos is well attested for the Arsinoites, and apparently refers to two distinct (at least from the Roman period) localities, one in the Herakleides division, the other in the Polemon division. The second one was called Ἱερὰ (Νῆσος) Νικολάου and may, or may not coincide with the Hiera Nesos connected to the Herakleopolites in the documents listed above[2]. None of these documents actually states that Ἱερὰ Νῆσος was *in* the Herakleopolites: its connection with this nome, and with the Ἄγημα toparchy in particular, are nevertheless obvious from the sources analysed here below. It seems possible that different localities, at no great distance from each other in the two neighbouring nomes, were called by the same name, with reference to the same features in the landscape, both natural (νῆσος: «newly-gained land»[3]) and human (ἱερά: a «sacred» place). This may be the case for the Arsinoite and the Herakleopolite Αὔηρις, too (see *s.v.*). See also *s.v.* KAINH.

ETYMOLOGY: νῆσος was the Greek (inaccurate) translation of the Egyptian word *m3j*, «new land»[4].

SB X 10540 and *P.Hib.* I 80: both documents concern exports of wine ἐκ Θμ[ο]ινεθύμεως τοῦ Ἡρακλε[ο]π[ο]λ[ί]του νομ[οῦ] εἰς Ἱε[ρὰν Νῆ[σον (*SB* X 10540,3-5).

In *P.Hels.* I 6 corn supplies for the army are also conveyed to Hiera Nesos (a safer place to keep them, thanks to its φρούριον) from the θησαυρός of Alilais (Ἄγημα ἄνω toparchy: the document refers to troubles in this area). *BGU* VIII 1808 confirms the connection between Hiera Nesos and Alilais (which recur at ll. 20 and 21 respectively), while *BGU* XIV 2429 includes Hiera Nesos after Petachor, at the end of a list of villages belonging almost exclusively to the Ἄγημα toparchy. Kollasoucha, Petachor and Hiera Nesos appear both in *BGU* XIV 2429 and in *BGU* VIII 1808: the connection between Hiera Nesos and Kollasoucha is confirmed by *P.Rain.Cent.* 40 (here, the φυλακίτης Herakleides is to be informed that two plots of land near Kollasoucha have been leased out: the relevant σύμβολον is kept at the λογευτήριον of Hiera Nesos).

BGU VIII 1784 is an official letter concerning preparations for the ποταμοφύλακες of the Πτολεμαικός canal to escort an οὐραγία (possibly the «rear-guard» of military troops) as far as Hiera Nesos, where their colleagues from the Troites (in the Memphites[5]) are to take over, and escort the οὐραγία to Χίη (in the Kynopolites).

---

[1] Ἱερὰ Νῆσος· ... ἔστι καὶ Αἰγύπτου Ἱερὰ Νῆσος κτλ.

[2] Only documents relevant to the connections of Hiera Nesos with the Herakleopolite nome are considered here. See also *Introduction*, p.10.

[3] Cf. *Introduction*, p.6.

[4] See *s.v.* ΘΜΟ().

[5] Τρωίτης must designate the surroundings (or the toparchy) of Troia, in the Memphite nome, apparently specializing in ship-building (cf. *BGU* VIII 1807, which also confirms its connection to the Herakleopolites). CALDERINI-DARIS, *Dizionario*, vol. V, p.34, lists several occurrences of Τρωίτης as an ethnic designation.

BGU VIII 1768 reports a visit of the strategos of the Herakleopolite nome: from Hiera Nesos he travels down the [....]μβατικὸς ποταμός to be met at a ὅρμος by the priests (a temple of Herakles is mentioned at l.8), the Greek military settlers (κάτοικοι ἱππεῖς and πεζοί), the whole Greek community (l.6: τοῦ σύμπαντος τῆς κατοικίας πλήθους), the foreigners who happened to be there at the time of the strategos' visit (τῶν κατὰ ξέ[νην]), and the local Egyptian population (λα[ός]). An Ἀρσινοεῖον and a γυμνάσιον are also mentioned.

A temple of the «powerful god Semarpochrates» appears in *BGU* VIII 1835 (ll.3-5): this is a petition from the priests who are apparently the only inhabitants left at Hiera Nesos, all others having left the village since August 51/50.

On the whole, the place gives the impression of a rather busy station on a traffic *route* along which food provisions, officials and military troops all travelled. *P.Hib.* I 110 *recto* shows that there was a guard-post (φυλακή: one is reminded of the φρούριον mentioned in *P.Hels.* I 6) and a shunting station for φυλακίται escorting corn from Hiera Nesos to Alexandria (see esp. ll.21-33). On the way to Alexandria, after the φυλακή at Hiera Nesos, there was another one at Memphis (one may recall the change-over to the ποταμοφύλακες of the Troites in *BGU* VIII 1784); the next one was at Σχεδία («on the canal connecting Alexandria with the Canopic branch of the Nile»[1]), before the final station at Alexandria. The reference to Phebichis (Koites) in the following section (ll.34-39: «Account taken with Plutarchus at Phebichis...») confirms the connection between Hiera Nesos and the Herakleopolites, as might the previous mention of an Ἡρακλεῖον (l.5; one may be reminded of the temple of Herakles in *BGU* VIII 1768).

ΙΕΡΚΙΝΚ[

VII-VIII A.D.	*Stud.Pal.* X 206,9

Apparently the name of a κλῆρος, listed with several others (see the *Reverse Index* at the end of this volume).

ΙΠΠΩΝΩΝ (κώμη)

I/II A.D.	*P.Hib.* II 218, col. III	
19 March 334 A.D.	*P.Lond.* VI 1913,2;9	ἀπὸ κώμης Ἱππώνων
about 343 A.D.	*SB* XVI 12814,4	ἀπὸ κώμης Ἱππώνων
IV A.D.	*P.Amh.* II 142,16	τ]ῷ πραιποσίτῳ τ[ῶ]ν κάστρων Ἱππώνων
VI A.D.	*P.Bad.* (=*VBP*) IV 55,6-7	ἐν τῷ ἀπηλιωτικο(ῦ) [πρ]ὸς τῆς Ἀραβίας περὶ φυλα[κὴν] Ἵππονος
VII-VIII A.D.	*SB* XVIII 13888,8	[χ(ωρίου)] Ἵππωνο(ς)
VII-VIII A.D.	*Stud.Pal.* X 203,9	χ(ωρίον) Ἱππῶνο(ς)[2]

---

[1] See *P.Hib.* I 110,25 n.

[2] Reading checked for me on the original by Johannes Diethart (letter of February 25, 1994): «χ() Ἱππῶνο(ς) scheint möglich».

CATALOGUE

VII-VIII A.D.   *Stud.Pal.* X 213,3   χ(ωρίον) Ἱππω.[[1]

Literary Sources

about 300 A.D.   *Itin. Anton.* 168,2   *Hipponon*
V A.D.   *Not.Dign.Or.*   *Hipponos*
                         XXVIII 32

TOPARCHY: Koites.

ETYMOLOGY: «the village of the stables» (ἱππών, -ῶνος = «place for horses, stable» but also «posting-house, station», as in XEN. *Cyr.* 8,6,17: cf. LSJ *s.v.*). Ἱππώνων, on the East bank of the Nile, was a station of the Roman army (see below): its name possibly refers to the stables for the horses of the cavalry, which most likely had one of its bases here during the Ptolemaic period, too; at the same time, the place may also have functioned as a shunting station for the postal service[2]. The plural form is obviously explained by assuming the existence of several stables, as one may expect in an army base, but also in a posting-house of some importance. The Byzantine documents of a later time, however, make the name a singular (see *s.v.* Ἀγκυρῶν κώμη for a similar shifting from plural to singular).

MODERN ARABIC NAME: Qarāra[3]. See *TAVO B 69* § 4.3 (O 12) and p.180: «Südlich des Dorfes befinden sich zwei koptische Friedhöfe, die durch einen islamischen getrennt sind. Die Gräber sind zum größten Teil ausgeplündert. ... Aufgrund der Raubgräberei in der Gegend von Qarāra seitens der Dorfbewohner begann die ägyptische Altertümerverwaltung im Jahr 1981, Ausgrabungen durchzuführen. Dabei legte man Bestattungen frei, die in die Spätzeit und danach zu datieren sind ... die Kalkstein-Fundamente eines Bauwerkes ... Möglicherweise wurde der Bau, nach einem hier gefundenen Kalksteinfragment mit dem Anfang der Kartusche eines ptolemäischen Herrschers zu schließen, in ptolemäischer Zeit errichtet». See also TIMM, *Das christlich-koptische Ägypten* III, p.1207 f., *s.v.* ʿIzbat Qarāra).

P.Lond. VI 1913: the priest Aurelius Pageus son of Horus, from Hipponon, informs the priors of the monastery of (P)hathor of the appointment of Amelius Gerontius, to take his place until his return from the Synod of Caesaraea. The appointment has been made in the presence of witnesses, among them a priest of Hipponon and the deacon of Thmoinpesla (also in Koites)[4].

Hipponon and Phathor also recur together in *SB* XVIII 13888, along with other villages of the southern Koites (Nokle, Thelbo) and the northern Oxyrhynchites (Kalamou, Ostrakinou).

Presumably, the location of the same monastery is given in *P.Bad.* IV 55 ([πρ]ὸς τῆς Ἀραβίας περὶ φυλα[κὴν] Ἱππονος), with reference to the military establishment also attested in the *Itinerarium Antonini* and the *Notitia Dignitatum* (station of the *Ala Apriana*).

P.Amh. II 142 contains a petition to the praefect of Augustamnica, written at Herakleopolis: the intervention of the πραιπόσιτος τῶν κάστρων Ἱππώνων is requested against intruders upon Aurelius Germanus' land, near Thmoiouthis.

---

[1] Ι[ ]ων[ ] *ed. pr.*: Johannes Diethart considers «Ἱππω.[möglich» (letter of February 25, 1994), which supports a conjecture Ἱππών[ων. Other villages mentioned in the same document were in the Agema toparchy (Petachor: ll.2 and 5; Kollasoucha: l.4)

[2] Ptolemaic postal service: STEPHEN R. LLEWELYN, «Did the Ptolemaic Postal System work to a Timetable?», *ZPE* 99, 1993, pp.41-56.

[3] Cf. FRIEDRICH BILABEL, *P.Bad.* IV, *Einleitung*, pp.3-4.

[4] There was a net of Meletian monasteries in the Koites, also including one at Ankyron. See *P.Neph.*, *Einleitung*, pp.20-21; BÄRBEL KRAMER, «Neuere Papyri zum frühen Mönchtum in Ägypten», in *Philanthropia kai eusebeia. Festschrift für Albrecht Dihle zum 70. Geburtstag*, hrsg. von G.W. Most, H. Petersmann und A.M. Ritter, Göttingen 1993, pp.217-231.

ΙΣΙΟΝ[1]

4 Oct. 698 A.D.	*CPR* VIII 76,2 (= *Stud.Pal.* VIII 1186)	ἀπὸ χ(ωρίου) Ἰσίου ὑπὲρ τ(ο–) χω(ρίο–) Λευκ(ο)γ(ίου)

Literary Sources

about 300 A.D.	*Itin. Anton.* 156,4	*Isiu*

ETYMOLOGY: «...either a sanctuary consecrated to Isis or a surrounding village which owes its existence to the sanctuary»[2].

Ἰσῖον must have been near Λευκόγιον[3]. An identification with *Isiu* of the *Itinerarium Antonini* was suggested by Amundsen, who also refers to *P.Hib.* I 167: however, this document (of about 245 B.C.) refers to an Ἰσεῖον in connection to Ταλαω, in the Northern toparchy of the Oxyrhynchites.

Κ.( )

I B.C.	*BGU* XIV 2441,201	περὶ Κ.( )

TOPARCHY: Tekmi.

Part of the land assigned to Apollonios son of Apollonios is surveyed as belonging to the Pyrgotos area, in the Tekmi toparchy (six arourae are in Skiron's fossil kleros). More land, held by the same man, is recorded περὶ Κ.( ).

Κ.ΑΡΜΟΥ

V A.D.	*Stud.Pal.* X 233, col. II,6	Κ.αρμου καὶ [±2]αρε.ως[4]

Κ̣[...].ΙΝ...

72/71 B.C.	*BGU* VIII 1739,12	περὶ κώμην Κ̣[...].ιν...

---

[1] The same place-name is also attested for other nomes: see CALDERINI-DARIS, *Dizionario*, vol.III, pp.38-40; DREW-BEAR, *Le nome Hermopolite*, p.135.

[2] Cf. LEIV AMUNDSEN, *O.Osl.*, pp.50 ff.

[3] Cf. *CPR* VIII 76,2 (with the Editor's note).

[4] «Κ.αρμου schlägt Hermann Harrauer vor» (letter from Johannes Diethart, of February 25, 1994). What follows looks like καὶ to me (cf. Απεριο(υ) καὶ Χορταςω, in the preceding line); after this, [..]αρε.ως, as in the *ed. pr.*

Περὶ κώμην Κ[...].ιν... is the location of a kleros in a παραχώρησις contract drawn up at Herakleopolis.

Κ..ΚΕΩΣ

V A.D.   *Stud.Pal.* X 9,5 [1]

Other Herakleopolite villages in this document were all in the northern part of the nome: Onnes and Mouchis (Tekmi toparchy), Sobthis, Phnebieus (Μέση toparchy).

ΚΑΘΟΛΙΚ[

VII A.D.	*CPR* X 63,6	ἀπὸ Καθολ(ικοῦ)
VII A.D.	*Stud.Pal.* X 22,4	χ(ωρίον) Καθολικ()
VIII A.D.	*Stud.Pal.* X 204,5	ὄρρ(ια) κώ[μ(ης)?] Κα[θολ]ικ[ο]ῦ [2]

ETYMOLOGY: presumably from the title (καθολικός = Latin *rationalis*) of the official who, from the third century A.D. onwards, supervised the accounts of all Egypt; in the Byzantine period, there were two καθολικοί (cf. ORSOLINA MONTEVECCHI, *La Papirologia*, Milano 1991², pp.153, 166).

BIBLIOGRAPHY: TIMM, *Das christlich-koptische Ägypten* III, p.1234.

Stud.Pal. X 22 lists, among other place-names, Sobthis ἡ μικρά, Charamou and Tokois (all in the περὶ Πόλιν toparchy).
The Editor of *CPR* X 63 notes that the handwriting of this document is very similar to that of *Stud.Pal.* X 22.

ΚΑΙΝΗ

| III B.C. | (?)*P.Tebt.* III 815, fr.3 verso,14 | Καινήν [3] |
| 51/50 B.C. | *BGU* VIII 1834,10 | ἐκ τῆς Καινῆς τοῦ Πέρα |

---

[1] «Κ..κεως, d.h., Κερκεως ist gut möglich» (Diethart, letter of February 25, 1994): as no village by this name is elsewhere attested for the Herakleopolites, this could perhaps be the Memphite Kerke, harbour of Philadelphia in the Fayūm: cf. WILLY CLARYSSE, «Philadelpheia and the Memphites in the Zenon Archive», in *Studies on Ptolemaic Memphis (Studia Hellenistica 24)*, pp.96-97; for the Roman period: ANN ELLIS HANSON, *ZPE* 47, 1982, pp.233-243, and *BASP* 21, 1984, pp.76-87.

[2] Ἡν[]ι *ed. pr.*: new reading by Johannes Diethart (letter of September 9, 1994).

[3] A very uncertain reading: see Edd. *ad loc.*

I B.C.	*BGU* VIII 1857,10	ἐπὶ τῆ φερούσηι εἰς τὴν Καινήν ὁδῶι (9-10)
I A.D.	(?)*P.Oxy.* XLII 3052,10	Κεν..[1]
202/203 A.D.	*SB* XVI 12612,2	ἀπὸ κώμης Καινῆς τοῦ Ἡρακλ[ε]οπολείτου ν[ο]μοῦ (2-3)
about 215 A.D.	*P.Brook.* 24,41	*Caene* (= Καινή?)
15 June 415 A.D. (cf. *BL* 7,261)	*Stud.Pal.* XX 90,4	ἐν κώμῃ Καινῆς (cf. *BL* 8,467)
475 A.D.	*P.Rain.Cent.* 106,5	ἀπὸ κώμης Καινῆς
17 Sept. 591 A.D. (cf. *BL* 7,47)	*P.Erl.* 67,8;19	ἀπὸ κώμ(ης) Καινῆς τοῦ Ἡρακλεοπολίτου ν[ο]μοῦ (8-9); ἀπὸ Καινῆς (19)
19 Sept. 596 A.D. (cf. *BL* 8,418)	*P.Strasb.* V 318,13	κλήρου Καινοῦ ἤτοι [ἐπὶ διώρ]υγος Πεχιτ (13-14)
VII A.D.	*Stud.Pal.* VIII 1305,1;3	Καινοῦ νοτ(ίνου) (1); [Καινοῦ] βορρ(ίνου) (3)
VII/VIII A.D.	*CPR* IV 2,13	Καιν'οῦ' ἐπ'ο'(ίκιον)
VII-VIII A.D.	*Stud.Pal.* X 16,1;2;3;4	ἀπὸ χ(ωρίου) Καιν'οῦ' Νοτί(νου) (καὶ) Καινοῦ Βορρ(ίνου) (4)
VII-VIII A.D.	*Stud.Pal.* X 292,4	Καινοῦ βορ(ρίνου)
VIII A.D.	*Stud.Pal.* X 169,11	Κ[α]ιν'ο(ῦ)' Νοτί[ν]'ου'
Byz.	*SB* I 5339,19	χω(ρίον) Καινοῦ Βορρ(ίνου)

Literary Sources

about 300 A.D.	*Itin. Anton.* 156,5	*Caene* (= Καινή?)

TOPARCHY: Πέραν (XIII *pagus*, according to an unpublished papyrus of the Benaki Museum in Athens, from the late IV A.D.[2]). There was a very well attested ὅρμος (with one or more πύλαι where customs duties had to be paid) called Καινή in the Polemon division of the Arsinoites, which was probably distinct from the Herakleopolite place (also a ὅρμος) bearing the same name.

ETYMOLOGY: this place-name evidently refers to a «new» foundation (a port) by the Greek settlers.

---

[1] The Editor suggests that this may conceal a misspelling for Καινή (station on a southward itinerary: the same as *Caene* in *Itin. Ant.* 156.5). See *s.v.* ΟΝΝΗΣ.

[2] As reported by EFSTATHIOS PAPAPOLYCHRONIOU, «The Papyri of the Benaki Museum in Athens», *21. Internationaler Papyrologenkongress (Berlin, 13.-19. August 1995)*.

MODERN ARABIC NAME: the identification with Qāi (suggested in the *TAVO Map BV 21* [1]) is phonetically inconsistent with the identification of the Panopolite Καινή with Qene [2] (cf. the very likely equivalence Καινή = *Caene* of the *Itinerarium Antonini*).

BGU VIII 1834, the earliest certain attestation to date for this place-name, locates Καινή in the Πέραν toparchy of the Herakleopolites: the ἀρχενδρωμίτης Ploutos has been given by the king the right to all ἐνόρμια to be paid at the port of Καινή (ll.11-15).

BGU VIII 1857 connects it to Tebetny (also in the Πέραν): these two villages also recur together in the Byzantine *SB* I 5339 (Tebetny is at l.9).

SB XVI 12612 is a sale contract (a donkey is being sold) between Petesouchos, from Καινή in the Herakleopolites, and Pabous, from Soknopaiou Nesos in the Arsinoites.

P.Strasb. V 318 is a lease-contract for land in the kleros Καινοῦ, which is further identified by reference to a nearby canal Πεχιτ: the parties are from Herakleopolis.

CPR IV 2 (a bilingual document in Coptic and Greek) lists Καινοῦ together with many villages of the central toparchies of the Herakleopolite nome (toponyms in Greek) [3]. This change of gender (from Καινή to Καινοῦ) is remarkable, but supported by other documents of the Byzantine period which mention a «southern» (as opposed to «northern») Καινοῦ. The «southern» Καινοῦ could coincide with the Herakleopolite (as opposed to the Arsinoite) Καινή, as the first appears together with Ἱερὰ (Νῆσος) Νικ(ο)λ(άου) (*Stud.Pal.* X 292), which in turn may (or may not: see *s.v.* Ἱερὰ Νῆσος) coincide with the Hiera Nesos sometimes mentioned in a Herakleopolite connection.

ΚΑΛΑΜΟΥΡΙΟΥ

VI/VII A.D.	*P.Oxy.* XVI 1939,1	Καλαμουρίου
VII/VIII A.D.	*SB* XVIII 13888,6	[χ(ωρίου)] Καλαμου(ρίου) [4]

ETYMOLOGY: the first element in this toponym (καλα– = Egyptian *gl*) is the same as in the word Καλάσιρις (Egyptian *Gl-šr*), which is already found in HDT. II 81 («a long Egyptian garment, with tassels or fringe at bottom»: LSJ *s.v.,I*). Herodotus (II 164 etc.) also attests the same word in the plural (οἱ Καλασίριες, as the name of «a branch of the military cast in Egypt» (LSJ *s.v.,II*); in some documents (e.g. *P.Petr.* III 99, after a reference to the Herakleopolite village of Philonikou) the same word apparently designates a police official (cf. JAN KRZYSZTOF WINNICKI, «Die Kalasirier in griechischen Papyri», *JJP* 22, 1992, pp.63-65).

BIBLIOGRAPHY: HUBERT METZGER-HERMANN HARRAUER, *ZPE* 60, 1985, pp.246 ff.; *P.Neph.*, *Einleitung*, p.14.

Other place-names appearing in *SB* XVIII 13888 point to the southern Koites (or to the northern

---

[1] This identification is dubitatively put forth in the *TAVO BV 21* Map (*Ägypten in hellenistisch-römischer Zeit*, Wiesbaden 1989), following JOHN BALL, *Egypt in the Classical Geographers*, Cairo 1942, p.143.

[2] This is generally accepted: cf. *L.Ä.*, Bd.V, col.48, *s.v.* «Qene»: «Griech. Καινὴ πόλις, moderne Stadt an der Mündung des Wadi Qena, evtl. Ausgangspunkt für altägyptische Expeditionen durch das Wadi zu einigen Goldminen. Vorptolemäisch ist Qene nicht nachgewiesen»; also PAULY-WISSOWA, *R.E.* Bd.X, col.1506, *s.v.* «Kainopolis».

[3] See *s.v.* ΝΙΝΩ.

[4] Καλάμου *ed. pr.*; Καλαμουρίου Daris (see CALDERINI-DARIS, *Dizionario*, Supplemento I, p.163, *s.v.*).

Oxyrhynchites [1]): Phathor (the seat of a monastery), Nokle, Ostrakinou, Thelbo, Hipponon.

P.Oxy. XVI 1939 concerns a payment made by some villagers.

ΚΑΛΑΤΗΣ

21 Oct. 163 B.C.	*P.Hels.* I 10,10	περὶ κώμην Καλατῆι (*BL* 9,65) [2]
7 April 335 A.D. (cf. *BL* 5,26)	*CPR* I 247,7	περὶ κώμην Καλατη (*BL* 9,65)

TOPARCHY: περὶ Πόλιν.

P.Hels. I 10: the ἀρχιφυλακίτης Eubios declares that he owns an empty dove-cote περὶ κώμην Καλατῆι.
CPR I 247: lease contract between two inhabitants of Herakleopolis for land near this village, in the kleros Μαχάτου.

ΚΑΣΑΝΟΥΠΕΩΣ

V A.D.	*Stud.Pal.* X 233, col. II,10	Κασανούπεως [3]
V/VI A.D.	*Stud.Pal.* III 354	βοηθ(ῷ) Κασανούπεως
VI A.D.	*MPER* XVII 2a,2	πόλεως καὶ Κασανούπεως [4]
VII-VIII A.D.	*Stud.Pal.* X 206,3	Κασανο'ύ'(πεως) [5]

ETYMOLOGY: Κοσανοῦφις is attested as a personal name in *P.Tebt.* III 1052,3;10;11 (mid-II B.C.; papyrus from a mummy-case whose cartonnage was made up of various documents originating from the Herakleopolite nome), and in *P.Köln Ägypt.* 4,4 (155 B.C.).

This place is called a κλῆρος in *Stud.Pal.* X 206.

---

[1] Καλάμου is in fact recorded by PRUNETI, *Centri abitati*, p.75, *s.v.*

[2] Καλαγῆι *ed.pr.* In both documents, however, the toponym seems to be undeclined.

[3] New reading by Johannes Diethart (letter of February 25, 1994), who also made me aware of the two other sources for the same village: «Kol. II 10 findet sich der dritte Beleg für das Dorf Κασανούπεως (Κεθανουπεως Wessely)».

[4] «Bei Κασανοῦπις dürfte es sich nach dem Zusammenhang um einen, bisher nicht bekannten, Ort im Herakleopolites handeln. Preisigke, *Namenbuch*, verzeichnet ihn aus *Stud.Pal.* III 354 als Personennamen (so auch *Pros.Ars.* I 2854): Ματαείῳ βοηθ(ῷ) Κασανούπεως weist angesichts des neuen Beleges auf eine Herkunftsangabe hin. Auch die Formulierung πόλεως καὶ Κασανούπεως im neuen Papyrus trägt zu der Auffassung als Ortsnamen bei. Dazu bereits *ZPE* 76 (1989) 110» (letter from Johannes Diethart, February 25, 1994).

[5] Κασανο'τ'( ) *ed.pr.*

ΚΑΤΩ   (ΑΓΗΜΑ)

254/253 B.C.	*PSI* V 510,2	τοῦ [οἰ]κονομ[ο]ῦ[ντος] τὴν Κάτω τοπαρχίαν
19 Oct. 163 B.C.	*P.Hels.* I 18,3	τῆς Κάτω τοπαρ[χίας]
mid-II B.C.	*P.Gen.* III 132,6	[πρὸς] τῆι σιτολογίαι [τῶ]ν Κάτω τόπων (5–6)
mid-II B.C.	*P.Gen.* III 134,4	εἰς τοὺς Κάτω Τόπους
I B.C.	*BGU* VIII 1778,6-7	τῷ ὑ[πο]στρατήγῳ τῆς Κάτω τοπαρ[χί]ας
I B.C. (after 84/83 B.C.)	*BGU* XIV 2370,26; (fr.1), 73	Κάτω τοπαρχίας (26); Κάτω τοπαρ[χ]ίας (73)
I B.C.	*BGU* XIV 2434,10	Κάτω τοπαρχ...
I B.C.	*BGU* XIV 2437,26	Ἀγήματος κάτω
I B.C.	*BGU* XIV 2438,89	Ἀγή(ματος) κάτω
I B.C.	*BGU* XIV 2440, 3	[Ἀγή(ματος) κάτ]ω

The reasons for identifying the Κάτω τοπαρχία (or τόποι) with the Ἄγημα κάτω are stated *s.v.* ΑΓΗΜΑ.

PSI V 510 deals with taxes to be paid by a bee-keeper from Bousiris upon request of the οἰκονομῶν in the Κάτω toparchy, where the bee-hives were presumably kept.

P.Gen. III 132 contains an order (presumably from the διοικητής) to the στρατηγός of the Herakleopolites, and to his subordinates, concerning the collection of the tax to be paid in grain in the Κάτω τόποι.

P.Gen. III 134 orders that provisions be sent for the prisoners (σώματα δέσμια) of the Κάτω τόποι: the order is addressed to a certain Herakleides, who could be the same one who must provide a boat for the transport of «the Mysians and of 41 more men» in *P.Gen.* III 131 (May 29th, 146 B.C.).

P.Hels. I 18 is a declaration of uncultivated land.

BGU VIII 1778: report by a λογχοφόρος, who has met one of the κάτοικοι ἱππεῖς settled at Tanchais, and consigned a letter to the ὑποστράτηγος of the Κάτω τοπαρχία.

BGU XIV 2370 (fr.1) is puzzling, in that the reference to a Κάτω τοπαρχία is apparently followed by the names of some villages known to be in the Koma toparchy (Koma, Toou, Thmoibastis). In this case, it seems reasonable[1] to assume a mistake on the part of the compiler of this text.

ΚΕΛΛΑΣ

I B.C.   *BGU* XIV 2437,34

TOPARCHY: Ἄγημα.
A village by the same name is also attested for the Arsinoites (*Stud.Pal.* X 55,5).

ETYMOLOGY: κέλλα is attested as the Greek transcription of the Latin word *cella* (cf. Κέλλια, plural of

---

[1] Cf. *BGU* XIV 2370,73 n.: «Hier liegt offensichtlich ein Fehler vor».

the diminutive κέλλιον): but this document is too early for a word derived from Latin to be used as a place-name. A gloss in Hesychios (*s.v.* κελλόν) reveals that an adjective κελλός existed, meaning στρεβλός, πλάγιος («crooked, athwart»), which could refer to some feature in the landscape. We cannot be sure that this was a Greek word, rather than the Greek rendering of an Egyptian toponym.

MODERN ARABIC NAME: Qilla? (topographically not quite convincing: see *Introduction*, p.11 n.3). No identification is offered in *TAVO B 69*, which records the place (M 103) but: «Es wurden keine antiken Relikte festgestellt» (*ibid.*, p.214).

Last village in a list of localities in Ἄγημα κάτω (l.26) also including: Peenameus (26), Korphotoi (28), Peenepsomphis (30), Peensemtheus (32).

ΚΕΡΚΕΣΗΣ

about 260 B.C.	*P.Hib.* I 112, 2;6;81	[Κε]ρκέσης (2)
		Κερκέσης (6)
		Κερκέση[ς (81)
mid-III B.C.[1]	*P.Fuad Crawford* 5, *verso*, 14	Κερκεσης

ETYMOLOGY: first element *grg-*, «foundation of» (cf. JEAN YOYOTTE, *RdE* 14, 1962, pp.84-86)[2].

TOPARCHY: Koites.

Listed with several villages of the Koites both in *P.Hib.* I 112 and in *P.Fuad Crawford* 5, *verso*.

ΚΕΡΚΕΣΗΦΙΣ

I B.C.	*BGU* XIV 2435,30	Κερκεσ(ήφις)[3]
I/II A.D.	*P.Hib.* II 218,14;18	Κερκεσήφεως
155 A.D.	*SB* V 7515,248 (= *P.Berl.Frisk* 1 = *P.Bankakten* 1)	Κερκεσήφ(εως)
25 Nov. 188 A.D.	*O.Wilck.* II 1100,2	σιτολ(όγοι) Κερκεσήφεως (?)
193 A.D.	*Stud.Pal.* XX 16,9-10	ἀπὸ κώμης Κερκεσήφεως

---

[1] On the re-dating of this document see *Introduction*, p.14 n.7.

[2] Information from Katelijn Vandorpe (letter of July 18, 1995).

[3] Κερκεσ( ) *ed. pr.*

193 A.D.	*O.Wilck.* II 1114, 3-4	Ἡρακ(λεοπολίτου) νο(μοῦ) Κερκεσήφεως
II/III A.D.	*O.Wilck.* II 1124,3	Κερκεσήφεως
II/III A.D.	(?) *P.Heid.* IV 303, II,6	ἀπὸ κ(ώμης) Κερκ(εσήφεως)[1]
463 A.D.	*Stud.Pal.* XX 127,2	ἐπὶ κώμης Κερκεσήφεως
V/VI A.D.	*P.Vind.Tand.* 16,25	Κερκεσύφεως
VI/VII A.D.	(?) *P.Heid.* VII 410,5	ἀπ[ὸ] Κερκεσύφε(ως)

TOPARCHY: Koites. A village by the same name is attested in the Polemon division of the Arsinoite nome.

ETYMOLOGY: *Grg-(n)-Hrj-šf*, «foundation of Eseph»[2].

Kerkesephis is mentioned in connection with Talae in *SB* V 7515 (mainly dealing with the Polemon division of the Arsinoites: the Herakleopolite villages include Kerkesephis, Talae, Philonikou) and in *P.Hib.* 218 (ll.15, 26), and together with Assya (which also appears in *P.Hib.* II 218) in *P.Vindob.Tand.* 16. It seems therefore possible to resolve Κερκεσ(ῆφις) in *BGU* XIV 2435, where this village is again linked with Assya, both places being administratively subordinated to Talae (Koites). A reference to Phebichis is found at the beginning of the same document, and in *Stud.Pal.* XX 127, an ἐγγύη given at Kerkesephis by Aurelius Victor Apasirios of Phebichis (but living ἐν ἐποικίῳ Πασηει).

Stud.Pal. X 16 is a receipt for a loan taken by an inhabitant of Kerkesephis: it was drawn up at Herakleopolis.

ΚΕΡΚΕΥΝΙΦΕΩΣ

10 May 174 B.C.[3]	*BGU* XIV 2382,14	ἐκ Κερκευνίφεως[4]

ETYMOLOGY: first component *grg*, «the foundation of» (see *s.v.* ΚΕΡΚΕΣΗΣ).

TOPARCHY: Μέση?

A contract is stipulated at Ποιμένων κώμη (l.11; Μέση toparchy): one of the parties involved, Eupolemos, is ἐκ Κερκευνίφεως.

---

[1] «Falls die Lesung richtig ist, kommen zur Auflösung folgende Ortsnamen in Betracht: Κερκέσης, Κερκεσῆφις, Κερκεφθᾶ und Κέρκυτος» (*ed. pr. ad loc.*). Κερκεσῆφις is more likely, as this document is concerned with the Koites: Ψῦχις is mentioned on l.2, and the document on the *recto* (= *P.Heid.* IV 301) is part of a τόμος συγκολλήσιμος containing a survey of land at Tosachmis.

[2] Information from Katelijn Vandorpe.

[3] Cf. RENATE ZIEGLER, *ZPE* 106, 1995, p.190.

[4] Reading checked for me by Günter Poethke (letter of December 8, 1994).

ΚΕΡΚΥΤΟΣ

161/160 B.C.	*P.Hels.* I 29,28	Κερκύτου
28 Sept.-27 Oct. 54 A.D.	*P.Vind.Tand.* 10,32	ἀπὸ κώμης Κερκύτου (cf. *BL* 7,279)
II-III A.D.	*P.Köln* II 99,3	Κερκύτου
227 A.D.	*CPR* I 64,7	ἐν κώμη⟨ι⟩ Κερκύτω⟨ι⟩
V A.D.	*Stud.Pal.* X 233, col. I B,6	Καρκύτου (cf. *BL* 8,459)

See also: .ρ..ατου.

TOPARCHY: Μέση.

ETYMOLOGY: first component *grg* : «the foundation of» (see *s.v.* ΚΕΡΚΕΣΗΣ).

P.Köln II 99 includes Kerkytos in a list of villages in the Middle toparchy (Phnebieus, Peenpibyk(is), Kerkytos, Phys, Thmoinothis).

CPR I 64 confirms this location: it is a παραχώρησις contract between Aurelius Sarapammon (from Herakleopolis but apparently living at Kerkytos) and a woman living at Thmoinothis; the woman acquires 9.5 arourae near Phys (in the fossil kleros of Ἄμμων) and a few more near Thmoinothis (in the fossil kleros of Ἀριστόμαχος). The contract is recorded at the office of the agoranomos of the Μέση toparchy at Peenameus.

P.Hels. I 29 enters Kerkytos after Thmoiphtha (24; Πέραν toparchy).

P.Vind.Tand. 10 (col.III: the best preserved part of a τόμος συγκολλήσιμος) contains an oath-declaration by two προστάται γεωργῶν, both ἀπὸ κώμης Κερκύτου, who are to supervise work on the οὐσίαι of Agrippina Augusta Minor (l.39) and of the Emperor Claudius (ll.40 ff., cf. ll.8 and 12). Claudius' οὐσία, previously belonging to Iulia Augusta = Livia, had perhaps originally belonged to C. Iulius Alexander (cf.l.10). In any case, according to the Editors, all οὐσίαι referred to in this document were in the vicinity of Euhemeria (Arsinoites).

ΚΕΦΑΛΑΙ

245 (244) B.C.	*P.Hib.* I 71,7	ἐκ τῆς ἐ[ν] Κεφαλαῖς λατομίας (6-7)
after 27 B.C.	*BGU* XVI 2599,5	ἀπὸ Κεφαλῶν
8/7 B.C.	*BGU* XVI 2570,5	Κεφαλαῖς
169-177 A.D. (cf. *BL* 9,32)	*BGU* XIII 2326, fr. **a**,3;6;10	εἰς προθμῖον [Κεφαλ– (3); εἰς πρ[ο]θμῖον Κε[φαλ– (6); εἰς προθμῖον Κεφαλ.[(10)

TOPARCHY: Koma.

ETYMOLOGY: this locality was presumably called after some landscape feature: κεφαλή can mean «extremity (of things, e.g. of a plot of land)» and also, in the plural, «source (of a river)» as in HDT. 4,91 (see *LSJ s.v.* κεφαλή II).
BIBLIOGRAPHY: TIMM, *Das christlich-koptische Ägypten* III, p.1235 f. (*s.v.* Kephalē II).

P.Hib. I 71: the λατομία of Κεφαλαί is mentioned in a letter to Dorion, head of police at Phebichis[1]. Quarries were near Ankyron, but also near Bousiris, and in *BGU* XVI 2570 reference is also made to Koma and to its komogrammateus. Besides, in *BGU* XIII 2326 (customs-house register covering five days) Κεφαλ.[appears along with Λευκόγιον (*passim*) and perhaps Bousiris (l.13).

BGU XVI 2599 is a petition from three farmers of Κεφαλαί, concerning their insufficiently flooded land-holdings (of seven arourae each) near the village of Taphthiris.

There was a προθμῖον (= πορθμεῖον, «place for crossing, ferry, ferry-boat») at Κεφαλαί (*BGU* XIII 2326).

ΚΗΡΑ ΜΙΚΡ(Α)[2]

V A.D.   *Stud.Pal.* X 233, col. II,7

ΚΗΤΣ

V A.D.   *P.Oxy.* VIII 1126,8   γίτονες νώτου τον ἀπὸ
                                              Τάλη λιβὸς λιδης
                                              Κήτς, ἀπη(λ)λιώτου
                                              λιδης .μεια (7-9)

See also: Κετη

P.Oxy. VIII 1126: lease of 4 ar. «in the holding called that of Tsabatoüs, ... the boundaries being on the south the land of the people of Τάλη, on the north ..., on the west λιδης Κήτς, on the east λιδης .μεια»[3]: Kets was near Talae, and north-west of it.

ΚΙΛΘΩ

216 A.D.   *Stud.Pal.* XX 22,6-7 (=   περὶ κώμην Κιλθω
                CPR I 35)

TOPARCHY: περὶ Πόλιν? Tekmi ?

---

[1] See the Editors' *Introduction* to this document.

[2] «Κηρα Μικρ(ά) schlägt Hermann Harrauer vor» (letter from Johannes Diethart, of February 25, 1994).

[3] According to the Editor *ad loc.*, the word λιδη/λιδης «seems from its repetition to be a common, not a proper name. Possibly it is for λιτή or –ῆς», which is an attribute of γαῖα in ALEX. AETOL. fr. 1 Powell (to which ORPH. A. 92 may be added: see *LSJ s.v.* λιτός). As regards the meaning of λιτή, a gloss in HESYCHIUS *s.v.* λιτὴ χθών· ἀπὸ τοῦ προσκυνεῖσθαι καὶ λιτανεύεσθαι, could perhaps be relevant: was this «sacred» land?

A lease contract between two sisters from Herakleopolis and an inhabitant of Pyrgotos (Tekmi toparchy) for land (belonging to the two sisters) περὶ κώμην Κιλθω.

ΚΛΕΩΝΟ(Σ)

VII/VIII A.D. *Stud.Pal.* X 209,1 χ(ωρίον) Κλέωνο(ς)

BIBLIOGRAPHY: TIMM, *Das christlich-koptische Ägypten* III, p.1276, s.v. *Kleōn(os)*.

Kollasoucha, Maiouma and Nois are mentioned in the same document.

ΚΟΒΑ

267-260 B.C. (cf.*BL* 5,46)	*P.Hib.* I 164 descr.	Κόβας
probably between 265 and 245 B.C.	*P.Hib.* I 123 descr.	ἐκ Κόβα
9 Dec. 249 B.C.	*P.Yale* I 35,6 (= *P.Hib.* I 56)	ἐκ Κόβα
mid-III B.C.(?)	*SB* X 10447 *recto*,43	Κόβα (cf. *BL* 6,168)
III B.C.	*P.Strasb.* VII 643,2	ἐν] κώμηι Κόβα τοῦ Κωείτου
about 138 B.C.	*P.Tebt.* III 860,61;64	
I A.D.	*P.Oxy.* VIII 1145,1	
I/II A.D.	*P.Hib.* II 218,17	
about 250 A.D.	*SB* I 1496,3	
about 250 A.D.	*SB* I 1501,3	
about 250 A.D.	*SB* I 1512,5	
24 March 261 A.D.	*O.Mich.* I 68,3	
III A.D.	*P.Oxy.* XII 1529,7	
411 A.D.	*Stud.Pal.* XX 117,1;2 (= *SB* I 5160)	ἐν κώμη Κόβα ιβ [πά]γου (1); ἀπὸ κώμης Κόβα δωδεκά[του] π[ά]γου (2) (cf. *BL* 7,262)
29 Sept. 457 A.D.	*P.Rain.Cent.* 101,4;6	ἀπὸ κώμης Κόβα (4); ἀπὸ τῆς αὐτῆς κώμης Κόβα (6)
484 A.D.	*PSI* III 183,1	ἐν κώμη Κόβα

CATALOGUE

1 Dec. 502 A.D.	*P.Oxy.* L 3600,5;32	ἀπὸ κώμης Κόβα (5); κώμ(ης) Κόβ[α] (32)
VI A.D.	*P.Princ.* II 105,1;6	βοηθ(ῷ) πρωτοκωμ(ητῶν) Κόβα
late VI or VII A.D.	*P.Oxy.* XVI 1910,8	ἀπὸ Κ[ό]βα
VI/VII A.D.	*Stud.Pal.* VIII 1346,4;6	ἀπὸ Κόβα
early VII A.D.	*P.Laur.* II 47,2	τῆς κώμης Κόβα
VII/VIII A.D.	*Stud.Pal.* X 202,15	χ'ω'(ρίον) Κόβα

TOPARCHY: Koites (XII *pagus*: *Stud.Pal.* XX 117).

The links between Koba and the Northern toparchy of the Oxyrhynchites were close: cf. *P.Yale* I 35 (the ἀρχιφυλακίτης of the Northern toparchy of the Oxyrhynchites orders the komogrammateus not to disturb an inhabitant of Koba); *P.Oxy.* L 3600 (Flavius Timotheus originates from Koba but now lives at Oxyrhynchus); *P.Princ.* II 105 (the πρωτοκωμῆται of Koba are instructed to entertain an official on his way to Oxyrhynchus); *Stud.Pal.* VIII 1346 and *P.Laur.* II 47 (Phebichis, in the Koites, Ἰσῖον κάτω and Talao, of the Oxyrhynchite nome, are mentioned in both documents together with Koba)[1].

However, the village is already assigned to the Koites in the III B.C. (*P.Strasb.* VII 643), and mentioned along with other villages of this toparchy in several documents: *SB* X 10447 (references to Koba, Phebichis, and the Koites); *P.Tebt.* III 860 (listed with a number of other Herakleopolite villages: Psebthonpenouph(is), Tilothis, Gemoun(is), Ἰβιὼν Ἀρσάμου, Pselemachis, Toemesis); *P. Hib.* II 218 (listing many villages of the Koites); *Stud.Pal.* XX 117 (Philonikou also mentioned); *Stud.Pal.* X 202 (with Thmoiphtha and Thelbonthis).

The Apion estates also extended to Koba (cf. *P.Oxy.* XVI 1910).

ΚΟΛ(Λ)ΑΣΟΥΧΑ / ΚΟΛΑΣΟΥΧΙΣ

22 Jan. 223 B.C.[2]	*P.Rain.Cent.* 40,2	περὶ Κολλασοῦχα[3]; cf. l.4: περὶ τὴν αὐτὴν (*scil.* κώμην)
96-94 or 63-61 B.C.	*BGU* XIV 2429,7	Κολασούχ(εων)[4]
after 52/51 B.C.	*BGU* VIII 1808,22	Κολασούχεων
9-7 B.C.	*BGU* XVI 2598,5	περὶ κώμην Κολασοῦχιν
I B.C.	*BGU* XIV 2434,4	[Κο]λασοῦχιν

---

[1] PRUNETI, *Centri abitati*, pp.86-87, includes this village among those belonging to the Oxyrhynchites. There must have been just one village by this name, very near the border between the two nomes, and assigned to one or the other district at different times. *P.Oxy.* VIII 1145 (I A.D.), for example, points to connections between Koba and various villages in the Oxyrhynchites. See also TIMM, *Das christlich-koptische Ägypten*, vol.III, p.1428.

[2] New dating by Willy Clarysse (letter of July 7, 1994): see above, p.90 n.1.

[3] New reading by Willy Clarysse (letter of July 7, 1994).

[4] Κολασούχ(εως) *ed. pr.*

I B.C.	*BGU* XIV 2438,20	Κολασού(χεων)¹
I/II A.D.	*P.Hib.* II 218,34	Κολασούχ(εων)
VII-VIII A.D.	*Stud.Pal.* X 209,2	χ(ωρίον) Κολασούχε()²
VII-VIII A.D.	*Stud.Pal.* X 213,4	χ(ωρίον) Κολασούχ()

TOPARCHY: Ἄγημα (ἄνω?).

ETYMOLOGY: first element: κολλ–³; second element: the name of the crocodile god Souchos (pointing to a Fayūm connection).

The plural Κολ(λ)ασουχα (gen. Κολλασουχεων) and the (apparently later) singular form Κολάσουχις are attested in the Greek rendering of this village name. Cf. the variant spellings Κερκέσουχος/Κερκέσουχα (Arsinoite nome)⁴.

P.Rain.Cent. 40: the φυλακίτης Herakleides is to be informed that two plots of land near Kollasoucha (one of them in the kleros Σατύρου) have been leased out: the relevant σύμβολον is kept at the λογευτήριον of Hiera Nesos. The connection between Kollasoucha and Hiera Nesos is confirmed by *BGU* XIV 2429 (see below).

BGU XIV 2438: Kollasoucha is listed with other places of the Ἄγημα toparchy: note especially Korphotoi (l.15), as these two villages are mentioned in two consecutive lines (22 and 23, respectively) in *BGU* VIII 1808.

Kollasoucha, Petachor, and Hiera Nesos are all mentioned in *BGU* XIV 2429, and in *BGU* VIII 1808, where Alilais also occurs; as *P.Hib.* II 218 also lists Alilais, Kollasoucha and Petachor in three consecutive lines (33-35), it seems likely that these villages were in the same area, i.e. in Ἄγημα ἄνω (where Alilais certainly belonged). Further support to this hypothesis is lent by *Stud.Pal.* X 209: here Kollasoucha recurs with Nois, a village of the περὶ Πόλιν toparchy which also recurs with Petachor in another document (*CPR* XIV 40): Alilais is therefore a highly plausible reading in *CPR* XIV 40, l.3. Kollasoucha and Petachor again recur together in *Stud.Pal.* X 213⁵ (ll.4 and 5).

ΚΟΛΛΕΩΣ

between 173 and 130-128 B.C. (cf. *BL* 7,273)	*P.Tebt.* III 890,81	ἐκ Κόλλεως

TOPARCHY: Μέση (?)

---

¹ Κολασού(χεως) *ed. pr.*

² χ(ωρίον) Κολασούχο(υ) *ed. pr.*, Johannes Diethart (letter of February 25, 1994): a genitive ending of the third declension is required here.

³ As in Kollasoucha, Koll(is), Kollinpetou, Kollintaathyr: κολλ– = *gl* ? (see *s.v.* ΚΑΛΑΜΟΥΡΙΟΥ).

⁴ I owe this comparison to Willy Clarysse.

⁵ *Stud.Pal.* X 211, 212 and 213, though published as separate documents, are in fact fragments of the same text, so that the villages mentioned in *Stud.Pal.* X 211 (Ogou, in the Tekmi toparchy), 212 (Thelbonthis, in the Techtho Nesos toparchy) and 213 (Petachor and Kollasoucha, in the Ἄγημα) may have been near each other.

ETYMOLOGY: the personal name Κολεύς is apparently attested in *P.Ryl.* II 72 (99/98 B.C., from the Arsinoites).

Bank accounts. Other villages mentioned are Tantoka (l.7) and Phnebieus (ll.74,75,100; Μέση toparchy).

ΚΟΛΛΙΝΠΕΤΩΥ

| I B.C. | *BGU* XIV 2441,67;79 | Κολλιν'πετων'⟦τααθυρ⟧ (67)[1]; Κολ[λ]ινπετ[ω]υ (79) |

TOPARCHY: Tekmi.

ETYMOLOGY: first element κολλ– (see *s.v.* ΚΟΛΛΑΣΟΥΧΑ) + -*n*- (genitive) + second element = Πετωύς (a common personal name).

In this survey of the land around Pyrgotos (Tekmi toparchy) some holdings are recorded that were split between this village and Kollinpetou: the fossil kleroi concerned are those of Ἄσανδρος (68), Σκίρων (71), Φιλώτας (77), Ἀλέξανδρος (78; with further reference to a Διονυσίον[2]).
Part of the ἀπόμοιρα from vine- and orchard-land collected in this area was due to the temple of Eseph at Tekmi.

ΚΟΛ(Λ)ΙΝΤΑ(Α)ΘΥΡ

139 B.C.	*P.Tebt.* III 988,15	περὶ Κολλιντααθύρ
139 B.C.	*P.Tebt.* III 991,2	[Κολιντααθ]υρ[3]
139 B.C.	*P.Tebt.* III 992	Κολιντααθύρ
after 52/51 B.C.	*BGU* VIII 1808,4	Κολλιντααθύρ (cf. *BL* 8,49)
I B.C.	*BGU* XIV 2437,1	Κολλιντααθύρ
I B.C.	*BGU* XIV 2441,67	Κολλιν⟦τααθύρ⟧'πετων'
28/29 A.D.	*P.Oxy.* XXIV 2412,74;156;185	Κολλιντ(αθύρ)
first half of III A.D.	*CPR* I 156,3;4	περὶ κώμην Κολιντααθύρ (3); Κολλιντααθύρ (4)[4]

---

[1] Kollintaathyr (which belonged to the same toparchy) was first written at l.67, and then altered into Kollinpetou.

[2] Presumably the same Διονυσίον also appears in *BGU* XIV 2440, fr.1, col.II, 74 (soon after a reference to the fossil kleros of Κόρραγος).

[3] The Editors based this supplement on *P.Tebt.* III 992, a document of the same type and date.

[4] New readings checked for me by Johannes Diethart (letter of February 25, 1994).

350 A.D.	*P.Oxf.* 6,5	ἀπὸ κώ]μης Κολινταθύρ (5)
VI A.D.	*Stud.Pal.* X 44,8	χ'ω'(ρίον) Κολλινταθηρ
VI-VII A.D.	*Stud.Pal.* X 5,6	τὸν βοηθ(ὸν) Κολινταθύρ
VII/VIII A.D.	*CPR* IV 2,13	χ(ωρίον) Κολιντα'θ'(ύρ)
VII-VIII A.D.	*Stud.Pal.* X 230,5	χ(ωρίον) Κολιντ'α'(θύρ)

TOPARCHY: Tekmi.

ETYMOLOGY: first element κολλ- (see *s.v.* ΚΟΛΛΑΣΟΥΧΑ) + -*n*- (genitive) + *ta* (feminine article) + the name of the goddess Hathor: «the (?) of the female one of Hathor».[1]

BGU XIV 2437 shows that this village belonged to the Tekmi toparchy: 60 arourae, making up a τοπογραμματικὸς κλῆρος, are entered under the heading περὶ Τέκμι· Κολλινταατθύρ; these were distributed among the following villages: Taemsis, Tou, Tochontou, Πεενε..() and Tekmi. Six centuries later, Kollintaathyr and Tou are found together again in *Stud.Pal.* X 244.

P.Oxy. XXIV 2412 contains accounts of money payments from six villages, all apparently in the Tekmi toparchy: Ogou, Tekmi, Kollintaathyr, Pyrgotos, Mouchis, Ibion (potters are mentioned in connection with Kollintaathyr). Ogou, Kollintaathyr, Pyrgotos and Mouchis also recur together in *CPR* IV 2[2]. The proximity of Ogou and Kollintaathyr, in particular, is confirmed by *P.Oxf.* 6, which concerns a conflict between the two petitioners, both from Kollintaathyr, and «the people of Ogou» for the ownership of five arourae. The petitioners assert that the land has been in their possession for twenty years, since they bought it from a senator; the inhabitants of Ogou have apparently tried to persuade the boundary inspectors that they were in fact the owners (and the petitioners, presumably, their lessees)[3].

ΚΟΛΛΟΥΘΟΥ

V A.D.	*Stud.Pal.* X 47,5	Κολλούθου (cf. *BL* 1,418)

BIBLIOGRAPHY: W.E. Crum, *Kollouthus: the Martyr and his Name*, Berlin 1929/30.

Stud.Pal. X 47: list of Herakleopolite villages, apparently proceeding from the north to the south: Onosis (l.1; περὶ Πόλιν toparchy); Mouchis (l.2; Tekmi toparchy); Tanaso (l.3); Tosachmis (l.4; Koites); Κολλούθου follows in the next line.

A κτῆμα with this name appears in three documents from the end of the III A.D.: *P.Oxy.* XLIX 3513,4; *P.Oxy.* XLIX 3515,4; *P.Oxy.* XLIX 3519,5. This could be identical with the κλῆρος κατοικικὸς (πρότερον) Κολλούθου Ἀπολλωνίου mentioned in *P.Oxy.* XLIX 3475,14-15: two superintendents of the dykes present an account of the work done on the dykes of the canals in the southern

---

[1] Etymology suggested by Willy Clarysse and Katelijn Vandorpe.

[2] *CPR* IV 2 is a bilingual document in Coptic and Greek (toponyms in Greek); it lists many villages of the central toparchies of the Herakleopolite nome (see also *s.v.* ΝΙΝΩ).

[3] See the Editor's comments *ad loc.*

section of the Western toparchy of the Oxyrhynchite nome (the document is dated to the 16th of March, A.D. 220).

ΚΟΜ..[

VII-VIII A.D.   *Stud.Pal.* X 206,8

Apparently the name of a κλῆρος, listed with several others (see the *Reverse Index* at the end of this volume).

ΚΟΜΑ

212/211 B.C.	*P.Lille* I 59,23;49;107	
III B.C.	*P.Cair.Zen.* III 59473,9	ἐγ Κομαι
III B.C.	*P.Cair.Zen.* IV 59782 (b),63;73;95	ἐκ ⟦Κ..ας⟧'Τμοιβάστιος ' (63); ἐκ Κομα (73;95)
II B.C.	*P.Mil.Vogl.* inv. 1299,3	ἐν κώμῃ Κόμαι τοῦ Ἡρακλεο[πολίτου[1]
ca. 160 B.C.	*P.Hels.* I 27,4	
136 B.C.	*P.Tebt.* III 931,2	παρ' Ἰμούθου τοῦ κωμογραμματέως Κόμα (1-2)
after 84/83 B.C.	*BGU* XIV 2370 (fr. 1),74	
after 52/51 B.C.	*BGU* VIII 1808,5	
I B.C.	*BGU* VIII 1789,8	[Π]ετεχῶντι καὶ Σαδά(λῳ) λογε(υταῖς) Κόμα
I B.C.	*BGU* XIV 2434,2	[πε]ρὶ Κόμα
I B.C.	*BGU* XIV 2437,44;46;48;49	περὶ Κόμα (44); τοῦ ἐν Κόμα ἱεροῦ (48); ἐν Κό[μα (49)
I B.C.	*BGU* XIV 2438,72	περὶ Κόμα
I B.C.	*BGU* XIV 2439,70	
I B.C.	*BGU* XIV 2440,51;53	περὶ Κόμα (51)
21/20 B.C.	*BGU* XVI 2655,22	εἰς Κόμα
21/20 B.C.-5 A.D.	*BGU* XVI 2641,10	
15/14 B.C.	*BGU* IV 1188,2	[γ]υμν[ασι]άρχου Κόμα
12/11 B.C.	*BGU* IV 1197,9	οἱ μὲν ἀπὸ Λινῆ καὶ Κόμα κωμῶν [ἱ]γερὶς

---

[1] Guido Bastianini kindly informed me of this new source for the present village. *P.Mil.Vogl.* inv.1299 was obtained from the same *cartonnage* containing a roll with Posidippus' epigrams: see *Introduction*, p.20 f.

13 Nov. 9 B.C.	*BGU* XVI 2610,5	τοῖς ἐπὶ λόγοις τῆς Κόμα
8 B.C.	*BGU* IV 1193,4	περὶ Κόμα
8/7 B.C.	*BGU* XVI 2562,2	σιτολόγοις Κόμα
8/7 B.C.	*BGU* XVI 2563,3;5	σιτολ[ό]γ[οι]ς Κόμα (2-3)
8/7 B.C.	*BGU* XVI 2570,7;8	τῆς Κόμα κωμογρα[μματ– (7)
6/5 B.C.	*SB* V 7537,2-3;5	ἀπ[ὸ Κο]μα (2-3); περὶ τὴν Κόμα (5)
26 June 4 B.C.	*BGU* XVI 2644,6;8	εἰς Κόμα (6); εἰς τὴν Κόμα (8)
26 Nov. 3 B.C.	*BGU* XVI 2573,3	σ[ιτολόγοις] Κόμα
25,26 Nov. 3 B.C.	*BGU* XVI 2569,2	[Κ]όμα
3/2 B.C.(?)	*BGU* XVI 2564,3	σιτολόγοις [Κ]όμα (2-3)
ca. 1 A.D.	*BGU* IV 1189,6	δεκανοὶ χώματος τοῦ κατὰ Κόμα
1-9 A.D.	*BGU* XVI 2559,1;2;7;12;14	σιτο'λ'(όγοι) Κόμα (1;6-7;12)
I/II A.D.	*P.Hib.* II 218,63	
II/III A.D.	*P.Köln* II 99,7;8	περὶ Κόμα (7)
late II or III A.D.	*P.Ryl.* II 225,49	περὶ Κόμα[1]
III A.D.	*P.Osl.* III 82,15	ἀπὸ κώ]μης Κόμα
IV A.D.	*P.Ross.Georg.* V 61 A,verso,9	ἐν Κόμα
534 A.D.	*P.Oxy.* I 142,1	ἀπὸ Κόμα
probably 565/566 A.D.	*P.Oxy.* XXVII 2480,66;76;93;111;112;115;117	τῆς Κόμα
566 A.D.	*P.Oxy.* LV 3804,149	ἀπὸ Κόμα
590 A.D.	*P.Oxy.* I 150,1 (= *Stud.Pal.* III 283)	βουκελλ(αρίοις) τῆς Ἡρακλέους (καὶ) Κόμα
VI A.D.	*SB* XX 14123, 6[2]	ἀπὸ Κώμα
VI A.D.	*P.Oxy.* XVI 1998,2;6	ἀπὸ Κώμα (2); προ(νοητοῦ) Κώμα(2); ἀπὸ Κώμα (6)

---

[1] The first Editor deciphered περὶ Κομαμαχόρ, which should be articulated as follows: περὶ Κόμα· Μαχόρ.

[2] First edition: ROSARIO PINTAUDI-PIETER J. SIJPESTEIJN, *Aegyptus* 70, 1990, p.50.

VI A.D.	*SB* VI 9608,2 [1]	ἀπὸ λόγου ἐκφορίων Κόμα
VI or VII A.D.	*P.Oxy.* XVI 1848,7	τὴν Κώμα
VI or VII A.D.	*P.Oxy.* XVI 1861,5	ἐπὶ τὴν Κόμα
VII A.D.	*Stud.Pal.* X 4,2	εἰ(ς) παράχωμ(α) τῆ(ς) Κόμα
VII/VIII A.D.	*Stud.Pal.* X 17,3	ἀπὸ χ'ω'(ρίου) Κόμα
708 A.D. (cf. *BL* 7,256)	*Stud.Pal.* III 448,2	ἀπὸ χωρίου Κόμα
VIII A.D.	*Stud.Pal.* X 223,5	ἀπὸ χ(ωρίου) Κομ( )
s.d.	*Ét.Fouad* 2,2 [2]	Ἡρακλᾶς εἰς Κόμα τοῦ Ἡρακλεοπολίτου (1-5)

Literary Sources

V A.D.	SOZOM. *h.e.* I 13,2 [3]

TOPARCHY: Koma.

A list of villages belonging to this toparchy is on p.293.

BIBLIOGRAPHY: FRIEDRICH ZUCKER, *Aegyptus* 11, 1931, p.491, n.3; IDEM, *Symbolae Osloenses*, 17, 1937, pp.54-55; TIMM, *Das christlich-koptische Ägypten*, V, pp.2154-2157.

MODERN ARABIC NAME: Qiman Al-'Arûs (about 7 kms SW of Al-Wasta) is identified with ancient Koma by TIMM (cited above).

The lists of villages in *P.Lille* I 59 and *P.Cair.Zen.* IV 59782 (b) coincide for the main part: besides Bousiris and Koma, they include other villages of the Koma toparchy (Krekis, Machor; in addition, *P.Cair.Zen.* IV 59782 (b) mentions Thmoiobastis and Tou), the Tilothis toparchy (Tilothis, Tanchais; in addition, *P.Lille* I 59 mentions Peenpasbyt(is) and Schnomthis) and the Tekmi toparchy (Onnes; in addition, *P.Lille* I 59 has Peenepsy). Much the same group of villages recurs in *BGU* XIV 2438: Tilothis, Schnomthis, Peenpasbyt(is), Tanchais, Koma, Toou (preceded by entries for the Ἄγημα κάτω, Μέση and Phebichis toparchies). Many of these villages are also recorded in *BGU* XIV 2370, fr.1, under the main entry Κάτω τοπαρ[χ]ίας; these are: Koma, Toou, Machor, Thmoiobastis, Onnes, Tilothis, Tanchais. A second fragment (*BGU* XIV 2370 fr.2) has a reference to Bousiris. These connections are confirmed by *P.Cair.Zen.* III 59473 (Onnes, Koma), *BGU* VIII 1808 (Tekmi, Koma, Onnes, Thmoiobastis, Bousiris), *BGU* VIII 1789 (ll.8-9: Koma, Toou, Krekis, listed one after the other), *BGU* XIV 2440, ll.41 ff. (entries for the Tekmi toparchy, including Onnes, precede those for the Koma toparchy, which comprise Toou, Koma and Thmoiobastis; there follow references to the Phebichis and Πέραν toparchies), *P.Hib.* II 218 (listing Koma, Krekis, Bousiris, Thmoiamoun(is) and Thmoiobastis in a sequence: ll.63-67) and *P.Ryl.* II 225 (Koma, Machor).

BGU IV 1189 is a petition submitted by the gymnasiarches on account of two inhabitants of Bousiris,

---

[1] On this document see AMPHILOCHIOS PAPATHOMAS, «Lexikographische Delenda im Geschäftsbrief *SB* VI 9608 und Erstedition der Versoseite», *Tyche* 10, 1995, pp.155-159.

[2] *Ed. pr.*: MICHEL CHAVEAU-FRANÇOIS KAYSER, «Cinq étiquettes de momies», *BIFAO* 91, 1991, pp.155-159.

[3] According to Timm (cited above), Sozomenos is the first to indicate Koma as St. Anthony's birthplace.

who are also δεκανοί of the χῶμα κατὰ Κόμα.

BGU IV 1193: petition to the komogrammateus from a κάτοικος whose land comprises parts of three fossil kleroi (those of Ῥόδων, Σάτοκος and Δημήτριος) near Koma.

BGU IV 1188: petition to the strategos from the gymnasiarches, the κάτοικοι, the ἄλλοι γεωργοί, and the βασιλικοὶ γεωργοί living at Koma.

BGU IV 1197: government allowances to the priests (note the spelling ἱγερῖς) from Line and Koma.

A number of documents concerning the delivery of grain are published in *BGU* XVI: *BGU* XVI 2562-2564, 2569, 2570 and 2573 contain orders for seed-grain (2570, in particular, also mentions Κεφαλαί); *BGU* XVI 2559 is a collection of extracts from sitologos receipts; *BGU* XVI 2644 concerns grain shipments that are impeded by the fact that all boats have been requisitioned by the army; *BGU* XVI 2610 also is a letter concerning wheat. In *BGU* XVI 2641 the villages of Koma, Tanchais, and Trikomia are referred to.

P.Ross.Georg. V 61: army supplies (food and clothes); many Ἡρακλεοπολῖται are listed, Koma and Taamorou are the only place-names mentioned.

ΚΟΡΡΑΣ

mid-III B.C.	*P.Strasb.* IX 802,19	Κόρρας

TOPARCHY: Koites?

P.Strasb. IX 802 is a list of Egyptian tax-payers and their villages, all of them probably in the Koites.

ΚΟΡΦΟΤΟΙ

III B.C.	*P.Lille* I 6,4	εἰς Κορφοτοῦν
96-94 or 63-61 B.C.	*BGU* XIV 2429,4	Κορφ(οτοι)
after 52/51 B.C.	*BGU* VIII 1808,23	Κολφατοί
I B.C.	*BGU* XIV 2436,11	
I B.C.	*BGU* XIV 2437,28; (fr.1),52	
I B.C.	*BGU* XIV 2438,15	
29 July 25 B.C.	*BGU* XVI 2590, I,5; II,5	πρεσβύτεροι τῶν ἀπὸ κώμης Κορφοτοι (I,4-5); ἀπὸ κώμης Κορφοτοι (II,4-5)
223 A.D.	*P.Ross.Georg.* V 20 *recto*,1;4;8	Κορφοτύ (1); κώμ(ης) Κ[ο]ρφοτύ (4); Κορφοτ̣ύ (8)

TOPARCHY: Ἄγημα.

ETYMOLOGY: the variant spelling Κολφατοι (*BGU* VIII 1808,23) is explained by the interchangeability of the sounds for *l* and *r* in the Egyptian language. The variant spellings Κορφοτουν/Κορφοτοι match

Πεονταμουν/Πεενσαμοι: in both cases, the –ουν ending is attested in the earliest source (III B.C.).

MODERN ARABIC NAME: Al-Gafādūn (most similar to the spelling Κορφοτουν, as attested in the earliest Greek source). No identification is suggested for this village in *TAVO B 69*, § 4.3 (W 29) (p.169) its name is «arabisch nicht etymologisierbar». See also *ibid.*, p.233: «Nach Auskunft des Bürgermeisters ... gab es im Dorf mehrere Kōms. Sie sind heute restlos abgetragen. Auch berichten Dorfbewohner, daß sie direkt westlich des Dorfes beim Graben Keramikscherben sowie gebrannte Lehmziegel gefunden hatten. Im Dorf befinden sich vier große Gefäße, ca.70 cm. hoch, aus Stein, in der Form eines Mörsers ... In den Dorfstraßen und westlich des Dorfes selbst wurden keine Keramikscherben gesehen».

BGU XIV 2437 enters Korphotoi in a list of villages of the Ἄγημα κάτω, together with Peenameus, Peenepsomphis (which again recurs with Korphotoi in *BGU* XIV 2437 fr.1), Peensemtheus, Kella. A location in the southern part of the toparchy, however, would be more compatible with the identification with modern Al-Gafādūn, and can be supported by *BGU* VIII 1808 and *BGU* XIV 2438: both these documents mention Korphotoi along with Kollasoucha, which was probably in Ἄγημα ἄνω.

P.Lille I 6: the petitioner has been robbed while on his way from Tebetny to Korphotoi (Διαβάντος μου ἐκ Τεβετνὺ εἰς Κορφοτοῦν ἐπισκέψασθαι τὴν ἀδελφὴν ...).

BGU XVI 2590 comprises two documents: one is a sworn agreement by the elders of Korphotoi to undertake maintenance work of the three public canals near the village; the second is the receipt of 120 drachmae from the toparches, to cover any costs for the work. The three χώματα are thus identified: τὸ λεγόμενον Ζανήριος, τὸ λεγόμενον Μεγάλης ὁδοῦ, and finally τὸ ἀπὸ λιβὸς το[ῦ .].ωνίου παραδείσου.

BGU XIV 2436, 10-11: the holding of a Ptolemaios jr. is split between Korphotoi and Peenpasbyt(is) (in the Tilothis toparchy).

Villages of the Techtho Nesos toparchy (Thmoinache) and the Koites (Thelbo, Phebichis) appear in the document on the *verso* of *P.Ross.Georg.* V 20.

ΚΡΗΚΙΣ

212/211 B.C.	*P.Lille* I 59,10;39;85;97;112;124	Κρήκεως
III B.C.	*P.Cair.Zen.* IV 59782 (b),30;71;93	ἐκ Κρίκεως (30,93); ἐκ Κρηκερ (71)[1]
30 B.C.-14 A.D.	*BGU* XVI 2577,72	Κρηκίτη[ς] (ethnic)
I B.C.	*BGU* VIII 1789,9	Κρή(κεως)[2]
I B.C.	*BGU* XIV 2437,44	Κρήκεως
I B.C.	*BGU* XIV 2438,72;75;76	Κρῆ(κις)[3]
I B.C.	*BGU* XIV 2439,20;62	[τ]ῆς Κρήκεως (20); Κρήκεως (62)

---

[1] The scribe wrote ἐκ ρηκερ, a haplography for ἐκ Κρηκερ (in other documents, graecisized as Κρῆκις): WILLY CLARYSSE, *Studia Hellenistica* 24, 1980, p.113 n.3.

[2] The Editors deciphered ...τοου κρη(), which can be understood as ... Τοου Κρη(κεως). Both these villages were in the Koma toparchy: note the reference to Koma in the preceding line.

[3] The Editor deciphered Κρη(): in my opinion, this is to be resolved as Κρῆ(κις).

I B.C.	*BGU* XVI 2674,3	Κρ'η'(κίτης) (ethnic)
I/II A.D.	*P.Hib.* II 218,64	Κρήκεως

TOPARCHY: Koma.

Krekis consistently appears in connection with Koma in almost all documents listed above. *BGU* XVI 2577, a tax-list, was presumably drawn at Herakleopolis (a μητρόπολις is referred to on l.203): two of the people listed apparently originated from Krekis and Onnes, respectively; *BGU* XVI 2674 is a document of a similar kind.

ΚΡΟΥΣΤΟΥ

VI A.D.	*Stud.Pal.* VIII 848,2	
VI A.D.	*Stud.Pal.* VIII 849 (+ 809)[1],1-2	πωμαρίου Κρούστου
VI A.D.	*Stud.Pal.* VIII 861,1	πωμαρίου Κρούστου
VIII A.D.	*Stud.Pal.* X 226,4	ἐποίκ(ιον) Μ(ε)γ(άλου) Κρούστ'ου'

Evidently an orchard (πωμάριον) to which a settlement was attached. In *Stud.Pal.* X 226 Κωπρυας is also entered (l.6).

ΚΤΗΜΑ

557 A.D.	*P.Oxy.* XVI 1911,164	τῆς μηχ(ανῆς) καλουμέ(νης) τοῦ Κτήματος
610-641 A.D.[2]	*P.Bodl.* I 73,4;5	ἀπὸ] Κτήματος τοῦ Ἡρακλεοπολίτου νομοῦ (4); ἀπὸ τοῦ αὐτοῦ Κτ[ήμα]τος τοῦ αὐτοῦ νομοῦ (5)
late VI A.D.	*P.Oxy.* XVI 1912,149	μ]ηχ(ανῆς) καλουμ(ένης) τοῦ Κτήμ(ατος)
VI-VII A.D.	*P.Oxy.* XIX 2244,76	μηχ(ανῆς) καλουμ(ένης) τοῦ Κτήμ(ατος)

---

[1] Cf. *BL* 7,256.

[2] The Editor indicates that this document should be dated to the reign of Fl. Heraklius (October 5, 610-February 11, 641: cf. ROGER S. BAGNALL - KLAAS A. WORP, *Regnal Formulas in Byzantine Egypt*, Missoula 1979, p.68).

CATALOGUE

P.Oxy. XVI 1911 and 1912 contain accounts concerning estates of the Apion family. *P.Oxy.* XIX 2244 is an account of axles supplied for water-wheels. *P.Bodl.* I 73 records a loan (of money?).

ΚΩ

30 Jan. 28 A.D.	*SB* XVI 12762,9 (= *P.Oxy.* II 352 descr.)	περὶ Κῶ τοῦ Ἡρακλεοπολ]είτου (9-10)[1]
20 Aug. 55 A.D.	(?)*P.Giss.Univ.* 19,10	ἐν Κου
16 March 102 A.D. (cf. *BL* 7,148)	(?)*P.Oxy.* XXII 2342,40	ἐν Κῶι
145 A.D.	(?)*P.Flor.* I 23,9	ἐκ τοῦ Λιβυ[ος?] κλ(ήρου) κωμογραμματείας Κωυ
14 February 484 A.D.	*P.Rain.Cent.* 107,4	ἀπὸ ἐποικίου Κόν
574 A.D.	*P.Berl. Zill.* 7, *recto*,8; *verso*,1	ἀπὸ κώμης Κῶς τοῦ Ἡρακλεοπολιτῶν νομοῦ (*recto*,8); ἀπὸ κώμης Κῶς (*verso*,1)
VI A.D.	(?)*Stud.Pal.* III 453,2	Κῶς[2] Μη(νᾶς) ἀπὸ ἐποικ(ίου) Ἀγκυρ(ῶνος)
VII/VIII A.D.	(?)*P.Batav.* XXV 80 B, col. II,3	χ(ωρίον) Κῶν

Literary Sources

II A.D.	PTOL. *Geogr.* IV 5,59	
V A.D.	STEPH. BYZ. *s.v.* Κῶς	... ἐστι καὶ ἐν Αἰγύπτῳ πόλις Κῶς

TOPARCHY: Koites.

MODERN ARABIC NAME: by combining the testimony of PTOL. *Geogr.* IV 5,59 with the fact of the existence of a toparchy called Κωίτης, Grenfell and Hunt argued for the existence of a place called Κῶ: their hypothesis is now supported by a handful of documents. On the other hand, Ptolemy seems to have confused Ko and the capital of the Kynopolite nome, Κυνῶν πόλις (*alias* Σκω: see below). In his description, these two places face each other: according to Ptolemy, their latitude is exactly the same (28° 40/60'), while the respective longitudes locate Ko further east (at 60° 50/60') than Κυνῶν πόλις (at 62°

---

[1] One might supply Ἀρσινοείτου, as there was a place called Kos in the Arsinoites: the present document, however, comes from Oxyrhynchus, and is more likely to refer to the Herakleopolite Ko. «Lo spazio per integrare [Ἡρακλεοπολ]είτου sembra però insufficiente, a meno di supporre qualche forma di abbreviazione, oppure che essendo parola nota, fosse scritta in maniera più contratta» (CARLA BALCONI, *Aegyptus* 84, 1984, pp.57).

[2] This may not be a toponym.

10/60'), which would thus actually be situated at the southern edge of the Herakleopolite island. However, if we assume that Ptolemy simply swapped the two, both would come to be in a more likely location, i.e. Ko at the southern extreme of the Herakleopolites (having in fact given its name to the southernmost toparchy of that name), while Κυνῶν πόλις would occupy a position east, and slightly south of Oxyrhynchus - just as is fitting for the capital of the Kynopolite nome. Κυνῶν πόλις is the Greek translation of one of the Egyptian names of this city (*Inpwt*, based on the name of the Dog-god of this district, *Inpw*, or Anubis): other names were *Hnw* and *S3k3*, which is also found in the Greek sources, being transliterated as Σκω. The similarity between the two place-names Σκω (*alias* Κυνῶν πόλις) and Κω could account for Ptolemy's confusion between the two. Finally, the ancient toponym *S3k3*/Σκω (= Κυνῶν πόλις) is behind the modern place-name Al Qais, a site provided with rich archaeological evidence[1]. The rarely attested Herakleopolite Ko seems to have perished[2].

SB XVI 12762: a shepherd registered as resident at Kos undertakes to pasture sheep and goats in the Thmoisepho toparchy of the Oxyrhynchites.

P.Oxy. XXII 2432: draft for a petition to the prefect, submitted by a wine-merchant from Oxyrhynchus; the petitioner kept this draft: the date on which the fair copy was submitted to the prefect was noted down on it: «Handed to the prefect ἐν Κωι, on the 20th of Phamenoth».

P.Berl.Zill. 7: lease-contract between an inhabitant of Oxyrhynchus and an inhabitant of Kos, for a μηχανή «called Ακεεις, to the north of the same village (Ko)».

It is clear that Ko gravitated towards the Oxyrhynchite nome.

ΚΩΙΤΗΣ (toparchy)

247/246 B.C.	*SB* III 7176,3	εἰς τὸν Κωίτην
244/243 B.C.	*P.Hib.* I 78,14	ἐκ τοῦ Κωίτου
240/239 or 215/214 B.C.	*P.Hib.* I 117,2	παρὰ Ἀροννώφριος [το]ῦ πρὸς τοῖς θη(σαυροῖς) τοῦ Κωίτου
29 June 228 B.C.	*P.Hib.* I 66 verso	τραπεζίτηι Κωίτου
227/226 B.C.	*P.Grad.* 3,8;10;22 (= *SB* III 6277)	Κλειτάρχ[ωι τραπεζ]ίτηι τοῦ Κωίτου (7-8); ἐγχειρίσαντα τοῦ Κωίτου (10, *supra lineam*); τραπεζίτηι τοῦ Κωίτου (22)

---

[1] Cf. *TAVO B 69*, p.74; BERNARD P. GRENFELL - ARTHUR S. HUNT, *P.Hib.* I, Introduction, p.9. See also NIKOS LITINAS, «Κυνῶν πόλις and Εὐεργητίς. Designation and location of the capital of the Cynopolite nome», *APF* 40, 1994, pp.143-155. It will be noted that Al Qais/Κυνῶν πόλις is about 25 km south of even the southernmost Herakleopolite villages: how could Ptolemy locate it on the same latitude as Ko? This, however, can be explained with measures wrongly assessed in the survey Ptolemy is relying upon (cf. *Introduction*, p.5 n.3): Ἀγκυρῶν πόλις, for instance, is located too far to the north. It is only fair to remark that blunders almost as serious as Ptolemy's have been detected in the maps published as part of the *Description de l'Égypte*: cf. *TAVO B 69*, p.30.

[2] An identification with Qāi, as suggested in *TAVO B 69* § 4.3 (M 119), would be inconsistent with the location of Ko in the southern Herakleopolites.

CATALOGUE

227/226 B.C.	*SB* III 6301,8;11	Κλειτάρχωι τραπε[ζίτηι τοῦ] Κω[ίτου (8); τὴν τράπεζαν το[ῦ Κωίτου] (11)[1]
226/225 B.C.	*P.Ross.Georg.* II 3,5;7	[τοῦ] Κωίτου
246-222 B.C.	*P.Hib.* II 203,15	ἀρχιφυλακίτου τοῦ Κωίτου
163-162 B.C.(?)	*P.Hels.* I 21,4	Κωίτου
2 Sept. 162 B.C.	*P.Hels.* I 26 A 3;6;11;23;24	τὸν Κωίτην καὶ τὴν Τεχθὼ Νῆσον καὶ τὸ Πέρα (2-4); Κωίτου (6;24); Κω(ίτου) (11); Κωίτ̣ου (23)
after 52/51 B.C.	*BGU* VIII 1808,16	Κωίτου
mid-I B.C.	*SB* VIII 9790,1	Ἀλεξάνδρωι στρατηγῶι Κωίτου
I B.C.	*BGU* VIII 1764,10	ἐκ τοῦ Κωίτου
I B.C.	*BGU* XIV 2434,8	[Κω]ί̣του
I/II A.D.	*P.Hib.* II 272,4	ἀπὸ κώμης Ψύχεως τοῦ κάτωι Κωίτου
4 June 109 A.D.	*P.Rein.* 98,4	[τοῦ] Κοείτου
3 July 138 A.D.	*P.Heid.* IV 320,1	οἱ δύο χωμ(ατεπιμεληταὶ) Κωϊτῶ(ν) δύο
18 Nov. 162, 20 Feb. 163 A.D.	*P.Heid.* IV 321,5	πρ(άκτορι) ἀργυρικ(ῶν) Κωίτου Ἄνω (4-5)
169-177 A.D. (cf. *BL* 8,410)	*PSI* XIII 1325,8	τοῦ Κωίτου
II-III A.D.[2]	*BGU* III 958a	Κωίτου ἄνω Ψωλε[
2 July 225 A.D.[3]	*P.Vind.Bosw.* 7,3	δι'ἐπιτηρητῶν ἀγ[ο]ρ[ανομίας] [Κωί]του κάτω τοῦ ὑπὲρ Μέμφ[ιν Ἡ]ρακλεοπολείτου
231 A.D.	*Stud.Pal.* XX 32,8	Κωίτου ἄνω

---

[1] «Der Papyrus stellt die Außenschrift dar, deren Innenschrift *SB* III 6277 (= *P.Grad.* 3) ist» (Ed. *ad loc.*).

[2] This papyrus was burnt in a fire in the port of Hamburg (see *Introduction*, p.27): it was assigned to the Roman period in the *editio princeps*, but this date can be narrowed down because of the reference to the southern Koites, since the earliest document attesting the distinction between a northern and a southern (κάτω and ἄνω) Koites is dated to 138 A.D.

[3] On this dating, see JEAN A. STRAUS, *Chr.d'Ég.* 69, 1994, pp.305-307.

241/242 A.D.	*P.Vind.Tand.* 11,15;40	Κωίτου (15); Κωίτου ἄνω (40)
III A.D. (first half)	*CPR* I 82,II,4	δι' ἐπιτηρ]ητῶν ἀγορανομίας Κωίτου κάτω [τοῦ ὑπὲρ Μέμφιν Ἡρακλεοπολείτου]
III A.D. (second half)[1]	*P.Lond.* II 171 b,8 (p.176)	τοῦ Κωίτου

As a rule, documents which mention the Koites in connection to one or more of its villages do not appear here: these are listed and discussed under the entries for the relevant villages. See p.293 for a list of the villages belonging to this toparchy.

Since the third century B.C., Phebichis (see *s.v.*) regularly appears as the main village in the Koites: the Phebichis toparchy of a number of documents dating from the first century B.C. should therefore be the same as, or at least part of the Koites. *SB* VIII 9790, a petition addressed to the strategos of the Koites, apparently indicates that the Koites was an independent district in the later Ptolemaic period (unless the ὑποστρατηγός was meant here).

A division into northern (Κάτω) and southern (Ἄνω[2]) Κωίτης is attested in the documents of the Roman period[3].

ΚΩΠΡΥΑΣ

VIII A.D.	*Stud.Pal.* X 226,6	ἐποί'κ'(ιον) Κωπρυας

ETYMOLOGY: this could be a misspelling of the copronym Κοπρίας, Κοπρέας, on which see OLIVIER MASSON, *ZPE* 112, 1996, pp.146-150. Cf. also SARAH B. POMEROY, «Copronyms and the Exposure of Infants in Egypt», in *Studies in Roman Law in Memory of A. Arthur Schiller*, Leiden 1986, pp.147-162; DEBORAH HOBSON, «Naming Practices in Roman Egypt», *BASP* 26, 1989, pp.163-164.

The ἐποίκιον Μ(ε)γ(άλου) Κρούστου is entered at l.4 of the same document.

Λ[±2].[±2]

VII-VIII A.D.	*Stud.Pal.* X 227,7	ἀπ[ὸ] χ(ωρίου) Λ[±2].[±2]η[4]

---

[1] See GUIDO BASTIANINI, *ZPE* 39, 1980, p.154 n.30.

[2] Cf. *SB* XVI 12814, 4-5: ἀπὸ κώμης Ἱππώνων τοῦ Ἡρακλεοπολείτου ἄνω.

[3] The denomination «second toparchy», apparently coinciding with περὶ Φέβιχιν, in a document later than 212 A.D. (*P.Lund.* VI 8,5 and 9,4-5: τοπαρχία β περὶ Φέβιχιν), if correctly deciphered, is an isolated case.

[4] ἀπὸ χ(ωρίου) Χ..... *ed.pr.* Reading checked by Johannes Diethart (letter of February 25, 1994).

CATALOGUE

ΛΕΒΕΤΡ...

| II/III A.D. | *O.Wilck.* II 1125,2 | σιτολ(όγοι) Λεβετρ... |

TOPARCHY: Bousiris.

Forty donkeys from Bousiris are employed in the transport of goods. The reference to σιτολόγοι Λεβετρ... has been added by a second hand.

ΛΕΙΘΕΩΣ

| I/II A.D. | *P.Hib.* II 218,43 | Λείθεως |

TOPARCHY: Koites.

Tosachmis precedes in the same list (1.42).

ΛΕΥΚΟΓΙΟΝ

I A.D.	*P.Oxy.* XLII 3052,10	⟦Λευκογε⟧
154 A.D.	*P.Mil.Vogl.* IV 214 verso,21;22	τῆς Λευκογ(ίου) (21); ἰς τ(ὴν) πόλ(ιν) Λευκ(ογίου) (22) (cf. *BL* 6,88) [1]
169-177 A.D. (cf. *BL* 9,32)	*BGU* XIII 2326, fr. **a**,4;7-9; fr. **b**,2;3;6-8;10-15;17	εἰς Λευκογῖον
23 July 297 A.D.	*O.Mich.* I 179,2-3	ἐπιμ(ελητὴς) ὅρμου Λευκογείου
late III/early IV A.D.	*O.Mich.* I 254,3	ἐπιμελητὴς θησαυρὸν (*sic*) Λευκογίου (2-3)
22 May 302 A.D.	*SB* VI 9632,3-4 (= *O.Mich.*I 253)	Λευ[κο(γίου)]
4 Jan. 304 or 312 A.D.	*O.Mich.* III 1079,4	εἰς ὅρμον Λευκογίου
17 Jan. 304 or 312 A.D.	*O.Mich.* I 525,3	εἰς ὅρμο(ν) Λευκογ(ίου)
17 Jan. 304 or 312 A.D.	*O.Mich.* I 526,3	εἰ]ς ὅρμον Λευκογίου
17 Jan. 304 or 312 A.D.	*O.Mich.* II 927,4	εἰς ὅρμον Λευκο(γίου) (3-4)
18 Sept. 304 or 312 A.D. (?)	*O.Mich.* III 1080,3	εἰς ὅρμον Λευκογ(ίου)

---

[1] The Editor's supplements are Λευκογ(αίου) and Λευκ(ογαίου), respectively at l.21 and l.22 - but I see no reason to postulate such a variant spelling in this document.

3 Sept. 307 A.D.	*P.Cair.Isid.* 46,2	ἐποικίου Λευκογίου
5 Sept. 308 A.D.(?)	*O.Mich.* I 516,7-8	ἐν ὅρμῳ Λευκογίου
308-310 A.D.	*P.Col.* VII 141,40	ἐν ὅρμῳ Λευκογίου
after 30 Nov. 309 A.D.	*P.Cair.Isid.* 9 *verso*,282;284	Λευκογίου
309 A.D.	*P.Cair.Isid.* 47,39;42	ὅρμου Λευκογίου (39); ἐν τῷ αὐτῷ ὅρμῳ Λευκογίου (42)
probably 309/310 A.D.	*O.Mich.* I 517,5	ἐν ὅρμῳ Λευκογίου (4-5)
28 Jan. 311 A.D.(?)	*O.Mich.* I 520,5	ἐν ὅρ(μῳ) Λευκο(γίου)
13 Jan. 312 A.D.	*O.Mich.* I 524,3	εἰς ὅρμον Λευκογ(ίου)
4 Nov. 312 A.D. (cf. *BL* 8,227)	*P.NYU* 4a,2;7	ἀποδέκται ὅρμο[υ] Λευκογίου (2); ἐν τῷ αὐτῷ ὅρμῳ Λευκογίου (6-7)
23 July 315 A.D. (cf. *BL* 8,528)	*O.Mich.* II 930,4	ἐν ὅρμῳ Λευκογείου
316 A.D.	*P.Mich.* IX 573,8;[13]	ἀποδέκταις ὅρμ[ου] Λευκογείου (8); ὅρμῳ Λε[υκογείῳ (13)
25 July 318 A.D.(?) (cf. also *BL* 8,527)	*O.Mich.* I 532,3	ἐν ὅρμου Λευκογίου
5-12 Sept. 324 A.D.	*P.Sakaon* 22,7;11 (= *P.Thead.* 34)	κωμάρχοι ἐποικίου Λευκογίου (7); Λευκογίου (11)
333 or 348 A.D.	*P.NYU* 11,2;6	ἐν ὅρμῳ Λευκογί[ου (2); ἐν ὅρμῳ Λευκογίου (5-6)
334/335 A.D.	*P.Col.* VII 144, 1-2;6;11;13;18;20	ἐν ὅρμ(ῳ) Λευκογ[ίο]υ (1-2); ἐν ὅρμου Λευκογίου (6); <ἐν ὅ>ρμου Λευκογίου (13); ἐν ὅρμου Λευκογίου (18); ἀπὸ Λευκογίου (20)
338-342 A.D. (cf. *BL* 8,227)	*P.NYU* 11a,12;26;30;69; 114;151;182;192;199	ἐν ὅρμῳ Λευκογίου (11-12;25-26; 29-30;114); ἐν ὅρμου Λευκογίου (69); ὑποδ(έκτων) ὅρμου Λευκωγίου (151); ὑποδέκτας ὅρμου Λευκωγίο[υ (182); ὅρμῳ Λευκογείου (192); ἐν Λευκογίῳ (199)

CATALOGUE

343-345 A.D.	*P.Col.* VII 152, 35;50-51	ἐν ὅρμου Λευκογίου (35); ἐν ὅρμου Λευκογίου (50-51)
345-351 A.D.	*P.Col.* VII 161,2;21	ἐν ὅρμ(ῳ) Λευκογίου (2); ἐν ὅρμῳ Λευκογίου (21)
345-354 A.D.	*P.Col.* VII 160,2;7;14-15;19-20;31;36;45-46;50-51;69	ἐν ὅρμου Λευκογίου (2;7;19-20;36;69); ἐν ὅρμῳ Λευκογίου (14-15;31;45-46;50-51)
348 A.D.	*P.Col.* VII 163,2	ἐν ὅρ]μου Λευκωγίου (1-2)
early IV A.D.	*O.Mich.* I 534,3-4	εἰς ὅρμον Λευκογίου
early IV A.D.	*O.Mich.* I 541,3	ἐν ὅρμῳ [Λε]υκογ[ίου]
early IV A.D.	*O.Mich.* I 545,5	ἐν ὅρμῳ Λευκογ(ίου)
early IV A.D.	*O.Mich.* II 931,4	ἐν ὅρμου Λευκογίου
early IV A.D.	*P.Mich.* XII 647,3	ἀποδέκται ὅρμου Λευκογίου
IV A.D.	*P.Abinn.* 11,12 (= *P.Lond.* II 405 [p.294])	ἐν τῷ Λευκοκίου
VI A.D.	*CPR* VI 7,6-7	ἀπὸ τοῦ Λευκογίου κτήματος
VI A.D.	*P.Dub.* 24,3	ἀπὸ τοῦ Λευκογίου κτήματος τοῦ Ἡρακλεουπολίτου νομοῦ
VI A.D.	*Stud.Pal.* X 234,2	ἀπὸ κώμης Λευκογίου
VI or VII A.D.	*P.Lond.* II 392 (p.333),3	Λευκωγίου (cf. *BL* 7,85)
VI/VII A.D.	*PUG* I 50,6	Λευκογίου (cf. *BL* 7,276)
611/612 A.D.?	*P.Dub.* 28,4;6	ἐν Λε(υκογίου) κ(ώμῃ) (4); ἀπὸ κ]ώμης Λευκογίου (6)
4 Oct. 698 A.D.	*CPR* VIII 76,2 (= *Stud.Pal.* VIII 1186)	ἀπὸ χ(ωρίου) Ἰσίου ὑπὲρ τ(οῦ) χω(ρίου) Λευκ(ο)γ(ίου)
VII A.D.	*SB* XX 15092,5;8 [1]	ἐν Λευκογίῳ (5); ἀπὸ κώμης Λευκογίου τοῦ Ἡρ[ακλεοπολί]του νομοῦ (8-9)
VII A.D.	*Stud.Pal.* III 68,3	ἀπὸ κώμης Λευκογίο'υ'

---

[1] *Ed. pr.*: ROBERT HÜBNER, *ZPE* 84, 1990, pp.31-43.

VII A.D.	*Stud.Pal.* VIII 952,2	Λευκογι( )
VII A.D.	*Stud.Pal.* X 149,8	Λευκ(ογίῳ)
VII/VIII A.D.	*SB* VI 9262,2	ἀπὸ χ(ωρίου) Λευκογ(ίου)
719 A.D.	*Stud.Pal.* III 258,4 (= *P.Grenf.* II 105)	ἀπὸ χ(ωρίου) Λευκ(ογίου)
719 A.D.	*Stud.Pal.* III 259,4 (= *P.Grenf.* II 106)	Λευκογεί(ο)'υ'
28 Oct. 729 A.D.	*SB* XX 14234,2 [1]	ἀπὸ χ(ωρίου) Λευκο(γίου)

TOPARCHY: first assigned to the Herakleopolites in the sixth century A.D. (see below); 5th *pagus* of the Arsinoite nome (*P.Cair.Isid.* 47,39)[2].

ETYMOLOGY: possibly from the adjective λευκόγειος =λευκόγαιος =λευκόγεως, «of white earth» (cf. *CPR* VI 7,6 n.)

BIBLIOGRAPHY: TIMM, *Das christlich-koptische Ägypten*, vol.III, p.1494.

First attested by *P.Oxy.* XLII 3052 (itinerary of a journey into the Arsinoites and further south), where the scribe began to write its name at 1.10, then crossed it out and wrote Κενη (= Καινή?) above it.

Λευκόγιον, «the southern Nile port for the Arsinoite nome»[3], is not assigned to the Herakleopolites before the sixth century A.D. (*Stud.Pal.* X 234). In the seventh century A.D., *Stud.Pal.* III 68 is a receipt for a payment by two inhabitants of Onnes (which was assigned to the Tekmi toparchy during the Ptolemaic period) to the owner of two arourae they lease from him: this man is ἀπὸ κώμης Λευκογίου τοῦ αὐτοῦ (*scil.* Ἡρακλεοπολείτου) νομοῦ[4]. *P.Dub.* 24 and *SB* XX 15092 (money loan) also assign Λευκόγιον to the Herakleopolites.

Most documents mentioning Λευκόγιον relate to payments in kind, or deliveries (wheat, barley, chaff, grass, etc.) to the officials of the ὅρμος. The documents point to close connections with the Arsinoites (Karanis, Theadelpheia) and to links with other ports (Κεφαλαί, in the Herakleopolites: *BGU* XIII 2326; Kerke, in the Memphites: *P.Cair.Isid.* 9 and 47; Ἀρσινοϊτῶν πόλις: *P.Col.* VII 152, 160, 161 and 163).

P.Lond. II 392 and *PUG* I 50 refer to a μονή Λευκογίου: in the second document, Abraham acknowledges the receipt of «the annual wage, for which I operate the water-wheel ... (in the land) of the monastery of Leukogion»[5]. People living in the nearby area may have had to pay *annonae* to those in charge of the maintenance of the μονή[6]. The Λευκογίου κτῆμα of *CPR* VI 7 may have been connected to the monastery. In *CPR* VIII 76 the *dux* Flavius Atias instructs that a priest ἀπὸ χ(ωρίου) Ἰσίου ὑπὲρ

---

[1] *Ed. pr.*: GÜNTER POETHKE - PIETER J. SIJPESTEIJN, *APF* 38, 1992, pp.34-35.

[2] «All'ingresso meridionale dell'Arsinoite» (CALDERINI-DARIS, *Dizionario, s.v.*)

[3] Cf. *P.Abinn.* 11,12 n.; see also LEIV AMUNDSEN, *O.Oslo*, p.51.

[4] The connection between Leukogion and Onnes is also supported by the fact that these two are the only Herakleopolite villages mentioned in the *P.Dub.* (though in different documents: Onnes appears in *P.Dub.* 25 and 26).

[5] Translation by HERBERT C. YOUTIE, *ZPE* 23, 1976, p.113.

[6] *Ibid.*, p.112 n.9.

τ(οῦ) χω(ρίου) Λευκ(ο)γ(ίου) should cultivate one aroura east of a kleros called Φαειμ (1.4): according to the Editors, this wording may either refer to the location of Ἴσιον («south of Λευκόγιον»), or it may indicate that Ἴσιον had «eine gewisse Haftung für Leukogion».

ΛΕΥΚΟΥ

| 26 Feb. 538 A.D. | P.Michael.126,10 | ἀπὸ κώμης Λευκοῦ |

An ὁμολογία document (for which «no satisfactory interpretation is possible», according to its Editor) drawn up at Tinteris: the parties are ἀπὸ Νίλου πόλει [τοῦ] Ἡρακλεοπολίτου νομοῦ and ἀπὸ Λευκοῦ τοῦ αὐτοῦ νομοῦ. The three place-names are all wrongly spelt (Λευκοῦ = Λευκ<ογί>ου?); besides, this document shows a number of other peculiar spelling mistakes[1]. A κώμη Λευκίου is attested in the Oxyrhynchite nome[2].

ΛΙΝΗ

| 12/11 B.C. | BGU IV 1197,I,9 | οἱ μὲν ἀπὸ Λινῆ καὶ Κόμα κωμῶν [ἱ]γερῖς |
| 2/1 B.C. | BGU IV 1200, [16], [20],24 | ἀπὸ [κ]ώμης Λινῆ] (16); [ἀπὸ Λινῆ] (20); ἀπὸ Λινῆ (24) |

TOPARCHY: Koma?

The two documents reveal a conflict between the priests (note the spelling ἱγερῖς) from Bousiris and those from Line and Koma about government allowances. According to BGU IV 1202 (18 B.C.) subsidies were granted to priests from Onnes (Tekmi toparchy), but it is unfortunately impossible to verify whether Onnes (often mentioned in connection with Bousiris) was written instead of Line: «BGU IV 1197 und 1200 sind seit dem letzten Krieg verschollen»[3].

ΛΙΝΥ..ΡΕΩΣ

| 19 Oct. 163 B.C. | P.Hels. I 15,7;14 | ἐκ κώμης Λινυ..ρέως (6-7); ἐν τῆι αὐ[τῆι] Λινυ....... (13-14)[4] |

---

[1] It is not among the P.Michael. recently acquired by the Cambridge University Library. On items from the Michaelides collection recently acquired by some European libraries see SARAH J. CLACKSON, ZPE 100, 1994, pp.223-226.

[2] See ROSARIO PINTAUDI-PIETER J. SIJPESTEIJN, «Prestito di grano (PL III/959)», Analecta Papyrologica 6, 1994, pp.145-147.

[3] Günter Poethke by letter (April 14, 1994).

[4] Very doubtful reading: «Der Dorfname war bisher nicht bekannt und ist schwer zu entziffern. Der erste Buchstabe ist kein Alpha, könnte aber ein Ny sein» (ed. pr. ad loc.).

The document is a declaration concerning orchards (one of them with palms in it).

ΛΟΛΛΙΑΝΟΥ

VII A.D.	*Stud.Pal.* X 214,2	ἐν τό'π'(ῳ) διόρ'υ'(γος) Λολλιανο[ῦ

The πεδία Περομ, Πουεν, Πλεμεδεου, Θαλμι, Μαλκουλι, Ψανατι, and the τόπος Πκατανω are also listed in this document.

ΜΑ[

VII-VIII A.D.	*Stud.Pal.* X 227,3	ἀπὸ [χ(ωρίου)] Μα[[1]

Talae (Koites) is among the villages listed in the same document.

ΜΑΓΔ[ ]Χ( ) or ΜΑΣΤ[ ]Χ( ) [2]

I/II A.D.	*P.Hib.* II 218,37

Sobthis (l.38), then Peenameus (l.39) follow in this long list of Herakleopolite place-names (most, but not all, in the Koites).

ΜΑΓΔΩΛΑ

96-94 or 63-61 B.C.	*BGU* XIV 2429,7	Μαγδῶ(λα)
I B.C.	*BGU* XIV 2436,1;14	Μαγδῶ(λα)
II/III A.D.	(?) *O.Wilck.* II 1124,5	Μαγδώλων [3]
late III A.D.	*BGU* XIII 2365,3	Μαγδ(ῶλα)
VII-VIII A.D.	*Stud.Pal.* X 200,3	χ'ω'(ρίον) Μαγδολον (cf. *BL* 8,459: *lege* Μαγδώλων)

---

[1] Μο[also possible, according to the Editor.

[2] A very uncertain reading: Μαγδωλ() is tempting, though deemed impossible in the *ed. pr.* If Μαστι]χ(), the fossil kleros Μαστιγοφόρου (*BGU* XI 2072,59,65,71; II A.D.; from the Arsinoites?) could be compared. *BGU* XI 2072 contains a register of fossil kleroi, many of them split and re-distributed by numbered κληρουχίαι, while recorded under the names of the present land-holders.

[3] There is a possibility (but no certainty) that this might be the Herakleopolite Magdola, as many of the ostraka published by Wilcken in this collection refer to Herakleopolite localities.

VIII A.D. *Stud.Pal.* X 204,1 χ'ω'(ρίον) Μαγδολ'ω'(ν)

TOPARCHY: Magdola seems to have been in the proximity of an intersection between the borders of the Tekmi, περὶ Πόλιν, Ἄγημα and Πέραν toparchies.
A homonymous village is well attested in the Arsinoites (modern Medinet Nehas).
ETYMOLOGY: *Mktl* (cf.*P.Köln Ägypt.* 5,7; see also note *ad loc.*): this is a place-name of Semitic origin, meaning «watch-tower»[1].

MODERN ARABIC NAME: Kōm Madīnat Gurāb? (See *Introduction*, p.10).

BGU XIV 2436, 1-3: Orestes' kleros is split between Magdola, an Ἰβιών locality, Pois, Ogou (Tekmi toparchy: in the same document with Magdola also in *Stud.Pal.* X 204) and Peensamoi, in the Πέραν toparchy. Another kleros, also near Magdola, is entered in *BGU* XIV 2436,14.

BGU XIV 2429 lists several villages, many in the Ἄγημα toparchy (among these Kollasoucha, on the same line with Magdola, Niseus and Nino), besides Sobthis, Mouchis (Tekmi toparchy), and Hiera Nesos (9).

ΜΑΙΟΥΜΑ

V A.D.	*Stud.Pal.* X 233, col. II,4	Μειουμα
540/541 A.D. (cf. *BL* 6,105)	*P.Oxy.* XVI 2032,41	προν(οητῇ) Μαειουμᾶ
VII-VIII A.D.	*Stud.Pal.* X 209,4	χ(ωρίον) Μαιουμα

ETYMOLOGY: «Le nom, dont on admet l'origine sémitique, ne se retrouve que sous graphie grecque, latine ou arabe. Son étymologie indiquerait ... un quartier maritime. Nous connaissons trois Maiouma en Palestine ... . En Égypte, il désignait peut-être certains endroits le long du Nil ou au bord d'un canal, où, à l'origine, des colonies juives s'étaient établies?»[2]

This is most likely the same village as the Maiouma attested, always in connection with the Apion estate, in several documents from the Oxyrhynchites[3]. *Stud.Pal.* X 233, however, certainly refers to the Herakleopolites (our village is listed immediately before Chortaso, possibly in the Πέραν toparchy); at least two Herakleopolite villages (Nois and Kollasoucha) are among those listed in *Stud.Pal.* X 209.
Maiouma must have been one of the villages near the boundary between the Herakleopolites and the Oxyrhynchites. This hypothesis is supported by an account of receipts and expenditure on one of the estates of Flavius Apion jr., where Maiouma is associated with «other outside places»[4].

---

[1] «Il désigne une tour de guet permettant de surveiller les abords du désert et de prévenir les incursions des Bédouins, en quête de pillage, qui menaçaient la sécurité des villages et des routes caravanières» (DREW-BEAR, *Le nome Hermopolite*, p.157); see also ALAN H. GARDINER, «The Ancient Military Road between Egypt and Palestine», *JEA* 6, 1920, pp.107-110.

[2] JOSEPH VAN HAELST, *Chr. d'Ég.* 67, 1959, p.297.

[3] Listed by PRUNETI, *Centri abitati*, s.v.

[4] *P.Oxy.* VI 999 (descr.): σὺν το(ῖς) ἄλλοις μέρ(εσι) (καὶ) Μα[ρ]γαρίτου καὶ ἄλλ(ων) ἐξωτικ(ῶν) τόπων.

ΜΑΚΑΙΤΟΝΟΣ

VII A.D.	*SB* VI 9590,[2];11;[16]	ἀπὸ Μακαίτ[(2); Μακαίτονος (11)[1]; Μακαιτ[(16)
VIII A.D.	*Stud.Pal.* X 204,2	χ'ω'(ρίον) Μακαι'δ'( )

ETYMOLOGY: this could be a late writing for the genitive of Μακεδών, Μακεδόνος, which is attested as a personal name in *P.Ryl.* II 227,18 (third century A.D.).

SB VI 9590: two arourae which Anatolios (from Herakleopolis) cedes to Pamoûn are apparently split between Makaitonos, Tebetny (Πέραν toparchy) and Chortaso, and situated to the west of the γήδια Ἀπαλά, ἐν κλήρῳ καλουμένῳ Τσαβα. These are ceded in exchange for two arourae near a κώμη (1.12) whose name is lost at the beginning of l.13: note, however, the reference to Noeris at l.22. The two witnesses are both from Herakleopolis.

Other villages listed in *Stud.Pal.* X 204 include: Magdola (1), Ogou (4; Tekmi toparchy), Psychis (B,2; Koites).

ΜΑΛΚΟΥΛΙ

VII A.D.	*Stud.Pal.* X 214,6	ἐν π(εδίῳ) Μαλκουλι( )

Peroe is on top of the list in this document.

ΜΑΡΩΝΟΣ

227 A.D.	*Stud.Pal.* XX 29,23

TOPARCHY: Koites.

One of several κλῆροι, including a κλῆρος Διδυμιανοῦ (entered on the same line) and some fossil kleroi[2], referred to in a sale contract for land near Tosachmis.

ΜΑΧΟΡ

mid-III B.C.[3]	*P.Cair.Zen.* IV 59782 (b),29;47;69;85(?);91	[ἐγ] Μαχόρ (29); ἐκ Μαχό[ρ (47); ἐγ Μαχόρ (69); ..[.]χορ...[(85); ἐγ Μαχόρ (91)

---

[1] «Sollte/könnte man bei diesem Wort nicht an "koptisch" geschriebenes Μακέδονος denken dürfen?» (Johannes Diethart, letter of September 13, 1994).

[2] See *s.v.* Νεπωτιανοῦ, and the list of *Fossil Kleroi* (below, pp.273 ff.).

[3] On the dating of this document see above, p.60 n.3.

CATALOGUE

212/211 B.C.	*P.Lille* I 59,57;92;105;116	
after 84/83 B.C.	BGU XIV 2370 (fr.1),75	Μ[α]χόρ [1]
61/60 B.C.	BGU VIII 1815,5	ἐκ κώμης Μαχόρ
60/59 B.C.	BGU VIII 1819,3	ἀπὸ Μαχόρ
I B.C.	BGU XIV 2439,26;97;103	Μαχ[ό]ρ (97)
12 B.C.	BGU IV 1167,48;72	περὶ κώ(μην) Μαχόρ (48); περὶ κώμη(ν) Μαχὸρ ἐκ τοῦ ⟦κλήρου⟧ Ἱεροξένο(υ) κλήρου (72)
8 B.C.	BGU IV 1104,30	κώ(μη..) Μαχόρ
I B.C.	BGU XVI 2674,40;58;137	Μαχορί'τ'(ης) (40); Μαχορ(ίτης) (58;137)
132 A.D.	*P.Bon.* 18, col.I,4; col.II,5; col.III,3-4	ἀπ[ὸ] κώμ(ης) Μαχόρ (I,4); [ἀπ]ὸ κώμ(ης) [Μ]αχ[όρ (II,5); [ἀπὸ κώμ(ης) Μα]χόρ (III,3-4)
late II or III A.D.	*P.Ryl.* II 225,49	Μαχόρ [2]
first half of III A.D.	*CPR* I 159,5	Μαχώρ [3]
V A.D.	*MPER* XV 103,17	πεδ(ίον) Μαχόρεως
V A.D.	*P.Oxy.* XVI 2017,5;14	Μαχόρεως [4]

TOPARCHY: Koma.

Machor is associated with Koma, Krekis and Toou in *P.Lille* I 59, *P.Cair.Zen.* IV 58782 b, *BGU* XIV 2439 and *BGU* XVI 2674 (accounts; possibly a tax-list); with Koma again in *P.Ryl.* II 225.

Two fossil kleroi are attested in the Machor area: Ἱεροξένου (*BGU* IV 1167) and [Ζ]ωί̣λ(ου) (*BGU* IV 1104) [5].

BGU VIII 1815 is a petition submitted to the strategos by the villagers left at Machor, asking for some relief from taxes and compulsory work after many other inhabitants have abandoned the village.

P.Bon. 18: fragment of a τόμος συγκολλήσιμος containing three census declarations: at least two of these concern Egyptian inhabitants of Machor [6].

---

[1] .[.]χορ *ed. pr.*, where two possible supplements are offered: χόρ[του] or Μ[α]χορ. As all other figures in this fragment refer to money payments, χόρ[του] seems unlikely to recur here. The immediately preceding reference to Toou further supports the reading Μ[α]χορ, as Machor recurs with Koma (also listed in this document) and Toou in other sources, too.

[2] περὶ Κομαμαχόρ *ed. pr.*: the correct word division should be περὶ Κόμα· Μαχόρ.

[3] Reading checked for me by Johannes Diethart (letter of February 25, 1994).

[4] My reading (checked for me by Revel A. Coles, letter of August 8, 1994: «clear in l.5; less clear in l.14»): Μαχόφεως (l.5), Μαχοφεως (l.14) *ed. pr.*

[5] A fossil kleros Ζωίλου is also mentioned in *BGU* XIV 2450 (ll.28,80,82).

[6] Corrections to cols. I and II of this document have been made by ROGER S. BAGNALL, *BASP* 28, 1991, pp.122-123.

ΜΕ[

between 173 and 130-128 B.C. (cf. *BL* 7,273)	*P.Tebt.* III 890,97	ἐκ Με[

TOPARCHY: Μέση?

Bank accounts. Other villages mentioned: Tantoka (l.7), Phnebieus (ll.74,75,100; Μέση), Koll(is) (l.81).

ΜΕΣΗ (toparchy)

161/160 B.C.	*P.Hels.* I 29,35	Μέσης
II B.C.	(?)*P.Münch.* III 61,22	
I B.C.	*BGU* VIII 1802,1	]τῆς Μέσης
about 7-4 B.C.	*BGU* XVI 2662,12	Μέσης
227 A.D.	*CPR* I 64,5 (= *SB* I 5165)	δι' ἐπιτηρητῶν ἀγορανομ[ίας] μερῶν Μέσης Πεενάμεως (4-5)
227 A.D.	*Stud.Pal.* XX 28,5 (= *CPR* I 7)	δι' ἐπιτηρητῶν ἀγορανομ[ίας] μερῶν Μέσης Πεε[ν]άμε(ως)(4-5)
228/229 A.D.	*SB* I 4370,5(?)	δι' ἐπιτηρητῶν ἀγορανομίας [Μέσης Πεενάμε(ως)] (4-5)

See also *s.v.* "ΑΓΗΜΑ.

A list of villages that can be assigned to this toparchy will be found on p.294.

Different documents, at a distance of about three centuries, assign the village of Peenameus first to Ἄγημα κάτω (in the first century B.C.: *BGU* XIV 2437), then to the Μέση toparchy: in A.D. 227 *Stud.Pal.* XX 28, a contract involving people from Peenpibyk(is) (in the Μέση), is registered δι'ἐπιτηρητῶν ἀγορανομίας μερῶν Μέσης Πεενάμεως; *CPR* I 64, also referring to villages of the Μέση toparchy (Thmoinothis, Kerkytos, Phys) issues from the same office. The fact that another contract (*Stud.Pal.* XX 47), again involving a party from Peenpibyk(is), was drawn up δι' ἐπιτηρητῶν ἀγορανομίας μερῶν τοπαρχίας Ἀγήμ[ατος, confirms the contiguity between the Μέση and Ἄγημα (Κάτω) toparchies. It seems however difficult to assume that the name Μέση actually stood for (Ἄγημα) Μέση, as there would then be little space left for the Ἄγημα κάτω, north of Peenameus and south of Herakleopolis.

The Μέση toparchy mentioned in *P.Münch.* III 61 is probably the Herakleopolite toparchy by this name (even though an Arsinoite, and an Oxyrhynchite village recur in the same document) because other papyri bearing related inventory numbers originate from the Herakleopolites (see *s.v.* Ἄνω τοπαρχία).

ΜΕΣΣΑΛΙΝΙΑΝΗ (οὐσία)

I A.D.	*P.Ryl.* IV 684,3	Μεσ]σαλεινιανῶν ἐδάφων
II A.D.	*P.Bodl.* I 61 (g)	
7 Oct. 225 A.D. (cf. *BL* 9,293)	*SB* XVI 12836,8 [1]	ἀπομισθώτης Μεσσαλι[νιανῆς] οὐσίας (8-9)
early III A.D.	*P.Ryl.* II 87,4;7	Μεσσαλινιανὰ [ἐδάφη] (4); Μεσσαλινιανὰ [ἐδάφη] (7)

See *s.v.* ΑΓΚΥΡΩΝ ΠΟΛΙΣ.

ΜΙΚΡΟΥΑΛΙΧ

683/684 A.D.   *CPR* X 135,10

Land ἐν διαφόροις κλήροις: a kleros Ἀκώρου is mentioned in the same line.

(?)ΜΙΚ( ) ΠΡΟΣ( )

VII-VIII A.D.   *Stud.Pal.* X 209,3   χ(ωρίον?) Μι'κ'() Προσ() [2]

Other villages in this document include Kollasoucha (l.2; Ἄγημα toparchy) and Nois (l.5; περὶ Πόλιν toparchy).

ΜΟΛΩΘΙΣ

mid-III B.C.	*P.Strasb.* IX 802,20	Μολῶθις [3]
mid-I B.C.	*SB* VIII 9790,9	περὶ Μολῶθιν

TOPARCHY: Koites.

MODERN ARABIC NAME: Malatiya (but previously Maltiya)? See *TAVO* B 69, p.202. The identification seems possible on account of the phonetic similarity between ancient and modern toponym, and in view of

---

[1] Re-edited by PIETER J. SIJPESTEIJN, *BASP* 21, 1984, pp.211 ff.

[2] Reading revised for me by Johannes Diethart (letter of February 25, 1994). The *ed. pr.* offered χ(ωρίον) Μι'κ'(ροῦ) Προσ(). It is not certain that this is a place-name.-

[3] My reading (checked on a photograph): Μρῶθις *ed.pr.*

the southern location of Molothis. However, «nach. Auskunft der Dorfbewohner sollen in Malatiya keine antiken Relikten vorhanden sein» (*TAVO* B 69, p.202).

SB VIII 9790: petition to the strategos of the Koites, submitted by a woman from Phebichis who had inherited a kleros near Molothis.

Most, or all, villages listed in *P.Strasb*. IX 802 were in the Koites.

ΜΟΥΗ

IV A.D.   *P.Neph*. 12,23   εἰς Μουὴ κώμη(ν)

See also: ΝΗΣΩΝ[1].

BIBLIOGRAPHY: TIMM, *Das christlich-koptische Ägypten* IV, p.1688 (*s.v.* Mouei).

Letter from the monk Serapion concerning his trip to Omboi (Upper Egypt). The same village is attested in *CPR* IV 176 (l.13), a Coptic document.

ΜΟΥΧΕΜΠ()'ΟΥ'

VI/VII A.D.   (?)*SB* XX 15072,9

ETYMOLOGY: *mhy* («the storehouse, depot»: see *s.v.* ΜΟΥΧΙΣ) + -*n*- (genitive) + (?).

The editor of this document[2] suggested the supplement Μουχεμπ(αμ)ού(νεως) (a village in the Lycopolites). The document may in fact mention at least another Lycopolite village (l.1: Τάσρεως): however, Herakleopolite and Arsinoite place-names are prevalent (Σωυχεως, l.2, and Daphne, l.7, were certainly in the Herakleopolites).

ΜΟΥΧΕΝΝΩΜΘΟΥ

237 A.D.   *Stud.Pal*. XX 36,3;7 = *SB* I   [κ]ώμης Μουχεννώμθου
                 5136 = *CPGr* II 78

ETYMOLOGY: *mhy* («the storehouse, depot»: see *s.v.* ΜΟΥΧΙΣ) + -*n*- (genitive) + second element (the same component – νωμθ – may recur in the toponyms Μουχεννωμθου and Σχνῶμθις).

---

[1] «Das Griechisch des Serapion ist desolat. ... Den Namen des Dorfes, zu dem das Kloster Hathor gehört, schreibt er zwar mit griechischen Buchstaben aber, wie wir glauben, in der koptischen Übersetzung: εἰς Μουὴ κώμη(ν) entspricht dem griechischen εἰς Νήσων κώμην. Aufgrund dieser Beobachtungen läßt sich vermuten, daß Serapions Muttersprache vielleicht Koptisch war» (*P.Neph., Einleitung*, p.74).

[2] PIETER J. SIJPESTEIJN, *ZPE* 81, 1990, pp.245-251.

ΜΟΥΧΙΝΕΜΒΗΣ[1]

about 260 B.C.   *P.Hib.* I 112,45

TOPARCHY: Koites.

ETYMOLOGY: *mhy* («the storehouse, depot»: see *s.v.* ΜΟΥΧΙΣ) + *-n-* (genitive) + second element εμβης (as in ΨΕΒΘΟΝΕΜΒΗΣ: see *s.v.*): «Embes' storehouse». Cf. JEAN YOYOTTE, *RdÉ* 15, 1963, p.108, n.10; cf. also JAN QUAEGEBEUR, in *Studia Hellenistica* 24, pp.75-76 (on the meaning of the personal name Embes, which he interprets as *Wn-Bs*, «the creature (?) Bes»).

Several other villages mentioned in the same document certainly belonged to the Koites: Pselemachis, Phebichis, Assya, Psychis.

ΜΟΥΧΙΝΘΑΗ( )

I/II A.D.   *P.Hib.* II 218,22;24;29

ETYMOLOGY: *mhy* («the storehouse, depot»: see *s.v.* ΜΟΥΧΙΣ) + *-n-* (genitive) + second element = personal name: «Thaesis'(?) storehouse».

ΜΟΥΧΙΝΠΑΓΕΙ

20 A.D.   *P.Ross.Georg.* II 11 (= *CPGr* II 3),2   Μουχινπάγει καὶ τῶν συγκυρουσῶν κωμῶν

TOPARCHY: Koites.

ETYMOLOGY: *mhy* («the storehouse, depot»: see *s.v.* ΜΟΥΧΙΣ) + *-n-* (genitive) + second element = «Pagis' storehouse». Pagis (= Pais) is attested as a personal name (cf. *PPt* 253).

P.Ross.Georg. II 11: death declaration addressed to the komogrammateus of Mouchinpagei «and villages under the same administration», from a man living at Ankyron; in the subscription, the same official calls himself the komogrammateus of Ankyron.

ΜΟΥΧΙΝΠΑΣΙΣ

about 260 B.C.   *P.Hib.* I 112,27   Μουχινπάσις[2]

TOPARCHY: Koites.

---

[1] My reading (checked on a photograph): Μοῦχιν Ἐμγῆς *ed.pr.*

[2] Μοῦχιν Πᾶσις *ed. pr.*

ETYMOLOGY: *mhy* («the storehouse, depot»: see *s.v.* ΜΟΥΧΙΣ) + -*n*- (genitive) + second element = common Egyptian personal name: «Pasis' storehouse».

Several other villages mentioned in *P.Hib.* I 112 certainly belonged to the Koites: Pselemachis, Phebichis, Assya, Psychis.

ΜΟΥΧΙΣ

96-94 or 63-61 B.C.	*BGU* XIV 2429,8	Μούχεως
21 June 51 B.C.(?)[1]	*BGU* VIII 1832,9	περὶ Μ̣[οῦχιν?][2]
49/48 B.C.	*SB* V 8756,6	περὶ Μοῦχιν
I B.C.	*BGU* XIV 2437,18; (fr.4),70	Μούχεως (18); Μοῦχιν (70)
I B.C.	*BGU* XIV 2441,208	περὶ Μοῦ(χιν)
28/27 B.C.	*BGU* XVI 2665,6	[πε]ρὶ Μοῦχιν
28/29 A.D.	*P.Oxy.* XXIV 2412,99	Μούχε̣[ως]
I/II A.D.	*P.Hib.* II 218, 41; col. III	Μούχεως
late or middle II A.D.	*P.Hib.* II 280,16	ἐν κώ(μῃ) Μούχει
V A.D.	*Stud.Pal.* X 9,4	Μούχεως
V A.D.	*Stud.Pal.* X 47,2	Μούχεως
V A.D.	*Stud.Pal.* X 233, col. I B,5	Μούχεως
565/566 A.D.	(?)*P.Oxy.* XXVII 2480,2	ἀπὸ Μούχεως
VII/VIII A.D.	*CPR* IV 2,15	χ(ωρίον) Μούχ'ε'(ως)[3]
VIII A.D.	(?)*SB* XX 14236,1	χωρ(ίου) Μούχ(εως)[4]

TOPARCHY: Tekmi.

ETYMOLOGY: formed on the stem *mhy*, «the storehouse, depot»[5].

Villages by the same name are attested in the Oxyrhynchites (see PRUNETI, *Centri abitati, s.v.*, pp.110-111), the Arsinoites and elsewhere (see CALDERINI-DARIS, *Dizionario, s.v.*, vol.III, pp.301-302; *Suppl.*, p.200).

---

[1] Cf. 1.20: (ἔτους) λ καὶ α Πα(ῦνι) κ («year 30 which is also year 1»); see THEODORE C. SKEAT, *The Reigns of the Ptolemies*, München 1954, p.18.

[2] «Anfang M oder A, schwerlich Τ̣[έκμι]» (*ed. pr. ad loc.*).

[3] Μούχ'ε'() *ed.pr.*

[4] Cf. GÜNTER POETHKE-PIETER J. SIJPESTEIJN, *APF* 38, 1992, p.36.

[5] Cf. KATELIJN VANDORPE, «Mouchis or the Storehouse» (forthcoming).

MODERN ARABIC NAME: Dimšuwīya: cf. *TAVO* B 69, § 4.3 (M109), even though «es wurden keine antiken Relikte festgestellt» (*ibid.*, p.215).

Listed, with other villages, as belonging to the Tekmi toparchy in *BGU* XIV 2437 (ll.1-25): ll.18-20, in particular, contain the record of 25 arourae privately owned by Dionysios son of Paniskos, and split between Mouchis and Τωυ.

BGU XIV 2441 records land ceded by Apollonios son of Apollonios to Apollonios son of Chairemon: it is entered under the heading for Pyrgotos (l.19), in the same toparchy, but part of the land ceded was in the Mouchis area (l.208).

Mouchis also recurs with other villages of the Tekmi toparchy (Ogou, Kollintaathyr, Pyrgotos, Tekmi) in *P.Oxy.* XXIV 2412. *BGU* XVI 2665 mentions it along with Ogou (l.4) again: Nois (περὶ Πόλιν) and Talae (Koites) follow (ll.16-17).

BGU XIV 2437, fr.4: holding split between Mouchis and Sobthis (in the περὶ Πόλιν toparchy). Sobthis and Mouchis are again found together in *Stud.Pal.* X 9 (ll.2 and 4, respectively): the other villages mentioned in this document include Onnes (1), Phnebieus (3), Kerkesephis (5).

CPR IV 2 (a bilingual document in Coptic and Greek) lists many villages of the central toparchies of the Herakleopolite nome (toponyms in Greek)[1].

ΜΟΥ.Ω( )

late or middle II A.D.   *P.Hib.* II 280,13   ἐν κώ(μῃ) Μου.ω( )
Χανηι

Ν....[

mid-III B.C.   *P.Strasb.* IX 802,14

TOPARCHY: Koites.

P.Strasb. IX 802 lists Egyptian tax-payers and their villages, all of them apparently in Koites.

ΝΑΝΗΟΥΕΙ

411 A.D.   *Stud.Pal.* X 117,5   ἐν [π]εδίοις Φιλονίκου
ἐν ἐδάφι καλ[ο]υμέν[ῳ]
Νανηουει

TOPARCHY: Koites.

Stud.Pal. X 117 is a sale-contract stipulated at Koba.

---

[1] See *s.v.* ΝΙΝΩ.

ΝΕ.[

V/VI A.D.   MPER XV 75,4   τραπεζ(ίτη) Νε.[[1]

ΝΕ.ΑΤΕΩΣ

I/II A.D.   P.Hib. II 218,69

ΝΕΑ ΑΓΟΡΑ

26 June 4 B.C.   BGU XVI 2644,10   ἀπὸ Νέας Ἀγορᾶ<ς>

ETYMOLOGY: «New Market».

Letter to Athenodoros, epistates and dioiketes, concerning grain shipments to Koma, which are impeded by the requisitioning of all boats for the army: this apparently affected the price of grain at New Market.

ΝΕΑ ΠΟΛΙΣ

V A.D.   Stud.Pal. X 233, col. I B,13   Νέας Πόλεως κ(α)ὶ Τάχεως [2]

This toponym is attested in Egypt as the name of a district in Alexandria[3], generally mentioned in connection with *horrea*. All, or most of the other toponyms listed in this document belong to Herakleopolite places.

ΝΕΘΙΣΕΙ

VI A.D.   Stud.Pal. X 228,6   ἐν τόπ(ῳ) Νεθισει

Cf. Νεχίσης?

Listed with Pargou (l.4), Piatimi (l.5), Neuela (l.7), Σουριυ (l.8), Πιακερ (l.9).

---

[1] Cf. Νειλ() at l.4?

[2] New reading by Johannes Diethart (letter of February 25, 1994).

[3] Cf. MARGARET MAEHLER, «Trouble in Alexandria in a Letter of the Sixth Century», GRBS 17, 1976, p.199.

ΝΕΙ[

I/II A.D.   *P.Hib.* II 218,97

TOPARCHY: Koites?

Most villages listed in *P.Hib.* II 218 were in the Koites.

ΝΕΙΛΟΥ ΠΟΛΙΣ   (see also: ΤΙΛΩΘΙΣ)

5 Sept. 103 A.D. (cf. *BL* 6,83)	*P.Mich.* IX 551,11	ἀπὸ Νίλου πόλεως τοῦ Ἡρακλεωπωλίτου νομοῦ (11-13)
I/II A.D.	(?) *P.Osl.* III 151, 11-12	ἐν τῇ Νεί[λου πόλει]
II A.D.	*CPR* I 238 (fr.1),6	ἀπὸ Νείλου πόλεως
second half of II A.D.	*P.Oxy.* XLVII 3362,18-19 (= *SB* XII 11045)	Ἡρακλεοπολ]είτου· Νειλο[πολείτο]υ (*scil.* νομοῦ)
late II/early III A.D.	*P.Batav.* XXV 49,9	Νειλο[πολ]είτου [1]
222-235 A.D.	*CPR* I 73,9	ἀπὸ Νείλου [πόλ]ε[ως
20 Jan. 225 A.D.	*SB* XIV 11277,3;4	ἐν Νείλου πόλει τῇ μητροπόλει (3); ἀπὸ Νείλου πόλεως (4); cf. 1.8: τῆς αὐτῆς πόλεως
14 May 261 A.D. (cf. *BL* 3,21)	*BGU* VII 1568,2	Ν[ειλο]πο[λ]εί[το]υ (*scil.* νομοῦ) [2]
III A.D.	*O.Theb.* 132,3 (= *O.Bodl.* 164)	Νιλούπολιν (cf. l.1: Ἡρα]κλεο[πολίτου)
III A.D.	*SB* XIV 11620,4	Νειλου[πολίτ]ης [3]
late III A.D.	*P.Oxy.* XXIV 2415,85	ἀ[πὸ] τοῦ Νειλ[οπολ(ίτου)] (*scil.* νομοῦ)
338-340 A.D. (cf. *BL* 6,65)	*P.Lond.* V 1823 descr.,1	Νειλοπολίτου

---

[1] Νειλο[υπολ]είτου *ed. pr.*: but the normal form should be Νειλοπολίτης (as Willy Clarysse pointed out to me); cf. also *SB* XIV 11620 and *P.Med.* I^2 66 (listed below).

[2] Ν[ειλου]πο[λ]εί[το]υ *ed. pr.*: see preceding note.

[3] Even though the normal form should be Νειλοπολίτης (see above n.1), the trace before the lacuna is more compatible with υ than with π. The document contained a list of nomes, the names of the districts being preceded by signs for which no explanation has been offered: PIETER I. SIJPESTEIJN (*ZPE* 55, 1984, p.155) tentatively suggested that they may be hieroglyphic or demotic.

343 A.D.	*P.Med.* I² 66,1;8 (*verso*) = *SB* VI 9510	π(αρὰ) Αὐρηλίου Διονυσίου ἐξάκτορος Νει[λοπολείτου] (1); ἐξ(άκτορος) Νειλοπολείτου (8)¹
V A.D.	*CPR* VI 79,4; 6-7	βου(λευτὴς) Νείλου πόλεως (4); ἐν τῇ αὐτῇ πόλει Νείλου πόλει (6-7)
V A.D.	*P.Oxy.* LI 3636,2	Νιλ(οπολίτου)
26 Feb. 538 A.D.	*P.Michael.* 126,7	ἀπὸ Νίλου πόλει [τοῦ] Ἡρακλεουπολίτου νομοῦ (7-8)²
582-602 A.D. (cf. *BL* 8,251)	*P.Oxy.* XVI 1909,8	(ὑπὲρ) [Ν]είλου πόλ(εως)
612 A.D.	*P.Oxy.* XVI 2045 descr.	Πέτρῳ Νειλουπολ(ίτῃ) (ethnic)
VI or VII A.D.	*P.Oxy.* VI 942,1 (= *P.Oxy.* I 162 descr.)	τὴν Νειλουπολιτῶν (*scil.* πόλιν; cf. l.4: τῆς πόλεως)
VI/VII A.D.	*SB* XVIII 13266,6	Νιλούπολις
Byz.	*SB* I 5337,5	ἀπὸ Νείλου πόλεως

Literary Sources

II A.D.	PTOL. IV,5,56-57 (ed. Nobbe)	Νείλου πόλις
III-IV A.D.	EUS. *Hist. Eccl.* VI,42,3	
IV A.D.	ATHAN. *c. Ar.* 71	
IV A.D.	ATHAN. *Ep.* 19	
V A.D.	STEPH. BYZ. *s.v.*	
VI A.D.	HIEROCLES, *Synecdemus* (ed. H. Gelzer) 729,2-730,4	
VII A.D.	GEORG. CYPR., *Descriptio Orbis Romani* (ed. H. Gelzer) 747	

---

¹ Νει[λοπόλεως] (l.1); π(αρὰ) Νειλοπόλ(εως) ἐξάκ(τορος) (l.8) *ed. pr.* The correct forms, however, should be Νειλοπολίτης and Νείλου πόλις, respectively (cf. above p.135 n.1). The new reading on l.8 has been checked and confirmed by Sergio Daris: «All'inizio e alla fine della riga di scrittura sul *verso* il papiro è molto danneggiato ma, per la parte che Le interessa, la nuova lettura è certa e suona così:]ἐξ(άκτορος) Νειλοπολείτου[. La lettura ἐξ(άκτορος) è assai probabile, e comunque da rigettare π(αρὰ); alla fine, dopo l'indicazione del nomos, non pare esserci altra traccia di scrittura» (letter of November 25, 1996).

² This is a contract, drawn up at Τίντυρις, between a man ἀπὸ Νίλου πόλει τοῦ Ἡρακλεουπολίτου νομοῦ and another from Λευκοῦ in the same nome. The spelling of all three place-names should be checked again, but I have not been able to locate this document (it is not among the *P.Michael.* recently acquired by the Cambridge University Library).

CATALOGUE

TOPARCHY: metropolis of its own nome from the III century A.D.

There were more than one Νείλου πόλις, including a very well attested one in the Arsinoite nome, at the northeast end of the Lake Moeris[1]. The Νείλου πόλις of DIOD.SIC. I 85 was probably in the Delta, like the Bousiris also mentioned there (see below, n. 1).

MODERN ARABIC NAME: Dalās.

The Coptic *Acts* of the Council held at Ephesos in 431 A.D.[2] enable us to identify Niloupolis = (Coptic) Tilodj = (Greek) Τίλωθις = (modern Arabic) Dalās: see also *s.v.* ΤΙΛΩΘΙΣ. The latest Greek papyrus recording the old toponym Τίλωθις dates from the late I B.C. or early I A.D. (*BGU* IV 1060), whereas the earliest source for Νείλου πόλις (explicitly stating that it was in the Herakleopolites) is dated to 103 A.D.[3]

The re-naming of Tilothis as Νείλου πόλις was probably related to the increasing importance of this centre in the Roman period. In the second half of the II A.D., Ptolemy (IV,5,56-57) refers to Niloupolis as still belonging to the Herakleopolite nome[4]: this is consistent with *P.Oxy.* XLVII 3362 (a list of nomes, also from the second half of the II A.D.), where the Nilopolites appears as part of the Herakleopolites. But *SB* XIV 11277 (a contract for the sale of a slave) was registered on January 20, 225 A.D., «at Niloupolis, the metropolis»: by this time, then, the Nilopolites had become an independent nome[5]. This is confirmed by later sources, beginning with *BGU* VII 1568,2 (of May 14, 261 A.D.)[6]. *P.Michael.* 126 seems to indicate that by 538 A.D. the Nilopolites had been reintegrated into the Herakleopolite nome. On the other hand, *P.Oxy.* XVI 1909, compiled during Mauricius' reign (582-602 A.D.), still seems to rank Niloupolis among the nome *metropoleis*, along with Oxyrhynchus, Kynopolis, and Herakleopolis itself: this papyrus is «part of a list of assessments on various cities, the imposts consisting of corn-dues, at an *adaeratio* of 1 *solidus* for 10 *artabae*, and gold taxes. Oxyrhynchus and Cynopolis are here assessed together, and it is noticeable that their combined quotas are only 2,000 *solidi* more than that of Herakleopolis»[7]: i.e. 59,500 as opposed to 57,500 *solidi*. Niloupolis is still considered separately, only the assessment for corn-dues being preserved (1,000 *solidi* for 10,000 artabae: somewhat less than one third of the 35,000 *solidi* due for the Herakleopolites for 350,000 artabae). *P.Oxy.* LI 3636 («from the account of the flat-bottomed boats») may be compared: it shows that the Oxyrhynchites paid the largest sum (298 *solidi*; the Kynopolites, here assessed separately, paid 62 5/6 *solidi*), followed by the Herakleopolites (251 1/6 *solidi*) and the

---

[1] On which see DANIELLE BONNEAU, «Niloupolis du Fayoum», *Actes du XVe Congrès International de Papyrologie (Bruxelles 1977)*, Quatrième Partie: *Papyrologie documentaire*, Bruxelles 1979, pp.258-273. The Niloupolis where the ritual of the enthroning of the new Apis bull was performed (DIOD. I 85,2) was probably *not* the Herakleopolite one (cf. ANNE BURTON, *Commentary on Diodorus Siculus* I, p.246), *pace* BONNEAU, *ibid.*, p.259.

[2] Cf. TIMM, *Das christlich-koptische Ägypten*, II, p.499 (with reference to H. MUNIER, *Recueil des listes épiscopales de l'Eglise copte*, Cairo 1943, p.16): «Unter den Teilnehmern des Konzils von Ephesus (431 A.D.) wird u.a. ein Bischof Eusebius von Νειλουπόλεως aufgeführt, das zur Provinz Arkadia (ἐπαρχία Ἀρκαδίας) rechnete ... Die koptischen Akten dieses Konzils geben als Name seines Bistums *Delati* oder *Telati*».

[3] *P.Mich.* IX 551 is a sale contract drawn up at Kerkesoucha (Arsinoites): a resident of Niloupolis sells a donkey to the veteran soldier Gaius Valerius Longus.

[4] On Ptolemy's description see *Introduction*, p.5.

[5] «... forse in conseguenza della politica di ampio favore concesso alle autonomie municipali, propria dell'età severiana» (GIOVANNI GERACI, *Aegyptus* 54, 1974, p.59). In the same period, the splitting of the Koites into two toparchies is attested by *P.Heid.* IV 320,1 (3 July 138 A.D.) and *P.Heid.* IV 321,5 (18 November 162 and 20 February 163 A.D.)

[6] The εἰρήναρχοι of the Arsinoites write to their colleagues of the Niloupolites, trying to recover a female donkey that had been requisitioned.

[7] From the *Introduction* in the *ed.pr.* of this document.

Nilopolites (with 170 2/3 *solidi*: but the reading is uncertain)[1]. The two taxes refer, of course, to completely different commodities, but a consistent picture does seem to emerge, whereby the Oxyrhynchite and Herakleopolite nomes were at this time (V-VI century A.D.) more or less balanced in their economic strength, both as regards their corn production, and their tax-payments on the flat-bottomed boats (taken as an indicator of trade in these districts). On the other hand, the relative economic strength of the Herakleopolites and the Nilopolites may be assessed on the basis of corn production (the Herakleopolites produces more than three times as much corn as the Nilopolites), but also by tax-payments on the flat-bottomed boats: compared to the Herakleopolites, the Nilopolites apparently pays little less than half. We may expect the Nilopolites to have been a busy area as far as trade is concerned. Its metropolis certainly owed its increasing importance to a strategic location on the routes leading westwards (to the Arsinoites) and southwards, to the Herakleopolites and beyond, along the Nile and the modern Bahr Yūsuf: «Then the river branches as it forms an island, the Herakleopolite nome, and in the island (is found) Niloupolis, inland ...» (so Ptolemy in his *Geographia*)[2]. The establishment of a bishopric there, which causes Niloupolis to be mentioned by some Christian authors, must have been another consequence of its convenient situation.

On account of the rather large figures given in *P.Oxy.* XVI 1909 and *P.Oxy.* LI 3636, it must be assumed that quite a wide area (presumably the whole northern part of the district, comprising the Koma and Bousiris toparchies, as well as the old Tilothis toparchy) was detached from the Herakleopolites and made into the autonomous Nilopolite nome.

Still a rather big place in the XIV century, with 5900 feddans land (= 2478 hectares)[3] surrounding it, and a tax-revenue of 20,000 dinars[4], Niloupolis nevertheless appeared much decayed to al-Idrîsî: «Du temps des anciens Égyptiens elle était comptée au nombre des villes les plus considerables, mais à présent elle est petite et n'a que peu d'habitants, son territoire ayant été pillé et ravagé par les Berbères de la tribu de Luwâtah et par les Arabes vagabonds»[5].

ΝΕΜΑΡΕΩΣ[6]

II-III A.D.	(?)*PSI* XIII 1332,10-11	Νεμαρίτου (ethnic)[7]

---

[1] The remaining districts pay as follows: Arsinoites (163 *solidi*), Aphroditopolites (72 *solidi*, if correctly read), Memphites (37 2/3 *solidi*), Theodosiopolites (13 1/6 *solidi*), Letopolites (7 1/2 *solidi*). *SB* XVIII 13266 (VI/VII; list of payments due for the *curiosus*) again lists Niloupolis (not the Arsinoite Niloupolis, I think) with Oxyrhynchus and Kynopolis, but Takona (certainly not a *metropolis*) is also included. *SB* I 5337 is another list of nome capitals, including Niloupolis.

[2] Trade by vessels in the Nilopolites: *P.Lond.* V 1823 *descr.*; *P.Oxy.* XXIV 2415. Niloupolis as a station for people travelling by land: *P.Oxy.* VI 942 («We reached Niloupolis on the 13th about the 6th hour, and after we had released the animals a letter was delivered to us from your brotherly Excellency...»). Ptolemy (IV,5,56-57) clearly indicates that Nilopolis was «inland» (μεσόγειος).

[3] 1 feddan = 0.42 hectares (cf. DOROTHY J. CRAWFORD, *Kerkeosiris. An Egyptian Village in the Ptolemaic Period*, Cambridge 1971, p.74 n.4).

[4] According to the *État des provinces et des villages de l'Égypte* (p.689), published by S. DE SACY as an Appendix to the *Relation de l'Égypte par Abd-Allatif, médecin de Bagdad* (quoted by É. Amélineau, *La Géographie de l'Égypte à l'époque copte*, Paris 1893, p.138). The *État ... de l'Égypte* was compiled in 1376, under the sultan Mélik al-Naser: «On y trouve ... chaque province et chaque territoire de ce pays, avec une liste alphabétique des villages qui devaient payer l'impôt annuel au sultan» (AMÉLINEAU, *cit.*, p.XVI).

[5] Quoted by J. MASPERO - G. WIET, *Matériaux pour servir à la géographie de l'Égypte*, Cairo 1919, p.51.

[6] A place called Νεμέρα/Νεμέρων is attested in the Μέση toparchy of the Oxyrhynchites: see PRUNETI, *Centri abitati*, *s.v.*

[7] «Θέων ὁ Νεμαρίτης ... may originate from this place» (PIETER J. SIJPESTEIJN, *ZPE* 81, 1990, p.248).

V/VI A.D.	*P.Köln* IV 192,1	ἀπὸ κώ]μης Ṇημάρ[ε]ως (cf. *BL* 9,113)
VI/VII A.D.	*SB* XX 15072,7 = *P.Lond.* III 1097¹	Δάφνης ὅρμου Νεμάρεως

In *P.Lond.* III 1097, the ὅρμος Νεμάρεως apparently functions as the port of Daphne.

ΝΕΜΗΟΥΕΙ

525/526 A.D.   *P.Rain.Cent.* 113,10   κ̣λήρου Νεμηουει

P.Rain.Cent. 113 is a contract drawn at Herakleopolis.

ṆΕṂΘΙΒΙΣ

mid-III B.C.[2]   *P.Fuad Crawford* 5 *recto*,11

ETYMOLOGY: second component *h(y)b*, «ibis».

Known villages listed in this document were in the Koites.

ΝΕΠΩΤΙΑΝΟΥ

227 A.D.   *Stud.Pal.* XX 29,20

TOPARCHY: Koites.

This is one of several kleroi[3] referred to in a contract for the sale of land.

ΝΕΥΑΚ[

VII-VIII A.D.   *Stud.Pal.* X 206,3

Apparently the name of a κλῆρος, listed with several others (see the *Reverse Index* at the end of this volume).

---

[1] The document has been published by PIETER J. SIJPESTEIJN, *ibid.*, pp.245-251.

[2] On the re-dating of this document see *Introduction*, p.14 n.7.

[3] See *s.vv.* Διδυμιανοῦ, Μάρωνος; see also the list of *Fossil Kleroi* (below, pp.273 ff.).

ΝΕΥΗΛΑ

VI A.D.	*Stud.Pal.* X 228,7	ἐν τόπ(ῳ) Νευηλα

Listed with Παργου (l.4), Πιατιμι (l.5), Νεθισει (l.6), Σουριυ (l.8), Πιακερ (l.9).

(?) ΝΕΧΙΣΗΙ

ca. 250 B.C.	*BGU* XIV 2391,7	ἐν Νεχισηι [1]
ca. 250 B.C.	*BGU* XIV 2392,5	ἐν Ν[εχισηι]

See also: ΝΕΘΙΣΕΙ.

This place-name is not attested elsewhere: in these two documents, it is mentioned with reference to a unit of volume adopted there. The Herakleopolite provenance of the two documents is also not certain: their origin might be the same as for *BGU* XIV 2380 (contract drawn at Κυνῶν πόλις in 265 B.C.)[2]. Note, however, the reference to the Ἄγημα toparchy in *BGU* XIV 2392.

ΝḚΧΟΣ

I B.C.	*BGU* XIV 2437,51

TOPARCHY: Koma.

ΝΗΣΩΝ

311/312-319/320 A.D.	*P.Neph.* 44,[2];6;[11];22	[ἀποδ(έκται) κώμης Νήσων] (2); ἀπ]οδέκται κώμης Νήσων (6); κωμάρχοι κώμης Ν[ήσων] (10-11); σιτολόγοις κώμης Νήσων (21-22)
315/316 or 330/331 A.D.	*P.Neph.* 43,2;15	ἀποδεκτῶν [κώ]μης Ν[ήσων] (1-2); ἀποδέκται κώμης Νήσω(ν) (15)

---

[1] «Addendum lexicis. Im Herakleopolites?» (*ed. pr. ad loc.*).

[2] The toponyms of the Kynopolites have been studied by NIKOS LITINAS, «Village and place-names of the Cynopolite Nome», *APF* 40, 1994, pp.157-164: he does not include Νεχιση in his list.

17 April 344 A.D.	*P.Neph.* 32,7	ἀπο κώμης Νήσων τοῦ αὐτοῦ (*scil.* Ἡρακλεοπολίτου) νομοῦ (6-7)
IV A.D.	*P.Neph.* 13,20	Νεφερῶτι πρ(εσ)β(υτέρῳ) τῆς Νήσου ἐν Φαθώρ
IV A.D.	*P.Neph.* 19,3	τὸ κοινόν[1] ἀπὸ κώμης Νήσων
IV A.D.	*P.Neph.* 20,5;9	ἀπὸ Νήσων
IV A.D.	*P.Neph.* 46, [1]	ἀποδεκτῶν κ[ώμης Νήσων τοῦ Ἡρακλεοπολίτου] νομοῦ (1-2)
V A.D.	*P.Oxy.* LIX 4004,10	ἐν τῇ Νήσων
V A.D.	*Stud.Pal.* X 233, col.I A,1	Νήσων[2]
VI A.D.	*P.Oxy.* XVI 1997,2	ὅρμου Νήσων
VI A.D.	*SB* I 1967,1	κώμ(ης) Νήσων
VI A.D.	*Stud.Pal.* III 399,1	βοηθὸς] κώμης Ετων τοῦτ'ἔστιν Νήσων[3]

See also: ΕΤΩΝ; ΜΟΥΗ[4].

TOPARCHY: Koites.

ETYMOLOGY: νῆσος was the Greek translation of the word *m3j* («new land»)[5].

The documents from the Nepheros archive show that the monastery of (P)hathor, in the southern Herakleopolites, was closely connected to this village.

P.Neph. 43, 44, 46 contain receipts for the payment of taxes (in money or in kind). *P.Neph.* 32 records a money-loan.

P.Neph. 20 is the report of a *speculator*, possibly addressed to a *riparius* of the Herakleopolites, on a conflict between the inhabitants of Νήσων and the police officials (εἰρήναρχοι) of Thelbo. The origin of the troubles seems to have been a mistake on the part of the πρεσβύτερος of Νήσων, who had wrongly effected a payment on account of the σύμμαχος of Thelbo.

P.Neph. 19: the κοινόν of Νήσων writes to Paulos (ll.1-2: τῷ κυρίῳ μου τιμιωτάτῳ πατρὶ Παύλῳ).

P.Oxy. LIX 4004: Theodoros invites Canopus and Valentinus to come and visit him at Νήσων: they

---

[1] «Das κοινόν ist wohl das Verwaltungsorgan (Ensemble der tätigen Beamten) des Dorfes und nicht mit der Bevölkerung als Gesamtheit identisch» (Edd. *ad loc.*).

[2] «Statt Ψνιω.. ist †Νήσων wohl zu lesen (vorgeschlagen von Hermann Harrauer)» (letter from Johannes Diethart, February 25, 1994).

[3] This document (a receipt) apparently indicates that Νήσων was also called Ετων.

[4] Cf. *P.Neph.* 12,23: according to the Editors, Μουὴ κώμη could be the Egyptian name of Νήσων/Νήσου κώμη.

[5] See *Introduction*, p.6.

are to travel by boat, ὅτι ἀνάβασίς ἐστιν (l.12: «because the river has risen»). *P.Oxy.* XVI 1997 shows that the village had a ὅρμος: it is the receipt for the payment of an ἐμβολή which was due εἰς τὸν ὀρθὸν ποταμὸν ὅρμου Νήσων. *SB* I 1967 belongs to a group of three payments for transport by boat.

P.Neph. 13 (letter from Lykarion to Nepheros) should refer to the same locality but, on this one occasion, in the singular.

ΝΙ[.].ΕΩΣ[1]

| I B.C. | *BGU* XIV 2433,54 |

TOPARCHY: Μέση.

Included in a list of villages (ll.46-55) belonging to the Μέση toparchy, among them Chennis, Phys and Peenepochra.

ΝΙΗΡΑ( )

| late III A.D. | *BGU* XIII 2365,7 | Νιηρα– |

ΝΙΝΩ

96-94 or 63-61 B.C.	*BGU* XIV 2429,6	Νίνωι
I B.C.	*BGU* XIV 2438,10; (fr.3),93	Νινω[(10); Νιν̣ω̣[(93)[2]
I/II A.D.	*P.Hib.* II 218,93	Νιν[ώ]
VI-VII A.D.	*Stud.Pal.* X 5,7	τὸν βοηθ(ὸν) Νινω
VII-VIII A.D.	*CPR* IV 2,11	χ(ωρίον) Νινω

See also: ΝΙΝΩΠΑΚΑΝ; ΝΙΤΩΜΙ̣; [±5].ΙΝΩ.

TOPARCHY: Ἄγημα κάτω.

MODERN ARABIC NAME: Ninā. See *TAVO B 69* § 4.3 (M 98) and p.213: «An einer höheren Stelle im Dorf liegen Keramikscherben aus spätantiker Zeit ... Die Türschwelle eines Hauses im Dorf besteht aus einem Stück Säulenschaft. Neben einem anderen Haus liegt ein korintisches Kapitell». See also TIMM, *Das christlich-koptische Ägypten*, IV, p.1777 (*s.v.* Ninā).

The villages listed in *BGU* XIV 2429 were for the most part in the Ἄγημα toparchy (Peenameus,

---

[1] «Es ist nicht Νιλεως oder Νισεως» (*ed. pr. ad loc.*).

[2] New readings (checked by me on a photograph, and on the original by William Brashear, who deems them «probable»); Νιλεύς *ed. pr.*

CATALOGUE

Peene, Peenepsomphis, Korphotoi, Kollasoucha, Niseus, Peensemtheus, Petachor). Nino should probably be assigned to the same toparchy, and this becomes a certainty if the new readings at *BGU* XIV 2438 are accepted, as fr.3 indicates that this was a village of the Ἄγημα Κάτω (it is listed after Peenepsomphis and Peensemtheus); at ll.10 ff. of the same document it is again entered with other villages of the Ἄγημα: Korphotoi (15), Niseus (17).

Onosis (περὶ Πόλιν toparchy), Tinteris and Kollintaathyr (Tekmi toparchy) recur with Nino in *Stud.Pal.* X 5, which also supports the supplement Νιν[ω] in *P.Hib.*II 218,93, where Onosis is mentioned at ll.90 and 92.

The village still appears, along with several others all belonging to the central toparchies of the Herakleopolites[1], in *CPR* IV 2, a bilingual document written in Coptic and Greek: all toponyms are written in Greek.

ΝΙΝΩΠΑΚΑΝ

IV A.D.	*CPR* I 42,12	περὶ Νινωπακαν

See also: ΝΙΝΩ.

TOPARCHY: περὶ Πόλιν?

CPR I 42, a lease contract in which all parties are from Herakleopolis, concerns 8 arourae near Sobthis ἡ μικρά (περὶ Πόλιν toparchy), 5 arourae at Σακαπρυ, 3 ar. at Νινωπακαν, 4 ar. at Noeris, 2 ar. «to the south of the mouth of the canal», and two thirds of an aroura to the west of a road. Because of the connections with Σῶβθις and the περὶ Πόλιν toparchy attested for Nino by the other documents, Νινωπακαν may either be the same village (presumably appearing here with its full name), or an "annexe" to it.

ΝΙΣΕΥΣ

III B.C.	*P.Lille* I 31,1	Νισεὺς καὶ Τερτονπετεχώνς
139 B.C.	*P.Tebt.* III 838,9	περὶ Νισέα
139 B.C.	*P.Tebt.* III 989,5	περὶ Νισέα
96-94 or 63-61 B.C.	*BGU* XIV 2429,9	Νισέως
I B.C.	*BGU* XIV 2438,17	Νισέως
I B.C.	*BGU* XIV 2440,65	περὶ Πέρα(ν) καὶ Νισέα
I/II A.D.	*P.Hib.* II 218,85	Νισέως

TOPARCHY: Ἄγημα (κάτω?)[2].

---

[1] In the Ἄγημα κάτω, περὶ Πόλιν, περὶ Τέκμι, Πέραν and Μέση toparchies: see the *Reverse Index* at the end of this volume.

[2] See: Ε....[, ΠΕΕΝΗ, ΤΕΡΤΟΝΠΕΤΕΧΩΝΣ.

Niseus is closely linked to Tertonpetechons (*P.Lille* I 31: accounts for the holding of the ἱλάρχης Antiphanes) and to the Πέραν toparchy (*BGU* XIV 2440; Peene appears at l.64).

BGU XIV 2438 enters it amid villages of the Ἄγημα toparchy: Korphotoi (15), Niseus (17), Kollasoucha (20); a reference to Hermes under the entry for Niseus is probably related to *BGU* XIV 2437, where sacred land of an Hermes sanctuary is recorded in the Πέραν toparchy (near Thmoiphtha: ll.36-40)[1].

BGU XIV 2429 confirms these connections, as it lists villages of the Ἄγημα (Peenameus, Peene, Peenepsomphis, Korphotoi, Nino, Kollasoucha, Niseus, Peensemtheus, Petachor), περὶ Τέκμι (Mouchis) and περὶ Πόλιν toparchies (Sobthis).

Niseus is also listed in *P.Hib.* II 218, where villages of the Koites are mostly included: this connection with the Koites may be supported by *P.Tebt.* III 838, where Tosachmis (Koites) also appears.

ΝΙΤΩΜΙ

I/II A.D.	*P.Hib.* II 218,36	
V/VI A.D.	*P.Heid.* III 246,9	ἐν κλήρου Νιτω.[.]

TOPARCHY: Koites?

Three villages of the Ἄγημα toparchy, i.e. Alilais (33), Kollasoucha (34), Petachor (35), precede Νιτωμι in *P.Hib.* II 218 (otherwise mostly listing villages of the Koites). A comparison with *BGU* XIV 2429, where Kollasoucha and Petachor also occur, might suggest a reading Νινω..: on the other hand, the name Νιτω.[.], attested for a kleros in the Ἄνω Κωίτης in *P.Heid.* III 246, may lend some support to the Editor's reading in *P.Hib.* II 218.

ΝΟ( )

64/63 B.C.	*BGU* VIII 1747,3	περὶ Νο( )[2]

As περὶ Τέκ(μι) is mentioned in the following line, περὶ Νο( ) may well refer to a toponym.

ΝΟ( ) or ΟΝ( )[3]

about 164 B.C.   *P.Tebt.* III 1044,65

---

[1] Also in the Tekmi toparchy: cf. ll.7-8.

[2] «ν ist recht deutlich» (Günter Poethke, letter of April 14, 1994).

[3] The Editor deciphers Νο() or Ον(), adding that this «might stand for Νό(κμου), Νο(κλή) or Ὀν(νή)». Νό(ηρις) (see *s.v.*) seems the most likely resolution here.

CATALOGUE

ΝΟΒ[[1]

I/II A.D.   *P.Hib.* II 218, col. III

ΝΟΗΡΙΣ

I B.C.	*BGU* XIV 2436,12	Νοῆ(ριν)
I/II A.D.	*P.Hib.* II 218,56	Νοήρεως
after 150 A.D.	*Stud.Pal.* XX 7,27 (= *CPR* I 22)	π]ερὶ τῆστε (*l.*-δε) τῆς Νοηρίου
IV A.D.	*CPR* I 42,14	περὶ Νοῆριν (13-14)
ca. 420-421 A.D.	*MPER* XV 63,16	ἀπὸ Νοήρεως
V A.D.	*Stud.Pal.* VIII 772,3	ἀπὸ Νοήρεω[ς]
V-VI A.D.	*CPR* VIII 59,3	ἀπὸ κώμης Νοήρεως
about 500 A.D. (cf. *BL* 8,343)	*SB* VI 9282,*verso*	ἀπὸ Νοήρεως
16 July 534 A.D.	*SB* VIII 9876,10	ἐν πεδίοις κώμης Νοήρεως [2]
VII A.D.	*SB* VI 9590,22	ἀπὸ Νοήρε(ως) (cf.*BL* 7,211)
VII/VIII A.D.	*CPR* IV 2,15	χ(ωρίον) Νοήρ'ε(ως)' [3]
VIII A.D.	*Stud.Pal.* X 84,3	χ(ωρίον) Νο[ή]ρε[ως]

See also: NO() or ON().

TOPARCHY: περὶ Πόλιν.

MODERN ARABIC NAME: An-Nuwaira [4].

The connection between this village and the metropolis, besides other villages of the περὶ Πόλιν toparchy, is consistently attested in our sources. Three documents attest links with Pois: in *BGU* XIV 2436, ll.11-12, Hierax' kleros is distributed between Tanchais (Tilothis toparchy), Noeris and Pois; in *P.Hib.* II 218 Tokois and Noeris are listed immediately before Pois; in *Stud.Pal.* X 84 Noeris, Pois and Peensamoi (Πέραν toparchy) recur in three consecutive lines, followed by Thmoinepsi.

CPR I 42 deals with a landholding split between Noeris, Sobthis and Ninopakan (all in the περὶ Πόλιν toparchy).

---

[1] Νοβ[«not Νοη[ρεως]») *ed. pr.*: one could think of Νοκ[λή, but I have not checked this.

[2] As read by HERMANN HARRAUER - PIETER J. SIJPESTEIJN, *Tyche* 3, 1988, p.113.

[3] Νοηρ'ε' *ed.pr.*

[4] This identification was already suggested by ULRICH WILCKEN, *APF* 2, 1903, p.325. See also *TAVO B 69* § 4.3 (M 113); and TIMM, *Das christlich-koptische Ägypten*, IV, p.1783 f. (*s.v.* «Noeris»).

Connection to the metropolis: *SB* VIII 9876 (lease contract between two women and the ἄββας Παῦλος, ἐπίσκοπος κ[αθολικῆς ἐ]κκλησίας of Herakleopolis, for land ἐν πεδίοις κώμης Νοήρεως); *CPR* VIII 59 (transaction between an inhabitant of Noeris and one of Herakleopolis); *MPER* XV 63 (payments in artabae and writing-exercises by a different hand; besides Noeris, Phys and Herakleopolis are mentioned)[1].

The connection to the Πέραν toparchy (Peensamoi also probably appears in the same document with Noeris in *P.Tebt.* III 1044[2]) is confirmed by *SB* VI 9590: two arourae which Anatolios (from Herakleopolis) cedes to Pamoûn are apparently split between Makaitonos, Tebetny (Πέραν toparchy) and Chortaso (also in the Πέραν?), and situated to the west of the γήδια Ἀπαλά, ἐν κλήρῳ καλουμένῳ Τσαβα; they are ceded in exchange for two arourae near a κώμη (l.12) whose name is lost at the beginning of l.13: this could be Noeris, referred to at l.22. The two witnesses are from Herakleopolis.

CPR I 22: dowry of a woman whose possessions are at Pharbaitha (in the Arsinoite nome), Philonikou (Koites) and Noeris.

CPR IV 2 (a bilingual document in Coptic and Greek) lists many villages of the central toparchies of the Herakleopolite nome (toponyms in Greek)[3].

ΝΟΚΛΗ

about 138 B.C.	*P.Tebt.* III 860,48;50	Νοκλέους (48); Νοκλεους (50)[4]
late II or III A.D.	*P.Ryl.* II 225,31	περὶ Νοκλή
VI A.D.	*P.Oxy.* XVI 1917,22;45;51	ἀπὸ Νόκλη (22); ἐποικ(ίου) Νόκλη (45); ἀπὸ Νόκλη(51)
VII/VIII A.D.	*SB* XVIII 13888,3	[χ(ωρίου) Ν]οκλή

TOPARCHY: Koites.

See also: ΝΟΚ[

There is little doubt that Nokle was in the Koites, where most of the villages listed with it in the sources were: it twice recurs with Pselemachis (*P.Tebt.* III 860; *P.Oxy.* XVI 1917) and Thelbo (*P.Ryl.* II 225; *SB* XVIII 13888), both villages of the Koites. The places mentioned in *SB* XVIII 13888 (Phathor, Ostrakinou, Thelbo, Hipponon), in particular, were close to the border between the Herakleopolites and the Oxyrhynchites.

---

[1] Cf. also *Stud.Pal.* X 59 (a Coptic document), where *Noeri* and *Hnes* (the Egyptian name of Herakleopolis) appear together.

[2] Peensamoi must have been meant at *Stud.Pal.* X 84, l.5, where Pois also appears at l.4, as well as Noeris (l.3; also found in *BGU* XIV 2436,l.12, again in connection with Pois). Peensamoi and Noeris are therefore the most likely solutions at *P.Tebt.* III 1044, ll.54 and 65.

[3] See *s.v.* ΝΙΝΩ.

[4] My readings (checked on a photograph); .οκλέους (l.48), Νόκμου (l.50) *ed. pr.*

CATALOGUE

(?) ΝΟΜΑΡΧΟΥ

| II A.D. | *P.Prag.* II 132,7-8 | ἐποικίου Νομάρχου λεγομένου |
| late III A.D. | *BGU* XIII 2365,16 | Νομαρχ() |

TOPARCHY: this could well be a locality in the Arsinoite nome: see *P.Prag.* II 132,7 n.

ΝΟΤΙΝΟΥ

| VII-VIII A.D. | *Stud.Pal.* X 200,4 | Νοτίνου ἐπ'οι'(κίου) |
| VIII A.D. | *Stud.Pal.* X 204,3 | Νο'τ'(ίνου)[1] ἐποικί'ου' |

Listed with Magdola (1.3) and Peene (1.6) in *Stud.Pal.* X 200; again with Magdola (1.1) and perhaps Peene (1.6), besides Ogou (1.4; Tekmi toparchy), in *Stud.Pal.* X 204.

ΝΩΙΣ

after 84/83 B.C.	*BGU* XIV 2370,5	ἐπὶ κώμης Νωεως
I B.C.	*BGU* XIV 2420,6	τῆς Νωυεως
I B.C.	*BGU* XIV 2425,7;27	Νωίτης (7); Νωείτης (27) (ethnic)
28/27 B.C.	*BGU* XVI 2665,16	περὶ Νῶϊν
V/VI A.D.	*CPR* XIV 40,2	[διὰ Ἰού]στου Ἠλεία βοηθ(οῦ) Νώεως
VII-VIII A.D.	*Stud.Pal.* X 209,5	χ(ωρίον) Νωεως

See also: ΝΩΥẸ..Σ

TOPARCHY: περὶ Πόλιν.

MODERN ARABIC NAME: Zawiet el Nâwya? (plausible on phonetical and topographical grounds).

BGU XIV 2370 assigns this village to the περὶ Πόλιν toparchy. Νωυις (*BGU* XIV 2420) should be a variant spelling.

Listed with villages of the Ἄγημα toparchy in *CPR* XIV 40 (Petachor[2]) and *Stud.Pal.* X 209 (Kollasoucha); and with villages of the Tekmi toparchy (Ogou, Mouchis) and the Koites (Talae) in *BGU* XVI 2665 (letter on poorly inundated land).

---

[1] The resolution is mine.

[2] There is also a possible reference to a βορριν(ῆς) Ἀλλ(αγῆς): a «nördliche Poststation» (cf. *BL* 9,76).

ΝΩΥΕ̣..Σ

169-164 B.C.　　　　　*P.Strasb.* II 99,3　　　　　ἐκ Νωυε̣..ς[1]

Petition to the sovereigns: an inhabitant of this village claims to be the rightful heir to his father's house at Ποιμένων κώμη (Μέση toparchy).

ΝΩΥΚΛΕΓΧΗΣ

mid-III B.C.[2]　　　　　*P.Fuad Crawford* 5, *recto*,3

TOPARCHY: Koites.

P.Fuad Crawford 5 *recto* lists several villages belonging to the Koites, including Pselemachis and Psychis.

ΝΩΥΠ

mid-III B.C.　　　　　*P.Strasb.* IX 802,2
TOPARCHY: Koites.

P.Strasb. IX 802 lists Egyptian tax-payers and their villages, all of them apparently in Koites.

ΟΓΟΥ

I B.C.	*BGU* XIV 2436,3	Ὄγου
28/27 B.C.	*BGU* XVI 2665,4	περὶ Ὄγου
28/29 A.D.	*P.Oxy.* XXIV 2412,96;164	Ὄγου (96); Ὀ[γ]ου (164)
350 A.D.	*P.Oxf.* 6,11;15;20	ἀπὸ Ὄγου (11); ἀπὸ ⟦κώμη⟧{ς} Ὄγου (15); ἀπὸ Ὄγου (20)
IV A.D.	*Stud.Pal.* X 236,1	Ὄγου
V A.D.	*Stud.Pal.* X 233, col. II,23	Ὄγου

---

[1] My reading: Νωυθσῦς *ed. pr.* A reading Νωυέως seems impossible, as the traces after θ are not compatible with an ω.

[2] On the re-dating of this document see *Introduction*, p.14 n.7.

VII/VIII A.D.	*CPR* IV 2,13	χ(ωρίον) Ὀγο(υ)[1]
VII-VIII A.D.	*Stud.Pal.* X 211,3	χ(ωρίον) Ὀγου
VIII A.D.	*Stud.Pal.* X 72,3	χ(ωρίον) Ὀγου
VIII A.D.	*Stud.Pal.* X 204,4	χ'ω'(ρίον) Ὀγου

TOPARCHY: Tekmi.

BGU XIV 2436 surveys a holding split among villages which, though presumably near each other, did not belong to the same toparchy; these are: Magdola (1), an Ἰβιών locality (2), Pois (2), Peens(amoi?) (3; Πέραν toparchy), Ogou (3). About eight centuries later, Magdola and Ogou again recur together in a list (*Stud.Pal.* X 204, ll.1 and 4 respectively; also note Πεε[at l.6: cf. Peens(amoi?) in *BGU* XIV 2436).

P.Oxy. XXIV 2412 includes Ogou in a group of six villages, all presumably in the Tekmi toparchy (Ogou, Tekmi, Kollintathyr, Pyrgotos, Mouchis, Ibion). The neighbourhood between Ogou and Kollintaathyr is confirmed by *P.Oxf.* 6: here the scribe deletes the κώμη qualification at l.15[2]. In *BGU* XVI 2665 (letter about poorly inundated land) Ogou is mentioned along with Mouchis (Tekmi toparchy), Nois (περὶ Πόλιν toparchy) and Talae (Koites). The village may have shrunk, or indeed it may not have been a proper village even at an earlier stage (older sources do not call it a κώμη): but it certainly was called a χωρίον in sources of the Byzantine period, such as *Stud.Pal.* X 72 (mentioning Ogou along with Hiera Nesos) and *Stud.Pal.* X 211. It should be noted that *Stud.Pal.* X 211, 212 and 213, though published as separate documents, are in fact fragments of one and the same source: therefore, the villages mentioned in all three may have been near each other; these are: Ogou, Thelbonthis (*Stud.Pal.* X 212; Techtho Nesos toparchy), Petachor and Kollasoucha (*Stud.Pal.* X 213; Ἄγημα toparchy).

CPR IV 2 (a bilingual document in Coptic and Greek) lists many villages of the central toparchies of the Herakleopolite nome (toponyms in Greek)[3].

ΟΔΟΣ ΒΑΣΙΛΙΚΗ

36/35 B.C.   *BGU* XIV 2376,19;38

A piece of garden-land near Sobthis (in περὶ Πόλιν) is located by reference to a διῶρυξ called ὀμφαλο.νια (south) and to this ὁδὸς βασιλική (north). References to a canal and a road, locating land near Sobthis, are also found in *CPR* I 42.

ΟΔΟΣ Η ΜΕΓΑΛΗ

1 August 25 B.C.   *BGU* XVI 2590,9-10   τὸ (*sc.* χῶμα) λεγόμενον Μεγάλης Ὁδοῦ

Sworn agreement by the elders of Korphotoi to undertake maintenance work of the three public canals near the village (see *s.v.* ΧΩΜΑ): one of these is identified by reference to the Μεγάλη Ὁδός.

---

[1] Ογο *ed. pr.*

[2] As noted in CALDERINI-DARIS, *Dizionario, s.v.*

[3] See *s.v.* ΝΙΝΩ.

ΟΙΝΑΛΕΓ( )

III A.D.	*BGU* XIII 2365,6	Οιναλεγ( )

ΟΛΩΝΘΕΩΣ

I B.C.	*BGU* XIV 2440,12	

TOPARCHY: Tekmi.

ΟΜΟΝΟΙΑ

V A.D.	*Stud.Pal.* X 233, col. II,9	Ομονοιας

ΟΝΝΗ(Σ) or ΟΝΝΕΟΥΣ (κώμη)

239/238 B.C.[1]	*P.Rain.Cent.* 44,5	ἐξ Ὀννέους
212/211 B.C.	*P.Lille* I 59,18;25;32;46;50;53;94 101;108;118	Ὀννέους
III B.C.	*P.Cair.Zen.* III 59473,4	ἐν Ὀννῆι
III B.C.	*P.Cair.Zen.* IV 59782 (b),28;45;67	ἐξ Ὀννέους (28); ἐξ Ὀννέ[ους (45); ἐξ Ὀννέους (67)
III B.C.	*PSI* VI 587,4	ἐξ Ὀννέους
early II B.C.	(?) *P.Tebt.* III 889,9	ἐν Ὀνῆι[2]
early II B.C.	*P.Tebt.* III 1082,35	ἐν τῆι Ὀ[ν]νῆι
after 84/83 B.C.	*BGU* XIV 2370 (fr.1),82;86; (fr.3),96	Ὀννέου[ς (82); εἰς Ὀννή (86); Ὀννέο[υς (96)[3]
after 52/51 B.C.	*BGU* VIII 1808,9	Ὀννέους λογευτῶν ε̄ ἀρχιφυλακίτο(υ) ε̄ (9-10)
I B.C.	*BGU* XIV 2440,44	Ὀννέους

---

[1] In my opinion, this document should be dated to the 9th year of Euergetes (239/238 B.C.). See the Editor's note on l.11; *P.Rain.Cent.* 44 comes from the same cartonnage as *P.Rain.Cent.* 43, which is dated to 236 B.C.

[2] My reading (checked on a photograph, where I can detect no τ: rather, a loop connecting η to the following ι) : ἐν Ὀνῆτι *ed. pr.* (derived from a nominative Ὀνῆς: see *Index of the geographical names* in the *ed.pr.*).

[3] I suggest this reading at l.96: Ονγ.. *ed. pr.*

CATALOGUE

30 B.C.-14 A.D.	*BGU* XVI 2577,80	Ὀννίτης (ethnic)
18 B.C.	*BGU* IV 1202,1	τοῖς ἀπ''Οννέους ἱερεῦσι
I A.D.	(?)*P.Oxy.* XLII 3052,10	Οὐεννε̣ [1]
August 199 A.D.	*O.Wilck.* II 1117,4	διὰ ὄνων Ἡρακλεοπ(ολίτου) νομ(οῦ) Ὀννή
205 A.D.	*Stud.Pal.* XX 18,3 (= *CPR* I 228)	ἀπὸ Ὀνν[έους [2]
late IV/early V A.D. (cf. *BL* 9,368)	*P.Vind.Tand.* 18,20	ἀπὸ Ὀννή
V A.D.	*Stud.Pal.* X 9,1	Ὀννή
V/VI A.D.	*Stud.Pal.* III 371,2	βοη(θὸς) κώμης Ὀννή
VI A.D.	*P.Rain.Cent.* 137,1	γρ(αμματεῖ) Ὀννή
VI/VII A.D.	*P.Dub.* 25,8	τῆς ἡμετέρας κώμης Ὀννή [3]
VI/VII A.D.	*P.Dub.* 26,1	ἀπὸ Ὀννή
25 Feb. 657 A.D. (cf. *BL* 8,353)	*SB* VIII 9750,3	ἀπὸ κώμης Ωννη τοῦ Ἡρ(ακλεο)π(ολίτου) νομοῦ
VII A.D.	*Stud.Pal.* III 68,2	ἀπὸ κώμης Ὀννή

Literary Sources

XII-XIII A.D.	(?) *Tabula Peutingeriana*	Venne

TOPARCHY: Tekmi.

ETYMOLOGY: Wilcken argued that this place-name should be understood as Ὀννέους (κώμη)[4]; however, early sources already employ Ὀννῆι for the dative (ἐν Ὀννῆι, rather than ἐν Ὀννέους κώμηι). Ὀνῆς is attested as a personal name in the Ptolemaic period at Abydos (*PPt* III 5656), Pathyris (*PPt* I 695) and Apollonospolis (*PPt* IV 8243; V 13329).

Onnes appears in a section of *BGU* XIV 2440 where land assigned to μάχιμοι is surveyed: these

---

[1] Is this a variant spelling for Οννη?

[2] My supplement: ἀπὸ Ὀνν[η *ed.pr.*

[3] There is also an intriguing reference to the πρωτοκώμιον τῆς αὐ[τῆς κώμης]: the «best part of town» (see Ed. *ad loc.*)?

[4] ULRICH WILCKEN, *APF* 5, 1913, p.432 (on *BGU* IV 1202): «Die beschenkten Priester heißen τοῖς ἀπ''Οννέους ἱερεῦσι. Dies Dorf kann nicht Onnes heißen, sondern nur Ὀννέους *scil.* κώμη. Vielleicht liegt derselbe Personenname zugrunde in der Ableitung Ὀννειτῶν, die im Fayûm begegnet».

μάχιμοι were also granted land at Tochontou (uncertainly read in the following line) which other sources locate in the Tekmi toparchy; reference to Tekmi itself is also made in the immediately preceding (1.41: land granted to φυλακῖται) and following (1.46: land assigned to ἐφοδοί) sections.

Much the same villages recur in *P.Lille* I 59 and in *P.Cair.Zen.*IV 59782 (b): in both documents Onnes is comprised between villages of the Tilothis and the Koma toparchies, while other villages of the Tekmi toparchy are also mentioned.

Often associated with Onnes in the sources are Koma, Bousiris, Thmoiobastis[1]. In *BGU* XVI 2577 (tax-list) the ethnics Κρηκίτης (from Krekis) and Ὀννίτης appear.

Journey along the river to Alexandria in *PSI* VI 587: Etearchos writes to Zenon and informs him that Diotimos is about to arrive at Philadelphia (Arsinoite nome)[2] from Onnes and Moiethymis (the modern Meidoum, in the Memphites); if Zenon wants to travel with him, he should get ready. This leads to the hypothesis that Onnes was a station on the journey down the Nile, to Alexandria, which in turn may support the identification with Οὐεννέ of *P.Oxy.* XLII 3052 (southward itinerary from Alexandria): Οὐεννέ was identified by the Editor as «the *Venne* mentioned by the *Tabula Peutingeriana* after Memphis and before Ptolemaidonar (= Ptolemais Hormou?) and Herakleo» (i.e. Herakleopolis); the following station in the itinerary may well be Κενή = Καινή.

If Ὀν(ν)ῆι can be read in *P.Tebt.* III 889,9 Naukratis also appears as a possible destination of a downstream journey *via* Onnes.

P.Tebt. III 1082 (part of an account) also mentions Tanis (in the Arsinoites) and Hiera (Nesos). Another connection with the Arsinoites is provided by *P.Dub.* 26, referring to somebody from the village of Onnes, but presently ἐν τῷ κτήματι Ταμαύεως (an Arsinoite locality). This is also consistent with *Stud.Pal.* III 68 (two men from Onnes lease two arourae from somebody ἀπὸ κώμης Λευκογίου)[3]. Besides, *Stud.Pal.* XX 18 (receipt by which Ammonios, ex-gymnasiarches and living at Herakleopolis, acknowledges the partial repayment of a loan by a woman from Onnes) points to a proximity of Onnes to the περὶ Πόλιν toparchy.

BGU IV 1202 is a letter from the topogrammateus of the Bousiris toparchy concerning the monthly provisions of ὄλυρα to the priests (from Onnes) of the temple of the «very great gods Μένδητος κ[α]ὶ Ἄ[μ]μων[ο]ς καὶ Χώνσιος καὶ Ἁρποχράτου»[4].

P.Rain.Cent. 137: 10.5 artabae σίτου κόκκ(ου) are to be given by Enoch (grammateus at Onnes) to the *liburnarius* Pamun: an order to this effect comes from Theodoros, son of Iakob, through the notarius Iohannes (note the obviously Jewish names).

Stud.Pal. XX 18: Ammonios, ex-gymnasiarches living at Herakleopolis, acknowledges the partial repayment of a loan by a woman from Onnes.

Stud.Pal. III 68: two men from Onnes lease two arourae from an inhabitant of Leukogion.

ΟΝΩΣΙΣ

I B.C.   *BGU* XIV 2440 (fr.7),95   Ὀνώσεως

---

[1] Koma: *P.Cair.Zen.* IV 59473 and 59782; *P.Lille* 59; *BGU* IV 1202; *BGU* VIII 1808; *BGU* XIV 2370 and 2440. Bousiris: *P.Lille* 59; *BGU* IV 1202; *BGU* VIII 1808; *BGU* XIV 2370; *P.Rain.Cent.* 44; *P.Vind.Tand.* 18. Thmoiobastis: *P.Cair.Zen.* IV 59782 (b); *P.Rain.Cent.* 44; *BGU* VIII 1808; *BGU* XIV 2370 and 2440.

[2] The connection between Onnes and the Arsinoites is confirmed by *O.Wilck.* 1117 (corn transport in the Arsinoites by means of donkeys requisitioned at Onnes).

[3] The connection between Leukogion and Onnes is also supported by the fact that these two are the only Herakleopolite villages mentioned in the *P.Dub.* papyri (though in different documents: Leukogion appears in *P.Dub.* 24 and 28).

[4] See above on the connection between Onnes and Bousiris.

I/II A.D.	*P.Hib.* II 218,54;90;92	Ὀνώσεως (54); Ὀνώ[σε]ως (90); Ὀνώ[σεως] (92)
IV A.D.	*P.Iand.* VI 124,5	εἰς Ὀνῶσιν
V A.D.	*Stud.Pal.* X 47,1	Ὀνώσεως
VI-VII A.D.	*Stud.Pal.* X 5,4	τὸν βοηθ(ὸν) Ὀνώσεως (cf. *BL* 1,418)
VII/VIII A.D.	*CPR* IV 2,15	χ(ωρίον) Ὀνώσ'ε'(ως) [1]
VIII A.D.	*Stud.Pal.* X 218,2	χ(ωρίον) Ὀνώσε'ω'(ς)
VIII A.D.	*Stud.Pal.* X 223,6	ἀπὸ χ(ωρίου) Ὀνώσ(εως) (cf. *BL* 1,419)

TOPARCHY: περὶ Πόλιν.

Assigned to the περὶ Πόλιν toparchy in *BGU* XIV 2440, Onosis is listed with at least two more villages of the same toparchy (Tokois, Noeris) in *P.Hib.* II 218.

CPR IV 2 (a bilingual document in Coptic and Greek) lists many villages of the central toparchies of the Herakleopolite nome (the toponyms are written in Greek)[2].

(?) ΟΞΥΡΥΓΧΟΣ

V A.D.	*Stud.Pal.* X 233, II,12	
VI-VII A.D.	*P.Oxy.* XIX 2244,57	ἐποίκιον Ὀξυρύγχο[υ]
VII A.D.	(?) *P.Lond.* V 1791,5;7	κατὰ τὴν Ὀξυρύγχο[υ κώμην?] (5)[3]; ἐπὶ Ὀξύρυγχον (7)
VII-VIII A.D.	*Stud.Pal.* X 56,4	ἀπὸ χωρ(ίου) Ὀξυρ(ύγ)χ(ου)
VIII A.D.	*Stud.Pal.* X 72,2	χ(ωρίον) [Ὀ]ξυ[ρύγχ(ου)]

TOPARCHY: Koites?

ETYMOLOGY: as is well known, the name refers to a fish which was especially venerated in the capital of the Oxyrhynchite nome[4].

---

[1] Ονωσ'ε' *ed.pr.*

[2] See *s.v.* ΝΙΝΩ.

[3] Harrauer's supplement; Ὀξυρυγχι[τῶν πόλιν *ed.pr.*

[4] Cf. DIETER HAGEDORN, *ZPE* 12, 1973, p.292, pointing out «daß die im heutigen Sprachgebrauch übliche Namensform der Stadt, Ὀξύρυγχος, die von den antiken literarischen Quellen ... ausschließlich verwendet wird, in den Papyri *nur ganz selten* bestätigt wird» (italics mine).

It has been suggested[1] that there was a village by this name in the Herakleopolites, too, besides one in the Arsinoites. This supposition is based especially on *Stud.Pal.* X 233, II,12 and on *Stud.Pal.* X 72, which otherwise list Herakleopolite toponyms only. On the other hand, none of the other χωρία appearing in *Stud.Pal.* X 56[2] seem to be elsewhere attested for the Herakleopolites, and the possibility cannot be excluded that either the Arsinoite village called Oxyrhynchus, or the capital of the Oxyrhynchite nome occasionally intruded in a list of Herakleopolite toponyms.

ΟΣΤΡΑΚΙΝΟΥ

VI A.D.	*P.Oxy.* XVI 1917,62	ἐποικ(ίου) Ὀστρακίνου
end of VI A.D.	*P.Oxy.* VI 998 descr.	Ὀστρακίνου
VII/VIII A.D.	*SB* XVIII 13888,6	[χ(ωρίου) Ὀ]στρακίνο(υ)

See also: ΟΤΡ()

BIBLIOGRAPHY: HUBERT METZGER-HERMANN HARRAUER, «Einige Giessener Papyri», *ZPE* 60, 1985, pp.246 ff.; *P.Neph.*, *Einleitung*, p.14.

Other place-names appearing in the same document point to the Koites: (P)hathor (the seat of a monastery), Nokle, Thelbo, Hipponon. All of these places were in the proximity of the border between the Herakleopolite and Oxyrhynchite nomes[3]. Nokle, with Taamorou and Pselemachis, also appears in *P.Oxy.* XVI 1917.

ΟΣΥΤΕΟΣ

See *s.v.* ΑΥΞΩΝΙΟΣ.

ΟΤΡ( )

VIII A.D.	*Stud.Pal.* X 109,5	ἐ(ν τῷ) χ(ωρίῳ) Οτρ()[4]

See also: Ο]ΣΤΡΑΚΙΝΟ(Υ).

The place-name immediately preceding Οτρ() is Taamorou (in the southern Koites; but other villages also listed were in other toparchies). If located in the Koites, this could well be the same locality as Ostrakinou (*q.v.*).

---

[1] Cf. HERMANN HARRAUER, «Ein drittes Oxyrhynchos», *Analecta Papyrologica* 3, 1991, pp.27-32.

[2] Namely: Φ[(1); Φο() (2); Φουρ. (3); Τζα[(5).

[3] Ὀστρακίνου is included in PRUNETI, *Centri abitati*, p.127.

[4] «Οτρ⁻ gut möglich, Ο[σ]τρ⁻ m.E. eher nicht» (Johannes Diethart, letter of February 25, 1994). The second reading would of course lead to Ostrakinou.

Π.[±6]

VI-VII A.D.　　　　　　　*Stud.Pal.* X 5,2　　　　　τὸν βοηθ(ὸν) Π.[±6] [1]

ΠΑΛΑΙ( ) [2]

late III A.D.　　　　　　*BGU* XIII 2365,5

Note Παλας, listed at l.2 of the same document.

ΠΑΛΑΣ

late III A.D.　　　　　　*BGU* XIII 2365,2

Note Παλαι( ), listed at l.5 of the same document.

ΠΑΛΕΤ[

VII-VIII A.D.　　　　　　*Stud.Pal.* X 206,11

Apparently the name of a κλῆρος, listed with several others (see the *Reverse Index* at the end of this volume).

ΠΑΠΑ

149 or 138 B.C. [3]	*SB* XVIII 13304,7	εἰς Πάπα
I/II A.D.	*P.Hib.* II 218,44;53	Πάπα (44); Πάμα (53)
298 A.D.	*P.Panop.Beatty* 1,121;161	ἀπὸ Πάπα (121); ἀπὸ Πάτα (161; *sic*) [4]

---

[1] «Vor der Lücke Π.» (Johannes Diethart, letter of February 25, 1994).

[2] The Editor indicates that Πελαγ( ) could also be read here.

[3] The date 157 B.C. suggested for this document in the *ed. pr.* (*BASP* 22, 1985, pp.243-246) may be wrong: according to GREGG WILLIAM SCHWENDNER, *ZPE* 72, 1988, pp.275-276, it should be dated to 149 or (preferably) 138 B.C.

[4] There is little doubt that one and the same locality is mentioned both at l.121 and at l.161. A scribal error seems more likely at l.161, where Πατα (instead of Παπα) may have been written by anticipating the τ of the following τοῦ. The other possibility would be for Παπα (at l.121) to have been written mistakenly by dittography - in which case Πατα (not attested elsewhere for the Herakleopolites) could be an abbreviation for Πατα(τωις) (see *s.v.*).

III A.D.	*P.Neph.* 28,6	ἀ]πὸ κώμ[η]ς Πάπα π[ερ]ὶ [[1]
late III A.D.	*BGU* XIII 2365,13	Πάπα
III-IV A.D.	*P.Neph.* 29,3	[ἐν κώμ]ῃ Πάπα
about 300 A.D.	*BGU* III 949,5	ἐν Πάπᾳ
313/314 A.D. (cf. *BL* 8,210)	*P.Michael.* 28,1	ἀπ]ὸ κώμης Πάπα
365-373 A.D.	*SB* XIV 11615,3	ἀπ]ὸ κώμης [Π]άπα τοῦ Ἡρακλεοπολίτου νομοῦ
IV A.D. (cf. *BL* 3,221)	*PSI* III 222,9	ἀπὸ κώμης Πάπα περὶ Φ( ) [2]
435 A.D.	*P.Select.* 15,5	ἀπὸ κώμης Πάπα μικρᾶς τοῦ Ἡρακλεοπολίτ[ου νομοῦ
VI/VII A.D.	*CPR* X 60,1	Γνῶσι(ς) Σολλομὼν ἐπικ(ειμέν)ου Πάπας
VI/VII A.D.	*P.Köln* VII 323,2	ἐν κώμῃ Πάπα Μεγάλης{ς} (2); ἀπὸ κώμης Πάπα Μεγάλης το[ῦ Ἡρα]κλεοπολίτου ν[ομο]ῦ (2-3)

TOPARCHY: Koites.

ETYMOLOGY: this village is attested in *P.Wilbour* (A 12,14; 13,23; 28,10; 30,2; 34,38; 34,41; 35,32(?); 43,10) with the double spelling *P3-m3* and *Pr-p3-m3* (Coptic *Papo*)[3], which explains the variant Greek spelling Παμα in *P.Hib.* II 218, l.53, as opposed to the normal Πάπα (also found in *P.Hib.* II 218,44).

MODERN ARABIC NAME: Bibā (older spelling: Babā). It seems probable that this village was the ancient Πάπα ἡ μεγάλη: to this all sources listed above are likely to refer, with the exception of *P.Select.* 15 and (possibly) *PSI* III 222.

SB XVIII 13304: the komogrammateus of Tekmi and Bichinthouth reports the arrival of the strategos Euphranor, «leading to Tekmi the troops that had been transferred to Papa».
P.Michael. 28 also lists Pselemachis and Philonikou (both in Koites).
Connection with Thelbo: *BGU* XIV 2365 (Techtho, Θμοιχ( ) also listed); *P.Hib.* II 218 (Thelbo is entered at l.52, Phebichis at l.46).
P.Beatty Panop. 1: letters from the strategos of the Panopolites, dealing with preparations for the

---

[1] The supplement π[ερ]ὶ [Φέβειχιν has been suggested by the Editors in their commentary (with reference to *P.Michael.* 28,1), but not accepted in their text, «denn es könnte ein weiteres Dorf desselben Namens in einen anderen Toparchie gegeben haben. Πάπα μεγάλης oder Πάπα μικρᾶς steht nicht da».

[2] As noted in the *ed. pr.*, a horizontal stroke above Φ, at the end of l.9, indicates that this was an abbreviated toponym, probably Φ(έβιχιν), as other documents show Papa to have been in the Koites. περὶ Φ[ε]β[ε]ῖχειν Daris (cf. *BL* 7,233; but on the original I could detect no β at the beginning of l.10).

[3] Cf. *TAVO B 69* p.92 (M 82) and p.123 (with nn.47 and 48).

forthcoming visit of the Emperor to Panopolis; one letter[1] reports the dispatch of two cargoes of charcoal from Papa to (presumably) Alexandria.

PSI III 222 deals with two unwilling tax-payers, one from Thmoiamounis (Koma toparchy), the other from Papa.

P.Select. 15: two γεωργοί from Papa ἡ μικρά sell barley and arakos to a baker from Herakleopolis.
P.Köln VII 323, referring to Papa ἡ μεγάλη, confirms the existence of two villages by the same name, at least in the Byzantine period.

ΠΑΡΓΟΥ

| VI A.D. | *Stud.Pal.* X 228,4 | ἐν τ[όπῳ] Πάργου[2] |

Listed with Πιατιμι (l.5), Νεθισει (l.6), Νευηλα (l.7), Σουριυ (l.8), Πιακερ (l.9).

ΠΑΣΗΕΙ

462 A.D.	*P.Vind.Sijp.* 7, 2;5;9; verso	ἐν ἐποικίο'υ' Πασῆει (2); ἀπὸ ἐποικίο'υ' Πασῆει (5); ἐν τῷ αὐτῷ ἐποικίο'υ' Πασῆει (9); ἀπὸ ἐπ[ο]ικίου(?) Πασηει (*verso*)[3]
463 A.D.	*Stud.Pal.* XX 127,6	ἐν ἐποικίου Πασῆει (cf. *BL* 9,346)
1 April-31 August 543 A.D.	*CPR* X 121,3	κεφαλαιωταὶ κτήματος Πασηει (*BL* 9,74)[4]

TOPARCHY: Koites.

Both *P.Vind.Sijp.* 7 and *Stud.Pal.* XX 127 are ἐγγύαι addressed to Φλάουιος Ὀλύμπιος ὁ λαμπροτάτος ἀπὸ πραίτορος. In *Stud.Pal.* XX 127 Aurelius Victor Apasirios of Phebichis gives security for Aurelius Ammianus: the document was drawn at Kerkesephis. All people involved apparently lived at Πασηει.

---

[1] Ll.120-127 were deleted by the scribe; but ll.160-166 are a slightly different version of the same text.

[2] Reading revised by Johannes Diethart (letter of February 25, 1994)

[3] Cf. JOHANNES M. DIETHART, *ZPE* 76, 1989, p.107.

[4] «Ob nur κτῆμα hier allerdings als Synonim für ἐποίκιον (oder χωρίον) zu gelten habe, möchte ich bezweifeln; vielleicht ist konkret, da es in dem letztgenannten Dokument um Belange eines Großgrundbesitzers geht, entweder das in diesem Dorfe befindliche Gut gemeint oder auch das Dorf selbst, aber in seiner Funktion als "Besitztum" (*ed. pr.*) in der Hand des Großgrundbesitzers» (cf. J. M. DIETHART, *ZPE* 76, 1989, p.107).

ΠΑ[ΣΤΟ]ΦΟΡΩΝ

| 256 (255) B.C. | *P.Yale* 31,6-7 (= *P.Hib.* I 87) | περὶ τὴν τῶν Πα[στο]φόρων [1] |
| about 250 B.C. | *P.Hib.* I 118,16 | [Παστο]φόρων |

ΠΑΤΑΜΟΥΣΟΥ

| early II A.D. | *P.Köln* II 98,24 | Παταμούσου |
| VII A.D. | *Stud.Pal.* X 220,1 | ἀπὸ χ(ωρίου) Παταμούσου[2] |

TOPARCHY: Πέραν? Koites?

ETYMOLOGY: Patamousos is a Thracian personal name [3]. It is certainly to be read at l.16 of *P.Tebt.* III 1045, too, where cleruchs of the Herakleopolites are apparently listed: cf. FRITZ UEBEL, *Die Kleruchen Ägyptens unter den ersten sechs Ptolemäern*, Berlin 1968 (Patamousos is no.1132 in his list). The reference to Peensamoi at this point of the document is particularly interesting, as Patamousos is also the name of a tax-farmer (?) in *P.Hels.* 26,A,33[4] (162 B.C.; an entry for Peensamoi recurs at l.28).

This was apparently, still in the II A.D., a "fossil" kleros (*P.Köln* II 98: mentioned with several other such kleroi) which eventually grew into a village.

ΠΑΤΑΤῶΙΣ

| I B.C. | *BGU* XIV 2436,15 | περὶ Πατατῶιν |

BGU XIV 2436 mentions villages belonging to different toparchies in the central and southern Herakleopolites.

---

[1] «The town near which the cleruchs have holdings is called τὴν τῶν Παστοφόρων. The reading is a restoration chosen by Grenfell and Hunt, and is something of a surprise. They pointed out that the name of this village does not occur elsewhere, unless it can be read in *P.Hib.* 118, I, 16, Παστο]φόρων». The kleruchs here are εἰκοσιπεντάρουροι (*P.Yale* I 31, Intro., p.87).

[2] Ταπαμ'γ'.[Wessely; but «In Z.1 der Liste ist ἀπὸ χ(ωρίου) Παπαμ'γ'()γ[zu lesen» (Johannes Diethart, letter of February 25, 1994): in place of two γ's, I propose to read the diphtong ου.

[3] Cf. LUDWIG KOENEN, *Eine agonistische Inschrift aus Ägypten und frühptolemäische Königsfeste*, Meisenheim am Glan 1977, pp.24-25, where he also argues for Παταμούσου to be read instead of Καταμούσου in *P.Tebt.* III 1045,15. On account of the recurrence of the name Πατάμουσος in the Herakleopolites, the inscription studied by Koenen is perhaps more likely to come from this nome. A photograph of this inscription is found in ÉTIENNE BERNAND, *Recueil des inscriptions grecques du Fayoum*, tome III, tav.42.

[4] ἐν Παταμ[ούσου (my supplement).

ΠΕ..[

I B.C.   *BGU* XIV 2429,18

ΠΕ[

II A.D.   *CPR* I 115 + 145,17[1]   περὶ Πε[

TOPARCHY: Koites?

Thmoinache (Koites) appears more than once in the same document (ll.1, 18 and 19).

ΠΕ.[

286 A.D.   *P.Wash.Univ.* I 18,25[2]   ἀπὸ Πε.[

Thneis (Koites) is mentioned in the same document.

ΠΕΕ[±4]

VIII A.D.   *Stud.Pal.* X 204,6   χ'ω'(ρίον) Πεε[±4][3]

ETYMOLOGY: presumably compounded with the prefix πεεν-(Egyptian *p.3-hr-n-*, «the portion, the plot of»: see below, *s.v.* ΠΕΕΜΠ(Α)'Θ'().

Other villages listed in the same document include Magdola (1), Νοτίνου (3), Ogou (4; Tekmi toparchy). A possible supplement is Πεε[νή, as this village appears in the same document with Magdola, in *BGU* XIV 2429 and in *Stud.Pal.* X 200 (Νοτίνου is also listed).

Another possible supplement is Πεε[νσαμοι, as Ogou also appears to have been contiguous to Peensamoi in *BGU* XIV 2436,3.

ΠΕΕΜΠ(Α)'Θ'( )

VI A.D.   *P.Batav.* XIX 23,3   πρωτωφήλακ(ος)
                                                                    πετιάτως (*l.*
                                                                    πρωτοφύλακος πεδιάδος)
                                                                    [ἀπὸ] νότου
                                                                    Πεεμπ(α)'θ'( )[4]

---

[1] «*CPR* I 115 ist mit *CPR* I 145 vereignit» (letter from Johannes Diethart, of February 25, 1994).

[2] Provenance of the document: «vielleicht Herakleopolites» (*BL* 8,509).

[3] Πεε[ναμεα *ed.pr.*: but Πεε[νσαμοί or Πεε[νή seem more likely supplements to me.

[4] «*P.Batav.* 23,3 ist m.E. Πεεμπ(α)'θ'() klar zu lesen» (Johannes Diethart, letter of September 13, 1994); Πεεμπθ() *ed.pr.*

| VI A.D. | *P.Batav.* XIX 23 bis,3 (= *Stud.Pal.* III 24 *recto*) | πρωτωφήλακ(ος) πετιάτως (*l*. πρωτοφύλακος πεδιάδος) <ἀ>πὸ νό(του) Πεεμπ.'θ'( )[1] |

ETYMOLOGY: first element *p3-hr* + *-n-* (genitive): «the plot of...»[2] (πεε-μ- before a labial sound).

This could be a Herakleopolite place-name because:
1. most toponyms with the prefix Πεεν-/Πεεμ- are Herakleopolite[3];
2. there is a good possibility for both documents (from the so-called Fayūm find) to originate from Herakleopolis[4].
Πεεμπ(ασβυ)'θ(εως)' is a possible supplement, especially if Πεεμπα'θ'( ) may be read in *P.Batav.* XIX 23 bis.

ΠΕΕΝ.[..

| I B.C. | *BGU* XIV 2429,16 | |

ETYMOLOGY: πεεν- = Egyptian *p3-hr-n-*: «the portion, the plot of»; see *s.v.* ΠΕΕΜΠ(Α)'Θ'().

ΠΕΕΝ.ΧΕΝΟΒΑ( )

| I B.C. | *BGU* XIV 2433,18 | ἀπὸ Πεεν.χενοβα( )[5] |

ETYMOLOGY: first component *p3-hr* + *-n-* (genitive)[6]: «the plot of...».

See also *s.v.* ΠΕΕΝΣΧΩΝ.

ΠΕΕΝΑΜΕΥΣ

| 157 B.C. | *UPZ* I 122,3 | ἐκ Παανάμεὺς τοῦ Ἡρακλεοπολίτου |

---

[1] The first Editor deciphered Πονπεε..π'θ'( ).

[2] Katelijn Vandorpe (letter of July 18, 1995).

[3] Cf. CALDERINI-DARIS, *Dizionario*, vol. IV, pp.82-84; *Suppl.* I, pp.221-224.

[4] See *Introduction*, p.26.

[5] The Editor indicates Πεεναχενοβα( ) or Πεενχενοβα( ) as possible readings.

[6] See *s.v.* ΠΕΕΜΠ(Α)'Θ'().

CATALOGUE

96-94 or 63-61 B.C.	*BGU* XIV 2429,2	Πεενάμεως
about 48/46 B.C.	*BGU* VIII 1849,6	ἐκ Ποενάμεως
I B.C.	*BGU* XIV 2435 *recto*, col. I,1 [1]	
I B.C.	*BGU* XIV 2437,26	Πεενάμεως
I B.C.	*BGU* XIV 2440,3	Πεενάμεως
I/II A.D.	*P.Hib.* II 218,39	Πεενάμεως
II A.D.	*CPR* I 111,7	κώ[μης] Πεενάμε[ως
225 A.D.	*CPR* I 36,3;7	κώμης Πεενάμεως (3); περὶ κώμην Πεενάμεα (6-7)
227 A.D.	*CPR* I 64,5 (= *SB* I 5165)	δι'ἐπιτηρητῶν ἀγορανομ[ίας] μερῶν Μέσης Πεενάμεως (4-5)
227 A.D.	*Stud.Pal.* XX 28,5 (= *CPR* I 7)	δι'ἐπιτηρητῶν ἀγορανομ[ίας] μερῶν Μέσης Πεε[ν]άμεως (4-5)
228/229 A.D.	*SB* I 4370,5;7;21	δι'ἐπιτηρητῶν ἀγορανομίας [Μέσης Πεενάμε(ως)] (4-5) [2]; [ἀπὸ] κώμ[η]ς Πεε[νάμε]ως (7); π[ερὶ] κώμ[ην] Πεε[νάμ]εα (21)
15 Oct. 251 A.D. (cf. *BL* 8,463)	*Stud.Pal.* XX 55,4 (= *CPR* I 37)	περὶ κώμην Πεενάμεα (3-4)
V A.D.	*Stud.Pal.* X 94,6	ἐποίκ(ιον) Πεενάμεως
V-VI A.D.	*CPR* XIV 6,5;15	ἀπὸ ἐποικίου Πεεν[άμεω]ς τοῦ Ἡρακλεοπολίτου νομ[ο]ῦ (5-6); ἀπὸ ἐποικ(ίου) Πεε[νάμεως] (15) [3]
VI-VII A.D.	*Stud.Pal.* X 237,1	Πεεν[αμ-] (?) [4]
VII A.D.	*Stud.Pal.* X 4,4	Ποιναμι

---

[1] Unpublished: see *BGU* XIV, p.131.

[2] My supplement; [περὶ Τέκμει] *ed. pr.*: but people living at Peenameus apparently acted through the ἐπιτηρηταί ἀγορανομίας of the Μέση toparchy: cf. *CPR* I 64 and *Stud.Pal.* XX 28.

[3] «The full name of the hamlet is missing both in this line and in the address, but ... Πεενᾶμις... appears the most probable restoration» (Editor's note *ad l.* 5). See also AMPHILOCHIOS PAPATHOMAS, «Textbeiträge zu *CPR* XIV», *Tyche* 10, 1995, p.145.

[4] My supplement. See p.163 n.1.

VII-VIII A.D.	*Stud.Pal.* X 17,10	ἀπὸ χ'ω'(ρίου) Ποιναμι[
Byz.	*SB* I 4727,2	[Πεε]νάμε(ως)

Literary Sources

V A.D.	STEPH.BYZ.	Πίναμυς· πόλις Αἰγύπτου κτλ.

TOPARCHY: Ἄγημα κάτω (I B.C.), then Μέση (III A.D.).

ETYMOLOGY: *p3-hr* + *-n-* (genitive) + *'Imn* («the plot of the shepherds»): this toponym recurs in *P.Wilbour* B 22,29 (variant spellings: B 15,13; A 20,26).

The village is also attested in Coptic sources, where it is called *Puōh(-n)-N(i)amēu* [1]: cf. GÉRARD ROQUET, *Toponymes et Lieux-dits égyptiens enregistrés dans le dictionnaire copte de W.E. Crum*, Cairo 1973, Nr.3. The Coptic *Life of the Apa Epima*, a martyr who lived in the fourth century A.D.[2], is a particularly important source: Apa Epima was taken to the port of *Pehnamoun* (this must be Peensamoi, *q.v.*), and then put to trial in *Puōh-Namēy* (Bohairic *Phouoh-n-Niamēy*).

The similarity between the village-names *Pehnamoun* and *Puōh-Namēy* has apparently given rise to some confusion. Thus, according to Timm (*cit.*) «das Verhältnis zwischen Pehnamoun und Pouōh-namēy ist noch zu klären. T. Mina [the Editor of the *Life of Apa Epima*] vermutete, daß es sich um zwei benachbarte Siedlungen handelte, wofür aber die Belege fehlen». Mina's opinion seems reasonable in the light of the Greek sources, attesting both Peenameus/*Pouōh Namēy*/Bahnamūh and Peensamoi/*Pehnamoun*/al-Bahsamūn (see *s.v.* ΠΕΕΝΣΑΜΟΙ).

The Map in *Tavo B 69* identifies Bahnamūh (correctly) with Greek Πεεναμις (actually Πεεναμευς: the wrong ending goes back to the Editors of *BGU* VIII) but also (wrongly, in my opinion) with Coptic *Pehnamoun*, which is probably no more than a variant spelling for *Pehṣamoun* = al-Bahsamūn: see *s.v.* ΠΕΕΝΣΑΜΟΙ.

This same place-name may have been translated into Greek in some sources: Ποιμένων κώμη (*q.v.*).

MODERN ARABIC NAME: Bahnamūh (cf. JEAN YOYOTTE, *apud* DREW-BEAR, *Le nome Hermopolite*, p.199 n.353).

BGU XIV 2437,26 assigns Peenameus to the Ἄγημα κάτω (followed by Korphotoi, Peenepsomphis, Peensemtheus, Kella) but about three centuries later *CPR* I 64 and *Stud.Pal.* XX 28 (contracts involving people from Thmoinothis and Peenpibyk(is), in the Μέση toparchy) are apparently drawn up in the agoranomos office of the Μέση toparchy at Peenameus. At least one village of the Μέση (Techymis) in fact appears at not great distance from Peenameus in *BGU* XIV 2440.

In *BGU* VIII 1849 a woman remembers her parents' journey from Peenameus to the temple of Herakles at Tilothis, and how she came to marry the brother of a priest of this temple. Her parents are said to have travelled north (κατελθόντων: down river, i.e. north), which is consistent with the identification of Peenameus and Tilothis with modern Bahnamūh and Dalās, respectively.

CPR I 111 (lease contract between two inhabitants of Herakleopolis) concerns land near Peenameus, in the fossil kleros Βίωνος.

---

[1] The Coptic name of the place would seem to postulate the prefix *p3-w3h*, «the residence», rather than *p3-hr*, «the plot». There are in fact signs of oscillation in the Greek rendering of the first element of this toponym: in the earliest document attesting it (*UPZ* I 122) this is transliterated as Παα–; later on, one finds Ποεναμεως (*BGU* VIII 1849) and Ποιναμι (*Stud.Pal.* X 4; X 17). Cf. HEINZ-JOSEF THISSEN, «Zu *P3-hr-n-'Imn* = Ποανεμουνις», *Enchoria* 1, 1971, pp.75-78 (on *p3-hr* = πεε– and *p3-w3h* = πο(υ)α–).

[2] Cf. TIMM, *Das christlich-koptische Ägypten* IV, pp.1872-1873 (*s.v.* «Pehnamoun»).

Stud.Pal. X 94: Peenameus is listed with Ἀννιανοῦ (near Sobthis), Daphne[1], Tosachmis. As this last village belonged to the Koites, it may be worth noting that Peenameus is also read at the top of the fifth column in a poorly preserved land-survey on the *verso* of *BGU* XIV 2435: the survey on the *recto* deals with the Phebichis area.

Stud.Pal. X 4: villagers from Ἀπίωνος (1), Poinami (2; variant spelling for Peenameus), Thmoiamounis (4; Koma toparchy), and Pkommatoei (5), are requested for compulsory work to be done on the dyke (παράχωμα) at Koma. Poinami recurs again with Koma (3) and Pkommatoei (13) in *Stud.Pal.* X 17.

ΠΕΕΝΒΕΝΔΗΤΕΩΣ

I B.C.   *BGU* XIV 2438,31   Πεενβενδήτεως

TOPARCHY: Μέση.

ETYMOLOGY: first component *p3-hr* + *-n-* (genitive)[2] + second component *b3-nb-dd* = Βένδης/Μένδης: «the plot of Mendes». On Mendes, «dieu bélier», see JAN QUAEGEBEUR, «Documents grecs et géographie historique. Le Mendésien», in *L'Égyptologie en 1979. Axes prioritaires de recherches (Colloques Internationaux du Centre National de la Recherche Scientifique. N° 595)*, Paris 1982, p.271.

Land-survey: the section on the Μέση toparchy includes Peenbendet(is) along with Phnebieus, Peenpibyk(is), Phys, Ποιμένων κώμη.

ΠΕΕΝΕ.'.'( )[3]

I B.C.   *BGU* XIV 2437,5

TOPARCHY: Tekmi.

ETYMOLOGY: first component *p3-hr* + *-n-* (genitive): «the plot of...»; see *s.v.* Πεεμπ(α)'θ'().

Part of a τοπογραμματικὸς κλῆρος was at Πεεν.'.'( ): it is recorded in *BGU* XIV 2437 (ll.1-8) under the heading περὶ Τέκμι· Κολλιντααθύρ. More land (to make up a 60 arourae holding) was in other places of the same toparchy (Taemsis, Tou, Tochontou, Tekmi).

ΠΕΕΝΕΠΟΧΡΑ

I B.C.   *BGU* XIV 2433,55   Πε[εν]έποχρα

---

[1] Πεεν[αμεύς] is therefore a likely supplement at *Stud.Pal.* X 237,1, as Daphne also appears in this document (l.3).

[2] See *s.v.* ΠΕΕΜΠ(Α)'Θ'().

[3] The *ed. pr.* offers Πεενεκ.( ), Πεενσκ.( ), or Πεενεσ.( ). A reading Πεενέπ(υς) also seems possible (checked on a photograph).

| I B.C. | *BGU* XIV 2440,56[1]; (fr.9),108; (fr.12),122 | περὶ Πεενέποχρα (122) |

TOPARCHY: Μέση.

ETYMOLOGY: first component *p3-hr* + *-n-* (genitive): «the plot of...»; see *s.v.* ΠΕΕΜΠ(Α)'Θ'().

BGU XIV 2433 includes Peenepochra in the same group (ll.48-55) with Chennis (48) and Phys (49), both of which were in the Μέση toparchy.

ΠΕΕΝΕΨΥ

212/211 B.C.	*P.Lille* I 59,12;43;98;126	Πεενέψυ
51/50 B.C.	*BGU* VIII 1779,2	παρ' Ἀρυ[ώτου] κ[ω]μογραμματέως Πεενέψυ[2]
50/49 B.C.	*BGU* VIII 1842,6	περὶ κώμην Πεενέπυς[3]
I B.C.	*BGU* VIII 1822,7	περὶ Πενεπυ[[4]

See also: Πεενε..( ).

TOPARCHY: Tekmi.

ETYMOLOGY: first component *p3-hr* + *-n-* (genitive): «the plot of...»; see *s.v.* ΠΕΕΜΠ(Α)'Θ'().

P.Lille 59 includes Peenepsy in a list of villages of the Koma, Tekmi and Tilothis toparchies.
BGU VIII 1842: Petechon, phylakites at Tekmi, has a 10 arourae kleros at Πεενέπυς.
BGU VIII 1822: Artemon, who leases land from an «Arab» in the Peenepsy area, petitions the strategos Paniskos against the local authorities at Tekmi.
BGU VIII 1779: petition written by the komogrammateus Haryotes on account of the inhabitants of Peenepsy, who complain of being charged excessively high taxes.

---

[1] New reading suggested after checking a photograph, and deemed «probable» by William Brashear, who checked the original for me (letter of August 22, 1994). Πεενωχρος.... *ed. pr.* (only the bottom parts of the letters are preserved).

[2] My reading (checked on a photograph). Τεσενεφῦ *ed. pr.*; Τεσενεψυ Günter Poethke (letter of April 14, 1994). The initial, very cursive, π differs from any other π in this document: toponyms, however, and especially standard prefixes such as πεεν–, were often written much more cursively than the rest of the document. The two shapes for a π coexist e.g. in *BGU* VIII 1824 (checked on a photograph), the cursive π being found in a large number of documents from Abū Sir Al-Malaq (published as *BGU* VIII, XIV and XVI).

[3] Πεενεπῦς according to the Editors: but the same toponym is indexed by them with a different accent (Πεενεπύς).

[4] Reading checked for me by Günter Poethke: περὶ Πενεπ.[*ed. pr.*

ΠΕΕΝΕΨΩΜΦΙΣ

96-94 or 63-61 B.C.	*BGU* XIV 2429,3	Πεενεψώ(μφεως)
63/62 B.C.	*BGU* VIII 1771,14	περὶ Πεενεψῶμφιν ἐν τοῖς Ἀρχαίοις
I B.C.	*BGU* XIV 2437,30; (fr.1),54; (fr.2),62	Πεενεψώμφεως (30); Πεενεψῶμφιν (54;62)
I B.C.	*BGU* XIV 2438 (fr.3),89	Πεενεψώμφεως
506/507 A.D.	*MPER* XV 62,1;4	πεδί(ου) Πεενεψόμθεως (1); πεδί(ου) Πεενεψό<μ>θεως (4)

TOPARCHY: Ἄγημα κάτω.

ETYMOLOGY: first component *p3-hr* + *-n-* (genitive)[1] + intermediate *e*[2] + second component *ṯnf* («temple dancer»[3]): «the plot of the temple dancer».

BGU XIV 2437 and 2438 assign this village to the Ἄγημα κάτω.

Peenepsomphis and Korphotoi appear as consecutive entries in *BGU* XIV 2429 (ll.3 and 4), 2437 (ll.28 and 30) and 2437 fr.1 (ll.52 and 54).

Near Peenepsomphis there was a settlement of Greek κάτοικοι, called οἱ Ἀρχαῖοι, contiguous to another such settlement called οἱ περὶ Αὐλήν, near Bichinthouth in the Tekmi toparchy (*BGU* VIII 1771).

ΠΕΕΝΗ

96-94 or 63-61 B.C.	*BGU* XIV 2429,3	Πεενηι.
I B.C.	*BGU* XIV 2440,62;64	περὶ Πε[ενή (62)[4]; περὶ Πεενή (64)
311 A.D.	*P.Oxy.* XIV 1708,3	ἀπὸ κώμης Πεννή[5]
381 A.D.	*P.Rain.Cent.* 87,2	ἀπὸ Πεενή
405 A.D.	*SB* VIII 9773,8	ἀπὸ κώ[μη]ς Π[ε]ενὴ

---

[1] See *s.v.* ΠΕΕΜΠ(Α)’Θ’( ).

[2] As in Θμοινεφθα (see *s.v.* ΘΜΟΙΦΘΑ).

[3] Cf. WILLY CLARYSSE-PIETER J. SIJPESTEIJN, «A Letter from a Dancer of Boubastis», *APF* 41, 1995, pp.57-61: they publish a Michigan papyrus (*P.Mich.* inv.no. 4394a, of the second or first century B.C.) which shows that there was a special link between σώμφεις (*ṯnf.w*, «dancers») and the cult of the goddess Bast, apparently well established in the Herakleopolites (see *s.v.* ΘΜΟΙΟΒΑΣΤΙΣ).

[4] περ Πε[*ed. pr.*: the supplement is mine, on the basis of l.64.

[5] On the variant spelling Πεννή see CALDERINI-DARIS, *Dizionario*, *s.v.* (where a comparison is drawn with the spellings Πεεννω/Πεννώ of an Oxyrhynchite place-name).

| V A.D. | *Stud.Pal.* X 233, col.I B,12 | Πεενή |
| VII-VIII A.D. | *Stud.Pal.* X 200,6 | χ'ω'(ρίον) Πεενή |

See also: Πεε[±4]

TOPARCHY: περὶ Πόλιν?

ETYMOLOGY: first component *p3-hr* + *-n-* (genitive): «the plot of...»; see *s.v.* Πεεμπ(α)'θ'().

MODERN ARABIC NAME: Bahā (on the analogy of Πεεναμεύς/Baanamūh, Πεενσαμου/Al-Bahsamūn; with loss of the *-n-* of the genitive, as in Al-Bahsamūn); this was Coptic *Paha*: see *TAVO B 69* § 4.3 (M117).

The villages listed in *BGU* XIV 2429 were for the most part in the Ἄγημα toparchy (Peenameus, Peenepsomphis, Korphotoi, Nino, Kollasoucha, Niseus, Peensemtheus, Petachor). Magdola, Hiera Nesos, Mouchis and Sobthis are also entered. Μαγδολον of *Stud.Pal.* 200 (l.3), where Peene also recurs, is probably just a different spelling for Μαγδωλα: the two villages would thus appear together in another, much later document.

BGU XIV 2440 (ll.62-66): private land of Berenike, the daughter of Eubios [1], situated περὶ Πεενή and περὶ Ε.... (ll.62-64); there follows a reference to περὶ Πέρα(ν) καὶ Νισέα (l.65: more of Berenike's property is being surveyed).

ΠΕΕΝΙΒΙΣ

| I/II A.D. | *P.Hib.* II 218,62 | Πεενίβ(εως) |

TOPARCHY: Μέση?

ETYMOLOGY: first component *p3-hr* + *-n-* (genitive) [2] + second component *h(y)b* («the plot of the ibis»)?

In *P.Hib.* II 218 Thmoinothis (58), Phnebieus (59), Chennis (60), in the Μέση toparchy, precede the entry for Peenibis; Koma (63), Krekis (64), Bousiris (65) follow it.

Πεεν- prefixes are well represented in the Μέση toparchy, while not attested in the Koma toparchy.

ΠΕΕΝΜΩ( ) [3]

| I B.C. | *BGU* XIV 2434,15 | |

---

[1] The same Berenike also appears in *BGU* XIV 2446 (ll.8,17), 2447 (l.9) and 2450 (l.35).

[2] See *s.v.* ΠΕΕΜΠ(Α)'Θ'( ).

[3] «Dorf, unbelegt» (*ed. pr.*). A very doubtful reading. One would not expect a village-name at this point of the document, unless it may be taken as an additional entry in the totals drawn at the end of this account of wheat revenues from the different toparchies of the Herakleopolite nome.

ETYMOLOGY: first component *p3-hr* + *-n-* (genitive)[1] + second component -μο( ): «the plot of...».

ΠΕΕΝΠΑΣΒΥΤΕΩΣ

212/211 B.C.	*P.Lille* I 59,8;35;121	Πεενπασβύτεως
29 Nov. 163 B.C.	*P.Hels.* I 8 (*Greek subscription*),2	Πεενπα[σ]β....[2]
after 84/83 B.C.	*BGU* XIV 2370,24	Πεενπασβύτεως
I B.C.	*BGU* XIV 2436,10	Πεενπασβῦ(τιν)
I B.C.	*BGU* XIV 2438,63	Πεενπασβύτεως
V A.D.	*Stud.Pal.* X 233, col.I B,14	Πεαμπασβύθεως (cf. *BL* 8,459)

See also ΠΕΕΜΠ(Α)'Θ'( ).

TOPARCHY: Tilothis.

ETYMOLOGY: first component *p3-hr* + *-n-* (genitive)[3] : «the plot of...».

Assigned to the Tilothis toparchy in *BGU* XIV 2370 and *BGU* XIV 2438, this village must have been near the Ἄγημα toparchy, too: the holding of a certain Ptolemaios jr. was in fact split between it and Korphotoi (which was in the Ἄγημα).

The lists of place-names of the Tilothis toparchy in *P.Lille* I 59 and *BGU* XIV 2438 coincide (Peenpasbyt(is), Schnomthis, Tanchais, Tilothis); both documents also mention Koma, and other villages of the Koma toparchy.

Stud.Pal. X 233 enters Peenpasbyt(is) three lines after Bousiris (which also recurs in *P.Lille* I 59).

ΠΕΕΝΠΙΒΥΚΕΩΣ

93-70 B.C.	*P.Yale* I 57,2	ἐν κώ]μηι Πεενπιβύκει τῆς [Μέσης] (cf. *BL* 8,513)
I B.C.	*BGU* VIII 1803,6	Πεενπιβυκε[
I B.C.	*BGU* XIV 2438,33; (fr.3),98	Πεενπιβύκεως (33); Πεενπιβύκ[εως (98)
II-III A.D.	*P.Köln* II 99,2	Πεενπιβύκ(εως)

---

[1] See *s.v.* ΠΕΕΜΠ(Α)'Θ'( ).

[2] Πϵεν... *ed.pr.*, Πεενπα... Clarysse (*JHS* 109, 1989, p.247). The traces as can be detected on the photograph are compatible with Πεενπα[σ]βυ.... .

[3] See *s.v.* ΠΕΕΜΠ(Α)'Θ'( ).

211-217 A.D.	*CPR* I 56,6	ἀγορανομίας Πεενπι]βύκεως (cf. *BL* 7,43)
227 A.D.	*Stud.Pal.* XX 28, 7-8	ἀπὸ κ[ώμης] Πεενπιβύκ[εως
236 A.D.(?) (cf. *BL* 8,463)	*Stud.Pal.* XX 47,5	ἀπὸ κώμης Πεενπιβύκεως (cf. *BL* 8,463)
first half of III A.D.	*CPR* I 92,9	Πεενπιβ]ύκεως (cf. *BL* 7,43)
IV/V A.D.	*Stud.Pal.* X 235,2	Πεενπιβύκεως
IV/V A.D.	*P.Rain.Cent.* 153,14	ἀπὸ Πεε]μπιβύκεως
V A.D.	*Stud.Pal.* X 233, col. II,19	Πεεμπιβύκεως
V/VI A.D.	*Stud.Pal.* VIII 1226,5	Πεενπ]ιβῦχ(ις)[1]
VI A.D.	*MPER* XV 113,1	ἀπὸ Πεεμπιβύκ[εως]
end of VI/VII A.D.	*P.Köln* VII 319,3	ἀπὸ κώμης Πεενπεβίχ[εως τ]οῦ Ἡρακλεοπολίτου νομοῦ
end of VI/VII A.D.	*P.Köln* VII 321,5	ἀπὸ κώμης Πεενπεβί[χεως τοῦ Ἡρ]ακλεοπο[λίτου νομοῦ

TOPARCHY: Μέση.

ETYMOLOGY: first component *p3-hr* (+ *-n-* of the genitive) :«the plot of...»[2].

This village often recurs in association with Phnebieus, which was the main centre in the Μέση toparchy (*BGU* VIII 1803,ll.2 and 6-7; *BGU* XIV 2438,22;96; *P.Köln* II 99,1).

Stud.Pal. XX 28 (παραχώρησις contract between two of its inhabitants, drawn up in the agoranomos office at Peenameus in the Μέση) confirms the location in this toparchy.

On the other hand, *Stud.Pal.* XX 47 is a παραχώρησις contract drawn up at the agoranomos office of the Ἄγημα toparchy, for land situated πε[ρ]ὶ κώμην Ὠτειριν, in the fossil kleros of Theodoros; the vendor is from Peenpibyk(is), the buyer probably from Alexandria (he is called an ἀστός). The contract was written by the same scribe who recorded *CPR* VI 73 (contract drawn up at the same agoranomos office, between parties from Tekmi and Herakleopolis)[3].

Stud.Pal. X 235 deals with wine production.

---

[1] The supplement is mine; the Editor offers Ψ]ιβυχ( ), otherwise unattested.

[2] See *s.v.* ΠΕΕΜΠ(Α)'Θ'( ).

[3] See *s.v.* ΠΕΡΑΦΘΙΣ.

ΠΕΕΝΣ[...]

Feb. 13 B.C.   *BGU* XVI 2585,1

ETYMOLOGY: first component *p3-hr* (+ *-n-* of the genitive): «the plot of...».

Declaration of sheep addressed to the agents of the official πρός τῷ ἐννομίῳ of the Herakleopolites.

ΠΕΕΝΣΑΜΟΙ

215/214 B.C.	*P.Strasb.* II 111, 5-6	Πεονταμοῦν (cf. *BL* 7,245)
about 164 B.C.	*P.Tebt.* III 1044,54	Πεενσα(μοί)[1]
about 164 B.C. (cf. *BL* 7,273)	*P.Tebt.* III 1045,14;45	περὶ Πεενσα(μοί) (14); περὶ] Πεενσα(μοί) (44-45)[2]
2 Sept. 162 B.C.	*P.Hels.* I 26 A,28	Πεενσαμοί
162 B.C.	*P.Tebt.* III 857,36	Πεενσα(μοί)[3]
I B.C.	*BGU* XIV 2436,3	Πεενσ(αμοί?)[4]
I B.C.	*BGU* XIV 2437,41	Πεενσαμοί
9 Jan. 13 B.C.	*BGU* XVI 2616,3	εἰς Π[εενσ]αμοί
9 Aug. 10 B.C.	*BGU* XVI 2640,3	ὁ τῆς Πεενσαμοί λογευτής
3/2 B.C.	*BGU* XVI 2565,4	ἀ[π]ὸ Πεεν<σ>αμοί[5]
192 A.D.	*P.Tebt.* II 353,4	κωμογρα(μματείας) Πεενσαμοί[6]
309 A.D.	*P.Hib.* II 219,11	[Πεενσ]αμοι[7]

---

[1] Πεενσά(κω) *ed.pr.*: the resolution here, as well as in *P.Tebt.* III 1044 and 1082 (see below), was based on the (wrong) reading at *P.Tebt.* II 353,5 (see below, n.6).

[2] Πεενσά(κω) *ed. pr.*: but see the preceding footnote.

[3] The resolution is mine: the Editors' note *ad loc.* records that «although the name might be read as Πεενσχ(ω), for which cf. *BGU* VIII 1827,26, Πεενσά(κω) is more probable; cf.[*P.Tebt.*] 1044,54; 1045,14» - where, however, just Πεενσα( ) can be read (see above, n.2).

[4] Πεενσ( ) *ed. pr.*

[5] Πεενᾶμοι Ed. (who hesitates between Πεενᾶμις and Πεενσαμοί).

[6] Πεενσακοι *ed. pr.* The new reading is mine (checked on a photograph).

[7] [±8]αμοι *ed. pr.*; [Πεενσ]αμοι is an attractive supplement, as this village of the Πέραν toparchy is elsewhere connected with Techtho (recurring at l.13).

421 A.D.	*P.Select.* 13,3; *verso*	ἀπὸ κώμης Πεενσαμοί ιγ πάγου τοῦ αὐτοῦ (*scil.* Ἡρακλεοπολίτου) νομοῦ (2-3); ἀπὸ Πεενσαμοί (*verso*; cf. *BL* 7,98)
V A.D.	*Stud.Pal.* X 233, col. I B,2	Πεενσαμοί (cf. *BL* 7,258)[1]
8 June 623 A.D. (cf. *BL* 9,244)	*SB* I 5681,19	ἐν τῇ καλουμένῃ κώμῃ Πεενσαμοί
VIII A.D.	*Stud.Pal.* X 84,5	χ(ωρίον) Π..αμοί[2]

See also: ΠΕΕ[±4].
TOPARCHY: Πέραν (XIII *pagus*: *P.Select.* 13).

ETYMOLOGY: *p3-hr* + *-n-* (genitive)[3] + -ταμουν/-σαμοι[4]: «the plot of...». The form -ταμουν is attested only once (along with a different vocalisation in the first component: Πεον- instead of Πεεν-), in the earliest source for this village [5].

The same village is attested in Coptic sources, where it is called *Pehsamoun* (cf. *CPR* IV 50,3,9; *CPR* IV 173,4) or *Pehnamoun* (in the *Life of Apa Epima*, where it is said to be a port: see *s.v.* ΠΕΕΝΑΜΕΥΣ).

MODERN ARABIC NAME: Al-Bahsamūn: cf. TIMM, *Das christlich-koptische Ägypten*, I, p.301. See also *TAVO B 69*, p.100 (site *W 36*: al-Kōm al-Ahmar/al-Bahsamūn): «Aus lautlichen und topographischen Gründen ist al-Bahsamūn mit dem koptischen *Pehsamoun* identisch. Der antike Ort lag jedoch wohl nicht an der Stelle des heutigen al-Bahsamūn, sondern am nahelegenen Kōm al-Ahmar» (no identification with a Greek toponym is offered); *ibid.*, p.239, on sites W 35 (al-Bahsamūn: «In den Dorfstraßen befinden sich zwei Säulenbasen sowie ein Kapitell»),W 36 («0,5 km nordwestlich von al-Bahsamūn liegt ein flacher Kom von 50 m Durchmesser, der wegen der großen Menge von Keramikscherben mit besonderem Recht den Namen al-Kōm al-Ahmar erhalten hat. Die nähere Untersuchung des Kōms zeigt deutlich, daß an dieser Stelle eine Keramikwerkstatt und Brennhöfen lagen. Die zahlreichen Keramikscherben sind in die spätantike Zeit zu datieren») and W 37 (Kōm Simūn: «Ca. 1,5 km westlich von al-Kōm al Ahmar/al-Bahsamūn. Hier liegen auf mehreren Plateaus unterschiedlicher Größe und Höhe Bestattungen. Die meisten gehören in die Spätantike, die Keramikscherben sind ebenfalls in spätantike Zeit zu datieren. Eine byzantinische Münze wurde auf dem großen Kōm gefunden»).

P.Hels. I 26 lists Peensamoi, Tebetny, Thmoiphtha, Thmoinausiris, as belonging to the Πέρα toparchy: the oikonomos deals with tax-arrears from the Koites, the Techtho Nesos and the Πέραν (*P.Hels.* I 21 almost certainly belongs to the same document). Peensamoi and Thmoiphtha again recur together in *BGU* XIV 2437. In *P.Strasb.* II 111 (farmers on strike have apparently fled from the first to the

---

[1] Πεενμαμοί in *BL* 7,258 (a misprint: cf. PIETER J. SIJPESTEIJN, «Addenda et corrigenda zu Wiener Texten», *ZPE* 24, 1977, p.96).

[2] Π̣ε̣γσαμοί seems possible here. Π̣[ ]αμοι *ed. pr.*; «vielleicht Π̣ο̣ταμοι» Diethart (letter of September 13, 1994).

[3] See *s.v.* ΠΕΕΜΠ(Α)'Θ'( ).

[4] The alternance τ/σ may suggest Egyptian *d* (information from Willy Clarysse).

[5] For a similar case, see *s.v.* ΚΟΡΦΟΤΟΙ.

second village) Clarysse's suggestion[1] that Πεονταμουν = Πεενσαμοι is therefore supported by the very likely reading Θμοι[ε]φθ[α] on the *verso*. Again, the same official (the oikonomos' agent, called Harmachis) who is in charge at Techtho (*P.Strasb.* II 563 and 113[2]), also supervises affairs at Πεονταμουν = Πεενσαμοι and Θμοι[ε]φθ[α] (both were villages of the Πέραν toparchy)[3]. In other words, there was an administrative connection between Techtho and Peensamoi (and with the Πέραν in general): this also accounts for the fact that these two villages appear one after another in *Stud.Pal.* X 233[4].

P.Hib. II 219 contains an assessment of linen-pieces to be produced by the λινούφοι of Ἀγκυρῶν πόλις, also on account of other villages, including Techtho (l.13).

In *P.Tebt.* III 857 Peensamoi and Pois are mentioned in two different fragments of the same document: this supports the resolution Πεενσ(αμοι) in *BGU* XIV 2436, 1-3, where Orestes' kleros is split between Magdola, an Ἰβιῶν locality, Pois, Ogou (Tekmi toparchy) and Peensamoi[5]. Peensamoi must have been meant at *Stud.Pal.* X 84, l.5, where Pois also appears at l.4, as well as Noeris (l.3, περὶ Πόλιν toparchy: also found in *BGU* XIV 2436,l.12, again in connection with Pois). Peensamoi and Noeris are therefore the most likely solutions at *P.Tebt.* III 1044, ll.54 and 65.

P.Tebt. II 353 (a receipt for tax-arrears paid to the agent of the komogrammateus of Peensamoi) was found among the ruins of a house at Tebtynis[6]; perhaps the payer had more than a single domicile, one at at Peensamoi (where he was in arrear with his taxes) and another at Tebtynis (where he may have kept this receipt): had he forgotten to pay his taxes because he was away or, rather, did he try not to pay them by moving to the neighbouring nome? In *SB* I 5681 Phoibammon, from Ἀρσινοιτῶν πόλις, has been living at Peensamoi for a long time, but still has business in the Arsinoites.

In the Coptic *Life of Apa Epima*, a martyr of the IV A.D., reference is made to the port of *Pehnamoun*[7].

ΠΕΕΝΣΕΜΘΕΥΣ

96-94 or 63-61 B.C.	*BGU* XIV 2429,10	Ποενσεμθεύς
after 84/83 B.C.	*BGU* XIV 2370,34	Πεενσεμθέως
I B.C.	*BGU* XIV 2437,32	Πεενσεμθέως
I B.C.	*BGU* XIV 2438 (fr.3),91	Πεενσεμ[θεως]
I B.C.	*BGU* XIV 2444,6	κώμης Πεενσεμθ(έως)[8]

See also: ΠΟ[..]ΟΜ( ).

TOPARCHY: Ἄγημα κάτω.

---

[1] *Ancient Society* 7, 1976, p.202.

[2] Both papyri were reedited by Clarysse, *ibid*.

[3] I suggest that εἰς τὸ Πέραν should in fact be read above l.21 in *P.Strasb.* II 111.

[4] Clarysse therefore suggested that Πεονταμουν was not far from Techtho.

[5] A resolution Πεενσ(εμθεύς) would imply the splitting of the name Semtheus.

[6] During the excavations of 1899/1900: see *P.Tebt.* II, *Preface*, p.V.

[7] Cf. TIMM, *Das christlich-koptische Ägypten*, IV, pp.1872-1873, *s.v.*

[8] My reading and supplement (checked on a photograph): Πεενσομ. *ed. pr.*

ETYMOLOGY: first component *p3-hr* + *-n-* (genitive)[1] + second component (Σεμθεύς: personal name, besides being the name of a god[2]): «the portion of Semtheus».

MODERN ARABIC NAME: on topographical grounds, an identification with Santūr is tempting; phonetically, however, this would imply the loss of the prefix *p3-hr -n-* /πεεν-, normally preserved in other toponyms (see *s.vv.* ΠΕΕΝΑΜΕΥΣ, ΠΕΕΝΣΑΜΟΙ).

BGU XIV 2370 assigns this village to a κάτω τοπαρχία which *BGU* XIV 2437 and 2438 name more precisely as the Ἄγημα κάτω. *BGU* XIV 2429 also comprises it in a group of villages in the Ἄγημα toparchy (Peenameus, Peenepsomphis, Korphotoi, Nino, Kollasoucha, Niseus, Peensemtheus, Petachor).

At least one land-grantee seems to have held land both at Peensemtheus and at Pyrgotos (Tekmi toparchy): this is Apollonios son of Chairemon (land at Peensemtheus: *BGU* XIV 2437,33; at Pyrgotos: *BGU* XIV 2441, 31 and 209[3]). A village of the Tekmi toparchy (Mouchis) appears in *BGU* XIV 2429, too. In the light of these connections between Peensemtheus and Tekmi, the reading Πεενσεμθ(έως), which I propose at *BGU* XIV 2444,6, seems plausible (the orchards and vineyards surveyed in this document pay their ἀπόμοιρα to the temple of Eseph at Tekmi).

ΠΕΕΝΣΧΩΝ

II B.C.	*BGU* IV 1244,6	Φνεβιέως καὶ Π[ε]ενσχων[4]
52/51 B.C.	*BGU* VIII 1827,26	κώμην Πεενσχώ[5]

TOPARCHY: Μέση.

ETYMOLOGY: first component *p3-hr* + *-n-* (genitive)[6]: «the plot of...».

The association with Phnebieus (the main centre in the Μέση toparchy) in *BGU* IV 1244 suggests the ascription to this toparchy. This is supported by *BGU* VIII 1827: a dispute between husband and wife

---

[1] See *s.v.* ΠΕΕΜΠ(Α)'Θ'( ). Note the alternative Greek spellings Ποεν–(*BGU* XIV 2429)/Πεεν–.

[2] «The great god Semtheus» (Σεμθεκεντωι θεοῦ μεγίστου: the final –κεντωι/–κομτωι is the Greek transcription of the Egyptian word for «great god», which is then also repeated in Greek words) had a temple at Tekmi (*BGU* VIII 1795,4-5). His προφήτης (called Semtheus son of Horus) was also the ἀρχιερεύς in the temple of Herakles at Sobthis. The god Semtheus has been recognized in a bronze statuette of a Belgian private collection by JAN QUAEGEBEUR, «Somtous l'Enfant sur le lotus», *CRIPEL* 13, 1991, pp.113-121.

[3] The entry immediately following (*BGU* XIV 2441,211) concerns Eubios son of Eubios, who also appears as a land-grantee at *BGU* XIV 2444,9 (first entry under Πεενσεμθέως).

[4] My reading (checked on a photograph) .[.]ενσχων Poethke (letter of February 14, 1994); ημενχων *ed. pr.* («Es folgt wohl ein zweiter Dorfname»). This toponym is found at the end of the line.

[5] κ]ώμην Πεενσχω... *ed. pr.* («Hinter dem Namen muß etwa folgen ἀρ(ουρῶν) ἀρ(ούρας) κ»: Edd. *ad loc.*). This reading has been checked for me by Tomasz Derda (letter of July 5, 1994): «What I can read is κ]ώμην or rather κώμην... In my opinion the toponym ends with *omega* and is Πεενσχω. After this there is some blank space with no traces of ink».

[6] See *s.v.* ΠΕΕΜΠ(Α)'Θ'( ).

concerning a piece of land near Πεενσχω is brought to the strategos, requesting him to write to a certain Nikarchos ἐν τ[οπαρ]χίᾳ Φνεβιεῖ, and to the ὑποστρατηγός, on this matter.

ΠΕΕΝΤΕΧΥ

| 30 Jan. 237 B.C. | *PUG* III 114,8 (= *SB* XVI 12979) | ἐκ Πεεντέχυ |
| 7 Dec. 227 A.D. (cf. *BL* 7,259) | *Stud.Pal.* XX 29,21 | περὶ Πεεντέχυ[.[1] |

TOPARCHY: περὶ Πόλιν? Tekmi?

ETYMOLOGY: first component *p3-hr* + -*n*- (genitive)[2]: «the plot of...».

PUG III 114: ναύκληρος declaration for the transport of corn from Peentechy, Taemsis (in the Tekmi toparchy) and Tanaso (περὶ Πόλιν toparchy) to Alexandria.

Stud.Pal. XX 29: some of the land ceded by a man from Tosachmis (Koites) to his wife (who is from Tanaso) is situated near Peentechy[3]: the connection between Peentechy and Tanaso is thus confirmed. The contract, however, was drawn up by the ἀγορανόμος of Tekmi.

ΠΕΕΝΦΡΙ...

| I B.C. | *BGU* XIV 2437 (fr.2),62 | Πεενφρι....[|
| I B.C. | *BGU* XIV 2438 (fr.3),94 | Πεενφρ[|

See also *s.v.* ΠΕΕΝΦΡΙΜΕΝΣΩΚΟΥ.

TOPARCHY: Ἄγημα κάτω.

ETYMOLOGY: first component *p3-hr* + -*n*- (genitive)[4] + second component *p3-hrj*: «the plot of the blessed» + third component (personal name?)[5].

Assigned to the Ἄγημα κάτω in *BGU* XIV 2438, where Peenepsomphis is entered at the beginning of the list. In *BGU* XIV 2437 Peenepsomphis also appears on the same line with Πεενφρι....[(which must therefore be the same village as Πεενφρ[in *BGU* XIV 2438).

---

[1] περὶ Πεεντε.[*ed. pr.* The new reading has been checked for me on the original by Johannes Diethart (letter of February 25, 1994).

[2] See *s.v.* ΠΕΕΜΠ(Α)'Θ'( ).

[3] Three kleroi are mentioned, in order to locate this landholding: Μάρωνος (l.23; south), Διδυμιανοῦ (l.23; north), Ἡλιοδώρου καὶ τοῦ ἀδελφοῦ (l.24; east and west).

[4] See *s.v.* ΠΕΕΜΠ(Α)'Θ'( ).

[5] φρι = *p3-hrj* is found in *UPZ* II 180a, XIV, 6-9: it meant «der Erhabene ... ein Ausdruck für den Verstorbenen» (HEINZ-JOSEF THISSEN, *Enchoria* 1, 1971, p.77).

ΠΕΕΝΦΡΙΜΕΝΣΩΚΟΥ

I B.C.	*BGU* XIV 2432,33	ἀπὸ Πεενφριμενσωκου

ETYMOLOGY: see *s.v.* ΠΕΕΝΦΡ...[1]. A personal name Σωκ(κ)εύς, or Σοκ(κ)εύς, is attested (cf. PIETER W. PESTMAN ET ALII, *A Guide to the Zenon Archive*, Leyden 1981, *Prosopography, s.v.*).

ΠΕΙΡΙΤΤΙΑΝΟΣ[2]

V A.D.	*Stud.Pal.* X 233, col. II,20

ΠΕΜΑΤΕ

after 13/12 B.C.	*BGU* XVI 2601,7	περὶ κώμην Πεματε [...] (7-8)

ΠΕΝΤΑΛ[ΕΩ]Σ

VI A.D.	*Stud.Pal.* X 44,5	χ(ωρίον) Πεντάλ[εω]ς (cf. *BL* 7,258)

ETYMOLOGY: first element *p3-hr* + *-n-* (genitive) + second element of Semitic origin (cf. *tell*): «the plot of the hill» (Coptic *Pehntal*); cf. JEAN YOYOTTE *apud* DREW-BEAR, *Le nome Hermopolite*, p.200 («l'établissement de la colline»).

MODERN ARABIC NAME: Badahl (on phonetical grounds). Badahl is «ein archäologisch bedeutender Ort mit einem sehr ausgedehnten, stellenweise im Abbau begriffenen Kōm. Die Keramikscherben sind in spätantike Zeit zu datieren. Im Dorf befinden sich eine ganze Reihe antiker Objekte, Ölpressen, Steinblöcke. Unter letzteren ist ein Kalksteinfragment mit griechischen Buchstaben hervorzuheben ... Im Haus des Elektroingenieurs Hatrī befinden sich zwei unterlebensgroße liegende Löwenstatuen ... auch das Fragment eines Gefäß - oder Opferständers ... Auf den Dächern einiger Häuser stehen Löwenfiguren, von denen wir vier gezählt haben» (*TAVO* B 69, p.210 f.).

Other localities listed in the same document include: Pois (1.4), Tou and Kollintaathyr (ll.7 and 8; Tekmi toparchy), Herakleopolis, Phnebieus (Middle toparchy), Tebetny (l.12; Πέραν toparchy).

---

[1] The Editor (*ad loc.*) remarks: «Eine sehr zweifelhafte Lesung. Allerdings ist es nicht dasselbe Dorf wie in *BGU* XIV 2437,62, wo die Spuren anders aussehen».

[2] «Wohl Πειριττιανος zu lesen» (Johannes Diethart, letter of February 25, 1994).

ΠΕΡΑΝ (toparchy)

215/214 B.C.	*P.Strasb.* II 111,21	'εἰς τὸ Πέραν'[1]
2 Sept. 162 B.C.	*P.Hels.* I 26A,4;15;20;26	τὸν Κωίτην καὶ τὴν Τεχθὼ Νῆσον καὶ τὸ Πέρα (3-4); Πέρα (15;26); [Π]έρα (20)
after 52/51 B.C.	*BGU* VIII 1808,14	Πέραν μεριδάρχο(υ)
I B.C.	*BGU* VIII 1805,1	[παρὰ] Πετειμούθου τοπογραμματέ[ως] τοῦ Πέραν
I B.C.	*BGU* XIV 2434,12	Πέραν
I B.C.	*BGU* XIV 2438,87	Πέραν κ...[2]
I B.C.	*BGU* XIV 2440,65	περὶ Πέρα(ν) καὶ Νισέα
about 7-4 B.C.	*BGU* XVI 2662,12	Πέρα
28 Jan. 5 B.C.	*BGU* XVI 2586,15	Πέρα
211-217 A.D.	*SB* XVIII 13858,12	δι' ἐπιτηρ(ητῶν) ἀγο(ρανομίας) Πέρα[3]

Documents which mention the Πέραν toparchy in connection to one or more of its villages do not appear here: these are listed and discussed under the entries for the relevant villages. A list of villages that can be assigned to this toparchy will be found on p.294.

The Πέραν and its villages are repeatedly associated in our sources to the Techtho Nesos toparchy (cf. e.g. *P.Hels.* I 26 A; *BGU* VIII 1808; *BGU* XIV 2434; *BGU* XVI 2586). Its connection with the Ἄγημα (and with the village of Niseus in particular: see *s.v.*) is most clearly shown in *BGU* XIV 2440

ΠΕΡΑΦΘΙΣ

222-235 A.D.	*CPR* VI 73,16	περὶ κώμην Περαφθιν

TOPARCHY: Tekmi? Ἄγημα?

---

[1] My reading (checked on a photograph); 'εἰς πε.α.ν' Clarysse (in his re-edition of this document: *Ancient Society* 7, 1976, pp.200-203). The reading εἰς τὸ Πέραν, inserted above l.21 presumably in order to clarify where «the (mansions of) Harsemtheus» (τὰ Ἀρσεμθέω[ς]: see *s.v.*) were, is further supported by the mention of two villages of the Πέραν in the same document: see *s.vv.* ΠΕΕΝΣΑΜΟΙ, ΘΜΟΙΦΘΑ.

[2] My reading (checked for me on the original, and deemed «probable» by William Brashear, letter of August 22, 1994); περαγκ..ου *ed.pr.*

[3] Cf. DIETER HAGEDORN, *ZPE* 34, 1979, pp.109-110 (re-edition of this document, which used to be *Stud.Pal.* II 19): «Mit einigen Bedenken möchte ich vorschlagen, Πέρα als (indeklinablen) Namen der Agoranomie im Genitiv aufzufassen. Eine Agoranomie dieses Namens ist zwar unbezeugt, doch gab es ... eine Toparchie Πέραν» (p.110). Documents of the same kind were issued through the agoranomiae of the Μέση and Ἄγημα toparchies: see *s.vv.*

Two sisters living at Tekmi sell some land (near Peraphthis), a 10 year old slave, and a μηχανή, to Aurelius Heron, also called Herakleios, σύνδικος and βουλευτής of Herakleopolis. The contract (apparently written by the same scribe who recorded *Stud.Pal.* XX 47[1]) was drawn up in the agoranomos office of the Ἅγημα toparchy.

ΠΕΡΕΜΘΕΩΣ[2]

| I B.C. | *BGU* XIV 2440 (fr.1),71 | |

ΠΕΡΟΗ

285/284 B.C. (cf. *BL* 4,39)[3]	*P.Hib.* I 84 a,7;22	ἐν κώμηι Περόηι
about 260 B.C.	*P.Hib.* I 112,14	Περόην
2 Sept. 162 B.C.	*P.Hels.* I 26 A,25;41	Περόηι (25; cf. *BL* 9,106); Περόηι (41)
I/II A.D.	*P.Hib.* II 218,2;16	
III/IV A.D.	*P.Mich.* XV 722,2;5;10;12;13;16	Περό(η)

TOPARCHY: Koites.

P.Hels. I 26 indicates that Peroe was in the Koites (ll.24-25); this village is again listed with localities of the Koites in *P.Hib.* I 112 (where it is entered after Psychis, Assya and Phebichis) and *P.Hib.* II 218.
P.Mich. XV 722: survey of land in the surroundings of Θμο() and/or Peroe.
P.Hib. 84 a: contract for the sale of 30 art. wheat between two Greek settlers living at Peroe.

ΠΕΡΟΜ'Ο'(Υ)

| VII A.D. | *Stud.Pal.* X 214,1 | π(ε)'δ'(ίον) Περόμ'ο'(υ)[4] |

Π(εδίον) Περόμ'ο'(υ) is written on top of the following list: ἐν τόπ(ῳ) διώρυ(γος) Λολλιανοῦ (l.2), ἐν π(εδίῳ) Πουεν (l.3), ἐν π(εδίῳ) Πλεμεδεου (l.4), ἐν π(εδίῳ) Θαλμι (l.5), ἐν π(εδίῳ) Μαλκουλι (l.6), ἐν τόπ(ῳ) Πκατανω (l.7), ἐν π(εδίῳ) Ψανατι (l.8). None of these localities is attested elsewhere.

---

[1] A παραχώρησις contract: the parties are from Peenpibyk(is), in the Μέση toparchy, and probably from Alexandria.

[2] Other possible readings (according to the *ed. pr.*): Πεμμθεως, Σελεμθεως. Also Πετεμθεως, Πε.εμθεως (William Brashear, letter of August 22, 1994).

[3] See also ALAN E. SAMUEL, *Ptolemaic Chronology*, München 1962, pp.11-12.

[4] «Ich möchte am liebsten Περομ'ο'(υ).... lesen» (Johannes Diethart, letter of September 13, 1994); Περομ *ed. pr.*

CATALOGUE

ΠΕΡΧΥΦΙΣ

about 260 B.C.	*P.Hib.* I 112,46	Περχύφις
mid-III B.C.	*P.Strasb.* IX 802,16	Περκῦφι[ς]

TOPARCHY: Koites.

Most, or all, villages listed in *P.Hib.* I 112 and *P.Strasb.* IX 802 belonged to the Koites.

ΠΕΣΕΝ

VII A.D.	*Stud.Pal.* XX 206,5	ἀπὸ χ(ωρίου) Πεσεν παγ(αρ)χ(ίας) Ἡρακλ(εοπολίτου)

See also: ΠΟΥΕΝ.

Other villages of the παγαρχία Ὀξυρυγχ(ίτου) are mentioned in the same document, including Τσιμιστεα (for which an identification with modern Sumustā al-Waqf has been suggested [1]).

ΠΕΤΑΧΟΡ

II B.C.	P.Mil.Vogl. inv. 1300,11	ἐκ Πεταρχ[ορ [2]
mid-II B.C.	*P.Tebt.* III 876,5	περὶ Πεταχόρ
96-94 or 63-61 B.C.	*BGU* XIV 2429,10;13	Πεταχόρ (10); Πεταχ(όρ) (13)
after 52/51 B.C.	*BGU* VIII 1808,17;33(?)	Πεταχόρ λογευτῶν ε ἀρχιφυλακίτο(υ) ε (17-19); Πεταχορ (33) [3]
I/II A.D.	*P.Hib.* II 218,35	Πεταχ(όρ)
3 Jan. 373 A.D. [4]	*P.Vind.Sijp.* 13,3	ἐν κώμῃ Πεταχόρ
V A.D.	*Stud.Pal.* X 233,col.I A,7	Πεταχωρεως
V-VI A.D.	*CPR* XIV 40,1	βοηθ(οῦ) Πεταχόρεως

---

[1] *TAVO B 69*, p.91.

[2] Guido Bastianini kindly informed me of this new source for the present village. *P.Mil.Vogl.* inv.1300 was obtained from the same *cartonnage* containing a roll with Posidippus' epigrams: see *Introduction*, p.20 f.

[3] My reading (checked on a photograph): Τ̣ε̣παχορ *ed. pr.*

[4] Cf. RENATE ZIEGLER, *ZPE* 106, 1995, p.193.

VII-VIII A.D.	*Stud.Pal.* X 213,2;5	Πεταχώρεως (2); χ(ωρίον) Πεταχω[ρ]εως (5)

TOPARCHY: Ἄγημα (ἄνω?).

Kollasoucha, Petachor and Hiera Nesos are all mentioned in *BGU* XIV 2429, and in *BGU* VIII 1808, where Alilais also occurs; Petachor and Kollasoucha also appear in consecutive lines in *Stud.Pal.* X 213[1] (ll.4 and 5). As *P.Hib.* II 218 also lists Alilais, Kollasoucha and Petachor in three consecutive lines (33-35), it seems likely that these villages were all in the same area, i.e. the Ἄγημα ἄνω (to which Alilais certainly belonged). Further support to this hypothesis is lent by *CPR* XIV 40, where Petachor recurs in the same document with Nois[2], a village in the περὶ Πόλιν toparchy which is also found with Kollasoucha in another document (*Stud.Pal.* X 209).

The following villages also recur with Petachor in one or the other document: Niseus (Ἄγημα toparchy, but very near the Πέραν; in the same line with Petachor: *BGU* XIV 2429,10; *P.Hib.* II 218,35; note also the entry Πέραν in *BGU* VIII 1808,14); Korphotoi (Ἄγημα κάτω toparchy; *BGU* VIII 1808,4; *BGU* XIV 2429,4); Peenameus (Ἄγημα κάτω, then Μέση toparchy); Phnebieus (Μέση toparchy; *BGU* VIII 1808,25; *P.Hib.* II 218,59). The location of Petachor in the proximity of the Πέραν may be safely inferred.

Proximity with the Tekmi toparchy may be deduced from the fact that Mouchis (*BGU* XIV 2429,7; *P.Hib.* II 218,41; *Stud.Pal.* X 233, col.I,B,5) also recurs in a number of sources, not too far from the entries for Petachor. *P.Vind.Sijp.* 13 is a loan contract drawn up at Petachor; both parties are from Herakleopolis.

BGU XIV 2429 apparently records 108 Egyptian, and 20 Greek (male) tax-payers at Petachor[3], which could be an interesting piece of information regarding the ratio of the Greek to the Egyptian population in this village.

P.Tebt. III 876 records it as a wine-producing area.

ΠΕΤΕΧΟΝ'Τ'

VII/VIII A.D.	*CPR* IV 2,15	χ(ωρίον) Πετεχον'τ'

See also: Τερτονπετεχωνς (same village?).

CPR IV 2 (a bilingual document in Coptic and Greek) lists many villages of the central toparchies of the Herakleopolite nome (toponyms in Greek)[4].

ΠΙ[

VI-VII A.D.	*Stud.Pal.* X 5,9	τὸν βοηθ(ὸν) Πι[

---

[1] *Stud.Pal.* X 211, 212 and 213, though published as separate documents, are in fact fragments of the same text, so that the villages mentioned in *Stud.Pal.* X 211 (Ogou, in the Tekmi toparchy), 212 (Thelbonthis, in the Techtho Nesos toparchy) and 213 (Petachor and Kollasoucha) may have been near each other.

[2] In *CPR* XIV 40,3 there is also a possible reference to a «nördliche Poststation», βορριν(ῆς) ἀλλ(αγῆς): cf. *BL* 9,76).

[3] See Brashear's introduction to this document (*BGU* XIV, p.114). The Egyptians are taxed at a higher rate.

[4] See *s.v.* ΝΙΝΩ.

CATALOGUE

List of the βοηθοί of several villages, including Onosis (περὶ Πόλιν toparchy), Nino (Ἄγημα toparchy), Tinteris (Koma toparchy) and Kollintaathyr (Tekmi toparchy).

ΠΙΑΔΕ.[.]ΕΥ

| VI-VII A.D. | CPR VIII 68,9-10 | ἐν κλήρῳ καλου(μένῳ) Πιαδε.[.]ευ ἤτοι λάκκου Αἰλοῦτος |

TOPARCHY: περὶ Πόλιν.
The κλῆρος was near Sobthis ἡ μικρά. The reference to a reservoir (λάκκος)[1] is meant to identify it more securely.

ΠΙΑΚΕΡ[2]

| VI A.D. | Stud.Pal. X 228,9 | ἐν τόπ(ῳ) Πιακερ[3] |

ETYMOLOGY: though only once, and at this late time, attested in the Greek documents, this must be the same place as *Pr-Jqr* («The House of *Jqr*») of *P.Wilbour* A 11,41; 13,30; 14,12; 17,8; 18,5; B 15,18; 21,25; 24,35[4].

Listed with Παργου (1.4), Πιατιμι (1.5), Νεθισει (1.6), Νευηλα (1.7), Σουριυ (1.8).

ΠΙΑΤΙΜΙ

| VI A.D. | Stud.Pal. X 228,5 | ἐν τόπ(ῳ) Πιατιμι[5] |

ETYMOLOGY: the prefix πια- means «a level irrigated place»[6].

Listed with Παργου (1.4), Νεθισει (1.6), Νευηλα (1.7), Σουριυ (1.8), Πιακερ (1.9).

ΠΙΕΝΕΚΑΜΟΥ

| VII-VIII A.D. | Stud.Pal. X 206,8 |

---

[1] See the Editors' comments *ad loc.*; see also below, *s.v.* ΠΕΧΙΤ.

[2] Could Πιακ[of *Stud.Pal.* X 79 (b),4 (VII/VIII B.C.; cf. *BL* 8,456) be the same village?

[3] Πιακερ() *ed.pr.*

[4] Cf. *TAVO* B 69, p.139; see also Preface, p.XII.

[5] Πιατεμι *ed. pr.*: new reading by Johannes Diethart (letter of September 13, 1994).

[6] Cf. LESLIE S.B. MACCOULL, *Dioscurus of Aphrodito*, Berkeley-Los Angeles-London 1988, p.14 and n.47.

Apparently the name of a κλῆρος, listed with several others (see the *Reverse Index* at the end of this volume).

ΠΙΜΕΙΝ

III A.D.   *P.Neph.* 28,8   περὶ κώ[μη]ν Πιμεῖν

Phebichis and Papa (both in the Koites) appear in the same document. The Nepheros archive is centered around the monastery of (P)hathor in the southern Herakleopolites.

ΠΙΝΗΧΕΩΣ

644/645 A.D.   *SB* VI 8987,6   ἐν κώμῃ Πινηχέως τοῦ
Ἡρακλεοπ[ο]λ[ίτου
νομο]ῦ

SB VI 8986-8988 and the (Coptic) Budge papyrus *P.Col.* inv. Nr.600 deal with the same dispute, which went on from 622 to 647 A.D.[1] *SB* VI 8987 is a deed to the property of a house-portion in Apollinopolis Magna (Edfu), which had been mortgaged to Philemon and his wife by its original owner, Thekla. She had then left to Great Beshin (possibly the Coptic name of Phebichis), and failed to repay her loan before her death. The property thus remained in the possession of Philemon and his wife. Thekla's heirs, now living ἐν κώμῃ Πινηχέως, in the Herakleopolite nome, having tried to claim it back, must eventually acknowledge the rights of the new owners.

ΠΚ[±3]

VII/VIII A.D.   *Stud.Pal.* X 17,6   ἀπὸ χ'ω'(ρίου) Πκ[±3] [2]

See also *s.v.* ΠΚΟΜΜΑΤΟΕΙ.

ΠΚΑΤΑΝΩ

VII A.D.   *Stud.Pal.* X 214,7   ἐν τό'π'(ῳ) Πκατάνῳ[3]

TOPARCHY: Koites?

See *s.v.* ΠΕΡΟΗ (heading the list in this document).

---

[1] See A. ARTHUR SCHILLER, «The Budge papyrus of Columbia University», *Journal of the American Research Centre in Egypt* 7, 1968, pp.79-118; IDEM, in *Studien zur Papyrologie und antiken Wirtschaftsgeschichte Fr. Oertel zum achtzigsten Geburtstag gewidmet*, Bonn 1964, pp.107-119; PIETER J. SIJPESTEIJN, ZPE 19, 1975, p.272.

[2] Pkommatoei is listed in the same document (l.12) and should perhaps be supplied here, too.

[3] Willy Clarysse suggests that this toponym could also be read as Πκατ ἄνω.

ΠΚΟΜΜΑΤΟΕΙ

after 52/51 B.C.	*BGU* VIII 1808,35	Π[κο]μματοέως¹
VII A.D.	*Stud.Pal.* X 4,5	Πκομματοεί
VII/VIII A.D.	*Stud.Pal.* X 17,12	ἀπὸ χ'ω'(ρίου) Κομματο[εί²

See also *s.v.* ΠΚ[.

TOPARCHY: Koma.

Stud.Pal. X 4: villagers from Ἀπίωνος (1), Ποιναμι (2; variant spelling for Πεεναμεύς, in the Ἄγημα κάτω toparchy), Thmoiamoun(is) (4; Koma toparchy), and Pkommatoei (5), are requested for compulsory work to be done on the dyke (παράχωμα) at Koma. Pkommatoei recurs again with Koma (3) and Poinami (10) in *Stud.Pal.* X 17.

In *BGU* VIII 1808 (where all Herakleopolite toparchies are represented) this place-name recurs at the end of the document, followed by the reference to an ἀρχεφοδεῖον (l.36: possibly a police-station in the village).

ΠΛ[.].[±2]Λ( )

VI-VII A.D.	*Stud.Pal.* X 5,11	τὸν βοηθ(ὸν) Πλ[.].[±2]λ( )³

List of the βοηθοί of several villages, including Onosis (περὶ Πόλιν toparchy), Nino (Ἄγημα toparchy), Tinteris (Koma toparchy) and Kollintaathyr (Tekmi toparchy).

(?) ΠΛΑΤΙΚ

I B.C.	*BGU* VIII 1824,18	ἀπὸ τῆς μεγάλης πλατικ⁴

A petition to the strategos, concerning assault and robbery on the part of people ἀπὸ τῆς μεγάλης πλατικ: the presence of the article (τῆς) makes it more likely for πλατικ to be the Greek transliteration of an Egyptian common name⁵. Tamphnouthis («wohl ein Dorfname», *ed. pr.*) is mentioned in the same document (l.8).

BGU VIII 1814, a petition to the same strategos written by the same hand, deals with land near Tebetny (Πέραν toparchy).

---

¹ My supplement; the reading has been checked for me by Günter Poethke (letter of April 14, 1994: «Ihr Vorschlag scheint gut zu sein»); Π[..]μματέως *ed. pr.*

² Johannes Diethart's reads Κομματα[(letter of February 25, 1994: «Vor κ ist Π m.E. eher unwahrscheinlich»); Wessely offered [Κ]ομματο[εί].

³ «Oder Πχ etc. oder Πελ etc.» (Johannes Diethart, letter of February 25, 1994).

⁴ «Eingeschoben. Nicht πλατείας! Auch κατοίκ(ων) unwahrscheinlich» (Ed. *ad loc.*).

⁵ This was pointed out to me by Willy Clarysse. The reading πλατικ, checked by me on the original, is correct.

ΠΛΕΜΕΔΕΟΥ

VII A.D.   *Stud.Pal.* X 214,4**a**   ἐν π(εδίῳ) Πλεμεδεου

See *s.v.* ΠΕΡΟΗ (heading the list in this document).

ΠΜΑΝΚΕΜ

VII-VIII A.D.   *Stud.Pal.* X 206,14   Ακακιητη Πμανκεμ

See *s.v.* ΑΚΑΚΙΗΤΗ.

ΠΟ[.]ΛΟΜ[

I/II A.D.   *P.Hib.* II 218,61

See also: Πο[..]ο̣μ()

TOPARCHY: Μέση ?

Listed after three villages of the Μέση toparchy.

ΠΟ[..]ΟΜ( )[1]

I/II A.D.   *P.Hib.* II 218,96

Sinary (89; Πέραν toparchy), Onosis (90,92; περὶ Πόλιν toparchy), and Techtho (91) precede in this list.

ΠΟΑΧΡΙΝΑ

late III A.D.   *BGU* XIII 2365,10

ETYMOLOGY: first component ποα- = *p3-w3h*, «the residence» (cf. HEINZ-JOSEF THISSEN, *Enchoria* 1, 1971, p.77).

---

[1] Πο[ενσ]ε̣μ(θεως) could be a possible supplement. Or this could be the same village as Πο[.]λομ[(l.61).

CATALOGUE

ΠΩΕΝΠΙΒΤΗΙ

I B.C.	*BGU* VIII 1733,6	ἀπὸ τοῦ κ[λήρου αὐτο]ῦ περὶ Ποενπίβτηι[1] τῶν ἐμ μιᾷ σφραγε[ῖδι] [τ]οῦ π[ρότ]ερον Φίλωνος [κλ]ήρου

TOPARCHY: Tekmi? περὶ Πόλιν?

A παραχώρησις contract, drawn up at Herakleopolis, deals with land near this village, more precisely located with reference to the fossil kleros of Σκίρων.

ΠΟΙΜΕΝΩΝ ΚΩΜΗ

10 May 174 B.C.[2]	*BGU* XIV 2382,11	ἐν Ποιμένων κώμῃ
169-164 B.C.	*P.Strasb.* II 99,5	ἐν Ποιμένων κώμηι
I B.C.	*BGU* XIV 2433,46	〚Ποιμέν[ω]ν κώμης〛
I B.C.	*BGU* XIV 2438,45	Ποιμένων κώ(μης)
27 April 15 B.C.	*BGU* XVI 2607,3-4	εἰς Ποιμένων
4 Feb. 13 B.C.	*BGU* XVI 2578,5	ἀπὸ Ποιμένων κώμης
9 June 192 A.D.	*O.Wilck.* II 1108,4	δι'ὄνω(ν) Ἡρακλεοπολ(ίτου) Ποιμένων (3-4)
about 245 A.D.(?)	*P.Oxy.* LVIII 3928,5-6	ἀπὸ κώμης Ποιμέ[νων]
VI A.D.	*Stud.Pal.* XX 148 *recto*,2; *verso*,1	Ποιμένων τοῦ Ἡρακλεοπολίτου νομοῦ (*recto*,2-3); ἀπὸ Ποιμένων (*verso*,1)
VII/VIII A.D.	*CPR* IV 2,11	Ποιμέν[ων[3]

TOPARCHY: Μέση.

ETYMOLOGY: «the shepherds' village» may be the translation of the Egyptian toponym Peenameus («the shepherds' plot»: see *s.v.*). Peenameus, which is assigned to the Ἄγημα κάτω by documents of the first century B.C., is in other documents (of the III A.D.) connected to the Μέση toparchy, where Ποιμένων κώμη is consistently located by the sources; besides, the two villages never recur in the same document.

At Herakleopolis there was a street called Ποιμένων λαύρα (*Stud.Pal.* VIII 1183, of the VII/VIII A.D.).

---

[1] περὶ ..π. ἐν Πίβτηι *ed. pr.* New reading checked on a photograph.

[2] Cf. RENATE ZIEGLER, *ZPE* 106, 1995, p.190.

[3] Ποιμεν[*ed.pr.*

Listed (but then crossed out) with villages of the Μέση toparchy in *BGU* XIV 2433 (including Chennis, Phys, Peenepochra), Ποιμένων κώμη is mentioned in the same document with Phnebieus (main centre of the Μέση) in *BGU* XVI 2607 (letter concerning the shipping of timber). It is also connected with localities of the περὶ Πόλιν toparchy in *P.Strasb.* II 99 (the petitioner, from Nois, has a claim on his father's house at Ποιμένων κώμη) and *Stud.Pal.* XX 148 (loan contract: the parties are from Ποιμένων κώμη and from Herakleopolis).

BGU XIV 2382 is a contract stipulated at Ποιμένων κώμη between Lysimachus and Eupolemos (who is from Kerkeuniphis).

BGU XVI 2578 is a declaration of sheep and goats.

CPR IV 2 (a bilingual document in Coptic and Greek) lists many villages of the central toparchies of the Herakleopolite nome (toponyms in Greek)[1].

ΠΟΛΙΤ( )

VII/VIII A.D.   *Stud.Pal.* X 217,5   ἐν κλ'ή'(ρῳ) Πολιτ( )

Near Daphne. A kleros Ψαννε( ) is also mentioned.

ΠΟΥΕΝ

VII A.D.   *Stud.Pal.* X 214,3   ἐν π(εδίῳ) Πουεν

ETYMOLOGY: *p3-w3h*: «the residence» (cf. HEINZ-JOSEF THISSEN, *Enchoria* 1, 1971, p.77)?

See *s.v.* ΠΕΡΟΗ (heading the list in this document).

ΠΟΥΛΗ

V A.D.   *Stud.Pal.* X 8,8   ἐποικίου Πουλη[2]

Choinothmis (Koites), Techtho, and Phnebieus (Μέση toparchy; immediately preceding Πουλη) appear in the same document.

ΠΡΑΝΙ

VII/VIII A.D.   *CPR* IV 2,12   χ(ωρίον) Πρανι

---

[1] See *s.v.* ΝΙΝΩ.

[2] «In der γνῶσις ἐμβολῆς κριθῶν aus dem 5. Jh. ist statt Wesselys ἐποικίου Ναυλη zu lesen ἐποικίου Πουλη, ein Ort, der bislang nicht belegt zu sein scheint» (Johannes Diethart, letter of February 25, 1994).

CATALOGUE

CPR IV 2 (a bilingual document in Coptic and Greek) lists many villages of the central toparchies of the Herakleopolite nome (toponyms in Greek)[1].

ΠΤΑΝ.

VIII A.D.   *Stud.Pal.* X 72,13   [χ(ωρίον)] Πταν.[2]

Other villages mentioned: Ogou (l.3; Tekmi toparchy), Ἁλμυρά (ll.11;12;14), Ἱερά (l.15).

ΠΤΕΝΝΕΩΣ

VI A.D.   *Stud.Pal.* X 210,1

Stud.Pal. X 210 is a list of inhabitants of this village.

ΠΤΟΛΕΜΑΙΚΟΣ   (*sc.* ΠΟΤΑΜΟΣ)

I B.C.   *BGU* VIII 1784,4   (ποταμοφύλαξι) 'τοῦ Πτολεμαικοῦ'

The ποταμοφύλακες of the Πτολεμαικός (canal) are to escort an οὐραγία (possibly the «rear-guard» of military troops) as far as Ἱερὰ Νῆσος (see *s.v.*), where their colleagues from the Troites are to take over.

ΠΥΡΓΩΤΟΣ

about 111 B.C.	*P.Tebt.* III 878,19	Πυργω(τός)[3]
I B.C.	*BGU* XIV 2437,14	Πυργωτοῦ[4]
I B.C.	*BGU* XIV 2440,129	περὶ Πυρ[γωτόν[5]
I B.C.	*BGU* XIV 2441,19	Πυρ[γ]ω[τ]οῦ[6]

---

[1] See *s.v.* ΝΙΝΩ.

[2] «Πταν. (Ausstrich), Πταν( ) oder Πτανι» (Diethart, letter of February 25, 1994).

[3] Πυργω( ) *ed. pr.*

[4] Πυργώτου *ed. pr.*

[5] περὶ Πυρ[γώτον is suggested with some doubts in the *ed. pr.*

[6] My reading (checked on a photograph with William Brashear): Ητρ.[.].ου *ed. pr.*

28/29 B.C.	*P.Oxy.* XXIV 2412,90;167;189	Πυργω(τός)¹
212 A.D.	*P.Rain.Cent.*64,5²	ἀπὸ κώμ(ης) Πυργώτου
216 A.D.	*Stud.Pal.* XX 22,1 (= *CPR* I 35)	ἀπὸ κώμης Πυργωτοῦ
490 A.D.	*P.Rain.Cent.* 110,5	ἀπὸ κώμης Πυργωτοῦ³
VII/VIII A.D.	*CPR* IV 2,11	χ(ωρίον) Πυργω(τοῦ) (11); Πυργω'τ'(οῦ) (18)⁴
VII-VIII A.D.	*Stud.Pal.* X 211,4	χ(ωρίον) Πυρ[γώτου (?)⁵
VIII A.D.	*Stud.Pal.* X 72,6	χ(ωρίον) Π[υ]ργ[ωτ]οῦ⁶
VIII A.D.	*Stud.Pal.* X 109,6	ἐν τ(ῷ) χ(ωρίῳ) [Π]υργω'τ'(ῷ)

TOPARCHY: Tekmi.

ETYMOLOGY: «made like a tower» (see *LSJ s.v.*); the name may bear reference to some kind of military building⁷.

MODERN ARABIC NAME: an identification with Al-Barqi would be topographically convenient (as suggested in the *Introduction*, p.8), though phonetically not particularly convincing.

P.Tebt. III 878 lists Psilichi (16), Pyrgotos (19), Bousiris (22), Toou (46).

BGU XIV 2437 connects Pyrgotos to περὶ Αὐλήν (Tekmi toparchy): this is consistent with the new reading Πυρ[γ]ω[τ]οῦ in *BGU* XIV 2441 (land-survey in the Tekmi toparchy).

P.Oxy. XXIV 2412 mentions six villages (Ogou, Tekmi, Kollintaathyr, Pyrgotos, Mouchis, Ἰβιών), all presumably in the Tekmi toparchy. Ogou and Pyrgotos again recur together in *Stud.Pal.* X 211.

P.Rain.Cent. 110 (loan contract) and *Stud.Pal.* XX 22 (land lease) both show people from Pyrgotos entering into a contract with inhabitants of Herakleopolis: the implication may well be that the Tekmi and περὶ Πόλιν toparchies were contiguous.

A temple dedicated to Stotoetis and (?)Herakles⁸, «very great gods», was in the Pyrgotos area.

---

¹ Πυργῶ(τος) *ed. pr.*

² *SB* I 5281 = ll.2-3 of this document.

³ Πυργώτου *ed. pr.*

⁴ Πυργω (11), Πυργω'τ' (18) *ed.pr.*

⁵ Reading suggested by Johannes Diethart (letter of September 13, 1994: «α ist m.E. wohl auszuschließen»); Παρ[*ed. pr.*

⁶ Reading checked for me by Johannes Diethart: «Π[υ]ργ[ωτ]ου ist nach den spärlichen Resten nicht auszuschließen» (letter of February 25, 1994).

⁷ Compare for instance the «Festungsbau im Gaue Herakleopolis» of *P.Berl. Zill.* 1-2 (156-155 B.C.).

⁸ See the Editor's note at *BGU* XIV 2441,108.

CATALOGUE

CPR IV 2 (a bilingual document in Coptic and Greek) lists many villages of the central toparchies of the Herakleopolite nome (toponyms in Greek)[1].

ΠΩΕΤ.[

| *ca.* 160 B.C. | *P.Hels.* I 27,3 | Πωετ.[|

Variant spelling for Πωις? Other villages listed: Phys, Ψεβχηθ[, Koma.

ΠΩΙΣ[2]

2 July 167 B.C.	*P.Hamb.* I 91,19;25	εἰς Πῶιν (19); ἐγ τῆι Πῶι (25); cf. ἐκ τῆς κώμης (23-24)
162 B.C.	*P.Tebt.* III 857,3	τὸν ἐμ Πώει θη(σαυρόν)
61-59 B.C.[3]	*BGU* VIII 1772,11	περὶ Πῶιν
60/59 B.C.	*BGU* VIII 1817,4-5	ἐν Πώει [τ]ῆι μεγάληι
after 52/51 B.C.	*BGU* VIII 1808,30	Πώεως
48/47 B.C.	*SB* V 7609,5 (=*BGU* VIII 1794c)	ἀπὸ Πώεως τῆς μεγάλης
I B.C.	*BGU* VIII 1777,6	νομογράφῳ τῶν ἐκ Πώεως
I B.C.	*BGU* XIV 2436,2;8;13	Πῶιν
4 Feb. 13 B.C.	*BGU* XVI 2579,6;13	ἀπὸ Πώεως (6); ἐν τῇ περὶ Πῶιν (13)
I/II A.D.	*P.Hib.* II 218,57;74	Πώεως
5 June 192 A.D.	*O.Wilck.* II 1106,3	διὰ ὄνο(υ) Ἡρακ(λεοπολίτου) Πώεως (2-3)
198/199 A.D.	*O.Wilck.* II 1116,3	διὰ Ἡρακλεοπολ(ίτου) Πώεως
ca. 250 A.D.	*SB* I 1500,2	διὰ κτη(νῶν) Πώεως

---

[1] See *s.v.* ΝΙΝΩ.

[2] There were several villages by this name in Egypt, and it is sometimes not clear which Pois is meant by the sources. Useful indications may derive from the type of document and the formulary adopted in it. Thus, though the provenance of *P.Michael.* 13 is unknown, the village meant at l.6 is probably Pois in the Hermoupolite nome, as argued by JOHANNES HERMANN, *Chr.d'Ég.* 63, 1957, p.121 («Die Urkunde stammt mit hoher Wahrscheinlichkeit aus dem hermopolitischen Gau. Diese unsere Annahme stützt sich hauptsächlich auf die Tatsache, dass Pachturkunden cheirographischer Fassung zu dieser Zeit für Hermopolis charakteristisch sind...»). Cf. also DREW-BEAR, *Le nome Hermopolite*, p.230, with regard to the village by this name attested by *SB* XII 10810,1;6 (second half of VI A.D.).

[3] Date according to THEODORE C. SKEAT, *The Reigns of the Ptolemies*, München 1954, p.38 (κα ἔτους: not κε).

ca. 250 A.D.	*SB* I 1508,2	Πώεως
250 A.D.	*SB* I 1515,3-4	διὰ δη(μοσίων) κτηνῶ(ν) Πώεως
24 March 261 A.D.	*O.Meyer* 51,4	Πώεως
mid-III A.D.	*P.Select.* 17,8;11	ἀπὸ κώμης Πόεως (8); [περὶ κώμην] Πόιν (11)
VI A.D.	*Stud.Pal.* X 44,4	Πώεως
VI/VII A.D.	(?)*SB* XX 15072,4 [1]	Πώεως
VII/VIII A.D.	*CPR* IV 2,12	χ(ωρίον) Πώε[ως] [2]
VIII A.D.	*Stud.Pal.* X 84,4	χ(ωρίον) Πώεως

See also: ΠΩΕΤ.[

TOPARCHY: Tilothis.

ETYMOLOGY: *p3-ihy* [3], «the precinct». Cf. the reference to a locality, denominated «the Palisade» in *P.Tebt.* III 857, a report about an investigation on thefts from the θησαυρός at Πῶις and «in the Palisade» (l.14: ἐν τῷ Χάρακι) [4].

MODERN ARABIC NAME: Būš; Coptic *Poušin*. Cf. *TAVO B 69* § 4.3 (M 118) and p.221: «Ein noch im Betrieb befindliches Kloster des Antonius und des Paulus bezeugt die koptische Zeit. ... Anhaltspunkte für Relikte aus älteren Perioden gibt es nicht». See also TIMM, *Das christlich-koptische Ägypten*, I, pp.455-457 (*s.v.* Būš); IV, p.1995 f. (*s.v.* Pois I).

SB V 7609: summons before a tribunal: Phibion and his brothers ἀπὸ Πώεως τῆς μεγάλης (ll.5-6) failed to appear on a previous occasion; the ὑποστράτηγος of the περὶ Πόλιν toparchy therefore bids them again to appear in front of the strategos Eurylochos within three days. The Herakleopolite Pois is styled ἡ μεγάλη, evidently in order to distinguish it from homonymous localities.
BGU VIII 1772 deals with a kleros assigned to an ex-gymnasiarches of Herakleopolis in Auletes' 12th regnal year (70/69 B.C.). Three of the kleroi surveyed in *BGU* XIV 2436 include land in the Pois area: at ll.1-3 Orestes' kleros is split between Pois, an Ἰβιών locality, Ogou (Tekmi toparchy), Magdola, and Peens(amoi), in the Πέραν toparchy; at ll.7-9, Ptolemaios' holding is split between Pois, Tanchais (Tilothis toparchy) and Tosachmis (Koites); finally, Hierax' kleros (ll.11-12) is distributed between Tanchais, Noeris (περὶ Πόλιν toparchy) and Pois. Pois recurs with one or other of these villages in the following documents:

---

[1] It is not certain that this is the Herakleopolite Pois: homonymous villages were in the Hermopolites, Memphites, Koptites, Apollonopolites, Lykopolites, and in the Mendesian nome (as indicated by PIETER J. SIJPESTEIJN, *ZPE* 81, 1990, pp.245-251, who published the entire document). Most of the localities mentioned in this text, however, were in the Arsinoite or Herakleopolite nomes.

[2] Πωε[?] *ed.pr.*

[3] Information from Katelijn Vandorpe. Cf. HEINZ-JOSEF THISSEN, *Enchoria* 1,1971, p.77 (*P3-hr-n-p3-ihj* = Ποενπῶις).

[4] «[Pois] peut désigner "un campement permanent de l'armée" et, plus fréquemment, "un terrain enclos destiné à la pâture du bétail», according to DREW-BEAR, *Le nome Hermopolite*, p.227 (with reference to JEAN YOYOTTE, *MDAIK* 16, 1958, pp.418-419 and to JAROSLAV CERNY, «Some Coptic Etymologies», *BIFAO* 57, 1958, pp.209-210). Παις, a dialectal variant of the same toponym, is also attested.

P.Tebt. III 857 (Peensamoi in a fragment from the same account mentioning Pois);

BGU VIII 1808 (entries for Tanchais, Pois, περὶ Πόλιν[1] in three consecutive lines, preceded by entries for Ἄγημα κάτω, περὶ Φέβιχιν and for Phnebieus in the Μέση toparchy);

BGU XIV 2440 (the place-names listed in the first column include Ἄγημα κάτω toparchy, Tilothis, Pois, Techymis in the Μέση toparchy, Tekmi toparchy and Koites, Phnebieus and Phebichis);

P.Hib. II 218 (Tokois and Noeris are listed immediately before Pois; Tosachmis and Phebichis appear at ll.42 and 46 respectively);

P.Select. 17 (lease contract[2] between a lessee from Pois and Aurelius Anoubion, βουλευτής at Herakleopolis, previously exegetes and *decaprotus* of περὶ Πόλιν and Ἄγημα, of Tokois and other villages);

Stud.Pal. X 84 (Noeris, Pois, Peensamoi in three consecutive lines, followed by Thmoinepsi).

Stud.Pal. X 44 confirms the connections between Pois, Herakleopolis (l.9), the Tekmi toparchy (Tou and Kollintaathyr are listed) and Phnebieus. Tebetny, appearing at the end of this list, was already associated to Pois in *P.Hamb.* I 91.

Κάτοικοι ἱππεῖς settled at Pois are mentioned in *BGU* VIII 1772 and 1817.

SB I 1550, 1508 and 1515, and *O.Meyer* 51[3], show that donkeys for the transport of corn to the θησαυρός of Theadelpheia (in the Arsinoites) were requisitioned from Pois, as well as from other villages of the Arsinoite, Memphite, Herakleopolite, Oxyrhynchite and Kynopolite nomes. Pois, however, had its own θησαυρός, as attested in *P.Tebt.* I 857.

BGU XVI 2579 is a declaration of sheep and goats by an inhabitant of the village.

CPR IV 2 (a bilingual document in Coptic and Greek) lists many villages of the central toparchies of the Herakleopolite nome (toponyms in Greek)[4].

Σ.ΟΥ[5]

I B.C.   *BGU* XIV 2446,1

TOPARCHY: Tekmi.

This place-name is the heading of a section of the land-survey in the Tekmi toparchy (*BGU* XIV 2441-2448 and 2449-2450). The following fossil kleroi are mentioned, which also appear at other points in the land-survey: Στράτωνος τοῦ Δημητρίου (4); Πολέμωνος τοῦ Δωρίωνος (5-6); Φιλίππου τοῦ Τιμοκράτου (6,13,22), Θεογένου<ς> (8,17).

ΣΑΓΑΡΟΣ[6]

V A.D.   *Stud.Pal.* X 233, col. II,2

---

[1] Cf. *BL* 7,22.

[2] The land (1.5 ar. near Pois) is located by reference to the fossil kleros of Laomedon.

[3] These four ostraka are part of a larger group, including *SB* I 1505-1516, *O.Meyer* 51-55 and *O.Fayûm Towns* 24-40.

[4] See *s.v.* ΝΙΝΩ.

[5] Τροῦ is attractive, but the traces (checked by me on a photograph, and by William Brashear on the original) do not quite fit.

[6] «Kol.II 2 nennt vielleicht das bisher unbekannte Dorf Σαγαρος» (letter from Johannes Diethart, February 25, 1994).

ΣΑΔΑΛΕΙΟΥ

51/50 B.C.	*BGU* VIII 1786, 4	τῶ[ν ἐκ τοῦ Σαδαλ]είου ἀνδρῶν (3-4)
51/50 B.C.	*BGU* VIII 1831,1;7	ἐκ τοῦ Σαδαλείου
I B.C.	*BGU* VIII 1763,10	κατὰ Σαδ'α'(λεῖον) (1; cf. *BL* 3,24); ἐκ τοῦ Σαδαλείου (7)

TOPARCHY: Koma? περὶ Πόλιν?

ETYMOLOGY: derived from the Thracian personal name Σαδάλας[1], which is elsewhere attested in the Koma toparchy: in *BGU* XIV 2390 (1.39) a Σαδάλας is among the six Thracian witnesses to a lease contract of the year 160/159 B.C.; in *BGU* XIV 2432 (1.23) Σαδάλας is the father of Σωσίπατρος, who is registered under the entry for Thmoiobastis, in the Koma toparchy; in *BGU* VIII 1789 (1.8) Σαδάλας is one of the two λογευταί at Koma. A Thracian cleruchy is attested in the Memphite nome, too: cf. Edgar's comments on *P.Cair.Zen.* III 59473 (also referring to Koma and Onnes, in the Herakleopolites). The -εῖον ending is commonly used for the name of a sanctuary[2].

A village by the name Σαδάλου is well attested in the Oxyrhynchite nome[3]. Stephanus of Byzantium records a Σαδάλις Αἰγυπτία πόλις.

Apparently a rather troublesome community (establishment of Thracian settlers?). People ἐκ τοῦ Σαδαλείου seem involved in a riot in *BGU* VIII 1763, while in *BGU* VIII 1831 the petitioner complains of damage he has suffered from Theophilos son of Nikobios, «one of those ἐκ τοῦ Σαδαλείου», apparently as a consequence of an intrusion in the land cultivated by the petitioner on account of Hierax (who also had land near Tokois, in the περὶ Πόλιν toparchy). This piece of land is located περὶ Αννης.

ΣΑΚΑΠΡΥ

IV A.D.	*CPR* I 42,11

TOPARCHY: περὶ Πόλιν.

Lease contract (both parties are from Herakleopolis) for land distributed between several villages: Sobthis (περὶ Πόλιν), Sakapry, Ninopakan, Noeris (περὶ Πόλιν). The land allotment is further located by reference to the mouth of a canal (στομίου, 1.13) and to a path (τρίβου, 1.14).

---

[1] For a discussion on this name see V. VELKOV - A. FOL, *Les Thraces en Égypte gréco-romaine* (Studia Thracica 4), Sofia 1977, p.14. Thracians in Egypt: JEAN BINGEN, «Les Thraces en Égypte ptolémaïque», in *Pulpuveda. Semaines philippopolitaines de l'histoire et de la culture thrace* 4 (Plovdiv 1980), Sofia 1983, pp.72-79; see also MARCEL LAUNEY, *Recherches sur les armées hellénistiques*, Paris 1949-1950, vol.I, pp.366-398.

[2] Cf. WILLY CLARYSSE-JAN QUAEGEBEUR, «Ibion, Isieion and Tharesieion in two Oslo Papyri», *Symbolae Osloenses* 57, 1982, p.77.

[3] See PRUNETI, *Centri abitati*, s.v.; also CALDERINI-DARIS, *Dizionario*, s.v. Cf. the inscription from Ṣafānīya (in the northern part of the ancient Oxyrhynchite nome, and probably to be dated to the mid-II B.C.) published by HEINZ HEINEN in *TAVO B 69*, pp.258-267 : it is a list of men belonging to a σύνοδος, including Λεόννατος Σαδάλου Θρᾷξ ἱερατευ[κ]ὼς τὴν σύνοδον (1.3). Another Thracian personal name (ending with -ζελμις) is mentioned in the inscription published *ibid.*, pp.251-258.

ΣΑΡΑΠΟΥΔΟΣ

V A.D.	*Stud.Pal.* X 233, col.I A,9	
VII-VIII A.D.	*Stud.Pal.* X 212,3	χ(ωρίον) Σαραπου'δ'(ος)
VII-VIII A.D.	*Stud.Pal.* X 227,4	ἀπὸ χ(ωρίου) Σαραπου'δ'(ος)

ETYMOLOGY: Σαραπούδος is the genitive of the female personal name Σαραποῦς (see PREISIGKE, *Namenbuch, s.v.*).

Mentioned in *Stud.Pal.* X 212 as part of the same διοίκησις to which Thelbonthis (which was in the Techtho Nesos toparchy) belongs. In *Stud.Pal.* X 227 Φρούριον and Talae (Koites) also appear.

ΣΙΘΕΩΣ[1]

| I B.C. | *BGU* XIV 2433,52 [2] |
| I B.C. | *BGU* XIV 2438,46 |

TOPARCHY: Μέση?

BGU XIV 2438 assigns this village to the περὶ Φέβιχιν toparchy, like Tosachmis (l.50). However, a list of villages in the Middle toparchy precedes (ll.40-45: Phys, Techymis, Ποιμένων κώμη), and a location in the Μέση would be consistent with *BGU* XIV 2433, where the place-name Σ[.].ινησιθεως (included in a list of villages of the Μέση with Chennis, Phys and Peenepochra: ll.47-55) can be made into two known villages: Σισινη (see *s.v.*) and Σιθεως.

ΣΙΝΑΡΥ

about 255 B.C.	*P.Hib.* I 132, descr.	Σινάρυ
about 250 B.C.	*P.Hib.* II 248, fr. III,9	Σινάρυ
about 245 B.C.	*P.Hib.* I 60,4	εἰς Σινάρυν
243-242 B.C.	*P.Hib.* I 34,2;4	ε[ἰς τὸ] ἐν Σινά[ρ]υ δεσμωτήριον (2); [ἐκ τοῦ ἐ]ν Σιναρ[υ] δεσμωτ[η]ρίου (4)
243-242 B.C.	*P.Hib.* I 73,[8];11	ἐν Σιναρυ
29 June 239 B.C.	*P.Strasb.* VII 662,20	ἐπὶ Σιναρύ

---

[1] The Editor suggests (see *Index*) Σιθεύς for the nominative.

[2] Σ[.].ινησιθεως *ed.pr.* (where the possibility is also suggested for this toponym to be divided into two parts).

mid-II B.C.	*P.Tebt.* III 876,51	ἐκ Σιναρύ
14 B.C.	*BGU* IV 1061,3;5;18	ἐκ Σιναρὺ τοῦ Πέραν (3); ἐκ τῆς Σιναρύ (5); αὐτῆι τῆι Σιναρύ (18)
I B.C.	*P.Oxy.* XLIX 3462,3	ἀπ]ὸ Σιναρύ
I/II A.D.	(?) *P.Hib.* II 218,89;95 [1]	

Literary Sources

| V A.D. | STEPH. BYZ. *s.v.* Ψένηρος [2] |

TOPARCHY: Sinary is consistently assigned to the Κάτω (i.e. northern) toparchy of the Oxyrhynchite nome [3] in the sources dating from the Roman and Byzantine periods [4]: however, *BGU* IV 1061 (14 B.C.) locates it in the Πέραν. Only the sources from the Ptolemaic period are discussed here: these, however, also point to connections mainly with the northern Oxyrhynchites.

ETYMOLOGY: *(p3-)šj* + *-n-* (genitive) + *Ḥr-wḏ3*: «(the) lake of Haryothes» (the personal name Haryothes being reduced to Hary) [5].

MODERN ARABIC NAME: Sinarā [6]. See *TAVO B 69*, p.232: «Der Ort liegt am alten Baḥr Yūsuf. (Grob

---

[1] *P.Oxy.* X 1281,15 (= *CPJ* II 414), of 21 A.D., is the earliest source which assigns Sinary to the Oxyrhynchite nome. The Editor of *P.Oxy.Hels.* 10 (34 A.D.) suggests that *P.Hib.* II 218, where Sinary appears (ll.89, 95) within a long list of Herakleopolite villages, should therefore be re-dated to the first part of the first century A.D. (this document was dated by Eric G. Turner, on palaeographical grounds, to the late first or early second century A.D.). It is however not surprising to find Sinary in such Herakleopolite company: most villages listed in *P.Hib.* II 218 were in the southernmost Herakleopolite toparchy (Koites), which bordered upon the Oxyrhynchites.

[2] Αἰγυπτία κώμη. τὸ ἐθνικὸν Ψενηρίτης τῷ τύπῳ τῆς χώρας.
Meineke thought that Ψένηρος («Ψενηρός *libri ὀξυτόνως contra usum nominum plus quam bysillaborum Aegyptiacorum*») could be the same place as Ψένυρις, which is entered next in Stephanus' lexicon, and should be identified with the northern Oxyrhynchite locality by this name: see PRUNETI, *Centri abitati, s.v.*); Sinary, on the other hand, is available for identification with Ψένηρος (same vocalisation as in the Coptic name for this village: *Psenaro*). This identification, first proposed by JOHN BALL (*Egypt in the Classical Geographers*, Bulâq 1942, p.174) is accepted in *TAVO B 69*, p.99.

[3] See PRUNETI, *Centri abitati, s.v.*; also CALDERINI-DARIS, *Dizionario, s.v.* To these references the following may now be added: *P.Col.* VIII 214,3 (about 86 A.D.); *P.Wash.Univ.* II 78, col.II,10; 16(?) (first half of I A.D.); *SB* XVIII 13958,5 (193/194 A.D.); *P.Wash.Univ.* II 84,5 (IV or V A.D.); *SB* XX 14235,1 (VIII A.D.; published by GÜNTER POETHKE - PIETER J. SIJPESTEIJN, *APF* 38, 1992, p.35).

[4] *SB* XVIII 13958, dated to 193/194 A.D. and containing a reference to a κώ]μη Σιναρ[, has been tentatively assigned by its Editor to the Herakleopolites, on account of «the occurrence of the name Ἀγχαροῦς in l.15 which occurs in only one other text, *Stud.Pal.* II p.27,10, and this papyrus originates from the Herakleopolite nome» (PIETER J. SIJPESTEIJN, *ZPE* 63, 1986, p.299).

[5] Etymology suggested by Katelijn Vandorpe.

[6] «Shenra, which is near the edge of the desert west of Fent may be the Oxyrhynchite Σιναρύ ... The boundary between Oxyrhynchites and Herakleopolites was perhaps slightly altered in Roman times ... somewhere between Feshn and Fent, and nearly opposite Hibeh, which lies on the East bank» (*P.Oxy.* XII 1416,13 n.). See also *P.Oxy.* LI 3638, 12 n.: the *ESM* of 1930 «shows Shinara on the Eastern bank of the old Baḥr Yusuf», which agrees with the new information provided by this papyrus «that land at Sinary was bounded on the west by the river Tomis» (Τῶμις ποταμός was the ancient name for the

geschätzt) 2 km nordwestlich des Dorfes kamen bei der Anlage eines neuen Drainage-Kanals zahlreiche Keramikscherben ans Tageslicht, auch sind gebrannte Lehmziegel und Mauerreste an dieser Stelle zu finden. Nach Aussage eines Ghafirs der Altertümerverwaltung sind der Landgewinnung viele antike Relikte zum Opfer gefallen. Eine andere Stelle mit Keramikscherben befindet sich (grob geschätzt) 500 m. westlich des Dorfes bei der Polizeistation. Keramikscherben beider Stellen datieren aus spätantiker Zeit». See also TIMM, *Das christlich-koptische Ägypten*, V, pp.2351-2353, *s.v.* Sinarā.

BGU IV 1061 reports an assault by robbers from Sinary against the παστοφόρος of the temple of Bousiris (this must be the village in the northern part of the Herakleopolite nome).

Dorion, the ἐπιστάτης who in *P.Hib.* I 72 was sent a ὑπόμνημα on the disappearance of the official seal belonging to the Herakles temple at Phebichis (Koites), also figures in the intricate case of a stolen donkey (*P.Hib.* 34 and 73: a petition to the king and a letter to the epistates, respectively)[1]. Following his instructions, the thief (a certain Kallidromos) had been put in prison at Sinary, but Patron the ἀρχιφυλακίτης of the Northern toparchy of the Oxyrhynchite nome (the same one to which Sinary is consistently assigned in the Roman and Byzantine sources) «then intervened, and not only released Callidromus from prison but himself took possession of the donkey»[2] which he now keeps at Takona. Here we may well have a conflict between different authorities of the two neighbouring nomes, possibly originating from the ambiguous location of Sinary.

More connections with Takona and other localities of the Northern, Western and Thmoisepho toparchies of the Oxyrhynchites: *P.Hib.* I 60, *P.Hib.* I 132, *P.Hib.* I 248, *P.Oxy.* XLIX 3462.

P.Tebt. III 876 lists Sinary with at least one Herakleopolite village (l.5: Petachor, in the Ἄγημα toparchy; Sinary, however, only occurs at l.51); Sinary and Petachor are both listed in *P.Hib.* II 218, too.

ΣΙΝΕΒ

| 185/186 A.D. | *O.Wilck.* II 1099,3 | Ἡρακ(λεοπολίτου) Σινεβ[3] |

Corn-transport by donkey from Σινεβ.

ΣΙΣΙΝΗ

| 25 Feb.-25 March 261 B.C. | *P.Hib.* I 101,6 | ἐν Σισίνῃ |
| I B.C. | *BGU* XIV 2433,52 | Σ[ι]σινη[4] |

TOPARCHY: Ἄγημα.

Bahr Yusuf).

[1] The ἐπιστάτης Dorion of *P.Hib.* I 73 is probably the same official as in *P.Hib.* I 34 and 72. Grenfell and Hunt (in the introduction to *P.Hib.* I 73) thought that these were different officials, presumably because in the first document Dorion appears to be ἐπιστάτης in the Herakleopolites, whereas in the other two papyri certain northern Oxyrhynchite localities are mentioned. In my opinion, however, this is sufficiently explained by the location of Sinary in the borderland between the two nomes.

[2] *P.Hib.* I 34, *Introduction* (p.173).

[3] «Lesung wahrscheinlich richtig, α statt ε kaum möglich» (Günter Poethke, letter of April 14, 1994).

[4] Σ[.].ινησιθεως *ed.pr.* (where the possibility is also suggested for this toponym to be made into two, i.e. Σισινη and Σιθεως).

ETYMOLOGY: Σισίνης was a Persian personal name: see *P.Heid.* VI, p.23[1]. See also *s.v.* ΙΒΙΩΝ ΑΡΣΑΜΟΥ ('Αρσάμης is also a Persian personal name).

P.Hib. I 101: receipt for rent paid to the sitologos of the Ἄγημα toparchy on account of land cultivated near Sisine. The same place is listed with villages of the Μέση toparchy (among them Chennis, Phys, Peenepochra) in *BGU* XIV 2433, 47-55: a similar shifting is attested for the village of Peenameus.

(?)ΣΚΥΠΙΩΝ

late III A.D.   *BGU* XIII 2365,9

Comprised in a list of toponyms, some of which certainly refer to Herakleopolite villages (Techtho, Papa, Thelbo).

ΣΟΥΡΙΥ

VI A.D.   *Stud.Pal.* X 228,8   ἐν τόπ(ῳ) Σουριυ[2]

This could be the same as Σοῦρις/Σοῦλις, a place-name in the Polemon division of the Arsinoites, well attested from the beginning of the II A.D. to the VII A.D. (see CALDERINI-DARIS, *Dizionario*, *s.vv.*).

ΣΟΥΧΕΩΣ

V A.D.	*Stud.Pal.* X 94,1	Σουχεως
VI/VII A.D.	(?)*SB* XX 15072,2	Σωυχεως

ETYMOLOGY: this place-name is presumably connected with the god Sobk.

A διῶρυξ Σουχιανοῦ is attested in 152 A.D. in the Arsinoites[3]. Also in the Arsinoites, there was an ἐποίκιον called Σουχᾶ (*SB* VI 9269; 297 A.D.?).

Σουχεως and Daphne recur in both documents. Villages also mentioned in *SB* XX 15072, which could be in the Herakleopolites: Ψῶβθις (l.2) and Pois (l.4), both in the περὶ Πόλιν toparchy; Νεμάρεως (l.7); Μουχεμπ(άγ)ου(?) (l.9). Other localities appearing in the same document belonged to the Arsinoite and possibly Lykopolite nomes.

---

[1] See also *CPJ* I 28,4 n. («Since there were Jewish settlers in Egypt under the Persian domination, Iranian names do not exclude the possibility of their bearers being Jews»).

[2] «In Z.8 der Liste von τόποι und ἄμματα aus dem 6. Jh. schreibt Wessely in der handschriftlich verfaßten Edition Σουρβ. Eine Überprüfung des Originals ergab die Lesung Σουριυ - und das steht auch auf dem Umschlag, in dem der Papyrus verwahrt ist, von Wesselys eigener Hand. Zu verstehen ist wohl Σουρί(ο)υ» (Johannes Diethart, letter of February 25, 1994). «Soll man ..."koptisches" *Souriou* verstehen?» (letter of September 13, 1994).

[3] *SB* XVI 12319: described in *P.Lond.* III, p.LXX, and published in *BASP* 16, 1979, p.134.

CATALOGUE

ΣΥΓΚΕΜΜ[..]ΕΙ

V A.D.	*P.Oxy.* XVI 2017,7

ΣΧΝΩΜΘΙΣ

212/211 B.C.	*P.Lille* I 59,29;41;61;114	Σχνώμθεως (29;41;114) Σχνόμθεως (61)
I B.C.	*BGU* XIV 2438,62	Σχνῶ(μθις)[1]
I B.C./I A.D.	*BGU* IV 1192,15	περὶ κώμην Σχμῶνθιν[2]
3 August 174 A.D.	*SB* XIV 11341,8 (= *P.Mich.* IX 531 re-ed.)	Σχμ..θιν[3]

TOPARCHY: Tilothis.

ETYMOLOGY: the same component –νωμθ– may recur in the toponyms Σχνῶμθις and Μουχεννωμθου.

MODERN ARABIC NAME: Ishmant (on phonetical and topographical grounds: see *Introduction*, p.8).

BGU XIV 2438 indicates that Schnomthis belonged to the Tilothis toparchy, along with Peenpasbyt(is) and Tanchais (entries for the Koma toparchy follow): the same four villages appear in *P.Lille* I 59 (with other villages of the Koma and Tekmi toparchies).

BGU IV 1192 (official report, apparently on arrears in the payment of taxes) mentions two strategoi of the Herakleopolite nome, Paniskos and Heliodoros, both well known from *BGU* VIII documents[4].

SB XIV 11341: «... Tastous has put herself down to appear before the archiereus [Ulpius Serenianus] with a request about land. ... Apparently she had failed to appear, and Serenianus had written to enquire about her. .. five months later, the scribe reports that she is in Alexandria»[5].

ΣΩΒΘΙΣ

early I A.D.	(?)*P.Corn.* 22,4;73	Σοβθίτης (4); Σωβθίτης (73) (ethnic)
I A.D.	*P.Oxy.* VIII 1145,19	Σόβθις
early II A.D.	*P.Köln* II 98,11	Σώβθεως

---

[1] It is difficult to establish whether the first letter is Σ or Ε (reading checked by me on a photograph, and by William Brashear on the original); Εχνω( ) *ed. pr.*

[2] But: «Papyrus hier schlecht erhalten. Σχνωμθιν kaum möglich» (Günter Poethke, letter of April 14, 1994).

[3] Σχ....ιν («perhaps Σχμ..θιν») Parsons; Σχεμῶνθιν Louise C.Youtie. See PETER J. PARSONS, «Ulpius Serenianus», *Chr. d'Ég.* 49, 1974, p.137.

[4] On the succession of the στρατηγοί of the Herakleopolite nome in the I B.C. see LUCIA CRISCUOLO, «Guerre civili e amministrazione tolemaica. Il caso degli strateghi dell'Herakleopolites», *Ancient Society* 22, 1991, pp.229-234.

[5] PETER J. PARSONS, *Chr. d'Ég.* 49, 1974, p.137.

17 April 395 A.D.	(?)*CEL* 231,3 (= *CPR* V 13, col. II + *P.Rain.Cent.* 165, col. I) ¹	*praef(ecto) k(astri) Psofthis*
396 A.D.	(?)*CEL* 232,3 (= *CPR* V 13, col. I)	*praef(ecto) k(astri) Psoftis*
IV A.D.	*MPER* XV 84,3	Σώβθεως
IV/V A.D.	*MPER* XV 83,10	ὑποδ(έκτου) Σώβθεως
401 A.D.	(?)*CEL* 233,3 (= *P.Rain.Cent.* 165, col. II)	*praef(ecto) k(astri) Ps[oft(h)is]*
VI A.D.	*Stud.Pal.* X 207,5	ἀπ'ὀ' Σώφ'θ'(εως)
VI/VII A.D.	*CPR* XIV 36,7	ἀπὸ Σώφθε(ως) Δ κωμ(ίας) ²
VI/VII A.D.	*SB* XX 15072,2	Ψώβθεως ³
26 Dec. 642 A.D.	(?) *SB* VI 9578,1;4	Ψώφθεως (1); ἀπὸ Σώ[φ]θε(ως) (4)
VII A.D.	*Stud.Pal.* X 220,8	ἀπὸ χ(ωρίου) Σώφ(θεως) ⁴

Literary Sources

V A.D.	*Not. Dign. Or.* XXVIII 33	*Sosteos*

ETYMOLOGY: *P3-sbt*, «the wall» ⁵.

---

¹ Cf. JOHN R. REA, *ZPE* 56, 1984, pp.79-84: *CPR* V 13 and *P.Rain.Cent.* 165 can be joined, so that «what we now have are the remains of a section of a roll containing three letters in a damaged but substantially comprehensible state, each from a different *comes et dux Aegypti* to three different prefects of the camp at a place in Egypt called Psoft(h)is. Each letter occupies a separate column. The earliest in date, 17 April A.D. 396, has the central position and is shared between the many fragments [...]. Next in date, A.D. 396, comes the letter [*CEL* 232] occupying the left-hand place [...]. Last in date, A.D. 401, [*CEL* 233] ... occupying the right-hand column» (p.79). It is not at all certain that this Sobthis was in the Herakleopolites.

² «Δ κωμ( ) could denote Τετρακωμία, which is the name of an Arsinoite village in *SPP* X 138 II 11 and *CPR* VI 82,7, or be resolved as Τετάρτη or Τέτταρες (Τέσσαρες) κώμη, by analogy with κώμ(η) Κ found for Εἴκοσι κώμη in *Stud.Pal.* III 617,2. The relationship of town and village to each other may best be brought out in the translation "Tetrakomia-by-Sophthis"» (Ed. *ad loc.*). This document also contains three references to the Herakleopolite village of Tanchais (ll.4;8;12).

³ The document has been published by PIETER J. SIJPESTEIJN, *ZPE* 81, 1990, pp.245-251, who indicates that villages by the name Psobthis are known in the Oxyrhynchite, Hermoupolite and Arsinoite nomes. Altough the spelling with initial Ψ does not seem to be otherwise attested for the Herakleopolites; my reason for including this reference is that another Herakleopolite locality is entered on the same line (Σωύχεως: see *s.v.* ΣΟΥΧΕΩΣ).

⁴ This must be the Herakleopolite Sobthis, as it appears here in the same list with Daphne, another Herakleopolite village also attested in *Stud.Pal.* X 94.

⁵ See JEAN YOYOTTE, «Sôphthis et le problème de Saft», *Rd'É* 15, 1963, pp.106-114, who derives this place-name from an Egyptian word attested since the XVIII Dinasty, to designate the «ramparts des villes fortifiées, ... murs de briques que l'on voit encore autour des temples»; cf. WILLY CLARYSSE - JAN QUAEGEBEUR, «Ibion, Isieion and Tharesieion in two Oslo Papyri», *Symbolae Osloenses* 57, 1982, p.79. See also PAULY-WISSOWA, *R.E.*, Bd. XVII, col. 1685; ARISTIDE CALDERINI, «Località dell'Ossirinchite del medesimo nome», *Rend. Ist. Lombardo* 58, 1925, pp.529-536; DREW-BEAR, *Le nome Hermopolite*, pp.331-332; PAOLA PRUNETI, *Aegyptus* 59, 1979, pp.98-101. Further comments: *CPR* V 13,3 n.; ANN ELLIS

Evidence from these sources is either insufficient or ambiguous, so that it is not possible to establish which of the two Herakleopolite villages called Sobthis (ἡ μεγάλη or ἡ μικρά: see *s.vv.*) is meant. Thus, connections with localities of the Koites as attested in *P.Oxy.* VIII 1145 (Koba) and *P.Köln* II 98 (Temenkyrkis) might be more likely for Sobthis ἡ μεγάλη, which was probably more to the south; such connections, however, are also attested in *P.Rain.Cent.* 82, which certainly concerns Sobthis of the περὶ Πόλιν toparchy, i.e. Σῶβθις ἡ μικρά.

SB XX 15072 and *Stud.Pal.* X 220 must refer to the same Sobthis, as the village of Daphne is mentioned in both documents. *SB* XX 15072 also contains a reference to Pois, which was probably in the Tilothis toparchy; a connection with this toparchy is also suggested by *CPR* XIV 36 (where Tanchais recurs three times).

The prefect of a fort *Psoftis* or *Psophtis* is the addressee of two letters in Latin contained in a military *dossier* of unknown provenance (*CEL* 232 = *CPR* V 13; see also *CEL* 231 and 233)[1]: in favour of a location in the Herakleopolites it may be argued that (a) these documents probably originate from Ihnāsiya al-Madīna/Herakleopolis[2]; (b) the Herakleopolites appears to have been well endowed with military establishments[3].

ΣΩΒΘΙΣ ἡ μεγάλη

V A.D.	*Stud.Pal.* X 8,3	Σώβθεως Μεγάλης
VI A.D.	*Stud.Pal.* XX 254,1	βοηθ(ῷ) Σώβθεως Μεγάλης

TOPARCHY: Κάτω toparchy of the Oxyrhynchite nome? (See *Introduction*, p.11).

ETYMOLOGY: *P3-sbt*, «the wall».

MODERN ARABIC NAME: Ṣafṭ al-Hirsa?

Other villages mentioned in *Stud.Pal.* X 8 include Choinotmis (on the same line with Sobthis ἡ μεγάλη), Ἁλμυρά, Techtho, Phnebieus (Μέση toparchy).

HANSON, *ZPE* 47, 1982, p.239.

[1] The fort should perhaps be identified with *Sosteos*, station of the *ala II Assyriorum* in the *Notitia Dignitatum*, and possibly with the κάστρον Ψώβθεως known from *P.Oxy.* XVI 1883 (504 A.D.) and *P.Oxy.* XVI 2004 (V A.D.). But, as noted by the Editor of *CPR* V 13, «the Oxyrhynchite nome is not a very likely provenance for this document». According to him, however, «there is a strong likelihood that the κάστρον Ψώβθεως, *Sosteos*, and our *Psoft(h)is* are all the same and that we are dealing here with the *ala II Assyriorum*, but it is less sure whether the fort should be located at one of the Oxyrhynchite villages called Psobthis or at one of the other similarly named places in the Herakleopolite and Arsinoite nomes». See also: KLAAS A. WORP, «Observations on some Military Camps and Place-Names in Lower Egypt», *ZPE* 87, 1991, pp.291-295; CONSTANTIN ZUCKERMANN, «Le camp de Ψῶβθις/Sosteos», *ZPE* 100, 1994, pp.199-202.

[2] See *Introduction*, p.29.

[3] *P.Berl. Zill.* 1 and 2, for instance, provide us with details about the building of a fort near Herakleopolis in the mid-second century B.C.

ΣΩΒΘΙΣ ἡ μικρά

mid-II B.C.	*P.Tebt.* III 876,66;87	'ἐν Σόφθει' (66); Σώβθεως (87)
96-94 or 63-61 B.C.	*BGU* XIV 2429,11	Σώβθ(εως)
64/63 B.C.	*BGU* VIII 1753,6	εἰς τὸν ἐν Σώβθει ἰβιῶνα
31 Dec. 57 B.C. (cf. *BL* 9,28)	*BGU* VIII 1821,15	ὁ λογευτὴς Σώβθεως
48/47 B.C.	*BGU* VIII 1795,6	ἐν Σώβθ(ει)
36/35 B.C.	*BGU* XIV 2376, 17;36	[ἐν κώμηι Σώβθει] (17); [ἐν] κώμηι Σώβ[θει] (36)
36/35 B.C.	*BGU* XIV 2377,42	ἐγ κώμηι Σώβθει
I B.C.	*BGU* XIV 2432,13	Σώβθεως
I B.C.	*BGU* XIV 2434,25	πε]ρὶ Σῶβθιν
I B.C.	*BGU* XIV 2437 (fr.4),70	Σ]ῶβθιν
I/II A.D.	*P.Hib.* II 218,38;80;87	Σώβθ(εως) (38); Σώβθ(εως) (80); Σώ[β]θ(εως) (87)
167/168 A.D.	*P.Berl.Leihg.* I 2 *recto*, 2	κώμης Σώβθεως
13 August (?) 176 A.D.	*P.Oxy. Hels.* 37,1	ἀπὸ Σώβθις
190 A.D.	*P.Tebt.* II 301,3	ἀπὸ κώμης Σώβθεως (2-3)
II A.D.	*P.Tebt.* II 575, descr.	εἰς Σῶβτιν
304/305 A.D.	*P.Rain.Cent.* 82,11	περὶ κώμην Σώβθιν
384/385 A.D. (cf.*BL* 7,16)	*BGU* III 938,3	περὶ πεδίον Σώβθεως μικρᾶ(ς)
IV A.D.	*CPR* I 42,9	περὶ κώμην Σῶβτιν μικρὰν κύκλω τοῦ χωρίου
V A.D.	*Stud.Pal.* X 9,2	Σώβθεως
V A.D.	*Stud.Pal.* X 233, col. II,13	Σώβθεως Μικρ(ᾶς) [1]
VI/VII A.D.	*CPR* VIII 68,3	ἀπο κώμης Σώβθεω[ς Μικ]ρᾶς (2-3); cf. ἐν πεδίοις τῆς αὐτῆς κώμης (8-9) [2]
VII A.D.	*Stud.Pal.* X 22,1	χ(ωρίον) Σώφ[θ(εως)] Μικρ(ᾶς)

---

[1] New reading by Johannes Diethart (letter of February 25, 1994).

[2] See *s.v.* ΑΙΛΟΥΤΟΣ.

TOPARCHY: this village is assigned to the περὶ Πόλιν until 304/305 A.D.: soon after this date, the *pagi* were instituted, so that a village was no longer to be identified by referring to its toparchy; as a consequence, the new denomination Sobthis ἡ μικρά, as opposed to Sobthis ἡ μεγάλη (*q.v.*), is found from the late fourth century A.D. onwards. The coincidence of Sobthis ἡ μικρά with Sobthis of the περὶ Πόλιν toparchy is assured by the fact that both are connected to Tokois, another village of the same toparchy (as shown by *BGU* VIII 1821 and *Stud.Pal.* X 22, respectively).

ETYMOLOGY: *P3-sbt*, «the wall» (see *s.v.* ΣΩΒΘΙΣ).

MODERN ARABIC NAME: Ṣaft Rašin? (See *Introduction*, p.11).

According to *TAVO B 69* (p.211), Ṣaft Rašin is one of the «archäologisch bedeutendsten Stätten zwischen Nil und Baḥr Yusūf. Das Geländerelief zeigt keinen besonders auffälligen Kōm. Keramikscherben sind nur wenige zu sehen. Es finden sich aber zahlreiche Steinblöcke, Säulentrommeln, Kapitelle und Basen sowie Ölpressen. In der Dorfmoschee sind drei ältere Säulen mit unterschiedlichen Kapitellen aus spätantiker und arabischer Zeit verbaut. Nach Auskunft des Bürgermeisters befand sich an der Stelle der Moschee früher eine Kirche. In Häusern finden sich zahlreiche Steinblöcke mit koptischen Ornamenten, zum Teil als Dekoration an den Eingangstüren angebracht» (*TAVO B 69*, p.211).

See also TIMM, *Das christlich-koptische Ägypten*, V, p.2230 f. (*s.v.* Ṣaft Rašin).

A village by the name Sobthis is assigned, or connected with the περὶ Πόλιν toparchy in *BGU* XIV 2376 (of which *BGU* XIV 2377 is a copy), *BGU* XIV 2432, *BGU* VIII 1753 (corn provisions for an ibis sanctuary at Sobthis) and, in 304/305 A.D., *P.Rain.Cent.* 82 (a lease contract for land in the fossil kleros of Ptolemaios near Sobthis in the περὶ Πόλιν toparchy: the lessors are from Choinothmis). In *BGU* XIV 2376 (= 2377) a piece of garden-land near Sobthis is located by reference to a διῶρυξ called ὀμφαλό.νια (south) and to the ὁδὸς βασιλική (north).

Other documents witnessing the connection of a Herakleopolite village called Sobthis with localities of περὶ Πόλιν and other toparchies in the northern Herakleopolites, besides relationships with the Arsinoite nome, are likely to refer to the same Sobthis. These include:

BGU VIII 1821 (Adrastos, who looks after his brother's holding at Tokois, complains about harassment by a λογευτής from Sobthis; Adrastos' brother is an ἐκλογιστής at Herakleopolis);

Stud.Pal. X 22 (again connection with Tokois);

BGU VIII 1795 (petition from Semtheus son of Horos, who was both προφήτης of the temple of Semthenkentôi at Tekmi, and ἀρχιερεύς of the temple of Herakles at Sobthis);

Stud.Pal. X 9 (connection with Mouchis, also in the Tekmi toparchy).

Of the documents explicitly referring to Sobthis ἡ μικρά, *BGU* III 938 is a lease contract for land in the surroundings of Ἀρριανοῦ; *CPR* VIII 68 is a lease contract for land near Sobthis, more precisely located with reference to «the kleros called Pia... or Ailous' reservoir» (the land-owner is from Herakleopolis).

P.Tebt. III 876 and *P.Oxy.Hels.* 37 apparently connect Sobthis with the port of Herakleopolis.

Connection with Phnebieus (Μέση toparchy): *BGU* XIV 2432; *BGU* XIV 2434; *Stud.Pal.* X 9.

Connection with Petachor (Ἄγημα): *BGU* XIV 2429; *P.Hib.* II 218; *P.Tebt.* III 876.

Connection with the Πέραν: *BGU* XIV 2432; *P.Tebt.* III 876 (Sinary).

Connection with the Arsinoite nome: *P.Tebt.* II 301 is a death notification sent to the komogrammateus of Tebtynis by the two guardians of a young priest (the guardians are: a priest of Isis and Serapis from Sobthis in the Herakleopolite nome, and a priest of «the famous temple of the village of Tebtynis»[1]); *P.Berl.Leihg.* I 2 recto concerns the transport of corn from the θησαυρός of the Themistos and Polemon divisions of the Arsinoite nome by the κτηνοτρόφοι of Sobthis (and of some villages in the Kynopolite nome).

---

[1] Other sanctuaries at Sobthis: *BGU* VIII 1753 and *BGU* VIII 1795 (both discussed above).

ΣΩΤΤΙΑΝΟΣ

V A.D.   Stud.Pal. X 233, col.II,11 [1]

Τ..[...]

135/134 B.C.   P.Münch. III 51,12;[14]   ἐκ Τ..[...] (12); ἐν τῆι
                                                            ἀ[ὐ]τ[ῆι] κ[ώ]μ[ηι Τ.....]
                                                            (14)

This petition is addressed to Euergetes II, Cleopatra II, and Cleopatra III, by a βασιλικὸς γεωργός from Sebennytos (Arsinoites, division of Herakleides). It concerns a property apparently located in the Herakleopolite nome: the people against whom the petition is directed originated from there.

Τ[..]λ[

VI-VII A.D.   Stud.Pal. X 5,3   βοηθ(ὸν) Τ[..]λ[[2]

Other villages listed in the same document: Onosis (1.4); Tinteris (1.5); Kolintaathyr (1.6); Nino (1.7).

Τα[....]

60/59 B.C.   BGU VIII 1818,2;28   περὶ Τα[....] (2) [3]; περὶ
                                                         Τα.[(28); cf. ll.17-18: τοῖς
                                                         τῆς κώμης φυλακίταις

Petition concerning a φυλακιτικὸς κλῆρος located near this village, where λινοκαλάμη had been sown. The *ed. pr.* suggested Τα[γχάιν] as a possible supplement at l.2: it may be noted that *P.Cair.Zen.* IV 59782(b), where Tanchais is listed with other villages, deals with the production of flax.

Τα..[....

200 A.D.   P.Oxy. VI 899,22

See also: ΤΑΤΑΡ( )

TOPARCHY: in the northern part of the nome.

---

[1] «Kol. II 11 ist der bisher unbekannte Dorf Σωττιανός (...ττια... Wessely) zu lesen» (Johannes Diethart, letter of February 25, 1994).

[2] According to Johannes Diethart (letter of September 13, 1994)

[3] Günther Poethke (letter of April 14, 1994) indicates Τα[...] or Τρ[....] as possible readings.

CATALOGUE

The document refers to land cultivated by the same person περὶ τε κώμην Βουσεῖρ[ι]ν καὶ Θιντῆριν καὶ Τα..ι[....].χος κώμας τοῦ Ἡρακλεοπολίτου.

ΤΑΑΜΗΧΕΩΣ

| 31 Jan. 49 A.D. | *P.Oxy.* XXXI 2582,4 | ἀπὸ κώμης Τααμήχεως τοῦ Κωίτου |

TOPARCHY: Koites.

The document records the sale of a slave at Euergetis (in the Herakleides division of the Arsinoites?): the seller is from Oxyrhynchus, the buyer is ἀπὸ κώμης Τααμήχεως, ἐν ἀγυιᾷ Εὐόρμῳ («in the street of the good moorings»).

ΤΑΑΜΟΡΟΥ

mid-III B.C. [1]	*P.Fuad Crawford* 5, recto,8	Τααμορους
mid-III B.C.	*P.Strasb.* IX 802,6	Τααμαρους
I/II A.D.	*P.Hib.* II 218,21	Τααμόρου
192/193 A.D.	*P.Langres* inv. 907.1.39 verso,1	Τααϰμωρο[υ]
29 Aug.-27 Sept. 241 A.D.	*CPR* VIII 14,3;12;20	[σιτολόγω]ν κώμης [Τααμορο]ῦ (2-3); ὑπ(ὲρ) πρ(ακτορείας) Τααμοροῦ [καὶ ἄλλω]ν κωμῶν (13); σιτ[ολόγος Τααμο]ροῦ κα[ὶ] [ἄλλων κωμῶν] (20-21)
241/242 A.D.	*P.Vind.Tand.* 11,[19];[24];43;47	κώμης Τααμοροῦ (43); τῆς α(ὐτῆς) Τααμοροῦ (47)
242 A.D.	*Stud.Pal.* XX 52,5	Τααμορου
May-June 335 A.D.(?)	*P.Lond.* VI 1914,58	ἀπὸ Ταμούρω; εἰς Ταμούρω
25 Feb. 381 A.D.	*P.Rain.Cent.* 86,4; verso,26 (= *Stud.Pal.* XX 103,4)	ἀπὸ κώμης Ταμωρῶ (4); Ταμμωρῶ (26)
IV A.D.	*P.Neph.* 12,11;17	Ταϩμουρώ (11); Ταϩμ[ο]υρού (17) [2]

---

[1] On the re-dating of this document see *Introduction*, p.14 n.7.

[2] «Das Griechisch des Serapion ist desolat ... Den Ortsnamen Tahmuro, der griechisch in den verschiedensten graphischen Varianten bezeugt ist, versieht er mit einem Koptischen Buchstaben ... Serapions Muttersprache [ist] vielleicht Koptisch» (*ed. pr. ad loc.*).

IV A.D.[1]	*P.Ross.Georg.* V 61 B recto 2;12; C verso 7;8;13; D recto 2;18; D verso 13	ἀπὸ Ταμουρώ (B recto 2;12; C verso 7;8;13; D recto 18); ἀπὸ κώμης Ταμουρώ (D recto 2); ἀπὸ Ταμ]ουρώ (D verso 13)
IV/V A.D.	*P.Laur.* II 42,7	Ταμμουρῷ (cf. *BL* 8,164)
VI A.D.	*P.Oxy.* XVI 1917,63;82;111;113	ἀπὸ Τααμώρου (63; 113); ἀπὸ Τααμ]ώρου (82); δ(ιὰ) τῶν πρωτοκ(ωμητῶν) Τααμώρου ὑπὲρ τῆς ἀνωρυχθ(είσης) διώρ(υγος) ἐξ ἀπηλιώτου Ψελεμάχεως (111-112)
VIII A.D.	*Stud.Pal.*X 109,4	Τααμώ(ρου) (cf. *BL* 7,258)

See also: ΙΒΙΩΝ ΤΑΜΜΩΡ[Ο]Υ.

TOPARCHY: Koites.

ETYMOLOGY: the "bilingual" spelling of *P.Neph.* 12 is most similar to Τααкμωρο[υ] of *P.Langres* inv. 907.1.39 (published by P. CAUDERLIER, *Chr.d'Ég.* 63, 1988, pp.317-322).

MODERN ARABIC NAME: Dahmarū: see *TAVO B* 69 § 4.3 (M 53), and p.202: «Ein Dorf mit einem großen Kōm. ... Die Oberflächenkeramik ist in spätantike Zeit zu datieren. Über dem Eingang des Scheichsgrabes ist ein Architekturfragment mit koptischen Ornamenten wiederverbaut. In der Nähe der Moschee wurden Säulenbasen gesehen, die vermutlich aus einer älteren Kirche Stammen...». See also TIMM, *Das christlich-koptische Ägypten*, VI, p.2464 f. (*s.v.* Tahmourō).

The border with the Oxyrhynchites must have been near Taamorou. A canal, which ran east of Pselemachis (Koites), probably ran past Taamorou, too (cf. *P.Oxy.* XVI 1917, also mentioning Nokle, and the Oxyrhynchite Ἰβιών and Palosis)[2]. Pselemachis is found in the same document with Taamorou since the III B.C. (*P.Strasb.* IX 802, listing various other villages in the Koites; *P.Fuad Crawford* 5, also mentioning Talae and Psychis); like Pselemachis, Taamorou is part of a net of Meletian monasteries attested in the Nepheros archive (*P.Neph.*12; *P.Lond.* VI 1914).

Philonikou and Taamorou are found together in *P.Hib.* II 218, *Stud.Pal.* XX 52[3], *Stud.Pal.* X 109.

ΤΑΑΜΨΕΩΣ

V A.D.   *Stud.Pal.* X 233, col. II,24

Ogou (Tekmi toparchy) precedes this village in the list.

---

[1] *P.Ross.Georg.* V 61 B *recto* is to be dated «nach der Mitte des 4. Jahrhunderts» (cf. *BL* 9,227).

[2] Cf. the Editors' comment on *P.Neph.* 13, ll.11 and 17. This Ἰβιών may well be the same as Ἰβιών Ταμμώρ[ο]υ (see *s.v.*) of *PSI* IX 1037.

[3] *P.Vind.Sijp.* 19 and *P.Vind.Worp* 4 (both mentioning Tebetny) are documents very similar to *Stud.Pal.* XX 52.

ΤΑΒΑ[

| 78/77 B.C. | *BGU* VIII 1737,18 | περὶ Ταβα[[1] |

See also *s.v.* ΤΑΒΟΚΛΙΣ

Reference to a βασιλικὴ ῥύμη is made at l.13.

ΤΑΒΟΚΛΙΣ

| I B.C. | *BGU* XIV 2440,17 | περὶ Ταβ(όκλιν) |
| 222 A.D. | *Stud.Pal.* XX 26,28 | ἀπὸ κώ(μης) Ταβόκλεως [2] |

See also: Ταβα[.

TOPARCHY: Tekmi.

Stud.Pal. XX 26: previous owners of a plot of land at Tanaso (περὶ Πόλιν toparchy) are listed up to A.D. 153: one from Taemsis (contract of sale drawn up by the ἀγορανόμος at Tekmi in 204), another from Tanaso (contract drawn up by the ἀγορανόμος of the περὶ Πόλιν toparchy in 196), a third one from Taboklis (contract drawn up by the ἀγορανόμος at Tekmi). It seems likely for these villages to have been in the border-area between the περὶ Πόλιν and the Tekmi toparchies.

BGU XIV 2440: ll.17-18 survey land granted to Herakleides son of Isidoros, partly in the Tekmi toparchy (uncultivated land near Ταβ( ), entered under Tochontou) and partly in the Koites (near Pselemachis).

ΤΑΓΧΑΙΣ

| 260-259 B.C. (cf. *BL* 9,282) | *SB* XVI 12387,4 | ἐ]ν κώμῃ Ταγχάϊ |
| 212/211 B.C. | *P.Lille* I 59,14;38;100;123 | Ταγχάεως [3] |

---

[1] The reading in the *ed. pr.* is correct (checked on a photograph). This may just be a different vocalisation for the place-name Taboklis.

[2] The *ed. pr.* dubitatively suggests Ταε(μσεα). Taemsis does in fact recur in connection with Tochontou in *BGU* XIV 2437 (cf. ll.1-6): both villages were in the Tekmi toparchy. However, the traces fit a β better, which leads to Ταβ(οκλιν), also a village in the Tekmi toparchy (reading checked by me on a photograph, and by William Brashear on the original).

[3] My readings (checked on Plate XII of the *editio princeps*): Τάγκλεως (14;38;100;123) *ed.pr.*; Ταγχλεως Hombert (cf. *BL* 2.2,78).

mid-III B.C.[1]	*P.Cair.Zen.* 59782 (b),26;65;83	ἐκ Ταγχά(εως)[2]
96-94 or 63-61 B.C.	*BGU* XIV 2429,9	Ταιχ( )[3]
after 84/83 B.C.	*BGU* XIV 2370 (fr.1),87	ἀπὸ Ταγχάεως
57 or 51/50 B.C. (cf. *BL* 8,48)	*BGU* VIII 1780,2	παρὰ Ἀρτεμιδώρου ὑποστρατήγο[υ] Ταγχάεως
after 52/51 B.C.	*BGU* VIII 1808,29;37	Ταγχάεως (29); Ταγχάεως λο(γευτῶν) η (37)
9 August 47 B.C.	*BGU* VIII 1811,6	ἀπὸ [Τ]αγχάεως
I B.C.	*BGU* VIII 1778,3-4	ἐγ Ταγχάεως
I B.C.	*BGU* VIII 1825,3-4	παρὰ Προίτου τοῦ Λυ[σα]νίου λογευτοῦ [Ταγ]χάεως
I B.C.	*BGU* VIII 1845,4	ἐν Ταγχάει
I B.C.	*BGU* XIV 2436,5;8;12	Τα<γ>χ(ᾶιν) (5); Ταγχ(ᾶιν) (8); Ταιχ(ᾶιν) (12)[4]
I B.C.	*BGU* XIV 2438,71	Ταγχάεως
21/20 B.C.-5 A.D.	*BGU* XVI 2641,11	Ταγχά'ε'(ως)
21 Dec. 10 B.C.	*BGU* XVI 2630,15	ἐν Ταγχάι
VI/VII A.D.	*CPR* XIV 36,4;8;12	ἀπὸ Ταγχάεως

See also: Ται'χ'( ); Τα[....].

TOPARCHY: Tilothis[5].

MODERN ARABIC NAME: Tansa Al-Malaq (on phonetical and topographical grounds: see *Introduction*).

BGU XIV 2438 assigns Tanchais to the Tilothis toparchy; *BGU* VIII 1808 (ll.36-38) apparently refers to an ἀρχεφοδεῖον there.

---

[1] On the dating of this document see above, p.60 n.3.

[2] ἐκ Τογχά *ed. pr.* I could not check this reading on a photograph, but it seems rather assured in view of the other place-names recurring in the same document (see below).

[3] A very doubtful reading: τ and α much effaced, ρ perhaps to be read instead of ι. If Ταιχ( ), this may be a variant spelling for Ταγχ(άεως) (see also next note).

[4] After checking a photograph, my opinion is that the scribe meant to write the same place-name in all three occurrences. Ταγχᾶ(ιν) can perhaps be read at l.12, too (reading checked for me by William Brashear).

[5] The Editors of *BGU* VIII 1780 and EDMOND VAN'T DACK, *Chr.d'Ég.* 23, 1948, p.151, infer from this document the existence of a toparchy περὶ Ταγχαιν, with a ὑποστράτηγος of its own. This, however, is not attested elsewhere: all other sources, including those dating (like *BGU* VIII 1870) from the I B.C., assign Tanchais to the Tilothis toparchy. The reference in *BGU* VIII 1780 perhaps simply identifies the place where the ὑποστράτηγος had the misadventure he is reporting to his superiors.

The lists of villages in *P.Lille* I 59 and *P.Cair.Zen.* IV 59782 (b) largely coincide: besides Bousiris, they include villages of the Koma toparchy (Koma, Krekis, Machor; in addition, *P.Cair.Zen.* IV 59782 (b) mentions Thmoiobastis and Tou), the Tilothis toparchy (Tilothis, Tanchais; in addition, *P.Lille* I 59 mentions Peenpasbyt(is) and Schnomthis) and the Tekmi toparchy (Onnes; in addition, *P.Lille* I 59 has Peenepsy). Many of these villages are recorded in *BGU* XIV 2370, fr.1; these are: Koma, Toou, Machor and Thmoiobastis (apparently under the main entry κάτω τοπαρ[χ]ίας), Onnes, Tilothis, Tanchais. A second fragment (*BGU* XIV 2370 fr.2), written by the same hand, has a reference to Bousiris. Much the same group of villages recurs in *BGU* XIV 2438: Tilothis, Schnomthis, Peenpasbyt(is), Tanchais, Koma, Toou (preceded by entries for the following toparchies: Ἄγημα κάτω, Μέση and περὶ Φέβιχιν). In *BGU* XVI 2630 (letter concerning the transport of grain) Bousiris, Tanchais and the Τρωΐτης are stations on the *route*. In *BGU* XVI 2641 (register of ten farmers) the names and/or villages of three farmers are preserved: Koma, Tanchais, Trikomia. These connections are confirmed in *BGU* VIII 1808: Tekmi, Koma, Trikomia, Onnes, Thmoiobastis, Bousiris again recur in a sequence; Tanchais appears a few lines below, following entries for the Πέραν, Techtho Nesos, Ἄγημα (Alilais, Kollasoucha, Korphotoi), περὶ Φέβιχιν and Μέση (Phnebieus), and immediately preceding Pois (there follows a reference to the περὶ Πόλιν toparchy: l.31). This is consistent with the information contained in *BGU* XIV 2436, where three land-holdings are surveyed: Kastor's is split between Tosachmis, Phebichis (both in the Koites) and Tanchais; Ptolemaios' is split between Pois, Tanchais and Tosachmis; Hierax' is distributed between Tanchais, Noeris (περὶ Πόλιν toparchy) and Pois. It also seems consistent with *BGU* XIV 2429, where some of the villages (Kollasoucha, Petachor, Hiera Nesos) also appearing in *BGU* VIII 1808 again appear in connection with Ταιχ( ) = Τάγχαις.

BGU VIII 1778 contains another hint at the connection (suggested by *BGU* XIV 2370 fr.1) between the (Ἄγημα) κάτω τοπαρχία and Tanchais: this is the beginning of a report by a λογχοφόρος who was to meet one of the κάτοικοι ἱππεῖς of Tanchais, and deliver a letter to the ὑποστράτηγος of the κάτω τοπαρχία. Κάτοικοι ἱππεῖς settled at Tanchais are also attested in *BGU* XIV 1845.

ΤΑΕΜΣΙΣ

30 Jan. 237 B.C.	*PUG* III 114,10	ἐκ Ταέμσεως
I B.C.	*BGU* XIV 2437,3	Ταέμσεα
23 Feb. 214 A.D.	*SB* XIV 11643,2;3 (= *SB* I 5163)	δι'ἐπιτηρητῶν ἀγορανομίας Ταέμσεως
222 A.D.	*Stud.Pal.* XX 26,15	ἀπὸ κώ(μης) Ταέμσεως
first half of III A.D.	*CPR* I 169,5 [1]	]κώμη Ταέμσεως(?) [2]
second half of III A.D.	*SB* XVI 12241,5;10;15	ἐν κώ(μῃ) Ταέμσει (5); ἐν τῇ (αὐτῇ) Ταέμσει (10); ἐν κώ(μῃ) Ταέμσει (15)

See also *s.v.* ΤΑΕΤΜΕΙ.

TOPARCHY: Tekmi.

BGU XIV 2437,1-6: a τοπογραμματικὸς κλῆρος, entered under the heading περὶ Τέκμι·

---

[1] *CPR* I 169 and *CPR* I 157 are part of the same document (cf. *P.Rain.Cent.*, vol.I, p.88).

[2] «Zeilenende, keine Kürzung angezeigt; vielleicht ist Ταέμ|σεως zu lesen» (Johannes Diethart, letter of February 25, 1994).

Κολλινταаθύρ, was distributed among several villages, all presumably in the Tekmi toparchy: Taemsis, Του, Tochontou, Πεενε.'.'( ), Tekmi itself.

Stud.Pal. XX 26: previous owners of a plot of land at Tanaso (περὶ Πόλιν toparchy) are listed up to A.D. 153: one from Taemsis (sale contract, drawn up by the ἀγορανόμος at Tekmi in 204), another from Tanaso (contract drawn up by the ἀγορανόμος of the περὶ Πόλιν toparchy in 196), a third one from Taboklis (contract drawn up by the ἀγορανόμος at Tekmi). The fact that successive owners of the same plot are from different toparchies (Tekmi, περὶ Πόλιν and Ἄγημα) suggests that these neighboured each other and that Tanaso (περὶ Πόλιν toparchy), Taemsis and Taboklis (both in the Tekmi toparchy) were presumably near the boundary between these two toparchies.

SB XIV 11643 was drawn up in the office of the agoranomos of Taemsis: it is the ἐκσφράγισμα of a declaration by a woman from Taemsis, but presently living at Herakleopolis, to invalidate a will she had previously made.

PUG III 114: ναύκληρος declaration for the transport of corn from Peentechy, Taemsis and Tanaso to Alexandria.

ΤΑΕΤΜΕΙ

235-238 A.D.(?)[1]   *CPR* I 84,6   ἐν κώμῃ Ταετμει[2]

See also *s.v.* ΤΑΕΜΣΙΣ.

TOPARCHY: Tekmi.

The document is a παραχώρησις contract, drawn up in the office of the agoranomos at Tekmi. This place-name could be understood as Ταετμ<σ>ει or Ταειμ<σ>ει (variant spelling for Ταεμσει): at least one of the parties in the contract comes from this village.

ΤΑΕΩΣ

I/II A.D.   *P.Hib.* II 218,49   Τάεως

Των (Tekmi toparchy) follows in this long list, otherwise mainly including villages of the Koites.

ΤΑΚΡΙΑΝ

683/684 A.D.   *CPR* X 135,7

Land ἐν διαφόροις κλήροις is surveyed in this document.

---

[1] Date uncertain: cf. *BL* 1,119 and 7,43 (with reference to *SB* I 4370); see also J.DAVID THOMAS, «*SB* XVI 13050 reconsidered», *ZPE* 88, 1991, p.124 and n.17.

[2] «ἐν κώμῃ Ταειμει oder Ταετμει: die Entscheidung ist schwierig» (Johannes Diethart, letter of February 25, 1994). ἐν κώμῃ Πεενάμει - suggested by Preisigke on the basis of a comparison with *SB* I 4370 where the same woman (called Thaesis) appears, seven years younger - cannot be read here.

ΤΑΛΑΗ/ΤΑΛΗ

264/263 or 263/262 B.C.	P.Hib. I 157 (descr.)	ἐκ [Τα]λάους
about 246 B.C.	SB XII 10783,7 (= P.Hib. 139 descr.)	ἐκ Ταλάη
246 (245) B.C.	P.Hib. I 106,7	ἐκ Ταλάη
244 (243) B.C.	P.Hib. I 107,6	ἐν [Ταλάη]
239 (238) or 214 (213) B.C.	P.Hib. I 117,8	ἐν Τάληι [1]
235 (234) B.C.	P.Hib. I 37,4;12	φυλακίτηι κώμης Ταλέου[ς (4); φυλακίτηι κώμης Ταλέ[ους] (12-13)
232 (231) B.C.	P.Hib. I 75,1;5	τοῖς ἐν Ταλάηι φυ(λακίταις) (1); ἐκ τοῦ Φιλοξένου κλ(ήρου) περὶ Ταλάην (5)
230/229 or 229/228 B.C.	P.Hib. I 144 descr.	φυλακίτης κώμης Τάλη
229 (228) B.C.	P.Hib. I 36,3;8	φυλακίτηι Ταλέους (3); φυλακίτηι Τάλη (8)
mid-III B.C. [2]	P.Fuad Crawford 5, recto,4	Ταλαης
mid-III B.C.(?)	SB X 10447 verso,27	εἰς Ταλήν (cf. BL 6,168)
I B.C.	BGU XIV 2431,8	ἐν Ταλῆ
I B.C.	BGU XIV 2435,25	Ταλέους
28/27 B.C.	BGU XVI 2665,17	τὸν περὶ Ταλὴ κλῆρον (16-17)
February 155 A.D.	SB V 7515,251 (= P.Berl.Frisk 1 = P.Bankakten 1)	Ṭαλαη[.] [3]
I/II A.D.	P.Hib. II 218,15;26;28;88	Τάλη (88: Τάλ[η])
IV A.D.	P.Rain.Cent. 147,6	μερ(ισμὸς) Ἀπίω[νος] στατι(ωναρίου) κώμης Ταλὴ σύμμαχ(ος) α (5-7; cf. BL 8,287)
IV/V A.D.	P.Rain.Cent. 153,7	ἀπὸ Ταλή

---

[1] Ταλει (dative according to the third declension) should perhaps be read.

[2] On the re-dating of this document see Introduction, p.14 n.7.

[3] I suggest this reading instead of Ṭαλλη[.] of the ed. pr. The Editor also notes ad loc.: «Ob etwas in der Lücke gestanden hat, ist sehr unsicher».

V A.D.	*P.Oxy.* VIII 1126,7	γίτονες νώτου τον ἀπὸ Τάλη λιβὸς λιδης Κητς, ἀπη]λιώτου λιδης .μεια (7-9)
VII A.D.	*Stud.Pal.* III 197,2	Ταλη
VII-VIII A.D.	*Stud.Pal.* X 227,5;6	ἀπὸ χ(ωρίου) Ταλη

TOPARCHY: Koites.

ETYMOLOGY: Ταλαη (possibly a more accurate rendering of the Egyptian place-name) is declined according to the first declension; Ταλη (spelling commonly adopted in the Roman period) follows the third declension (genitive Ταλέους)[1].

MODERN ARABIC NAME: Ṭalā[2].

P.Hib. I 106 and 107: the agents of Taembes, who lives at Talae, pay the beer-tax into the *logeuterion* of Phebichis. Talae is also connected to Phebichis in *BGU* XIV 2431.
P.Hib. I 117: account of corn (138 1/2 art. olyra; 12 art. wheat) compiled by an official in charge of the State granaries of the Koites (presumably at Phebichis); the olyra is paid at Talae, on account of holdings at Psychis and Assya.
BGU XIV 2435: Assya again recurs as administratively subordinated to Talae, along with Kerkes(ephis?), as in *SB* V 7515 (mainly dealing with the Polemon division of the Arsinoites: κτηνοτρόφοι from Kerkesephis, Philonikou and Talae, in the Herakleopolite nome, are also involved). Talae and Kerkesephis are both included in other lists of villages in the Koites (*P.Fuad Crawford* 5; *P.Hib.* II 218).
BGU XVI 2665 is a letter from a woman to her son, concerning land at Ogou, Mouchis (both in the Tekmi toparchy), Nois (περὶ Πόλιν) and Talae.
P.Rain.Cent. 153: villages of the Koites (Talae, Thmoinpesla and Thneis), the Middle toparchy (Phys, Peenpibykis) and the northern part of the Oxyrhynchite nome (Palosis) appear in the same accounts.
In *P.Oxy.* VIII 1126 Koba is also mentioned.

(?)ΤΑΜΕΡΣΟΦΩ( )

VI/VII A.D.	*SB* XX 15072,5[3]

Other villages mentioned include Psobthis, Pois, Daphne.

ΤΑΜΦΝΟΥΘΙΣ

I B.C.	*BGU* VIII 1824,8	Ταμφνοῦθιν

---

[1] See *P.Hib.* I 36,3 n.

[2] As already suggested by Bernard P. Grenfell and Arthur S. Hunt, *P.Oxy.* XII 1416,13 n. In *P.Hib.* I 117 Psychis (modern Absūg, about 4.5 km SE of modern Ṭalā) appears to depend administratively on Talae. See also *Introduction*, p.11.

[3] The document has been published by PIETER J. SIJPESTEIJN, *ZPE* 81, 1990, pp.245-251. It is not at all certain that Ταμερσοφω( ) was a village in the Herakleopolites: our source mentions several villages, which can be located in the Arsinoite, Herakleopolite, and apparently also Lykopolite and Aphroditopolite nomes.

A petition to the strategos, concerning assault and robbery on the part of people ἀπὸ τῆς μεγάλης πλατικ. *BGU* VIII 1814, a petition to the same strategos written by the same hand, deals with land near Tebetny (Πέραν toparchy).

ΤΑΝ[..].Α̣.[

| III A.D. | *P.Neph.* 28,4 | ἀπὸ κώμ]ης Ταν[..].α.[[1] |

This fragment of a contract also mentions the villages of Papa, Phebichis, Pimein. Ταν[τοκ]α seems a possible supplement.

ΤΑΝΑΣΩ

30 Jan. 237 B.C.	*PUG* III 114,11	ἐκ Τανασῶν
139 B.C.	*P.Tebt.* III 838,4	ὁ σιτολογῶν Τα[νασώ περὶ Πόλιν (ll.4-5) [2]
139 B.C.	*P.Tebt.* III 986,3	ὁ σιτολογῶν Τανασώ πε[ρ]ὶ Π[όλιν (ll.2-3) [3]
222 A.D.	*Stud.Pal.* XX 26,20; 31-32 (= *Chr.M.* 200)	ἀπὸ κώ(μης) Τανασώ (19-20); πε[ρὶ κώ(μην) Τα]νασώ
7 Dec. 227 A.D. (cf. *BL* 7,259)	*Stud.Pal.* XX 29,12	ἀπὸ κώμης Τανασώ
II/III A.D.	*P.Alex.* inv. 563 (p.32),5	Τανασώ
III A.D.	*CPR* I 66,10	ἐν τῇ αὐτῇ κώμῃ Τανασώ
V A.D.	*Stud.Pal.* X 47,3	Τανασώ

TOPARCHY: περὶ Πόλιν? περὶ Τεκμι?

Tanaso and Taemsis (Tekmi toparchy) recur together in *PUG* III 114 (ναύκληρος declaration for corn transport from Peentechy, Taemsis and Tanaso) and in *Stud.Pal.* XX 26: here Marcus Aurelius Horseus applies to the βιβλιοφύλαξ ἐγκτήσεων of the περὶ Πόλιν toparchy for an official statement concerning a plot of land he owns at Tanaso, in the fossil kleros Θεοδμ[ήτου] (l.32); this is to be sent to the ἀγορανόμος of the Ἄγημα toparchy [4]. Previous owners of the plot are listed up to A.D. 153: one from

---

[1] «Dieses Dorf braucht allerdings nicht im Herakleopolites gelegen zu haben» (Ed. *ad loc.*).

[2] Τα[*ed.pr.* Τα[νασώ seems a likely supplement, as this must have been the same village as in *P.Tebt.* III 986,3 (where Ταν.. is read in the *ed.pr.*, and the indication of the toparchy can in turn be supplied on the basis of *P.Tebt.* III 838): no other village-name beginning with Ταν- is attested in the περὶ Πόλιν toparchy.

[3] See preceding note.

[4] Presumably in order that he could then draw up a contract of sale: it may be that the buyer (not mentioned, in this document) originated from the Ἄγημα. Cf. however HANS JULIUS WOLFF, *Das Recht der griechischen Papyri Ägyptens.*

Taemsis (contract of sale drawn up by the ἀγορανόμος at Tekmi in 204), another from Tanaso (contract drawn up by the ἀγορανόμος of the περὶ Πόλιν toparchy in A.D. 196), a third one from Taboklis (contract drawn up by the ἀγορανόμος at Tekmi).

Connection between Tanaso and Peentechy: *PUG* III 114 (see above) and *Stud.Pal.* XX 29 (παραχώρησις contract drawn up in the agoranomos office at Tekmi: some of the land ceded by a man from Tosachmis to his wife, who is from Tanaso, is near Peentechy).

Connection between Tanaso and Tosachmis: *Stud.Pal.* XX 29 (see above) and *Stud.Pal.* X 47, a list of villages including Onosis (l.1; περὶ Πόλιν toparchy), Mouchis (l.2; Tekmi toparchy), Tanaso and Tosachmis (l.4; Koites). This connection is corroborated by *P.Alex.* inv. 563, where Phebichis is also entered (l.7).

ΤΑΝΙΣ

mid-III B.C.   *P.Strasb.* IX 802,12   Τᾶνις[1]

TOPARCHY: Koites.

There was a well attested Tanis in the Herakleides division of the Arsinoites[2], and a famous one in the Delta (cf. *L.Ä.*, Bd.II, 194-209).

Most, or all villages listed in *P.Strasb.* IX 802 were in the Koites.

ΤΑΝΤΟΚΑ

between 173 and 130-128   *P.Tebt.* III 890,7   ἐκ Ταντόκα
B.C. (cf. *BL* 7,273)

early II B.C.   *P.Tebt.* III 1044,62   Ταντό(κα)

See also *s.v.* TAN[..].Ạ.[

TOPARCHY: Μέση?

A village called Τοκα is attested in the Oxyrhynchites (see PRUNETI, *Centri abitati, s.v.*).

P.Tebt. III 890: bank accounts also mentioning Phnebieus (ll.74,75,100), Kolleus (l.81), Με[(l.97).
P.Tebt. III 1044: advances of wheat and barley to cleruchs; Peensamoi (Πέραν toparchy) also mentioned.

Zweiter Band. Organisation und Kontrolle des privaten Rechtsverkehrs, München 1978, p.25 (with reference to our document): «Offenbar ohne jegliche Einschränkung ihrer örtlichen Zuständigkeit konnten die Urkundsämter auch solche Vorgänge zu notariellem Protokoll nehmen, deren handelnde Personen oder Objekte außerhalb ihres Sprengels lebten bzw. belegen waren. ..... Die Beteiligung verschiedener Agoranomeia an aufeinander folgenden Veräußerungen ein und derselben Liegenschaft bezeugt die herakleopolitische Eingabe *Stud.Pal.* XX 26». As remarked by Wolff (p.18, n.48), local dependencies of the central ἀγορανόμος office of the Herakleopolites are well attested in the III A.D.: ἐπιτηρηταί were in charge of them.

[1] «Plutôt que Τᾶσις» (*ed. pr. ad loc.*).

[2] See WILLY CLARYSSE, *Studia Hellenistica* 24 (1980), p.105. The Arsinoite Tanis is also referred to in *P.Bodl.* I 150,6;13.

ΤΑΠΑΜΕ[

VII-VIII A.D.   *Stud.Pal.* X 206,14

Apparently the name of a κλῆρος, listed with several others (see the *Reverse Index* at the end of this volume).

ΤΑΠΙΑΜΠΕΣΗΤ

VII-VIII A.D.   *Stud.Pal.* X 206,11;12

Apparently the name of a κλῆρος, listed with several others (see the *Reverse Index* at the end of this volume).

ΤΑΠΟΥΡΣΗΕΙ

VI A.D.   *Stud.Pal.* III 86,1;4   ἀπὸ ἐποικίου
Ταπουρσηει τοῦ
Ἡρακλεοπολίτου νομοῦ
(1-2); ἐποικίου
Ταπουρσηει (4)

See also: ΤΑΠΡΟΥΣ[.

ΤΑΠΡΟΥΣ[

VII A.D.   *Stud.Pal.* X 22,3   χ(ωρίον) Ταπρουσ[[1]
See also: ΤΑΠΟΥΡΣΗΕΙ.

TOPARCHY: περὶ Πόλιν.

Stud.Pal. X 22 lists, among other place-names, Sobthis ἡ μικρά, Tokois and Charamou (all in the περὶ Πόλιν toparchy).

ΤΑΡΕΤΤΑΡΥ

16 July 534 A.D.   *SB* VIII 9876,10-11   κλήρου Ταρέτταρυ

TOPARCHY: περὶ Πόλιν.

Near Noeris.

---

[1] «Ob eine Metathesis für Ταπουρσηει!? An und für sich kein Problem. Es könnte aber auch schon Wortende sein, was sich aber nicht sagen läßt» (Johannes Diethart, letter of September 13, 1994).

ΤΑΡΩΤ

| May-June 335 A.D.(?) | P.Lond. VI 1914,57 | ἀπὸ Τεροτ |
| end of VI/VII A.D. | P.Köln VII 322,7 | [ἐν τόπῳ κα]λουμένῳ Ταρωτ |

ETYMOLOGY: see s.v. TEPTON().

MODERN ARABIC NAME: according to the Editor of P.Lond. VI 1914 (ad l.57), «no doubt to be identified with the Coptic *Terot*»: he offers Derût esh-Sherîf and the nearby district capital Derût («close to the junction of the Bahr Yusûf and the Ibrâhîmîyah Canal») as equally possible identifications for Τεροτ. On the whole, Τεροτ = Derût esh-Sherîf seems more likely; Derût (the modern district capital) could be ancient Τερυθις (in the Oxyrhynchite nome).

P.Köln VII 318-326 are all part of the same roll, which assembled several different documents: the place-names mentioned there (Papa, in the Koites; Peenpibyk(is), in the Μέση) point to the Herakleopolites. In P.Lond. VI 1914 Taamorou (in the border-area between Koites and Oxyrhynchites) and Τουμνακων are also mentioned.

P.Köln VII 322 contains a lease of land (six arourae) with all its attachments: λάκκος, ὕδρευμα, μηχανή, μηχανοστάσιον, μηχανικὰ ὄργανα, πύργος (ll.7-8). Borders: to the north a public road (δημοσία ὁδός), to the south the local canal (ἡ ἐκεῖ διῶρυξ), to the east another landholding (l.9).

ΤΑΣΑΥΤΗΣ

| V A.D. | Stud.Pal. X 233, col. I B,9 | ἐποίκ(ιον) Τασαυτης[1] |

TOPARCHY: Koma.

This place-name recurs between Thmoiobastis and Thmoiamoun(is), both in the Koma toparchy.

ΤΑΤΑΡ( )

| VIII A.D. | Stud.Pal. X 218,4 | χ(ωρίον) Ταταρ( ) |

See also: Τα̣..[.....

Other villages listed in Stud.Pal. X 218 include Onosis (περὶ Πόλιν toparchy) and Tinteris. It may be that Ταταρ( ) is the same village as Τα̣..[..... of P.Oxy. VI 899.

---

[1] Ταυαυτης ed. pr.; reading revised by Johannes Diethart (letter of February 25, 1994).

CATALOGUE

ΤΑΥΡΟΣ

VII A.D. Stud.Pal. X 66,3 χ(ωρίον) Ταῦρος[1]

Philonikou (Koites) is entered at l.5.

ΤΑΦΘΙΡΙΣ

after 27 B.C. BGU XVI 2599,6 περὶ Ταφθίριν

Petition from three farmers from Κεφαλαί, who claim that their respective seven-arourae kleroi (all near Taphthiris) have been insufficiently inundated.

ΤΑΧΕΩΣ

V A.D. Stud.Pal. X 233, col. I B,13 Νέας Πόλεως κ(α)ὶ Τάχεως[2]

ΤΑΧΟΝΠΑΧΝΟΥΒ / ἸΒΙΩΝ ΠΑΧΝΟΥΒΙΣ[3]

mid-III B.C. P.Strasb. IX 802,8 Ταχονπαχνοῦβ
131 A.D. P.Oxy. IV 715,21 περὶ κώμην Ἰβιῶνα Παχνοῦβιν

TOPARCHY: Koites.

ETYMOLOGY: Ταχο-ν-παχνουβ is transliterated from the Egyptian *T3-ᶜhj-n-Pa-Ḥnm* (no Greek case-ending): «the ibis-sanctuary[4] of (founded/sponsored by) Pachnoum».

Ἰβιών is the Greek translation of the Egyptian *t3-ᶜhj* (otherwise transliterated as ταχο/ε), in combination with the same Egyptian personal name: Πάχνουβ(ις). As might have been expected, the

---

[1] Reading suggested by Johannes Diethart: «Z.3 vermeine ich χ(ωρίον) Ταῦρος zu lesen, einen Ort im Herakleopolites, der bisher nicht bekannt war» (letter of February 25, 1994). The first Editor deciphered Τοπρ[?] or Ταυρ[ινου].

[2] New reading by Johannes Diethart (letter of February 25, 1994).

[3] VBP II 21 (March-April 117 A.D.) refers to an Ἰβιὼν Πα.[(1.12) which could be the Herakleopolite Ἰβιὼν Παχνουβεως, but also the Hermopolite Ἰβιὼν Πανεκτύρεως (referred to in VBP II 26): cf. P.Heid. IV p.77 n.10.

[4] See K.A.D. SMELIK, «The Cult of the Ibis in the Graeco-Roman Period with Special Attention to the Data from the Papyri», in *Studies in Hellenistic Religions (EPRO 78)*, 1979, pp.225-243. The Greek ταχο/ε transliterates the Egyptian *t3-ᶜhj*: Vandorpe (p.116) thinks that: «Une signification "réserve d'oiseaux" est plausible, vu l'origine du mot ... Là où le contexte nous apprend quelque chose au sujet de ces ᶜhj, il s'agit toujours du culte de l'ibis, auquel le culte du faucon est parfois associé». The meaning for ᶜhj was first postulated by PAOLO GALLO, «A proposito del termine demotico ᶜhj.t e dell'eventuale corrispondenza greca ἰβιών», EVO 9, 1986, pp.45-48.

earlier source attests the Egyptian place-name transliterated into Greek, whereas the hellenised place-name is found in a much later source.

BIBLIOGRAPHY: KATELIJN VANDORPE, «Les villages des Ibis dans la toponymie tardive», *Enchoria*, 18, 1991, pp.115-122, esp. pp.119-120

P.Oxy. IV 715: the property inherited by two brothers living at Toemesis included some land in the «fossil kleros» of Zoilos and Noumenios, near Ἰβιῶν Πάχνουβις, and some more in the «fossil kleros» of Menippos and Artemidoros, near Pselemachis. The same villages already appeared in three consecutive lines in *P.Strasb.* IX 802: Pselemachis (7), Tachonpachnoub (8)[1], Toemesis (9). As there is no doubt that Pselemachis was in the Koites, we can also be assured of the situation of Ταχονπαχνουβ/Ἰβιῶν Πάχνουβις in the same toparchy.

Another centre named after an ibis sanctuary near Pselemachis was Ἰβιῶν Ἀρσάμου; see also: Ἰβιῶν ... (*P.Fuad Crawford* 5, verso, 10).

TH()

VII-VIII A.D.   *Stud.Pal.* X 206,4

Apparently the name of a κλῆρος, listed with several others (see the *Reverse Index*, at the end of this volume).

ΤΕΒΕΤΝΥ

247/246 B.C.	*SB* III 7203,11	ἐν Τεβέτνυ
III B.C.	*P.Lille* I 6,4	ἐκ Τεβέτνου
2 July 167 B.C.	*P.Hamb.* I 91,4	ἐν Τεβέτνοι
2 Sept. 162 B.C.	*P.Hels.* I 26 A,15;26	Τεβέτνοι
II B.C.	*P.Münch.* III 49,2	ἐν] Τεβέτνοι
61/60 B.C.	*BGU* VIII 1814,7	περὶ Τεβέτνοι
I B.C.	*BGU* VIII 1857,8	ἐν τοῖς τῆς Τεβέτνοι πεδίοις
I B.C.	*BGU* XIV 2432,15	Τεβέτνοι
232/233 A.D.	*Stud.Pal.* XX 34,5;16	ἀπὸ κώμ[ης] Τεβέτνυ (5); περὶ τὴν αὐτὴν Τεβέτνυ (16)
233/234 A.D.	*P.Vind.Sijp.* 19,6	σιτολόγων κώμης Τεβετνῦ
234 A.D.	*P.Vind.Worp* 4,5	σιτολ(όγων) κώμης Τεβετνυ
446 A.D.	*P.Rain.Cent.* 95,6	[Τεβέ]τνυ τοῦ Ἡρακ[λεοπολίτου

---

[1] Vandorpe points out that the tax-payer referred to under the entry for Ταχονπαχνουβ is called Πῐβις, a variant spelling for Φῐβις (Egyptian *p3-hb*, «the ibis»).

CATALOGUE

16 Oct. 599 A.D.	*P.Köln* III 158,13	ἀπὸ κώμης Τεβέτνυ
VI A.D.	*Stud.Pal.* X 44,14	χ'ω'(ρίον) Τεβετνη
VII A.D.	*SB* VI 9590,11;22;*verso*	Τεβέτνυ
VII/VIII A.D.	*CPR* IV 2,12	χ(ωρίον) Τεβετνη
Byz.	*SB* I 5339,9	χωρ(ίον) Τεβέτνυ

TOPARCHY: Πέραν.

A Tebetny (modern Dafadnu) in the Polemon division of the Arsinoites is very well attested throughout the Graeco-Roman period (see also *P.Vind.Worp* 4,5 n.).

BIBLIOGRAPHY: TIMM, *Das christlich-koptische Ägypten* II, pp.491-492 (*s.v.* Dafadnū).

Both *P.Hels.* I 26 and *BGU* XIV 2432 mention Tebetny and Thmoiphtha as belonging to the Πέραν toparchy (in *P.Hels.* I 26, Peensamoi and Thmoinausiris are also assigned to the same toparchy).

Assuming that both Thmoinothis and Bousiris referred to in *SB* III 7203 were the Herakleopolite villages thus named, the Tebetny also mentioned there is likely to have been in the Herakleopolites (note, however, that various Arsinoite localities appear in the same document, too).

Tebetny in the Herakleopolites is also attested in some sources of the third century A.D. (*Stud.Pal.* XX 34: an inhabitant of Tebetny applies to the strategos of the Herakleopolites for a grant of seed-corn; *P.Vind.Sijp.* 19 and *P.Vind.Worp* 4: monthly reports from the sitologos of Tebetny to the strategos of the Herakleopolites[1]), and of the sixth/seventh century A.D. (*Stud.Pal.* X 44: several other Herakleopolite villages are listed, including Pois, Tinteris, Tou, Kollintaathyr, Phnebieus; *SB* VI 9590: two arourae which Anatolios cedes to Pamoûn are apparently split between Makaitonos, Tebetny and Chortaso).

P.Münch. III 49 *recto* contains an address [τοῖς ἐν] Τεβέτνοι πρεσβυτέρο[ι]ς τῶν Ἰουδαίων (l.2), while on the *verso* an address to ἄρχοντες of Herakleopolis is found (l.1: ἄρχου[σι), who may or may not be «chiefs of the Jews»[2], and may or may not coincide with the «elders of the Jews» of Tebetny[3]. There is anyway little doubt that the two texts, on the *recto* and *verso* of the same papyrus and both referring to Jews, are related, and thus offer a link between (the Jewish communities of?) Tebetny and Herakleopolis. The proximity of the Arsinoite Tebetny to Samareia, «probably a military establishment of Syrian soldiers (particularly Jews and Samaritans)»[4], may suggest a Jewish origin for the place-name Tebetny.

BGU VIII 1814 is a petition to the strategos Paniskos from a κάτοικος ἱππεύς holding a kleros at Tebetny. *BGU* VIII 1857 reports a serious offence: the petitioner's brother has been robbed and murdered on the way from Tebetny to Καινή (also in the Πέραν, as attested by *BGU* VIII 1834; the two villages also recur together in the Byzantine *SB* I 5339). A similar crime, though not with such tragic consequences, was already reported in the III B.C.: the petitioner survived to complain of having been assaulted while on his way from Tebetny to Korphotoi (in the Ἄγημα κάτω), where he was to visit his sister. *P.Hamb.* I 91, again a petition to the strategos of the Herakleopolites (this is Kydias, who was in charge in 167 B.C.), apparently indicates Tebetny as the place where «spoils» were shared (ll.3-4: ἀπὸ τῶν γενομένων σκύλ[ω]ν ἐν Τεβέτνοι)[5]; the petitioner apparently complains about the loss of his

---

[1] Cf. the similar *Stud.Pal.* XX 52 (place-names mentioned there: Taamorou, Philonikou).

[2] There is no way of knowing whether ἄρχου[σι was the last word in the line, and thus linked to τῶν Ἰουδαίων (which follows in the next line).

[3] See the introduction to *P.Monac.* III 49 (p.9).

[4] See *CPJ* I 22,6 n.

[5] According to the Editor of this text, the occasion might have been a clash of opposed factions in the conflict between Ptolemy VI Philometor and Ptolemy VIII Euegetes II. See THEODOR C. SKEAT, *The Reigns of the Ptolemies*, München

share, consisting of four female slaves: one of these, retrieved on the slave-market at Memphis, apparently managed to escape to Pois.

CPR IV 2 (a bilingual document in Coptic and Greek) lists many villages of the central toparchies of the Herakleopolite nome (toponyms in Greek)[1].

(?) ΤΕΚΒΗ[2]

36/35 B.C.	*BGU* XIV 2376,18;38	Τέκ]βη (18); Τέκβη[ς] (38)
36/35 B.C.	*BGU* XIV 2377,22;45	Τέκβης

BGU XIV 2376 and 2377 are copies of the same document, which concerns a confiscation procedure.

ΤΕΚΜΙ

246-221 B.C.	*P.Strasb.* VII 642,5	κώμηι Τ[έ]κμει
163/162 B.C. (?)	*P.Hels.* I 24,1;6	τὸ ἐν Τέκμι λο(γευτήριον) (1); περὶ Τεκμι (6)
149 or 138 B.C.[3]	*SB* XVIII 13304,1;6	κωμογραμματέως Τέκμι καὶ Βιχινθωύθ[4]
64/63 B.C.	*BGU* VIII 1747,4	περὶ Τέκ(μι)
63/62 B.C.	*BGU* VIII 1771,16;20	περὶ Τέκ(μι) (16); περὶ Τέκ(μι) (20)
21 June 51 B.C.(?)[5]	*BGU* VIII 1832,7;13	οἱ ἐκ τῆς ἐφοδείας κώμης Τέκμι (6-7); εἰς χορτοθήκην ἐν κώμηι Τέκμι (12-13)
51/50 B.C.	*BGU* VIII 1838,4	ἐκ κώμης Τέκμι
50/49 B.C.	*BGU* VIII 1842,4	φυλακίτου κώμης Τέκμι (3-4)

1954, p.33 f. and, more recently, *C.Ptol.Sklav.* I, pp.315 ff.

[1] See *s.v.* ΝΙΝΩ.

[2] Cf. *BGU* XIV 2376,19 n.: «[καὶ Τέκ]βης d.h. γῆ. Auch am Zeilenende verstehe man καὶ γῆ (πρότερον) Εὐμήλου»: according to the Editor, then, Τέκβη is probably the present landholder's name - *not* a place-name.

[3] The date 157 B.C. suggested by the first Editors (ROYCE L. B. MORRIS-JOHN F. OATES, «An official Report», *BASP* 22, 1985, pp.243-246) is wrong: cf. GREGG WILLIAM SCHWENDNER, *ZPE* 72, 1988, pp.275-276, suggesting the dates 149 or (preferably) 138 B.C.

[4] Cf. DIETER HAGEDORN, *ZPE* 68, 1987, pp.84-85.

[5] Cf. l.20: (ἔτους) λ καὶ α Πα(ῦνι) κ («year 30 which is also year 1»); see THEODOR C. SKEAT, *The Reigns of the Ptolemies*, München 1954, p.18.

CATALOGUE

48/47 B.C.	*BGU* VIII 1795,2;5	περὶ Τέκ(μι) (2); ἐν Τέκμι (4-5)
I B.C.	*BGU* VIII 1789,1	[περὶ Τ]έκμι τοπ[αρχία[1]
I B.C.	*BGU* VIII 1807,9	κατὰ Τέκμι (8-9)
I B.C.	*BGU* VIII 1808,1	Τέκμει λογευτῶν ε ἀρχιφυλακίτου ε Πέρσου υἱῶν ε (1-3)
I B.C.	*BGU* VIII 1822,21	τῆς Τέκμει
I B.C.	*BGU* XIV 2434,11	περὶ Τέκμι
I B.C.	*BGU* XIV 2437,1;5;7;12;23	περὶ Τέκμι (1)
I B.C.	*BGU* XIV 2440,12;41;46	περὶ Τέκμι (11;46)
I B.C.	*BGU* XIV 2441,53;58;75	[Τέκ]μι (53); εἰς τὸ ἐν Τέκ(μι) ἱερὸν Εσηφκόμτωι θε(οῦ) με(γίστου) (58); Τ[ε]κμι(75)
I B.C.	*BGU* XIV 2444,7;25;81;82	ἐν Τέκ(μι)
I B.C.	*BGU* XIV 2449,40	ἐν Τέκμι
I B.C.	*BGU* XIV 2450 (fr.1),5	ἐν Τέκ(μι)
about 14/13 B.C.	*BGU* XVI 2670,II,1	περὶ Τεκμί
28/29 A.D.	*P.Oxy.* XXIV 2412,34;135;173	
II A.D.	*P.Mil.Vogl.* VI 287,13	ἐν Τέκμει
193-211 A.D.	*CPR* I 50,b,3	περὶ Τέκμει
1 August 204 A.D.	*O.Wilck.* II 1121,1	σιτολ(όγοι) Τεκμι
218 A.D.	*Stud.Pal.* XX 25,5	δι'ἐπιτη[ρητῶν] ἀγορανομίας περὶ Τέκμει
222 A.D.	*PSI XV* estr. 1546,30	[δι'ἐπιτηρητῶν ἀγορανομίας μερῶ]ν τοπαρχίας περὶ Τεκμεὶ τοῦ ὑπὲρ Μέμφιν [Ἡρακλεοπολίτου] (30)

---

[1] «Tekmi ganz zw.» *ed. pr.*

222 A.D.	Stud.Pal. XX 26,12;26	δι' ἐπιτηρητ(ῶν) ἀγορ(ανομίας) περὶ Τέκμει (11-12); δι' ἀγορ(ανομίας) περὶ Τέκμει (26)
222-235 A.D. (emperor Severus Alexander)	CPR I 76,5 [1]	[δι' ἐπιτηρητῶν ἀγορανομίας περὶ Τέκμε]ι
222-235 A.D.	CPR VI 73,8	ἀ[πὸ κώμης] Τέκμει (7-8)
7 Dec. 227 A.D. (cf. BL 7,259)	Stud.Pal. XX 29,6	δι' ἐπιτηρ[η]τῶν [ἀγορανομί]ας περὶ Τέκμει
235-238 A.D.(?) [2]	CPR I 84,4	περὶ [Τέ]κμει
first half of III A.D.	CPR I 83,2	περὶ Τέκμει
first half of III A.D.	CPR I 90,2	περὶ Τέ[κμει
III A.D.	CPR I 66,4	περὶ] Τέκμει
III A.D.	CPR I 87,6	περὶ Τέκμει
25 April 664 or 679 A.D. (cf. BL 8,451)	Stud.Pal. VIII 1198,2	ἀπὸ χ(ωρίου) Τέκμι παγ(αρ)χ(ίας) Ἡρακλ(εοπολείτου)

TOPARCHY: Tekmi was the main centre of its own toparchy.

A list of the villages that can be assigned to this toparchy is found on p.294.
Several documents, ranging from the second century B.C. to the third century A.D., show that Tekmi was the main administrative centre of its own toparchy: *P.Hels.* 24 (tax payments at the logeuterion of Tekmi); *SB* XVIII 13304 (the village scribe of Tekmi and Bichinthouth reports the arrival of the strategos Euphranor, «leading to Tekmi the troops that had been transferred to Papa»); *BGU* XIV 2441-2448 and 2449-2450 (land-survey in the Tekmi toparchy); *Stud.Pal.* XX 25, *PSI* XV estr. 1546, *Stud.Pal.* XX 26, *CPR* I 76 and *Stud.Pal.* XX 29 (agoranomos office at Tekmi where a number of παραχώρησις contracts are drawn up).

BGU XIV 2441-2450 contain frequent references to the temple of Eseph at Tekmi. According to *BGU* VIII 1795, there was at Tekmi also a temple of the less well-known god Σεμθεκεντωι; Semtheus, son of Horos, is προφήτης there, but also ἀρχιερεύς of Herakles' temple at Sobthis (περὶ Πόλιν toparchy). Sacred land belonging to a temple of Hermes is surveyed in *BGU* XIV 2437: some of it is in the Tekmi area (l.17), some more at Thmoiphta, in the Πέραν toparchy.

BGU VIII 1807 deals with cargo-vessels: one of them was apparently made in the Troites [3], another seems to be identified by reference to its owner (l.7: Κράτωνος) and its present whereabouts (l.8-9: φόρτακος τοῦ κατὰ Τέκμι).

BGU XVI 2670 contains an account of contributions by individuals and groups of workers or craftsmen in view of the visit of a certain Lupus (presumably the nome strategos): other place-names mentioned are Φαινίππου (also in the Tekmi toparchy) and Thmoiamoun(is).

---

[1] *CPR* I 76 and *CPR* I 79 are part of one and the same document.

[2] Cf. *BL* 1,119 and 7,43; see also J.DAVID THOMAS, «SB XVI 13050 reconsidered», *ZPE* 88, 1991, p.124 and n.17.

[3] In the Memphite nome: cf. *BGU* VIII 1784 (see *s.v.* Ἱερὰ Νῆσος).

ΤΕΜΕΝΚΥΡΚΕΩΣ

I B.C.	*BGU* XIV 2438,[49]	〚Τεμενκύρκεως〛
I B.C.	*BGU* XIV 2440,60	Τεμενκύρκεως
early II A.D.	*P.Köln* II 98,34	Τεμενκύρκεως

TOPARCHY: Koites.

ETYMOLOGY: «the Hunting-Place»[1].

BGU XIV 2438 and 2440 indicate that this village was περὶ Φέβιχιν: Tosachmis is listed with it in the first document, Peene in the second.

P.Köln II 98: taxes to be paid upon land-holdings near Temenkyrkis and Sobthis.

ΤΕΡΟΥΦΕΩΣ

| I/II A.D. | *P.Hib.* II 218,45 |

TOPARCHY: Koites.

Most toponyms listed in this document belong to the Koites; the entry for Τερουφεως comes after Papa (l.44) and before Phebichis (l.46).

ΤΕΡΤΟΝ( )

| mid-III B.C. | *P.Strasb.* IX 802,22 | Τέρτον()[2] |

TOPARCHY: Koites.

ETYMOLOGY: two possible etymologies for the prefix Τερτον- are discussed by DREW-BEAR, *Le nome Hermopolite*, p.289, s.v. *Terōt* : (1) a point where the river branches («dérivation, division», as already suggested by Champollion), or else (2) a «colline végétante» (as tentatively suggested by Jean Yoyotte).

MODERN ARABIC NAME: cf. DREW-BEAR, *ibid.* («La correspondance entre ces toponymes et les bourgades appellées Deirout demeure très probable»).

Most or all villages listed in this document were in the Koites.

---

[1] See JEAN YOYOTTE, *Rd'É* 14, 1962, p.84; also quoted by DREW-BEAR, *Le nome Hermopolite*, p.276: «(Yoyotte) retrouve la racine *grg*, au sens de "poser un filet de chasse, un piège, une nasse" dans le toponyme Τεμενκῦρκις, qui signifie "le *dijm* de chasse"; le premier élément du mot représente *time* en Copte, c'est-à-dire "la place, le village"».

[2] Checked on a photograph: the decipherment of the second τ and the following ο appears very uncertain.

[Τ]ΕΡΤΟΝΑΛ( )

I/II A.D.   P.Hib. II 218,70

TOPARCHY: Koites?

ETYMOLOGY: see *s.v.* TEPTON( ).

Most documents listed in this document belong to the Koites.

ΤΕΡΤΟΝΙΧ( )

I/II A.D.   P.Hib. II 218,40;48;79;83   Τερτονιχ( ) (48);
                                                        Τερτ[ο]νιχ( ) (79);
                                                        Τερτονιχ( ) (83)

See also: ΤΕΡΤΟΝΠΕΤΕΧΩΝΣ.

TOPARCHY: Ἄγημα.

ETYMOLOGY: see TEPTON( ).

This place-name is included in a series of villages of the Ἄγημα (Alilais, Kollasoucha, Petachor, Peenameus), περὶ Πόλιν (Sobthis) and περὶ Τεκμι (Mouchis) in *P.Hib.*II 218 *verso*, ll.33-41: Tosachmis (Koites) follows (l.42). The connection with Sobthis and Tosachmis is confirmed in ll.79-87, where Thmoinache (l.85: also appearing soon after Τερτονιχ( ) at l.48) and Niseus are also entered. A close connection between Niseus and Tertonpetechons (in the Ἄγημα κάτω) is attested (see *s.vv.*).

ΤΕΡΤΟΝΠΕΤΕΜΟΥΝ

I B.C.   BGU XIV 2437 (fr.5),77   Τερτονπετεμουν[1]

ETYMOLOGY: see *s.v.* TEPTON().

ΤΕΡΤΟΝΠΕΤΕΧΩΝΣ

III B.C.   P.Lille I 31,1   Νισεὺς καὶ
                                                        Τερτονπετεχώνς

I B.C.   BGU XIV 2438 (fr.3),95   Τερτον[πετεχών][2]

---

[1] Τερτονπετεχων *ed. pr.*, but: «Now, 20 years later, I read quite clearly (I would even omit all the dots now): Τερτονπετεμουν in l.74» (letter from William M. Brashear, November 10, 1995).

[2] Τερτον.[*ed. pr. BGU* XIV 2438 (fr.3) lists villages of the Ἄγημα κάτω toparchy: this in my opinion makes the

4 Aug. 2 B.C.	*BGU* XVI 2591,1	ἀπὸ τῆς Τερτονπετεχῶν τοῦ Ἀγήματος
222 A.D.	*PSI* XV estr.1546,36	ἀπὸ Τ]ερτονπετεχών[1]

See also *s.vv.* ΤΕΡΤΟΝΙΧ( ); ΤΕΡΤΟΝΠΕΤΕΜΟΥΝ;].ΠΕΤΕΧΩΝ.

TOPARCHY: Ἄγημα κάτω.

ETYMOLOGY: see *s.v.* ΤΕΡΤΟΝ( ).

BGU XVI 2591 indicates that Tertonpetechons was in the Ἄγημα: this village in fact appears on the same line with Niseus (Ἄγημα toparchy) in *P.Lille* 31.
PSI XV estr.1546 comprises two παραχώρησις contracts: in the first one Thmoinache (in the Techtho Nesos toparchy) and Tekmi (where the agoranomos office was) are mentioned; Tertonpetechons appears in the second contract.

ΤΕΧΘΩ (ΝΗΣΟΣ)

III B.C.	*P.Hamb.* III 202,2;4;17-18	τοπ[άρ]χηι τῆς Τεχθὼ νήσου (1-2); ἐκ Τεχθώ (4); εἰς [Τε]χθώ (17-18)
second quarter of III B.C.[2]	*P.Hib.* II 198,128	Τεχθώ
15 Nov. 215 B.C.	*P.Strasb.* VI 563,9	Τεχθῶι (cf. *BL* 7,252)
9 Dec. 215 B.C.	*P.Strasb.* II 113,10	ἐκ θησα<υ>ροῦ Τεχθώ (9-10) (cf. *BL* 7,246)
4,11,12 Jan. 210 B.C. (cf. *BL* 9,324)	*P.Strasb.* II 103,5;15;26[3]	ἐν τῷ ἐν Τεχθὼ φρουρίῳ (5;15); ἐν Τεχθώ (26)
11 Jan. 210 B.C. (cf. *BL* 9,324)	*P.Strasb.* II 104,8	ἐν τῶι ἐν Τεχθ[ὼ] φρουρίῳ (8-9)
163/162 B.C. (?)	*P.Hels.* I 21,9	τῆς κατὰ Τεχθώ[4]

---

supplement Τερτον[πετεχών] very likely (Phnebieus, which follows at l.96, belonged to the Middle toparchy).

[1] ἀπὸ Τ]έρτον Πετεχῶν *ed.pr.*: «... è preferibile scrivere in una sola parola Τ]ερτονπετεχων, ... il sigma alla fine poteva anche non essere registrato nella traslitterazione dall'egiziano (cfr. Παχωνς/Παχων): infatti nel *PSI* 1546 non c'è» (Manfredo Manfredi, letter of September 25, 1994).

[2] The references in ll.147 and 160 are to 272/271 and 271/270 B.C., respectively (cf. *BL* 9,109).

[3] Cf. *Addendum* after *P.Strasb.* VII 622 (p.32).

[4] τῆς κατὰ Τεχθὼ <τοπαρχίας> *ed.pr.* (cf. *P.Hamb.* III 202): «der im Bereich des Dorfes Techtho (Toparchie)». One could also understand τῆς κατὰ Τεχθὼ <νήσου>.

2 Sept. 162 B.C.	*P.Hels.* I 26 A,4;12;21;37; B,13;19	τὸν Κωίτην καὶ τὴν Τεχθὼ Νῆσον καὶ τὸ Πέρα (A,4); [Τ]εχθὼ Νήσου (A,12); Τεχθὼ Νή(σου) (A,21); Τεχθὼ Νή[σου] (A,37); ἐν Τεχθώ (B,13); Τεχθώ (B,19)
first half of II B.C.	*P.Tebt.* III 920,20	ἐκ Τεχθω..
18 March 86 B.C.	(?)*BGU* XIV 2424,6	Διονῦς Τεχθ( )[1]
after 52/51 B.C.	*BGU* VIII 1808,15	Τεκθώ (cf. *BL* 7,22)
I B.C.	*BGU* XIV 2434,13	Τεχθώ
I B.C.	*BGU* XIV 2440,38	Τεχθώ
5 Aug. 28 B.C.	*BGU* XVI 2589,3	ἀπὸ κώμης Τεχθ[ω]ι
about 14/13 B.C.	*BGU* XVI 2602,1	ἀπὸ Τεχθώ
after 8/7 B.C.	*BGU* XVI 2632,5	εἰς Τεχθώ
about 7-4 B.C.	*BGU* XVI 2662,13	περὶ Τεχθῶι
I/II A.D.	*P.Hib.* II 218,71;78;91	Τέχθωι (71); Τέχθ(ωι) (78); Τέχ[θωι] (91)
late III A.D.	*BGU* XIII 2365,12	Τεχθώ
309 A.D.	*P.Hib.* II 219,13	π]ερὶ Τέχθω
V A.D.	*Stud.Pal.* X 8,5	
V A.D.	*Stud.Pal.* X 233, col. I,B,1	

See also *s.v.* ΙΒΙΩΝ ΤΕΧΘΩ.

TOPARCHY: Τεχθω (Νῆσος).

See p.294 for a list of the villages that can be assigned to this toparchy.

MODERN ARABIC NAME: Daštūt [2].

This identification is phonetically and topographically convincing: note especially the recurring connection between Peensamoi/Al-Bahsamūn and Techtho/Daštūt: the second village is 6 kms south of the first, almost in direct line. Cf. *TAVO B 69* p.212 (M92): «Nach Auskunft der Dorfbewohner sollen keine antiken Relikte vorhanden sein, jedoch wurden spätantike Keramikscherben gefunden».

See also TIMM, *Das christlich-koptische Ägypten*, VI, p.2469 f. (*s.v.* Taḥtut).

P.Hamb. III 202 (petition to Tryphon, «toparches of Techtho Nesos») indicates that Techtho already

---

[1] The Editor suggests the translation: «Dionys, (aus?) Techtho (?)»

[2] As is apparent from the *Map* at the end of this volume, this goes against the identification with *Teudzoi/T3j.w-ḏ3j.t*, near Al-Hība (see *Catalogue*, *s.v.* Ἀγκυρῶν πόλις), which I was inclined to accept in «The Herakleopolite Nome: Internal and External Borders», *Proceedings of the 20th International Congress of Papyrologists. Copenhagen, 23-29 August, 1992*, p.207 f. A strong objection against this identification was already made by Yoyotte *apud* WILLY CLARYSSE, *Ancient Society* 7, 1976, p.191: the Egyptian *w* is never rendered by the Greek χ.

had its own toparchy in the III B.C. A possible reference to this toparchy is also found in a II B.C. document (*P.Hels.* I 21), and there is a reference to it in *BGU* XVI 2662 (end of the I B.C.). Techtho still occurs as a separate entry in I B.C. documents such as *BGU* XIV 2434 and 2440[1].

P.Strasb. II 113 and 563 deal with the shipping of wheat from the θησαυρός at Techtho to Alexandria: Harmachis, the oikonomos' agent in charge at Techtho, also superintends affairs at Thmoiphta and Peontamoun (= Peensamoi), both villages of the Πέραν toparchy[2]. This connection is confirmed by *P.Hels.* I 26 (*P.Hels.* I 21 almost certainly belongs to the same document): the same official deals with tax-arrears from the Koites, the Techtho Nesos and the Πέραν. In turn, this is consistent with *BGU* VIII 1808 (entries for Πέραν and Techtho in a sequence: ll.14-15), *BGU* XIV 2440 (ll.12-13: entries for Πέραν and Techtho in consecutive lines), *P.Hib.* II 219 (where [Πεενσ]αμοι should be supplied at l.11; Techtho follows at l.13), *Stud.Pal.* X 233, col.I B (Techtho mentioned immediately before Peensamoi)[3].

BGU XVI 2602: οἱ ἀπὸ Τεχθὼ γεωργοί write to the epistates and dioiketes Athenodoros reporting that one of his men has come from Thmoinache to stop a functionary of the strategos who was trying to compel them to do canal work. *BGU* XVI 2632 is a letter from Aphrodisios to Athenodoros concerning wine brought to Techtho. In *BGU* XVI 2589 an inhabitant of Techtho swears that he will renounce his claims on land ἐν τῷ Πογχήους πεδίου.

P.Tebt. III 920 (fragment of a report about a conflict with robbers) mentions people from Techtho and Phebichis. Techtho is included in a list of guard-posts appended to a royal ordinance on security measures along the Nile (*P.Hib.* II 198; this φρούριον is also mentioned in *P.Strasb.* II 103 and 104, recording monthly payments to the soldiers of the garrison stationed there).

ΤΕΧΥΜΙΣ

21 Oct. 163 B.C.	*P.Hels.* I 13,9	ἐν κώμηι Τεχύμει (8-9)
about 160 B.C.	*P.Hels.* I 34,8	'Τεχύ(μεως)'
I B.C.	*BGU* VIII 1802,3	περὶ Τεχῦμιν
I B.C.	*BGU* XIV 2438,44	Τεχύμεως
I B.C.	*BGU* XIV 2440,10	Τεχύμεως
late II A.D.	*P.Oxy.* XLIV 3168,12	Τεχύμ(εως)[4]

TOPARCHY: Μέση.

BGU VIII 1802 indicates that Techymis belonged to the Μέση toparchy: this is confirmed in *BGU* XIV 2438, where Techymis is mentioned in association with Phys, as already in *P.Hels.* I 34.

P.Hels. I 13 is a petition submitted to the oikonomos by an Egyptian woman who owns a βαλανεῖον at Techymis.

---

[1] See *ed. pr. ad loc.*

[2] See WILLY CLARYSSE, *Ancient Society* 7, 1976, pp.185-207.

[3] Cf. WILLY CLARYSSE, *ibid.*, p.202.

[4] WILLIAM BRASHEAR, *ZPE* 60, 1985, p.239, recognised this as a place-name, to be located either in the Herakleopolites or in the Hermopolites. The Hermopolite provenance was considered «virtually assured» for this document by its Editor (who, however, treated Τεχύμεως as a personal name) because of the reference to ἀναίτητος γῆ and the use of a specific siglum for «catoecic land» (both apparently exclusive of the Hermopolites). A third argument, i.e. that «three of the names of κλῆροι given recur in other Hermupolite texts» is counterbalanced by the fact that Herakleopolite κλῆροι also bear the same names. As no Τέχυμις is attested for the Hermopolites, I take this to refer to the Herakleopolite village.

P.Oxy. XLIV 3168 is a land-survey; several fossil kleroi are referred to: at least that of Φιλίσκου is also attested in other sources for the Herakleopolites[1]. BGU VIII 1802 deals with catoecic land near Techymis (but no kleros name is preserved there).

ΤΙ[..].ΟΜ( )

| I/II A.D. | P.Hib. II 218,94 | |

Other villages listed in this part of the document are Sinary (ll.85,95; Πέραν toparchy); Onosis (ll.90,92; περὶ Πόλιν toparchy); Techtho (l.91).

ΤΙΛΩΘΙΣ

212/211 B.C.	P.Lille I 59,17;45;103	Τιλώθεως
mid-III B.C.	P.Cair.Zen. IV 59782 (b),66	ἐκ Τιλώ<θ>ιος[2]
ca. 138 B.C.	P.Tebt. III 860,59	Τιλώθεως
after 84/83 B.C.	BGU XIV 2370,16;17; (fr.1) 86	περὶ Τι[λώ]θιν (16) Τιλώθεως (17); ἀπὸ Τιλώθεως (86)
64/63 B.C.	BGU VIII 1742,2	[±8 ἀντι]γρα(φεῖ) θη(σαυροῦ) περὶ Τιλῶθιν
64/63 B.C.	BGU VIII 1752,5	τοῖς ἐν Τιλώθει ἱερεῦσι
60/59 B.C.	BGU VIII 1817,12	ἐκ Τιλώθεως
ca. 48-46 B.C.	BGU VIII 1848,4	ἐκ κώμης Τιλώθεως
ca. 48-46 B.C.	BGU VIII 1849,4;6	τοῦ πτεραφόρου ἱερέως τοῦ ἐν Τιλώ[θ]ει ἱεροῦ Ἡρακλέους θεοῦ μεγίστου (4-5); ἐν τῇ Τιλώθει (6)
I B.C.	BGU VIII 1734,5;8	[περὶ Τιλ]ῶθιν (4-5); ἐν Τιλώθει (8)
I B.C.	BGU VIII 1796,1	κωμογραμματεὺ[ς Τι]λώθεως
I B.C.	BGU VIII 1852,4	ἐν Τιλώ[θει

---

[1] Cf. the list of Fossil Kleroi in the Herakleopolite Nome, s.v.

[2] My supplement: Τιλώιος ed. pr. On the redating of this document, see p.60 n.3.

I B.C.	*BGU* XIV 2434,3;24	[π]ερὶ Τιλῶθιν (3); περὶ Τιλῶ(θιν) (24)
I B.C.	*BGU* XIV 2438,55; (fr.2),84	Τιλώθεως (55); περὶ Τιλῶθι[ν] (84)
I B.C.	*BGU* XIV 2440,8	Τιλώθεω[ς
Jan.-Feb. 13 B.C.	*BGU* XVI 2587,1;17	Τιλώθε'ω'(ς) (1); [περ]ὶ Τιλῶθιν (16-17)
17 Dec. 10 B.C.	*BGU* XVI 2611,9;16	εἰς Τιλῶθ{ε}ιν (9); εἰς Τ{ι}λῶθ{ε}ιν (16)
19 Dec. 9 B.C.	*BGU* XVI 2663,1	διὰ Ἀδράστου προστάτου Τιλώθεως
about 7 B.C.	*BGU* XVI 2608,3	εἰς Τ{ι}λῶθ{ε}ιν
about 7-4 B.C.	*BGU* XVI 2662,15	[περὶ Τι]λῶθιν
I B.C./I A.D.	*BGU* IV 1060,16	ἐν τοῖς περὶ τὴν Τιλῶθιν πεδίοις (cf. *BL* 2.2,23)

Literary Sources

| X A.D. | *Suda* s.v. Ἡρακλέων[1] | ἀπὸ κώμης Τιλώτεως οὔσης ὑπὸ τῇ Ἡρακλέους πόλει |

See also: ΝΕΙΛΟΥ ΠΟΛΙΣ; Τ[.]Λ[.

TOPARCHY: Tilothis was the main centre in its own toparchy.
See p.294, for a list of the villages that can be assigned to this toparchy.

ETYMOLOGY: Coptic: *Tilodj*[2]; JEAN YOYOTTE, *RdÉ* 13, 1961, p.97 (on a map) indicates the equivalence with *T3 ᶜi3t-rṯ* «ohne jedoch eine Erläuterung hierfür zu liefern» (*TAVO B 69*, p.96).

MODERN ARABIC NAME: Dalās[3]. For the triple identification Τίλωθις = Νείλου πόλις = Dalās, see *s.v.* Νείλου πόλις.
The latest Greek papyri mentioning Tilothis date from the Augustan period, while the earliest source for the Herakleopolite Νείλου πόλις is dated to 103 A.D. (*P.Mich.* IX 551). The Egyptian toponym, however, must have remained current outside the official records: it is even found in the *Suda* entry on

---

[1] Cf. HANS HAUBEN, *ZPE* 8, 1971, p.271 n.6.

[2] Cf. E. AMÉLINEAU, *La Géographie de l'Égypte à l'époque copte*, Paris 1893, s.v. «Delâs»: «Les Actes d'Epimé de Pankoleus, or Benkolaos, parlent d'un chrétien nommé Petsiri, natif de la ville de Tilodj [*Mss.Copt.Vat. LXVI* fol. 119 recto]. Dans un fragment sa'idique publié par Mingarelli, il est fait mention de la montagne de Tilodj [Mingarelli, *Aegypt.Cod. Reliquiae*, p.165]; de même dans l'éloge de Pisentios [E. Amélineau, *Étude sur le christianisme en Égypte au VII siècle. Vie de Pisentios*, p.133]».

[3] The identification Tilothis = Dalās was first put forward by JEAN YOYOTTE, «Études géographiques I», *RdÉ* 13, 1961, p.97, fig.5.

Ἡρακλέων[1], a γραμματικός from Tilothis who became a teacher in Rome; he was the author of commentaries on Homer and Greek lyric poetry.

BIBLIOGRAPHY: TIMM, *Das christlich-koptische Ägypten*, II, pp.498-502 (*s.v.* Dalās); *TAVO B 69* (M 122), p.96.

The lists of villages in *P.Lille* I 59 and *P.Cair.Zen.* IV 59782 (b) largely coincide: besides localities of the Tilothis toparchy (Tilothis, Tanchais; in addition, *P.Lille* I 59 mentions Peenpasbyt(is) and Schnomthis) they include Bousiris, villages of the Koma toparchy (Koma, Krekis, Machor; in addition, *P.Cair.Zen.* IV 59782 (b) mentions Thmoiobastis and Toou) and of the Tekmi toparchy (Onnes; in addition, *P.Lille* I 59 has Peenepsy). Many of these villages recur in *BGU* XIV 2438 (Tilothis, Schnomthis, Peenpasbyt(is), Tanchais, Koma, Toou; these are preceded by entries for the Ἄγημα κάτω, Μέση and περὶ Φέβιχιν toparchies) and in *BGU* XIV 2370, fr.1 (Koma, Toou, Machor, Thmoiobastis, recorded under the main entry κάτω τοπαρ[χ]ίας; references to Onnes, Tilothis and Tanchais follow; Bousiris appears in fr.2). Two consecutive entries for the Koma and the Tilothis toparchies appear in *BGU* XIV 2434.

P.Tebt. III 860 associates Tilothis with villages of the Koites, such as Koba, Pselemachis and Toemesis: the third locality (spelt Τέμησις) recurs in the same document with Tilothis in the first column of *BGU* XIV 2440, too (ll.8 and 14, respectively) which also mentions Phebichis, besides listing villages of the Ἄγημα κάτω, Μέση, and Tekmi toparchies.

BGU VIII 1734, a παραχώρησις contract, refers to some fossil kleroi in the Tilothis area (Νικάνορος, Πολέμωνος, Περιγένου, [Ἀλ]εξάνδρου) and to a Φιλώτου προπυργίον. The fossil kleroi of Πολέμων, Ἀλέξανδρος and Φιλώτης are also attested in *BGU* XIV 2441-2450 (land-survey of the Tekmi toparchy).

In *BGU* VIII 1849 Tasemthis remembers her parents' journey from Peenameus to the temple of Herakles at Tilothis, and how she came to marry Horos, the brother of a feather-bearing (πτεραφόρος) priest of this temple[2]. Her parents are said to have travelled north (κατελθόντων: down river), which is consistent with the identification of Peenameus and Tilothis with modern Bahnamūh and Dalās, respectively: these two villages also appear together in *BGU* XIV 2440 (ll.3 and 8).

A significant number of documents refer to people travelling by boat to Tilothis (see the above mentioned *BGU* VIII 1849), or away from it, to Alexandria: so do the run-away husband of *BGU* VIII 1848, and the untrustworthy travel companion of a κάτοικος ἱππεύς from Pois of *BGU* VIII 1817. *BGU* VIII 1742 contains instructions for the shipment of wheat from the θησαυρός at Tilothis to Alexandria. In *BGU* XVI 2611 (a letter from Herakleides to the epistates and dioiketes Athenodoros concerning corn deliveries) Bousiris and Alexandria are also mentioned.

In *BGU* XVI 2608 Herakleides writes to Athenodoros (these are the same people as in *BGU* XVI 2611) about beer-brewers in Tilothis.

BGU XVI 2587 is a declaration of sheep pasturing «around Tilothis and all over the nome» (ll.15-17).

BGU XVI 2663 contains a reference to (the cult of?) Isis Λοχιάς; the (probably Arsinoite) village of Kerke is also mentioned (l.8).

ΤΙΝΤΗΡΙΣ

50/49 B.C.	*BGU* VIII 1843,3	ἐκ κώμης Τιντήρεως

---

[1] Personal names deriving from Ἡρακλῆς were very common in the Herakleopolite nome: cf. e.g. the indexes of personal names in the *BGU* VIII and especially *BGU* XIV volumes.

[2] *BGU* VIII 1752 deals with food provisions for priests residing at Tilothis.

CATALOGUE

200 A.D.	*P.Oxy.* VI 899,22	περὶ τε κώμην Βουσεῖρ[ι]ν καὶ Θιντῆριν καὶ Τα..[....].χος κώμας τοῦ Ἡρακλεοπολείτου (22-23)
26 February 538 A.D.	*P.Michael.* 126,5	ἐν κώμῃ Τιντύρεως[1]
VI A.D.	*Stud.Pal.* X 44,6	χ'ω'(ρίον) Τιγτήλ[ε]ως[2]
VI-VII A.D.	*Stud.Pal.* X 5,5	τὸν βοηθ(ὸν) Τιντήρεως
VIII A.D.	*Stud.Pal.* X 109,7	ἐν τ(ῷ) χ(ωρίῳ) Τιντ'ή'(ρεως)
VIII A.D.	*Stud.Pal.* X 218,7	χ(ωρίον) Τιντήρ'ε'(ως)

TOPARCHY: in the northern Herakleopolites: περὶ Πόλιν?[3]

ETYMOLOGY: second component: *ntr.w* («gods»)[4]. The interchangeability of *l* and *r*, quite common in Egyptian[5], accounts for the variant spelling of *Stud.Pal.* X 44.

MODERN ARABIC NAME: Dandīl (phonetically and geographically likely); cf. *TAVO B 69*, p.221: «Etwa 2 km westlich des Dorfes am Südhang des Gabal Abū Ṣir befindet sich ein älterer Steinbruch, bei dem gebrannte Lehmziegel und Spätantike Keramikscherben liegen».

P.Oxy. VI 899 refers to land cultivated by the same person περὶ τε κώμην Βουσεῖρ[ι]ν καὶ Θιντῆριν καὶ Τα..[....].χος κώμας τοῦ Ἡρακλεοπολίτου. Tinteris was in the northern part of the nome; in our sources, it is associated with:

Onosis (περὶ Πόλιν toparchy) in *Stud.Pal.* X 5 (also mentioning Nino, which was in the Ἄγημα κάτω) and *Stud.Pal.* X 218;

Kollintaathyr (Tekmi toparchy) in *Stud.Pal.* X 5 and *Stud.Pal.* X 44 (villages belonging to the same διοίκησις; also listed: Pois and Τωυ, which was in the Tekmi toparchy);

Phnebieus (Μέση toparchy) in *Stud.Pal.* X 44 and *Stud.Pal.* X 109 (also mentioning Pyrgotos, again in the Tekmi toparchy, besides some villages of the Koites).

BGU VIII 1843 is a petition to the strategos: the βασιλικοὶ γεωργοί «and others» ask, presumably, for a remission of taxes as a consequence of an ἀβροχία which has occurred in the Herakleopolite nome.

---

[1] The document is a contract, drawn up at Tinteris, between a man ἀπὸ Νίλου πόλει [τοῦ] Ἡρακλεοπολίτου νομοῦ and another from the village of Λευκοῦ in the same nome. It is not among the *P.Michael.* recently acquired by the Cambridge University Library.

[2] New reading, checked for me by Johannes Diethart (letter of February 25, 1994): «Statt Τιστηχ[ι]ας (Wessely) ist die Form Τιγτήλ[ε]ως für Τιντήρεως zu lesen: λ/ρ Wechsel».

[3] Cf. *Introduction*, p.8.

[4] Information from Katelijn Vandorpe.

[5] The λ/ρ exchange is also found in *BGU* VIII 1808,21 ('Αριλάεως for 'Αλιλάεως).

ΤΙΩΒΑΣΤΙ

III A.D.　　　　　　　　*SB* XIV 12193,2-4　　　ἀπὸ κώμης Τιωβάστι
　　　　　　　　　　　　　　　　　　　　　　　τοῦ Ἡρακλεοπολίτου
　　　　　　　　　　　　　　　　　　　　　　　νομοῦ[1]

Two mummy labels, possibly «borderaux d'expedition»[2]. One may suspect a wrong spelling for Τμοιόβαστις (see *s.v.* ΘΜΟΙΟΒΑΣΤΙΣ).

ΤΚΟΥΝΣΩΣΕΙ

VII-VIII A.D.　　　　　　*Stud.Pal.* X 206,9

Apparently the name of a κλῆρος, listed with several others (see the *Reverse Index* at the end of this volume).

ΤΛΕΣΙΔΟΣ

V A.D.	*Stud.Pal.* X 233, col.III,3	Τλεσιδος
V-VI A.D.	*Stud.Pal.* VIII 955,1	Τλεσίδος (cf. *BL* 8,448)[3]
VI A.D.	*Stud.Pal.* XX 148,1	Τλεσιδος[4]
VII/VIII A.D. (cf. *BL* 8,439)	*Stud.Pal.* III 356,2	ἀπὸ ἐποικίου Τλ]εσιδος; cf. ἐν τ(ῷ) αὐτ(ῷ) ἐποικίῳ (3)
VII-VIII A.D.	*Stud.Pal.* XX 249 *verso*,2	χ(ωρίου) Τλεσιδ(ος)

This village appears as the last entry in *Stud.Pal.* X 233 (a very long list of Herakleopolite toponyms). It is again assigned to the Herakleopolites by *Stud.Pal.* III 356.

Stud.Pal. XX 148 is a loan contract between an inhabitant of Ποιμένων κώμη, in the Μέση toparchy and an inhabitant of Herakleopolis: Τλεσιδος appears at the beginning of the document as it is preserved (*mutilus in initio*).

ΤΜΟΙΕΝΕΤΙΣ

Aug.-Sept. 224 B.C.　　　*P.Coll.Youtie* I 7,5　　　κατὰ Τμοιενέτιν

---

[1] This reading is confirmed by a photograph kindly provided by Bernard Boyaval (letter of August 18, 1994).

[2] See BERNARD BOYAVAL, «Deux bordereaux d'expedition de momies?», *ZPE* 31, 1978, pp.118-120.

[3] The reading Τλεσιδος shows that this document comes from the Herakleopolites (the first Editor indicated the Hermopolites as the possible provenance).

[4] The Editor indicates a Hermopolite provenance for this document. However, no village by this name appears in DREW-BEAR, *Le nome Hermopolite*: the provenance of *Stud.Pal.* XX 148 is therefore most likely the Herakleopolite nome.

CATALOGUE

ETYMOLOGY: first component *t3-m3j* («new, newly gained land»): see *s.v.* ΘΜΟ().

P.Coll.Youtie I 7 contains a report concerning an assault and robbery: «le [bateau] d'Asonides ... sur lequel se trouvait Dorion ainsi que le pilote Erobastis, comme il se dirigeait vers l'amont, dans les parages de Tmoienetis, a intercepté une barge sur laquelle se trouvaient des femmes ...» (Editor's translation).

ΤΟΕΜΗΣΙΣ

mid-III B.C.	*P.Strasb.* IX 802,9	Τọεμῆσις[1]
2 Sept. 162 B.C.	*P.Hels.* I 26, A,24; B,8	Τοεμήσεως (A,24); Θọεμήσεως (B,8)
about 138 B.C.	*P.Tebt.* III 860,109	φυ(λακίτου) Τοεμήσεọς
I B.C.	*BGU* XIV 2432,18	Τεμήσεως
I B.C.	*BGU* XIV 2440,14	Τεμήσεως
131 A.D.	*P.Oxy.* IV 715,6;13;14	ἀπὸ κώμης Τοεμίσεως (5-6); ἀπὸ τῆς αὐτῆς Τοεμίσεως (12-13); ἐν τῇ αὐτῇ Τοεμίσει (14)
late II A.D.	P.Vindob. G 23035,1 [2]	σιτολ(όγοις) Τοεμήσεως
242 A.D. (cf. *BL* 8,108)	*CPR* VII 12,5	σιτολ(όγων) κώμης Τοεμήσεως (3-5)
544-559 A.D.(?)	*P.Rain.Cent.* 118,4	[ἀ]πὸ κώμης Τọεμέσε[ως

TOPARCHY: Koites.

ETYMOLOGY: *t3-whm.t-(n-)Is.t*, «the dyke of Isis»[3].

Two variant spellings are attested for this toponym: Θοέμησις (*P.Hels.* I 26) and Τέμησις (*BGU* XIV 2432 and 2440).

P.Hels. 26 indicates that Toemesis was in the Koites. This is confirmed by *P.Tebt.* III 860 (taxation returns and accounts), recording a payment effected at Psebthonpenouphis on account of a phylakites from Toemesis: Pselemachis appears at l.104, and the connection between these two villages is corroborated by *P.Oxy.* IV 715, an ἀπογραφή addressed to the βιβλιοφύλαξ ἐγκτήσεων (declaration by two brothers who have inherited part of a house at Toemesis, some catoecic land near Ἰβιὼν Πάχνουβις in the fossil kleros of Zoilos and Noumenios, and some more land near Pselemachis in the fossil kleros of Menippos and Artemidoros). As a matter of fact, the three villages already appeared in three consecutive lines in *P.Strasb.* IX 802: Pselemachis (7), Ταχονπαχνουβ (8; Ἰβιὼν Πάχνουβις is the hellenised name of the same locality), Toemesis (9).

A reference to Ἰβιὼν Τεχθώ is found in *BGU* XIV 2432 (l.20); a connection with Tilothis is attested in *P.Tebt.* III 860 and *BGU* XIV 2440.

---

[1] My reading (checked on a photograph): Παμῆσις *ed. pr.*

[2] *Editio princeps*: ROSARIO PINTAUDI, «Appunto (Etichetta, Memorandum?) per i sitologi», *Analecta Papyrologica* 5, 1993, pp.141-142.

[3] Etymology tentatively suggested by Katelijn Vandorpe.

CPR VII 12: monthly report from the sitologos of Toemesis to the strategos of the Herakleopolite nome.

ΤΟΕΝΕΓΟΥΣ[1]

about 260 B.C.   *P.Hib.* I 112,43

TOPARCHY: Koites.

The other villages mentioned in *P.Hib.* I 112 belong to the Koites.

ΤΟΘΙΣ

mid-III B.C.   *P.Strasb.* IX 802,18   Τοθις

TOPARCHY: probably Koites.

ETYMOLOGY: the name of the god Thoth is clearly recognizable in this toponym.

P.Strasb. IX 802: list of Egyptian tax-payers from several villages in the Koites. Tothis could well be the same place as Thmoitothis (see *s.v.*)[2].

ΤΟΚΩΙΣ

31 Dec. 57 B.C. (cf. *BL* 9,28)	*BGU* VIII 1821,13	εἰς Τοκῶιν
51/50 B.C.	*BGU* VIII 1761,8	ἀπὸ κώμης Τοκόεως
I B.C.	*BGU* IV 1187,4	ἐκ κώμης Τοκώεως
I/II A.D.	*P.Hib.* II 218,55	Τοκώεως
mid-III A.D.	*P.Select.* 17,5	Αὐρήλιος Ἀγ[ο]υβίων ἐξηγητεύσας βουλ(ευτὴς) Ἡρακλέου[ς] πόλεως δεκάπρωτ[ο]ς ἐν τοπα⟨ρ⟩χείᾳ μετροπόλεως καὶ Ἀγήματος[3] Τοκόεως καὶ ἄλλων κωμῶ[ν (1-5)
Oct. 300 A.D. (cf.*BL* 3,47)	*CPR* I 40,8	περὶ κώμην Τοκῶιν

---

[1] According to the Editor, this «seems to be a village rather than a personal name».

[2] This possibility is suggested in the *ed. pr.*

[3] ἀπηλιώτου *ed. pr.*: see *s.v.* Ἄγημα.

CATALOGUE

347 A.D.	*P.Athen.* 34,14	κ]ώμης Τοκώε[ω]ς (cf. *BL* 7,229 f.)
IV A.D.	*Stud.Pal.* X 221,1	Τοκώεως
end of IV A.D.	*SB* VI 9597,5;11	ἐν τε κώμῃ Τοκώει καὶ ἐν ἄλλαις κώμαις (5); [ἐν τῇ] κώμῃ Τοκώει κ[αὶ ἐ]ν ταῖς ἄλλαις κώμαις (11)
V A.D.	*Stud.Pal.* X 233, col.I B,4	Τοκώεως
V-VI A.D.	*SB* XX 14580,1	Τοκώεως βορρι(νῆς) [1]
VI A.D.	*Stud.Pal.* VIII 1257,3	Τοκώεως
VII A.D.	*Stud.Pal.* X 22,6	χ(ωρίον) Τοκώ[εως

TOPARCHY: περὶ Πόλιν.

Connection with Pois: *P.Hib.* II 218 (Onosis, Tokois and Noeris are listed immediately before Pois); *P.Select.* 17 (lease contract[2] between a lessee from Pois and Aurelios Anoubion, βουλευτής at Herakleopolis, previously an exegetes, *decaprotus* of the περὶ Πόλιν toparchy and of the Ἄγημα, Tokois «and other villages»[3]).

Connection with Herakleopolis: *P.Select.* 17; *CPR* I 40 (lease contract between two inhabitants of Herakleopolis for 50 arourae in the fossil kleros of Πρῶτος, near Tokois).

Connection with Sobthis: *BGU* VIII 1821 (Adrastos, who looks after his brother's holding at Tokois, complains about harassment by a λογευτής from Sobthis; Adrastos' brother is an ἐκλογιστής at Herakleopolis); *Stud.Pal.* X 22.

P.Athen. 34 is the report of a physician after an inspection effected ἅμα τῷ αὐτῷ ὑπερέτῃ| κ]ώμης Τοκώε[ω]ς (ll.13-14); the document also contains a reference to a βουλευτής of Herakleopolis.

ΤΟΛΕΩΣ

VI A.D.	*Stud.Pal.* X 207,3	ἀπ'ὸ' Τόλεως; cf. ἀπὸ τῆς αὐτ(ῆς) κώμ(ης)(4)

There is a reference to Sobthis at l.5 of the same document.

ΤΟΟΥ

212/211 B.C.	*P.Lille* I 59,28;31;47;55;83; 90;104;109;110;117	Τοου

---

[1] Document published in *P.Laur.* XIX.2, pp.451-453. «Eine Präzisierung Τοκῶις βορρινή - etwa als Ortsteil - ist bisher nicht bekannt» (*ibid.*, p.452, n.1); cf. also l.2: ὁμοίως βορρι(νῆς).

[2] The plot, near Pois, is located by reference to the fossil kleros of Laomedon.

[3] Note the same wording («Tokois and the other villages») in *SB* VI 9597.

mid-III B.C.[1]	*P.Cair.Zen.* IV 59782 (b),55;80	ἐκ Τ̣ο̣ύ (55); ἐκ Τού (80)
ca. 111 B.C.	*P.Tebt.* III 878,46	Τ̣ού
after 84/83 B.C.	*BGU* XIV 2370 (fr.1),75	Τοού
I B.C.	*BGU* VIII 1789,9	Τοού[2]
I B.C.	*BGU* XIV 2438,74	Τοού
I B.C.	*BGU* XIV 2439,84	Τοού
I B.C.	*BGU* XIV 2440,51	Τοού
8/7 B.C.	*BGU* XVI 2560,7	περὶ Τοού
8/7 B.C.	*BGU* XVI 2561,7	περὶ Το[ο]ύ
7 Aug. 218 A.D.	(?)*SB* XVIII 13151,6;17	Τοο[ύ (6); χω( ) Τοοὺ ὑ(πὲρ) νησ( ) το( ) [α(17)[3]
III A.D.	*P.Laur.* IV 174, recto,4	προνοη[τοῦ περὶ Τοού (3-4); περὶ τὴν α(ὐτὴν) [κώ(μην)] (5)[4]
III A.D.	*P.Oxy.* VII 1068,17	εἰς Τοού

See also: Σ.ΟΥ.

TOPARCHY: Koma.

ETYMOLOGY: *ḏw*, «desert cliffs» (hence: any «secluded place; monastery»)[5]. This toponym is also attested in the Aphroditopolite, Hermopolite and Oxyrhynchite nomes[6].

Toou is consistently mentioned in connection with Koma (*P.Lille* I 59; *P.Cair.Zen.* IV 59782 b; *BGU* VIII 1789; *BGU* XIV 2370, 2438, 2439 and 2440). In *P.Tebt.* III 878 it is listed with Psilichi and Pyrgotos (Tekmi toparchy), and with Bousiris.

BGU XVI 2560 and 2561 are orders for seed grain; some fossil kleroi in the Toou area are recorded: Πτολεμαίου (*BGU* XVI 2560,7; 2561,8), Θεοδωρίδου Ἀγήνορος (*BGU* XVI 2560, 8-9), Ἐπιφανίου (*BGU* XVI 2560,9), Πύθωνος (*BGU* XVI 2561,8), Σεύθ(ου) (*BGU* XVI 2561,10).

The sender of *P.Oxy.* VII 1068 is in charge of the transport of a mummy from the Arsinoites to Alexandria; delays have intervened, and his assistants have «determined on account of a pressing need to

---

[1] On the re-dating of this document, see p.60 n. 3.

[2] The Editors deciphered ...τοου κρη( ), which I propose to resolve as ...Τοου Κρη(κεως). Both these villages were in the Koma toparchy: there is a reference to Koma at l.8.

[3] According to the Editor, χω( ) may be understood as an abbreviation for χωματεπιμελητής, χωματεπείκτης, χωματεκβολεύς, or be resolved simply as χώματα or χωμάτων. ὑ(πὲρ) νησ() το() α can also be read at l.9: the Editor suggests that νησ( ) may be referred to an «island» or its inhabitants (νησιώτης, νησῖτις, νῆσος), and το( ) may stand for τοπαρχίας, τόπου; finally, α could be a numeral.

[4] This document comes from the Heroneinos archive.

[5] See DREW-BEAR, *Le nome Hermopolite*, p.305.

[6] See TIMM, *Das christlich-koptische Ägypten* VI, s.v. Tōou.

go to Toou»; it is perhaps more likely that this was the Herakleopolite Toou, nearer the Arsinoite nome, rather than the Hermopolite village by the same name.

ṬỌṢAΓAΛHN

| 21 March 8 B.C. | BGU XVI 2647,4 | εἰς τọσαγάλην (3-4) |

Letter to the epistates and dioketes Athenodoros, asking him to take care of Hieronikes who is being confronted with charges of shipwreck and loss of a cargo.

ΤΟΣΑΧΜΙΣ

139 B.C.	P.Tebt. III 838,13;16	περὶ Τοσάχμιν
I B.C.	BGU XIV 2436,4;9	περὶ Τοσάχμιν
I B.C.	BGU XIV 2438,50	Τοσάχμεως
12 Feb. 13 B.C.	BGU XVI 2580,1;2;12	Το]σάχμεως (1); Τοσ]άχμιν (2); περὶ Τοσάχμιν (12)
I/II A.D.	P.Hib. II 218,42;86	Τοσάχ(μεως)
192 A.D.	P.Heid. IV 301,II,15; III,11	ἀγορ(ανόμοις) περὶ Φεβ(ῖχιν) Τοσάχμεως (II,14-15); Τοσάχ(μεως)(III,11)
7 Dec. 227 A.D. (cf. BL 7,259)	Stud.Pal. XX 29,8;25	ἀπὸ κώμης Τοσάχμεως (8); περὶ τὴν αὐτὴν Τοσάχμιν (25)
V A.D.	Stud.Pal. X 47,4	Τοσάχμεως
V A.D.	Stud.Pal. X 94,8	Τοσάχμεως
V/VI A.D.	P.Amst. I 83,2	ἀπ]ὸ Τοσάχμεως
VI/VII A.D.	SB VI 9593,3;9	[ἐπὶ κώ]μης Τοσάχμεως (3); ἀπὸ κώμης Τοσάχμεως (9)
VII A.D.	Stud.Pal. III 67,2	ἀπὸ χ(ωρίου) Τωσάχμε(ως)

TOPARCHY: περὶ Φέβιχιν.

ETYMOLOGY: t3-shm.t, «the land of Sachmet»[1].

---

[1] Etymology suggested by Katelijn Vandorpe; cf. ULRICH WILCKEN, APF 7, 1923, p.101: «In dem Dorfnamen Tosachmis steckt ... die Göttin Sachmis».

The lion-goddess Sachmet was often assimilated to the cat-goddess Bast[1], whose presence in the Herakleopolites is revealed by a place-name like Θμοιόβαστις (see s.v.). The main centre for the cult of Sachmet was in Memphis. A village by the name Σάχμις is also attested in the Letopolite nome[2].

BGU XIV 2438 assigns Tosachmis to the περὶ Φέβιχιν. This is confirmed by *P.Heid.* IV 301 (part of a τόμος συνκολλήσιμος containing προσαγγελίαι: contract recorded through the ἀγορανόμος of Phebichis).

BGU XIV 2436: Kastor's holding is split between Tosachmis, Phebichis and Tanchais; the holding of Ptolemaios senior is split between Tosachmis, Tanchais and Pois.

Stud.Pal. XX 29: a man from Tosachmis cedes four parcels of land to his wife (who is from Tanaso, in the περὶ Πόλιν toparchy): all parcels were near Tosachmis, except one which was near Peentechy[3]: the contract was drawn up in the office of the agoranomos at Tekmi. The connection between Tosachmis and Tanaso is confirmed by *Stud.Pal.* X 47 (list including Onosis, Mouchis, Tanaso, Tosachmis, Kollouthou).

P.Hib. II 218: Tosachmis listed after Mouchis (l.47; Tekmi toparchy) and, at another point in the same document, after Niseus (l.85; Ἄγημα toparchy). *P.Tebt.* III 838: police-tax from περὶ Πόλιν (l.5), περὶ Νισέα (l.9), περὶ Τόσαχμιν (ll.13, 16). *Stud.Pal.* X 94 also mentions Peenameus (l.6; Ἄγημα toparchy).

ΤΟΧΟΝΤΩΥ

I B.C.	*BGU* XIV 2437,4;22	
I B.C.	*BGU* XIV 2440,17;45(?)	Τοχοντων (17); [Το]χ[ο]ντων (45)(?)
21/20 B.C.	*BGU* XVI 2597,2	παρ' Ὥρου κωμογραμματέως Τωὺ καὶ Τοχοντωύ (1-2)

TOPARCHY: Tekmi.
ETYMOLOGY: Τοχο-ν-τωυ: assuming that τοχο- = ταχο- (see s.v. Ταχονπαχνουβ), this would be «the ibis sanctuary of Τωυ».

As is shown by its name, this locality was closely connected to Τωυ: these two places share the same komogrammateus in *BGU* XVI 2597 (they are in fact considered as one village: ἐκ τῆς κώμης, l.3) and twice recur one after another in *BGU* XIV 2437.

The readings in *BGU* XIV 2440, though uncertain, are on the whole safe: at l.45, Tochontou is included in a whole section dealing with the Tekmi toparchy (ll.41-49); at l.17, it is associated with Taboklis (which may be assigned to the same toparchy).

---

[1] Cf. *L.Ä.*, Bd.V, col.324.

[2] *UPZ* I 72,14-15 n.: «In dem Dorfnamen steckt der Name der Göttin, die die Griechen der Λητώ gleichsetzen. Es ist die Göttin Shmt ... vgl. *P.Gurob* 22,43 (Fajjum), wo ein Σαχμιεῖον erscheint, ein Tempel der Sachmis neben einem Tempel ihres und des Ptah Sohnes Nefer-tem, einem Νεφθιμιεῖον»

[3] Several kleroi (including some fossil kleroi) are mentioned, in order to locate the different parcels being sold: Ἀπολλωνίου (l.18), Νεπωτιανοῦ (l.20), Θεοδώρου (ll.20-21), Μάρωνος (l.23), Διδυμιανοῦ (l.23), Ἡλιοδώρου (l.24), Διονυσίου (l.25), Ἡσιο..... (l.26), Ὑπερβάστου (l.28).

ΤΡΙΚΩΜΙΑ

about 152/151 B.C.	*UPZ* I 70,24	ἐν τῇ Τρικομίαι
mid-II B.C.	*UPZ* I 76,5	τ[ὴ]ν Τρικομίαν
52/51 B.C.	*BGU* VIII 1808,8	Τρικωμίας
21/20 B.C.-5 A.D.	*BGU* XVI 2641,12	Τρικ(ωμίας)

TOPARCHY: Koma? Tekmi?

ETYMOLOGY: this toponym obviously refers to the συνοικισμός of three originally distinct villages: in view of the *Greek* new toponym, this must have taken place in the Ptolemaic period.
Cf. Δικωμία (also in the Herakleopolite nome).

In his comment to *UPZ* I 70 and 76 (respectively: a letter from Apollonios to the recluse Ptolemaios, and the draft for another letter by Apollonios) Wilcken favoured the possibility that the Τρικωμία mentioned in these documents might be located in the Herakleopolites, and thus distinguished from the homonymous village in the Arsinoites[1]. His hypothesis is supported by *BGU* VIII 1808, which includes Τρικωμία in a group of Herakleopolite villages that recur together in several other documents, from the III B.C. to the V A.D.: Koma (5), Thmoiobastis (11), Bousiris (13), Onnes (9: Tekmi toparchy). It is further confirmed by *BGU* XVI 2641 (l.12), which contains a list of ten farmers: the names and/or villages (Koma, Tanchais, Trikomia) of three of them are preserved.

ΤΣΑΒΑ

| VII A.D. | *SB* VI 9590,7 | [ἐν κλή]ρῳ καλουμέ(νῳ) Τσαβα |

See also *s.v.* ΤΣΑΒΑΤΩΟΥ.

A cession of land: one of the parties is the ὑποδιάκονος Anatolios, from Herakleopolis. The villages of Makaitonos, Chortaso, Ἀπαλά and Tebetny are also mentioned.

ΤΣΑΒΑΤΩΟΥ

| V A.D. | *P.Oxy.* VIII 1126,5 | ἐν κλήρου καλουμένου Τσαβατώου |

See also *s.v.* ΤΣΑΒΑ.

TOPARCHY: Koites?

The villages of Talae and Kets are mentioned while describing the boundaries of this kleros.

---

[1] «Dieser auf Synoikismus von drei Dörfern hinweisende Dorfname ist uns aus dem Faijûm schon für das III Jahrh. v. Chr. mehrfach bezeugt. ... Aller Wahrscheinlichkeit nach ist damit nicht das ferne Dorf in Faijûm gemeint, sondern, da es im Leben des Apollonios und seiner Brüder offenbar eine Rolle spielt, ein Dorf im Herakleopolites (vgl. Ψιχις)» (*UPZ*, vol. I, p.336). See *CPR* XIII, *Einleitung*, pp.26-28, on the Arsinoite Τρικωμία.

ΤΣΗ[

VII-VIII A.D.   *Stud.Pal.* X 206,13

Apparently the name of a κλῆρος, listed with several others (see the *Reverse Index* at the end of this volume).

ṬΩΛ( )

VI A.D.   (?)*Stud.Pal.* III 24 *verso*,12   ἀπὸ Ṭωλ ( )[1]

Stud.Pal. III 24 *verso* contains a λόγος προβάτων. The village of Ṭωλ ( ) has been identified in CALDERINI-DARIS, *Dizionario* (vol. V, p.43) with Τωλλα, apparently on the basis of *CPR* I 156 (whose Herakleopolite provenance is certain), where the reading is also doubtful: see *s.v.* ΤΩΛΛ[.]. The village of Πεεμπα'θ'( ) is mentioned on the *recto* (re-edited as *P.Batav.* XIX 23 bis).

ΤΩΛΛ[.]

first half of III A.D.   *CPR* I 156,2   περὶ κώ[μη]ν Τωλλ[.][2]

See also *s.v.* ṬΩΛ( ).

TOPARCHY: Tekmi.

This document deals with the παραχώρησις of one aroura, whose location is given with reference to two fossil kleroi (Βίωνος and Κλεάνορος), respectively περὶ κώ[μη]ν Τωλλ[.] and περὶ κώμην Κολλιντααθυρ (Tekmi toparchy).

ΤΩΥ

about 51-49 B.C.	*BGU* VIII 1846,3	ἐκ κώμης Τωῦ
I B.C.	*BGU* XIV 2437,3;4;20;21	Τωύ
I B.C.	*BGU* XIV 2440,9	Τωέως[3]
21/20 B.C.	*BGU* XVI 2597,2	παρ' Ὥρου κωμογραμματέως Τωὺ καὶ Τοχοντωύ (1-2)

---

[1] «Τωλ( ) ist sehr unsicher, aber nicht auszuschließen» (Johannes Diethart, letter of February 25,1994).

[2] «λλ sehr unsicher» (Johannes Diethart, letter of February 25, 1994).

[3] Ṭωέως *ed. pr.* Reading checked on a photograph.

CATALOGUE

I/II A.D.	*P.Hib.* II 218,50	Τωύ
IV A.D.	*P.Lond.* III 985,11 (p.229)	ἀπὸ κώμης Τώου
IV/V A.D.	*P.Rain.Cent.* 154,2	πράκ(τωρ) Τωοῦ
VI A.D.	*Stud.Pal.* X 44,7	χ'ω'(ρίον) Τωου

TOPARCHY: Tekmi.

MODERN ARABIC NAME: Tuwa? Cf.*TAVO B 69*, p.213 (M 100): «Im Dorf ein im Abbau begriffener Kōm schwer zu schätzender Ausdehnung ... An einem Abbruch findet sich etwas Keramik. Außer einer kleinen ionischen Säulenbasis aus Kalkstein wurden keine weiteren Werksteine festgestellt».

BGU XIV 2437 and *Stud.Pal.* X 44 attest the connection between Των and Kollintaathyr (Tekmi toparchy).

BGU VIII 1846: petition to the strategos from the κατοικοῦντες at Των, who declare to be εἰς τέλος ἐξησθ[ε]νηκότες) and complain of too high taxes.

P.Lond. III 985: Flavius Papnuthis acknowledges the receipt of 30 solidi from the epimeletes Cyrillus, as payment for his military service.

P.Rain.Cent. 154: survey of land in the possession of Sarapion, praktor at Των; the following fossil kleroi are mentioned: Ἀσκληπιάδου, Ἡρακλείδου, Ἡγησιστράτου, Ἑρμώνακτος, Ἡρακλείδου, Εὐπολέμου, Ἀριστομάχου.

Φ[±3?]

VII-VIII A.D.	*Stud.Pal.* X 227,11	ἀ[πὸ χ(ωρίου)] Φ[±3]

This could be the same as Φρουρίου (ll.1 and 2 in the same document).

Φ..ΓΕΛ( )

VIII A.D.	*Stud.Pal.* X 109,8	ἐν τ(ῷ) χ(ωρίῳ) Φ..γελ( )[1]

The other villages mentioned in the document were either in southern Koites (Taamorou, l.4; Philonikou, l.10) or in the Tekmi toparchy (Pyrgotos, l.6).

Φ...ΡΥΓΕΛ

VIII A.D.	*Stud.Pal.* X 109,3	ἀπὸ χ(ωρίου) Φ...ρυγελ( )[2]

---

[1] A doubtful reading, checked for me by Johannes Diethart (letter of February 25, 1994). See next note.

[2] A doubtful reading, checked for me by Johannes Diethart (letter of February 25, 1994). He pointed out to me that the place-name Φ..γελ( ), recurring at l.8, is of a different length.

This village is listed between Tinteris (l.7) and Thneis (Koites; l.9). The other villages mentioned in the document were either in the Koites (Taamorou, l.4; Philonikou, l.10) or in the Tekmi toparchy (Pyrgotos, l.6).

ΦΑΕΙΝ

4 Oct. 698 A.D.	*CPR* VIII 76,4 (= *Stud.Pal.* VIII 1186)	κλήρου ἐξ ἀπηλιώτ(ου) Φαειμ
VII-VIII A.D.	*Stud.Pal.* VIII 1183,2	ἐν τ(ῷ) χ(ωρίῳ) Φν'ε(βι)' κλ'ή(ρου)' Φαειν
VII-VIII A.D.	*Stud.Pal.* X 206,10	κλ'ή'(ρος) Φαεινο[

TOPARCHY: Μέση.

The place is connected to Phnebi(eus) in *Stud.Pal.* VIII 1183.

ΦΑΘΩΡ

323 A.D. (cf. *BL* 9,174)	*P.Neph.* 48,4;5;9	[ἐν ὄρι καλου]μένῳ [Φα]θὼρ τοῦ Ἡρακλ[εοπολίτου νομοῦ] (4); μοναχῷ τῷ αὐτῷ ὄ[ρι Φαθώρ] (5); ἐξ] ἀπηλιώτου τοῦ μεγάλου π[ο]ταμοῦ [ἐν τῷ αὐτ]ῷ ὄρι Φαθώρ (9)
19 March 334 A.D.	*P.Lond.* VI 1913,3	τοῖς προεστῶσ[ι]' μονῆς μοναχῶν [καλ]ουμένης "Αθορ οὔσης ἐν τῷ ἀπηλιωτικῷ ὄρι τοῦ ἄνω Κυνοπολείτου (cf. *BL* 9,148)
about 330-340 A.D.	*P.Lond.* VI 1920,2	Φαθῶρ
IV A.D.	*P.Neph.* 11,4;27	πρεσβυτέροις νομῆς (*l.*μονῆς) Ἀθύρτι (3-4); [μονῆς] Ἀθύριος (27)
IV A.D.	*P.Neph.* 13,20	Νεφερῶτι πρ(εσ)β(υτέρῳ) τῆς Νήσου ἐν Φαθώρ
IV A.D.	*P.Neph.* 49,2	Φα]θώρ
V/VI A.D.	*P.Heid.* III 246,13	ἐν κλήρου Ἀθώρ
VII/VIII A.D.	*SB* XVIII 13888,1;9	δια(κόνου) ἀπὸ χ(ωρίου) Φαθώρ (1); [χ(ωρίου) Φ]αθώρ(9)

CATALOGUE

TOPARCHY: Koites.

ETYMOLOGY: «House of Hathor» (*Pr-hw.t-hrw, Pr-h.t-h*)[1].

BIBLIOGRAPHY: BÄRBEL KRAMER, «Neuere Papyri zum frühen Mönchtum in Ägypten», in *Philanthropia kai eusebeia. Festschrift für Albrecht Dihle zum 70. Geburtstag*, hrsg. von G.W. Most, H. Petersmann und A.M. Ritter, Göttingen 1993, pp.217-231.

The Nepheros archive offers a wealth of information on the monastery of (P)hathor, in the southernmost part of the Herakleopolites. A μονή by the same name is attested in the Kynopolites by *P.Lond.* VI 1913 (obviously the same as in *P.Lond.* VI 1920): a possible explanation could be that the border (to the east of the Nile) between the Herakleopolite and Kynopolite nomes altered between 323 and 334 A.D.

About four centuries later, *SB* XVIII 13888 mentions the same place-name as a χωρίον: the other villages listed (all of them near the border between the Herakleopolites and the Oxyrhynchites) are: Nokle, Kalamou, Ostrakinou, Thelbo, Hipponon.

ΦΑΙΝΙΠΠΟΥ

III B.C.	*P.Enteux.* 61,2	τ]ὴν Φαιν[ί]ππου κώμην
about 14/13 B.C.	*BGU* XVI 2670,II,2	
II A.D.	*CPR* I 238,3	ἐν κώμῃ Φαι[νίππ]ου
211-217 A.D.	*SB* XVIII 13858,15 (= *Stud.Pal.* XX 19,15)	ἀπὸ κώ'μ'(ης) Φαινίππου
222-235 A.D.	*CPR* I 73,12;17	Φ]αινί[ππ]ου (12); κώμης Φ]αινίππου (17)
III A.D. (first half)	*CPR* I 82, II,4	ἀπὸ κώμη]ς Φαινίππου
VII/VIII A.D.	*CPR* IV 2,17	χ(ωρίον) Φαινίππ'ου'

TOPARCHY: Tekmi.

ETYMOLOGY: a Φαινίππου κλῆρος, located περὶ κώμην Π[ε]εννώ (in the Middle toparchy of the Oxyrhynchites[2]) appears in a cession of land sworn in August 57 B.C. (*P.Oxy.* LV 3777,15). The Φαίνιππος who since the III B.C. gave his name to the Herakleopolite village, however, must have been a higher-ranking man, being entitled to a whole κώμη. Two men called Φαίνιππος are recorded in the *Prosopographia Ptolemaica*: one (*PPt* I 105) may have been connected to the dioiketes Apollonios in some way[3]; the other (*PPt* VI 16721), a τραγῳδιῶν ποιητής, was one of the τεχνῖται οἱ περὶ τὸν Διόνυσον καὶ θεοὺς Ἀδελφούς who caused an inscription to be put up at Ptolemais Hermiou in honour

---

[1] Cf. *P.Neph.*, Einl., p.11 n.1: «Zur Form Ἀθώρ bzw. Ἀθύρ, d.h. zur Weglassung des anlautenden Π konnte es vermutlich nur dadurch kommen, daß dieses als Artikel mißverstanden und somit als überflüssig angesehen wurde».

[2] See PRUNETI, *Centri abitati*, s.v. Πεεννω.

[3] *P.Tebt.* III 918,22-24 (early second century B.C.) Φαινίππου τοῦ [προστ?]άντος τῶν Ἀπολλωνίου τοῦ [διοικη?]σαντος.

of their benefactor Lysimachos, son of Ptolemaios[1].

BGU XVI 2670 shows that Φαινίππου was in the Tekmi toparchy: this is an account of contributions from individuals and groups of workers or artisans in view of the visit by a certain Lupus, presumably the nome strategos; the place-name Thmoiamoun(is) occurs in the next column.
CPR I 238, *CPR* I 73, *CPR* I 82: contracts involving people from Φαινίππου; *CPR* I 73 and 238 also refer to Herakleopolis and Νείλου πόλις, while *CPR* I 82 is to be recorded through the ἀγορανομία Κωίτου κατωτέρου (ll.4-5).
SB XVIII 13858 (= *Stud.Pal.* XX 19): προσαγγελία effected through the ἐπιτηρηταί ἀγο(ρανομίας) Πέρα (l.12)[2].
CPR IV 2 (a bilingual document in Coptic and Greek) lists many villages of the central toparchies of the Herakleopolite nome (toponyms in Greek)[3].

ΦΑΜΕΙΘΟΥ[4]

V A.D.   *Stud.Pal.* X 233, col. II,8

ΦΑΜΤΩΝΝΕΣΩΟΥ

683/684 A.D.   *CPR* X 135,9   κλήρου Φαμτωννεσωου
(or later)

Land ἐν διαφόροις κλήροις (see *Reverse Index* at the end of this volume).

ΦΑΡΣΕΣΙ

64/63 B.C.   *BGU* VIII 1749,11   τοῖς ἀποτεταγμένο<ι>ς
                                         σοι ἐν Φάρσεσι
                                         Θεβαίων ε ἀρ(ο)ύ(ρων)
                                         ἀνδ(ράσι) υη
                                         (11-12)

BGU VIII 1749: corn-provisions for 408 Theban 5-arourae-holders[5] stationed ἐν Φάρσεσι, at the disposal of the strategos of the Herakleopolites.

---

[1] *SB* V 8855 (= *OGIS* I 51),32 (the inscription is to be dated between 279 and 239 B.C.).

[2] New reading suggested «mit einigen Bedenken» by DIETER HAGEDORN, *ZPE* 34, 1979, p.110.

[3] See *s.v.* ΝΙΝΩ.

[4] Ψ..θο'υ' *ed. pr.* «Die Lesung ist schwierig. M.E. ist vielleicht Φαμειθου möglich (jedenfalls scheint mir Φ am Anfang besser als Ψ)» (Johannes Diethart, letter of February 25, 1994).

[5] Cf. also ll.6-7 of the same document.

ΦΕΒΙΧΙΣ ἡ μεγάλη

about 270 B.C.	*P.Hib.* I 110 *recto*, 36	ἐμ Φεβίχι
265/264 B.C. (cf. *BL* 8,427)	*P.Strasb.* VII 641,4	ἐμ Φεβίχι
263/262 (262/261) B.C.	*P.Hib.* I 88, [5]	[ἐμ Φεβίχι τοῦ Κωίτου][1]
263/262 B.C.	*P.Hib.* II 209,5	ἐμ Φεβ[ί]χι [το]ῦ Κωίτ[ου]
about 260 B.C.	*P.Hib.* I 112,4;13;30;38;48;54;60;79;84;91	
259 (258) B.C.	*P.Hib.* I 96,3;19	ἐμ Φεβ[ί]χι τοῦ Κωίτ[ου] (3); ἐ]μ Φεβίχι τοῦ Κ[ω]ίτου (19)
about 246 B.C.	*SB* XII 10783,2 (= *P.Hib.* I 139)	[ἐπὶ τὸ] ἐμ Φεβίχει λο(γευτήριον) τοῦ Κωίτου (2-3)
246 (245) B.C.	*P.Hib.* I 106,3	τὸ ἐμ Φεβίχι λογευτήριον τοῦ Κωίτου
246 (245) B.C.	*P.Hib.* I 138 *descr*	
about 245 B.C.	*P.Hib.* I 131 *descr.*	
244 (243) B.C.	*P.Hib.* I 107,3	τὸ ἐμ] Φεβίχει λο(γευτήριον) (2-3)
244 (243) B.C.	*P.Hib.* I 136 descr.	
26 April 241 B.C. (cf. *BL* 2.2,76)	*P.Hib.* I 72,2	παρὰ Πετοσίριος τοῦ ἀρχιερέως τοῦ ἐμ Φεβίχει Ἡρακλέους Εὐθε.[........]ἱεροῦ(?) (1-2)
239 (238) or 215 (214) B.C.	*P.Hib.* I 117,15	[ἐν Φεβί]χει
232/231 or 231/230 B.C.	*P.Hib.* I 143 *descr.*	
229 B.C.(?)	*P.Fuad Crawford* App. I, 3 (and 4),8	ἐπὶ τοῦ ἐμ Φεβίχι τοῦ Κωίτου λογευτηρίου
mid-III B.C.	*P.Strasb.* IX 802,21	
mid-III B.C.(?)	*SB* X 10447 *recto*,60; *verso*,35	Φεβῖχ[ις
after 168/167 B.C.	*P.Hels.* I 4 D, col. II, 1	Φεβίχεως τοῦ Κωίτου
2 Sept. 162 B.C.	*P.Hels.* I 26 B,3	Φεβίχεως

---

[1] «The restorations of the lacunae in ll.2-5 are derived from a fairly complete but much effaced agreement (unpublished) concerning a payment of rent, which belonged to the same piece of cartonnage and preserves nearly all the protocol» (*P.Hib.* I, p.251).

first half of II B.C.	*P.Tebt.* III 920,21	[ἐκ] Φεβίχεως
64/63 B.C.	*BGU* VIII 1748,3	ἀντιγρα(φεῖ) θη(σαυροῦ) [π]ερὶ Φεβέχ(ιν)
after 52/51 B.C.	*BGU* VIII 1808,24	περὶ Φεβῖχιν
I B.C.	*BGU* XIV 2419,2	τῆς Φεβίχεως
I B.C.	*BGU* XIV 2431,1	Φεβίχεως
I B.C.	*BGU* XIV 2435,1	Φεβίχεως
I B.C.	*BGU* XIV 2436,5	Φεβῖχιν
I B.C.	*BGU* XIV 2438,46	περὶ Φεβῖχιν
I B.C.	*BGU* XIV 2440,16;19;60; (fr.5),84	Φεβίχεως (16); περὶ Φε(βῖχιν) (19;84); περὶ Φεβῖχ(ιν) (60)
mid-I B.C.	*SB* VIII 9790,3	ἀπὸ Φεβίχεως
20 Feb. 13 B.C.	*BGU* XVI 2582,1;7	Φεβίχεως Κωεί'τ'(ου) (1); ἀπὸ Φεβ[ί]χεως τοῦ Κωείτου (7-8)
I B.C./I A.D.[1]	*BGU* XVI 2593,1	Φεβίχεως
late I A.D.	*P.Oxy.* XLVII 3357,14	ἀπὸ Φεβείχεως
I/II A.D.	*P.Hib.* II 218,46;59	Φεβε[ί]χ[εω]ς (46); Φ[εβείχεως]νεβιέως (59)
I/II A.D.	*PSI* VIII 967,19	Φεβηχίτης (ethnic)
169-177 A.D. (cf. *BL* 8,410)	*PSI* XIII 1325,8;22 (= *SB* V 7630)	ἐν κώμῃ Φεβίχι τοῦ Κωίτου (8); περὶ κώμην Φεβ[ῖ]χιν (22)[2]
192 A.D.	*P.Heid.* IV 301, II,14; III,10	περὶ Φεβ(ῖχιν)
II A.D.	*P.Petaus* 28,6	οἱ ἀπὸ Φεβῖχις
II/III A.D.	P.Alex. inv. 536 (p.32),7	Φεβίχεως[3]
after 212 A.D.	*P.Lund* VI 8,5 (= *SB* VI 9358, I)	τοπαρχ(ίας) β περὶ .... Φεβεῖχιν
after 212 A.D.	*P.Lund* VI 9,4-5 (= *SB* VI 9358, II)	τοπαρχ(ίας) β Ἡρακλ(εοπολίτου) καὶ περὶ Φεβῖχιν[4]

---

[1] Another (apparently still unpublished) document from the same piece of cartonnage, and mentioning Phebichis, is referred to in *BGU* XIV, *Appendix*, p.222: it dates from the 25th year of Augustus.

[2] The supplement at l.22 is suggested in the *ed. pr.*, on the basis of l.8.

[3] Φ.εβίχεως *ed.pr.*

[4] JEAN BINGEN, *Chr.d'Ég.* 29, 1954, p.153, writes: «Les deux textes (*P.Lund* VI 8 and 9) sont écrits en une cursive particulièrement difficile et plusieurs lectures restent incertaines; à la ligne 4 du n° 9, p.ex., je ne crois pas pouvoir lire

CATALOGUE

222 A.D.	*PSI* XV estr. 1546,8	τοπαρχίας περὶ Φεβ[ῖ]χιν¹
223 A.D.	*P.Ross.Georg.* V 20 *verso*, col. II,4	
6 May 252 A.D. (cf. *BL* 2.2,61)	*P.Gen.* I 9,2	ἐν κώμῃ Φεβε[ί]χει
second half of III A.D.²	*P.Lond.* II 171 b (p.176),7	ἐν κώμῃ Φεβε[ῖ]χι τοῦ Κωίτου (cf. *BL* 1,258)
III A.D.	*P.Erl.* 48,29-30	[Φε]βείχεως
III A.D.	*P.Neph.* 28,5	Φεβεῖ[χι]ν
313/314 A.D.	*P.Michael.* 28,1	περὶ Φεβεῖχιν
8 August 323 A.D.	*P.Gen.* I 10,2;5;7	ἐν κώμῃ Φεβείχι ια πάγου (2-3); ἐπὶ τῆς αὐτῆς [κώ]μης Φεβείχεως (4-5); ἐπὶ τῆς αὐτῆς [Φεβείχ]εως (6-7)
IV A.D.	(?) *PSI* III 222,9	ἀπὸ κώμης Πάπα περὶ Φ(εβῖχιν³)
IV or early V A.D.	*P.Amh.* II 147,2;4	ἀπὸ κώμης Φεβείχι ια πάγου (2); ἀπὸ τῆς αὐτῆς Φεβείχε(ως) (4)
459 A.D.	*P.Rain.Cent.* 102,5	Φε]βίχεως μεγάλης
463 A.D.	*Stud.Pal.* XX 127,5	ἀπὸ κώμης Φεβίχεως Μεγάλης Μεγάλης (cf. *BL* 1,42)
15-23 June 478 A.D.	*P.Rain.Cent.* 123,3;9 (= *CPR* V 15)	ἐγ κώμης Φεβίχεως μεγάλ[ης] (3); ἀπὸ κώμης Φεβίχεως (9)
VI/VII A.D.	*P.Oxy.* XVI 1866,2	ἀπὸ Φεβίχεως
VI/VII A.D.	*Stud.Pal.* VIII 1346,1	Φεβίχεως
beginning of VII A.D.	*P.Laur.* II 47,3	Φυβύχεως
VII A.D.	*Stud.Pal.* VIII 1326,1	ἀπὸ χ(ωρίου) Φεβίχ(εως) Με(γάλης)

Ἡρακλ(εοπολίτου)». On this document see also DIETER HAGEDORN, *ZPE* 1, 1967, p.196.

[1] A new fragment has been added since the first edition of this document. The new reading has been checked for me by Isabella Andorlini: Manfredo Manfredi then provided me with a new transcription (letter of September 25, 1994).

[2] Cf. GUIDO BASTIANINI, *ZPE* 39, 1980, p.154, n.30.

[3] As noted in the *ed. pr.*, a horizontal stroke above Φ, at the end of l.9, indicates that this was an abbreviated toponym, probably Φ(εβῖχιν)· see *s.v.* ΠΑΠΑ. The reading περὶ Φ[ε]β[ε]ῖχειν was suggested by Sergio Daris for ll.9-10: cf. *BL* 7,233; but on the original I could detect no β at the beginning of l.10).

Byz.	*SB* I 5338,11	Πεβίχον[1]

See also: ΙΒ[Ι]ΧΕΩΣ; Φ( ); [±8]ΧΕΩΣ.

TOPARCHY: Koites (XI *pagus* :*P.Gen.* 10; *P.Ahm.* II 147).

MODERN ARABIC NAME: Al-Fašn[2]. *TAVO B 69*, p.89 (M 64) offers the identification of Al-Fašn with Coptic *Pbešin*[3], which I propose to identify with Greek Φέβιχις: this seems very likely from a topographical point of view; phonetically, however, the absence of the sound *n* in the Greek toponym is not easily accounted for. The location of *Pbešin* in the Herakleopolites was already suggested by the editor of the Coptic *Budge Papyrus P.Col.* inv.Nr. 600 (see *s.v.* ΠΙΝΕΞΕΩΣ).

Cf. *TAVO B 69*, p.206: «Im Dorf befindet sich ein ausgedehnter Kōm mit einer Höhe bis zu (grob geschätzt) 5 m. Teile davon wurden neuerdings abgetragen, um Platz zu schaffen für eine Schule und ein Verwaltungsgebäude. Die reichlich vorhandene Oberflächenkeramik ist in Spätantike sowie arabische Zeit zu datieren. Nach Auskunft von Bewohnern sind keine antiken Architekturteile vorhanden. Es wurde auch in den begangenern Bereichen keine gesehen». Cf. also TIMM, *Das christlich-koptische Ägypten*, II,p.946 f. (*s.v.* al-Fašn).

The chief centre in northern Koites since the III B.C. In the V century it is sometimes styled ἡ μεγάλη (earliest source: *P.Rain.Cent.* 102), apparently to distinguish it from Φέβιχις ἡ μικρά (*q.v.*)[4].

P.Hib. I 106; 107; 136; 138; *SB* XII 10783 (= *P.Hib.* I 139): beer-tax payments on account of the same producer (Taembes, living at Talae) into the logeuterion of Phebichis («a kind of centre of the finance administration of the Koites»)[5]. *P.Hib.* I 112 was «perhaps written at the logeuterion of Phebichis, recording money payments for various taxes at different villages of the Koites»[6].

The θησαυρός of Φέβιχις is mentioned in *BGU* VIII 1748, and an agoranomos office in *P.Heid.* IV 301.

P.Lund. VI 8 and 9: χειρόγραφα of the πράκτορες σιτικῶν at Phebichis.

Connections with the northern Oxyrhynchites: *BGU* XIV 2419; *P.Oxy.* XVI 1866; *P.Laur.* II 47 (Apion estate). Phebichis and Ἰσῖον κάτω (in the Northern toparchy of the Oxyrhynchites[7]) recur together in the last two documents, and in *Stud.Pal.* VIII 1346 (Koba also appears both in *P.Laur.* II 47 and *Stud.Pal.* VIII 1346).

P.Tebt. III 920 (fragment of a report about a conflict with robbers) mentions people from Techtho and Phebichis.

P.Hib. I 96: agreement between two military settlers from Phebichis; at least one of them is a Jew.

The *verso* of *P.Hib.* I 110 preserves part of the day-book of a post-office in an intermediate station on

---

[1] «Wohl Φεβίχων (?)» Preisigke (*ad loc.*).

[2] This identification is further supported by the equation Ταλαη/Ταλη (near Phebichis) = modern Tala (not far from Al-Fašn): cf. *Introduction*, p.11.

[3] «Der koptische Name dürfte auf altägyptisch *P3bhn* zurückgehen. Die 2. Sektion des P.Wilbour, die die entsprechende Gegend umfaßt, führt mehrere Orte dieses Namens auf, so daß eine eindeutige Identifikation nicht möglich ist» (*TAVO B 69*, p.89).

[4] Where no special designation appears in the documents dating from this period, I assume that Phebichis ἡ μεγάλη is meant.

[5] Cf. *P.Hib.* I, p.280.

[6] *P.Hib.* I, p.296.

[7] See PRUNETI, *Centri abitati*, *s.v.*

the *route* from Alexandria to southern Egypt and the Thebaid (and back)[1]: what is left of this text does not indicate where this station was, but the two Editors appear to consider Phebichis a suitable location, as this is one of the place-names appearing on the *recto* (account of corn, some of which was transported to Alexandria)[2].

There was a temple of Herakles/Eseph at Phebichis (*P.Hib.* I 72); *P.Hib.* I 131 mentions the ἀρχιερεύς of Phebichis.

ΦΕΒΙΧΙΣ ἡ μικρά

V A.D.	*Stud.Pal.* X 233, col.II,16	Φεβίχε[ως] Μικρ(ᾶς)[3]
VIII A.D.	*Stud.Pal.* X 199,3	χ(ωρί)ον Φ<ε>βίχεως Μικ(ρᾶς)[4]

The designation ἡ μικρά, in connection with Phebichis, only recurs in *Stud.Pal.* X 233 and, later on, in *Stud.Pal.* X 199[5].

ΦΕΛΕ( )

VII-VIII A.D.	*Stud.Pal.* X 208 *verso*,3	Φελ'ε'( )

According to Johannes Diethart the reading Φελ^ε «dürfte stimmen»[6]. One might perhaps assume a scribal error for Ψελ'έ'μαχις.

ΦΕΝΑΜΕΝΙ

April-August 42 A.D.	*P.Mich.* II 121 *recto*, col.IV. 1,2	ἀπὸ κώμη(ς) Φεναμενι τοῦ ὑπὲρ Μέμφι<ν> Ἡρακλεοπολ(ίτου)

This is one of the abstracts from the ἀναγραφαί of the γραφεῖον of Tebtynis and Kerkesouchon Oros[7].

---

[1] The document has been re-examined by STEPHEN R. LLEWELYN, *ZPE* 99, 1993, pp.41-56.

[2] See the introduction to this document (*P.Hib.* I, p.287). Hiera Nesos, also mentioned on the *recto*, is another possibility.

[3] Reading checked for me on the original by Johannes Diethart (letter of February 25, 1994).

[4] This reading was checked for me by Johannes Diethart (letter of February 25, 1994): «In dieser Steuerliste aus dem 8.Jh. hat Wessely in seiner Edition nur eine Nachzeichnung des Ortes in Z.3 gebracht, auf dem Original läßt sich χ^ο Φ<ε>βίχεως Μικρ(ᾶς) lesen».

[5] Cf. JOHANNES DIETHART, *Tyche* 10, 1995, p.239.

[6] Letter of February 25, 1994.

[7] Cf. A.E.R. BOAK, «The Anagraphai of the Grapheion of Tebtunis and Kerkesouchon Oros», *JEA* 9, 1923, pp.164-167.

ΦΙ....[1]

223 A.D.   *P.Ross.Georg.* V 20, *verso*, col. II,5

TOPARCHY: Koites.

This is a census list, also mentioning Thmoinache, Thelbo, Phebichis (all in the Koites). On the *recto*, reference to Korphotoi ("Αγημα toparchy).

(?) ΦΙΛΑΔΕΛΦΟΣ

88-81 B.C.   *BGU* XIV 2374,6   ἐν Φιλαδέλφωι[2]

This is presumably the same locality attested for the Arsinoites in *SB* I 1214 (mummy label; undated).

ΦΙΛΟΝΙΚΟΥ[3]

III B.C.	*P.Petr.* III 99 *recto*,10;17;28[4]	περὶ τὸ Φ[ιλονίκου] ἐ[πο]ίκιον (10-11); ἐκ τ[οῦ Φ]ιλονίκου ἐποικί[ο]υ (17); περὶ τὸ Φιλονίκου ἐπ[οίκιον (28)
I/II A.D.	*P.Hib.* II 218,6;11;20;23	Φιλονείκ(ου) (11;23)
after 150 A.D.	*Stud.Pal.* XX 7,12 (= *CPR* I 22)	[περὶ Φιλ]ονεικίου[5]
155 A.D.	*SB* V 7515,223 (= *P.Berl.Frisk* = *P.Bankakten* 1)	κώ(μης) Φιλονίκου
early II A.D.	*P.Oxy.* III 504,7	ἀπὸ Φιλονίκου

---

[1] According to the *ed. pr.*, not Φιλονείκου.

[2] «Die Lesung ist sehr unsicher... . Ein Dorf, genannt Philadelphos, ist in *SB* I 1214,6 für den Arsinoites belegt, aber eins für den Herakleopolites fehlt bisher» (*ed.pr.*).

[3] The toponym Φιλονίκου is also attested on an inscription (*SB* I 2246,6-7): cf. BERNARD P. GRENFELL - ARTHUR S. HUNT, *Egypt Exploration Fund. Arch. Report*, 1901/1902, p.5; also *P.Hib.* I, *Introduction*, p.4:«An inscription rudely carved on a block of limestone measuring 50 x 30 cm. records the death of] Ὀρ[σ]ενεφοιῶτος Ἀπίωνος τῶν ἀπὸ κώμης Φιλονίκου (ἐτῶν) γ».

[4] Clarysse's new reading at l.12 ('Ἡρακλεοπ[ολίτου instead of Ἡρακλεωτ[; cf. JAN KRZYSZTOF WINNICKY, *Orientalia Lovaniensia Periodica* 17, 1986, p.19 and n.10) confirms that this papyrus refers to Herakleopolite localities.

[5] «ι kann wohl gelesen werden» (Johannes Diethart, letter of February 25, 1994).

late II or III A.D.	*P.Ryl.* II 225,37	περὶ Φιλονείκου
231 A.D.	*Stud.Pal.* XX 32,8;14	[σιτο]λόγων Κωίτου Ἄνω Φιλονείκου (7-8; cf. *BL* 2.2,158); ἐκ θησαυρῶν τῆς αὐτῆς Φιλονείκ[ου (14)
242 A.D.	*Stud.Pal.* XX 52,15	
III A.D.	*P.Oxy.* VI 965, descr.	πράκτορσ[ι] σιτικῶν Φιλονείκου
III A.D.	*P.Oxy.* VIII 1156,4	ἀπὸ Φιλονίκου
313/314 A.D.	*P.Michael.* 28,11	κωμάρχου τῆς Φιλονίκου
4 April 328 A.D.	SB XVIII 13260, [8];22	οὐετρ[α]νοῦ ἀπὸ [χωρίου] |[Φιλονίκου] (7-8); οὐετρανῷ [ἀπὸ χωρίου] Φιλονίκου (21-22)
17 April 344 A.D.	*P.Neph.* 32,5	ἀπὸ κώμης Φιλονείκου τοῦ ὑπὲρ Μέμφιν Ἡρακλεοπολίτου νομοῦ
IV A.D.	*P.Lond.* VI 1924,5	ἀπὸ Φιλονίκου
411 A.D.	*Stud.Pal.* XX 117,5	ἐν [π]εδίοις Φιλονίκου
V A.D.	SB XII 10939,7	ἀπὸ [χωρ]ί[ο]υ Φιλ[ον]ίκου [τ]οῦ Ἡ[ρα]κ[λ]εουπολίτ[ου νομο]ῦ[1]
V A.D.	*Stud.Pal.* X 233, col. I A,3	Φιλονίκου
VI A.D.	SB VI 9139,18	Φιλονίκ(ου)
VII A.D.	*Stud.Pal.* X 66,5	χ(ωρίον) Φιλονί[κου][2]
beginning of VIII A.D. (719/720 or 734/735 A.D.?)	SB XVIII 13870,2	ἀπὸ χ(ωρίου) Φιλονίκου παγαρχ(ίας) Ἡρακλε(οπολίτου)
VIII A.D.	*Stud.Pal.* X 109,10	ἀπὸ χ(ωρίου) Φιλονίκο'υ'
VIII A.D.	*Stud.Pal.* X 199,5	χ(ωρίον) Φοιλωνίκ'ου'

TOPARCHY: Koites (XII *pagus*: *P.Michael.* 28).

ETYMOLOGY: like the κώμη called Φαινίππου, this ἐποίκιον Φιλονίκου must have been named after

---

[1] My reading (checked on the photograph in the *editio princeps*): Φιλονίκου η[..]..[.]εου πολιτάρχο]υ *ed. pr.*

[2] «Φιλονί[κου] ist sicher» (Johannes Diethart, letter of February 25, 1994).

some (arguably less important) Greek person; however, no Φιλόνικος appears in the *Prosopographia Ptolemaica*.

Philonikou recurs in the same document with Thelbo in *P.Ryl.* II 225 (Nokle, Koma, Machor also mentioned), *P.Michael.* 28 (Papa, Pselemachis and other villages also listed) and in *P.Hib.* II 218 (with many other villages, mostly in the Koites). It also appears in two documents of the IV A.D.: *P.Neph.* 32 (here Νήσων κώμη is mentioned as well) and *P.Lond.* VI 1924, which both belong to dossiers relating to «apparently influential monks»[1] (Nepheros and Papnouthios, respectively) in two monasteries of the Herakleopolites.

Stud.Pal. XX 52: the sitologoi of Taamorou acknowledge the receipt of corn from Philonikou[2]: both villages also recur in *P.Hib.* II 218.

More sitologoi receipts: *SB* V 7515 (mainly dealing with the Polemon division of the Arsinoites: Herakleopolite villages include Kerkesephis, Talae, Philonikou); *Stud.Pal.* XX 52. Πράκτορες σιτικῶν appear in *P.Oxy.* VI 965.

A naukleros receipt: *Stud.Pal.* XX 32 (corn shipped at the θησαυρός of Philonikou, to be transported to Alexandria).

Stud.Pal. XX 7: marriage contract; the bride's dowry comprises land at Pharbaitha (in the Arsinoites) and more possessions at Philonikou.

Stud.Pal. XX 117: sale of land located ἐν [π]εδίοις Φιλονίκου ἐν ἐδάφι καλ[ο]υμέν[ῳ] Νανηουει.

ΦΝΕΒΙΕΥΣ[3]

17 Jan. 245 B.C.[4]	*P.Petr.* III 43 (2), col. III,30 (= *Chr.W.* 387)	τὴν γέφυραν τὴν ἐν Φνεβγει καὶ τὴν ἄγουσαν εἰς Χανααναιν (30)[5]
III B.C.	*P.Petr.* III 62 b,4	εἰς τὸ ἱπποτρόφιον Φενεβιεως (cf. *BL* 7,162)[6]
between 173 and 130-128 B.C.	*P.Tebt.* III 890,74;75;100	ἐκ Φν[εβιέως (74); ἐκ Φ[νεβιέως (75); ἐκ Φνεβιέως (100)
II B.C.	*BGU* VI 1244,6;38	Φνεβιέως καὶ Π[ε]ενοχων (6)[7]; ἐπιστάτης Φνεβιέως (38)

---

[1] On these monks and their monasteries see PETER VAN MINNEN, «The Roots of Egyptian Christianity», *APF* 40/41, 1994, pp.79 ff.

[2] *P.Vind.Sijp.* 19 and *P.Vind.Worp* 4 (both mentioning Tebetny) are documents very similar to *Stud.Pal.* XX 52.

[3] The place-name Πνεβῆβις, attested in the lexicon of Stephanus of Byzantium, may perhaps be compared.

[4] See ALAN E. SAMUEL, *Ptolemaic Chronology*, München 1962, p.92.

[5] Reading checked for me by Brian McGing: «Φνεβγεῖ quite clearly right» (letter of 8 September 1994).

[6] Reading checked for me by Brian McGing: «Φενεβιέως absolutely clear» (letter of 8 September 1994).

[7] Φνεβιεως («hier auch möglich?») καὶ .[.]ενοχων (see *s.v.* Πεενοχών) read by Günter Poethke (letter of April 14, 1994), who checked this reading for me.

after 84/83 B.C.	*BGU* XIV 2370 (fr.1),79	Φνεβιεῖ
52/51 B.C.	*BGU* VIII 1827,6	Νικάρχωι τῶι ἐν τ[οπαρ]χίᾳ Φνεβιεῖ ὄντι καὶ τῶι ὑπο[σ]τρατήγωι (6-7)[1]
52/51 B.C.	*BGU* VIII 1828,4;8	τοῦ ἐν Φνεβιεῖ δεσμωτηρίου (4-5); ἀπὸ τῆς πρότερον Ἀπικκίου προσόδου περὶ Φνεβιέα ἐν τῶι πρότερον Ἀγελάου κλήρωι (7-9)
51/50 B.C.	*BGU* VIII 1837,4	τῶν ἐκ κώμη[ς] Φνεβιέως κτηνοτρόφων βασιλίσσης (3-5)
after 52/51 B.C.	*BGU* VIII 1808,25	Φνεβ'ι'έως (cf. *BL* 7,22)
I B.C.	*BGU* VIII 1798,1	ἀρχιφυλακίτηι Φνεβιέως
I B.C.	*BGU* VIII 1803,3;6-7	Φνεβιέα (3); [Φνε]βιέα (6-7)
I B.C.	*BGU* VIII 1855,2	Φνεβιέως
I B.C.	*BGU* XIV 2432,11	Φνειβι
I B.C.	*BGU* XIV 2434,28	περὶ Φεβιέ(α) (*l.* Φνεβιέα)
I B.C.	*BGU* XIV 2438,22; (fr.3),96	Φνεβιέως (22); Φνεβιέω[ς (96)
I B.C.	*BGU* XIV 2440,15	[Φεβ]νιέως[2]
27 April 15 B.C.	*BGU* XVI 2607,14	ἐ<ν> Φνέβι
5 Feb. 13 B.C.	*BGU* XVI 2583,1;8;21	Φνεβι(έως) (1); ἀπὸ Φνε[βιέως] (8); περὶ Φνεβιέα (21)
II/III A.D.	*P.Köln* II 99,1[3]	Φνεβιέως
V A.D.	*Stud.Pal.* X 8,7	χ(ωρίου) Φνεβιέως

---

[1] «τοπαρχία nur Vermutung; diese Toparchie ist nicht belegt. Nikarchos muß eine hohe Person sein, die ohne weiteres dem Hypostrategen übergeordnet erscheint» (*ed. pr.*).

[2] ...νιεως *ed.pr.*; the reading [Φεβ]νιέως is supported by the fact that this village recurs twice more in the same document with Pois (*BGU* VIII 1808; *Stud.Pal.* X 44). Besides, references to the Ἄγημα κάτω and the Koites are found both in *BGU* VIII 1808 and in the first column of *BGU* XIV 2440. All three documents also mention villages of the Tekmi toparchy.

[3] «Vielleicht vor Z.1 [περὶ Φνεβιέα]» (*ed. pr.*).

V A.D.	Stud.Pal. X 9,3	Φνεβιέως
VI A.D.	Stud.Pal. III 341,1	ἀπὸ ἐ]πο(ικίου) Φνεβι τοῦ Ἡρ(ακλεο)π(ολίτου) νομοῦ
VI A.D.	Stud.Pal. X 44,10	χ'ω'(ρίον) Φνεβι
VII A.D.	Stud.Pal. III 202,2	Φνεβι[1]
VII/VIII A.D.	CPR IV 2,18	χ(ωρίον) Φνεβι
VII-VIII A.D.	Stud.Pal. VIII 1183,2	ἐν τ(ῷ) χ(ωρίῳ) Φνε(βι)
VII-VIII A.D.	Stud.Pal. X 208 verso,2	Φνεβι
VIII A.D.	Stud.Pal. X 109,12	ἐν τ(ῷ) χ(ωρίῳ) Φνεβι

TOPARCHY: Μέση[2].

ETYMOLOGY: a few variant spellings are attested for this place-name: Φνεβγεύς (P.Petr. III 43.2) and Φενεβιεύς (P.Petr. III 62b), both attested only once, may result from different attempts at rendering the Egyptian original; the (apparently simplified) spelling Φνεβιεύς prevails in the documents of the later period. In BGU XIV 2432, the reading Φνειβι is uncertain: if correct, Φνεγβι (lege Φνεβγει, as in P.Petr. III 43.2) was perhaps meant by the scribe; and Φνεβι (found in the sources from the VI A.D. onwards) seems to be a simpler form of this spelling.

A locality called «the Mound of P-nebi» is attested in P.Wilbour B 13,20; is this the same as Per-nebit mentioned in the «inscription of Shoshenq I» (Journal d'entrée du Musée égyptien du Caire no.39410, l.24; mid-X B.C.)[3]?

P.Petr. III 43 (2), coll. III-IV: contract for maintenance work on bridges and canals; the work has been given out (after proclamation by a herald) at Κροκοδείλων πόλις (Arsinoites) by the oikonomos, in the presence of the chief architect and the basilikos grammateus. It is to be performed in several localities, some of which may have been either in the Herakleopolites (like Φνεβγεύς) or along the border between the Herakleopolites and the Arsinoites: like Hiera Nesos (col.III,ll.23;26) and Tebetny (col.IV,l.8).

BGU VIII 1827: a dispute between husband and wife concerning a plot of land near Peenscho is brought in front of the strategos, with the request that he should write to a certain Nikarchos ἐν τ[οπαρ]χίᾳ (?) Φνεβι, and to the ὑποστράτηγος, about it. Phnebieus was in fact the main centre of the Μέση toparchy, appearing in almost all documents where other localities of the same toparchy are mentioned (P.Tebt. III 890; BGU VIII 1803; BGU XIV 2370 and 2438; P.Köln II 99).

The connection with Peenscho is confirmed in BGU IV 1244 (petition submitted by a brewer from Phnebieus).

BGU VIII 1798 is addressed to the ἀρχιφυλακίτης of Phnebieus, where there was also a prison

---

[1] My reading: Φνευι[..]η[...]ιμ[ed. pr.

[2] One (or two) villages with a similar name are attested in the Arsinoites. The «northern» (κάτω) Φνεβίη (see CALDERINI-DARIS, Dizionario, s.v.; cf. also GENEVIÈVE HUSSON, Proceedings of the XIXth International Congress of Papyrology. Cairo 2-9 September 1989, Cairo 1992, vol. I, p.100) is connected to Memphis in the sources. Another, «southern» (ἄνω) Φνεβίη could coincide with the Phnebieus of the Petrie Papyri, which I am inclined to assign to the Herakleopolites (see also Introduction, p.9f.): it is read doubtfully (περὶ Φνεβιε[.]σιν ἄνω) in PUG III 103,11 (219 B.C.?). SERGIO DARIS, Aegyptus 64, 1984, pp.118-119, suggests the reading Φνεβίη ἄνω in P.IFAO III 42,3 (II/III A.D.), where Hiera Nesos and Tebetny also appear (the Arsinoite Kerkesis also recurs in both documents).

[3] Cf. PAUL TRESSON, «L'inscription de Chechanq Ier, au Musée du Caire», Mélanges Maspero I. Orient Ancien (MIFAO 66), Le Caire 1935-1938.

(*BGU* VIII 1828).

BGU VIII 1837 is a petition submitted by the κτηνοτρόφοι of the Queen at Phnebieus.

BGU XVI 2607 concerns the shipping of timber, also mentioning the place-name Ποιμένων κώμη (in the same toparchy).

BGU XVI 2583 is a declaration of sheep and goats νεμόμενα καὶ ποτιζόμενα καὶ αὐλιζόμενα περὶ Φνεβιέα καὶ δι' ὅλου τοῦ νομοῦ: their owner lives at Phnebieus.

CPR IV 2 (a bilingual document in Coptic and Greek) lists many villages of the central toparchies of the Herakleopolite nome (toponyms in Greek)[1].

ΦΡΟΥΡΙΟΝ

V A.D.	*Stud.Pal.* X 233, col. I A,5	Φρουρίου
VII A.D.	*Stud.Pal.* X 66,4	χ(ωρίον) Φ[ρ]ουρί[ου
VII-VIII A.D.	*Stud.Pal.* X 227, 1;2	ἀπὸ χ(ωρίου) Φρου[ρίου (1); ἀπὸ χ(ωρίου) Φρο[υρίου (2)

TOPARCHY: Koites?

ETYMOLOGY: «guarding post».

Talae (Koites) is among the villages listed in *Stud.Pal.* X 227, Philonikou (Koites) among those appearing in *Stud.Pal.* X 66.

Guarding posts (φρούρια) in the Herakleopolites are attested at Techtho and Herakleopolis (*P.Berl.Zill.* 1 and 2). A reference to a φρούριον in the Herakleopolites is also found in *SB* I 5137,5 (237 A.D.).

ΦΥΣ

259 B.C.	*P.Mich.Zen.* 30a,10; (?)b,2	ἐν Φῦς
probably 259/258 or 249/248 B.C. (cf. *BL* 3,84)	*P.Hib.* I 108,2	ἐν Φῦς λογευτήριον
4 July 238 B.C.	*SB* III 7179,6	τῶι ἐμ Φῦς τραπεζίτηι
(?)23 Oct. 163 B.C.	(?)*P.Hels.* I 9,8	....[...].[.]Φ..[2]
about 160 B.C.	*P.Hels.* I 27,1	Φῦς
about 160 B.C.	*P.Hels.* I 34,10	'Φῦ(ς)'
159 B.C.	*P.Hels.* I 38,5	Φῦς
49/48 B.C.	*SB* V 8755,4	ἐκ Φῦς (cf. 1.7: περὶ τὴν κώμην)

---

[1] See *s.v.* ΝΙΝΩ.

[2] «In der Lücke könnte man den Dorfnamen erwarten, z.B. ἐν κώμηι Φῦς» (*ed. pr.*).

I B.C.	*BGU* XIV 2433,49	Φῦς
I B.C.	*BGU* XIV 2438,40	Φῦς
I B.C.	*BGU* XIV 2439,104	Φῦς
I B.C.	*BGU* XIV 2440,26	Φῦς
21/20 B.C.-5 A.D.	*BGU* XVI 2592,3;6	ἐγ κώμη Φῦς (3); ἐν [κώμ]η Φῦς (6)
21/20 B.C.-5 A.D.	*BGU* XVI 2669,3	ἐν τῆι ἐ[v] τῶι ὅρμωι οἰκία ἐπὶ τῶι Φῦς ἐν οἰκίσκῳ (ll.2-4)
185 A.D.	*P.Bon.* 25,9	ἀπὸ κώμης Φῦς
227 A.D.	*CPR* I 64,12	περὶ κώμην Φῦς
II-III A.D.	*P.Köln* II 99,4	Φῦς
IV-V A.D.	*MPER* XV 91,3	Φῦς
IV-V A.D.	*P.Rain.Cent.* 153,9	ἀπὸ Φῦς
late IV/early V A.D. (cf. *BL* 9,368)	*P.Vind.Tand.* 18,34 (*bis*)	Φῦς
about 420/421 A.D.	*MPER* XV 63,25;49	πεδ(ίου) Φῦς (25); ἐπὶ πεδί(ον) Φῦς (49)
V A.D.	*CPR* X 105a,2	ἐποικίου Φῦ[ς
V A.D.	*Stud.Pal.* X 233, col. I B,7	Φῦς
V A.D.	*P.Vind.Sijp.* 9,7	ἐν πεδίῳ Φῦς ἐν κλήρῳ Ψαννέ
VI/VII A.D.	*SB* XX 14705,14 [1]	[ἐν] Φῦ(?)
14 Jan. 653 A.D.	*SB* VIII 9756,1	ἀπὸ χω(ρίου) Φῦς
VII/VIII A.D.	*CPR* IV 2,14	χ(ωρίον) Φ(ῦς) [2]

TOPARCHY: Μέση.

Assigned to the Μέση toparchy in *BGU* XIV 2438 (where it is listed with Phnebieus, Peenbendet(is), Peenpibyk(is), Ποιμένων κώμη, Techymis) Phys recurs with some of the same villages in *BGU* XIV 2433 (Ποιμένων κώμη, Chennis), *P.Köln* II 99 (Phnebieus, Peenpibyk(is), Kerkytos, Thmoinothis), *P.Hels.* I 34 (Techymis). The attribution is confirmed by *CPR* I 64, a παραχώρησις contract recorded in the agoranomos office of the Μέση toparchy at Peenameus between Aurelius Sarapammon (from Herakleopolis but apparently living at Kerkytos) and a woman living at Thmoinothis (cf. *P.Köln* II 99): the woman acquires 9.5 arourae near Phys (in the fossil kleros of Ἄμμων) and a few more near Thmoinothis (in the fossil kleros Ἀριστομάχου).

Phys and Peenpibyk(is) appear once more together in *P.Rain.Cent.* 153,9, which also lists villages of the Koites (Talae, Thmoinpesla, Thneis; Palosis of the northern Oxyrhynchites). In *BGU* XIV 2438 the list

---

[1] Published by PIETER J. SIJPESTEIJN, *Tyche* 5, 1990, pp.171-174.

[2] Φ(ῦς) seems the most likely resolution here; Φ* (*sic*) ed. pr.

of villages of the Μέση toparchy is followed by sections devoted to the περὶ Φέβιχιν), Tilothis and Koma toparchies.

Other documents point to a connection with the περὶ Πόλιν toparchy: *MPER* XV 63 contains a reference to Noeris (l.16; περὶ Πόλιν toparchy); *P.Vind.Sijp.* 9 is a lease contract for land in the plain of Phys (the land-owner is from Herakleopolis); in *P.Bon.* 25 two inhabitants of Phys act as mutual sureties, as they borrow 100 silver drachmae from Nemesianus, ex-γυμνασιάρχης, ἀρχιερεύς at Herakleopolis. *BGU* XVI 2592: oath sworn by a man from Herakleopolis but residing (κατοικῶν) at Phys, concerning timber for house-building.

Possible connection with the Koma toparchy: *BGU* XIV 2439 registers Phys at the end of a document otherwise devoted to the Koma toparchy; *MPER* XV 91 also includes references to the πεδ(ίον) Βουσίρεως (ll.34,37) and to the Herakleides division of the Arsinoite nome; *P.Vind.Tand.* 18 (accounts drawn by Victor, βοηθός at Phys, and Hierax: payments in gold are recorded; one of the payers is from Bousiris, another from Onnes, in the Tekmi toparchy).

P.Hib. I 108: tax on baths paid at the λογευτήριον of Phys.

SB V 8755: corn loan granted to a βασιλικὸς γεωργός from Phys.

BGU XVI 2669: inventory list of various objects «in a room in the house in the port at Phys» (ll.2-4), including a Βῆσις κασσιτερίνη (a tin statue of Bes, l.28).

CPR X 105 is part of a small archive consisting of eight documents concerning a man called Odysseus[1].

CPR IV 2 (a bilingual document in Coptic and Greek) lists many villages of the central toparchies of the Herakleopolite nome (toponyms in Greek)[2].

ΦΥΧΙΤΗΣ

| 20 Feb. 13 B.C. | *BGU* XVI 2582,12;14 | Φυχίτης (12); [Φ]υχίτης (14) |

Declaration of sheep: the owners are from Phebichis and perhaps from nearby Psychis (assuming a scribal error at l.12: Φυχίτης for Ψυχίτης). A derivation from Φυς seems unlikely.

ΦΦ

| V A.D. | *MPER* XV 103,5 | ἀπὸ πεδ(ίου) Φφ |

A kleros belonging to a certain Φοιβάμμων was in this πεδίον. Reference to the πεδίον Μαχόρ (a village assigned to the Koma toparchy in some I B.C. sources) at l.17.

(?) ΧΑΝΑΑΝΑΙΣ

| 17 Jan. 245 B.C.[3] | *P.Petr.* III 43 (2), col. III,30 | τὴν γέφυραν τὴν ἐν Φνέβγει καὶ τὴν ἄγουσαν εἰς Χανααναιν |

---

[1] See BRIGITTE ROM, *ZPE* 56, 1984, pp.103-106.

[2] See *s.v.* ΝΙΝΩ.

[3] See ALAN E. SAMUEL, *Ptolemaic Chronology*, München 1962, p.92.

ETYMOLOGY: a place-name of Jewish origin[1].

This could be a locality in the Polemon division of the Arsinoites[2].

ΧΑΡΑΜΟΥ

| V A.D. | *Stud.Pal.* X 233, col. I B,3 | Χαραμ....ς[3] |
| VII A.D. | *Stud.Pal.* X 22,2 | χ(ωρίον) Χαραμού[4] |

TOPARCHY: περὶ Πόλιν.

ETYMOLOGY: «Etymologisch ist das Wort wohl durch das in einer Glosse des Hesych genannte χαραμός· ἡ τῆς γῆς διάστασις, οἷον χηραμός: "Auseinanderklaffen der Erde, wie Erdspalt" zu fassen»[5].

Stud.Pal. X 22 lists, among other place-names, Sobthis ἡ μικρά and Tokois (both in the περὶ Πόλιν toparchy, according to I B.C. sources). Tokois immediately follows Χαραμ....ς in *Stud.Pal.* X 233, too.

ΧΑΡΜΙ'Κ'( )

| VII/VIII A.D. | *CPR* IV 2,14 | χ(ωρίον) Χαρμι'κ'() |

CPR IV 2 (a bilingual document in Coptic and Greek) lists many villages of the central toparchies of the Herakleopolite nome (toponyms in Greek)[6].

ΧΕΝΝΙΣ

| I B.C. | *BGU* XIV 2433,48 | Χεννi[εω]ς |

---

[1] See A. KASHER, *The Jews in Hellenistic and Roman Egypt*, p.67 n.166.

[2] See *P.Tebt.* II, *Appendix*, pp.359, 409.

[3] My reading (checked on a photograph). Χαραμμειτος Wessely; «vielleicht Χαραμειγεως» Diethart (letter of February 25, 1994).

[4] Λαράμου *ed. pr.*: new reading by Johannes Diethart (letter of September 13, 1994).

[5] JOHANNES DIETHART, *Tyche* 10, 1995, p.239.

[6] See *s.v.* ΝΙΝΩ.

I B.C.	*BGU* XIV 2438,101	Χ̣εννεως¹
17 July 8 B.C.	*BGU* XVI 2594,9	οἱ δέκα τῶν ἀπὸ Χέννεως θηρατ[ ].......οἱ θηρατῶν πάντες(8-9)
I/II A.D.	*P.Hib.* II 218,60	Χέννεως²
VII/VIII A.D.	*CPR* IV 2,13	χ(ωρίον) Χένν'ε'(ως)³

See also: ..NIN.

TOPARCHY: Μέση.

BIBLIOGRAPHY: TIMM, *Das christlich-koptische Ägypten*, vol.I, p.482.

Chennis appears in *BGU* XIV 2433 with villages certainly belonging to the Μέση, like Ποιμένων κώμη and Phys. It is therefore safe to read the same place-name in *BGU* XIV 2438, which assigns it to the Μέση (along with Phnebieus, Peenbendet(is), Peenpibyk(is), Phys, Techymis, Ποιμένων κώμη, etc.), and in *P.Hib.* II 218 (note the immediately preceding entry for Phnebieus).

BGU XVI 2594: sale contract (translated from Egyptian κατὰ τὸν δυνατόν, l.2) : part of a house is apparently being sold by ten men, who are said to be hunters.

CPR IV 2 (a bilingual document in Coptic and Greek) lists many villages of the central toparchies of the Herakleopolite nome (toponyms in Greek)⁴.

ΧΟΙΒΝΩΤΜΙΣ

about 260 B.C.	*P.Hib.* I 112,26;86	Χοιβν[ῶτμις (86)
21 May 247 B.C.	*SB* VIII 9841,3;17	ἐκ Χοινώτβιος (3); ἐκ Χοινώτβιος (17)
about 228 B.C.	*P.Hib.* I 68,3	ἐν Χοιβνώτμει
mid-III B.C.⁵	*P.Fuad Crawford* 5, *recto*,6; *verso*,15	Χοιβνῶτμις (*verso*,15)⁶
mid-III B.C.	*P.Strasb.* IX 802,11	
4 Aug. 13 B.C.	*BGU* XVI 2600,2	μελισσουργοὶ Χοινώ[θ]μεως

---

¹ Χ̣εννεως seems to fit the traces, as suggested in the *ed. pr.* : «Vom ersten Buchstaben sind allerdings nur einige Punkte vorhanden» (Johannes Diethart, letter of September 13, 1994).

² I suggest this reading, which I could not check on a photograph: Χο̣ννεως *ed. pr.*

³ Χεvv'ε' *ed.pr.*

⁴ See *s.v.* ΝΙΝΩ.

⁵ On the re-dating of this document see *Introduction*, p.14 n.7.

⁶ Χ̣οιβ...μις *ed. pr.*

3 July 138 A.D.	*P.Heid.* IV 320,10	εἰς τὸ κατὰ Χ[οι]νῶθμ(ιν) χῶμα
138-161 A.D.	*P.Hib.* II 277,12	ἀπὸ κώμης Χοινώ[θεως(?)
about 165/166 A.D.	*P.Oxy.* LIX 3975,6	ἀπὸ κώμης Χυνώθμεως τοῦ Ἡρακλεοπολείτου νομοῦ
215 A.D.	*P.Oxy.* XII 1463,8	ἀπὸ Χοινώθεως
217 A.D.	*PSI* XII 1229,8	ὀνηλ(άται) κώμης Χοινώθμεως (7-8)
304/305 A.D.	*P.Rain.Cent.* 82,5-6 (= *CPR* I 41)	κωμάρχαις κώμης Χοινώθμεως
V A.D.	*Stud.Pal.* X 8,2	Χοινώθμεως
566 A.D. or later	*P.Oxy.* LV 3805,91	δ(ιὰ) Παλεοῦτος μείζ(ονος) Χοινόθμεως ὑ(πὲρ) τῶν παλαι(ῶν) χωρ(ίων) Σέφθα

TOPARCHY: Koites.

ETYMOLOGY: in the spelling Χοινωτβις (only attested in *SB* VIII 9841, of the III B.C.) the β, coming after -νωτ- (rather than before it, as in the more common spelling Χοιβνωτμις) also assimilates the following μ. In later documents (from the late I B.C. onwards) the β is dropped altogether, and in at least one case (*P.Oxy.* XII 1463), the final μ is also missing; at the same time, a θ replaces the τ of the earlier spellings.

Listed with villages of the Koites in *P.Hib.* I 112, *P.Strasb.* VII 802, *P.Fuad Crawford* 5, *Stud.Pal.* X 8.

BGU XVI 2600: petition from the bee-keepers of Chennis, who claim to have duly paid their taxes seven years before.

P.Heid. IV 320: the two χωμ(ατεπιμεληταί) of the two Κῶίται (i.e. Ἄνω and Κάτω, southern and northern Koites) acknowledge payment of the ναύβιον-tax by twenty inhabitants of Ankyron, for maintenance-work on the dyke near Choinotmis.

P.Hib. I 68: weavers living at Choinotmis are to be paid for the manufacturing of cloths of various kinds (weaving is also attested at nearby Ankyron). Both Choinotmis and Ankyron also recur in *P.Hib.* I 112 and *P.Fuad Crawford* 5.

P.Oxy. LIX 3975 contains the beginning of a sworn declaration by Klemens, skipper of a private riverboat, originating from the village of Choinotmis but residing in Sesphtha in the Oxyrhynchite nome.

P.Oxy. XII 1463: application to the nomarches of Antinoupolis for examination (ἀνάκρισις) of a slave to be sold by the owner (from Choinotmis) to an inhabitant of Oxyrhynchus[1].

P.Rain.Cent. 82: land near Sobthis of the περὶ Πόλιν toparchy, in the fossil kleros of Ptolemaios, is assigned for compulsory cultivation to the villagers of Choinotmis.

---

[1] Connections between this area and the Oxyrhynchite nome and Antinoupolis: see s.v. ΑΓΚΥΡΩΝ ΠΟΛΙΣ.

ΧΟΡΤΑΣΩ

V A.D.	*Stud.Pal.* X 233, col. II,5	Απεριο(υ) (?) καὶ Χορτασω[1]
second half of VI A.D.	P.Berol.inv. 25009,5 [2]	ἐπὶ τὴν Χορτασό
VII A.D.	*SB* VI 9590,4;11;22;*verso*	Χορτασώ (4;11); Χορτασο (22)

Literary Sources

| V A.D. | STEPH. BYZ. s.v. Χορτασώ |

TOPARCHY: Πέραν ?

A place by this name (modern Qartasā: TIMM, *Das christlich-koptische Ägypten*, V, p.2017 f.) is attested in Lower Egypt, between Hermoupolis Parva and Alexandria: cf. *Pauly-Wissowa R.E.*, Bd.III, Kol.2444, *s.v. Chortaso* (Sethe): «Auf der neuerdings zu Madeba in Moab aufgefundenen antiken Mosaiklandkarte ist die Stadt im nordwestlichen Teile des Deltas, nordwestlich von Hermopolis (heute Damanhur) angegeben» (cf. M.-G. LAGRANGE, «La Mosaique géographique de Madeba», *Revue Biblique* 6, 1897, pp.165-184).

ETYMOLOGY: Stephanus of Byzantium offers what may well be a pseudo-Greek etymology from the future of the verb χορτάζω (from χόρτος: hay and other green fodder, used especially to feed horses and cattle): according to his lemma (presumably originating from the *Aegyptiaca* of Alexander Polyhistor) this place-name commemorated the inhabitants' cooperativeness with a queen Cleopatra on the occasion of an unspecified war [3].

SB VI 9590: two arourae which Anatolios (from Herakleopolis) cedes to Pamoûn are apparently split between Makaitonos, Tebetny (Πέραν toparchy) and Chortaso, and situated to the west of the γήδια Ἀπαλά, ἐν κλήρῳ καλουμένῳ Τσάβα. These are ceded in exchange for two arourae near a κώμη (l.12) whose name is lost at the beginning of l.13: note, however, the reference to Noeris at l.22. The two witnesses are from Herakleopolis.

This village already appeared in *Stud.Pal.* X 233, col. II, where it is associated with Απεριο(υ), of uncertain reading and otherwise unknown: the first entry (Ψυχεωνος?) in the same column may refer to Psychis, which was in the Koites; Thmoinepsi (l.14 in the same column) is connected with Noeris (περὶ Πόλιν toparchy), Pois and Peensamoi (Πέραν toparchy) in *Stud.Pal.* X 84.

---

[1] A very uncertain reading; «Απεριο(υ) (?) καὶ Χορτασω durchaus möglich» (Johannes Diethart, letter of February 25, 1994).

[2] This document was published by MARGARET MAEHLER, *GRBS* 17, 1976, pp.197-203 (reference from Peter Van Minnen).

[3] Πόλις Αἰγύπτου. ἀπὸ μέλλοντος ὁ σχηματισμός. ὡς γὰρ τοῦ καλύψω ἡ Καλυψώ οὕτω καὶ τοῦ χορτάσω Χορτασώ. Ἱστοροῦσι («Alexander, ut opinor, in *Aegyptiacis*»: Meineke *ad loc.*) γὰρ Κλεοπάτραν εἰς πόλεμον μὴ ἔχειν σιτία, τοῖς δ' οἰκοῦσι τόν τόπον τοσαύτην παράσχεσθαι τούτου τὴν ἀφθονίαν ὥστε χορτάσαι πᾶσαν τὴν στρατίαν καὶ ὄνομα τῇ πόλει παρ' αὐτῆς ἐντεῦθεν τεθῆναι.

ΧΩΜΑ

1 August 25 B.C.	*BGU* XVI 2590,9	τὸ λεγόμενον Ζανήριος
1 August 25 B.C.	*BGU* XVI 2590,9-10	τὸ λεγόμενον Μεγάλης Ὁδοῦ
1 August 25 B.C.	*BGU* XVI 2590,10	τὸ ἀπὸ λιβὸς το[ῦ .] .ωνίου
3 July 138 A.D.	*P.Heid.* IV 320,10	τὸ κατὰ Χ[οι]γῶθμιν χῶμα

BGU XVI 2590 contains a sworn agreement by the elders of Korphotoi to undertake maintenance work of the three public canals near the village.

P.Heid. IV 320, a receipt for maintenance-work on a dyke near Choinotmis, was issued by Phanias and Atreus, οἱ δύο χωμ(ατεπιμεληταί) Κωιτῶ(ν) δύο: it appears therefore that this canal ran across both Northern and Southern Koites.

ΨΑΝΑΤΙ( )

VII A.D.	*Stud.Pal.* X 214,8	ἐν π(εδίῳ) Ψανατι()
VII-VIII A.D.	*Stud.Pal.* X 206,13	Ψαντι

TOPARCHY: Koites?

Listed as a κλῆρος in *Stud.Pal.* X 206 (with several others: see the *Reverse Index* at the end of this volume), and referred to as a πεδίον in *Stud.Pal.* X 214 (where Peroe appears at the head of the following list of toponyms).

ΨΑΝΝΕ

V A.D.	*P.Vind.Sijp.* 9,8	ἐν πεδίῳ Φῦς ἐν κλήρῳ Ψαννέ
VII/VIII A.D.	*Stud.Pal.* X 217,4	ἐν κλ'ή'(ρῳ) Ψαννέ

TOPARCHY: Μέση.

A kleros in the πεδίον around Phys (Μέση toparchy), according to *P.Vind.Sijp.* 9, Psanne is connected to the village of Daphne in *Stud.Pal.* X 217.

ΨΕΒΘΟΝΕΜΒΗΣ

245 (244) B.C.	*P.Hib.* I 33,7-8	ἐν κώμηι Ψεπθονέμβη τοῦ Κωείτ[ο]υ

CATALOGUE

| III B.C.(?) | P.Fuad Crawford App. II, 66 recto,9 | Ψεβθονέμβης |
| I/II A.D. | P.Hib. II 218,27;30 | Ψεβθονέμβ(ης) |

TOPARCHY: Koites.

ETYMOLOGY: *P3-sbt-n-jnb.t* «the wall of Embes»[1]. The second component of this toponym is also found in the place-name Μουχινεμβης (*q.v.*); on the first component *p3-sbt*, see *s.v.* ΣΩΒΘΙΣ. Cf. also RENATE MÜLLER-WOLLERMANN, «Zur Lokalisierung von Orten in Mittelägypten», *Proceedings of the XIXth International Congress of Papyrology (Cairo 2-9 September 1989)*, Cairo 1992, vol.I, p.716.

MODERN ARABIC NAME: to be identified with Ṣaft alʿUrafā (see *Introduction*, p.11 f.)? Cf. *TAVO* B 69 § 4.3 (M 65), and p.206: «Im Dorf befindet sich ein flacher, ausgedehnter Kōm. In der Nähe der Dorfmoschee liegen ein ca. 2,5 m. langer Säulenschaft aus dunklem Stein, eine Säulenbasis sowie andere Blöcke und Fragmente aus Stein. Die an dieser Stelle des Dorfes befindlichen Keramikscherben sind in Spätantike und arabische Zeit zu datieren».

P.Hib. I 33: a Thracian military settler (Aroimeotes) owns eight sheep at Psebthonembes.

ΨΕΒΘΟΝΠΕΝΟΥΦ(ΙΣ)

| about 260 B.C. | P.Hib. I 112,25 | Ψεβθον(πενούφις)[2] |
| about 138 B.C. | P.Tebt. III 860,21;105 | Ψεβθονπενού(φεως) (21); ἐν Ψεβθον[π]ενούφει (105) |

TOPARCHY: Koites.

ETYMOLOGY: *P3-sbt-n-P3-nfr*, «the wall of Penoufis»[3]. On the first component *p3-sbt*, see *s.v.* ΣΩΒΘΙΣ; the second component is a personal name.

MODERN ARABIC NAME: to be identified with Ṣaft alʿUrafā? Or with Izben Ṣaft? See *Introduction*, p.11 f.

P.Tebt. III 860 records a payment effected on account of a φυλακίτης from Toemesis (l.105); at l.104, Pselemachis is also mentioned (as in *P.Hib.* I 112).

ΨΕΒΧΗΘ[

| about 160 B.C. | P.Hels. I 27,2 |

In the same document: Phys (l.1; Middle toparchy) and Koma.

---

[1] Information from Katelijn Vandorpe.

[2] Ψεβθον(έμβη) was suggested, rather dubitatively, by the Editor: but in *P.Tebt.* III 860 Ψεβθονπενουφ(ις) is attested in conjunction with Pselemachis, which also recurs in *P.Hib.* I 112.

[3] Information from Katelijn Vandorpe (letter of July 18, 1995).

ΨΕΛΕΜΑΧΙΣ

about 260 B.C.	P.Hib. I 112,36	περὶ κώμη[ν Ψελεμάχιν (35-36)
mid-III B.C. [1]	P.Fuad Crawford 5 recto,2; verso,13	Ψελεμαχις (recto,2); Ψελεμαχις (verso,13)
mid-III B.C.	P.Strasb. IX 802,7	
about 138 B.C.	P.Tebt. III 860,104	περὶ Ψελεμάχιν
I B.C.	BGU XIV 2440,18	περὶ Ψελεμάχιν
131 A.D.	P.Oxy. IV 715,24	περὶ Ψελεμάχ(ιν) ἐκ τοῦ Μεγίππου καὶ Ἀρτεμιδώρου κλ(ήρου) γῆς κατοικ[ι]κῆ[ς (24-25)
313/314 A.D.	P.Michael. 28,8	κ]ώμης Ψελεμάχεως
IV A.D.	P.Neph. 11,19;21	ἐν Ψελλεμά[χει (19); εἰς Ψελλεμάχιν (21)
VI A.D.	P.Oxy. XVI 1917,93;94;100;112;114	δ(ιὰ) τῶν πρωτοκ(ωμητῶν) Ψελεμάχεως (93); Ψελεμάχεως (94;100); δι(ὰ) τῶν πρωτοκ(ωμητῶν) Τααμώρου ὑπὲρ τῆς ἀνωρυχθ(είσης) διώρ(υγος) ἐξ ἀπηλιώτου Ψελεμάχεως (111-112); ἀπὸ Ψελεμάχεως (114)

See also: ΦΕΛ'Ε'( ); ΨΩΛΕ[.

TOPARCHY: Koites (XII *pagus*: *P.Michael.* 28).

Listed with villages of the Koites in *P.Hib.* I 112, *P.Strasb.* IX 802, *P.Tebt.* III 860, and *P.Fuad Crawford* 5.

P.Tebt. III 860 (taxation returns and accounts) records a payment effected at Psebthonpenouph(is) on account of a phylakites from Toemesis: Pselemachis appears at l.104, and the connection between these two villages is corroborated by *P.Oxy.* IV 715, an ἀπογραφή addressed to the βιβλιοφύλαξ ἐγκτήσεων (two brothers have inherited part of a house at Toemesis, some catoecic land near Ἰβιὼν Πάχνουβις, in the fossil kleros of Zoilos and Noumenios, and some more land near Pselemachis, in the fossil kleros of Menippos and Artemidoros). The three villages also appear in three consecutive lines in *P.Strasb.* IX 802: Pselemachis (7), Ταχονπαχνουβ (=Ἰβιὼν Πάχνουβις; l.8), Toemesis (9); they are followed by Choinotmis (11), which also recurs in the same document with Pselemachis in *P.Fuad Crawford* 5 and in *P.Hib.* I 112.

P.Neph. 11: a monk of the monastery of (P)hathor writes to the πρεσβύτεροι there, to inform them

---

[1] On the re-dating of this document see *Introduction*, p.14 n.7.

that he has been robbed of his clothes at Pselemachis. A net of Meletian monasteries in the southern Koites (at (P)hathor, Taamorou, Ankyron, Νήσων κώμη, Pselemachis) has been postulated by the Editors of the Nepheros archive[1]. A connection between Pselemachis and Taamorou is suggested in *P.Oxy.* XVI 1917: a canal originating east of Pselemachis apparently reached Taamorou.

Stud.Pal. X 208 *verso*: Pselemachis listed after Phnebieus and Θμοιν( ).

ΨΙΛΙΧΙ

about 111 B.C.　　　*P.Tebt.* III 878,16　　　Ψιλῖχι

TOPARCHY: Tekmi?

The document contains an account of receipts in money. The following villages are also mentioned: Pyrgotos (19; Tekmi toparchy), Bousiris (22) and Toou (46; Koma toparchy). In the lines preceding the entry for Psilichi, reference is made to the ἱερὰ γῆ Ἑρμοῖ (8), which is also attested in the Tekmi and Πέραν toparchies (*BGU* XIV 2437,7-8; 37-38).

ΨΙΝΑΠΕΛΕΥ[2]

mid-III B.C.[3]　　　*P.Fuad Crawford* 5, *recto*,10

TOPARCHY: Koites.

ETYMOLOGY: first component + genitive: *p3-sy-n-* («the lake of»)[4].

The other villages mentioned in the same document belong to the Koites.

ΨΥΧΕΩΝΟΣ[5]

V A.D.　　　*Stud.Pal.* X 233, col. II,1

ΨΥΧΙΣ[6]

about 260 B.C.　　　*P.Hib.* I 112,11;57

---

[1] See *P.Neph., Einleitung*, pp.17-18.

[2] According to the Editor, Φ (instead of Ψ) could also be read at the beginning of this village name.

[3] On the re-dating of this document see *Introduction*, p.14 n.7.

[4] Information from Katelijn Vandorpe.

[5] «Hermann Harrauer schlägt Ψυχεῶνος vor» (letter from Johannes Diethart, February 25, 1994).

[6] The Psychis mentioned in *BGU* VI 1216 (ll.3, 134, 167) is assigned to the Memphite nome in CALDERINI-DARIS, *Dizionario*, s.v. Ψῦχις/2 (where other sources for the Memphite village are also listed); this may well be correct, but it is worth pointing out that this document surveyed cult-places etc. in the Memphite, Aphroditopolite and Herakleopolite nomes.

239 (238) or 214 (213) B.C.	*P.Hib.* I 117,8;10	περὶ Ψῦχιν
mid-III B.C.[1]	*P.Fuad Crawford* V, *recto*,5	Ψῦχις
2 Sept. 162 B.C.	*P.Hels.* I 26 A,19	Ψύχεως
9-10 Oct. 162 B.C.	*P.Hels.* I 19,5	περὶ κώμην Ψῦχιν
161/160 B.C.	*UPZ* I 9,5	ἐν Ψίχει τοῦ Ἡρα[κλεο]πολίτου
160/159 B.C.	*UPZ* I 10,7	περὶ κώμην Ψίχιν τοῦ Ἡρακλεοπολίτου
160 B.C.	*UPZ* I 11,6	π[ερὶ κ]ώμην <Ψίχ>ιν τοῦ Ἡρακλεοπολίτου[2]
29 A.D.(?)	*P.Oxy.* XXXVIII 2842,5	Ψύχ(εως)
I-II A.D.	*P.Hib.* II 272,4	ἀπὸ κώμης Ψύχεως τοῦ κάτωι Κωίτου
I/II A.D.	*SB* XX 14115,3[3]	ἐν Ψύχει
II/III A.D.	*P.Heid.* IV 303, II,2	Ψύχεως
October 210 A.D.	*P.Hamb.* I 17,II,5; III,1	Ψύχεως
beginning of III A.D.	*P.Erl.* 48,20	Ψύχεως[4]
419 A.D.	*P.Oxy.* XVI 1953,2	μέχρι Ψύχεως
V A.D.	*Stud.Pal.* X 233, col. I A,4	Ψύχεως
VII A.D.[5]	*Stud.Pal.* VIII 1309,1	ἀπὸ χ(ωρίου) Ψείχ(εως) Μεγ[ά]λ(ης)
VIII A.D.	*Stud.Pal.* X 204 B,2	χωρί'ο'(ν) Ψύχ'ε(ως)'

TOPARCHY: Koites (northern Koites: *P.Hib.* II 272).

MODERN ARABIC NAME: Absūg.[6]

BIBLIOGRAPHY: AURORA LEONE, «Psychis: un villaggio egiziano dell'Herakleopolites», *Tempo Nuovo* 30, 1985, pp.16-29.

Listed with villages of the Koites in *P.Hib.* I 112, *P.Fuad Crawford* 5, *P.Erl.* 48, *Stud.Pal.* X 233.

---

[1] See above, p.261 n.3.

[2] Cf. *UPZ, Einleitung*, p.145: «Da das Original nicht auffindbar war, konnte Brunet de Presle nur die ihm vorliegende Transkription von Letronne reproduzieren. Auch mir bleibt nichts anderes übrig ...».

[3] A letter from a certain Herakleides to Sarapion, published by PIETER J. SIJPESTEIJN, *Aegyptus* 70, 1990, p.36. There were villages called Psychis in the Herakleopolites, Memphites, Kynopolites and Hermopolites. It may be noted that the personal name Herakleides is especially well attested in the Herakleopolites; Sarapion is also frequent there (see for example *BGU* XIV, Index III, *Personennamen, s.vv.*).

[4] Reading checked on a photograph: Ψύλεως *ed. pr.*; «vielleicht » Ψύχεως *BL* 8,120.

[5] «Quittung wohl aus dem 7. Jh.» (Johannes Diethart, letter of February 25, 1994). Wessely dated it to the VII-VIII A.D.

[6] In *P.Hib.* I 117 Psychis appears to depend administratively on Talae (modern Talā about 4.5 km NW of Absug); the identification was suggested by BERNARD P. GRENFELL - ARTHUR S. HUNT *ad P.Oxy.* 1416,13.

CATALOGUE

UPZ I 9-11: Ptolemaios son of Glaukias, Macedonian by descent, the recluse in the Serapeion at Memphis, originated from Psychis in the Herakleopolites [1].

ΨΩBTON( )

mid-III B.C. *P.Strasb.* IX 802,13 Ψωβτον( ) [2]

ETYMOLOGY: on *P3-sbt* («the wall») see *s.v.* ΣΩΒΘΙΣ.

TOPARCHY: Koites.

Most, if not all, villages listed in *P.Strasb.* IX 802 were in the Koites: Ψωβτον() here might be shortened either for Psebthonembes or Psebthonpenouph(is), both in the Koites.

ΨΩΛΕ[

II-III A.D. [3] *BGU* III 958a Κωίτου ἄνω Ψώλε[

TOPARCHY: southern Koites.

Because the original of this document was burnt, it is impossible to verify the reading of this toponym. One might think of a wrong decipherment for Ψελέ[μαχις], whose connections with the southern Koites are attested.

ΩΤΕΙΡΙΣ

236 A.D.(cf. *BL* 7,259) *Stud.Pal.* XX 47,7 (= *CPR* I 6,7) πε[ρ]ὶ κώμην Ωτειριν

TOPARCHY: "Αγημα.

A παραχώρησις contract drawn up at the agoranomos office of the "Αγημα toparchy, for land situated πε[ρ]ὶ κώμην Ωτειριν, in the fossil kleros of Theodoros. The vendor is from Peenpibyk(is) (Μέση toparchy), the buyer is called an ἀστός (from Alexandria, presumably). This contract was written by the same scribe who recorded *CPR* VI 73 (contract drawn up at the same agoranomos office, between parties from Tekmi and Herakleopolis) [4].

A fossil kleros Θεοδώρου is also mentioned in *Stud.Pal.* XX 29, among the neighbours of some land to be sold near Tosachmis (Koites).

---

[1] See DOROTHY J. THOMPSON, *Memphis under the Ptolemies*, Princeton 1988, pp.213-231.

[2] Ψῶντον *ed. pr.*

[3] On the dating of this papyrus, see *s.v.* ΚΩΙΤΗΣ.

[4] See *s.v.* ΠΕΡΑΦΘΙΣ.

Acephalous Toponyms

[± 3]ΑΓΕΩΣ

I B.C.   *BGU* XIV 2440,48

TOPARCHY: Tekmi.

BGU XIV 2440, ll.41-49, surveys land granted to φυλακῖται, μάχιμοι and ἐφοδοί in the Tekmi toparchy. Euphrates son of Epimachos, who is granted 24 arourae at]αγεως, must have been an ἐφοδός.

..[±3]ΑΙ

VIII A.D.   *Stud.Pal.* X 84,6   χ(ωρίον) ..[±3]αι[1]

...ΑΙΝΕΩΣ

I B.C.   *BGU* XIV 2438,36

TOPARCHY: Μέση.

Comprised in a group of villages of the Μέση toparchy, with Phnebieus, Peenbendet(is), Peenpibyk(is), Phys, Techymis, Ποιμένων κώμη.

[...].ΑΡΑΠΕΩΣ

I B.C.   *BGU* XIV 2437,15

TOPARCHY: Tekmi.

This place-name appears under the main entry Τέκμι· περὶ Αὐλήν (1.12); a reference to Πυργωτός (in the same toparchy) precedes (1.14).

[± 2]ΑΡΕ.ΩΣ

V A.D.   *Stud.Pal.* X 233, col. II,6   Κ.αρμου καὶ
                                                                      [±2]αρε.ως[2]

---

[1]]μι *ed.pr.*; X..[±3]αι («gut möglich; nach der Klammer kein μ») or Ψ[...]αι («es kann sich aber nach der Art der Unterlänge um den unteren Rest eines μ, ρ oder φ handeln») Johannes Diethart (letters of February 25 and September 13, 1994).

[2] «Κ.αρμου schlägt H. Harrauer vor» (letter from Johannes Diethart, February 25, 1994). What follows looks like καὶ

[±4]ẠT

VII-VIII A.D.   *Stud.Pal.* X 206,7

Apparently the name of a κλῆρος, listed with several others (see the *Reverse Index* at the end of this volume).

[...]ΑΤΜΥ[

223 A.D.   *P.Ross.Georg.* V 20 *verso*, col. II,6

Included in a list of villages with Thmoinache (Techtho toparchy) and Phebichis (Koites).

[.]Ε[..]ΒΕΩΣ

I B.C.   *BGU* XIV 2433,51

TOPARCHY: Μέση.

Listed in a group of villages belonging to the Μέση toparchy, among them Phys (l.49).

[.]Ẹ[.]Λ[

VII-VIII A.D.   *Stud.Pal.* X 206,4

Apparently the name of a κλῆρος, listed with several others (see the *Reverse Index* at the end of this volume).

..ΕṆΕ( ) ΜΕΓΑΛΗΣ

V A.D.   *Stud.Pal.* X 233, col. I A,6

[±4]ΕΤΑ

VII-VIII A.D.   *Stud.Pal.* X 206,6

Apparently the name of a κλῆρος, listed with several others (see the *Reverse Index* at the end of this volume).

---

to me (cf. Απεριο(υ) καὶ Χορτασω in the preceding line); after this, [..]αρε.ως, as in the *ed. pr.*

[...]ΘΕ.. [Μ]ΙΚΡ( )

V A.D.   Stud.Pal. X 233, col. II,13

[± 5].ΙΝΩ

V A.D.   Stud.Pal. X 94,4 [1]

Cf. Νινω.

[.]..ΚΑΚ...[....]Ν

14/13 B.C.   BGU XVI 2581,6   ἀπὸ [.]..κακ...[....]ν (cf. περ[ὶ] τὴν κ[ώμη]ν: ll.15-16)

Declaration of sheep and goats.

..ΚΕΝΗ

III A.D.   BGU III 927,2   κώ]μης ..κενη

....ΛΣΙΟΥ

I B.C.   BGU XIV 2440,97

TOPARCHY: Techtho Nesos.

Thelbonthis and Thmoin(ache), in the Techtho Nesos toparchy, are apparently subordinated to ....λσιου: after a blank space, an entry for Olonthis follows.

.( ) Μ(Ε)'Γ(ΑΛΗ?)'

VII A.D.   Stud.Pal. X 231,2

TOPARCHY: Koites?

---

[1] [ ]χω ed. pr.: new reading by Johannes Diethart (letter of September 13, 1994).

Thelbo (Koites) is listed at l.1. In the Herakleopolites, we know of a Φέβιχις ἡ μεγάλη, a Σῶβθις ἡ μεγάλη, and a Παπα ἡ μεγάλη.

.ΜΕΙΑ

V A.D.   *P.Oxy.* VIII 1126,9   γίτονες νώτου τον ἀπὸ
Τάλη λιβὸς λιδης Κήτς,
ἀπη{λ}λιώτου λιδης
.μεια (7-9)

See *s.v.* ΚΗΤΣ.

[...] ΝΕΑ

VI-VII A.D.   *Stud.Pal.* III 25,1   ἀπὸ κώμης ...] Νέας τοῦ
Ἡρ(ακλεο)π(ολίτου)
νομοῦ

[± 8]ΝΕΑΣ[[1]

309 A.D.   *P.Hib.* II 219,10

TOPARCHY: Koites.

Assessment of linen-pieces to be produced by the λινοῦφοι of Ankyron (ll.4, 12), also on account of other villages, including Techtho (l.13).

..ΝΙΝ

I B.C.   *BGU* XIV 2434,27   περὶ ..νιν

See also *s.v.* ΧΕΝΝΙΣ

Χέννιν might be a possible reading (note the reference to περὶ Φ<νε>βιέα in the following line).

---

[1] «Or]νηας. Perhaps there is nothing lost after the ς» (Ed. *ad loc.*).

[±5]ΝΟΣ

313-314 A.D   P.Michael. 28,7   [κωμάρχοις
                                               ±5]νος¹

TOPARCHY: Koites (XII *pagus*).

The document is a contract of hire between a ναύτης and the κωμάρχαι of seven villages in the 12th *pagus*², including Papa, Pselemachis, Thelbo, Philonikou (all of them belonging to the Koites).

[± 8]ΟΥΝΕΩΣ

309 A.D.   P.Hib. II 219,15

Assessment of linen-pieces to be produced by the λινούφοι of Ankyron (ll.4, 12) also on account of other villages (including Techtho l.13). [Θμοιαμ]ούνεως could be an attractive supplement, but this was a village in the Koma toparchy, whereas this document apparently deals with villages of the southern Herakleopolites.

.ΠΕΙ.'Α'

VII-VIII A.D.   Stud.Pal. X 206,5

Apparently the name of a κλῆρος, listed with several others (see the *Reverse Index* at the end of this volume).

].ΠΕΤΕΧΩΝ

I B.C.   BGU XIV 2437 (fr.5),74

The supplement Τερτο]υπετεχων is tempting, but «it is impossible to say what the trace before the initial *pi* in -πετεχων might be. It is too ambiguous»³.

.Ρ..ΑΤΟΥ

I B.C.   BGU XIV 2438,34   .ρ..ατου

---

¹ [κωμάρχοις κώμης .]ωνος *ed. pr.* (on the analogy of ll.3 and 9 in the same document, but leaving little room to supply a village-name here). «Man könnte .]ωνος zu Ἀγκυρ]ῶνος ergänzen» (cf. *P.Neph., Einleitung*, p.129 n.4). I can detect no trace of ω on the photograph I have checked.

² Cf. B. R. REES, *CR* 70, 1956, p.235.

³ Letter from William M. Brashear (November 10, 1995).

See also *s.v.* ΚΕΡΚΥΤΟΣ[1].

TOPARCHY: Μέση.

Included in a list of villages of the Μέση toparchy (mentioning Phys, Phnebieus, Peenpibyk(is) and other localities).

[.....]ΡΕΩΣ

191 A.D.   *P.Mert.* II 78,3   ἀπὸ κώ[μης .....]ρεως

TOPARCHY: περὶ Πόλιν?

Two persons ἀπὸ κώ[μης .....]ρεως borrow 600 drachmae from the ex-*gymnasiarches* of Herakleopolis [2].

(?) [....]ΣΕΙ

224/225 A.D.   *SB* XVI 12836,12 (= *CPR* I 243)   ἀπὸ ἐδαφ[ῶν τῆς] προκιμένης [ο]ὐσίας π[ερὶ(?)....]σει ἐκ τοῦ Μενελάου κλήρου[3]

.[.]ΤΑΕΩΣ

I B.C.   *BGU* XIV 2370 (fr.2),94

Reference to Bousiris at l.92.

[±4]ΤΙΟΜ

VII-VIII A.D.   *Stud.Pal.* X 206,10

Apparently the name of a κλῆρος, listed with several others (see the *Reverse Index* at the end of this volume).

---

[1] .ρ..ατου *ed. pr.* Κερκύτου might perhaps fit the traces (reading checked by me on a photograph, and by William Brashear on the original).

[2] Another document of the same kind (two years later): *Stud.Pal.* XX 16.

[3] π[.......]σει *ed. pr.* The οὐσία in question is the Μεσσαλινιανὴ οὐσία. «Vielleicht handelt es sich um eine nähere geographische Bestimmung» (Ed. *ad ll.*11-12).

[.]Υ[

VIII A.D. *Stud.Pal.* X 72,1 χ(ωρίον) [.]υ[[1]

[± 8]ΥΨΗ[..]Ν( )

309 A.D. *P.Hib.* II 219,9

TOPARCHY: Koites.

Assessment of linen-pieces to be produced by the λινοῦφοι of Ankyron (ll.4, 12), also on account of other villages (including Techtho, l.13).

.ΦΗΕΩΣ

I B.C. *BGU* XIV 2435,19

TOPARCHY: Koites.

BGU XIV 2435 is part of a land-survey concerning villages in the Koites, as shown by the entries for Phebichis(l.1) and Talae (l.25).

[± 8]ΧΕΩΣ

309 A.D. *P.Hib.* II 219,7

Assessment of linen-pieces to be produced by the λινοῦφοι of Ankyron (ll.4, 12), also on account of other villages (including Techtho, l.13). [Φεβί]χεως seems the most likely supplement here.

[....].ΧΟΣ

200 A.D. *P.Oxy.* VI 899,23

περὶ τε κώμην
Βουσεῖρ[ι]ν καὶ
Θιντῆριν καὶ Τα..
[....].χος κώμας (22-23)

The document refers to land cultivated by the same person περί τε κώμην Βουσεῖρ[ι]ν καὶ Θιντῆριν καὶ Τα.. [....].χος κώμας.

---

[1] The Editor offers the supplement [Ο]υ[, for no apparent reason.

[...].Ω

IV/V A.D.   *P.Rain.Cent.* 153,13   ἀπὸ [...].ω

TOPARCHY: Koites? Μέση?

The other villages listed in this document were either in the Koites (Talae, Thmoinpesla, Thneis) or in the Μέση (Phys, Peenpibykis). Palosis (in the Oxyrhynchite nome, near the border with the Herakleopolites) is also mentioned.

2 Fossil Kleroi[1]

The names of the first Graeco-Macedonian settlers in the Egyptian χώρα stayed as topographical indications in the records of the Graeco-Roman administration, long after their bearers had given up the land they had been granted. I shall refer to these as *fossil kleroi*. The officials in charge of the survey and re-distribution of land (an on-going process) obviously found it convenient to refer back to the first mapping of the newly conquered land by the Ptolemaic administrators. The final disappearance of fossil kleroi must have coincided with the re-organisation of the χώρα into *pagi*, at the beginning of the IV A.D.[2].

Fossil Kleros	Location	Source	Date
Α.νευδ()	Talae	BGU XIV 2435,25	I B.C.
Ἀγαθ..()	Koma toparchy	BGU XVI 2563,6	8/7 B.C.
Ἀγαθοκλέους	Pyrgotos	BGU XIV 2441,98;104; 109;122;213; 241	I B.C.
		BGU XIV 2443,29	I B.C.
		BGU XIV 2447,39	I B.C.
		BGU XIV 2448,45;58	I B.C.
		BGU III 922,8	286 A.D.
Ἀγαθοκ(λέους) Ταυρω()	Techymis	P.Oxy. XLIV 3168,9	late II A.D.
Ἀγάθωνος	Kerkes(ephis)	BGU XIV 2435,40	I B.C.
Ἀγελάου (= Ἀπικκίου)	Phnebieus	BGU VIII 1828,9	52/51 B.C.
	Ogou	BGU XVI 2665,4	28/27 B.C.

---

[1] Only fossil kleroi certainly located in the Herakleopolites are included in this list; villages referred to under the heading **Location** are those mentioned in the source in which the kleros also appears. Cf. also F. ZUCKER, *Beobachtungen zu den permanenten Klerosnamen, Festschrift Oertel,* (cited on p.180 n.1), pp.101-106.

[2] Byzantine documents also refer to κλῆροι: these, however, are usually no *fossil* kleroi: see the list of *Other Kleroi in the Herakleopolite Nome* (below, p.289).

Ἀλεξάνδρου	Tilothis	**BGU** VIII 1734,7	I B.C.
	Pyrgotos, Kollinpetou[1]	**BGU** XIV 2441,78;84;118;132	I B.C.
		BGU XIV 2447,63	I B.C.
		BGU XIV 2448,59	I B.C.
Ἀλκίμου	Phebichis	**BGU** XIV 2435,10	I B.C.
Ἄμμωνος[2]	Phys	**CPR** I 64,12	227 A.D.
Ἀμύντα	Phys	**BGU** XIV 2438,40	I B.C.
Ἀνδρονίκου	Sobthis, Temenkyrkis	**BGU** XIV 2443,32[3]	I B.C.
		P.Köln II 98,24[4]	II A.D.
Ἀνικήτου		**BGU** XIV 2444,119;135	I B.C.
		BGU XIV 2445, 19;38	I B.C.
Ἀντιπάτρου	Peensemtheus	**BGU** XIV 2444,26;41;43;44;68 70;78;95;100	I B.C.
		BGU XIV 2445,25	I B.C.
Ἀπολλ'ω'()	Peensamoi	**BGU** XVI 2565,7	3/2 B.C.
Ἀπολλοδώρου	Koma	**BGU** XVI 2570,9	8/7 B.C.
Ἀπολλωνίου Μέλανος	Nokle, Thelbo, Koma, Machor, Philonikou	**P.Ryl.** II 225,32	II-III A.D.
Ἀπο]λλωνίου καὶ Στοτοήτιος	Thmoinache	**CPR** I 115+ +145,20	II A.D.

---

[1] The land assigned to Apollonios and Herak() is split between Pyrgotos (about one aroura in the fossil kleros of Φιλώτας) and Kollinpetou (5+ arourae), plus some land ἐν περιμέτρῳ Ἀλεξάνδρου (further located by reference to a Διονυσῖον, possibly the same as in *BGU* XIV 2440,74).

[2] Παραχώρησις contract: the land being ceded was split between Phys and Thmoinothis (in the fossil kleros of Ἀριστόμαχος).

[3] Ἀνδ.νι.() *ed.pr.*

[4] Spelt Ἀνδρονείκου in this document.

Ἀπολλωνίου	Bousiris	**BGU** XVI 2662,14	about 7-4 B.C.
		P.Hib. II 282,21 [1]	I/II A.D.
	Tosachmis	**Stud.Pal.** XX 29,18	227 A.D.
Ἀργαίου	Herakleopolis	**PSI** XIII 1325,29	176-180 A.D.
Σοφοκλέους καὶ Ἀρείου	Pyrgotos	**BGU** XIV 2441,82;155; 158;165;219; 246	I B.C.
Ἀρ...	Pyrgotos	**BGU** XIV 2441,46	I B.C.
Ἀριστοδήμου	See: Μενοίτου		
Ἀριστομάχου	Thmoinothis	**CPR** I 64,15 [3]	227 A.D.
	Των (ι κοίτη) [2]	**P.Rain.Cent.** 154,10 [4]	IV/V A.D. [5]
Ἀριστονείκου	Herakleopolis	**BGU** III 929 B 3	II/III A.D.
Ἀρομβ()	Techymis	**P.Oxy.** XLIV 3168,13	late II A.D.
Μενίππου καὶ Ἀρτεμιδώρου	Toemesis Pselemachis	**P.Oxy.** IV 715,24-25	131 A.D.
Ἀρχεπόλεως	Pyrgotos	**BGU** XIV 2441,20;42;50;56;66 83;106;129;218;230 248	I B.C.
Ἀσάνδρου	Pyrgotos	**BGU** XIV 2441,68;176;222	I B.C.
		BGU XIV 2447,40;53	I B.C.
Ἀσκλ()	Kerkes(ephis)	**BGU** XIV 2435,39	I B.C.

---

[1] The papyrus reads τοῦ Ἀμέως το(ῦ) Ἀπολλωνίου κλ(ήρου).

[2] A κοίτη was «a topographical section in which the land was divided, especially for purposes of ἐπίσκεψις» (*P.Oxy.* XXXVIII 2847,col.II,18 n.).

[3] Ἀριστ[...]α[.]ος *ed.pr.* This is a παραχώρησις contract, also concerning land near Phys (see above *s.v.* Ἄμμωνος).

[4] *P. Rain. Cent.* 154 records land belonging to Sarapion, son of Serenus, previously ἄρξας [Ἀν]τι(νόου) πόλεως, but presently πράκτωρ Τωου: one may wonder whether this place should rather be located in the Hermopolites, but the spelling differs from Τοου, which is in fact attested there (see DREW-BEAR, *Le nome Hermopolite, s.v.*). Besides, two of the fossil kleroi out of which Sarapion's land is made up are attested for the Herakleopolites (Ἀριστομάχου, Ἀσκληπιάδου).

[5] This dating seems to be in contrast with the reference to several fossil kleroi, as these were as a rule no longer referred to in documents later than the creation of the *pagi*.

Ἀσκληπιάδου[1]		**BGU** XIV 2449,58;64;87	I B.C.
	Των α κοίτη	**P.Rain.Cent.** 154,4 [2]	IV/V A.D.
Βακχίου		**BGU** XIV 2444,5	I B.C.
Βαλλήρου	Assya	**BGU** XIV 2435,29	I B.C.
Βίωνος	Peenameus	**CPR** I 111,4	II A.D.
	Τωλλ[.]	**CPR** I 156,2	III A.D. (first half)
Βοήθου	Ἄγημα	**BGU** XVI 2572,4	6/5 B.C.
Γλε[	Herakleopolis	**PSI** XIII 1325,28	176-180 A.D.
Δαλίσκου		**BGU** XIV 2441,11,17	I B.C.
		BGU XIV 2442,14	I B.C.
		BGU XIV 2443,41;53	I B.C.
		BGU XIV 2448,63	I B.C.
Δερ()	Kerkesephis	**BGU** XIV 2435,43	I B.C.
Δημ()	Phebichis	**BGU** XIV 2435,3	I B.C.
Δημητρίου	Κωμα	**BGU** IV 1193,7	8 B.C.
	Herakleopolis	**BGU** VIII 1732,5	I B.C.
	Herakleopolis	**BGU** VIII 1856,2	I B.C.
	Herakleopolis	**BGU** VIII 1872,19	51/50 B.C.
Δ]ημοστρ()	Herakleopolis	**PSI** XIII 1325,31	176-180 A.D.
Δι...		**BGU** XIV 2445,20	I B.C.
Διδ()		**BGU** XIV 2445,14	I B.C.
Διοδώρου	Ἄγημα	**BGU** XVI 2562,7	8/7 B.C.
Διον()	.φηεως	**BGU** XIV 2435,24	I B.C.
Διονυσίου τοῦ Σαραπίωνος	Sinary	**PSI** VIII 897,68	93 A.D.

---

[1] A fossil kleros Ἀσκληπιάδου is also attested in the neighbouring Polemon division of the Arsinoites: *P.Mil.Vogl.* II 87,9; 88,9 (150/151 A.D.).

[2] See above, p.275 n.4.

Δωριέως	Peensemtheus	**BGU** XIV 2444,14;77;98;101	I B.C.
		BGU XIV 2445,28	I B.C.
Δωρίονος	Tekmi	**CPR** I 90,12 (cf. **BL** 1,452)	III A.D.
Ε[	Pyrgotos	**BGU** XIV 2441,108	I B.C.
Ἐμπεδοκλέους	Pyrgotos	**BGU** XIV 2441,105;114;120; 236;243;250	I B.C.
		BGU XIV 2447,20;49;55	I B.C.
Επιαραλ.[	Koma	**BGU** XVI 2569,2	3 B.C.
Ἐπιφανίου	Toou	**BGU** XVI 2560,10	8/7 B.C.
Ἐπιχάρο(υς)	Techymis	**P.Oxy.** XLIV 3168,37	late II A.D.
Ἑρμώνακτος	Τωυ [1] (ζ κοίτη)	**P.Rain.Cent.** 154,7	IV/V A.D.
Ἕρμωνος	Tilothis	**BGU** VIII 1796,8	I B.C.
Εὐ..()	Ἄγημα	**SB** V 7611,14;15 (cf. *BL* 7,195)	50/49 B.C.
Εὐάνδρου	Krekis	**BGU** XIV 2439,22	I B.C.
Εὐβίου	Techymis	**P.Oxy.** XLIV 3168,9	late II A.D.
Εὐδόξου	Peenepochra	**BGU** XIV 2440,122	I B.C.
Εὐμήλου	Sobthis/ Herakleopolis	**BGU** XIV 2376,19;39	I B.C.
	Sobthis/ Herakleopolis	**BGU** XIV 2377,45	I B.C.
	Pyrgotos	**BGU** XIV 2441,83	I B.C.
	Σ.ου	**BGU** XIV 2444,13;17;64;113	I B.C.
		BGU XIV 2445,30	I B.C.
Εὐπολέμου	Τωυ [2] (θ κοίτη)	**P.Rain.Cent.** 154,9	IV/V A.D.

---

[1] See above, p.275 n.4.

[2] See above, p.275 n.4.

Εὐτίμου	Pyrgotos	**BGU** XVI 2441,105;124; 126;131	I B.C.
		BGU XIV 2447,18	I B.C.
Εὐτύχωνος	Peensemtheus	**BGU** XIV 2444,137	I B.C.
Εὐφράνορο[ς		**P.Strasb.** VIII 782,5 [1]	II B.C.
Εὔφρονος		**P.Strasb.** VIII 782,8 [2]	II B.C.
Ζωίλου		**BGU** XIV 2450,28;80;82	I B.C.
	Machor	**BGU** IV 1104,30 [3]	8 B.C.
Ζωίλου καὶ Νουμηνίου	Ἰβιὼν Πάχνουβις	**P.Oxy.** IV 715,21-23	131 A.D.
Ἡγησίνου		**BGU** XIV 2442,6	I B.C.
Ἡγησιδήμου		**BGU** XIV 2441,18	I B.C.
		BGU XIV 2443,16;42	I B.C.
Ἡγησίππου		**BGU** XIV 2441,10	I B.C.
Ἡγησιστράτου	Τωυ [4] (ϛ κοίτη)	**P.Rain.Cent.** 154,6	IV/V A.D.
Ἡλιο[		**BGU** XVI 2575,5	6/5 B.C.
Ἡλιοδώρου	Tosachmis	**Stud.Pal.** XX 29,24	227 A.D.
Ἡρακλείδου	Τωυ [5] (η κοίτη)	**P.Rain.Cent.** 154,8	IV/V A.D.
Ἡρακλείδου α[	Τωυ [6] (ε κοίτη)	**P.Rain.Cent.** 154,5	IV/V A.D.
Ἡρακλείου	Techtho	**BGU** XVI 2662,13	about 7-4 B.C.

---

[1] This Strasbourg papyrus from cartonnage may well originate from the Herakleopolites (see *Introduction*, p.14); no certainly Herakleopolite place-name recurs in this document, but a kleros Νικοστράτου (as in l.3: see *s.v.*) is attested in the Herakleopolite nome.

[2] See preceding note.

[3] [Ζ]ωίλ(ου) *ed.pr.*

[4] See above, p.275 n.4.

[5] See above, p.275 n.4.

[6] See above, p.275 n.4.

Ἡρακλ[....] τοῦ Κίσσου[1]	Πέραν	**BGU** VIII 1805,5	I B.C.
Ἡρακλέους τοῦ Καλλιστράτου	Sinary	**PSI** VIII 897,65-66	93 A.D.
	Sinary	**P.Oxy.** II 348 descr.[2]	late I A.D.
		P.Oxy. XLVII 3365,34[3]	after May 22, 241 A.D.
Θ[		**BGU** XIV 2447,9	I B.C.
Θεο[		**BGU** XIV 2448,35	I B.C.
Θεο.....		**BGU** XIV 2450,40	I B.C.
Θεογένους	Σ.ου	**BGU** XIV 2446,8;17	I B.C.
		BGU XIV 2449,5	I B.C.
		BGU XIV 2450,24;30;49	I B.C.
Θεοδμ[ήτου]	Taemsis, Tanaso, Taboklis, Ἄγημα	**Stud.Pal.** XX 26,32	222 A.D.
Θεοδωρίδου Ἀγήνορος[4]	Toou	**BGU** XVI 2560,10	8/7 B.C.
Θεοδώρου	Tosachmis	**Stud.Pal.** XX 29,20-21	227 A.D.
	Oteiris	**Stud.Pal.** XX 47,7	236 A.D. (cf. *BL* 7,259)
Ἱεροξένου	Machor	**BGU** IV 1167,50;74	12 B.C.
Ἱππονίκου τοῦ Πρωτεσιλάου	Pois	**BGU** VIII 1772,11;16[5]	57/56 B.C.
Κ[		**BGU** XIV 2448,50	I B.C.

---

[1] «Die Erg. Ἡρακλέους paßt zum Raume besser als Ἡρακλείδου», Edd. *ad loc.*: Ἡρακλ[είου] would fit the space equally well.

[2] «...payment of the tax upon the mortgage ... of catoecic land near Psobthis ... and of other land near Σιναχ in the κλῆροι of Herakles and Callistratus...»: there is little doubt that Σιναρυ, not Σιναχ, is to be read here.

[3] Other kleroi are mentioned, all of them in the Northern toparchy of the Oxyrhynchite nome.

[4] Some arourae located within the limits of this fossil kleros are «put down» to a certain Epiphanius: ὑποτε(θεμένας) Ἐπιφανίου.

[5] Ἱππονίκου τοῦ Πρωτεσιλ[ά]ου τοῦ Πρωτεσιλάου [ἱπ]πικὸ[ν κλῆ]ρον (l.16).

Καλλιάδου	Nokle, Thelbo, Koma, Machor, Philonikou	**P.Ryl.** II 225,35	II-III A.D.
Καλλινίκου	Herakleopolis	**P.Flor.** III 385,25	II-III A.D.
Καλλίππου	Kerkesephis	**BGU** XIV 2435,47	I B.C.
		BGU XIV 2450,46	I B.C.
Καλλίστου		**BGU** XIV 2449,131	I B.C.
Καλλιστράτου	Phnebieus (l.100)	**P.Tebt.** III 890,191	II B.C.
Κασσάνδρου	Herakleopolis	**P.Tebt.** III 827,19	about 170 B.C.
[Κ]άστορος	Peensamoi	**BGU** XVI 2565,8	3/2 B.C.
Κιλλέους (or: Κιαλέους)		**BGU** XIV 2449,106	I B.C.
Κλε.()	Pyrgotos	**BGU** XIV 2441,56	I B.C.
Κλεάνορος	Kollintaathyr	**CPR** I 156,3	III A.D. (first half)
Κλειτάρχ[ου	Techymis	**P.Oxy.** XLIV 3168,35	late II A.D.
Κλεοδήμου	Phebichis	**BGU** XIV 2435,6;8	I B.C.
Κλεοκράτους	Peensemtheus	**BGU** XIV 2444,13;56	I B.C.
Κλεομαντρίδου		**BGU** XIV 2443,20	I B.C.
Κλεοξένου		**BGU** XIV 2449,70	I B.C.
Κλέωνος	Sobthis Temenkyrkis	**P.Köln** II 98,9	II A.D.
Κοινοῦ		**BGU** XIV 2444,2	I B.C.
Κορράγου	Pyrgotos	**BGU** XIV 2441,87;106; 130;190;199; 225;233;235	I B.C.
		BGU XIV 2447,18;59	I B.C.
		BGU XIV 2450,39	I B.C.
Κυδρέως [1]	Herakleopolis	**PSI** XIII 1325,14;30	176-180 A.D.
Λα[		**BGU** XIV 2448,51	I B.C.
Λαβοῦτος		**BGU** XIV 2441,9	I B.C.

---

[1] A fossil kleros Κυδρέους is attested near Tholthis, in the Northern toparchy of the Oxyrhynchites: cf. PAOLA PRUNETI, «I ΚΛΗΡΟΙ del nomo Ossirinchite», *Aegyptus* 55, 1975, pp.186-187.

Λακύδους		**BGU** XIV 2443,24;35;37;43	I B.C.
		BGU XIV 2447,31	I B.C.
Λαομέδοντος	Pois	**P.Select** 17,10-11	mid-III A.D.
Λαομήδους	Peensemtheus	**BGU** XIV 2444,71	I B.C.
		BGU XIV 2445,4	I B.C
Λεωνίδου		**BGU** XIV 2445,34	I B.C.
Λιβυ[	Ko?	**P.Flor.** I 23,8-9	145 A.D.
Λογγίνου		**BGU** III 741,22	143/144 A.D.
Μ...ειδου		**BGU** XV 2447,64	I B.C.
Μαχαίτου	Kalates	**CPR** I 247,7	346 A.D.
Μελανθίου		**P.Hels.** I 31,6;10 [1]	160 B.C.
Μέλανος	Phebichis	**BGU** XIV 2435,11;15	I B.C.
Μενδ()	Pyrgotos	**BGU** XIV 2441,232	I B.C.
Μενελάου	Herakleopolis	**P.Tebt.** III 827,15	about 170 B.C.
	Ankyron (Μεσσαλινιανὴ οὐσία)	**P.Ryl.** II 87,3	III A.D.
	Ankyron (Μεσσαλινιανὴ οὐσία)	SB XVI 12836,12	224/225 A.D.
Μενίππου	See: Ἀρτεμιδώρου		
Μενοίτου τοῦ Ἀριστοδήμου	Peensemtheus	**BGU** XIV 2444,30;57;79;139	I B.C.
		BGU XIV 2445,15	I B.C.
		BGU XIV 2447,42	I B.C.
Μένω(νος)	Techymis	**P.Oxy.** XLIV 3168,46	late II A.D.
Μη()		**BGU** XIV 2441,14	I B.C.
Μι()		**BGU** XIV 2441,15	I B.C.
Μοσχίω(νος)		**P.Oxy.** XLIV 3168,34;47	late II A.D.

---

[1] Other papyri from the same cartonnage point to a Herakleopolite origin (see *Introduction*, p.18).

Νέωνος	Peensemtheus	**BGU** XIV 2444,11;12;76;94	I B.C.
		BGU XIV 2445,31	I B.C.
Νικαίου	Pyrgotos	**BGU** XIV 2441,93;109; 119;204;221; 227;247;249; 255	I B.C.
		BGU XIV 2442,18	I B.C.
Νικάνορος	Tilothis	**BGU** VIII 1734,5	I B.C.
	Sobthis Temenkyrkis	**P.Köln** II 98,22	II A.D.
Νικίου καὶ Πτολεμαίου καὶ ἄλλων	Tebetny	**Stud.Pal.** XX 34,16-17	232/233 A.D.
Νικολάου		**BGU** XIV 2449,15;45;53;55;57 127;165	I B.C.
Νικομάχου		**BGU** XIV 2449,138	I B.C.
Νικοστράτου		**P.Strasb.** VIII 782,3 [1]	II B.C.
	.φηεως; Assya	**BGU** XIV 2435,20;28	I B.C.
Νικοφῶντος	Peensemtheus	**BGU** XIV 2444,15;57;95; 99;102	I B.C.
Νουμηνίου	see: Ζωίλου		
Ξενοφῶντος	Tekmi	**Stud.Pal.** XX 25,13	218 A.D.
Ξένωνος	Sinary	**P.Oxy.** IV 810 *descr.*	134/135 A.D.
	Sinary	**P.Oxy.** XIV 1751 *descr., recto*	IV A.D. *in.*
Πα()	Phebichis	**BGU** XIV 2435,12	I B.C.

---

[1] See above, p.278 n.1.

Παγκράτου	Peensemtheus	**BGU** XIV 2444,34;53;98;107;108	I B.C.
		BGU XIV 2445,1;5;10;33	I B.C.
	Thmoinache	**CPR** I 115+145,21	II A.D.
Παμφίλου	Sobthis Temenkyrkis	**P.Köln** II 98,16;25	II A.D.
Πανίσκου	Peensemtheus	**BGU** XIV 2444,69	I B.C.
Πάρι(δος)	Techymis	**P.Oxy.** XLIV 3168,21	late II A.D.
Παρμε()		**BGU** XIV 2445,38	I B.C.
Παρμε()	Techymis	**P.Oxy.** XLIV 3168,17	late II A.D.
Παρμενίσκου	Peensemtheus	**BGU** XIV 2444,111	I B.C.
Παρμενίωνος	Nokle, Thelbo, Koma, Machor, Philonikou	**P.Ryl.** II 225,31	late II or III A.D.
Παρμένοντος	Peensemtheus	**BGU** XIV 2444,17;75	I B.C.
		BGU XIV 2445,41	I B.C.
Πασ[.......	Peenameus	**SB** I 4370,21	228/229 A.D.
Πολέμωνος καὶ Περιγένου	Tilothis	**BGU** VIII 1734,6	I B.C.
Περικλέους[1]		**P.Strasb.** VIII 782,7 [2]	II B.C.
Περίτου	Kerkesephis	**BGU** XIV 2435,36;37	I B.C.
Πλ..()	Pyrgotos	**BGU** XIV 2441,101	I B.C.
Πολεμάρχου	Peensemtheus	**BGU** XIV 2444,23	I B.C.
Πολέμωνος καὶ Περιγένου	see: Περιγένου		
Πολέμωνος	Σ.ου	**BGU** XIV 2446,5	I B.C.
		BGU XIV 2449,31;42;75;132	I B.C.

---

[1] «La lecture Περικλέους (plus rare) l'emporte sur Περιγένους» (Ed. *ad loc.*).

[2] See above, p.278 n.1..

Πολυδάμαντος	Peensemtheus	**BGU** XIV 2444,10;16;18;20;27	I B.C.
Πολυκ()	Techymis	**P.Oxy.** XLIV 3168,8;24	late III A.D.
Πολυνίκου	Kerkesephis	**BGU** XIV 2435,31;35	I B.C.
Πρωτογένους	Pyrgotos	**BGU** XIV 2441,33;44;85	I B.C.
		BGU XIV 2442,4	I B.C.
		BGU XIV 2445,18;35;39	I B.C.
Πρωτολάου		**BGU** XIV 2443,29	I B.C.
Πρῶτος	Tokois	**CPR** I 40,9	300 A.D.
Πτολ() Μενεβούλ(ου)	Techymis	**P.Oxy.** XLIV 3168,12	late II A.D.
Πτολ() Μιθ()	Techymis	**P.Oxy.** XLIV 3168,29	late II A.D.
Πτολεμαίου	Pyrgotos	**BGU** XIV 2441,125;198;258	I B.C.
		BGU XIV 2447,18	I B.C.
	Απρηλ()	**BGU** XIV 2450,40	I B.C.
		BGU XIV 2450,58	I B.C.
	Τοου	**BGU** XVI 2560,7	8/7 B.C.
	Τοου	**BGU** XVI 2561,8	8/7 B.C.
	Πέραν	**BGU** XVI 2662,12	about 7-4 B.C.
	Sobthis (περὶ Πόλιν), Choibnotmis	**P.Rain.Cent.** 82,12-13	304/305 A.D.
	(see also: Νικίου)		
Πύθωνος	Τοου	**BGU** XVI 2561,8	8/7 B.C.
Ῥώδωνος	Koma	**BGU** IV 1193,4	8 B.C.
Σαραπίου	Herakleopolis	**BGU** XIV 2390,42	160/159 B.C.
Σαραπίωνος		**BGU** XVI 2662,15	about 7-4 B.C.
Σατόκου	Koma	**BGU** IV 1193,6	8 B.C.

Σατύρου	Kollasoucha	**P.Rain.Cent.** 40,3-4	223 B.C.
Σελεύκου	Peensemtheus	**BGU** XIV 2444,77;84	I B.C.
		BGU XIV 2445,22	I B.C.
		BGU XIV 2448,54	I B.C.
	Sobthis, Temenkyrkis	**P.Köln** II 98,25	II A.D.
Σεύθου	Toou	**BGU** XVI 2561,10	8/7 B.C.
Σιμίου	.φηεως	**BGU** XIV 2435,23	I B.C.
Σκίρωνος	Pyrgotos	**BGU** XIV 2441,36;46;71;83;86 103;121;150;153; 159;175;177;180; 187;191;193;195; 201;204;206;216; 239;240;258	I B.C.
		BGU XIV 2447,41;77	I B.C.
		BGU XIV 2448,57	I B.C.
Σοφοκλέους καὶ Ἀρείου	see: Ἀρείου		
Στρ() τοῦ Αμν()		**BGU** XIV 2449,59	I B.C.
Στρα()		**BGU** XIV 2450,27;81	I B.C.
Στράτωνος τοῦ Νικοστράτου		**BGU** XIV 2449,73	I B.C.
Στράτωνος τοῦ Δημητρίου	Σ.ου	**BGU** XIV 2446,4	I B.C.
		BGU XIV 2449,67	I B.C.
Συμμάχου		**BGU** XIV 2445,17	I B.C.
Στεφάνου	Koites	**P.Rein.** 98,12	109 A.D.
Ἀπο]λλωνίου καὶ Στοτοήτιος	see: Ἀπολλωνίου		
Στράτωνος	Techymis	**P.Oxy.** XLIV 3168,4	late II A.D.
Στρούθου	Thmoinache	**CPR** I 115+145,17	II A.D.
Σωκράτους καὶ Καλλιτ[	see: Καλλιτ[		
Σωννόμου		**BGU** XIV 2445,37	I B.C.

Σωσιβίου	Koites	**P.Tebt.** III 860,17;19;20;61;66;67	about 138 B.C.
		BGU XIV 2444,105	I B.C.
		BGU XIV 2447,26	I B.C.
		BGU XIV 2450,12	I B.C.
Σωσιπάτρου	Sobthis (περὶ Πόλιν), Temenkyrkis	**P.Köln** II 98,19	II A.D.
Σωστράτου	Thmoinausiris	**P.Hels.** I 11,12	163 B.C.
	Thmoinausiris	**P.Hels.** I 14,9	163 B.C.
Σωτ()	.φηεως	**BGU** XIV 2435,22	I B.C.
Σωτερίχου		**BGU** XIV 2450,26	I B.C.
Τ[......]		**BGU** VIII 1813,8	I B.C.
Τιμοκράτου	Peensemtheus	**BGU** XIV 2444,13;50;56;104;114	I B.C.
		BGU XIV 2445,34;36	I B.C.
		BGU XIV 2449,118	I B.C.
Τρ.()	Peensemtheus	**BGU** XIV 2444,76	I B.C.
Τρύφωνος	Techymis	**P.Oxy.** XLIV 3168,3	late II A.D.
Τύχωνος	Peensemtheus	**BGU** XIV 2444,56;76;100;112	I B.C.
Ὑπέρβαστος	Tosachmis	**Stud.Pal.** XX 29,28	227 A.D.
Φ..()	Pyrgotos	**BGU** XIV 2441,40	I B.C.
Φίδωνος	Bousiris	**BGU** VIII 1773,6	59/58 B.C.

Φιλίππου τοῦ Τιμοκράτου	Σ.ου	**BGU** XIV 2446,6;13;22	I B.C.
		BGU XIV 2447,14;52	I B.C.
		BGU XIV 2448,47;62	I B.C.
		BGU XIV 2449,20;25;37;47;50 58;59;130;143;151	I B.C.
		BGU XIV 2450,35;51;76	I B.C.
Φιλίσκου		**P.Hels.** I 16,12-13 [1]	163 B.C.
	Techymis	**P.Oxy.** XLIV 3168,8	late II A.D.
Φιλω()	Phebichis	**BGU** XIV 2435,7	I B.C.
Φιλω()	Pyrgotos	**BGU** XIV 2441,172;174	I B.C.
Φίλωνος [2]	Poenpibtei	**BGU** VIII 1733,6	I B.C.
		BGU XIV 2449,61	I B.C.
Φιλώτου [3]	Pyrgotos	**BGU** XIV 2441,45;62;77; 154	I B.C.
	Sobthis (περὶ Πόλιν), Temenkyrkis	**P.Köln** II 98,24	II A.D.
Χαιρε()	Assya	**BGU** XIV 2435,28	I B.C.
Χαρισίο[υ		**P.Strasb.** VIII 782,1 [4]	II B.C.
]δου		**BGU** XIV 2450,77	I B.C.
..ε()	Pyrgotos	**BGU** XIV 2441,105	I B.C.
]...ε()	Peensemtheus	**BGU** XIV 2444,58	I B.C.

---

[1] See above, p.281 n.1.

[2] A kleros Φίλωνος is attested in *P.Köln* IV 194,14, too (I A.D.; provenance unknown), and in the Oxyrhynchites (see PRUNETI, «I ΚΛΗΡΟΙ del nomo Ossirinchite», pp.204-205).

[3] There is a reference to a Φιλώτου προπύργιον, located at Tilothis, in *BGU* VIII 1734,8 (I B.C.).

[4] See above, p.278 n.1.

[..]ει..()	Pyrgotos	**BGU** XIV 2441,49	I B.C.
...ειου		**BGU** XIV 2448,16	I B.C.
....ιου	Pyrgotos	**BGU** XIV 2441,105	I B.C.
.....λειχους	Ankyron (Μεσσαλινιανὴ οὐσία)	**P.Ryl.** II 87,6	early III A.D.
...νιεω()	Peensemtheus	**BGU** XIV 2444,108	I B.C.
]νίου	Ἄγημα	**BGU** XVI 2662,13	about 7-4 B.C.
].ου	Pyrgotos	**BGU** XIV 2441,199	I B.C.
.πλάρχου	Kerkesephis	**BGU** XIV 2435,33	I B.C.
]..που		**BGU** XIV 2443,26	I B.C.
]που		**BGU** XIV 2448,55	I B.C.
]ρέους		**Stud.Pal.** XX 29,22	227 A.D.
]ρηνου	Σ.ου	**BGU** XIV 2446,15	I B.C.
....σ()	Pyrgotos	**BGU** XIV 2441,56	I B.C.
...ωνος		**BGU** XIV 2447,77	I B.C.
...[	Απρηλ()	**BGU** XIV 2450,41	I B.C.
[name lost]	Ankyron (Μεσσαλινιανὴ οὐσία)	**P.Ryl.** II 87,4	early III A.D.

3 Other Kleroi

I list here those toponyms that are referred to as κλῆροι in the sources of the Roman and Byzantine periods (full reference to the relevant sources is found in the *Catalogue*, under the appropriate entries). These were different from the *fossil kleroi* (see *Appendix 1*) which disappeared from all records at the time of the institution of the *pagi*. In one case, the denomination τόπος is employed for what is elsewhere called a κλῆρος (see *s.v.* Ψαννε); in another case, what may be the same toponym (Νανηουει/Νεμηουει) is once identified as an ἔδαφος (*Stud.Pal.* XX 117) and another time as a κλῆρος (*P.Rain.Cent.* 113); finally, a κλῆρος Ἀθωρ is mentioned in *P.Heid.* III 246,13: this was presumably connected with the homonymous ὄρος, μονή, or χωρίον (see *Catalogue*, *s.v.* Φαθωρ). Κασάνουπ(ις), though attested in four different documents, is only once termed a κλῆρος. I also include the Μεσσαλινιανὴ (οὐσία), and the toponym Ακεεις, designating a μηχανή, i.e. a plot of land inclusive of an irrigation machine.

Ακακιητη
Ακεεις
Ἀκώτου
Διδυμιανοῦ
Ιερκινκ[
Καινοῦ
Κασανου'π'(ις)
Κλέωνος
Κομ..[
Λολλιανοῦ
Μάρωνος
Μεσσαλινιανὴ (οὐσία)
Μικρουαλιχ
Νανηουει
Νεμηουει
Νεπωτιανοῦ
Νευακ[
Παλιετ[
Πιαοε.[.]ευ
Πιενεκαμου

Πμανκεμ
Πολιτ( )
Τακριαν
Ταπαμε[
Ταπιαμπεσητ
Ταρετταρυ
Τη( )
Τκουνσωσει
Τσαβα
Τσαβατωου
Τση[
Φαειν
Φαμτωννεσωου
Ψαννε
Ψαντι
[±4]ατ
[.]ε.]λ[
[±4]ετα
.πει.'α'
[±4]τιομ

INDEXES

1 Villages arranged by Toparchy

ΑΓΗΜΑ

ΑΛΙΛΑΙΣ
ΑΜΦΙΩ(ΝΟΣ?)
οἱ ΑΡΧΑΙΟΙ
ΚΕΛΛΑΣ
ΚΟΛΛΑΣΟΥΧΑ
ΚΟΡΦΟΤΟΙ
ΝΙΝΩ
ΝΙΣΕΥΣ
ΠΕΕΝΑΜΕΥΣ (see also: **ΜΕΣΗ**)
ΠΕΕΝΕΨΩΜΦΙΣ
ΠΕΕΝΣΕΜΘΕΥΣ
ΠΕΕΝΦΡΙ...
ΠΕΤΑΧΟΡ
ΣΙΣΙΝΗ (see also: **ΜΕΣΗ**)
ΤΕΡΤΟΝΙΧ()
ΤΕΡΤΟΝΠΕΤΕΧΩΝΣ
ΩΤΕΙΡΙΣ

περὶ **ΒΟΥΣΙΡΙΝ**

ΒΟΥΣΙΡΙΣ (see also περὶ ΚΟΜΑ)

περὶ **ΚΟΜΑ**

ΒΟΥΣΙΡΙΣ (see also περὶ ΒΟΥΣΙΡΙΝ)
ΘΜΟΙΑΜΟΥΝ(ΙΣ)
ΘΜΟΙΟΒΑΣΤΙΣ
ΚΕΦΑΛΑΙ
ΚΟΜΑ
ΚΡΗΚΙΣ
ΛΙΝΗ
ΜΑΧΟΡ
ΠΚΟΜΜΑΤΟΕΙ
ΤΟΟΥ

ΚΩΙΤΗΣ/περὶ **ΦΕΒΙΧΙΝ**

ΑΓΚΥΡΩΝ πόλις/κώμη

ΑΝΑΤΙΕΥ
ΑΣΣΥΑ
ΑΤΤΟΝ()
ΓΕΜΟΥΝ(ΙΣ)
ΘΕΛΒΩ
ΘΜΟΙΝΕΘΥΜΙΣ
ΘΜΟΙΝΠΕΣΛΑ
ΘΜΟΙΤΟΘΙΣ
ΘΝΗΙΣ
ΙΒΙΩΝ ΑΡΣΑΜΟΥ
ΙΠΠΩΝΩΝ κώμη
ΚΕΡΚΕΣΗΣ
ΚΕΡΚΕΣΗΦΙΣ
ΚΟΒΑ
ΚΩ
ΜΟΛΩΘΙΣ
ΜΟΥΧΙΝΕΜΒΗΣ
ΜΟΥΧΙΝΠΑΣΙΣ
ΝΟΚΛΗ (?)
ΝΩΥΚΛΕΓΧΗΣ
ΠΕΡΟΗ
ΠΕΡΧΥΦΙΣ
ΣΙΘΕΩΣ
ΣΩΒΘΙΣ ἡ μεγάλη
ΤΑΑΜΗΧΕΩΣ
ΤΑΑΜΩΡΟΥ
ΤΑΛΑΗ
ΤΑΧΟΝΠΑΧΝΟΥΒ
ΤΕΜΕΝΚΥΡΚΙΣ
ΤΟΕΜΗΣΙΣ
ΤΟΣΑΧΜΙΣ
ΦΕΒΙΧΙΣ
ΦΙΛΟΝΙΚΟΥ
ΧΟΙΒΝΩΤΜΙΣ
ΨΕΒΘΟΝΕΜΒΗΣ
ΨΕΒΘΟΝΠΕΝΟΥΦΙΣ
ΨΕΛΕΜΑΧΙΣ
ΨΙΝΑΠΕΛΕΥ
ΨΥΧΙΣ

ΜΕΣΗ

ΑΥΗΡΙΣ
ΑΥΞΩΝΙΟΥ
ΘΜΟΙΝΩΘΙΣ
ΚΕΡΚΕΥΝΙΦ(ΙΣ)
ΚΕΡΚΥΤΟΣ
ΠΕΕΝΑΜΕΥΣ (see also: **ΑΓΗΜΑ**)
ΠΕΕΝΒΕΝΔΗΤ(ΙΣ)
ΠΕΕΝΕΠΟΧΡΑ
ΠΕΕΝΙΒΙΣ
ΠΕΕΝΠΙΒΥΚ(ΙΣ)
ΠΕΕΝΣΧΩΝ
ΠΟΙΜΕΝΩΝ κώμη
ΣΙΣΙΝΗ (see also: **ΑΓΗΜΑ**)
ΤΑΝΤΟΚΑ?
ΤΕΧΥΜΙΣ
ΦΝΕΒΙΕΥΣ
ΦΥΣ
ΧΕΝΝΙΣ

ΠΕΡΑΝ

ΕΛΑΣΙΜΗΣ
ΘΜΟΙΝΑΥΣΙΡΙΣ
ΘΜΟΙΦΘΑ
ΠΕΕΝΣΑΜΟΙ
ΤΕΒΕΤΝΥ
ΧΟΡΤΑΣΩ

περὶ ΠΟΛΙΝ

ΑΡΤΕΜΙΔΟΣ   ΟΡΜΟΣ
ΘΜΟΙΝΕΨΙ
ΝΟΗΡΙΣ
ΝΩΙΣ
ΟΝΩΣΙΣ
ΠΕΕΝΗ
ΠΕΕΝΤΕΧΥ
ΣΩΒΘΙΣ ἡ μικρά
ΤΑΝΑΣΩ
ΤΙΝΤΗΡΙΣ
ΤΟΚΩΙΣ

περὶ ΤΕΚΜΙ

ΑΝΑ()
ΑΣΚΑΙΑΤΑΣ
περὶ ΑΥΛΗΝ
ΒΙΧΙΝΘΩΥΘ
ΚΟΛΛΙΝΠΕΤΩΥ
ΚΟΛΛΙΝΤΑΑΘΥΡ
ΜΟΥΧΙΣ
ΟΓΟΥ
ΟΛΩΝΘ(ΙΣ)
ΟΝΝΗΣ
ΠΕΕΝΕΨΥ
ΠΥΡΓΩΤΟΣ
ΤΑΒΟΚΛΙΣ
ΤΑΕΜΣΙΣ
ΤΑΕΤΜΕΙ
ΤΕΚΜΙ
ΤΟΧΟΝΤΩΥ
ΤΩΥ
ΦΑΙΝΙΠΠΟΥ
ΨΙΛΙΧΙ

ΤΕΧΘΩ   ΝΗΣΟΣ

ΘΕΛΒΩΝΘΙΣ
ΘΜΟΙΝΑΧΗ
ΤΕΧΘΩ

περὶ ΤΙΛΩΘΙΝ

ΝΕΙΛΟΥ ΠΟΛΙΣ (= ΤΙΛΩΘΙΣ)
ΠΕΕΝΠΑΣΒΥΤ(ΙΣ)
ΠΩΙΣ (?)
ΣΧΝΩΜΘΙΣ
ΤΑΓΧΑΙΣ
ΤΙΛΩΘΙΣ (= Νείλου πόλις)

2 Chronological Index

III-III/II B.C.

P.Bad. (= VBP) IV 82	237 B.C.	P.Hib. I 136 descr.	244 B.C.
BGU X 1911	III B.C.	P.Hib. I 138 descr.	245 B.C.
BGU XIV 2391	about 250 B.C.	P.Hib. I 143 descr.	231 B.C.
BGU XIV 2392	about 250 B.C.	P.Hib. I 144 descr.	230/229 B.C.
P.Cair.Zen. II 59151	256 B.C.	P.Hib. I 157 descr.	264/263 B.C.
P.Cair.Zen. III 59473	III B.C.	P.Hib. I 163 descr.	229 B.C.
P.Cair.Zen. III 59368	240 B.C.	P.Hib. I 164 descr.	267-260 B.C.
P.Cair.Zen. IV 59753	III B.C.	P.Hib. I 167 descr.	about 245 B.C.
P.Cair.Zen. IV 59767	III B.C.	P.Hib. II 198	III B.C.
P.Cair.Zen. IV 59782(b)	mid-III B.C.	P.Hib. II 203	246-222 B.C.
P.Coll. Youtie I 7	224 B.C.	P.Hib. II 209	263/262 B.C.
P.Enteux. 61	III B.C.	P.Hib. II 248,fr.III	about 250 B.C.
P.Fuad Crawford. 5	III B.C. ?	P.Lille I 6	III B.C.
P.Fuad Crawford (*App.* I)	229 B.C.?	P.Lille I 31	III B.C.
P.Fuad Crawford (*App.* II)	III B.C. ?	P.Lille I 59	212/211 B.C.
P.Grad. 3	227/226 B.C.	P.Lond. VII 1972	254 B.C.
P.Hamb. III 202	III B.C.	P.Mich.Zen. 30 a	259 B.C.
P.Hib. I 33	245 B.C.	P.Mich.Zen. 87	III B.C.
P.Hib. I 34	243/242 B.C.	P.Petr. III 43(2),col.III	245 B.C.
P.Hib. I 36	229 B.C.	P.Petr. III 62 b	III B.C.
P.Hib. I 37	235 B.C.	P.Petr. III 99 *recto*	III B.C.
P.Hib. I 47	256 B.C.	P.Rain.Cent. 40	223 B.C.
P.Hib. I 60	about 245 B.C.	P.Rain.Cent. 44	III/II B.C.
P.Hib. I 66	228 B.C.	P.Ross.Georg.II 3	226/225 B.C.
P.Hib. I 67	228/227 B.C.	SB III 6301	227/226 B.C.
P.Hib. I 68	about 228 B.C.	SB III 7176	247/246 B.C.
P.Hib. I 70(b)	about 228 B.C.	SB III 7179	238 B.C.
P.Hib. I 71	245 B.C.	SB III 7203	247/246 B.C.
P.Hib. I 72	241 B.C.	SB VIII 9841	247 B.C.
P.Hib. I 73	244/243 B.C.	SB X 10447 *recto*	mid-III B.C.
P.Hib. I 75	232 B.C.	SB X 10540	251/250 B.C.
P.Hib. I 78	244/243 B.C.	SB X 10783	about 246 B.C.
P.Hib. I 80	250 B.C.	SB XVI 12387	260-255 B.C.
P.Hib I 84(a)	285/284 B.C.	PSI V 510	254/253 B.C.
P.Hib. I 88	263/262 B.C.	PSI VI 587	III B.C.
P.Hib. I 96	259/258 B.C.	P.Strasb. II 103	after 210 B.C.
P.Hib. I 100	267 B.C.	P.Strasb. II 104	after 210 B.C.
P.Hib. I 101	261 B.C.	P.Strasb. II 111	215/214 B.C.
P.Hib. I 106	245 B.C.	P.Strasb. II 113	215 B.C.
P.Hib. I 107	244 B.C.	P.Strasb. VI 563	mid-III B.C.
P.Hib. I 108	259/258 or 249/248 B.C.	P.Strasb. VII 641	215 B.C.
P.Hib. I 110 *recto*	about 270 B.C.	P.Strasb. VII 642	265/264 B.C.
P.Hib. I 112	about 260 B.C.	P.Strasb. VII 643	246-221 B.C.
P.Hib. I 116	about 245 B.C.	P.Strasb. VII 662	III B.C.
P.Hib. I 117	240/239 or 215/214 B.C.	P.Strasb. IX 802	239 B.C.
P.Hib. I 118	about 250 B.C.	PUG III 114	237 B.C.
P.Hib. I 123 descr.	265-245 B.C. (probably)	P.Yale I 31	257/256 B.C.
P.Hib. I 131 descr.	about 245 B.C.	P.Yale I 35	249 B.C.
P.Hib. I 132 descr.	about 255 B.C.		

II B.C.

BGU VI 1216	110 B.C.	**P.Münch.** III 49	II B.C.
BGU VI 1244	II B.C.	**P.Münch.** III 51	135/134 B.C.
BGU XIV 2382	174 B.C.	**P.Münch.** III 55	II B.C.
BGU XIV 2389	172 B.C.	**P.Münch.** III 56	II B.C.
BGU XIV 2390	160/159 B.C.	**P.Münch.** III 61	II B.C.
P.Duk. inv. 605	mid-II B.C.	**SB** XIV 12089	130 B.C.
P.Gen. III 132	mid-II B.C.	**SB** XVIII 13304	138 B.C.?
P.Gen. III 134	mid-II B.C.	**P.Strasb.** II 99	169-164 B.C.
P.Hamb. I 91	167 B.C.	**P.Strasb.** VIII 781	mid-II B.C.
P.Hels. I 4	II B.C. (after 168/167 B.C.)	**P.Strasb.** VIII 782	II B.C.
P.Hels. I 6	164 B.C.	**P.Tebt.** III 827	about 170 B.C.
P.Hels. I 8	163 B.C.	**P.Tebt.** III 838	139 B.C.
P.Hels. I 9	163 B.C.	**P.Tebt.** III 857	162 B.C.
P.Hels. I 10	163 B.C.	**P.Tebt.** III 860	about 138 B.C.
P.Hels. I 11	163 B.C.	**P.Tebt.** III 876	mid-II B.C.
P.Hels. I 12	163 B.C.	**P.Tebt.** III 878	about 111 B.C.
P.Hels. I 13	163 B.C.	**P.Tebt.** III 890	173-130/128 B.C.
P.Hels. I 14	163 B.C.	**P.Tebt.** III 920	II B.C. (first half)
P.Hels. I 15	163 B.C.	**P.Tebt.** III 931	136 B.C.
P.Hels. I 16	163 B.C.	**P.Tebt.** III 986	139 B.C.
P.Hels. I 18	163 B.C.	**P.Tebt.** III 987	139 B.C.
P.Hels. I 19	162 B.C.	**P.Tebt.** III 988	139 B.C.
P.Hels. I 20	163 B.C.	**P.Tebt.** III 989	139 B.C.
P.Hels. I 21	163/162 B.C.	**P.Tebt.** III 991	139 B.C.
P.Hels. I 24	163/162 B.C.?	**P.Tebt.** III 992, descr.	139 B.C.
P.Hels. I 26	162 B.C.	**P.Tebt.** III 1043, descr.	about 170 B.C.?
P.Hels. I 27	160 B.C.	**P.Tebt.** III 1044	early II B.C.
P.Hels. I 29	161/160 B.C.	**P.Tebt.** III 1045	about 164 B.C.
P.Hels. I 31	160 B.C.	**P.Tebt.** III 1082	early II B.C.
P.Hels. I 32	160 B.C.	**UPZ** I 9	161/160 B.C.
P.Hels. I 34	about 160 B.C.	**UPZ** I 10	160/159 B.C.
P.Hels. I 38	159 B.C.	**UPZ** I 11	160 B.C.
P.Hels. I 40 *verso*	about 160 B.C.	**UPZ** I 70	152/151 B.C.
P.Merton II 59	154 or 143 B.C.	**UPZ** I 76	mid-II B.C.
P.Mil.Vogl. inv.1299	II B.C.	**UPZ** I 122	157 B.C.
P.Mil.Vogl. inv.1300	II B.C.		

I B.C.

BGU VI 1285	I B.C.	**BGU** VIII 1764	I B.C.
BGU VIII 1732	I B.C.	**BGU** VIII 1768	I B.C.
BGU VIII 1733	I B.C.	**BGU** VIII 1771	63/62 B.C.
BGU VIII 1734	I B.C.	**BGU** VIII 1772	61-59 B.C.
BGU VIII 1737	78/77 B.C.	**BGU** VIII 1773	59/58 B.C.
BGU VIII 1739	72/71 B.C.	**BGU** VIII 1777	I B.C.
BGU VIII 1742	64/63 B.C.	**BGU** VIII 1778	I B.C.
BGU VIII 1747	64/63 B.C.	**BGU** VIII 1779	51/50 B.C.
BGU VIII 1748	64/63 B.C.	**BGU** VIII 1780	57 or 51/50 B.C.
BGU VIII 1749	64/63 B.C.	**BGU** VIII 1784	I B.C.
BGU VIII 1752	64/63 B.C.	**BGU** VIII 1786	51/50 B.C.
BGU VIII 1753	64/63 B.C.	**BGU** VIII 1789	I B.C.
BGU VIII 1761	51/50 B.C.	**BGU** VIII 1795	48/47 B.C.
BGU VIII 1763	I B.C.	**BGU** VIII 1796	I B.C.

BGU VIII 1798	I B.C.	**BGU** XIV 2370	I B.C.		
BGU VIII 1802	I B.C.	**BGU** XIV 2374	88/81 B.C.		
BGU VIII 1803	I B.C.	**BGU** XIV 2376	36/35 B.C.		
BGU VIII 1805	I B.C.	**BGU** XIV 2377	36/35 B.C.		
BGU VIII 1807	I B.C.	**BGU** XIV 2419	I B.C.		
BGU VIII 1808	I B.C.	**BGU** XIV 2420	I B.C.		
BGU VIII 1811	47 B.C.	**BGU** XIV 2424	86 B.C.		
BGU VIII 1813	I B.C.	**BGU** XIV 2425	I B.C.		
BGU VIII 1814	61/60 B.C.	**BGU** XIV 2429	96-94 or 63-61 B.C.		
BGU VIII 1815	61/60 B.C.	**BGU** XIV 2431	I B.C.		
BGU VIII 1817	60/59 B.C.	**BGU** XIV 2432	I B.C.		
BGU VIII 1818	60/59 B.C.	**BGU** XIV 2433	I B.C.		
BGU VIII 1819	60/59 B.C.	**BGU** XIV 2434	I B.C.		
BGU VIII 1821	I B.C.	**BGU** XIV 2435	I B.C.		
BGU VIII 1822	I B.C.	**BGU** XIV 2436	I B.C.		
BGU VIII 1824	I B.C.	**BGU** XIV 2437	I B.C.		
BGU VIII 1825	I B.C.	**BGU** XIV 2438	I B.C.		
BGU VIII 1827	52/51 B.C.	**BGU** XIV 2439	I B.C.		
BGU VIII 1828	52/51 B.C.	**BGU** XIV 2440	I B.C.		
BGU VIII 1831	51/50 B.C.	**BGU** XIV 2441	I B.C.		
BGU VIII 1832	51 B.C.?	**BGU** XIV 2442	I B.C.		
BGU VIII 1834	51/50 B.C.	**BGU** XIV 2443	I B.C.		
BGU VIII 1835	I B.C.	**BGU** XIV 2444	I B.C.		
BGU VIII 1837	51/50 B.C.	**BGU** XIV 2445	I B.C.		
BGU VIII 1838	51/50 B.C.	**BGU** XIV 2446	I B.C.		
BGU VIII 1842	50/49 B.C.	**BGU** XIV 2447	I B.C.		
BGU VIII 1843	50/49 B.C.	**BGU** XIV 2448	I B.C.		
BGU VIII 1845	I B.C.	**BGU** XIV 2449	I B.C.		
BGU VIII 1846	about 50-49 B.C.	**BGU** XIV 2450	I B.C.		
BGU VIII 1848	about 48-46 B.C.	**SB** V 7609	48/47 B.C.		
BGU VIII 1849	about 48-46 B.C.	**SB** V 7611	50/49 B.C.		
BGU VIII 1852	I B.C.	**SB** V 8755	49/48 B.C.		
BGU VIII 1855	I B.C.	**SB** V 8756	49/48 B.C.		
BGU VIII 1856	I B.C.	**SB** VI 9065	50/49 B.C.		
BGU VIII 1857	I B.C.	**SB** VIII 9790	mid-I B.C.		
BGU VIII 1872	51/50 B.C.	**P.Yale** I 57	93-70 B.C.		
BGU VIII 1888	I B.C.				

I B.C./I A.D.

BGU IV 1060	I B.C./I A.D.	**BGU** XVI 2560	8/7 B.C.
BGU IV 1061	14 B.C.	**BGU** XVI 2561	8/7 B.C.
BGU IV 1104	8 B.C.	**BGU** XVI 2562	8/7 B.C.
BGU IV 1138	19/18 B.C.	**BGU** XVI 2563	8/7 B.C.
BGU IV 1167	12 B.C.	**BGU** XVI 2564	3/2 B.C.?
BGU IV 1187	I B.C.	**BGU** XVI 2565	3/2 B.C.
BGU IV 1188	15/14 B.C.	**BGU** XVI 2569	3 B.C.
BGU IV 1189	about 1 A.D.	**BGU** XVI 2570	8/7 B.C.
BGU IV 1192	I B.C./I A.D.	**BGU** XVI 2572	6/5 B.C.
BGU IV 1193	8 B.C.	**BGU** XVI 2573	3 B.C.
BGU IV 1196	about 11/10 B.C.	**BGU** XVI 2575	6/5 B.C.
BGU IV 1197	12/11 B.C.	**BGU** XVI 2577	30 B.C.-14 A.D.
BGU IV 1198	5/4 B.C.	**BGU** XVI 2579	13 B.C.
BGU IV 1200	2/1 B.C.	**BGU** XVI 2580	13 B.C.
BGU IV 1202	18 B.C.	**BGU** XVI 2581	14/13 B.C.
BGU IV 1208	27/26 B.C.	**BGU** XVI 2582	13 B.C.

BGU XVI 2583	13 B.C.	**BGU** XVI 2616	13 B.C.
BGU XVI 2584	13 B.C.	**BGU** XVI 2630	10 B.C.
BGU XVI 2585	13 B.C.	**BGU** XVI 2632	after 8/7 B.C.
BGU XVI 2586	5 B.C.	**BGU** XVI 2640	10 B.C.
BGU XVI 2587	13 B.C.	**BGU** XVI 2641	21/20 B.C.-5 A.D.
BGU XVI 2589	28 B.C.	**BGU** XVI 2643	9/8 B.C.
BGU XVI 2591	2 B.C.	**BGU** XVI 2644	4 B.C.
BGU XVI 2592	21/20 B.C.-5 A.D.	**BGU** XVI 2646	3 B.C.
BGU XVI 2593	I B.C./I A.D.	**BGU** XVI 2647	8 B.C.
BGU XVI 2594	8 B.C.	**BGU** XVI 2655	21/20 B.C.
BGU XVI 2597	21/20 B.C.-5 A.D.	**BGU** XVI 2662	about 7-4 B.C.
BGU XVI 2598	9-7 B.C.	**BGU** XVI 2663	9 B.C.
BGU XVI 2599	after 27 B.C.	**BGU** XVI 2665	28/27 B.C.
BGU XVI 2600	13 B.C.	**BGU** XVI 2669	21/20 B.C.-5 A.D.
BGU XVI 2601	after 13/12 B.C.	**BGU** XVI 2670	about 14/13 B.C.
BGU XVI 2602	about 14/13 B.C.	**BGU** XVI 2674	I B.C.
BGU XVI 2607	15 B.C.	(?)**P.Oxy.** IV 742	2 B.C.
BGU XVI 2608	about 7 B.C.	**SB** V 7537	6/5 B.C.
BGU XVI 2610	9 B.C.	**SB** XVI 12312	25 B.C.
BGU XVI 2611	10 B.C.		

I A.D.

BGU IV 1201	2 A.D.	**P.Oxy.** XLVII 3357	late I A.D.
BGU XVI 2559	1-9 A.D.	**P.Oxy.** XXIV 2412	28/29 A.D.
P.Corn. 22	early I A.D.	**P.Oxy.** XXXI 2582	49 A.D.
P.Giss.Univ. 19	55 A.D.	**P.Oxy.** XXXVIII 2842	29 A.D.?
P.Heid. IV 326	98 A.D.	**P.Oxy.** LV 3807	about 26-28 A.D. ?
P.Mich. II 121 *recto*, col.IV.I,2	42 A.D.	**P.Ross.Georg.** II 11	19 A.D.
P.Oxy. II 348 descr.	late I A.D.	**SB** XVI 12762	28 A.D.
P.Oxy. IV 814 descr.	17/18 A.D. (probably)	**PSI** VIII 897	93 A.D.
P.Oxy. VIII 1145	I A.D.	**P.Tebt.** II 535 descr.	early I A.D.
P.Oxy. XLII 3052	I A.D.	**P.Vind.Tand.** 10	54 A.D.

I/II A.D.

P.Erl. 58	I/II A.D.	**P.Osl.** III 151	I/II A.D.
P.Hib. II 218	I/II A.D.	**P.Princ.** inv. AM 15960 B(1)	I/II A.D.
P.Hib. II 272	I-II A.D.	**PSI** VIII 967	I/II A.D.
P.Hib. II 282	I/II A.D.		

II A.D.

P.Aberd. 42(h)	189 A.D.	**BGU** III 741	143/144 A.D.
P.Bad. (= **VBP**) IV 75a	133 A.D.	**BGU** XIII 2326	168-176 or 180-193 A.D.
P.Bad. (= **VBP**) IV 74	138 A.D.	**P.Bodl.** I 61 (g)	II A.D.
P.Bad. (= **VBP**) IV 75	147 A.D.	**P.Bodl.** I 150	191 A.D.
P.Bad. (= **VBP**) IV 77	II A.D.	**P.Bon.** 18	132 A.D.
P.Berl.Leihg. I 2, *recto*	167/168 A.D.	**P.Bon.** 25	185 A.D.

CHRONOLOGICAL INDEX

P.Corn. 17	147 A.D.	P.Oxy. XXII 2342	102 A.D.
CPR I 50,b	193-211 A.D.	P.Oxy. XLIV 3168	late II A.D.
CPR I 111	II A.D.	P.Oxy. LIX 3975	about 165/166 A.D.
CPR I 115+145	II A.D.	P.Petaus 28	II A.D.
CPR I 238	II A.D.	P.Prag. II 132	mid-II A.D.
P.Fayum 23	II A.D.	P.Rein. 98	109 A.D.
P.Flor. I 23	145 A.D.	SB V 7515	155 A.D.
P.Flor. III 385	II/III A.D.	SB XII 11262	139 A.D.
P.Heid. IV 297	172-175 A.D.	SB XIV 11341	174 A.D.
P.Heid. IV 301	192 A.D.	SB XIV 11958	117 A.D.
P.Heid. IV 320	138 A.D.	SB XIV 11959	142 A.D.
P.Heid. IV 321	162, 163 A.D.	PSI VIII 962	131/132 A.D.
P.Heid. IV 322	182 A.D.	PSI XIII 1325	169-177 A.D.
P.Hib. II 237+217	177-180 A.D.	P.Strasb. V 356	II A.D.
P.Hib. II 277	138-161 A.D.	Stud.Pal. XX 16	193 A.D.
P.Hib. II 278	176-180 A.D.	Stud.Pal. XX 7	after 150 A.D.
P.Hib. II 280	II A.D.	P.Tebt. II 301	190 A.D.
P.Iand. III 33	180-192 A.D.	P.Tebt. II 353	192 A.D.
P.Köln II 98	early II A.D.	P.Tebt. II 575, descr.	II A.D.
P.Langres inv.907.1.39 verso	192/193 A.D.	P.Vind.Sal. 6	192 A.D.
P.Merton II 78	191 A.D.	P.Vindob. inv. G 23035	late II A.D.
P.Mich. IX 551	103 A.D.	O.Wilck. II 1099	185/186 A.D.
P.Mil.Vogl. IV 214 verso	154 A.D.	O.Wilck. II 1100	188 A.D.
P.Mil.Vogl. VI 287	II A.D.	O.Wilck. II 1104	190/191 A.D.
P.Oxy. Hels. 37	176 A.D.	O.Wilck. II 1106	192 A.D.
P.Oxy. III 504	early II A.D.	O.Wilck. II 1108	192 A.D.
P.Oxy. IV 715	131 A.D.	O.Wilck. II 1114	193 A.D.
P.Oxy. IV 810 descr.	134/135 A.D.	O.Wilck. II 1116	198/199 A.D.
P.Oxy. XIV 1751	134/135 A.D.	O.Wilck. II 1117	199 A.D.
P.Oxy. XX 2272	II A.D.		

II/III A.D.

P.Batav. XXV 49,9	II/III A.D.	P.Oxy. LIX 3993	II/III A.D.
BGU III 929	II/III A.D.	P.Ryl. II 225	II/III A.D.
BGU XI 2073	II/III A.D.	PSI VI 928	II/III A.D.
P.Alex. inv. 563	II/III A.D.	PSI XIII 1332	II-III A.D.
P.Heid. IV 303	II/III A.D.	O.Wilck. II 1124	II/III A.D.
P.Köln II 99	II/III A.D.	O.Wilck. II 1125	II/III A.D.

III A.D.

BGU III 922	286 A.D.	CPR I 76 (+ CPR I 79)	222-235 A.D.
BGU III 927	III A.D.	CPR I 78	221 A.D.? 225/226 A.D.?
BGU VII 1568	261 A.D.	CPR I 82	III A.D. (first half)
BGU XIII 2365	late III A.D.	CPR I 83	III A.D. (first half)
CPR I 36	225 A.D.	CPR I 84	235-238 A.D.
CPR I 56	211-217 A.D.	CPR I 86	III A.D. (first half)
CPR I 61	218-222 A.D.	CPR I 87	III A.D.
CPR I 62	218-222 A.D.	CPR I 88	III A.D. (first half)
CPR I 64	227 A.D.	CPR I 90	III A.D. (first half)
CPR I 66	III A.D.	CPR I 92	III A.D. (first half)
CPR I 73	222-235 A.D.	CPR I 96	III A.D. (first half)

CPR I 98	III A.D. (first half)	**SB** I 1515	250 A.D.
CPR I 156	III A.D. (first half)	**SB** I 4370	228/229 A.D.
CPR I 159	III A.D. (first half)	**SB** XIV 11277	225 A.D.
CPR I 169 (+ **CPR** I 157)	III A.D. (first half)	**SB** XIV 11643	214 A.D.
CPR VI 73	222-235 A.D.	**SB** XIV 12193	III A.D.
CPR VII 12	242 A.D.	**SB** XVI 12241	III A.D. (second half)
CPR VIII 14	241 A.D.	**SB** XVI 12612	202/203 A.D.
P.Erl. 48	III A.D. (beginning)	(?)**SB** XVI 12836	224/225 A.D.
P.Flor. III 364	III A.D.	**SB** XVI 12837	225-233 A.D.
P.Gen. I 9	252 A.D.	(?)**SB** XVIII 13151	218 A.D.
P.Hamb. I 17	210 A.D.	**SB** XVIII 13858	211-217 A.D.
P.Köln II 88	200 A.D.	**P.Select.** 17	mid-III A.D.
P.Laur. IV 174,*recto*	III A.D.	**PSI** I 32	208 A.D.
P.Lond. II 171 b	III A.D. (second half)	**PSI** III 184	292 A.D.
P.Lund VI 8	after 212 A.D.	**PSI** XV estr. 1546	222 A.D.
P.Lund VI 9	after 212 A.D.	**PSI** XII 1229	217 A.D.
P.Neph. 28	III A.D.	**Stud.Pal.** II p.28	217 A.D.
P.Osl. II 82	III A.D.	**Stud.Pal.** XX 18	205 A.D.
P.Oxy. VI 899	200 A.D.	**Stud.Pal.** XX 22	216 A.D.
P.Oxy. VI 965 descr.	III A.D.	**Stud.Pal.** XX 25	218 A.D.
P.Oxy. VII 1068	III A.D.	**Stud.Pal.** XX 26	222 A.D.
P.Oxy. VIII 1156	III A.D.	**Stud.Pal.** XX 28	227 A.D.
P.Oxy. XII 1463	215 A.D.	**Stud.Pal.** XX 29	227 A.D.
P.Oxy. XII 1529	III A.D.	**Stud.Pal.** XX 32	231 A.D.
P.Oxy. XLVII 3365	after May 22, 241 A.D.	**Stud.Pal.** XX 34	232/233 A.D.
P.Oxy. LVIII 3928	about 245 A.D. ?	**Stud.Pal.** XX 36	237 A.D.
P.Panop.Beatty 1	298 A.D.	**Stud.Pal.** XX 47	236 A.D.?
P.Rain.Cent. 64	212 A.D.	**Stud.Pal.** XX 52	242 A.D.
P.Ross.Georg. V 20 *verso*	223 A.D.	**Stud.Pal.** XX 55	251 A.D.
P.Ryl. II 87 *recto*	early III A.D.	**P.Vind.Bosw.** 7	221 A.D.
P.Ryl. II 351 descr.	III A.D.	**P.Vind.Sijp.** 19	233/234 A.D.
SB I 1495	about 250 A.D.	**P.Vind.Tand.** 11	241/242 A.D.
SB I 1496	250 A.D.	**P.Vind.Worp** 4	234 A.D.
SB I 1497	about 250 A.D.	**P.Wash.Univ.** I 18	286 A.D.
SB I 1500	about 250 A.D.	**O.Meyer** 51	261 A.D.
SB I 1501	about 250 A.D.	**O.Mich.** I 179	297 A.D.
SB I 1508	about 250 A.D.	**O.Mich.** I 68	261 A.D.
SB I 1511	about 250 A.D.	**O.Theb.** 132	III A.D.
SB I 1512	about 250 A.D.	**O.Wilck.** II 1121	204 A.D.

IV A.D.

P.Abinn. 11	IV A.D.	**P.Col.** VII 161	345-351 A.D.
P.Amh. II 142	IV A.D.	**P.Col.** VII 163	348 A.D.
P.Athen. 34	347 A.D.	**CPR** I 40	300 A.D.
BGU III 938	384/385 A.D.	**CPR** I 42	IV A.D.
BGU III 949	about 300 A.D.	**CPR** I 247	335 A.D.
P.Cairo Isid. 9,*verso*	about 309 A.D.	**CPR** X 107a	396 A.D.
P.Cairo Isid. 46	307 A.D.	**P.Gen.** I 10	IV A.D.
P.Cairo Isid. 47	309 A.D.	**P.Hib.** II 219	309 A.D.
CEL 231	395 A.D.	**P.Hib.** II 220	335 A.D.
CEL 232	396 A.D.	**P.Iand.** VI 124	IV A.D.
P.Col. VII 141	308-310 A.D.	**P.Lond.** III 985	IV A.D.
P.Col. VII 144	334/335 A.D.	**P.Lond.** VI 1913	334 A.D.
P.Col. VII 152	343-345 A.D.	(?)**P.Lond.** VI 1914	335 A.D.(?)
P.Col. VII 160	345-354 A.D.	**P.Lond.** VI 1920	about 330-340 A.D.

P.Lond. VI 1924	mid-IV A.D.	P.Ross Georg. V 61 A *verso*	IV A.D.
P.Med. I² 66, *verso*	343 A.D.	P.Ross Georg. V 61 B *recto*;	
P.Mich. IX 573	316 A.D.	C *verso*; D *recto*; D *verso*	IV A.D.
P.Mich. XII 647	IV A.D. (beginning)	P.Sakaon 22	324 A.D.
P.Mich. XV 722	III/IV A.D.	SB VI 9597	IV A.D. (end)
P.Michael. 28,1	313-314 A.D.	SB VI 9632	302 A.D.
MPER XV 84	IV A.D.	SB VIII 9683	IV A.D. (end)
MPER XV 101	IV A.D.	SB XIV 11615	365-373 A.D.
P.Neph. 3	IV A.D.	SB XVI 12814	343 A.D.
P.Neph. 6	IV A.D.	SB XVIII 13260	328 A.D.
P.Neph. 11	IV A.D.	PSI III 222	IV A.D.
P.Neph. 12	IV A.D.	PSI IX 1037	301 A.D.
P.Neph. 13	IV A.D.	Stud.Pal. X 221	IV A.D.
P.Neph. 19	IV A.D.	Stud.Pal. X 236	IV A.D.
P.Neph. 20	IV A.D.	P.Vind.Sijp. 13	372 A.D.
P.Neph. 29	III-IV A.D.	O.Mich. I 254	III/IV A.D.
P.Neph. 32	344 A.D.	O.Mich. I 516	308 A.D.?
P.Neph. 43	330/331 A.D.	O.Mich. I 517	309/310 A.D.(probably)
P.Neph. 44	311/312-319/320 A.D.	O.Mich. I 520	311 A.D.?
P.Neph. 45	320/321-321/322 A.D.	O.Mich. I 524	312 A.D.?
P.Neph. 46	IV A.D.	O.Mich. I 525	304 or 312 A.D.
P.Neph. 48	323 A.D.	O.Mich. I 526	304 or 312 A.D.
P.Neph. 49	IV A.D.	O.Mich. I 532	318 A.D.
P.NYU 11	333 or 348 A.D.	O.Mich. I 534	early IV A.D.
P.NYU 11 a	338-342 A.D.	O.Mich. I 541	early IV A.D.
P.NYU 4 a	312 A.D.	O.Mich. I 545	early IV A.D.
P.Oxf. 6	350 A.D.	O.Mich. II 927	304 or 312 A.D.
P.Oxy. XIV 1708	311 A.D.	O.Mich. II 930	315 A.D.
P.Rain.Cent. 82	304/305 A.D.	O.Mich. II 931	early IV A.D.
P.Rain.Cent. 86	381 A.D.	O.Mich. III 1079	304 or 312 A.D.
P.Rain.Cent. 87	381 A.D.	O.Mich. III 1080	304 or 312 A.D.?
P.Rain.Cent. 147	IV A.D.		

IV/V A.D.

P.Amh. II 147	IV/V A.D.	MPER XV 91	IV/V A.D.
P.Batav. XXV 65	IV/V A.D.	P.Rain.Cent. 153	IV/V A.D.
P.Flor. I 11	IV-V A.D.	P.Rain.Cent. 154	IV/V A.D.
P.Laur. II 42	IV/V A.D.	P.Vind.Tand. 18	IV/V A.D.
MPER XV 82	IV/V A.D.	P.Vind.Tand. 19	IV/V A.D.
MPER XV 83	IV/V A.D.	Stud.Pal. X 235	IV/V A.D.

V A.D.

CEL 233	401 A.D.	P.Oxy. XVI 1953	419 A.D.
CPR VI 79	V A.D.	P.Oxy. XVI 1961	487 A.D.
CPR X 105a	V A.D.	P.Oxy. XVI 2017	V A.D.
P.Köln III 151	423 A.D.	P.Oxy. XX 2268	late V A.D.
MPER XV 103	V A.D.	P.Oxy. LIX 4004	V A.D.
MPER XV 13	V A.D.	P.Rain.Cent. 95	446 A.D.
MPER XV 63	about 420/421 A.D.	P.Rain.Cent. 101	457 A.D.
P.Oxy. VIII 1126	V A.D.	P.Rain.Cent. 102	459 A.D.

P.Rain.Cent. 106	475 A.D.	Stud.Pal. X 8	V A.D.
P.Rain.Cent. 107	484 A.D.	Stud.Pal. X 9	V A.D.
P.Rain.Cent. 110	490 A.D.	Stud.Pal. X 47	V A.D.
P.Rain.Cent. 123	478 A.D.	Stud.Pal. X 50	V A.D.
P.Rain.Cent. 124	492 A.D.	Stud.Pal. X 94	V A.D.
P.Select. 13,*verso*	421 A.D.	Stud.Pal. X 233	V A.D.
P.Select. 15	435 A.D.	Stud.Pal. XX 90	415 A.D.
SB VIII 9773	405 A.D.	Stud.Pal. XX 117	411 A.D.
SB XII 10939	V A.D.	Stud.Pal. XX 127	463 A.D.
(?)PSI I 80	V A.D.	P.Vind.Sijp. 7	462 A.D.
PSI III 183	484 A.D.	P.Vind.Sijp. 9	V A.D.
Stud.Pal. VIII 772	V A.D.		

V/VI A.D.

P.Amst. I 83	V/VI A.D.	SB I 1945	V/VI A.D.
CPR VIII 59	V/VI A.D.	SB XVIII 14004	V/VI A.D.
CPR XIV 6	V-VI A.D.	SB XVIII 14005	V/VI A.D.
CPR XIV 40	V/VI A.D.	SB XX 14580	V-VI A.D.
P.Heid. III 246	V/VI A.D.	Stud.Pal. III 371	V/VI A.D.
P.Köln IV 192	V/VI A.D.	Stud.Pal. VIII 955	V-VI A.D.
P.Merton I 46	V/VI A.D.	Stud.Pal. VIII 1226	V-VI A.D.
MPER XV 75	V/VI A.D.	Stud.Pal. XX 124	V-VI A.D.
P.Oxy. XVI 1834	V/VI A.D.	P.Vind.Sijp. 16	V/VI A.D.
P.Rain.Cent. 133	V/VI A.D.	P.Vind.Tand. 16	V/VI A.D.

VI A.D.

P.Bad. (= VBP) IV 55	VI A.D.	P.Oxy. LV 3804	566 A.D.
P.Batav. 23	VI A.D.	P.Oxy. LV 3805	566 A.D. (or later)
P.Batav. 23 bis	VI A.D.	P.Princ. II 105	VI A.D.
P.Berl.Zill. 7,*recto; verso*	574 A.D.	P.Rain.Cent. 113	525/526 A.D.
CPR VI 7	VI A.D.	P.Rain.Cent. 118	544-559 A.D.?
CPR X 121	543 A.D.	P.Rain.Cent. 137	VI A.D.
P.Dub. 24	VI A.D.	SB I 1967	VI A.D.
P.Erl. 67	591 A.D.	SB VI 9139	VI A.D.
P.Köln III 158	599 A.D.	SB VI 9282 *verso*	about 500 A.D.
P.Mich. X 591	VI A.D.	SB VI 9608	VI A.D.
P.Michael. 126	538 A.D.	SB VIII 9876	534 A.D.
MPER XV 62	506/507 A.D.	SB XVIII 13949	541 A.D.
MPER XV 113	VI A.D.	SB XX 14123	VI A.D.
MPER XXII 2 a	VI A.D.	P.Strasb. V 318,13	596 A.D.
P.Oxy. I 142	534 A.D.	Stud.Pal. III 24 *verso*	VI A.D.
P.Oxy. I 150	590 A.D.	Stud.Pal. III 66	VI A.D.
P.Oxy. XVI 1909	582-602 A.D.	Stud.Pal. III 86	VI A.D.
P.Oxy. XVI 1911	557 A.D.	Stud.Pal. III 341	VI A.D.
P.Oxy. XVI 1912	late VI A.D.	Stud.Pal. III 399	VI A.D.
P.Oxy. XVI 1917	VI A.D.	Stud.Pal. III 453	VI A.D.
P.Oxy. XVI 1997	VI A.D.	Stud.Pal. VIII 1257	VI A.D.
P.Oxy. XVI 1998	VI A.D.	Stud.Pal. X 44	VI A.D.
P.Oxy. XVI 2018	VI A.D.	Stud.Pal. X 207	VI A.D.
P.Oxy. XXVII 2480	565/566 A.D. (probably)	Stud.Pal. X 210	VI A.D.
P.Oxy. L 3600	502 A.D.	Stud.Pal. X 228	VI A.D.

… CHRONOLOGICAL INDEX

Stud.Pal. X 234	VI A.D.	**Stud.Pal.** XX 148	VI A.D.
Stud.Pal. X 258	VI A.D.	**Stud.Pal.** XX 254	VI A.D.
Stud.Pal. XX 137	522 A.D.	**P.Wash.Univ.** II 103	VI A.D.

VI/VII A.D.

CPR VIII 68	VI/VII A.D.	**P.Oxy.** XVI 1910	VI/VII A.D.
CPR X 60	VI/VII A.D.	(?)**P.Oxy.** XIX 2244,57	VI/VII A.D.
CPR XIV 36	VI/VII A.D.	**P.Oxy.** LVI 3870	VI/VII A.D.
P.Dub. 25	VI/VII A.D.	**SB** I 5681	VI-VII A.D.
P.Heid. VII 410,5	VI/VII A.D.	**SB** VI 9146	VI/VII A.D.
P.Köln VII 319	VI/VII A.D.	**SB** VI 9593	VI/VII A.D.
P.Köln VII 321	VI/VII A.D.	**SB** XVIII 13266	VI/VII A.D.
P.Köln VII 322	VI/VII A.D.	**SB** XX 14705	VI/VII A.D.
P.Köln VII 323	VI/VII A.D.	**SB** XX 15072	VI/VII A.D.
P.Lond. II 392	VI-VII A.D.	**Stud.Pal.** III 25	VI-VII A.D.
P.Lond. III 1097	VI/VII A.D.	**Stud.Pal.** VIII 1346	VI/VII A.D.
P.Oxy. VI 922	VI/VII A.D.	**Stud.Pal.** X 5	VI-VII A.D.
P.Oxy. VI 942	VI-VII A.D.	**Stud.Pal.** X 237	VI-VII A.D.
P.Oxy. XVI 1848	VI-VII A.D.	**PUG** I 50	VI/VII A.D.
P.Oxy. XVI 1861	VI-VII A.D.	**P.Vind.Tand.** 17	VI-VII A.D.
P.Oxy. XVI 1866	VI/VII A.D.		

VII A.D.

P.Bodl. I 73	610-641 A.D.	**Stud.Pal.** III 67	VII A.D.
CPR VII 51	629 A.D.	**Stud.Pal.** III 68	VII A.D.
CPR VIII 76	698 A.D.	**Stud.Pal.** III 197	VII A.D.
CPR X 63	VII A.D.	**Stud.Pal.** III 202	VII A.D.
CPR X 135	683/684 A.D.	**Stud.Pal.** VIII 952	VII A.D.
P.Dub. 28	611/612 A.D.?	**Stud.Pal.** VIII 1198	664 or 679 A.D.
P.Laur. II 47	VII A.D. (beginning)	**Stud.Pal.** VIII 1309	VII A.D.
(?)**P.Lond.** V 1791	VII A.D.	**Stud.Pal.** VIII 1326	VII A.D.
P.Mich. inv.489	VII A.D.	**Stud.Pal.** X 4	VII A.D.
SB I 4497	616 A.D.	**Stud.Pal.** X 22	VII A.D.
SB VI 8987	644/645 A.D.	**Stud.Pal.** X 66	VII A.D.
SB VI 9578	642 A.D.	**Stud.Pal.** X 149	VII A.D.
SB VI 9590	VII A.D.	**Stud.Pal.** X 214	VII A.D.
SB VIII 9750	657 A.D.	**Stud.Pal.** X 220	VII A.D.
SB VIII 9756	653 A.D.	**Stud.Pal.** X 231	VII A.D.
SB XVIII 13771	677 or 707 A.D.	**Stud.Pal.** X 263	VII A.D.
Stud.Pal. III 64	VII A.D.	**Stud.Pal.** XX 206	VII A.D.

VII/VIII A.D.

CPR IV 2	VII/VIII A.D.	**Stud.Pal.** III 356	VII/VIII A.D.
P.Batav. XXV 80 B	VII/VIII A.D.	**Stud.Pal.** VIII 1183	VII/VIII A.D.
SB VI 9262	VII/VIII A.D.	**Stud.Pal.** X 17	VII/VIII A.D.
SB XVIII 13888	VII/VIII A.D.	(?) **Stud.Pal.** X 56	VII-VIII A.D.

Stud.Pal. X 200	VII-VIII A.D.	**Stud.Pal.** X 212	VII-VIII A.D.
Stud.Pal. X 202	VII-VIII A.D.	**Stud.Pal.** X 213	VII-VIII A.D.
Stud.Pal. X 203	VII-VIII A.D.	**Stud.Pal.** X 217	VII-VIII A.D.
Stud.Pal. X 206	VII-VIII A.D.	**Stud.Pal.** X 227	VII-VIII A.D.
Stud.Pal. X 208	VII-VIII A.D.	**Stud.Pal.** X 230	VII-VIII A.D.
Stud.Pal. X 209	VII-VIII A.D.	**Stud.Pal.** X 232	VII/VIII A.D.
Stud.Pal. X 211	VII-VIII A.D.	**Stud.Pal.** XX 249 *verso*	VII-VIII A.D.

VIII A.D.

SB XVIII 13870	VIII A.D. (beginning)	**Stud.Pal.** X 84	VIII A.D.
SB XX 14234	729 A.D.	**Stud.Pal.** X 109	VIII A.D.
SB XX 14236	VIII A.D.	**Stud.Pal.** X 119	VIII A.D.
Stud.Pal. III 258	719 A.D.	**Stud.Pal.** X 199	VIII A.D.
Stud.Pal. III 259	719 A.D.	**Stud.Pal.** X 204	VIII A.D.
Stud.Pal. III 343	VIII A.D.	**Stud.Pal.** X 218	VIII A.D.
Stud.Pal. III 448	708 A.D.	**Stud.Pal.** X 223	VIII A.D.
Stud.Pal. X 72	VIII A.D.	**Stud.Pal.** X 226	VIII A.D.

Byz.

SB I 4727,2	Byz.	**SB** I 5338,11	Byz.
SB I 5337,5	Byz.		

s.d.

Ét.Fouad 2,1	**SB** I 2246,6-7

3 Reverse Index[1]

P.Aberd. 42(h),2	ΚΑΙΝΗ	BGU IV 1193,6	ΣΑΤΟΚΟΥ (fossil kleros)
P.Abinn. 11,12	ΛΕΥΚΟΓΙΟΝ	BGU IV 1193,7	ΔΗΜΗΤΡΊΟΥ (fossil kleros)
P.Alex. inv. 563,5 (p.32)	ΤΑΝΑΣΩ	BGU IV 1196,27	ΒΟΥΣΙΡΙΣ
P.Alex. inv. 563,7 (p.32)	ΦΕΒΙΧΙΣ	BGU IV 1197,I,4	ΒΟΥΣΙΡΙΣ
P.Amh. II 142,4	ΘΜΟΙΤΟΘΙΣ	BGU IV 1197,I,9	ΚΟΜΑ
P.Amh. II 142,16	ἹΠΠΩΝΩΝ κώμη	BGU IV 1197,I,9	ΛΙΝΗ
P.Amh. II 147,2;4	ΦΕΒΙΧΙΣ	BGU IV 1198,6	ΒΟΥΣΙΡΙΣ
P.Amst. I 83,2	ΤΟΣΑΧΜΙΣ	BGU IV 1200,3	ΒΟΥΣΙΡΙΣ
P.Athen. 34,14	ΤΟΚΩΙΣ	BGU IV 1200,16;20;24	ΛΙΝΗ
P.Bad. (= VBP) IV 55,6-7	ἹΠΠΩΝΩΝ κώμη	BGU IV 1201,4	ΒΟΥΣΙΡΙΣ
P.Bad. (= VBP) IV 74,7;12	ἈΓΚΥΡΩΝ πόλις/κώμη	BGU IV 1202,1	ΒΟΥΣΙΡΙΣ
P.Bad. (= VBP) IV 75a,3	ἈΓΚΥΡΩΝ πόλις/κώμη	BGU IV 1202,1	ΟΝΝΗΣ
P.Bad. (= VBP) IV 75b,5	ἈΓΚΥΡΩΝ πόλις/κώμη	BGU IV 1202,11	ΘΑΛ...
P.Bad. (= VBP) IV 77,8	ἈΓΚΥΡΩΝ πόλις/κώμη	BGU IV 1208,21	ΔΙΚΩΜΙΑ
P.Bad. (= VBP) IV 82,8	ἈΓΚΥΡΩΝ πόλις/κώμη	BGU VI 1216,68;70	περὶ ΑΥ̓ΛΗΝ
* P.Batav. XIX 23,3	ΠΕΕΜΠ(Α) 'Θ'	* BGU VI 1244,6	ΠΕΕΝΣΧΩΝ
P.Batav. XIX 23 bis,3	ΠΕΕΜΠ(Α) 'Θ'	* BGU VI 1244,6;38	ΦΝΕΒΙΕΥΣ
P.Batav. XXV 49,9	ΝΕΙ͂ΛΟΥ ΠΟΛΙΣ	BGU VI 1285,9	ΘΜΟΙΦΘΑ
P.Batav. XXV 65,9	ΒΟΥΣΙΡΙΣ	BGU VII 1568,2	ΝΕΙ͂ΛΟΥ ΠΟΛΙΣ
P.Batav. XXV 80 B,II,3	ΚΩ	BGU VIII 1732,5	ΔΗΜΗΤΡΊΟΥ (fossil kleros)
P.Berl.Leihg. I 2,recto,2	ΣΩΒΘΙΣ	BGU VIII 1733,6	ΦΊΛΩΝΟΣ (fossil kleros)
P.Berl.Zill. 7,recto,8; verso,1	ΚΩ	* BGU VIII 1733,6	ΠΟΕΝΠΙΒΤΗΙ
P.Berl.Zill. 7,recto,13; verso,1	ΑΚΕΕΙΣ	BGU VIII 1734,5;8	ΤΙΛΩΘΙΣ
BGU III 741,22	ΛΟΓΓΊΝΟΥ (fossil kleros)	BGU VIII 1734,5	ΝΙΚΑΝΟΡΟΣ (fossil kleros)
BGU III 922,8	ἈΓΑΘΟΚΛΕΟΥΣ (fossil kleros)	BGU VIII 1734,6	ΠΟΛΕΜΩΝΟΣ καὶ ΠΕΡΙΓΈΝΟΥ(fossil kleros)
BGU III 927,2	]ΚΕΝΗ		
BGU III 929 B,3	ἈΡΙΣΤΟΝΕΊΚΟΥ (fossil kleros)	BGU VIII 1734,7	ἈΛΕΞΑΝΔΡΟΥ (fossil kleros)
BGU III 938,3	ΣΩΒΘΙΣ ἡ μικρά	* BGU VIII 1737,18	ΤΑΒΑ[
BGU III 938,4	ἈΡΡΙΑΝΟΥ͂	BGU VIII 1739,12	Κ[...].ΙΝ...
BGU III 949,5	ΠΑΠΑ	BGU VIII 1742,2	ΤΙΛΩΘΙΣ
BGU III 958a	ΚΩΙΤΗΣ	* BGU VIII 1747,3	ΝΟ( )
BGU III 958a	ΨΩΛΕ[	BGU VIII 1747,4	ΤΕΚΜΙ
BGU IV 1060,16	ΤΙΛΩΘΙΣ	BGU VIII 1748,3	ΦΕΒΙΧΙΣ
BGU IV 1061,3;5;18	ΣΙΝΑΡΥ	BGU VIII 1749,11	ΦΑΡΣΕΣΙ
BGU IV 1061,8	ΒΟΥΣΙΡΙΣ	BGU VIII 1752,5	ΤΙΛΩΘΙΣ
BGU IV 1104,30	ΜΑΧΟΡ	BGU VIII 1753,6	ΣΩΒΘΙΣ
BGU IV 1104,30	ΖΩΊΛΟΥ (fossil kleros)	BGU VIII 1761,8	ΤΟΚΩΙΣ
BGU IV 1138,2	ΘΕΛΒΩΝΘΙΣ	BGU VIII 1763,10	ΣΑΔΑΛΕΙΟΝ
BGU IV 1167,48;72	ΜΑΧΟΡ	BGU VIII 1764,10	ΚΩΙΤΗΣ
BGU IV 1167,50;74	ἹΕΡΟΞΕΝΟΥ (fossil kleros)	BGU VIII 1768,1	ἹΕΡΑ ΝΗ͂ΣΟΣ
BGU IV 1187,4	ΤΟΚΩΙΣ	BGU VIII 1771,13	῎ΑΓΗΜΑ
BGU IV 1188,2	ΚΟΜΑ	BGU VIII 1771,14	ΠΕΕΝΕΨΩΜΦΙΣ
BGU IV 1189,3;9	ΒΟΥΣΙΡΙΣ	BGU VIII 1771,14	οἱ ἈΡΧΑΙ͂ΟΙ
BGU IV 1189,6	ΚΟΜΑ	BGU VIII 1771,16	ΒΙΧΙΝΘΩΥΘ
BGU IV 1192,15	ΣΧΝΩΜΘΙΣ	BGU VIII 1771,16	περὶ ΑΥ̓ΛΗΝ
BGU IV 1193,4	ΚΟΜΑ	BGU VIII 1771,16;20	ΤΕΚΜΙ
BGU IV 1193,4	ῬΩΔΩΝΟΣ (fossil kleros)	BGU VIII 1772,11	ΠΩΙΣ

---

[1] Documents marked with an asterisk are those for which a new dating or a new reading is proposed. See also (for documents in the Wien collection) JOHANNES DIETHART, «Korr.Tyche 148-162», *Tyche* 10,1995, pp.237-241.

BGU VIII 1772,11;16	ἹΠΠΟΝΊΚΟΥ ὁ ΠΡΩΤΕΣΙΛΆΟΥ (fossil kleros)	BGU VIII 1822,21	ΤΕΚΜΙ
		BGU VIII 1824,8	ΤΑΜΦΝΟΥΘΙΣ
BGU VIII 1773,5;8	ΒΟΥΣΙΡΙΣ	BGU VIII 1824,18	ΠΛΑΤΙΚ
BGU VIII 1773,6	ΦΊΔΩΝΟΣ (fossil kleros)	BGU VIII 1825,3-4	ΤΑΓΧΑΙΣ
BGU VIII 1777,6	ΠΩΙΣ	BGU VIII 1827,6	ΦΝΕΒΙΕΥΣ
BGU VIII 1778,3-4	ΤΑΓΧΑΙΣ	* BGU VIII 1827,26	ΠΕΕΝΣΧΩΝ
BGU VIII 1778,6-7	ΚΆΤΩ (ἌΓΗΜΑ)	BGU VIII 1828,4;8	ΦΝΕΒΙΕΥΣ
* BGU VIII 1779,2	ΠΕΕΝΕΨΥ	BGU VIII 1828,9	ἈΓΕΛΆΟΥ (fossil kleros; later ἈΠΙΚΚΊΟΥ)
BGU VIII 1780,2	ΤΑΓΧΑΙΣ		
BGU VIII 1784,5	ἹΕΡΑ ΝΗΣΟΣ	BGU VIII 1831,1;7	ΣΑΔΑΛΕΪΟΝ
BGU VIII 1786,4	ΣΑΔΑΛΕΪΟΝ	BGU VIII 1831,9	ΑΝΝΗΣ
BGU VIII 1789,1	ΤΕΚΜΙ?	BGU VIII 1832,7;13	ΤΕΚΜΙ
BGU VIII 1789,8	ΚΟΜΑ	BGU VIII 1832,9	ΜΟΥΧΙΣ ?
* BGU VIII 1789,9	ΚΡΗΚΙΣ	BGU VIII 1834,10	ΚΑΙΝΗ
* BGU VIII 1789,9	ΤΟΟΥ	BGU VIII 1835,3-4	ἹΕΡΆ ΝΗΣΟΣ
BGU VIII 1795,2;5	ΤΕΚΜΙ	BGU VIII 1837,4	ΦΝΕΒΙΕΥΣ
BGU VIII 1795,6	ΣΩΒΘΙΣ	BGU VIII 1838,4	ΤΕΚΜΙ
BGU VIII 1796,1	ΤΙΛΩΘΙΣ	BGU VIII 1842,4	ΤΕΚΜΙ
BGU VIII 1796,8	ἝΡΜΩΝΟΣ (fossil kleros)	BGU VIII 1842,6	ΠΕΕΝΕΨΥ
BGU VIII 1798,1	ΦΝΕΒΙΕΥΣ	BGU VIII 1843,3	ΤΙΝΤΗΡΙΣ
BGU VIII 1802,1	ΜΕΣΗ	BGU VIII 1845,4	ΤΑΓΧΑΙΣ
BGU VIII 1802,3	ΤΕΧΥΜΙΣ	BGU VIII 1846,3	ΤΩΥ
BGU VIII 1803,3;6-7	ΦΝΕΒΙΕΥΣ	BGU VIII 1848,4	ΤΙΛΩΘΙΣ
BGU VIII 1803,6	ΠΕΕΝΠΙΒΥΚ(ΙΣ)	BGU VIII 1849,4;6	ΤΙΛΩΘΙΣ
BGU VIII 1805,1	ΠΕΡΑΝ	BGU VIII 1849,6	ΠΕΕΝΑΜΕΥΣ
BGU VIII 1805,5	ἩΡΑΚΛ[....] ὁ ΚΊΣΣΟΥ (fossil kleros)	BGU VIII 1852,4	ΤΙΛΩΘΙΣ
BGU VIII 1807,9	ΤΕΚΜΙ	BGU VIII 1855,2	ΦΝΕΒΙΕΥΣ
BGU VIII 1808,1	ΤΕΚΜΙ	BGU VIII 1856,2	ΔΗΜΗΤΡΊΟΥ (fossil kleros)
BGU VIII 1808,4	ΚΟΛΛΙΝΤΑΑΘΥΡ	BGU VIII 1857,8	ΤΕΒΕΤΝΥ
BGU VIII 1808,5	ΚΟΜΑ	BGU VIII 1857,10	ΚΑΙΝΗ
BGU VIII 1808,8	ΤΡΙΚΩΜΊΑ	BGU VIII 1872,19	ΔΗΜΗΤΡΊΟΥ (fossil kleros)
BGU VIII 1808,9	ΟΝΝΙΙΣ	BGU VIII 1888,3	ΘΜΟΙΝΑΥΣΙΡΙΣ
BGU VIII 1808,12	ΘΜΟΙΟΒΑΣΤΙΣ	BGU X 1911,7	ΔΙΚΩΜΊΑ
BGU VIII 1808,13	ΒΟΥΣΙΡΙΣ	BGU XI 2073,2	ἈΓΚΥΡΩΝ πόλις/κώμη
BGU VIII 1808,14	ΠΕΡΑΝ	BGU XIII 2326,fr.a,3;6;10	ΚΕΦΑΛΑΪ
BGU VIII 1808,15	ΤΕΧΘΩ	BGU XIII 2326,fr.a,4;7-9;fr.b,2;3;6-8;10-15;17	ΛΕΥΚΟΓΙΟΝ
BGU VIII 1808,16	ΚΩΊΤΗΣ		
* BGU VIII 1808,17;33	ΠΕΤΑΧΟΡ	BGU XIII 2326,fr.a,13	ΒΟΥΣΙΡΙΣ
BGU VIII 1808,20	ἹΕΡΆ ΝΗΣΟΣ	BGU XIII 2365,1	ΑΜΦ.Δ()
* BGU VIII 1808,21	ΑΛΙΛΑΙΣ	BGU XIII 2365,2	ΠΑΛΑΣ
BGU VIII 1808,22	ΚΟΛΛΑΣΟΥΧΑ	BGU XIII 2365,3	ΜΑΓΔΩΛΑ
BGU VIII 1808,23	ΚΟΡΦΟΤΟΙ	BGU XIII 2365,4	ΑΤΤΟΝ()
BGU VIII 1808,24	ΦΕΒΙΧΙΣ	BGU XIII 2365,5	ΠΑΛΑΙ()
BGU VIII 1808,25	ΦΝΕΒΙΕΥΣ	BGU XIII 2365,6	ΟΙΝΑΛΕΓ()
BGU VIII 1808,27	ΑΦΛΩΘΙΣ	BGU XIII 2365,7	ΝΙΗΡΑ()
BGU VIII 1808,29;37	ΤΑΓΧΑΙΣ	BGU XIII 2365,8	ΒΑΣΙΛ()
BGU VIII 1808,30	ΠΩΙΣ	BGU XIII 2365,9	ΣΚΥΠΙΩΝ
* BGU VIII 1808,35	ΠΚΟΜΜΑΤΟΕΙ	BGU XIII 2365,10	ΠΟΑΧΡΙΝΑ
BGU VIII 1811,6	ΤΑΓΧΑΙΣ	BGU XIII 2365,12	ΤΕΧΘΩ
BGU VIII 1813,6;8	ΒΟΥΣΙΡΙΣ	BGU XIII 2365,13	ΠΑΠΑ
BGU VIII 1813,8	Τ[......] (fossil kleros)	BGU XIII 2365,14	ΘΕΛΒΩ
BGU VIII 1814,7	ΤΕΒΕΤΝΥ	BGU XIII 2365,15	ΘΜΟΙΧ()?
BGU VIII 1815,5	ΜΑΧΟΡ	BGU XIII 2365,16	ΝΟΜΑΡΧ()
BGU VIII 1817,4-5	ΠΩΙΣ	BGU XIV 2370,5	ΝΩΙΣ
BGU VIII 1817,12	ΤΙΛΩΘΙΣ	BGU XIV 2370,16;17;86	ΤΙΛΩΘΙΣ
BGU VIII 1818,2;28	ΤΑ[or ΤΡ[	BGU XIV 2370,24	ΠΕΕΝΠΑΣΒΥΤ(ΙΣ)
BGU VIII 1819,3	ΜΑΧΟΡ	BGU XIV 2370,24	ΠΕΕΝΣΕΜΘΕΥΣ
BGU VIII 1821,13	ΤΟΚΩΙΣ	BGU XIV 2370,26;73	ΚΆΤΩ (ἌΓΗΜΑ)
BGU VIII 1821,15	ΣΩΒΘΙΣ	BGU XIV 2370,37	ἌΓΗΜΑ
* BGU VIII 1822,7	ΠΕΕΝΕΨΥ	BGU XIV 2370,38	ΑΛΙΛΑΙΣ

REVERSE INDEX

BGU XIV 2370,74	ΚΟΜΑ	BGU XIV 2433,48	ΧΕΝΝΙΣ
* BGU XIV 2370,75	ΜΑΧΟΡ	BGU XIV 2433,49	ΦΥΣ
BGU XIV 2370,75	ΤΟΟΥ	BGU XIV 2433,51	].Ε[..]ΒΕΩΣ
BGU XIV 2370,77	Β[..]ΟΥ	BGU XIV 2433,52	ΣΙΣΙΝΗ
BGU XIV 2370,78	ΘΜΟΙΟΒΑΣΤΙΣ	BGU XIV 2433,52	ΣΙΘΕΥΣ
BGU XIV 2370,79	ΦΝΕΒΙΕΥΣ	BGU XIV 2433,53	ΒΕ[.]Υ
BGU XIV 2370,80	ΆΥΗΡΙΣ	BGU XIV 2433,54	ΝΙ[.].ΕΩΣ
* BGU XIV 2370,82;86;96	ΟΝΝΗΣ	BGU XIV 2433,55	ΠΕΕΝΕΠΟΧΡΑ
BGU XIV 2370,87	ΤΑΓΧΑΙΣ	BGU XIV 2433,71	περὶ ΑΥΛΗΝ
BGU XIV 2370,92	ΒΟΥΣΙΡΙΣ	BGU XIV 2434,2	ΚΟΜΑ
BGU XIV 2370,94	.[.]ΤΑΕΩΣ	BGU XIV 2434,3;24	ΤΙΛΩΘΙΣ
BGU XIV 2374,6	ΦΙΛΑΔΕΛΦΟΣ	BGU XIV 2434,4	ΚΟΛΛΑΣΟΥΧΑ
BGU XIV 2376,17;36	ΣΩΒΘΙΣ	BGU XIV 2434,8	ΚΩΪΤΗΣ
BGU XIV 2376,18;38	ΤΕΚΒΗ (?)	BGU XIV 2434,10	ΚΆΤΩ (ΆΓΗΜΑ)
BGU XIV 2376,19;39	ΕΥΜΗΛΟΥ (fossil kleros)	BGU XIV 2434,11	ΤΕΚΜΙ
BGU XIV 2377,22;45	ΤΕΚΒΗ (?)	BGU XIV 2434,12	ΠΕΡΑΝ
BGU XIV 2377,42	ΣΩΒΘΙΣ	BGU XIV 2434,13	ΤΕΧΘΩ
BGU XIV 2377,45	ΕΥΜΗΛΟΥ (fossil kleros)	BGU XIV 2434,15	ΠΕΕΝΜΟ()
BGU XIV 2382,11	ΠΟΙΜΕΝΩΝ κώμη	BGU XIV 2434,25	ΣΩΒΘΙΣ
BGU XIV 2382,14	ΚΕΡΚΕΥΝΙΦΙΣ	BGU XIV 2434,27	..ΝΙΝ
BGU XIV 2389,2;17	ΘΜΟΙΝΑΥΣΙΡΙΣ	BGU XIV 2434,28	ΦΝΕΒΙΕΥΣ
BGU XIV 2390,42	ΣΑΡΑΠΙΟΥ (fossil kleros)	BGU XIV 2435,1	ΦΕΒΙΧΙΣ
BGU XIV 2391,7	ΝΕΧΙΣΗ	BGU XIV 2435,6,8	ΚΛΕΟΔΗΜΟΥ (fossil kleros)
BGU XIV 2392,2	ΆΓΗΜΑ	BGU XIV 2435,7	ΦΙΛΩ() (fossil kleros)
BGU XIV 2392,5	ΝΕΧΙΣΗ	BGU XIV 2435,10	ΆΛΚΙΜΟΥ (fossil kleros)
BGU XIV 2419,12	ΦΕΒΙΧΙΣ	BGU XIV 2435,11;15	ΜΕΛΑΝΟΣ (fossil kleros)
BGU XIV 2420,6	ΝΩΙΣ	BGU XIV 2435,12	ΠΑ() (fossil kleros)
BGU XIV 2424,6	ΤΕΧΘΩ (?)	BGU XIV 2435,19	.ΦΗΕΩΣ
BGU XIV 2425,7;27	ΝΩΙΣ	BGU XIV 2435,20;28	ΝΙΚΟΣΤΡΑΤΟΥ (fossil kleros)
BGU XIV 2429,2	ΠΕΕΝΑΜΕΥΣ	BGU XIV 2435,22	ΣΩΤ() (fossil kleros)
BGU XIV 2429,3	ΠΕΕΝΕΨΩΜΦΙΣ	BGU XIV 2435,23	ΣΙΜΙΟΥ (fossil kleros)
BGU XIV 2429,3	ΠΕΕΝΗ	BGU XIV 2435,24	ΔΙΟΝ() (fossil kleros)
BGU XIV 2429,4	ΆΜΦΙΩ(ΝΟΣ?)	BGU XIV 2435,25	ΤΑΛΑΗ
BGU XIV 2429,4	ΚΟΡΦΟΤΟΙ	BGU XIV 2435,25	Α.ΝΕΥΔ() (fossil kleros)
BGU XIV 2429,6	ἸΒΙΩΝ ...	BGU XIV 2435,26	ΑΣΣΥΑ
BGU XIV 2429,6	ΝΙΝΩ	BGU XIV 2435,28	ΧΑΙΡΕ() (fossil kleros)
BGU XIV 2429,7	ΚΟΛΛΑΣΟΥΧΑ	BGU XIV 2435,29	ΒΑΛΛΗΡΟΥ (fossil kleros)
BGU XIV 2429,7	ΜΑΓΔΩΛΑ	BGU XIV 2435,30	ΚΕΡΚΕΣ(ΗΦΙΣ)
BGU XIV 2429,8	ΆΝΑ(ΒΩΛΙΑ)	BGU XIV 2435,31;35	ΠΟΛΥΝΙΚΟΥ (fossil kleros)
BGU XIV 2429,8	ΜΟΥΧΙΣ	BGU XIV 2435,33	.ΠΛΑΡΧΟΥ (fossil kleros)
BGU XIV 2429,9	ΝΙΣΕΥΣ	BGU XIV 2435,36;37	ΠΕΡΙΤΟΥ (fossil kleros)
* BGU XIV 2429,9	ΤΑΓΧΑΙΣ	BGU XIV 2435,39	ΆΣΚΛ() (fossil kleros)
BGU XIV 2429,10;13	ΠΕΤΑΧΟΡ	BGU XIV 2435,40	ΆΓΑΘΩΝΟΣ (fossil kleros)
BGU XIV 2429,10	ΠΕΕΝΣΕΜΘΕΥΣ	BGU XIV 2435,43	ΔΕΡ() (fossil kleros)
BGU XIV 2429,11	ἹΕΡΑ ΝΗΣΟΣ	BGU XIV 2435,47	ΚΑΛΛΙΠΠΟΥ (fossil kleros)
BGU XIV 2429,11	ΣΩΒΘΙΣ	BGU XIV 2435, col.I,1	ΠΕΕΝΑΜΕΥΣ
BGU XIV 2429,16	ΠΕΕΝ.[..	BGU XIV 2436,1;14	ΜΑΓΔΩΛΑ
BGU XIV 2429,18	ΠΕ..[	BGU XIV 2436,2	ἸΒΙΩΝ ...
BGU XIV 2431,1	ΦΕΒΙΧΙΣ	BGU XIV 2436,2;8;13	ΠΩΙΣ
BGU XIV 2431,8	ΤΑΛΑΗ	BGU XIV 2436,3	ΟΓΟΥ
* BGU XIV 2432,11	ΦΝΕΒΙΕΥΣ	* BGU XIV 2436,3	ΠΕΕΝΣΑΜΟΙ
BGU XIV 2432,13	ΣΩΒΘΙΣ	BGU XIV 2436,4;9	ΤΟΣΑΧΜΙΣ
BGU XIV 2432,15	ΤΕΒΕΤΝΥ	BGU XIV 2436,5	ΦΕΒΙΧΙΣ
BGU XIV 2432,17	ΘΜΟΙΦΘΑ	* BGU XIV 2436,5;8;12	ΤΑΓΧΑΙΣ
BGU XIV 2432,18	ΤΕΜΗΣΙΣ	BGU XIV 2436,10	ΠΕΕΝΠΑΣΒΥΤ(ΙΣ)
BGU XIV 2432,20	ἸΒΙΩΝ ΤΕΧΘΩ	BGU XIV 2436,11	ΚΟΡΦΟΤΟΙ
BGU XIV 2432,22	ΘΜΟΙΟΒΑΣΤΙΣ	BGU XIV 2436,12	ΝΟΗΡΙΣ
BGU XIV 2432,33	ΠΕΕΝΦΡΙΜΕΝΣΩΚΟΥ	BGU XIV 2436,15	ΠΑΤΑΤΩΙΝ
BGU XIV 2433,18	ΠΕΕΝ.ΧΕΝΟΒΑ()	BGU XIV 2437,1	ΚΟΛΛΙΝΤΑΑΘΥΡ
BGU XIV 2433,46	ΠΟΙΜΕΝΩΝ κώμη	BGU XIV 2437,1;5;7;12;23	ΤΕΚΜΙ

BGU XIV 2437,3	ΤΑΕΜΣΙΣ	BGU XIV 2439,70	ΚΟΜΑ
BGU XIV 2437,3;4;20;21	ΤΩΥ	BGU XIV 2439,84	ΤΟΟΥ
BGU XIV 2437,4;22	ΤΟΧΟΝΤΩΥ	BGU XIV 2439,104	ΦΥΣ
* BGU XIV 2437,5	ΠΕΕΝΕ.'.'()	BGU XIV 2440,3	ΚΑΤΩ (ΑΓΗΜΑ)
BGU XIV 2437,12	περὶ ΑΥΛΗΝ	BGU XIV 2440,3	ΠΕΕΝΑΜΕΥΣ
BGU XIV 2437,13	ΑΣΚΑΙΑΤΑΣ	BGU XIV 2440,8	ΤΙΛΩΘΙΣ
BGU XIV 2437,14	ΠΥΡΓΩΤΟΣ	BGU XIV 2440,9	ΤΩΥ
BGU XIV 2437,15	[...].ΑΡΑΠΕΩΣ	BGU XIV 2440,10	ΤΕΧΥΜΙΣ
BGU XIV 2437,18;70	ΜΟΥΧΙΣ	BGU XIV 2440,12	ΟΛΩΝΘΙΣ
BGU XIV 2437,26	ΚΑΤΩ (ΑΓΗΜΑ)	BGU XIV 2440,12;41;46	ΤΕΚΜΙ
BGU XIV 2437,26	ΠΕΕΝΑΜΕΥΣ	BGU XIV 2440,14	ΤΕΜΗΣΙΣ
BGU XIV 2437,28;51	ΚΟΡΦΟΤΟΙ	* BGU XIV 2440,15	ΦΝΕΒΙΕΥΣ
BGU XIV 2437,30;54;62	ΠΕΕΝΕΨΩΜΦΙΣ	BGU XIV 2440,16;19;60;84	ΦΕΒΙΧΙΣ
BGU XIV 2437,32	ΠΕΕΝΣΕΜΘΕΥΣ	* BGU XIV 2440,17	ΤΑΒΟΚΛΙΣ
BGU XIV 2437,34	ΚΕΛΛΑΣ	BGU XIV 2440,17;45	ΤΟΧΟΝΤΩΥ
BGU XIV 2437,36	ΘΜΟΙΦΘΑ	BGU XIV 2440,18	ΨΕΛΕΜΑΧΙΣ
BGU XIV 2437,38	ΙΒΙΩΝ ΘΜΟΙΦΘΑ	BGU XIV 2440,26	ΦΥΣ
BGU XIV 2437,41	ΠΕΕΝΣΑΜΟΙ	BGU XIV 2440,38	ΤΕΧΘΩ
BGU XIV 2437,44	ΚΡΗΚΙΣ	BGU XIV 2440,44	ΟΝΝΗΣ
BGU XIV 2437,44;46;48;49	ΚΟΜΑ	BGU XIV 2440,48	]ΑΓΕΩΣ
BGU XIV 2437,51	ΝΕΧΟΣ	BGU XIV 2440,51;53	ΚΟΜΑ
BGU XIV 2437,62	ΠΕΕΝΦΡΙ....[	BGU XIV 2440,51	ΤΟΟΥ
BGU XIV 2437,70	ΣΩΒΘΙΣ	* BGU XIV 2440,56;108;122	ΠΕΕΝΕΠΟΧΡΑ
* BGU XIV 2437,74	ΤΕΡΤΟΝΠΕΤΕΜΟΥΝ	BGU XIV 2440,58	ΘΜΟΙΟΒΑΣΤΙΣ
* BGU XVI 2437,77	].ΠΕΤΕΧΩΝ	BGU XIV 2440,60	ΤΕΜΕΝΚΥΡΚ(ΙΣ)
* BGU XIV 2438,10;93	ΝΙΝΩ	* BGU XIV 2440,62;64	ΠΕΕΝΗ
BGU XIV 2438,15	ΚΟΡΦΟΤΟΙ	BGU XIV 2440,63	Ε....[
BGU XIV 2438,17	ΝΙΣΕΥΣ	BGU XIV 2440,65	ΠΕΡΑΝ
BGU XIV 2438,20	ΚΟΛΛΑΣΟΥΧΑ	BGU XIV 2440,65	ΝΙΣΕΥΣ
BGU XIV 2438,22;96	ΦΝΕΒΙΕΥΣ	* BGU XIV 2440,71	ΠΕΡΕΜΘ(ΙΣ)
BGU XIV 2438,31	ΠΕΕΝΒΕΝΔΗΤΙΣ	BGU XIV 2440,95	ΟΝΩΣΙΣ
BGU XIV 2438,33;98	ΠΕΕΝΠΙΒΥΚ(ΙΣ)	BGU XIV 2440,97	....ΑΣΙΟΥ
* BGU XIV 2438,34	ΚΕΡΚΥΤΟΥ(?)	* BGU XIV 2440,97	ΘΜΟΙΦΘΑ (?)
BGU XIV 2438,36	...ΑΙΝΕΩΣ	BGU XIV 2440,98	(Θ)ΕΛΒΩΝΘΙΣ
BGU XIV 2438,40	ΦΥΣ	BGU XIV 2440,122	ΕΥΔΟΞΟΥ (fossil kleros)
BGU XIV 2438,40	ΑΜΥΝΤΑ (fossil kleros)	BGU XIV 2440,129	ΠΥΡΓΩΤΟΣ
BGU XIV 2438,44	ΤΕΧΥΜΙΣ	BGU XIV 2441,9	ΛΑΒΟΥΤΟΣ (fossil kleros)
BGU XIV 2438,45	ΠΟΙΜΕΝΩΝ κώμη	BGU XIV 2441,10	ΗΓΗΣΙΠΠΟΥ (fossil kleros)
BGU XIV 2438,46	ΣΙΘΕΥΣ	BGU XIV 2441,11;17	ΔΑΛΙΣΚΟΥ (fossil kleros)
BGU XIV 2438,46	ΦΕΒΙΧΙΣ	BGU XIV 2441,14	ΜΗ() (fossil kleros)
BGU XIV 2438,49	ΤΕΜΕΝΚΥΡΚΙΣ	BGU XIV 2441,15	ΜΙ() (fossil kleros)
BGU XIV 2438,50	ΤΟΣΑΧΜΙΣ	BGU XIV 2441,18	ΗΓΗΣΙΔΗΜΟΥ (fossil kleros)
BGU XIV 2438,55;84	ΤΙΛΩΘΙΣ	* BGU XIV 2441,19	ΠΥΡΓΩΤΟΣ
BGU XIV 2438,62	ΣΧΝΩΜΘΙΣ	BGU XIV 2441,20, passim	ΑΡΧΕΠΟΛΕΩΣ (fossil kleros)
BGU XIV 2438,63	ΠΕΕΝΠΑΣΒΥΤ(ΙΣ)	BGU XIV 2441,33;44;85	ΠΡΩΤΟΓΕΝΟΥΣ (fossil kleros)
BGU XIV 2438,71	ΤΑΓΧΑΙΣ	BGU XIV 2441,36, passim	ΣΚΙΡΩΝΟΣ (fossil kleros)
BGU XIV 2438,72	ΚΟΜΑ	BGU XIV 2441,40;62;77;154	Φ..() (fossil kleros)
* BGU XIV 2438,72;75;76	ΚΡΗΚΙΣ	BGU XIV 2441,45	ΦΙΛΩΤΟΥ (fossil kleros)
BGU XIV 2438,74	ΤΟΟΥ	BGU XIV 2441,46	ΑΡ... (fossil kleros)
* BGU XIV 2438,87	ΠΕΡΑΝ	BGU XIV 2441,49	[..]ΕΙ..() (fossil kleros)
BGU XIV 2438,89	(ΚΑΤΩ) ΑΓΗΜΑ	BGU XIV 2441,53;58;75	ΤΕΚΜΙ
BGU XIV 2438,89	ΠΕΕΝΕΨΩΜΦΙΣ	BGU XIV 2441,56	ΚΛΕ.()
BGU XIV 2438,91	ΠΕΕΝΣΕΜΘΕΥΣ	BGU XIV 2441,56	....Σ() (fossil kleros)
BGU XIV 2438,94	ΠΕΕΝΦΡ[	BGU XIV 2441,67	ΚΟΛΛΙΝΤΑΑΘΥΡ
BGU XIV 2438,95	ΤΕΡΤΟΝΠ[	BGU XIV 2441,67;79	ΚΟΛΛΙΝΠΕΤΩΥ
BGU XIV 2438,100	ΑΥΗΡΙΣ	BGU XIV 2441,68;176;222	ΑΣΑΝΔΡΟΥ (fossil kleros)
BGU XIV 2438,101	ΧΕΝΝΙΣ	BGU XIV 2441,78;84;118;132	ΑΛΕΞΑΝΔΡΟΥ (fossil kleros)
BGU XIV 2439,20;62	ΚΡΗΚΙΣ		
BGU XIV 2439,22	ΕΥΑΝΔΡΟΥ (fossil kleros)	BGU XIV 2441,82;155;158;165;219;246	ΣΟΦΟΚΛΕΟΥΣ
BGU XIV 2439,26;97;103	ΜΑΧΟΡ		καὶ ΑΡΕΙΟΥ (fossil kleros)

REVERSE INDEX

BGU XIV 2441,83	ΕΥΜΗΛΟΥ (fossil kleros)
BGU XIV 2441,87; passim	ΚΟΡΡΑΓΟΥ (fossil kleros)
BGU XIV 2441,93; passim	ΝΙΚΑΪΟΥ (fossil kleros)
BGU XIV 2441,101	ΠΛ..() (fossil kleros)
BGU XIV 2441,105	..Ε() (fossil kleros)
BGU XIV 2441,105	....ΙΟΥ (fossil kleros)
BGU XIV 2441,105;114;120;236;243;250	ΕΜΠΕΔΟΚΛΕΟΥΣ (fossil kleros)
BGU XIV 2441,105;124;126;131	ΕΥΤΙΜΟΥ (fossil kleros)
BGU XIV 2441,108	Ε[(fossil kleros)
BGU XIV 2441,125;198;258	ΠΤΟΛΕΜΑΪΟΥ (fossil kleros)
BGU XIV 2441,172;174	ΦΙΛΩ() (fossil kleros)
BGU XIV 2441,199	].ΟΥ (fossil kleros)
BGU XIV 2441,201	Κ.()
BGU XIV 2441,208	ΜΟΥΧΙΣ
BGU XIV 2441,232	ΜΕΝΔ() (fossil kleros)
BGU XIV 2442,4	ΠΡΩΤΟΓΕΝΟΥΣ (fossil kleros)
BGU XIV 2442,6	ΗΓΗΣΙΝΟΥ (fossil kleros)
BGU XIV 2442,14	ΔΑΛΙΣΚΟΥ (fossil kleros)
BGU XIV 2442,18	ΝΙΚΑΪΟΥ (fossil kleros)
BGU XIV 2443,16;42	ΗΓΗΣΙΔΗΜΟΥ (fossil kleros)
BGU XIV 2443,20	ΚΛΕΟΜΑΝΤΡΙΔΟΥ (fossil kleros)
BGU XIV 2443,24;35;37;43	ΛΑΚΥΔΟΥΣ (fossil kleros)
BGU XIV 2443,26	]..ΠΟΥ (fossil kleros)
BGU XIV 2443,29	ΑΓΑΘΟΚΛΕΟΥΣ (fossil kleros)
BGU XIV 2443,29	ΠΡΩΤΟΛΑΟΥ (fossil kleros)
BGU XIV 2443,32	ΑΝΔΡΟΝΙΚΟΥ (fossil kleros)
BGU XIV 2443,41;53	ΔΑΛΙΣΚΟΥ (fossil kleros)
BGU XIV 2444,2	ΚΟΙΝΟΥ (fossil kleros)
BGU XIV 2444,5	ΒΑΚΧΙΟΥ (fossil kleros)
* BGU XIV 2444,6	ΠΕΕΝΣΕΜΘΕΥΣ
BGU XIV 2444,7;25;81;82	ΤΕΚΜΙ
BGU XIV 2444,10;16;18;20;27	ΠΟΛΥΔΑΜΑΝΤΟΣ (fossil kleros)
BGU XIV 2444,11;12;76;94	ΝΕΩΝΟΣ (fossil kleros)
BGU XIV 2444,13;17;64;113	ΕΥΜΗΛΟΥ (fossil kleros)
BGU XIV 2444,13;50;56;104;114	ΤΙΜΟΚΡΑΤΟΥ (fossil kleros)
BGU XIV 2444,13;56	ΚΛΕΟΚΡΑΤΟΥΣ (fossil kleros)
BGU XIV 2444,14;77;98;101	ΔΩΡΙΕΩΣ (fossil kleros)
BGU XIV 2444,15;57;95;99;102	ΝΙΚΟΦΩΝΤΟΣ (fossil kleros)
BGU XIV 2444,17;75	ΠΑΡΜΕΝΟΝΤΟΣ (fossil kleros)
BGU XIV 2444,23	ΠΟΛΕΜΑΡΧΟΥ (fossil kleros)
BGU XIV 2444,26;41;43;44;68;70;78;95;100	ΑΝΤΙΠΑΤΡΟΥ (fossil kleros)
BGU XIV 2444,30;57;79;139	ΜΕΝΟΙΤΟΥ καὶ ΑΡΙΣΤΟΔΗΜΟΥ (fossil kleros)
BGU XIV 2444,34;53;98;107;108	ΠΑΓΚΡΑΤΟΥ (fossil kleros)
BGU XIV 2444,56;76;100;112	ΤΥΧΩΝΟΣ (fossil kleros)
BGU XIV 2444,69	ΠΑΝΙΣΚΟΥ (fossil kleros)
BGU XIV 2444,71	ΛΑΟΜΗΔΟΥΣ (fossil kleros)
BGU XIV 2444,76	ΤΡ.() (fossil kleros)
BGU XIV 2444,77;84	ΣΕΛΕΥΚΟΥ (fossil kleros)
BGU XIV 2444,105	ΣΩΣΙΒΙΟΥ (fossil kleros)
BGU XIV 2444,108	...ΝΙΕΩ() (fossil kleros)
BGU XIV 2444,111	ΠΑΡΜΕΝΙΣΚΟΥ (fossil kleros)
BGU XIV 2444,119;135	ΑΝΙΚΗΤΟΥ (fossil kleros)
BGU XIV 2444,137	ΕΥΤΥΧΩΝΟΣ (fossil kleros)
BGU XIV 2445,1;5;10;33	ΠΑΓΚΡΑΤΟΥ (fossil kleros)
BGU XIV 2445,4	ΛΑΟΜΗΔΟΥΣ (fossil kleros)
BGU XIV 2445,14	ΔΙΔ() (fossil kleros)
BGU XIV 2445,15	ΜΕΝΟΙΤΟΥ καὶ ΑΡΙΣΤΟΔΗΜΟΥ (fossil kleros)
BGU XIV 2445,17	ΣΥΜΜΑΧΟΥ (fossil kleros)
BGU XIV 2445,18;35;39	ΠΡΩΤΟΓΕΝΟΥΣ (fossil kleros)
BGU XIV 2445,19;38	ΑΝΙΚΗΤΟΥ (fossil kleros)
BGU XIV 2445,20	ΔΙ... (fossil kleros)
BGU XIV 2445,22	ΣΕΛΕΥΚΟΥ (fossil kleros)
BGU XIV 2445,25	ΑΝΤΙΠΑΤΡΟΥ (fossil kleros)
BGU XIV 2445,28	ΔΩΡΙΕΩΣ (fossil kleros)
BGU XIV 2445,30	ΕΥΜΗΛΟΥ (fossil kleros)
BGU XIV 2445,31	ΝΕΩΝΟΣ (fossil kleros)
BGU XIV 2445,34	ΛΕΩΝΙΔΟΥ (fossil kleros)
BGU XIV 2445,34;36	ΤΙΜΟΚΡΑΤΟΥ (fossil kleros)
BGU XIV 2445,37	ΣΩΝΝΟΜΟΥ (fossil kleros)
BGU XIV 2445,38	ΠΑΡΜΕ() (fossil kleros)
BGU XIV 2445,41	ΠΑΡΜΕΝΟΝΤΟΣ (fossil kleros)
BGU XIV 2446,1	Σ.ΟΥ
BGU XIV 2446,4	ΣΤΡΑΤΩΝΟΣ τοῦ ΔΗΜΗΤΡΙΟΥ (fossil kleros)
BGU XIV 2446,5	ΠΟΛΕΜΩΝΟΣ (fossil kleros)
BGU XIV 2446,6;13;22	ΦΙΛΙΠΠΟΥ τοῦ ΤΙΜΟΚΡΑΤΟΥ (fossil kleros)
BGU XIV 2446,8;17	ΘΕΟΓΕΝΟΥΣ (fossil kleros)
BGU XIV 2446,15	]ΡΗΝΟΥ (fossil kleros)
BGU XIV 2447,9	Θ[(fossil kleros)
BGU XIV 2447,14;52	ΦΙΛΙΠΠΟΥ τοῦ ΤΙΜΟΚΡΑΤΟΥ (fossil kleros)
BGU XIV 2447,18	ΕΥΤΙΜΟΥ (fossil kleros)
BGU XIV 2447,18	ΠΤΟΛΕΜΑΪΟΥ (fossil kleros)
BGU XIV 2447,18;59	ΚΟΡΡΑΓΟΥ (fossil kleros)
BGU XIV 2447,20;49,55	ΕΜΠΕΔΟΚΛΕΟΥΣ (fossil kleros)
BGU XIV 2447,26	ΣΩΣΙΒΙΟΥ (fossil kleros)
BGU XIV 2447,31	ΛΑΚΥΔΟΥΣ (fossil kleros)
BGU XIV 2447,39	ΑΓΑΘΟΚΛΕΟΥΣ (fossil kleros)
BGU XIV 2447,40;53	ΑΣΑΝΔΡΟΥ (fossil kleros)
BGU XIV 2447,41;77	ΣΚΙΡΩΝΟΣ (fossil kleros)
BGU XIV 2447,42	ΜΕΝΟΙΤΟΥ καὶ ΑΡΙΣΤΟΔΗΜΟΥ (fossil kleros)
BGU XIV 2447,63	ΑΛΕΞΑΝΔΡΟΥ (fossil kleros)
BGU XIV 2447,64	Μ...ΕΙΔΟΥ (fossil kleros)
BGU XIV 2447,77	...ΩΝΟΣ (fossil kleros)
BGU XIV 2448,16	..ΕΙΟΥ (fossil kleros)
BGU XIV 2448,35	ΘΕΟ((fossil kleros)
BGU XIV 2448,45;58	ΑΓΑΘΟΚΛΕΟΥΣ (fossil kleros)
BGU XIV 2448,47;62	ΦΙΛΙΠΠΟΥ τοῦ ΤΙΜΟΚΡΑΤΟΥ (fossil kleros)
BGU XIV 2448,50	Κ[(fossil kleros)
BGU XIV 2448,51	ΛΑ[(fossil kleros)
BGU XIV 2448,54	ΣΕΛΕΥΚΟΥ (fossil kleros)
BGU XIV 2448,55	]ΠΟΥ (fossil kleros)
BGU XIV 2448,57	ΣΚΙΡΩΝΟΣ (fossil kleros)
BGU XIV 2448,59	ΑΛΕΞΑΝΔΡΟΥ (fossil kleros)
BGU XIV 2448,63	ΔΑΛΙΣΚΟΥ (fossil kleros)
BGU XIV 2449,5	ΘΕΟΓΕΝΟΥΣ (fossil kleros)
BGU XIV 2449,15;45;53;55;57;127;165	ΝΙΚΟΛΑΟΥ (fossil kleros)

THE HERAKLEOPOLITE NOME

BGU XIV 2449,20;25;37;47;50;58;59;130;143;151		
	ΦΙΛΙΠΠΟΥ τοῦ ΤΙΜΟΚΡΑΤΟΥ (fossil kleros)	
BGU XIV 2449,31;42;75;132	ΠΟΛΕΜΩΝΟΣ (fossil kleros)	
BGU XIV 2449,40	ΤΕΚΜΙ	
BGU XIV 2449,58;64;87	ΑΣΚΛΗΠΙΑΔΟΥ (fossil kleros)	
BGU XIV 2449,59	ΣΤΡ() τοῦ ΑΜΝ() (fossil kleros)	
BGU XIV 2449,61	ΦΙΛΩΝΟΣ (fossil kleros)	
BGU XIV 2449,67	ΣΤΡΑΤΩΝΟΣ τοῦ ΔΗΜΗΤΡΙΟΥ (fossil kleros)	
BGU XIV 2449,70	ΚΛΕΟΞΕΝΟΥ (fossil kleros)	
BGU XIV 2449,73	ΣΤΡΑΤΩΝΟΣ τοῦ ΝΙΚΟΣΤΡΑΤΟΥ (fossil kleros)	
BGU XIV 2449,106	ΚΙΛΛΕΟΥΣ/ΚΙΑΛΕΟΥΣ (fossil kleros)	
BGU XIV 2449,118	ΤΙΜΟΚΡΑΤΟΥ (fossil kleros)	
BGU XIV 2449,131	ΚΑΛΛΙΣΤΟΥ (fossil kleros)	
BGU XIV 2449,138	ΝΙΚΟΜΑΧΟΥ (fossil kleros)	
BGU XIV 2450,5	ΤΕΚΜΙ	
BGU XIV 2450,12	ΣΩΣΙΒΙΟΥ (fossil kleros)	
BGU XIV 2450,24;30;49	ΘΕΟΓΕΝΟΥΣ (fossil kleros)	
BGU XIV 2450,26	ΣΩΤΕΡΙΧΟΥ (fossil kleros)	
BGU XIV 2450,27;81	ΣΤΡΑ() (fossil kleros)	
BGU XIV 2450,28;80;82	ΖΩΙΛΟΥ (fossil kleros)	
BGU XIV 2450,35;51;76	ΦΙΛΙΠΠΟΥ τοῦ ΤΙΜΟΚΡΑΤΟΥ (fossil kleros)	
BGU XIV 2450,39	ΑΠΡΗΛ()	
BGU XIV 2450,39	ΚΟΡΡΑΓΟΥ (fossil kleros)	
BGU XIV 2450,40	ΘΕΟ..... (fossil kleros)	
BGU XIV 2450,40;58	ΠΤΟΛΕΜΑΙΟΥ (fossil kleros)	
BGU XIV 2450,41	...[(fossil kleros)	
BGU XIV 2450,46	ΚΑΛΛΙΠΠΟΥ (fossil kleros)	
BGU XIV 2450,77	]ΔΟΥ (fossil kleros)	
BGU XVI 2559,1;2;7;12;14	ΚΟΜΑ	
BGU XVI 2560,7	ΤΟΟΥ	
BGU XVI 2560,7	ΠΤΟΛΕΜΑΙΟΥ (fossil kleros)	
BGU XVI 2560,10	ΕΠΙΦΑΝΙΟΥ (fossil kleros)	
BGU XVI 2560,10	ΘΕΟΔΩΡΙΔΟΥ ΑΓΗΝΟΡΟΣ (fossil kleros)	
BGU XVI 2561,7	ΤΟΟΥ	
BGU XVI 2561,8	ΠΤΟΛΕΜΑΙΟΥ (fossil kleros)	
BGU XVI 2561,8	ΠΥΘΩΝΟΣ (fossil kleros)	
BGU XVI 2561,10	ΣΕΥΘΟΥ (fossil kleros)	
BGU XVI 2562,2	ΚΟΜΑ	
BGU XVI 2562,6	ΑΓΗΜΑ	
BGU XVI 2562,7	ΔΙΟΔΩΡΟΥ (fossil kleros)	
BGU XVI 2563,3;5	ΚΟΜΑ	
BGU XVI 2563,6	ΑΓΑΘ..() (fossil kleros)	
BGU XVI 2564,3	ΚΟΜΑ	
BGU XVI 2565,4	ΠΕΕΝΣΑΜΟΙ	
BGU XVI 2565,8	[Κ]ΑΣΤΟΡΟΣ (fossil kleros)	
BGU XVI 2569,2	ΚΟΜΑ	
BGU XVI 2569,2	ΕΠΙΡΑΛ.[(fossil kleros)	
BGU XVI 2570,5	ΚΕΦΑΛΑΙ	
BGU XVI 2570,7;8	ΚΟΜΑ	
BGU XVI 2570,9	ΑΠΟΛΛΟΔΩΡΟΥ (fossil kleros)	
BGU XVI 2572,3	ΑΓΗΜΑ	
BGU XVI 2572,4	ΒΟΗΘΟΥ (fossil kleros)	
BGU XVI 2573,3	ΚΟΜΑ	
BGU XVI 2575,5	ΗΛΙΟ[(fossil kleros)	
BGU XVI 2577,72	ΚΡΗΚΙΣ	
BGU XVI 2577,80	ΟΝΝΗΣ	
BGU XVI 2578,5	ΠΟΙΜΕΝΩΝ κώμη	
BGU XVI 2579,6;13	ΠΩΙΣ	
BGU XVI 2580,1;2;12	ΤΟΣΑΧΜΙΣ	
BGU XVI 2581,6	[.]..ΚΑΚ...	
BGU XVI 2582,1;7	ΦΕΒΙΧΙΣ	
BGU XVI 2582,12;14	ΦΥΧΙΤΗΣ	
BGU XVI 2583,1;8;21	ΦΝΕΒΙΕΥΣ	
BGU XVI 2584,6	ΤΙΛ....ΕΥ	
BGU XVI 2585,1	ΠΕΕΝΣ[...]	
BGU XVI 2586,1	ΤΗΝ...[	
BGU XVI 2586,12	ΒΟΥΣΙΡΙΣ	
BGU XVI 2586,15	ΠΕΡΑΝ	
BGU XVI 2587,1;17	ΤΙΛΩΘΙΣ	
BGU XVI 2589,3	ΤΕΧΘΩ	
BGU XVI 2589,6	ΠΟΓΧΗΟΥΣ πεδίον	
BGU XVI 2590,I,5;II,5	ΚΟΡΦΟΤΟΙ	
BGU XVI 2591,1	ΤΕΡΤΟΝΠΕΤΕΧΩΝΣ	
BGU XVI 2592,3;6	ΦΥΣ	
BGU XVI 2593,1	ΦΕΒΙΧΙΣ	
BGU XVI 2594,9	ΧΕΝΝΙΣ	
BGU XVI 2597,1	ΤΩΥ	
BGU XVI 2597,2	ΤΟΧΟΝΤΩΥ	
BGU XVI 2598,5	ΚΟΛΛΑΣΟΥΧΑ	
BGU XVI 2599,5	ΚΕΦΑΛΑΙ	
BGU XVI 2599,6	ΤΑΦΘΙΡΙΣ	
BGU XVI 2600,2	ΧΟΙΒΝΩΤΜΙΣ	
BGU XVI 2601,7	ΠΕΜΑΤΕ	
BGU XVI 2602,1	ΤΕΧΘΩ	
BGU XVI 2602,12	ΘΜΟΙΝΑΧΗ	
BGU XVI 2607,3-4	ΠΟΙΜΕΝΩΝ κώμη	
BGU XVI 2607,14	ΦΝΕΒΙΕΥΣ	
BGU XVI 2608,3	ΤΙΛΩΘΙΣ	
BGU XVI 2610,5	ΚΟΜΑ	
BGU XVI 2611,6;8	ΒΟΥΣΙΡΙΣ	
BGU XVI 2611,9;16	ΤΙΛΩΘΙΣ	
BGU XVI 2616,3	ΠΕΕΝΣΑΜΟΙ	
BGU XVI 2630,11	ΒΟΥΣΙΡΙΣ	
BGU XVI 2630,15	ΤΑΓΧΑΙΣ	
BGU XVI 2632,5	ΤΕΧΘΩ	
BGU XVI 2640,3	ΠΕΕΝΣΑΜΟΙ	
BGU XVI 2641,10	ΚΟΜΑ	
BGU XVI 2641,11	ΤΑΓΧΑΙΣ	
BGU XVI 2643,10	ΒΟΥΣΙΡΙΣ	
BGU XVI 2644,6;8	ΚΟΜΑ	
BGU XVI 2644,10	ΝΕΑ ΑΓΟΡΑ	
BGU XVI 2646,14	ΒΟΥΣΙΡΙΣ	
BGU XVI 2647,4	ΤΟΣΑΓΑΛΗ	
BGU XVI 2647,9	ΒΟΥΣΙΡΙΣ	
BGU XVI 2655,22	ΚΟΜΑ	
BGU XVI 2662,12	ΜΕΣΗ	
BGU XVI 2662,12	ΠΕΡΑΝ	
BGU XVI 2662,12	ΠΤΟΛΕΜΑΙΟΥ (fossil kleros)	
BGU XVI 2662,13	ΑΓΗΜΑ	
BGU XVI 2662,13	ΗΡΑΚΛΕΙΟΥ (fossil kleros)	
BGU XVI 2662,13	]ΝΙΟΥ (fossil kleros)	
BGU XVI 2662,14	ΑΠΟΛΛΩΝΙΟΥ (fossil kleros)	
BGU XVI 2662,15	ΣΑΡΑΠΙΩΝΟΣ (fossil kleros)	
BGU XVI 2663,1	ΤΙΛΩΘΙΣ	
BGU XVI 2665,4	ΟΓΟΥ	
BGU XVI 2665,4	ΑΓΕΛΑΟΥ (fossil kleros; later ΑΠΙΚΚΙΟΥ)	

REVERSE INDEX

BGU XVI 2665,6	ΜΟΥΧΙΣ	CPR I 64	ἈΡΙΣΤΟΜΑΧΟΥ (fossil kleros)
BGU XVI 2665,7	ἈΠΟΛΛΩ() (fossil kleros)	CPR I 66,4	ΤΕΚΜΙ
BGU XVI 2665,16	ΝΩΙΣ	CPR I 66,10	ΤΑΝΑΣΩ
BGU XVI 2665,17	ΤΑΛΑΗ	CPR I 73,9	ΝΕΙΛΟΥ ΠΟΛΙΣ
BGU XVI 2669,3	ΦΥΣ	CPR I 73,12;17	ΦΑΙΝΙΠΠΟΥ
BGU XVI 2670,II,1	ΤΕΚΜΙ	CPR I 76,5 (+ CPR I 79)	ΤΕΚΜΙ
BGU XVI 2670,II,2	ΦΑΙΝΙΠΠΟΥ	CPR I 78,4	ἈΓΗΜΑ
BGU XVI 2670,III,1	ΘΜΟΙΑΜΟΥΝ(ΙΣ)	CPR I 82,4	ΚΩΙΤΗΣ
BGU XVI 2674,3	ΚΡΗΚΙΣ	CPR I 82,II,4	ΦΑΙΝΙΠΠΟΥ
BGU XVI 2674,40;58;137	ΜΑΧΟΡ	CPR I 83,2	ΤΕΚΜΙ
P.Bodl. I 61 (g)	ΜΕΣΣΑΛΙΝΙΑΝΗ οὐσία	CPR I 84,4	ΤΕΚΜΙ
P.Bodl. I 73,4;5	ΚΤΗΜΑ	* CPR I 84,6	ΤΑΕΤΜΕΙ
P.Bodl. I 150,6;13	ΤΑΝΙΣ	CPR I 86,3	ἈΓΗΜΑ
P.Bon. 18,I,4;II,5;III,3-4	ΜΑΧΟΡ	CPR I 87,2-3	ἈΓΗΜΑ
P.Bon. 25,9	ΦΥΣ	CPR I 88,1 (+ CPR I 132)	ἈΓΗΜΑ
P.Cair.Isid. 9,verso,282;284	ΛΕΥΚΟΓΙΟΝ	CPR I 90,2	ΤΕΚΜΙ
P.Cair.Isid. 46,2	ΛΕΥΚΟΓΙΟΝ	CPR I 90,12	ΔΩΡΙΩΝΟΣ (fossil kleros)
P.Cair.Isid. 47,39;42	ΛΕΥΚΟΓΙΟΝ	CPR I 92,9	ΠΕΕΝΠΙΒΥΚ(ΙΣ)
P.Cair.Zen. II 59151,1	ΒΟΥΣΙΡΙΣ	CPR I 96,2	ἈΓΗΜΑ
P.Cair.Zen. III 59368,23	ΒΟΥΣΙΡΙΣ	CPR I 98,3	ἈΓΗΜΑ
P.Cair.Zen. III 59473,4	ΟΝΝΗΣ	CPR I 111,4	ΒΙΩΝΟΣ (fossil kleros)
P.Cair.Zen. III 59473,9	ΚΟΜΑ	CPR I 111,7	ΠΕΕΝΑΜΕΥΣ
P.Cair.Zen. IV 59753,14;51	ΒΟΥΣΙΡΙΣ	* CPR I 115+145,1;18;19	ΘΜΟΙΝΑΧΗ
P.Cair.Zen. IV 59767,6	ΒΟΥΣΙΡΙΣ	* CPR I 115+145,17	ΠΕ[
* P.Cair.Zen. IV 59782(b),24;63;81;88(?)	ΘΜΟΙΟΒΑΣΤΙΣ	CPR I 115+145,17	ΣΤΡΟΥΘΟΥ (fossil kleros)
* P.Cair.Zen. IV 59782(b),26;65;83	ΤΑΓΧΑΙΣ	CPR I 115+145,20	ἈΠΟ]ΛΛΩΝΙΟΥ καὶ
* P.Cair.Zen. IV 59782(b),28;45;67	ΟΝΝΗΣ		ΣΤΟΤΟΗΤΙΟΣ (fossil kleros)
* P.Cair.Zen. IV 59782(b),29;47;69;85(?);91	ΜΑΧΟΡ	CPR I 115+145,21	ΠΑΓΚΡΑΤΟΥ (fossil kleros)
* P.Cair.Zen. IV 59782(b),30;71;93	ΚΡΗΚΙΣ	* CPR I 156,2	ΤΩΛΛ[.]
* P.Cair.Zen. IV 59782(b),53;78	ΒΟΥΣΙΡΙΣ	CPR I 156,2	ΒΙΩΝΟΣ (fossil kleros)
* P.Cair.Zen. IV 59782(b),55;80	ΤΟΟΥ	* CPR I 156,3;4	ΚΟΛΛΙΝΤΑΑΘΥΡ
* P.Cair.Zen. IV 59782(b),63(?);73;95	ΚΟΜΑ	CPR I 156	ΚΛΕΑΝΟΡΟΣ (fossil kleros)
* P.Cair.Zen. IV 59782(b),66	ΤΙΛΩΘΙΣ	* CPR I 159,5	ΜΑΧΟΡ
CEL 231,3	ΣΩΒΘΙΣ	* CPR I 169,5 (+ CPR I 157)	ΤΑΕΜΣΙΣ (?)
CEL 232,3	ΣΩΒΘΙΣ	CPR I 238,3	ΦΑΙΝΙΠΠΟΥ
CEL 233,3	ΣΩΒΘΙΣ	CPR I 238,fr.1,6	ΝΕΙΛΟΥ ΠΟΛΙΣ
P.Col. VII 141,40	ΛΕΥΚΟΓΙΟΝ	CPR I 247,7	ΚΑΛΑΤΗΣ
P.Col. VII 144,1-2;6;11;13;18;20	ΛΕΥΚΟΓΙΟΝ	CPR I 247,7	ΜΑΧΑΙΤΟΥ (fossil kleros)
P.Col. VII 152,35;50-51	ΛΕΥΚΟΓΙΟΝ	CPR IV 2,11	ΝΙΝΩ
P.Col. VII 160,2; passim	ΛΕΥΚΟΓΙΟΝ	CPR IV 2,11	ΠΥΡΓΩΤΟΣ
P.Col. VII 161,2;21	ΛΕΥΚΟΓΙΟΝ	CPR IV 2,11	ΠΟΙΜΕΝΩΝ κώμη
P.Col. VII 163,1-2	ΛΕΥΚΟΓΙΟΝ	CPR IV 2,12	ΠΩΙΣ
P.Coll.Youtie I 7,5	ΤΜΟΙΕΝΕΤΙΣ	CPR IV 2,12	ΤΕΒΕΤΝΥ
P.Corn. 22,4;73	ΣΩΒΘΙΣ	CPR IV 2,12	ΘΜΟΙΝΕΨΙ
CPR I 36,3;7	ΠΕΕΝΑΜΕΥΣ	CPR IV 2,12	ΠΡΑΝΙ
CPR I 40,8	ΤΟΚΩΙΣ	CPR IV 2,13	ΚΑΙΝΗ
CPR I 40,9	ΠΡΩΤΟΣ (fossil kleros)	CPR IV 2,13	ΟΓΟΥ
CPR I 42,9	ΣΩΒΘΙΣ	CPR IV 2,13	ΚΟΛΛΙΝΤΑΑΘΥΡ
CPR I 42,11	ΣΑΚΑΠΡΥ	CPR IV 2,13	ΧΕΝΝΙΣ
CPR I 42,12	ΝΙΝΩΠΑΚΑΝ	CPR IV 2,14	ΦΥΣ
CPR I 42,14	ΝΟΗΡΙΣ	CPR IV 2,14	ΧΑΡΜΙΚ()
CPR I 50,b,3	ΤΕΚΜΙ	CPR IV 2,14	ΘΜΟΙΝ()
CPR I 56,6	ΠΕΕΝΠΙΒΥΚ(ΙΣ)	CPR IV 2,15	ΟΝΩΣΙΣ
CPR I 61,4	ἈΓΗΜΑ	CPR IV 2,15	ΜΟΥΧΙΣ
* CPR I 62,4	ΑΣΣΥΑ	CPR IV 2,15	ΝΟΗΡΙΣ
CPR I 64,5	ΠΕΕΝΑΜΕΥΣ	CPR IV 2,15	ΠΕΤΕΧΟΝΤ()
CPR I 64,7	ΚΕΡΚΥΤΟΣ	CPR IV 2,17	ΦΑΙΝΙΠΠΟΥ
CPR I 64,9;15	ΘΜΟΙΝΩΘΙΣ	CPR IV 2,17	ΔΙΟΝ()
CPR I 64,12	ΦΥΣ	CPR IV 2,17	ΑΙΛΙΑΝΟΥ
CPR I 64,12	ἈΜΜΩΝΟΣ (fossil kleros)	CPR IV 2,17	ΔΙΑΣΗΜΩΤΑΤΟΥ

CPR IV 2,18	ΠΥΡΓΩΤΟΣ	* P.Fuad Crawford 5 verso,12		ΘΜΟΙΤΩΘΙΣ
CPR IV 2,18	ΦΝΕΒΙΕΥΣ	* P.Fuad Crawford 5 verso,14		ΚΕΡΚΕΣΗΣ
CPR VI 7,6-7	ΛΕΥΚΟΓΙΟΝ	P.Fuad Crawford (App. I) 3 and 4,8		ΦΕΒΙΧΙΣ
CPR VI 73,4-5	῎ΑΓΗΜΑ	P.Fuad Crawford (App. II) 66 recto,9		ΨΕΒΘΟΝΕΜΒΗ
CPR VI 73,8	ΤΕΚΜΙ	P.Gen. I 9,2		ΦΕΒΙΧΙΣ
CPR VI 73,16	ΠΕΡΑΦΘΙΣ	P.Gen. I 10,2;5;7		ΦΕΒΙΧΙΣ
CPR VI 79,4;6-7	ΝΕΙΛΟΥ ΠΟΛΙΣ	P.Gen. III 132,6	ΚΑΤΩ	(῎ΑΓΗΜΑ)
CPR VII 12,5	ΤΟΕΜΗΣΙΣ	P.Gen. III 134,4	ΚΑΤΩ	(῎ΑΓΗΜΑ)
CPR VII 51,21	ΑΛΙΛΑΙΣ	P.Giss.Univ. 19,10		ΚΩ
CPR VIII 14,3;12;20	ΤΑΑΜΟΡΟΥ	P.Grad. 3,6;20		ΘΜΟΙΝΕΨΙ
CPR VIII 51,2	ΑΙΛΙΑΝΟΥ̂	P.Grad. 3,8;10;22		ΚΩΙΤΗΣ
CPR VIII 59,3	ΝΟΗΡΙΣ	P.Hamb. I 17,II,5; III,1		ΨΥΧΙΣ
CPR VIII 68,3	ΣΩΒΘΙΣ	P.Hamb. I 91,4		ΤΕΒΕΤΝΥ
CPR VIII 68,9-10	ΠΙΑΔΕ.[.]ΕΥ	P.Hamb. I 91,19;25		ΠΩΙΣ
CPR VIII 76,2	ΛΕΥΚΟΓΙΟΝ	P.Hamb. III 202,2;4;17-18		ΤΕΧΘΩ
CPR VIII 76,2	ἸΣΙΕ͂ΙΟΝ	P.Heid. III 246,9		ΝΙΤΩΜΙ
CPR VIII 76,4	ΦΑΕΙΜ	P.Heid. III 246,13		(Φ)ΑΘΩΡ
CPR X 60,1	ΠΑΠΑ	P.Heid. IV 297,4	ἈΓΚΥΡΩ͂Ν	πόλις/κώμη
CPR X 63,6	ΚΑΘΟΛΙΚ[	P.Heid. IV 301,II,14;III,10		ΦΕΒΙΧΙΣ
CPR X 105a,2	ΦΥΣ	P.Heid. IV 301,II,15;III,11		ΤΟΣΑΧΜΙΣ
CPR X 107a,5(?);9	ΘΕΡ	P.Heid. IV 303,II,2		ΨΥΧΙΣ
CPR X 121,3	ΠΑΣΗΕΙ	* P.Heid. IV 303,II,6		ΚΕΡΚ(ΕΣΗΦΙΣ)
CPR X 135,7	ΤΑΚΡΙΑΝ	P.Heid. IV 320,1		ΚΩΙΤΗΣ
CPR X 135,9	ΦΑΜΤΩΝΝΕΣΩΟΥ	P.Heid. IV 320,9-10	ἈΓΚΥΡΩ͂Ν	πόλις/κώμη
CPR X 135,10	ΑΚΩΤΟΥ	P.Heid. IV 320,10		ΧΟΙΒΝΩΤΜΙΣ
CPR X 135,10	ΜΙΚΡΟΥΑΛΙΧ	P.Heid. IV 321,5		ΚΩΙΤΗΣ
CPR XIV 6,5;15	ΠΕΕΝΑΜΕΥΣ	P.Heid. IV 322,5	ἈΓΚΥΡΩ͂Ν	πόλις/κώμη
CPR XIV 36,1;5;9;13	ΒΟΥΣΙΡΙΣ	P.Heid. IV 326,2	ἈΓΚΥΡΩ͂Ν	πόλις/κώμη
CPR XIV 36,4;8;12	ΤΑΓΧΑΙΣ	P.Heid. VII 410,5		ΚΕΡΚΕΣΗΦΙΣ
CPR XIV 36,7	ΣΩΒΘΙΣ	P.Hels. I 4d,II,1		ΦΕΒΙΧΙΣ
CPR XIV 40,1	ΠΕΤΑΧΟΡ	P.Hels. I 6,2	῎ΑΝΩ	(῎ΑΓΗΜΑ)
CPR XIV 40,2	ΝΩΙΣ	P.Hels. I 6,6		ἹΕΡΑ ΝΗ͂ΣΟΣ
CPR XIV 40,3	ΑΛΙΛΑΙΣ	P.Hels. I 6,7		ΑΛΙΛΑΙΣ
P.Dub.24,3	ΛΕΥΚΟΓΙΟΝ	P.Hels. I 8,2		ΠΕΕΝΠΑΣΒΥΤ(ΙΣ)
P.Dub.25,8	ΟΝΝΗΣ	P.Hels. I 9,8		ΦΥΣ (?)
P.Dub.25,8	ΟΝΝΗΣ	P.Hels. I 10,10		ΚΑΛΑΤΗΣ
P.Dub.28,4;6	ΛΕΥΚΟΓΙΟΝ	P.Hels. I 11,11		ΘΜΟΙΝΑΥΣΙΡΙΣ
P.Duk. inv. 605	ΘΜΟΙΝΑΥΣΙΡΙΣ	P.Hels. I 11,12	ΣΩΣΤΡΑΤΟΥ	(fossil kleros)
P.Enteux. 61,2	ΦΑΙΝΙΠΠΟΥ	P.Hels. I 12,7		ΒΟΥΣΙΡΙΣ
* P.Erl. 48,20	ΨΥΧΙΣ	P.Hels. I 13,9		ΤΕΧΥΜΙΣ
P.Erl. 48,23	ΘΜΟΙΝ.()	P.Hels. I 14,7-8		ΘΜΟΙΝΑΥΣΙΡΙΣ
* P.Erl. 48,28	ΘΜΟΙΝΕΘΥΜΙΣ	P.Hels. I 14,9	ΣΩΣΤΡΑΤΟΥ	(fossil kleros)
P.Erl. 48,29-30	ΦΕΒΙΧΙΣ	P.Hels. I 15,7;14		ΔΙΝΥ..ΡΕΩΣ
P.Erl. 58,3	Ε...]ΦΕ	P.Hels. I 16,12-13	ΦΙΛΙΣΚΟΥ	(fossil kleros)
P.Erl. 67,8;19	ΚΑΙΝΗ	P.Hels. I 18,3	ΚΑΤΩ	(῎ΑΓΗΜΑ)
Ét.Fouad 2,1	ΚΟΜΑ	P.Hels. I 19,5		ΨΥΧΙΣ
P.Flor. I 11,8	ΚΩΣ	P.Hels. I 20,13		ΘΝΗΙΣ
P.Flor. I 23,8-9	ΛΙΒΥ̂ (fossil kleros)	P.Hels. I 21,4		ΚΩΙΤΗΣ
P.Flor. III 385,25	ΚΑΛΛΙΝΙΚΟΥ̂ (fossil kleros)	P.Hels. I 21,9		ΤΕΧΘΩ
* P.Fuad Crawford 5 recto,2; verso,13	ΨΕΛΕΜΑΧΙΣ	P.Hels. I 24,1;6		ΤΕΚΜΙ
* P.Fuad Crawford 5 recto,3	ΝΩΥΚΛΕΓΧΗΣ	P.Hels. I 26 A,3;6;11;23;24		ΚΩΙΤΗΣ
* P.Fuad Crawford 5 recto,4	ΤΑΛΑΗ	P.Hels. I 26 A,4;12;21;37;B,13,19		ΤΕΧΘΩ
* P.Fuad Crawford 5 recto,5	ΨΥΧΙΣ	P.Hels. I 26 A,4;15;20;26		ΠΕΡΑΝ
* P.Fuad Crawford 5 recto,6; verso,15	ΧΟΙΒΝΩΤΜΙΣ	P.Hels. I 26 A,9; B,9		ΘΜΟΙΝΕΘΥΜΙΣ
* P.Fuad Crawford 5 recto,8	ΤΑΑΜΟΡΟΥ	P.Hels. I 26 A,13;21		(Θ)ΕΛΒΩΝΘΙΣ
* P.Fuad Crawford 5 recto,10	ΨΙΝΑΠΕΛΕΥ	P.Hels. I 26 A,14;17; B,20		ΘΜΟΙΝΑΧΗ
* P.Fuad Crawford 5 recto,11	ΝΕΜΘΙΒΙΣ	P.Hels. I 26 A,15;26		ΤΕΒΕΤΝΥ
* P.Fuad Crawford 5 verso,3	ΘΜΟΙΝΕΘΥΜΙΣ	P.Hels. I 26 A,19		ΨΥΧΙΣ
* P.Fuad Crawford 5 verso,7	ἈΓΚΥΡΩ͂Ν πόλις/κώμη	P.Hels. I 26 A,20;29		ΘΜΟΙΝΑΥΣΙΡΙΣ
* P.Fuad Crawford 5 verso,10	ἸΒΙΩ͂Ν ...	P.Hels. I 26 A,24; B,8		ΤΟΕΜΗΣΙΣ

REVERSE INDEX

P.Hels. I 26 A,25;41	ΠΕΡΟΗ	P.Hib. I 112,43	ΤΟΕΝΕΓΟΥΣ
P.Hels. I 26 A,27	ΘΜΟΙΦΘΑ	* P.Hib. I 112,45	ΜΟΥΧΙΝΕΜΒΗΣ
P.Hels. I 26 A,28	ΠΕΕΝΣΑΜΟΙ	P.Hib. I 112,46	ΠΕΡΧΥΦΙΣ
P.Hels. I 26 A,31	ἈΓΚΥΡΩ͂Ν πόλις/κώμη	P.Hib. I 112,74	ἈΓΚΥΡΩ͂Ν πόλις/κώμη
* P.Hels. I 26 A,33	ΠΑΤΑΜ[ΟΥ͂ΣΟΥ	P.Hib. I 116,2	ΒΟΥΣΙΡΙΣ
P.Hels. I 26 B,3	ΦΕΒΙΧΙΣ	P.Hib. I 117,2	ΚΩΪΤΗΣ
* P.Hels. I 26 B,19	ΘΕΡ	* P.Hib. I 117,8	ΤΑΛΑΗ
P.Hels. I 27,1	ΦΥΣ	P.Hib. I 117,8;10	ΨΥΧΙΣ
P.Hels. I 27,2	ΨΕΒΧΗΘ	P.Hib. I 117,8;10	ΑΣΣΥΑ
P.Hels. I 27,3	ΠΩΙΣ (?)	P.Hib. I 117,15	ΦΕΒΙΧΙΣ
P.Hels. I 27,4	ΚΟΜΑ	P.Hib. I 117,15-16	ἈΓΚΥΡΩ͂Ν πόλις/κώμη
P.Hels. I 29,18	ΘΝΗΙΣ	P.Hib. I 118,16	ΠΑΣΤΟΦΟΡΩΝ (?)
* P.Hels. I 29,19	ΕΛΑΣΙΜΗΣ	P.Hib. I 123 descr.	ΚΟΒΑ
P.Hels. I 29,24	ΘΜΟΙΦΘΑ	P.Hib. I 131 descr.	ΦΕΒΙΧΙΣ
P.Hels. I 29,28	ΚΕΡΚΥΤΟΣ	P.Hib. I 132 descr.	ΣΙΝΑΡΥ
P.Hels. I 29,35	ΜΕΣΗ	P.Hib. I 136 descr.	ΦΕΒΙΧΙΣ
P.Hels. I 31,6;10	ΜΕΛΑΝΘΙΟΥ (fossil kleros)	P.Hib. I 138 descr.	ΦΕΒΙΧΙΣ
P.Hels. I 32,4	ΒΟΥΣΙΡΙΣ	P.Hib. I 143 descr.	ΦΕΒΙΧΙΣ
P.Hels. I 34,8	ΤΕΧΥΜΙΣ	P.Hib. I 144 descr.	ΤΑΛΑΗ
P.Hels. I 34,10	ΦΥΣ	P.Hib. I 157 descr.	ΤΑΛΑΗ
P.Hels. I 38,5	ΦΥΣ	P.Hib. I 163 descr.	ΘΜΟΙΝΕΘΥΜΙΣ
P.Hels. I 40 verso,1;2;4;6	ΒΕ()	P.Hib. I 164 descr.	ΚΟΒΑ
P.Hib. I 33,7-8;15	ΨΕΒΘΟΝΕΜΒΗ	P.Hib. II 198,128	ΤΕΧΘΩ
P.Hib. I 34,2;4	ΣΙΝΑΡΥ	P.Hib. II 203,15	ΚΩΪΤΗΣ
P.Hib. I 36,3;8	ΤΑΛΑΗ	P.Hib. II 209,5	ΦΕΒΙΧΙΣ
P.Hib. I 37,4;12	ΤΑΛΑΗ	P.Hib. II 218, col.III	ΑΣΣΥΑ
P.Hib. I 47,29	ΔΙΚΩΜΙΑ	P.Hib. II 218, col.III	ἹΠΠΩΝΩΝ κώμη
P.Hib. I 60,4	ΣΙΝΑΡΥ	* P.Hib. II 218, col.III	ΝΟΚΛΗ (?)
P.Hib. I 66 verso	ΚΩΪΤΗΣ	P.Hib. II 218, col.III;41	ΜΟΥΧΙΣ
P.Hib. I 67,4	ἈΓΚΥΡΩ͂Ν πόλις/κώμη	P.Hib. II 218,2;16	ΠΕΡΟΗ
P.Hib. I 68,3	ΧΟΙΒΝΩΤΜΙΣ	P.Hib. II 218,6;11;20;23	ΦΙΛΟΝΙΚΟΥ
P.Hib. I 70(b),8-9	ΘΜΟΙΝΕΘΥΜΙΣ	P.Hib. II 218,9;13	ἈΓΚΥΡΩ͂Ν ΠΟΛΙΣ
P.Hib. I 71,7	ΚΕΦΑΛΑΪ	P.Hib. II 218,14;18	ΚΕΡΚΕΣΗΦΙΣ
P.Hib. I 72,2	ΦΕΒΙΧΙΣ	P.Hib. II 218,15;26;28;88	ΤΑΛΑΗ
P.Hib. I 73,8;11	ΣΙΝΑΡΥ	P.Hib. II 218,17	ΚΟΒΑ
P.Hib. I 75,1;5	ΤΑΛΑΗ	P.Hib. II 218,21	ΤΑΑΜΟΡΟΥ
P.Hib. I 78,14	ΚΩΪΤΗΣ	P.Hib. II 218,22;24;29	ΜΟΥΧΙΝΘΑΗ()
P.Hib. I 80,7-8	ΘΜΟΙΝΕΘΥΜΙΣ	P.Hib. II 218,27;30	ΨΕΒΘΟΝΕΜΒΗ
P.Hib. I 84(a),7;22	ΠΕΡΟΗ	P.Hib. II 218,33	ΑΛΙΛΑΙΣ
P.Hib. I 88,5	ΦΕΒΙΧΙΣ	P.Hib. II 218,34	ΚΟΛΛΑΣΟΥΧΑ
P.Hib. I 96,3;19	ΦΕΒΙΧΙΣ	P.Hib. II 218,35	ΠΕΤΑΧΟΡ
P.Hib. I 100,12	ΑΝΑΤΙΕΥ	P.Hib. II 218,36	ΝΙΤΩΜΙ
P.Hib. I 101,6	ΣΙΣΙΝΗ	P.Hib. II 218,37	ΜΑΣΤΙ[Χ] or ΜΑΓΔ[.]Χ()
P.Hib. I 106,3	ΦΕΒΙΧΙΣ	P.Hib. II 218,38;80;87	ΣΩΒΘΙΣ
P.Hib. I 106,7	ΤΑΛΑΗ	P.Hib. II 218,39	ΠΕΕΝΑΜΕΥΣ
P.Hib. I 107,3	ΦΕΒΙΧΙΣ	P.Hib. II 218,40;48;79;83	ΤΕΡΤΟΝΙΧ()
P.Hib. I 107,6	ΤΑΛΑΗ	P.Hib. II 218,42;86	ΤΟΣΑΧΜΙΣ
P.Hib. I 108,2	ΦΥΣ	P.Hib. II 218,43	ΛΕΙΘΕΩΣ
P.Hib. I 110 recto,36	ΦΕΒΙΧΙΣ	P.Hib. II 218,44	ΠΑΠΑ
P.Hib. I 111,3	ἌΓΗΜΑ	P.Hib. II 218,45	ΤΕΡΟΥΦΕΩΣ
P.Hib. I 112,2;6;81	ΚΕΡΚΕΣΗΣ	P.Hib. II 218,46;59	ΦΕΒΙΧΙΣ
P.Hib. I 112,4; passim	ΦΕΒΙΧΙΣ	P.Hib. II 218,47;68	ΓΑΠΑΣΩ(ΙΣ)
P.Hib. I 112,5;12;52	ΑΣΣΥΑ	P.Hib. II 218,49	ΤΑ(ΙΣ)
P.Hib. I 112,11;57	ΨΥΧΙΣ	P.Hib. II 218,50	ΤΩΥ
P.Hib. I 112,14	ΠΕΡΟΗ	P.Hib. II 218,51;66;84	ΘΜΟΙΝΑΧΗ
* P.Hib. I 112,25	ΨΕΒΘΟΝ(ΠΕΝΟΥΦΙΣ)	P.Hib. II 218,52	ΘΕΛΒΩ
P.Hib. I 112,26;86	ΧΟΙΒΝΩΤΜΙΣ	P.Hib. II 218,53	ΠΑΜΑ (= ΠΑΠΑ)
* P.Hib. I 112,27	ΜΟΥΧΙΝΠΑΣΙΣ	P.Hib. II 218,54;90;92	ΟΝΩΣΙΣ
P.Hib. I 112,36	ΨΕΛΕΜΑΧΙΣ	P.Hib. II 218,55	ΤΟΚΩΙΣ
P.Hib. I 112,39;56;88	ΘΜΟΙΤΟΘΙΣ	P.Hib. II 218,56	ΝΟΗΡΙΣ

P.Hib. II 218,57;74	ΠΩΙΣ	P.Köln IV 192,1	ΝΕΜΑΡΕΩΣ
P.Hib. II 218,58	ΘΜΟΙΝΩΘΙΣ	P.Köln VII 319,3	ΠΕΕΝΠΙΒΥΚ(ΙΣ)
* P.Hib. II 218,60	ΧΕΝΝΙΣ	P.Köln VII 321,5	ΠΕΕΝΠΙΒΥΚ(ΙΣ)
P.Hib. II 218,61	ΠΟ[.]ΛΟΜ[	P.Köln VII 322,7	ΤΑΡΩΤ
P.Hib. II 218,62	ΠΕΕΝΙΒΙΣ	P.Köln VII 323,2	ΠΑΠΑ
P.Hib. II 218,63	ΚΟΜΑ	P.Laur. II 42,7	ΤΑΑΜΟΡΟΥ
P.Hib. II 218,64	ΚΡΗΚΙΣ	P.Laur. II 47,2	ΚΟΒΑ
P.Hib. II 218,65;76	ΒΟΥΣΙΡΙΣ	P.Laur. II 47,3	ΦΕΒΙΧΙΣ
* P.Hib. II 218,66	ΘΜΟΙΑΜΟΥΝ(ΙΣ)	P.Laur. IV 174,recto,4	ΤΟΟΥ
P.Hib. II 218,67	ΘΜΟΙΟΒΑΣΤΙΣ	P.Lille I 6,4	ΚΟΡΦΟΤΟΙ
P.Hib. II 218,69	ΝΕ.ΑΤ(ΙΣ)	P.Lille I 6,4	ΤΕΒΕΤΝΥ
P.Hib. II 218,70	ΤΕΡΤΟΝΑΛ()	P.Lille I 31,1	ΝΙΣΕΥΣ
P.Hib. II 218,71;78;91	ΤΕΧΘΩ	P.Lille I 31,1	ΤΕΡΤΟΝΠΕΤΕΧΩΝΣ
P.Hib. II 218,85	ΝΙΣΕΥΣ	P.Lille I 59,6; passim	ΒΟΥΣΙΡΙΣ
P.Hib. II 218,89;95	ΣΙΝΑΡΥ	P.Lille I 59,8;35;121	ΠΕΕΝΠΑΣΒΥΤ(ΙΣ)
P.Hib. II 218,93	ΝΙΝΩ	P.Lille I 59,10;39;85;97;112;124	ΚΡΗΚΙΣ
P.Hib. II 218,94	ΤΙ[..].ΟΜ()	P.Lille I 59,12;43;98;126	ΠΕΕΝΕΨΥ
* P.Hib. II 218,96	ΠΟ[..]ΟΜ()	* P.Lille I 59,14;38;100;123	ΤΑΓΧΑΙΣ
P.Hib. II 218,97	ΝΕΙ[	P.Lille I 59,17;45;103	ΤΙΛΩΘΙΣ
P.Hib. II 219,4;12	ἈΓΚΥΡΩΝ πόλις/κώμη	P.Lille I 59,18; passim	ΟΝΝΗΣ
P.Hib. II 219,7	[±8]ΧΕΩΣ	P.Lille I 59,23;49;107	ΚΟΜΑ
P.Hib. II 219,9	[±8]ΥΨΗ[..]Ν()	P.Lille I 59,28; passim	ΤΟΟΥ
P.Hib. II 219,10	[±8]ΝΕΑΣ	P.Lille I 59,29;41;61;114	ΣΧΝΩΜΘΙΣ
P.Hib. II 219,11	[ΠΕΕΝΣ]ΑΜΟΙ	P.Lille I 59,57;92;105;116	ΜΑΧΟΡ
P.Hib. II 219,13	ΤΕΧΘΩ	P.Lond. II 171 b,7 (p.176)	ΦΕΒΙΧΙΣ
P.Hib. II 219,15	[±8]ΟΥΝΕΩΣ	P.Lond. II 171 b,8 (p.176)	ΚΩΙΤΗΣ
P.Hib. II 220,5	ἈΓΚΥΡΩΝ πόλις/κώμη	P.Lond. II 392,3 (p.333)	ΛΕΥΚΟΓΙΟΝ
P.Hib. II 237+217,17	ἈΓΚΥΡΩΝ πόλις/κώμη	P.Lond. III 985,11 (p.229)	ΤΩΥ
P.Hib. II 248,fr.III,9	ΣΙΝΑΡΥ	P.Lond. V 1791,5;7	ΟΞΥΡΥΓΧΟΣ
P.Hib. II 272,4	ΚΩΙΤΗΣ	P.Lond. VI 1913,2;9	ἹΠΠΩΝΩΝ κώμη
P.Hib. II 272,4	ΨΥΧΙΣ	P.Lond. VI 1913,3	(Φ)ΑΘΩΡ
P.Hib. II 277,12	ΧΟΙΒΝΩΤΜΙΣ	P.Lond. VI 1913,10	ΘΜΟΙΝΠΕΣΛΑ
P.Hib. II 277,19	ΑΓΥΦΑΛΟΣ	P.Lond. VI 1914,57	ΤΑΡΩΤ
P.Hib. II 278,2-3	ΑΣΣΥΑ	P.Lond. VI 1914,58	ΤΑΑΜΟΡΟΥ
* P.Hib. II 280,3	ΘΜΟΥΑ...[	(?)P.Lond. VI 1914,61	ΘΜΟΙΝΑΧΗ
P.Hib. II 280,13	ΜΟΥ.Ω	P.Lond. VI 1920,2	(Φ)ΑΘΩΡ
P.Hib. II 280,16	ΜΟΥΧΙΣ	P.Lond. VI 1924,5	ΦΙΛΟΝΙΚΟΥ
P.Hib. II 282,21	ἈΠΟΛΛΩΝΙΟΥ (fossil kleros)	P.Lond. VII 1972,1	ΘΜΟΙΟΒΑΣΤΙΣ
P.Iand. III 33,7	ΒΟΥΣΙΡΙΣ	P.Lund VI 8,5	ΦΕΒΙΧΙΣ
P.Iand. VI 124,5	ΟΝΩΣΙΣ	P.Lund VI 9,4-5	ΦΕΒΙΧΙΣ
P.Köln II 88,4	ΒΟΥΣΙΡΙΣ	P.Med. I² 66,1;8(verso)	ΝΕΙΛΟΥ ΠΟΛΙΣ
P.Köln II 98,9	ΚΛΕΩΝΟΣ (fossil kleros)	P.Mert. I 46,2	ΓΕΣΣΙΑΣ
P.Köln II 98,11	ΣΩΒΘΙΣ	P.Mert. II 59,20	ΒΟΥΣΙΡΙΣ
P.Köln II 98,16;25	ΠΑΜΦΙΛΟΥ (fossil kleros)	P.Mert. II 78,2-3	[.....]ΡΕΩΣ
P.Köln II 98,19	ΣΩΣΙΠΑΤΡΟΥ (fossil kleros)	P.Mich. II 121 recto, col.IV.I,2	ΦΕΝΑΜΕΝΙ
P.Köln II 98,22	ΝΙΚΑΝΟΡΟΣ (fossil kleros)	P.Mich. IX 551,11	ΝΕΙΛΟΥ ΠΟΛΙΣ
P.Köln II 98,24	ΠΑΤΑΜΟΥΣΟΥ	P.Mich. IX 573,8;13	ΛΕΥΚΟΓΙΟΝ
P.Köln II 98,24	ἈΝΔΡΟΝΙΚΟΥ (fossil kleros)	P.Mich. X 591,1	ΘΜΟΙΝΕΨΙ
P.Köln II 98,24	ΦΙΛΩΤΟΥ (fossil kleros)	P.Mich. XII 647,3	ΛΕΥΚΟΓΙΟΝ
P.Köln II 98,25	ΣΕΛΕΥΚΟΥ (fossil kleros)	P.Mich. XV 722,1;3;4;7;8;15;22	ΘΜΟ()
P.Köln II 98,34	ΤΕΜΕΝΚΥΡΚ(ΙΣ)	P.Mich. XV 722,2;5;10;12;13;16	ΠΕΡΟΗ
* P.Köln II 98,40	ΘΜΟΙΟΝΠΡΟΦ[	P.Mich.Zen. 30 a,10	ΦΥΣ
P.Köln II 99,1	ΦΝΕΒΙΕΥΣ	P.Michael. 28,1	ΠΑΠΑ
P.Köln II 99,2	ΠΕΕΝΠΙΒΥΚ(ΙΣ)	P.Michael. 28,1	ΦΕΒΙΧΙΣ
P.Köln II 99,3	ΚΕΡΚΥΤΟΣ	* P.Michael. 28,7	ἈΓΚΥΡΩΝ πόλις/κώμη
P.Köln II 99,4	ΦΥΣ	P.Michael. 28,8	ΨΕΛΕΜΑΧΙΣ
P.Köln II 99,5	ΘΜΟΙΝΩΘΙΣ	P.Michael. 28,9	ΘΕΛΒΩ
P.Köln II 99,7;8	ΚΟΜΑ	P.Michael. 28,9	ΘΝΗΙΣ
P.Köln III 151,34	ΘΜΟΙΝΠΕΣΛΑ	P.Michael. 28,11	ΦΙΛΟΝΙΚΟΥ
P.Köln III 158,13	ΤΕΒΕΤΝΥ	P.Michael. 126,5	ΤΙΝΤΗΡΙΣ

REVERSE INDEX

P.Michael. 126,7	ΝΕΊΛΟΥ ΠΌΛΙΣ	P.Oxy. I 142,1	ΚΟΜΑ
* P.Michael. 126,10	ΛΕΥΚΟΥ͂	P.Oxy. I 150,1	ΚΟΜΑ
* P.Mil.Vogl. IV 214 verso,21;22	ΛΕΥΚΟΓΙΟΝ	P.Oxy. II 348 descr.	ἩΡΑΚΛΈΟΥΣ τοῦ
P.Mil.Vogl. VI 287,13	ΤΕΚΜΙ		ΚΑΛΛΙΣΤΡΆΤΟΥ (fossil kleros)
P.Mil.Vogl. inv.1299,3	ΚΟΜΑ	P.Oxy. III 504,7	ΦΙΛΟΝΊΚΟΥ
P.Mil.Vogl. inv.1300,11	ΠΕΤΑΧΟΡ	P.Oxy. IV 715,6;13;14	ΤΟΕΜΗΣΙΣ
MPER XV 13,1	ΣΥΝΟΡΘΟΥ	P.Oxy. IV 715,21	ἸΒΙΩ͂Ν ΠΑΧΝΟΥΒΙΣ
MPER XV 13,2	ΒΟΥΣΙΡΙΣ	P.Oxy. IV 715,21-23	ΖΩΪΛΟΥ καὶ
MPER XV 62,1;4	ΠΕΕΝΕΨΩΜΦΙΣ		ΝΟΥΜΗΝΊΟΥ (fossil kleros)
MPER XV 63,16	ΝΟΗΡΙΣ	P.Oxy. IV 715,24	ΨΕΛΕΜΑΧΙΣ
MPER XV 63,25;49	ΦΥΣ	P.Oxy. IV 715,24-25	ΜΕΝΊΠΠΟΥ καὶ
MPER XV 75,4	ΝΕ.[		ἈΡΤΕΜΙΔΏΡΟΥ (fossil kleros)
MPER XV 82,3;4	ΒΟΥΣΙΡΙΣ	P.Oxy. IV 742,17	ΝΟΚΛΗ
MPER XV 83,10	ΣΩΒΘΟΙΣ	P.Oxy. IV 810 descr.	ΞΈΝΩΝΟΣ (fossil kleros)
MPER XV 84,3	ΣΩΒΘΟΙΣ	P.Oxy. IV 814 descr.	ΘΕΛΒΩ
MPER XV 91,3	ΦΥΣ	P.Oxy. VI 899,22	ΒΟΥΣΙΡΙΣ
MPER XV 91,4	ἸΒΙΩ͂Ν	P.Oxy. VI 899,22	ΤΙΝΤΗΡΙΣ
MPER XV 91,5	ΑΤΡΤ..	P.Oxy. VI 899,22	ΤΑ..[.....
MPER XV 91,34;37	ΒΟΥΣΙΡΙΣ	P.Oxy. VI 899,23	[....].ΧΟΣ
MPER XV 101,2;13	ΒΟΥΣΙΡΙΣ	P.Oxy. VI 922,1	ΑΣΚΛΟΥ
MPER XV 103,5	ΦΦ	P.Oxy. VI 942,1	ΝΕΊΛΟΥ ΠΌΛΙΣ
MPER XV 103,17	ΜΑΧΟΡ	P.Oxy. VI 965 descr.	ΦΙΛΟΝΊΚΟΥ
MPER XV 113,1	ΠΕΕΝΠΙΒΥΚ(ΙΣ)	P.Oxy. VII 1068,17	ΤΟΟΥ
MPER XVII 2 a,2	ΚΑΣΑΝΟΥΠ(ΙΣ)	P.Oxy. VIII 1126,5	ΤΣΑΒΑΤΩΟΥ
P.Münch. III 49,2	ΤΕΒΕΤΝΥ	P.Oxy. VIII 1126,7	ΤΑΛΑΗ
P.Münch. III 51,12;14	Τ.[...]	P.Oxy. VIII 1126,8	ΚΗΤΣ
P.Münch. III 55,3	ΘΜΟΙΝΑΧΗ	P.Oxy. VIII 1145,1	ΚΟΒΑ
P.Münch. III 56,6	ἌΝΩ (ἌΓΗΜΑ)	P.Oxy. VIII 1145,19	ΣΩΒΘΟΙΣ
P.Münch. III 61,22	ΜΈΣΗ	P.Oxy. VIII 1156,4	ΦΙΛΟΝΊΚΟΥ
P.Neph. 3,11	ἈΓΚΥΡΩ͂Ν πόλις/κώμη	P.Oxy. XII 1463,8	ΧΟΙΒΝΩΤΜΙΣ
P.Neph. 6,24	ἈΓΚΥΡΩ͂Ν πόλις/κώμη	P.Oxy. XII 1529,7	ΚΟΒΑ
P.Neph. 11,4;27	(Φ)ΑΘΩΡ	P.Oxy. XII 1529,7	ΑΣΣΥΑ
P.Neph. 11,19;21	ΨΕΛΕΜΑΧΙΣ	P.Oxy. XIV 1708,3	ΠΕΕΝΗ
P.Neph. 12,11;17	ΤΑΑΜΟΡΟΥ	P.Oxy. XIV 1751 recto	ΞΈΝΩΝΟΣ (fossil kleros)
P.Neph. 12,23	ΜΟΥΗ	P.Oxy. XVI 1834,3;5	ΓΕΣΣΙΑΣ
P.Neph. 13,20	ΝΗ͂ΣΩΝ κώμη	P.Oxy. XVI 1848,7	ΚΟΜΑ
P.Neph. 13,20	(Φ)ΑΘΩΡ	P.Oxy. XVI 1861,5	ΚΟΜΑ
P.Neph. 19,3	ΝΗ͂ΣΩΝ κώμη	P.Oxy. XVI 1866,2	ΦΕΒΙΧΙΣ
P.Neph. 20,5;9	ΝΗ͂ΣΩΝ κώμη	P.Oxy. XVI 1909,8	ΝΕΊΛΟΥ ΠΌΛΙΣ
P.Neph. 20,6;8;13	ΘΕΛΒΩ	P.Oxy. XVI 1910,8	ΚΟΒΑ
P.Neph. 28,4	ΤΑΝ[..].Α.[	P.Oxy. XVI 1911,164	ΚΤΗ͂ΜΑ
P.Neph. 28,5	ΦΕΒΙΧΙΣ	P.Oxy. XVI 1912,149	ΚΤΗ͂ΜΑ
* P.Neph. 28,6	ΠΑΠΑ	P.Oxy. XVI 1917,22;45;51	ΝΟΚΛΗ
P.Neph. 28,8	ΠΙΜΕΙΝ	P.Oxy. XVI 1917,63;82;111;113	ΤΑΑΜΟΡΟΥ
P.Neph. 29,3	ΠΑΠΑ	P.Oxy. XVI 1917,93;94;100;112;114	ΨΕΛΕΜΑΧΙΣ
P.Neph. 32,5	ΦΙΛΟΝΊΚΟΥ	P.Oxy. XVI 1939,1	ΚΑΛΑΜΟΥΡΙΟΥ
P.Neph. 32,7	ΝΗ͂ΣΩΝ κώμη	P.Oxy. XVI 1953,2	ΨΥΧΙΣ
P.Neph. 43,2;15	ΝΗ͂ΣΩΝ κώμη	* P.Oxy. XVI 1961,9	ΙΒΙΧΕΩΣ
P.Neph. 44,2;6;11;21-22	ΝΗ͂ΣΩΝ κώμη	P.Oxy. XVI 1997,2	ΝΗ͂ΣΩΝ κώμη
P.Neph. 45,19	ΘΜΟΙΝΠΕΣΛΑ	P.Oxy. XVI 1998,2;6	ΚΟΜΑ
P.Neph. 46,1	ΝΗ͂ΣΩΝ κώμη	P.Oxy. XVI 2017,1;2;4;6;12	ΘΜΟΙΑΜΟΥΝ(ΙΣ)
P.Neph. 48,4;5;9	(Φ)ΑΘΩΡ	* P.Oxy. XVI 2017,5;14	ΜΑΧΟΡ
P.Neph. 49,2	(Φ)ΑΘΩΡ	P.Oxy. XVI 2017,7	ΣΥΓΚΕΜΜ[..]ΕΙ
P.NYU 4 a,2;7	ΛΕΥΚΟΓΙΟΝ	P.Oxy. XVI 2018,6;21;22	ΜΑΙΟΥΜΑ
P.NYU 11,2;6	ΛΕΥΚΟΓΙΟΝ	P.Oxy. XIX 2244,57	ΟΞΥΡΥΓΧΟΣ
P.NYU 11 a,12; passim	ΛΕΥΚΟΓΙΟΝ	P.Oxy. XIX 2244,76	ΚΤΗ͂ΜΑ
P.Osl. III 82,15	ΚΟΜΑ	P.Oxy. XX 2268,6	ΓΕΣΣΙΑΣ
P.Osl. III 151,11-12	ΝΕΊΛΟΥ ΠΌΛΙΣ	P.Oxy. XX 2272,13;16	ΒΟΥΣΙΡΙΣ
P.Oxf. 6,5	ΚΟΛΛΙΝΤΑΑΘΥΡ	P.Oxy. XXII 2342,40	ΚΩ
P.Oxf. 6,11;15;20	ΟΓΟΥ	P.Oxy. XXIV 2412,34;135;173	ΤΕΚΜΙ

P.Oxy. XXIV 2412,72	ἸΒΙΩΝ	P.Rain.Cent. 82,5-6	ΧΟΙΒΝΩΤΜΙΣ
P.Oxy. XXIV 2412,74;156;185	ΚΟΛΛΙΝΤΑΑΘΥΡ	P.Rain.Cent. 82,11	ΣΩΒΘΟΙΣ
P.Oxy. XXIV 2412,90;167;189	ΠΥΡΓΩΤΟΣ	P.Rain.Cent. 82,12-13	ΠΤΟΛΕΜΑΙΟΥ (fossil kleros)
P.Oxy. XXIV 2412,96;164	ΟΓΟΥ	P.Rain.Cent. 86,4	ΤΑΑΜΟΡΟΥ
P.Oxy. XXIV 2412,99	ΜΟΥΧΙΣ	P.Rain.Cent. 87,2	ΠΕΕΝΗ
P.Oxy. XXVII 2480,2	ΜΟΥΧΙΣ	P.Rain.Cent. 95,6	ΤΕΒΕΤΝΥ
P.Oxy. XXVII 2480,66;76;93;111;112;115;117	ΚΟΜΑ	P.Rain.Cent. 101,4-5;6	ΚΟΒΑ
P.Oxy. XXXI 2582,4	ΤΑΑΜΗΧΙΣ	P.Rain.Cent. 101,10	ἈΓΚΥΡΩΝ πόλις/κώμη
P.Oxy. XXXVIII 2842,5	ΨΥΧΙΣ	P.Rain.Cent. 102,5	ΦΕΒΙΧΙΣ
P.Oxy. XLII 3052,10	ΚΑΙΝΗ (?)	P.Rain.Cent. 106,5	ΚΑΙΝΗ
P.Oxy. XLII 3052,10	ΛΕΥΚΟΓΙΟΝ	P.Rain.Cent. 107,4	ΚΩ
P.Oxy. XLII 3052,10	ΟΝΝΗΣ	P.Rain.Cent. 110,5	ΠΥΡΓΩΤΟΣ
P.Oxy. XLIV 3168,3	ΤΡΥΦΩΝΟΣ (fossil kleros)	P.Rain.Cent. 113,10	ΝΕΜΗΟΥΕΙ
P.Oxy. XLIV 3168,4	ΣΤΡΑΤΩΝΟΣ (fossil kleros)	P.Rain.Cent. 118,4	ΤΟΕΜΗΣΙΣ
P.Oxy. XLIV 3168,8	ΦΙΛΙΣΚΟΥ (fossil kleros)	P.Rain.Cent. 123,3;9	ΦΕΒΙΧΙΣ
P.Oxy. XLIV 3168,8;24	ΠΟΛΥΚ() (fossil kleros)	P.Rain.Cent. 124,6-7;9-10	ΒΟΥΣΙΡΙΣ
P.Oxy. XLIV 3168,9	ἈΓΑΘΟΚ(ΛΕΟΥΣ) ΤΑΥΡΩ() (fossil kleros)	P.Rain.Cent. 133,2	ΑΙΛΙΑΝΟΥ
P.Oxy. XLIV 3168,12	ΤΕΧΥΜΙΣ	P.Rain.Cent. 137,1	ΟΝΝΗΣ
P.Oxy. XLIV 3168,12	ΠΤΟΛ() ΜΕΝΕΒΟΥ(ΛΟΥ) (fossil kleros)	P.Rain.Cent. 147,6	ΤΑΛΑΗ
		P.Rain.Cent. 147,8	ΑΣΣΥΑ
P.Oxy. XLIV 3168,13	ἈΡΟΜΒ() (fossil kleros)	P.Rain.Cent. 153,7	ΤΑΛΑΗ
P.Oxy. XLIV 3168,17	ΠΑΡΜΕ() (fossil kleros)	P.Rain.Cent. 153,9	ΦΥΣ
P.Oxy. XLIV 3168,21	ΠΑΡΙΔΟΣ (fossil kleros)	P.Rain.Cent. 153,10	ΘΜΟΙΝΠΕΣΛΑ
P.Oxy. XLIV 3168,29	ΠΤΟΛ() ΜΙΘ() (fossil kleros)	P.Rain.Cent. 153,12	ΘΝΗΙΣ
P.Oxy. XLIV 3168,34;47	ΜΟΣΧΙΩ(ΝΟΣ) (fossil kleros)	P.Rain.Cent. 153,13	[...].Ω
P.Oxy. XLIV 3168,35	ΚΛΕΙΤΑΡΧΟΥ (fossil kleros)	P.Rain.Cent. 153,14	ΠΕΕΝΠΙΒΥΚ(ΙΣ)
P.Oxy. XLIV 3168,37	ἘΠΙΧΑΡΟ(ΥΣ) (fossil kleros)	P.Rain.Cent. 154,2	ΤΩΥ
P.Oxy. XLIV 3168,46	ΜΕΝΩΝΟΣ (fossil kleros)	P.Rain.Cent. 154,4	ἈΣΚΛΗΠΙΑΔΟΥ (fossil kleros)
P.Oxy. XLVII 3357,14	ΦΕΒΙΧΙΣ	P.Rain.Cent. 154,5	ἩΡΑΚΛΕΙΔΟΥ Α[(fossil kleros)
P.Oxy. XLVII 3365,34	[ἩΡΑΚΛΕΟΥΣ] τοῦ ΚΑΛΛΙΣΤΡΑΤΟΥ (fossil kleros)	P.Rain.Cent. 154,6	ἩΓΗΣΙΣΤΡΑΤΟΥ (fossil kleros)
		P.Rain.Cent. 154,7	ἙΡΜΩΝΑΚΤΟΣ (fossil kleros)
P.Oxy. XLIX 3462,3	ΣΙΝΑΡΥ	P.Rain.Cent. 154,8	ἩΡΑΚΛΕΙΔΟΥ (fossil kleros)
P.Oxy. L 3600,5;32	ΚΟΒΑ	P.Rain.Cent. 154,9	ΕΥΠΟΛΕΜΟΥ (fossil kleros)
P.Oxy. LV 3804,149	ΚΟΜΑ	P.Rain.Cent. 154,10	ἈΡΙΣΤΟΜΑΧΟΥ (fossil kleros)
P.Oxy. LV 3805,91	ΧΟΙΒΝΩΤΜΙΣ	P.Rein. 98,4	ΚΩΙΤΗΣ
P.Oxy. LV 3807,35	ΔΙΚΩΜΙΑ	P.Rein. 98,12	ΣΤΕΦΑΝΟΥ (fossil kleros)
P.Oxy. LVI 3870,3	ΘΜΟΙΝΕΨΙ	P.Ross.Georg. II 3,5;7	ΚΩΙΤΗΣ
P.Oxy. LVIII 3928,5-6	ΠΟΙΜΕΝΩΝ κώμη	P.Ross.Georg. II 11,2	ΜΟΥΧΙΝΠΑΣΙΣ
P.Oxy. LIX 3975,6	ΧΟΙΒΝΩΤΜΙΣ	P.Ross.Georg. II 11,5;6;15	ἈΓΚΥΡΩΝ πόλις/κώμη
P.Oxy. LIX 3993,7	ΔΙΚΩΜΙΑ	P.Ross.Georg. V 20 recto,1;4;8	ΚΟΡΦΟΤΟΙ
P.Oxy. LIX 4004,10	ΝΗΣΩΝ κώμη	P.Ross.Georg. V 20 verso,col.II,1	ΘΜΟΙΝΑΧΗ
P.Oxy. Hels. 37,1	ΣΩΒΘΟΙΣ	P.Ross.Georg. V 20 verso,col.II,2	ΘΕΛΒΩ
* P.Panop.Beatty 1,121;161	ΠΑΠΑ	P.Ross.Georg. V 20 verso,col.II,4	ΦΕΒΙΧΙΣ
P.Petaus 28,6	ΦΕΒΙΧΙΣ	P.Ross.Georg. V 20 verso,col.II,5	ΦΙ....
P.Petaus 28,6;20	ΘΜΟΙΝΑΧΗ	P.Ross.Georg. V 20 verso,col.II,6	[...]ΑΤΜΥ
P.Petr. III 43(2),col.III,28	ΘΜΟΙΝΩΘΙΣ	P.Ross.Georg. V 61 A verso,9	ΚΟΜΑ
P.Petr. III 43(2),col.III,30	ΦΝΕΒΙΕΥΣ	P.Ross.Georg. V 61 B recto,2;12; C verso,7;8;13; D recto,2;18;D verso,13	ΤΑΑΜΟΡΟΥ
P.Petr. III 43(2),col.III,30	ΧΑΝΑΑΝΑ(ΙΣ)		
P.Petr. III 62 b,4	ΦΝΕΒΙΕΥΣ	P.Ryl. II 87,3	ΜΕΝΕΛΑΟΥ (fossil kleros)
P.Petr. III 99 recto,10;17;28	ΦΙΛΟΝΙΚΟΥ	P.Ryl. II 87,4	[name lost] (fossil kleros)
P.Prag. II 132,7-8	ΝΟΜΑΡΧΟΥ	P.Ryl. II 87,5	ἈΓΚΥΡΩΝ πόλις/κώμη
P.Princ. II 105,1;6	ΚΟΒΑ	P.Ryl. II 87,6	......ΔΕΙΧΟΥΣ (fossil kleros)
* P.Rain.Cent. 40,2	ΚΟΛΛΑΣΟΥΧΑ	P.Ryl. II 87 recto, col.II(see P.Ryl. II, p.51)	ΑΛΙΔΑΙΣ
P.Rain.Cent. 40,3-4	ΣΑΤΥΡΟΥ (fossil kleros)	P.Ryl. II 87 recto, col.II(see P.Ryl. II, p.51)	ΘΜΟΙΝΑΧΗ
* P.Rain.Cent. 40,7	ἹΕΡΑ ΝΗΣΟΣ	P.Ryl. II 225,31	ΝΟΚΛΗ
P.Rain.Cent. 44,5	ΟΝΝΗΣ	P.Ryl. II 225,31	ΠΑΡΜΕΝΙΩΝΟΣ (fossil kleros)
P.Rain.Cent. 44,6	ΘΜΟΙΟΒΑΣΤΙΣ	P.Ryl. II 225,32	ἈΠΟΛΛΩΝΙΟΥ ΜΕΛΑΝΟΣ (fossil kleros)
P.Rain.Cent. 44,9-10;13	ΒΟΥΣΙΡΙΣ	P.Ryl. II 225,35	ΚΑΛΛΙΑΔΟΥ (fossil kleros)
P.Rain.Cent. 64,5	ΠΥΡΓΩΤΟΣ	P.Ryl. II 225,36	ΘΕΛΒΩ

REVERSE INDEX

P.Ryl. II 225,37	ΦΙΛΟΝΊΚΟΥ	SB VIII 9756,1	ΦΥΣ
* **P.Ryl.** II 225,49	ΚΟΜΑ	SB VIII 9773,8	ΠΕΕΝΗ
* **P.Ryl.** II 225,49	ΜΑΧΟΡ	SB VIII 9790,1	ΚΩΊΤΗΣ
P.Ryl. II 351 descr.	ΘΕΛΒΩ	SB VIII 9790,3	ΦΕΒΙΧΙΣ
P.Sakaon 22,7;11	ΛΕΥΚΟΓΙΟΝ	SB VIII 9790,9	ΜΟΛΩΘΙΣ
SB I 1495,4	ΔΙΚΩΜΊΑ	SB VIII 9841,3;17	ΧΟΙΒΝΩΤΜΙΣ
SB I 1496,3	ΚΟΒΑ	SB VIII 9876,10	ΝΟΗΡΙΣ
SB I 1497,1	ΔΙΚΩΜΊΑ	SB VIII 9876,10-11	ΤΑΡΕΤΤΑΡΥ
SB I 1500,2	ΠΩΙΣ	SB X 10447 recto,43	ΚΟΒΑ
SB I 1501,3	ΚΟΒΑ	SB X 10447 recto,60; verso,35	ΦΕΒΙΧΙΣ
SB I 1508,2	ΠΩΙΣ	SB X 10447 verso,27	ΤΑΛΑΗ
SB I 1511,4	ΔΙΚΩΜΊΑ	SB X 10540,3	ΘΜΟΙΝΕΘΥΜΙΣ
SB I 1512,5	ΚΟΒΑ	SB X 10783,2	ΦΕΒΙΧΙΣ
SB I 1515,3-4	ΠΩΙΣ	SB X 10783,7	ΤΑΛΑΗ
SB I 1945,6	ΘΜΟΙΝΕΨΙ	SB XII 10939,7	ΦΙΛΟΝΊΚΟΥ
SB I 1967,1	ΝΉΣΩΝ κώμη	SB XII 11262,11;18	ἈΓΚΥΡΩΝ πόλις/κώμη
SB I 2246,6-7	ΦΙΛΟΝΊΚΟΥ	SB XIV 11277,3;4	ΝΕΊΛΟΥ ΠΟΛΙΣ
* SB I 4370,5;7;21	ΠΕΕΝΑΜΕΥΣ	* SB XIV 11341,8	ΣΧΝΩΜΘΙΣ
SB I 4370,21	ΠΑΣ...... (fossil kleros)	SB XIV 11615,3	ΠΑΠΑ
SB I 4497,7	ΑΛΙΛΑΙΣ	SB XIV 11643,2;3	ΤΑΕΜΣΙΣ
SB I 4727,2	ΑΛΙΛΑΙΣ	SB XIV 11958,27;29	ἈΓΚΥΡΩΝ πόλις/κώμη
SB I 5337,5	ΝΕΊΛΟΥ ΠΟΛΙΣ	SB XIV 11959,12;23	ΒΟΥΣΙΡΙΣ
SB I 5338,11	ΦΕΒΙΧΙΣ	SB XIV 12089,2	ΘΜΟΙΟΒΑΣΤΙΣ
SB I 5338,15	ἈΛΜΥΡΆ	SB XIV 12193,2-3	ΤΙΩΒΑΣΤΙ
SB I 5681,19	ΠΕΕΝΣΑΜΟΙ	SB XVI 12241,5;10;15	ΤΑΕΜΣΙΣ
SB III 6301,6	ΘΜΟΙΝΕΨΙ	SB XVI 12312,col.II,5-6	ἌΓΗΜΑ
SB III 6301,8;11	ΚΩΊΤΗΣ	SB XVI 12387,4	ΤΑΓΧΑΙΣ
SB III 7176,3	ΚΩΊΤΗΣ	SB XVI 12612,2	ΚΑΙΝΉ
SB III 7179,6	ΦΥΣ	SB XVI 12762,9	ΚΩ
SB III 7203,8	ΘΜΟΙΝΩΘΙΣ	SB XVI 12814,4	ἹΠΠΩΝΩΝ κώμη
SB III 7203,11	ΒΟΥΣΙΡΙΣ	SB XVI 12836,2-3;7;37	ἈΓΚΥΡΩΝ πόλις/κώμη
SB V 7515,223	ΦΙΛΟΝΊΚΟΥ	* SB XVI 12836,12	Π[....]ΣΕΙ
SB V 7515,248	ΚΕΡΚΕΣΗΦΙΣ	SB XVI 12836,12	ΜΕΝΕΛΆΟΥ (fossil kleros)
* SB V 7515,251	ΤΑΛΑΗ	SB XVI 12837,8	ἈΓΚΥΡΩΝ πόλις/κώμη
SB V 7537,2-3;5	ΚΟΜΑ	(?)SB XVIII 13151,6;17	ΤΟΟΥ
SB V 7609,5	ΠΩΙΣ	SB XVIII 13260,8;22	ΦΙΛΟΝΊΚΟΥ
SB V 7611,1	ἌΓΗΜΑ	SB XVIII 13266,6	ΝΕΊΛΟΥ ΠΟΛΙΣ
SB V 7611,14;15	ΕΥ..() (fossil kleros)	SB XVIII 13304,1;6	ΤΕΚΜΙ
SB V 8755,4	ΦΥΣ	SB XVIII 13304,2	ΒΙΧΙΝΘΩΥΘ
SB V 8756,6	ΜΟΥΧΙΣ	SB XVIII 13304,7	ΠΑΠΑ
SB VI 8987,6	ΠΙΝΗΧΕΩΣ	SB XVIII 13771,10	ἈΠΊΩΝΟΣ
SB VI 9065,11	ἸΒΙΩΝ (3)	SB XVIII 13858,12	ΠΈΡΑΝ
SB VI 9139,18	ΦΙΛΟΝΊΚΟΥ	SB XVIII 13858,15	ΦΑΙΝΊΠΠΟΥ
SB VI 9146,5;13	ΘΜΟΙΑΜΟΥΝ(ΙΣ)	SB XVIII 13870,2	ΦΙΛΟΝΊΚΟΥ
SB VI 9262,2	ΛΕΥΚΟΓΙΟΝ	SB XVIII 13888,1;9	(Φ)ΑΘΩΡ
SB VI 9282 verso	ΝΟΗΡΙΣ	SB XVIII 13888,3	ΝΟΚΛΗ
SB VI 9578,1;4	ΣΩΒΘΙΣ	SB XVIII 13888,5	ΚΑΛΑΜΟΥΡΙΟΥ
* SB VI 9590,2;11;16	ΜΑΚΑΙΤΟΝΟΣ	SB XVIII 13888,6	ΟΣΤΡΑΚΙΝΟΥ
SB VI 9590,4;11;22;verso	ΧΟΡΤΑΣΩ	SB XVIII 13888,7	ΘΕΛΒΩ
SB VI 9590,4;16;22	ἈΠΑΛΆ	SB XVIII 13888,8	ἹΠΠΩΝΩΝ κώμη
SB VI 9590,7	ΤΣΑΒΑ	SB XVIII 13949,5	ἈΜΜΩΝΙΑΝΟΥ
SB VI 9590,11;22	ΤΕΒΕΤΝΥ	SB XVIII 14004,2	ΒΟΥΣΙΡΙΣ
SB VI 9590,22	ΝΟΗΡΙΣ	SB XVIII 14005,2	ΒΟΥΣΙΡΙΣ
SB VI 9593,3;9	ΤΟΣΑΧΜΙΣ	SB XX 14115,3	ΨΥΧΙΣ
SB VI 9597,5;11	ΤΟΚΩΙΣ	SB XX 14123,6	ΚΟΜΑ
SB VI 9608,2	ΚΟΜΑ	SB XX 14234,2	ΛΕΥΚΟΓΙΟΝ
SB VI 9632,3-4	ΛΕΥΚΟΓΙΟΝ	SB XX 14236,1(?)	ΜΟΥΧΙΣ
SB VIII 9683,6;12	ἈΓΚΥΡΩΝ πόλις/κώμη	SB XX 14304,3	ἈΓΚΥΡΩΝ πόλις/κώμη
SB VIII 9683,16	ΘΕΛΒΩ	SB XX 14580,1;2	ΤΟΚΩΙΣ
SB VIII 9750,3	ΟΝΝΗΣ	SB XX 14705,14	ΦΥΣ

THE HERAKLEOPOLITE NOME

SB XX 15072,2	ΣΩΥΧ(ΙΣ)	P.Strasb. VIII 781,8	ΘΜΟΙΝΩΘΙΣ
SB XX 15072,2	ΣΩΒΘΙΣ	P.Strasb. VIII 782,1	ΧΑΡΙΣΙΟΥ (fossil kleros)
SB XX 15072,4	ΠΩΙΣ	P.Strasb. VIII 782,3	ΝΙΚΟΣΤΡΑΤΟΥ (fossil kleros)
SB XX 15072,5	ΤΑΜΕΡΣΟΦΩ()	P.Strasb. VIII 782,5	ΕΥΦΡΑΝΟΡΟΣ (fossil kleros)
SB XX 15072,7	ΔΑΦΝΗ	P.Strasb. VIII 782,7	ΠΕΡΙΚΛΕΟΥΣ (fossil kleros)
SB XX 15072,7	ΝΕΜΑΡΕΩΣ	P.Strasb. VIII 782,8	ΕΥΦΡΟΝΟΣ (fossil kleros)
SB XX 15072,9	ΜΟΥΧΕΜΠ(ΑΓ)ΟΥ (?)	P.Strasb. IX 802,2	ΝΩΥΠ
SB XX 15092,5;8	ΛΕΥΚΟΓΙΟΝ	P.Strasb. IX 802,3;24	ΘΜΟΙΝΕΘΥΜΙΣ
SB XX 15130,2	ΘΕΛΒΩ	P.Strasb. IX 802,4	ΘΜΟΙΤΑΩΥΣ
P.Select. 13,3;verso	ΠΕΕΝΣΑΜΟΙ	P.Strasb. IX 802,5	ΘΝΗΙΣ
P.Select. 15,5	ΠΑΠΑ	P.Strasb. IX 802,6	ΤΑΑΜΟΡΟΥ
* P.Select. 17,4	ΆΓΗΜΑ	P.Strasb. IX 802,7	ΨΕΛΕΜΑΧΙΣ
P.Select. 17,5	ΤΟΚΩΙΣ	P.Strasb. IX 802,8	ΤΑΧΟΝΠΑΧΝΟΥΒ
P.Select. 17,8;11	ΠΩΙΣ	* P.Strasb. IX 802,9	ΤΟΕΜΗΣΙΣ
P.Select. 17,10-11	ΛΑΟΜΕΔΟΝΤΟΣ (fossil kleros)	P.Strasb. IX 802,11	ΧΟΙΒΝΩΤΜΙΣ
PSI I 32,3;8	ΆΓΚΥΡΩΝ πόλις/κώμη	P.Strasb. IX 802,12	ΤΑΝΙΣ
(?)PSI I 80,4	ΘΜΟΙΝΑΧΗ	* P.Strasb. IX 802,13	ΨΕΒΘΟΝΠΕΝΟΥΦΙΣ
PSI III 183,1	ΚΟΒΑ	P.Strasb. IX 802,14	Ν....[
PSI III 184,4	ΒΟΥΣΙΡΙΣ	P.Strasb. IX 802,16	ΠΕΡΧΥΦΙΣ
PSI III 222,7	ΘΜΟΙΑΜΟΥΝ(ΙΣ)	P.Strasb. IX 802,18	ΤΟΘΙΣ
PSI III 222,9	ΠΑΠΑ	P.Strasb. IX 802,19	ΚΟΡΡΑΣ
* PSI III 222,9-10	ΦΕΒΙΧΙΣ	* P.Strasb. IX 802,20	ΜΟΛΩΘΙΣ
PSI V 510,2	ΚΑΤΩ (ΆΓΗΜΑ)	P.Strasb. IX 802,21	ΦΕΒΙΧΙΣ
PSI V 510,4;11	ΒΟΥΣΙΡΙΣ	P.Strasb. IX 802,22	ΤΕΡΤΟΝ()
PSI VI 587,4	ΟΝΝΗΣ	Stud.Pal. II p.28,6;11;12;13-14	ΆΓΚΥΡΩΝ πόλις/κώμη
PSI VI 928,12	ΆΓΚΥΡΩΝ πόλις/κώμη	* Stud.Pal. III 24 verso,12	ΤΩΛ()
PSI VIII 897,65-66	ΉΡΑΚΛΕΟΥΣ τοῦ ΚΑΛΛΙΣΤΡΑΤΟΥ (fossil kleros)	Stud.Pal. III 25,1	[...]ΝΕΑΣ
PSI VIII 897,68	ΔΙΟΝΥΣΙΟΥ τοῦ ΣΑΡΑΠΙΩΝΟΣ (fossil kleros)	Stud.Pal. III 64,2	ΕΥΑΓΟΥΣ (fossil kleros)
		Stud.Pal. III 66,1	ΘΜΟΙΝΕΨΙ
PSI VIII 962,25	ΘΜΟΙΦΘΑ	Stud.Pal. III 67,2	ΤΟΣΑΧΜΙΣ
PSI VIII 967,19	ΦΕΒΙΧΙΣ	Stud.Pal. III 68,2	ΟΝΝΗΣ
PSI IX 1037,9	ΤΑΑΜΟΡΟΥ	Stud.Pal. III 68,3	ΛΕΥΚΟΓΙΟΝ
PSI XII 1229,8	ΧΟΙΒΝΩΤΜΙΣ	Stud.Pal. III 86,1;4	ΤΑΠΟΥΡΣΗΕΙ
PSI XIII 1325,8	ΚΩΪΤΗΣ	Stud.Pal. III 197,2	ΤΑΛΑΗ
PSI XIII 1325,8;22	ΦΕΒΙΧΙΣ	Stud.Pal. III 202,2	ΦΝΕΒΙΕΥΣ
PSI XIII 1325,14;30	ΚΥΔΡΕΩΣ (fossil kleros)	Stud.Pal. III 258,4	ΛΕΥΚΟΓΙΟΝ
PSI XIII 1325,28	ΓΛΕ[(fossil kleros)	Stud.Pal. III 259,4	ΛΕΥΚΟΓΙΟΝ
PSI XIII 1325,29	ΆΡΓΑΙΟΥ (fossil kleros)	Stud.Pal. III 341,1	ΦΝΕΒΙΕΥΣ
PSI XIII 1325,31	Δ]ΗΜΟΣΤΡ() (fossil kleros)	Stud.Pal. III 343,1	ΘΕΛΒΩ
PSI XIII 1332,10-11	ΝΕΜΑΡΕΩΣ	Stud.Pal. III 356,2	ΤΛΕΣΙΔΟΣ
PSI XV estr. 1546,5;14	ΘΜΟΙΝΑΧΗ	Stud.Pal. III 371,2	ΟΝΝΗΣ
PSI XV estr. 1546,8;30	ΤΕΚΜΙ	Stud.Pal. III 399,1	ΕΤΩΝ
PSI XV estr. 1546,36	ΤΕΡΤΟΝΠΕΤΕΧΩΝΣ	Stud.Pal. III 448,2	ΚΟΜΑ
* P.Strasb. II 99,3	ΝΩΥΕ..Σ	Stud.Pal. III 453,2	ΆΓΚΥΡΩΝ πόλις/κώμη
P.Strasb. II 99,5	ΠΟΙΜΕΝΩΝ κώμη	(?)Stud.Pal. III 453,2	ΚΩ
P.Strasb. II 103,5;15;26	ΤΕΧΘΩ	Stud.Pal. VIII 772,3	ΝΟΗΡΙΣ
P.Strasb. II 104,8	ΤΕΧΘΩ	Stud.Pal. VIII 952,2	ΛΕΥΚΟΓΙΟΝ
P.Strasb. II 111,5-6	ΠΕΕΝΣΑΜΟΙ	* Stud.Pal. VIII 955,1	ΤΛΕΣΙΔΟΣ
* P.Strasb. II 111,21	ΠΕΡΑΝ	Stud.Pal. VIII 1183,2	ΦΑΕΙΝ
* P.Strasb. II 111,23	ΘΜΟΙΦΘΑ	Stud.Pal. VIII 1183,2	ΦΝΕΒΙΕΥΣ
P.Strasb. II 113,10	ΤΕΧΘΩ	Stud.Pal. VIII 1198,2	ΤΕΚΜΙ
P.Strasb. V 318,13	ΚΑΙΝΗ	* Stud.Pal. VIII 1226,5	ΠΕΕΝΠΙΒΥΚ(ΙΣ)
P.Strasb. V 318,13	ΠΕΧΙΤ	Stud.Pal. VIII 1257,3	ΤΟΚΩΙΣ
P.Strasb. V 356,3	ΘΜΟΙ[	Stud.Pal. VIII 1309,1	ΨΥΧΙΣ
P.Strasb. VI 563,9	ΤΕΧΘΩ	Stud.Pal. VIII 1309,4	ΆΛΜΥΡΑ
P.Strasb. VII 641,4	ΦΕΒΙΧΙΣ	Stud.Pal. VIII 1309,4	ΔΙΑΣΗΜΩΤΑΤΟΥ
P.Strasb. VII 642,5	ΤΕΚΜΙ	Stud.Pal. VIII 1326,1	ΦΕΒΙΧΙΣ
P.Strasb. VII 643,2	ΚΟΒΑ	Stud.Pal. VIII 1346,1	ΦΕΒΙΧΙΣ
P.Strasb. VII 662,20	ΣΙΝΑΡΥ	Stud.Pal. VIII 1346,4;6	ΚΟΒΑ
		Stud.Pal. X 4,2	ΚΟΜΑ

REVERSE INDEX

Stud.Pal. X 4,2	ἈΠΙΩΝΟΣ	Stud.Pal. X 84,3	ΝΟΗΡΙΣ
Stud.Pal. X 4,4	ΠΕΕΝΑΜΕΥΣ	Stud.Pal. X 84,4	ΠΩΙΣ
Stud.Pal. X 4,5	ΠΚΟΜΜΑΤΟΕΙ	* Stud.Pal. X 84,5	ΠΕΕΝΣΑΜΟΙ
Stud.Pal. X 4,6	ΘΜΟΙΑΜΟΥΝ(ΙΣ)	* Stud.Pal. X 84,6	..[±3]ΑΙ
* Stud.Pal. X 5,2	Π.[±6]	* Stud.Pal. X 84,7	ΘΜΟΙΝΕΨΙ
* Stud.Pal. X 5,3	Τ[.]Λ[.	Stud.Pal. X 94,1	ΣΟΥΧ(ΙΣ)
Stud.Pal. X 5,4	ΟΝΩΣΙΣ	Stud.Pal. X 94,2	ἈΝΝΙΑΝΟΥ̑
Stud.Pal. X 5,5	ΤΙΝΤΗΡΙΣ	Stud.Pal. X 94,3	ΕΛΑΣΙΜΗΣ
Stud.Pal. X 5,6	ΚΟΛΛΙΝΤΑΑΘΥΡ	* Stud.Pal. X 94,4	].ΙΝΩ
Stud.Pal. X 5,7	ΝΙΝΩ	* Stud.Pal. X 94,5	ΓΕΣΣΙΑΣ
Stud.Pal. X 5,9	ΠΙ[	Stud.Pal. X 94,6	ΠΕΕΝΑΜΕΥΣ
Stud.Pal. X 5,10	ΓΕΛ[	Stud.Pal. X 94,7	ΔΑΦΝΗ
* Stud.Pal. X 5,11	ΠΛ[.].[±2]Λ	Stud.Pal. X 94,8	ΤΟΣΑΧΜΙΣ
Stud.Pal. X 8,2	ΧΟΙΒΝΩΤΜΙΣ	* Stud.Pal. X 109,3	Φ...ΡΥΓΕΛ
Stud.Pal. X 8,2	ΣΩΒΘΙΣ	Stud.Pal. X 109,4	ΤΑΑΜΟΡΟΥ
Stud.Pal. X 8,4	ἉΛΜΥΡΆ	* Stud.Pal. X 109,5	ΟΤṚ()
Stud.Pal. X 8,5	ΤΕΧΘΩ	Stud.Pal. X 109,6	ΠΥΡΓΩΤΟΣ
Stud.Pal. X 8,7	ΦΝΕΒΙΕΥΣ	Stud.Pal. X 109,7	ΤΙΝΤΗΡΙΣ
* Stud.Pal. X 8,8	ΠΟΥΛΗ	* Stud.Pal. X 109,8	Φ..ΓΕΛ()
Stud.Pal. X 9,1	ΟΝΝΗΣ	Stud.Pal. X 109,9	ΘΝΗΙΣ
Stud.Pal. X 9,2	ΣΩΒΘΙΣ	Stud.Pal. X 109,10	ΦΙΛΟΝΙΚΟΥ
Stud.Pal. X 9,3	ΦΝΕΒΙΕΥΣ	Stud.Pal. X 109,12	ΦΝΕΒΙΕΥΣ
Stud.Pal. X 9,4	ΜΟΥΧΙΣ	Stud.Pal. X 119,2	ΘΜΟΙΟΒΑΣΤΙΣ
* Stud.Pal. X 9,5	Κ..ΚΕΩΣ	Stud.Pal. X 149,8	ΛΕΥΚΟΓΙΟΝ
Stud.Pal. X 17,1	ΘΡΥΩΝΟΣ	Stud.Pal. X 199,1	ΒΟΑΦΡΕΩΣ
Stud.Pal. X 17,3	ΚΟΜΑ	* Stud.Pal. X 199,3	ΦΕΒΙΧΙΣ
Stud.Pal. X 17,6	ΠΚ[	* Stud.Pal. X 199,4	ΑΣΣΥΑ
Stud.Pal. X 17,8	Α.[	Stud.Pal. X 199,5	ΦΙΛΟΝΙΚΟΥ
Stud.Pal. X 17,10	ΠΕΕΝΑΜΕΥΣ	Stud.Pal. X 200,3	ΜΑΓΔΩΛΑ
* Stud.Pal. X 17,12	ΠΚΟΜΜΑΤΟΕΙ	Stud.Pal. X 200,4	ΝΟΤΙΝΟΥ
Stud.Pal. X 22,1	ΣΩΒΘΙΣ	Stud.Pal. X 200,4	ΑΛΗ (?)
* Stud.Pal. X 22,2	ΧΑΡΑΜΟΥ	Stud.Pal. X 200,6	ΠΕΕΝΗ
* Stud.Pal. X 22,3	ΤΑΑΠΡΟΥΣ[	Stud.Pal. X 202,7	ΘΜΟΙΦΘΑ
Stud.Pal. X 22,4	ΚΑΘΟΛΙΚ[	Stud.Pal. X 202,11	(Θ)ΕΛΒΩΝΘΙΣ
Stud.Pal. X 22,5	ΘΜΟΙΝ()	Stud.Pal. X 202,15	ΚΟΒΑ
Stud.Pal. X 22,6	ΤΟΚΩΙΣ	Stud.Pal. X 203,1	(Θ)ΕΛΒΩΝΘΙΣ
Stud.Pal. X 44,4	ΠΩΙΣ	Stud.Pal. X 203,2	ΘΕΛΒΩ
Stud.Pal. X 44,5	ΠΕΝΤΑΛ[ΕΩ]Σ	Stud.Pal. X 203,3	ΘΑΛΛΟΥΣ
* Stud.Pal. X 44,6	ΤΙΝΤΗΡΙΣ	Stud.Pal. X 203,4	ΘΜΟΙΟΒΑΣΤΙΣ
Stud.Pal. X 44,7	ΤΩΥ	Stud.Pal. X 203,5	ΘΜΟΙΝ()
Stud.Pal. X 44,8	ΚΟΛΛΙΝΤΑΑΘΥΡ	Stud.Pal. X 203,6	ΘΜΟΙΑΜΟΥΝ(ΙΣ)
Stud.Pal. X 44,10	ΦΝΕΒΙΕΥΣ	Stud.Pal. X 203,7	ΘΜΟΙΝΕΨΙ
Stud.Pal. X 47,1	ΟΝΩΣΙΣ	Stud.Pal. X 203,8	ΘΜΟΙΝΩΘΙΣ
Stud.Pal. X 47,2	ΜΟΥΧΙΣ	* Stud.Pal. X 203,9	ἹΠΠΩΝΩΝ κώμη
Stud.Pal. X 47,3	ΤΑΝΑΣΩ	Stud.Pal. X 204,1	ΜΑΓΔΩΛΑ
Stud.Pal. X 47,4	ΤΟΣΑΧΜΙΣ	Stud.Pal. X 204,2	ΜΑΚΑΙΤΟΝΟΣ
Stud.Pal. X 47,5	ΚΟΛΛΟΥΘΟΥ	* Stud.Pal. X 204,3	ΝΟΤΊΝΟΥ
Stud.Pal. X 50,1;50	ΓΕΜΟΥΝ(ΙΣ)	Stud.Pal. X 204,4	ΟΓΟΥ
Stud.Pal. X 50,4	ἈΜΗΤΙΑΝΌΣ	* Stud.Pal. X 204,5	ΚΑΘΟΛΙΚ[
Stud.Pal. X 50,6	ΒΟΥΝΩΝ	* Stud.Pal. X 204,6	ΠΕΕ[
Stud.Pal. X 56,4	ΟΞΥΡΥΓΧΟΣ	Stud.Pal. X 204 B,2	ΨΥΧΙΣ
* Stud.Pal. X 66,2	ΑΜΜΙΑΝ[..]	Stud.Pal. X 206,3	ΚΑΣΑΝΟΥΠ(ΙΣ)
* Stud.Pal. X 66,3	ΤΑΥΡΟΣ	Stud.Pal. X 206,3	ΝΕΥΑΚ[
Stud.Pal. X 66,4	Φ[Ρ]ΟΥΡΊ[ΟΥ	Stud.Pal. X 206,4	ΤΗ()
* Stud.Pal. X 66,5	ΦΙΛΟΝΙΚΟΥ	Stud.Pal. X 206,4	[.]Ε[.]Λ[
* Stud.Pal. X 72,1	[.]Υ̣	Stud.Pal. X 206,5	.ΠΕΙ.ʹΑʹ
Stud.Pal. X 72,3	ΟΓΟΥ	Stud.Pal. X 206,6	[±4]ΕΤΑ
* Stud.Pal. X 72,6	ΠΥΡΓΩΤΟΣ	Stud.Pal. X 206,7	[±4]ΑΤ
Stud.Pal. X 72,11;12;14	ἉΛΜΥΡΆ	Stud.Pal. X 206,8	ΠΙΕΝΕΚΑΜΟΥ
* Stud.Pal. X 72,13	ΠΤΑΝ.	Stud.Pal. X 206,8	ΚΟΜ.[

Stud.Pal. X 206,9	ΤΚΟΥΝΣΩΣΕΙ	Stud.Pal. X 227,3	ΜΑ[
Stud.Pal. X 206,9	ΙΕΡΚΙΝΚ[	Stud.Pal. X 227,4	ΣΑΡΑΠΟΥΔΟΣ
Stud.Pal. X 206,10	[±4]ΤΙΟΜ	Stud.Pal. X 227,5;6	ΤΑΛΑΗ
Stud.Pal. X 206,10	ΦΑΕΙΝ	* Stud.Pal. X 227,7	Λ[±2].[±2]Η
Stud.Pal. X 206,11;12	ΤΑΠΙΑΜΠΕΣΕΤ	Stud.Pal. X 227,8	Θ[±3?]
Stud.Pal. X 206,11	ΠΑΛΙΕΤ[	Stud.Pal. X 227,11	Φ[±3?]
Stud.Pal. X 206,13	ΨΑΝΤΙ	* Stud.Pal. X 228,4	ΠΑΡΓΟΥ
Stud.Pal. X 206,13	ΤΣΗ[	* Stud.Pal. X 228,5	ΠΙΑΤΙΜΙ
Stud.Pal. X 206,14	ΑΚΑΚΙΗΤΗ	Stud.Pal. X 228,6	ΝΕΘΙΣΕΙ
Stud.Pal. X 206,14	ΠΜΑΝΚΕΜ	Stud.Pal. X 228,7	ΝΕΥΗΛΑ
Stud.Pal. X 206,14	ΤΑΠΑΜΕ	* Stud.Pal. X 228,8	ΣΟΥΡΙΥ
Stud.Pal. X 207,3	ΤΟΛΕΩΣ	Stud.Pal. X 228,9	ΠΙΑΚΕΡ
Stud.Pal. X 207,5	ΣΩΒΘΙΣ	Stud.Pal. X 230,2	ἉΛΜΥΡΑ
Stud.Pal. X 208,2	ἈΠΙΩΝΟΣ	Stud.Pal. X 230,3	ΑἸΛΙΑΝΟΥ
Stud.Pal. X 208,3	ΘΜΟΙΑΜΟΥΝ(ΙΣ)	Stud.Pal. X 230,4	ἈΝΑΒΩΛΙΑ?
Stud.Pal. X 208,4	ΘΡΥΩΝΟΣ	Stud.Pal. X 230,5	ΚΟΛΛΙΝΤΑΑΘΥΡ
Stud.Pal. X 208 verso,1	ΘΜΟΙΝ()	Stud.Pal. X 231,1	ΘΕΛΒΩ
Stud.Pal. X 208 verso,2	ΦΝΕΒΙΕΥΣ	Stud.Pal. X 231,2	.() ΜΕΓΑ()
* Stud.Pal. X 208 verso,3	ΦΕΛΕ()	Stud.Pal. X 232,1	ΘΜΟΙΑΜΟΥΝ(ΙΣ)
Stud.Pal. X 209,1	ΚΛΕΩΝΟΣ	* Stud.Pal. X 233, col.I A,1	ΝΗΣΩΝ
* Stud.Pal. X 209,2	ΚΟΛΛΑΣΟΥΧΑ	Stud.Pal. X 233, col.I A,2	ΘΝΗΙΣ
* Stud.Pal. X 209,3	ΜΙΚ() ΠΡΟΣ()	Stud.Pal. X 233, col.I A,3	ΦΙΛΟΝΙΚΟΥ
Stud.Pal. X 209,4	ΜΑΙΟΥΜΑ	Stud.Pal. X 233, col.I A,4	ΨΥΧΙΣ
Stud.Pal. X 209,5	ΝΩΙΣ	Stud.Pal. X 233, col.I A,5	ΦΡΟΥΡΙΟΥ
Stud.Pal. X 210,1	ΠΤΕΝΝΕΩΣ	Stud.Pal. X 233, col.I A,5	..ΕΝΕ ΜΕΓΑΛΗ
Stud.Pal. X 211,3	ΟΓΟΥ	Stud.Pal. X 233, col.I A,7	ΠΕΤΑΧΟΡ
* Stud.Pal. X 211,4	ΠΥΡΓΩΤΟΣ	Stud.Pal. X 233, col.I A,8	ΘΜΟΙΝΑΧΗ
Stud.Pal. X 211,5	ΗΛΙ()	Stud.Pal. X 233, col.I A,9	ΣΑΡΑΠΟΥΔΟΣ
Stud.Pal. X 212,2	(Θ)ΕΛΒΩΝΘΙΣ	Stud.Pal. X 233, col.I B,1	ΤΕΧΘΩ
Stud.Pal. X 212,3	ΣΑΡΑΠΟΥΔΟΣ	* Stud.Pal. X 233, col.I B,2	ΠΕΕΝΣΑΜΟΙ
Stud.Pal. X 213,2;5	ΠΕΤΑΧΟΡ	* Stud.Pal. X 233, col.I B,3	ΧΑΡΑΜΟΥ
* Stud.Pal. X 213,3	ἹΠΠΩΝΩΝ κώμη	Stud.Pal. X 233, col.I B,4	ΤΟΚΩΙΣ
Stud.Pal. X 213,4	ΚΟΛΛΑΣΟΥΧΑ	Stud.Pal. X 233, col.I B,5	ΜΟΥΧΙΣ
* Stud.Pal. X 214,1	ΠΕΡΟΜΟΥ	Stud.Pal. X 233, col.I B,6	ΚΕΡΚΥΤΟΣ
Stud.Pal. X 214,2	ΛΟΛΛΙΑΝΟΥ	Stud.Pal. X 233, col.I B,7	ΦΥΣ
Stud.Pal. X 214,3	ΠΟΥΕΝ	Stud.Pal. X 233, col.I B,8	ΘΜΟΙΟΒΑΣΤΙΣ
Stud.Pal. X 214,4a	ΠΛΕΜΕΔΕΟΥ	* Stud.Pal. X 233, col.I B,9	ΤΑΣΑΥΤΗΣ
Stud.Pal. X 214,5	ΘΑΛΜΙ	Stud.Pal. X 233, col.I B,10	ΘΜΟΙΑΜΟΥΝ(ΙΣ)
Stud.Pal. X 214,6	ΜΑΛΚΟΥΛΙ	Stud.Pal. X 233, col.I B,11	ΒΟΥΣΙΡΙΣ
Stud.Pal. X 214,7	ΠΚΑΤΑΝΩ	Stud.Pal. X 233, col.I B,12	ΠΕΕΝΗ
Stud.Pal. X 214,8	ΨΑΝΑΤΙ()	* Stud.Pal. X 233, col.I B,13	ΝΕΑ ΠΟΛΙΣ
Stud.Pal. X 217,1	ΔΑΦΝΗ	* Stud.Pal. X 233, col.I B,13	ΤΑΧΕΩΣ
Stud.Pal. X 217,4	ΨΑΝΝΕ	Stud.Pal. X 233,col.I B,14	ΠΕΕΝΠΑΣΒΥΤ(ΙΣ)
Stud.Pal. X 217,5	ΠΟΛΙΤ()	* Stud.Pal. X 233, col.II,1	ΨΥΧΕΩΝΟΣ
Stud.Pal. X 218,2	ΟΝΩΣΙΣ	* Stud.Pal. X 233, col.II,2	ΣΑΓΑΡΟΣ
Stud.Pal. X 218,4	ΤΑΤΑΡ()	Stud.Pal. X 233, col.II,3	Ἐ...]ΕΡ()
Stud.Pal. X 218,5	ΘΜΟΙΝ()	Stud.Pal. X 233, col.II,4	ΜΑΙΟΥΜΑ
* Stud.Pal. X 218,6	ἈΡΧ(ΑΓΓΕΛΟΣ) ΜΙΧ(ΑΗΛ)	* Stud.Pal. X 233, col.II,5	ἈΠΕΡΙΟ(Υ) (?)
Stud.Pal. X 218,7	ΤΙΝΤΗΡΙΣ	* Stud.Pal. X 233, col.II,5	ΧΟΡΤΑΣΩ
* Stud.Pal. X 220,1	ΠΑΤΑΜΟΥΣΟΥ	* Stud.Pal. X 233, col.II,6	Κ.ΑΡΜΟ(Υ)
Stud.Pal. X 220,2	ΔΑΦΝΗ	* Stud.Pal. X 233, col.II,6	[±2]ΑΡΕ.ΩΣ
Stud.Pal. X 220,8	ΣΩΒΘΙΣ	* Stud.Pal. X 233, col.II,7	ΚΕΡΑ ΜΙΚΡ(Α)
Stud.Pal. X 221,1	ΤΟΚΩΙΣ	* Stud.Pal. X 233, col.II,8	ΦΑΜΕΙΘ'ΟΥ'
Stud.Pal. X 223,1	ἉΛΜΥΡΑ	Stud.Pal. X 233, col.II,9	ὉΜΟΝΟΙΑ
Stud.Pal. X 223,3	ΘΜΟΙΝ()	* Stud.Pal. X 233, col.II,10	ΚΑΣΑΝΟΥΠ(ΙΣ)
Stud.Pal. X 223,5	ΚΟΜΑ (?)	* Stud.Pal. X 233, col.II,11	ΣΩΤΤΙΑΝΟΣ
Stud.Pal. X 223,6	ΟΝΩΣΙΣ	* Stud.Pal. X 233, col.II,13	ΣΩΒΘΙΣ ἡ μικρά
Stud.Pal. X 226,4	Μ(Ε)Γ(ΑΛΟΥ) ΚΡΟΥΣΤ'ΟΥ'	Stud.Pal. X 233, col.II,14	ΘΜΟΙΝΕΨΙ
Stud.Pal. X 226,6	ΚΩΠΡΥΑΣ	Stud.Pal. X 233, col.II,15	ἈΜΜΙΑΝ[..]
Stud.Pal. X 227,1;2	ΦΡΟΥΡΙΟΥ	* Stud.Pal. X 233, col.II,16	ΦΕΒΙΧΙΣ

REVERSE INDEX

* Stud.Pal. X 233, col.II,17	ΔΙΑΣΗΜΟΤΑΤΟΥ	Stud.Pal. XX 117,5	ΦΙΛΟΝΙΚΟΥ
Stud.Pal. X 233, col.II,19	ΠΕΕΝΠΙΒΥΚ(ΙΣ)	Stud.Pal. XX 117,5	ΝΕΜΗΟΥΕΙ
Stud.Pal. X 233, col.II,20	ΣΩΤΤΙΑΝΟΣ	Stud.Pal. XX 124,1	ΆΛΜΥΡΑ
* Stud.Pal. X 233, col.II,21	ΑΓΚΗΡΜΕΙ	Stud.Pal. XX 127,2	ΚΕΡΚΕΣΗΦΙΣ
Stud.Pal. X 233, col.II,23	ΟΓΟΥ	Stud.Pal. XX 127,5	ΦΕΒΙΧΙΣ
Stud.Pal. X 233, col.II,24	ΤΑΑΜΨΕΩΣ	Stud.Pal. XX 127,6	ΠΑΣΗΕΙ
* Stud.Pal. X 233, col.III,1	ΒΑΥΚΑΛΙ	Stud.Pal. XX 137,9	ΑΝΙΠΙΑΡ
Stud.Pal. X 233, col.III,2	ΆΝΑΒΩΛΙΑ	Stud.Pal. XX 148,1	ΤΛΕΣΙΔΟΣ
Stud.Pal. X 233, col.III,3	ΤΛΕΣΙΔΟΣ	Stud.Pal. XX 148 recto,2;verso,1	ΠΟΙΜΕΝΩΝ κώμη
Stud.Pal. X 234,2	ΛΕΥΚΟΓΙΟΝ	Stud.Pal. XX 206,5	ΠΕΣΕΝ
Stud.Pal. X 235,2	ΠΕΕΝΠΙΒΥΚ(ΙΣ)	Stud.Pal. XX 249 verso,2	ΤΛΕΣΙΔΟΣ
Stud.Pal. X 236,1	ΟΓΟΥ	Stud.Pal. XX 254,1	ΣΩΒΘΙΣ
* Stud.Pal. X 237,1	ΠΕΕ[ΝΑΜΕΥΣ?]	P.Tebt. II 301,4	ΣΩΒΘΙΣ
Stud.Pal. X 237,3	ΔΑΦΝΗ	* P.Tebt. II 353,4	ΠΕΕΝΣΑΜΟΙ
Stud.Pal. X 258,2	ΘΜΟΙΟΒΑΣΤΙΣ	P.Tebt. II 575	ΣΩΒΘΙΣ
Stud.Pal. X 263,1	ΘΜΟΙΟΒΑΣΤΙΣ	P.Tebt. III 827,15	ΜΕΝΕΛΑΟΥ (fossil kleros)
Stud.Pal. XX 7,12	ΦΙΛΟΝΙΚΟΥ	P.Tebt. III 827,19	ΚΑΣΣΑΝΔΡΟΥ (fossil kleros)
Stud.Pal. XX 7,27	ΝΟΗΡΙΣ	P.Tebt. III 838,9	ΝΙΣΕΥΣ
Stud.Pal. XX 16,9-10	ΚΕΡΚΕΣΗΦΙΣ	P.Tebt. III 838,13;16	ΤΟΣΑΧΜΙΣ
* Stud.Pal. XX 18,3	ΟΝΝΗΣ	P.Tebt. III 857,3	ΠΩΙΣ
Stud.Pal. XX 22,1	ΠΥΡΓΩΤΟΣ	* P.Tebt. III 857,36	ΠΕΕΝΣΑΜΟΙ
Stud.Pal. XX 22,6-7	ΚΙΛΘΩ	P.Tebt. III 857,37	ΑΠΙ()
Stud.Pal. XX 25,5	ΤΕΚΜΙ	P.Tebt. III 860,17;19;20;61;66;67	ΣΩΣΙΒΙΟΥ
Stud.Pal. XX 25,13	ΞΕΝΟΦΩΝΤΟΣ (fossil kleros)		(fossil kleros)
Stud.Pal. XX 26,12;26	ΤΕΚΜΙ	P.Tebt. III 860,21;105	ΨΕΒΘΟΝΠΕΝΟΥΦΙΣ
Stud.Pal. XX 26,15	ΤΑΕΜΣΙΣ	* P.Tebt. III 860,22	ΘΜΟΙΤΟΘΙΣ
Stud.Pal. XX 26,20	ΤΑΝΑΣΩ	* P.Tebt. III 860,48;50	ΝΟΚΛΗ
Stud.Pal. XX 26,28	ΤΑΒΟΚΛΙΣ	P.Tebt. III 860,59	ΤΙΛΩΘΙΣ
Stud.Pal. XX 26,32	ΘΕΟΔΜ[ΗΤΟΥ (fossil kleros)	P.Tebt. III 860,61;64	ΚΟΒΑ
Stud.Pal. XX 26,40;49	ΆΓΗΜΑ	P.Tebt. III 860,65	ΓΕΜΟΥΝΙΣ
Stud.Pal. XX 28,5	ΠΕΕΝΑΜΕΥΣ	P.Tebt. III 860,103	ΊΒΙΩΝ ΑΡΣΑΜΟΥ
Stud.Pal. XX 28,7-8	ΠΕΕΝΠΙΒΥΚ(ΙΣ)	P.Tebt. III 860,104	ΨΕΛΕΜΑΧΙΣ
Stud.Pal. XX 29,6	ΤΕΚΜΙ	P.Tebt. III 860,109	ΤΟΕΜΗΣΙΣ
Stud.Pal. XX 29,8;25	ΤΟΣΑΧΜΙΣ	P.Tebt. III 876,5	ΠΕΤΑΧΟΡ
Stud.Pal. XX 29,12	ΤΑΝΑΣΩ	P.Tebt. III 876,51	ΣΙΝΑΡΥ
Stud.Pal. XX 29,18	ΆΠΟΛΛΩΝΙΟΥ (fossil kleros)	P.Tebt. III 876,66;87	ΣΩΒΘΙΣ
Stud.Pal. XX 29,20	ΝΕΠΩΤΙΑΝΟΣ	P.Tebt. III 878,16	ΨΙΛΙΧΙ
Stud.Pal. XX 29,20-21	ΘΕΟΔΩΡΟΥ (fossil kleros)	* P.Tebt. III 878,19	ΠΥΡΓΩΤΟΣ
* Stud.Pal. XX 29,21	ΠΕΕΝΤΕΧΥ	P.Tebt. III 878,22	ΒΟΥΣΙΡΙΣ
Stud.Pal. XX 29,22	]ΡΕΟΥΣ (fossil kleros)	P.Tebt. III 878,46	ΤΟΟΥ
Stud.Pal. XX 29,23	ΔΙΔΥΜΙΑΝΟΥ	* P.Tebt. III 889,9	ΟΝΝΗΣ
Stud.Pal. XX 29,23	ΜΑΡΩΝΟΣ	P.Tebt. III 890,7	ΤΑΝΤΟΚΑ
Stud.Pal. XX 29,24	ΉΛΙΟΔΩΡΟΥ (fossil kleros)	P.Tebt. III 890,74;75;100	ΦΝΕΒΙΕΥΣ
Stud.Pal. XX 29,26	ΉΣΙΟ.... (fossil kleros)	P.Tebt. III 890,81	ΚΟΛΛΕΥΣ
Stud.Pal. XX 29,28	ΥΠΕΡΒΑΣΤΟΣ	P.Tebt. III 890,97	ΜΕ
Stud.Pal. XX 32,8	ΚΩΙΤΗΣ	P.Tebt. III 890,191	ΚΑΛΛΙΣΤΡΑΤΟΥ (fossil kleros)
Stud.Pal. XX 32,8;14	ΦΙΛΟΝΙΚΟΥ	P.Tebt. III 920,20	ΤΕΧΘΩ
Stud.Pal. XX 34,5;16	ΤΕΒΕΤΝΥ	P.Tebt. III 920,21	ΦΕΒΙΧΙΣ
Stud.Pal. XX 34	ΝΙΚΙΟΥ καὶ ΠΤΟΛΕΜΑΙΟΥ καὶ ἄλλων (fossil kleros)	P.Tebt. III 931,2	ΚΟΜΑ
Stud.Pal. XX 36,3;7	ΜΟΥΧΕΝΝΩΜΘΟΥ	P.Tebt. III 987,5	ΆΓΗΜΑ
Stud.Pal. XX 47,3-4	ΆΓΗΜΑ	P.Tebt. III 988,15	ΚΟΛΛΙΝΤΑΑΘΥΡ
Stud.Pal. XX 47,5	ΠΕΕΝΠΙΒΥΚ(ΙΣ)	P.Tebt. III 989,5	ΝΙΣΕΥΣ
Stud.Pal. XX 47,7	ΩΤΕΙΡΙΣ	P.Tebt. III 991,2	ΚΟΛΛΙΝΤΑΑΘΥΡ
Stud.Pal. XX 47,7	ΘΕΟΔΩΡΟΥ (fossil kleros)	P.Tebt. III 991,8	ΑΣΣΥΑ
Stud.Pal. XX 52,5	ΤΑΑΜΟΡΟΥ	P.Tebt. III 992, descr.	ΚΟΛΛΙΝΤΑΑΘΥΡ
Stud.Pal. XX 52,15	ΦΙΛΟΝΙΚΟΥ	P.Tebt. III 1043, descr.	ΒΟΥΣΙΡΙΣ
Stud.Pal. XX 55,4	ΠΕΕΝΑΜΕΥΣ	* P.Tebt. III 1044,54	ΠΕΕΝΣΑΜΟΙ
Stud.Pal. XX 90,4	ΚΑΙΝΗ	P.Tebt. III 1044,62	ΤΑΝΤΟΚΑ
Stud.Pal. XX 117,1;2	ΚΟΒΑ	* P.Tebt. III 1044,65	ΝΟ(?) ΟΝ(?)
		* P.Tebt. III 1045,14;45	ΠΕΕΝΣΑΜΟΙ

P.Tebt. III 1082,35	ΟΝΝΗΣ	P.Wash. Univ. II 103,6	ΘΜΟΙΝΕΨΙ
PUG I 50,6	ΛΕΥΚΟΓΙΟΝ	P.Yale I 31,6-7	ΠΑΣΤΟΦΟΡΩΝ
PUG III 114,8	ΠΕΕΝΤΕΧΥ	P.Yale I 35,6	ΚΟΒΑ
PUG III 114,10	ΤΑΕΜΣΙΣ	P.Yale I 57,2	ΠΕΕΝΠΙΒΥΚ(ΙΣ)
PUG III 114,11	ΤΑΝΑΣΩ	O.Meyer 51,4	ΠΩΙΣ
UPZ I 9,5	ΨΥΧΙΣ	O.Mich. I 68,3	ΚΟΒΑ
UPZ I 10,7	ΨΥΧΙΣ	O.Mich. I 179,2-3	ΛΕΥΚΟΓΙΟΝ
UPZ I 11,6	ΨΥΧΙΣ	O.Mich. I 254,3	ΛΕΥΚΟΓΙΟΝ
UPZ I 70,24	ΤΡΙΚΩΜΙΑ	O.Mich. I 516,7-8	ΛΕΥΚΟΓΙΟΝ
UPZ I 76,5	ΤΡΙΚΩΜΙΑ	O.Mich. I 517,4-5	ΛΕΥΚΟΓΙΟΝ
UPZ I 122,3	ΠΕΕΝΑΜΕΥΣ	O.Mich. I 520,5	ΛΕΥΚΟΓΙΟΝ
P.Vind.Bosw. 7,3	ΚΩΙΤΗΣ	O.Mich. I 524,3	ΛΕΥΚΟΓΙΟΝ
P.Vind.Bosw. 7,11	ΑΓΗΜΑ	O.Mich. I 525,3	ΛΕΥΚΟΓΙΟΝ
P.Vind.Sal. 6,7	ΑΛΙΛΑΙΣ	O.Mich. I 526,3	ΛΕΥΚΟΓΙΟΝ
P.Vind.Sijp. 7,2;5;9	ΠΑΣΗΕΙ	O.Mich. I 532,3	ΛΕΥΚΟΓΙΟΝ
P.Vind.Sijp. 9,2	ΟΣΥΤΕΟΣ	O.Mich. I 534,3-4	ΛΕΥΚΟΓΙΟΝ
P.Vind.Sijp. 9,2	ΑΥΞΩΝΙΟΣ	O.Mich. I 541,3	ΛΕΥΚΟΓΙΟΝ
P.Vind.Sijp. 9,7	ΦΥΣ	O.Mich. I 545,5	ΛΕΥΚΟΓΙΟΝ
P.Vind.Sijp. 9,8	ΨΑΝΝΕ	O.Mich. II 927,4	ΛΕΥΚΟΓΙΟΝ
P.Vind.Sijp. 13,3	ΠΕΤΑΧΟΡ	O.Mich. II 930,4	ΛΕΥΚΟΓΙΟΝ
P.Vind.Sijp. 16,4	ΒΟΥΣΙΡΙΣ	O.Mich. II 931,4	ΛΕΥΚΟΓΙΟΝ
P.Vind.Sijp. 19,6	ΤΕΒΕΤΝΥ	O.Mich. III 1079,4	ΛΕΥΚΟΓΙΟΝ
P.Vind.Tand. 10,3;61	ΑΤ.[	O.Mich. III 1080,3	ΛΕΥΚΟΓΙΟΝ
P.Vind.Tand. 10,32	ΚΕΡΚΥΤΟΣ	O.Theb. 132,3	ΝΕΙΛΟΥ ΠΟΛΙΣ
P.Vind.Tand. 11,15;40	ΚΩΙΤΗΣ	O.Wilck. II 1099,3	ΣΙΝΕΒ
P.Vind.Tand. 11,19;24;43;47	ΤΑΑΜΟΡΟΥ	O.Wilck. II 1100,2	ΚΕΡΚΕΣΗΦΙΣ
P.Vind.Tand. 16,24	ΑΣΣΥΑ	* O.Wilck. II 1104,3	ΕΕΒΗΚΙΣ
P.Vind.Tand. 16,25	ΚΕΡΚΕΣΗΦΙΣ	O.Wilck. II 1106,3	ΠΩΙΣ
P.Vind.Tand. 17,17;18	ΘΜΟΙΟΒΑΣΤΙΣ	O.Wilck. II 1108,4	ΠΟΙΜΕΝΩΝ ΚΩΜΗ
P.Vind.Tand. 18,16	ΒΟΥΣΙΡΙΣ	O.Wilck. II 1114,3-4	ΚΕΡΚΕΣΗΦΙΣ
P.Vind.Tand. 18,20	ΟΝΝΗΣ	O.Wilck. II 1116,3	ΠΩΙΣ
P.Vind.Tand. 18,34	ΦΥΣ	O.Wilck. II 1117,4	ΟΝΝΗΣ
P.Vind.Tand. 19,6;7	ΘΜΟΙΝΕΨΙ	O.Wilck. II 1121,1	ΤΕΚΜΙ
P.Vind.Worp 4,5	ΤΕΒΕΤΝΥ	O.Wilck. II 1124,3	ΚΕΡΚΕΣΗΦΙΣ
P.Vind.inv. G 23035,1	ΤΟΕΜΗΣΙΣ	O.Wilck. II 1124,5	ΜΑΓΔΩΛΑ
P.Wash. Univ. I 18,17	ΘΝΗΙΣ	O.Wilck. II 1125,2	ΛΕΒΕΤΡ...
P.Wash. Univ. I 18,25	ΠΕ.[	O.Wilck. II 1125,3	ΒΟΥΣΙΡΙΣ

4 Variant Spellings

Variant Spelling	Catalogue Entry
ΑΓΚΥΡΩΝΟΣ	ΑΓΚΥΡΩΝ ΠΟΛΙΣ
ΑΓΚΥΡΩΝΩΝ ΠΟΛΙΣ	ΑΓΚΥΡΩΝ ΠΟΛΙΣ
ΑΜΙΑ...	ΑΜΜΙΑΝ[..]
ΑΝΑΒΑΛ'Ε'	ΑΝΑΒΩΛΙΑ
ΒΑΣΙΛΙΚΗ	see: ΟΔΟΣ
ΕΛΒΩΝΘΙΣ	ΘΕΛΒΩΝΘΙΣ
ΖΑΝΗΡΙΟΣ	see: ΧΩΜΑ
ΘΜΟΙΒΑΣΤΙΣ	ΘΜΟΙΟΒΑΣΤΙΣ
ΘΜΟΙΕΦΘΑ	ΘΜΟΙΦΘΑ
ΘΜΟΙΝΕΦΘΑ	ΘΜΟΙΦΘΑ
ΘΟΕΜΗΣΙΣ	ΤΟΕΜΗΣΙΣ
ΙΠΠΩΝΟΣ	ΙΠΠΩΝΩΝ
ΚΑΙΝΟΥ	ΚΑΙΝΗ
ΚΕΝ..	ΚΑΙΝΗ
ΚΟΛΑΣΟΥΧΙΣ	ΚΟΛΛΑΣΟΥΧΑ
ΚΟΛΙΝΤΑΘΥΡ	ΚΟΛΛΙΝΤΑΑΘΥΡ
ΚΟΡΦΟΤΟΥΝ	ΚΟΡΦΟΤΟΙ
ΜΑΚΑΙ'Δ'()	ΜΑΚΑΙΤΟΝΟΣ
ΜΑΣΤ[.]Χ()	ΜΑΓΔ[.]Χ()
ΜΕΓΑΛΗ	see: ΟΔΟΣ
ΝΟΗΡΙΟΥ	ΝΟΗΡΙΣ
ΟΜΦΑΛΟ.ΝΙΑ	see: ΔΙΩΡΥΞ
ΟΝΝΕΟΥΣ	ΟΝΝΗΣ
ΟΝΝΗ	ΟΝΝΗΣ
ΠΑΜΑ	ΠΑΠΑ
ΠΑΤΑ	ΠΑΠΑ
ΠΕΕΝΕΨΩΜΘ(ΙΣ)	ΠΕΕΝΕΨΩΜΦΙΣ
ΠΕΕΝΠΕΒΙΧΙΣ	ΠΕΕΝΠΙΒΥΚΙΣ
ΠΕΝΕΠΥ	ΠΕΕΝΕΨΥ

Variant Spelling	Catalogue Entry
ΠΕΝΝΗ	ΠΕΕΝΗ
ΠΕΟΝΤΑΜΟΥΝ	ΠΕΕΝΣΑΜΟΙ
ΠΟΙΝΑΜΙ	ΠΕΕΝΑΜΕΥΣ
Σ[.].ΙΝΗΣΙΘ(ΕΥΣ)	ΣΙΣΙΝΗ; ΣΙΘ(ΕΥΣ)
ΣΧΜ..ΘΙΣ	ΣΧΝΩΜΘΙΣ
ΣΧΜΩΝΘΙΣ	ΣΧΝΩΜΘΙΣ
ΣΩΥΧ(ΙΣ)	ΣΟΥΧ(ΙΣ)
ΤΑΕΙΜΕΙ	ΤΑΕΤΜΕΙ
ΤΑΙΧ( )	ΤΑΓΧΑΙΣ
ΤΑΛΗ	ΤΑΛΑΗ
ΤΕΜΗΣΙΣ	ΤΟΕΜΗΣΙΣ
ΤΙΝΤΗΛΙΣ	ΤΙΝΤΗΡΙΣ
ΤΙΝΤΥΡΙΣ	ΤΙΝΤΗΡΙΣ
ΤΝΗΙΣ	ΘΝΗΙΣ
ΤΟΕΜΙΣΙΣ	ΤΟΕΜΗΣΙΣ
ΦΕΝΕΒΙ(ΕΥΣ)	ΦΝΕΒΙΕΥΣ
ΦΙΛΟΝΕΙΚΟΥ	ΦΙΛΟΝΙΚΟΥ
ΦΝΕΒΓΕΙ	ΦΝΕΒΙΕΥΣ
ΦΝΕΒΙ	ΦΝΕΒΙΕΥΣ
ΧΟΙΝΩΘΜΙΣ	ΧΟΙΒΝΩΤΜΙΣ
ΧΟΙΝΩΤΒΙΣ	ΧΟΙΒΝΩΤΜΙΣ
ΧΥΝΩΘΜΙΣ	ΧΟΙΒΝΩΤΜΙΣ
ΨΙΧΙΣ	ΨΥΧΙΣ
.ΩΝΙΟΥ	see: ΧΩΜΑ